Whitman Encyclopedia of Mexican Money

Volume 2: Modern Coins of Mexico, 1905 to Date

Don and Lois Bailey

Research editor *Diana Plattner*
Foreword by *Beth Deisher*

www.whitman.com

Whitman Encyclopedia of Mexican Money
Volume 2

www.whitman.com

© 2015 Whitman Publishing, LLC
3101 Clairmont Road · Suite C · Atlanta GA 30329

All rights reserved, including duplication of any kind and storage in electronic or visual retrieval systems. Permission is granted for writers to use a reasonable number of brief excerpts and quotations in printed reviews and articles, provided credit is given to the title of the work and the author. Written permission from the publisher is required for other uses of text, illustrations, and other content, including in books and electronic or other media.

Correspondence concerning this book may be directed to the publisher, attn: Encyclopedia of Mexican Money, at the address above.

ISBN: 0794839541
Printed in Mexico

Disclaimer: Expert opinion should be sought in any significant numismatic purchase. This book is presented as a guide only. No warranty or representation of any kind is made concerning the completeness of the information presented. The authors are professional numismatists who regularly buy, sell, and sometimes hold certain of the items discussed in this book.

Caveat: The value estimates given are subject to variation and differences of opinion. Before making decisions to buy or sell, consult the latest information. Past performance of the rare-coin market or any coin or series within that market is not necessarily an indication of future performance, as the future is unknown. Such factors as changing demand, popularity, grading interpretations, strength of the overall coin market, and economic conditions will continue to be influences.

For a complete listing of numismatic reference books, supplies, and storage products, visit Whitman Publishing online at www.whitman.com, or scan the QR code on the inside front cover of this book.

WCG™   Whitman®   OCG™

CONTENTS

Foreword *by Beth Deisher* iv
How to Use This Book..v

1. An Overview of Mexican Numismatics 1
2. Coinage Reform of 1905 8
3. Coinage Reform of 1992 89
4. Commemorative Coinage...170
5. Mint and Proof Sets...309
6. Silver Bullion Coinage...316
7. Gold Bullion Coinage..326
8. Platinum Bullion Coinage 336
9. Libertads: Silver, Gold, and Platinum..339
10. Pre-Columbian Collections..371
   Aztec...*372*
   Central Veracruz *386*
   Maya *397*
   Olmec *406*
   Teotihuacán...*416*
   Toltec *425*

Appendix A: Bullion Values of Gold and Silver Coins 434
Appendix B: The Calendar Stone on Mexican Coinage 436
Appendix C: Eagle Styles on Mexican Coinage 441
Glossary 448
Bibliography...455
Image Credits...455
Acknowledgments...458
About the Authors 458
Index 460

FOREWORD
by Beth Deisher

Mexico's coins are captivating—but many people, especially Americans, imagine they lack the depth of historical knowledge necessary to collect them. With the book you hold in your hands, however, authors Don and Lois Bailey remove any preconceived barriers to entry.

Don's vast knowledge was gained in part through his advisory roles with both the mint and the Banco de México (the nation's central bank, which has marketing responsibility for Mexico's numismatic programs). He and Lois take you on a visually inviting adventure, guiding you through the rich imagery of ancient cultures and introducing you to the heroes, heroines, and historical events depicted on Mexico's coins. Their in-depth survey of the coinage reforms of 1905 and 1992 explain the circulating denominations and the factors that precipitated the changes to the coins Mexicans have used in everyday commerce for the past 110 years. Their coverage of the circulating and non-circulating commemorative coins and bullion issues is especially comprehensive.

The Baileys' table at major coin shows was always easy to spot, thanks to the big Mexican flag that marked it as the location of the full gamut of historic and rare Mexican coins, paper money, medals, and historic documents. In 1982 Mexico's launch of the silver Libertad, followed by its extensive 1985 and 1986 series honoring Mexico's hosting of the FIFA World Cup Fútbol Games, propelled Mexico onto the world-coin stage—and into the Baileys' bourse offerings.

When I became editor of *Coin World* in 1985, I sought to expand its coverage of world coins, particularly those of Canada and Mexico. However, direct communications proved challenging, especially in Mexico. At Don's urging I traveled to Mexico City for annual conventions of the Sociedad Numismatica de México to get to know the collectors and establish working relationships with mint and bank officials. Don was at my side every step of the way, helping *Coin World* expand its coverage of Mexican numismatics.

I encouraged Don to reach out to American collectors through in-depth feature articles. His first, "The Numismatics of Spanish Colonial Mexico," was the cover story for *Coin World*'s monthly *World Coins* supplement in November 1987. He also began regularly reporting on new issues, especially Mexico's commemorative programs, which rocketed to the forefront as major mints competed for shares of the numismatic market around the world. When *Coin World* re-launched its "Trends of Mexico" in 1993, I once again called on Don's knowledge and market savvy. As market analyst, he provided up-to-date pricing and insights into the health of the market for the next 20 years.

Don's driving vision for the last 40 years has been to share his knowledge and to entice others to become as smitten with Mexican numismatics as he was. Don and Lois (his wife and numismatic research partner) can take pride in knowing they've succeeded. The *Whitman Encyclopedia of Mexican Money: Modern Coins of Mexico, 1905 to Date* is a must-have reference for anyone interested in collecting or investing in modern Mexican coins. Once you open its pages, you'll become smitten, too.

Beth Deisher
Editor, *Coin World*, 1985–2012

HOW TO USE THIS BOOK

Volume 2 is written to be user-friendly for the beginning collector as well as useful for the advanced numismatist. Regular-issue coinage is discussed first, in chronological order, beginning with issues of the Coinage Reform of 1905. Subjects that were touched upon in volume 1 are enlarged upon here in catalog format, with expanded historical information, date listings, illustrations, and technical information such as weights, sizes, mintages, and so on (where available). Numismatic valuations are also provided.

Coin Legends. The *Whitman Encyclopedia of Mexican Money* contains a unique typeface that attempts to reproduce the devices in the coin legends as closely as possible. For example, the nine-punch appears as ⚚, and the mintmarks traditionally depicted in books as **Mo**, **Go**, and **Oa** appear as M̊, G̊, and O̊, respectively. These characters are general representations of the characters in coin legends and mintmarks. The reader should keep in mind that the positions of dots, annulets, rondules, and so forth, relative to other elements on the coin, can vary. When legends are reproduced in the regular text, they are in a slightly bolder typeface.

In descriptions of coin legends, a **forward slash** indicates a line break or a separation of the legend by another element of the design (e.g., the base of a statue). Circular legends, unless specified otherwise, are assumed to be read clockwise. If **and** appears in the text description of a circular legend, it indicates that the following characters switch direction so the legend can be read without turning the coin. If the entire legend is read in a **counterclockwise** direction, it is described as such in the text.

Obverse vs. Reverse. For many years, U.S. auction catalogs and dealer price lists have sought to accommodate American collectors by using the words "obverse" and "reverse" as would be expected for U.S. coins. Although these catalogs usually note that U.S. definitions are being used, when those definitions conflict with standard Mexican numismatics, confusion can result. In this encyclopedia, we apply the terms according to correct Mexican numismatic usage, as defined in *Numismatic History of Mexico* (Alberto Francisco Pradeau, 1938).

Symbols in Charts. In the year-by-year valuation charts, a **forward slash** refers to an overstrike, whether of date or mintmark. The term **Unconfirmed** refers to coins that are said to exist or are listed in other catalogs, but have not been verified by the authors or contributors. **BV** stands for bullion value; to determine the bullion value of a circulating gold or silver coin, see appendix A.

Attribution Numbers. BW numbers are from the Bailey-Whitman classification system, developed for this encyclopedia. **KM** numbers are from the system developed by Chet Krause and Clifford Mishler. Other numbering systems that are relevant to this encyclopedia (but not necessarily this volume) are explained in the glossary.

Historical Information. Every effort has been made to explain subjects with which American readers might not be familiar: people, mythological figures, historical events, and so forth. Many of these subjects (e.g., the serpent god Quetzalcóatl) appear on multiple coins and across multiple chapters; if the subject is not explained near the coin of interest, the reader should check the index.

The subjects covered in the other three volumes of this encyclopedia are as follows.

Volume 1: An Illustrated History of Mexican Coins and Currency

1. An Overview of Mexican Numismatics
2. Media of Exchange in the Anáhuac Era
3. Carlos and Johanna Coinage
4. Cob Coinage
5. Milled Coinage
6. Coinage of the War of Independence
7. Coinage of Augustín de Iturbide
8. Republic Reales Coinage
9. State and Federal Copper Coinage
10. Coinage of Emperor Maximilian
11. Republic Decimal Coinage
12. Coinage of the Revolution
13. The Coinage Reform of 1905
14. The Coinage Reform of 1992
15. Commemoratives of the Coinage Reforms of 1905 and 1992
16. Mint and Proof Sets
17. Silver Bullion Coinage
18. Gold Bullion Coinage
19. Libertads: Silver, Gold, and Platinum
20. Pre-Columbian Collections
21. Tokens of Mexico
22. Variety and Error Coins
23. Patterns, Trial Strikes, and Experimental Pieces
24. Medals of Mexico
25. Orders and Decorations of Mexico
26. Bullion Values of Silver and Gold Coins
27. Paper Money of Mexico

Volume 3: Early Numismatics

1. An Overview of Mexican Numismatics
2. Media of Exchange in the Anáhuac Era
3. Carlos and Johanna Coinage
4. Cob Coinage
5. Milled Coinage
6. Coinage of the War of Independence
7. Coinage of Agustín de Iturbide
8. Republic Reales Coinage
9. State and Federal Coppers
10. Coinage of Emperor Maximilian
11. Republic Decimal Coinage

Volume 4: The Mexican Revolution

1. An Overview of Mexican Numismatics
2. Estado de Aguascalientes
3. Estado de Chihuahua
4. Estado de Durango
5. Estado de Guerrero
6. Estado de Jalisco
7. Estado de México
8. Estado de Morelos
9. Estado de Oaxaca
10. Estado de Puebla
11. Estado de Sinaloa
12. Estado de Zacatecas

An Overview of Mexican Numismatics

The history of any country can be viewed from a study of its coinage, and Mexico is no exception. The various conflicts in Mexico's history, both political and economic, present a wealth of numismatic subjects for the collector to pursue. A study of these conflicts reveals the entwinement of the histories of Mexico and the United States, including the War with Texas (1836–1845); the Mexican War (1846–1848); the 1914 conflict at Veracrúz; the 1916 invasion of Columbus, New Mexico, by Pancho Villa; and the Mexican Revolution of 1910 to 1920.

Long before the United States and Mexico were heard of, however, before the arrival of Hernán Cortés and the lengthy period of colonial rule in the Americas, the indigenous peoples used other media of exchange. During the period now called the Anáhuac era, these items included cacao beans, strings of colored shells, patolquechtli (small squares of woven cotton material), and gold-filled quills, as well as *tajaderas* (now referred to as "Aztec hoe money") made of copper in T-shapes of various sizes. In later years, tokens were often used as local "necessity" money within Mexico. In most cases, they filled a need for small coins in the rural areas, and they were used by haciendas and merchants. Some were overstruck on earlier copper state coins.

In 1536, Mexico (then the Viceroyalty of New Spain) issued the first coinage of the Americas. Mexican coins were used in U.S. commerce and were legal tender in the United States, by statute, until 1857. Mexican coinage then ceased to be official legal tender in the U.S.A., although it continued to circulate in rural areas. The only Mexican coinage issued under Spanish rule within what would later be part of the United States was the copper 1/2 real known as the Texas jola, issued in 1818. They were struck in San Fernándo de Bexar (San Antonio, Texas) by José Antonio de la Garza.

A half-real of San Fernándo de Bexar / San Antonio, Texas, also known as a *Texas jola*. (BW-62.1, KM-Tn1, 16 mm)

The Carlos and Johanna coinage series covers the period from 1536 to 1572. Its coins were issued in silver and copper, with denominations of 1/2, 1, 2, 3, 4, and 8 reales in silver, and 2 and 4 maravedies in copper.

An early-series Carlos and Johanna 1 real. (No date; BW-5.1, Nesmith 9, KM-7, 23 mm)

The Codex Mendoza

In the Codex Mendoza (left), the eagle stands on a flowering or fruiting cactus, which sprouts from the Aztec glyph for *rock*. Below the rock is a shield backed by arrows—the Aztec glyph for *war*. The *ihuiteteyo* (down balls) on the shield represent the power of Tenochtitlán.

The 25 pesos of 1968 below depicts an eagle that is similar in style to the Codex eagle. Below the cactus and the simplified depiction of the rock glyph are stylized waves with series of dots that echo the dots on the shield.

Mexico's national emblem, the eagle, derives from an image found most famously on the opening page of the Codex Mendoza—a 71-page manuscript commissioned in Mexico City around 1541 by the Spanish conquerors. Possibly intended to explain the history and ways of the conquered Mexica (Aztecs) to King Charles V, it is also a depiction of the Aztecs' lives from their own point of view. The Codex consists of three separate sections: the history of the Aztec empire; the "tribute roll," or records of the tributes regularly paid by Moctezuma II's 400 subject towns; and the culture and daily details of Aztec life. The sections were drawn in vividly colored pictograms by Aztec scribes, then annotated in Spanish.

The first folio of the Codex, shown above, depicts the founding of the Aztec city Tenochtitlán: a legend in which the wandering Mexica people knew they'd reached their home when they found an eagle (symbol of the sun god Huitzilopochtli) perched on a cactus growing from a stone. The eagle, cactus, and stone appear at the center of a blue cross representing Tenochtitlán's canals; the cross divides the field into four parts, representing the city's four main wards or neighborhoods.

As is often the case with cultural stories, different versions of Tenochtitlán's foundation story exist and are found on later codices and elsewhere. Some, but not all, of these depictions include a snake, the meaning of

An Overview of Mexican Numismatics

which has been variously interpreted. In any case, since the time of Mexico's independence from Spain, all Mexican coats of arms have featured the eagle, cactus, and stone, and often the water surrounding the stone; the snake became a standard element very early, on the coins of the First Republic.

Cob coinage followed the Carlos and Johanna series. These coins were issued from approximately 1580 to 1732, under six different Spanish rulers from Philip II to Luis I. The origin of the word "cob" is debated among numismatists; some say it derives from the Spanish term *cabo de barra*, or "end of the bar"—and the planchets for cob coins were, indeed, cut from the ends of bars of metal, clipped to the required weight, and hand-stamped with die punches. Others say the term comes from the old, English word "cob," which refers, in essence, to a small, rough lump of something (e.g., cob horses are small, thick, sturdy animals, noted for their practicality rather than their beauty). Many cob coins are, indeed, quite crude, with a good portion of the design missing. "Royal strikes" are an exception to the rule during this era. Struck carefully on perfectly round discs, probably for presentation to the king, royal strikes are very rare. Both gold and silver coins were struck in the cob series.

A Philip IV one-real cob coin. (1627 D; BW-12.c, KM-28, 20 mm)

Cob coinage was replaced by milled coinage, so called because it was minted on a screw press rather than hand stamped like the cob coinage. Milled coins were issued from 1732 through 1771 in the Pillar series, and from 1772 through 1821 in the Portrait (or Bust) series, under five Spanish rulers from Philip V to Ferdinand VII. Pillar and Portrait coins were issued in bronze, silver, and gold. The milled coinage is historically and numismatically important to U.S. collectors, as some pieces circulated in the United States as legal tender in the nation's early days.

An early-date, milled 8 reales of Philip V—also known as a *Pillar dollar* or *piece of eight*. Along with their fractional equivalents (one-half, one, two, and four reales), Pillar dollars not only circulated in Mexico but also were the principal coins of the American colonists. Produced at the first mint in the New World, they were the forerunners of the American dollar. (1741 M-F; BW-28.1, KM-103, 40 mm)

Milled Coinage

"Milled" coinage, simply put, is coinage produced by a mechanical device (or mill) rather than by hand-striking. A *milled edge* is one that is impressed with a pattern by a machine. On early Mexican milled coinage, the blanks were run through a Castaing machine (named for its inventor, Jean Castaing) to impart a design to the edges before being sent to the screw press for striking. (For more information, see the sidebar on pages 316 and 317.)

An illustration of a Castaing machine from the 18th-century *Encyclopaedia, or a Systematic Dictionary of the Sciences, Arts, and Crafts,* edited by Denis Diderot.

A *Castaing machine* is most easily described as a flat surface or table bearing a track, slightly narrower than the coin's diameter, between two rectangular bars of metal. One of the bars is fixed to the surface; the other bar moves parallel to the fixed bar by means of a crank. The inner edge of each bar is inscribed with the design intended for the edge of the coin: lettering, flowers, reeds, or any pattern that is regular enough to make it obvious if someone has clipped away part of the metal. The operator places the blank flat on the surface in the track and turns the crank, rolling the blank between the two bars under enough pressure to leave each bar's design impressed on the edge.

In addition to the colonial coinage discussed to this point, the proclamation medals issued to honor Spanish rulers and the events during their reigns are also collectible. Pattern, experimental, and trial pieces, dating from the 18th century to the modern era, are collected by specialists.

The War of Independence, 1810 to 1820, brought about the next era of Mexican coinage. Mexico's fight to obtain independence from Spanish rule was led by the heroic Father Miguel Hidalgo y Costilla, with his September 16, 1810, call for

A proclamation medal minted in Zacatecas, announcing the ascension of Ferdinand VII to the throne of Spain. (1808; G-F199a, 41 mm)

War of Independence: a Royalist 8 reales of 1812 from Oaxaca. (BW-60, KM-168, 39mm)

War of Independence: an Insurgent issue, Supreme National Congress 8 reales of 1811. (BW-153.1, KM-206, 39 mm)

Augustín de Iturbide 4 escudos, 1823-M̊, JM. (BW-167, KM-312, 30 mm)

liberty: "Viva Mexico! Viva independence! Viva the Virgin of Guadalupe!" Many numismatic oddities—cast coinage, counterstamped and double-counterstamped by both the Royalist and the Insurgent sides of the conflict—were issued during this time.

The end of the War of Independence brought Mexico the short-lived empire of Agustín de Iturbide in 1822 and 1823. The first paper money of Mexico was issued during Iturbide's reign, along with coinage of copper, silver, and gold.

After the abdication of Iturbide, Mexico became a republic; its coinage was issued from 1823 through 1897 in denominations of reales and escudos. Within the period of 1824 through 1872, a wide variety of state and federal issues of the real denomination were struck in copper and brass. Those from the state mints were originally authorized by the federal government, but they proliferated to the point that the government finally put a halt on their production. The French intervention of 1863 to 1867, under Emperor Maximilian, interrupted the Republic coinage and resulted in Imperial decimal coinage of copper, silver, and gold. Even so, coinage of the Republic design continued to be struck at some mints during the French occupation.

After the June 1867 execution of Maximilian by Benito Juárez García, Republic coinage was officially restored. This was the Republic's first decimal coinage, and it continued until the Coinage Reform of 1905, with the Liberty Cap pesos continuing into 1909. The Republic decimal series, like the Republic real series, offers bronze, silver, and gold coinages of several types.

Republic reales coinage of the Hookneck Eagle style: 8 reales, Looped Tail (Type II) on snake, 1823-M, JM. (BW-206.11H, KM-A376.2, 38 mm)

Republic 2 escudos, Upright Eagle style, 1863-M, TH. (BW-209.7, KM-380.7, 23 mm)

A state copper coin from Chihuahua: 1/8 real of 1855. (DB-110, BW-176.1, KM-319, 20 mm)

Maximilian 20 pesos, 1866-M. (BW-231, KM-389, 35 mm)

Republic decimal coinage: 50 centavos, 1869-Mo, C. (BW-257.7, KM-407.6, 30 mm)

All of the early coinage of Mexico, from the Anáhuac era through the Republic decimal issues, is summarized in volume 1 and presented in greater depth in volume 3.

The 20th century, which is the subject of the present volume, brought the development of a wealth of new coin types and production concepts. Under the Coinage Reform of 1905, the gold standard was introduced, all the branch mints were closed, and ESTADOS UNIDOS MEXICANOS replaced REPUBLICA MEXICANA on the coinage. After this reform all of the coinage was struck at the Mexico City mint, except for a few occasions when some coins were struck outside the country. They all bear the famous mintmark of M̊. Today's coinage is struck at the modern mint at San Luis Potosí, using the M̊ mintmark to denote the Casa de Moneda de México.

The Coinage Reform of 1992 introduced the temporary *nuevo peso* (new peso) denominations, along with the subsequent issues that are in circulation today. Both coinage reforms embraced the idea of commemorative (non-circulating legal tender) coinage, which is made to very high standards and sold to collectors at a premium above face value. Similar numismatic items that have been produced for sale to the public are Mint and Proof sets; silver and gold bullion coinage; the Libertad series, in silver, gold, and platinum; and the extensive coinage of the Pre-Columbian Collections Program.

The violent era of the Mexican Revolution of 1910 through 1920 generated a vast variety of coins, tokens, and paper money, all of which is widely collected today. Coinage of this era is treated in-depth in volume 4 of this encyclopedia.

A copper bucket of gold planchets for 50-peso coins, Apartado Mint, Mexico City, 1980— a pot of gold at the end of the rainbow of Mexico's fascinating history.

THE COINAGE REFORM OF 1905

At the beginning of the 20th century, the coinage of Mexico was in disarray. All the branch mints were under private contracts, the copper coins were too large and too expensive to mint for their face value, and gold and silver coins were of finenesses not in general use by other countries. This complicated trade: Mexican silver coinage before the reform was 0.9027 fine, whereas British sterling was 0.925 and the common fineness in the United States and most Latin American countries was 0.900. Mexican gold coins were 0.875 fine; elsewhere, gold coins were almost universally 0.900 fine.

Leading up to the 1905 reform, the branch mints' contracts were beginning to come up for renewal—at San Luis Potosí and Oaxaca in 1893, and elsewhere in 1905. This was Mexico's opportunity to close the branch mints and move all minting operations to Mexico City, at the Apartado Mint, which had been founded by decree on May 11, 1535. The Apartado Mint had first been located at Casa de Axayácatl, which is now the location of the Nacional Monte de Piedad (National Pawnshop); it later moved to the location now occupied by the Palacio Nacional (National Palace). The mint was moved again in 1569 to a location on Calle de Moneda (Coin Street). In March 1848 construction of the new Apartado Mint began, and the first coinage from this mint was produced on June 1, 1850.

The coinage reform of 1905 changed the status of the Apartado Mint from the Mexico *City* Mint to the Mexico Mint. The Legaria Mint opened in 1970, utilizing all state-of-the-art equipment to strike silver, gold, and platinum commemorative coinage as well as circulation coinage. In 1983 the San Luis Potosí Mint began supplementing the increased need for coinage minted at the Legaria facility, and continued to play a supplementary role until 1999, when minting operations were moved from Legaria to San Luis Potosí. Today, this minting facility is the only plant that strikes coinage for Mexico displaying the famous M̥ mintmark.

Over the years, Mexican coinage has also been struck at various mints outside the country, including the U.S. mints in New Orleans and San Francisco and the Heaton Mint in Birmingham, England (see sidebar).

Due to the price fluctuations of precious metals, and the changing economic conditions of Mexico over the years, the size and fineness of various coins have changed from time to time to fit existing circumstances. Because of these conditions, the selections of denominations issued have also changed.

Mexican Coins, Foreign Mints

The building formerly housing the Benziger Brothers operation in Brooklyn, New York.

The portion of the former Birmingham Mint facing Icknield Street. The mint closed in 2003 and the facilities are undergoing residential renovation.

The New Orleans Mint, ca. 1900.

The old San Francisco Mint, ca. 1906.

The Denver Mint, ca. 1906.

The Philadelphia Mint, ca. 1905.

On several occasions, non-Mexican mints have struck Mexican coinage—not just specialty items like the silver Bullion Commemorative Series or the gold mini-Libertad coinage (both produced under private contract between the Casa de Moneda and a Texas firm), but also circulating legal tender.

> These foreign mints included the New Orleans, Denver, San Francisco, and Philadelphia facilities of the U.S. Mint; the Brooklyn, New York, location of the Benziger Brothers operation; and The Mint, Birmingham, Ltd. (the "Birmingham mint"), operated by the Heaton family in England. The following is a list of known 20th-century coins produced by these mints, along with their mintages. The coins were struck with the M̊ mintmark, and were in all respects identical to their Mexican-made counterparts.
>
> **1 centavo, Type 1 (bronze).** *Birmingham mint*—50 million coins in 1906 and 1907, all dated 1906.
>
> **2 centavos, Type 1 (bronze).** *Birmingham mint*—5 million coins in 1906 and 1907, all dated 1906.
>
> **5 centavos, Type 1 (nickel).** *Birmingham mint*—A large portion of the 1906 and 1911 mintage, and all of the 1907–1910 mintage.
>
> **20 centavos, Type 1 (.800 fine silver).** *New Orleans*—5,434,619 pieces dated 1907 (apparently the only foreign order this branch mint produced).
>
> **50 centavos, Type 1 (.800 fine silver).** *San Francisco*—3,800,000 in 1906, and 8,642,000 in 1907. *Denver*—8,642,000 in 1907.
>
> **50 centavos, Type 4 (.420 fine silver).** *San Francisco*—18,000,000. *Denver*—17,000,850. *Philadelphia*—25,000,000. All dated 1935.
>
> **5-peso gold (.900 fine).** *Philadelphia*—4,000,000 pieces dated 1906.
>
> **10-peso gold (.900 fine).** *Philadelphia*—1,000,000 pieces dated 1906.

In this chapter, for each denomination we list the basic types, along with the common terms (if any) by which those types are known to collectors. We limit varieties, for the most part, to overdates, positioning of dates, and other results of the minting process.

The numerous varieties in the 1905 and 1992 coinage reforms can also be found in the *Illustrated Price Guide of the Modern Mexican Coins 1905 to Date*, by Carlos Abel Amaya Guérra.

Note: Values of common-date silver and gold coins have been based on bullion prices of $20 per ounce and $1,200 per ounce, respectively, and may vary with prevailing spot prices. To determine the bullion value (BV, or intrinsic value) of common silver and gold coins, see appendix A.

1 CENTAVO

Centavos under the Reform of 1905 fall into six basic types:

> Type 1—Monogram (with the value depicted as a numeral superimposed on a horizontally shaded centavo symbol, ¢—i.e., forming a "monogram")

The Nopal Cactus

An extremely useful plant, the nopal cactus *(Opuntia ficus)* depicted in the national emblem was cultivated in Mesoamerica long before the Spanish conquest. More than 100 species are known in Mexico, most of them edible. It is widely grown for food; the pads of the young cactus can be eaten before or after the spines form, and the fruit, called a *tuna* or prickly pear, is also edible. It plays a role in traditional medicine and is an excellent fodder for animals.

Nopal is widely cultivated in Mexico, from the family farm to the industrial level. It is particularly valuable to subsistence farmers due to its ease of propagation, minimal soil and water requirements, and low-tech farming needs. In many cases it is cultivated using the same methods as in ancient Mesoamerica.

The nopal has been part of the national emblem since independence. On the 1 centavos of Type 1 through Type 4 it is quite small, and the eagle can appear to be standing on a dry tree-branch.

One of many nopal farms in rural Mexico.

Type 2—Zapatista (like Type 1, but struck at the Mexico City Mint while it was under the control of Emiliano Zapata's Revolutionary troops; distinguishable from Type 1 coins of 1915 by their smaller size)

Type 3—Monogram (like Type 1, but with less tin and more zinc in the composition)

Type 4—Monogram (like Type 3, but with even less tin and more zinc in the composition)

Type 5—Brass (with a wheat-ear design instead of a monogram on the reverse)

Type 6—Brass, Reduced (same as Type 5, but 3 mm smaller in diameter)

Type 1 (Monogram). BW-501, KM-415.

Composition: 0.950 copper, 0.040 tin, 0.010 zinc. *Weight:* 3 g. *Obverse:* The national coat of arms with the eagle facing forward, head to the right, above a spray of oak and laurel; above, the legend **ESTADOS UNIDOS MEXICANOS**. *Reverse:* At the center, within an open wreath of laurel, a large number 1 superimposed on a horizontally shaded centavo symbol (¢). At the top, between the wreath tips, the date; below the wreath, the mintmark M̊. *Diameter:* 20 mm. *Edge:* Smooth.

	Mintage	F	VF	EF	UNC	BU
1905	6,040,000	$4.25	$5.75	$10.50	$55.00	$70.00
1906, Wide Date	67,505,000	0.45	1.20	2.85	11.50	15.00
1906, Narrow Date	*	0.45	0.60	1.90	9.50	12.50
1910	8,799,000	1.70	2.85	7.75	65.00	85.00
1911, Wide Date	16,450,000	0.95	1.90	5.75	15.00	25.00
1911, Narrow Date	*	0.70	1.20	3.80	13.00	24.00
1912	12,650,000	0.70	0.95	2.85	25.00	30.00
1913	12,850,000	0.70	0.95	2.85	25.00	30.00
1914, Narrow Date	17,350,000	0.60	0.95	3.80	20.00	28.00
1914, Wide Date	*	0.60	0.95	3.80	16.00	24.00
1915	2,276,947	9.50	24.00	70.00	165.00	215.00

* Included above.

Type 2 (Zapatista). BW-502, KM-416.

Composition: 0.950 copper, 0.025 tin, 0.025 zinc. *Weight:* 1.5 g. *Obverse:* The national coat of arms with the eagle facing forward, head to the right, above a spray of oak and laurel; above, the legend **ESTADOS UNIDOS MEXICANOS**. *Reverse:* At the center, within an open wreath of laurel, a large number 1 superimposed on a horizontally shaded centavo symbol (¢). At the top, between the wreath tips, 1915; below the wreath, the mintmark M̊. *Diameter:* 16 mm. *Edge:* Smooth.

	Mintage	F	VF	EF	UNC	BU
1915, Narrow Date, Thick 1	179,048	$19.00	$32.00	$70.00	$120.00	$165.00
1915, Wide Date, Thin 1	*	19.00	32.00	70.00	120.00	165.00

Type 3 (Monogram). BW-501.1, KM-415.

Composition: 0.950 copper, 0.025 tin, 0.025 zinc. *Weight:* 3 g. *Obverse:* The national coat of arms with the eagle facing forward, head to the right, above a spray of oak and laurel; above, the legend **ESTADOS UNIDOS MEXICANOS**. *Reverse:* At the center, within an open wreath of laurel, a large number 1 superimposed on a horizontally shaded centavo symbol (¢). At the top, between the wreath tips, the date; below the wreath, the mintmark M̥. *Diameter:* 20 mm. *Edge:* Smooth.

	Mintage	F	VF	EF	UNC	BU
1916, Narrow Date	500,000	$28.00	$60.00	$120.00	$710.00	$1,000.00
1916, Wide Date	*	28.00	60.00	120.00	710.00	1,000.00
1920	1,433,000	20.00	50.00	100.00	300.00	380.00
1921	3,470,000	4.75	14.00	42.00	235.00	285.00
1922	1,880,000	9.50	19.00	50.00	260.00	310.00
1923	4,800,000	1.90	2.85	4.75	16.00	24.00
1924	2,000,000	2.85	9.50	24.00	165.00	215.00
1924, 4 Over 3	*	55.00	140.00	235.00	430.00	570.00
1925	1,550,000	3.80	9.50	24.00	165.00	215.00
1926	5,000,000	0.95	1.90	3.80	24.00	30.00
1927	6,000,000	0.95	1.90	4.75	32.00	38.00
1927, 7 Over 6	*	19.00	38.00	70.00	145.00	190.00
1928	5,000,000	0.60	0.95	3.80	22.00	28.00
1929	4,500,000	0.60	0.95	1.90	14.00	19.00
1930	7,000,000	0.75	1.20	2.85	19.00	25.00
1933	10,000,000	0.25	0.45	1.90	16.00	20.00
1934	7,500,000	0.70	1.40	3.80	30.00	38.00
1935	12,400,000	0.45	0.95	1.90	7.75	10.50
1936	20,100,000	0.10	0.25	0.95	7.75	10.50
1937	20,000,000	0.10	0.25	0.70	3.35	5.75
1938	10,000,000	0.20	0.45	1.20	2.85	4.75
1939	30,000,000	0.15	0.35	0.70	1.90	3.80
1940	10,000,000	0.25	0.45	0.95	5.75	7.75
1941	15,800,000	0.20	0.45	1.20	2.85	4.75
1942	30,400,000	0.15	0.35	0.70	1.90	3.80
1943	4,310,000	0.95	1.90	2.85	10.50	14.00

* Included above.

Type 4 (Monogram). BW-503, KM-415.

Composition: 0.950 copper, 0.040 tin, 0.010 zinc. *Weight:* 3 g. *Obverse:* The national coat of arms with the eagle facing forward, head to the right, above a spray of oak and laurel; above, the legend **ESTADOS UNIDOS MEXICANOS**. *Reverse:* At the center, within an open wreath of laurel, a large number 1 superimposed on a horizontally shaded centavo symbol (¢). At the top, between the wreath tips, the date; below the wreath, the mintmark M̊. *Diameter:* 20 mm. *Edge:* Smooth.

	Mintage	F	VF	EF	UNC	BU
1944	5,645,000	$0.25	$0.45	$0.95	$5.75	$7.75
1945	26,375,000	0.10	0.20	0.45	1.20	2.85
1946	42,135,000	0.10	0.10	0.15	0.65	1.20
1947	13,445,000	0.10	0.10	0.15	0.65	1.20
1948	20,040,000	0.10	0.10	0.25	0.95	1.90
1949	6,235,000	0.25	0.45	0.95	2.85	4.75

Type 5 (Brass). BW-504, KM-417.

Composition: 0.850 copper, 0.150 zinc. *Weight:* 2 g. *Obverse:* Above a spray of oak and laurel, the national coat of arms depicting the eagle in profile to the left, with stylized, leaf-like feathers and very large feet. Above, the legend **ESTADOS UNIDOS MEXICANOS**. *Reverse:* A stylized sprig of wheat with three ears. One ear points horizontally to the left, the other horizontally to the right; the central, vertical ear divides the denomination 1 / C. At bottom left, the date; at bottom right, the mintmark M̊. *Diameter:* 16 mm. *Edge:* Smooth.

	Mintage	F	VF	EF	UNC	BU
1950	12,815,000	$0.10	$0.10	$0.25	$0.95	$1.90
1951	25,740,000	0.10	0.10	0.45	0.80	1.40
1952	24,610,000	0.10	0.10	0.25	0.45	0.70
1953	21,160,000	0.10	0.10	0.25	0.45	0.70
1954	25,675,000	0.10	0.10	0.45	0.80	1.40
1955	9,820,000	0.10	0.10	0.25	0.80	1.40
1956	11,285,000	0.10	0.10	0.15	0.60	1.40
1957	9,805,000	0.10	0.10	0.25	0.70	1.50
1958	12,155,000	0.10	0.10	0.25	0.50	0.95
1959	11,875,000	0.10	0.10	0.25	0.50	0.95

	Mintage	F	VF	EF	UNC	BU
1960	10,360,000	0.10	0.10	0.25	0.50	0.95
1961	6,385,000	0.10	0.10	0.25	0.50	0.95
1962	4,850,000	0.10	0.10	0.20	0.45	0.70
1963	7,775,000	0.10	0.10	0.15	0.25	0.40
1964	4,280,000	0.10	0.10	0.15	0.25	0.40
1965	2,225,000	0.10	0.10	0.15	0.25	0.40
1966	1,760,000	0.10	0.10	0.25	0.50	0.95
1967	1,290,000	0.10	0.10	0.20	0.45	0.70
1968	1,000,000	0.10	0.10	0.25	0.50	0.95
1969	1,000,000	0.10	0.10	0.25	0.50	0.95

Type 6 (Brass, Reduced). BW-505, KM-418.

Composition: 0.850 copper, 0.150 zinc. *Weight:* 1.5 g. *Obverse:* Above a spray of oak and laurel, the national coat of arms depicting the eagle in profile to the left, with the feathers and other elements drawn as outlines instead of in full relief. Above, the legend ESTADOS UNIDOS MEXICANOS. *Reverse:* A stylized sprig of wheat with three ears. One ear points horizontally to the left, the other horizontally to the right; the central, vertical ear divides the denomination 1 / C. At bottom left, the date; at bottom right, the mintmark M̊. *Diameter:* 13 mm. *Edge:* Smooth.

	Mintage	F	VF	EF	UNC	BU
1970	1,000,000	$0.10	$0.15	$0.45	$1.65	$1.90
1972, 2 Over 2	**	0.45	0.95	2.85	3.80	5.75
1972	1,000,000	0.10	0.15	0.45	1.90	2.85
1973	1,000,000	0.35	1.40	1.90	11.50	15.00

** Included below.

2 CENTAVOS

The 2 centavos under the Reform of 1905 fall into three basic types:

Type 1—Bronze (with the value depicted as a numeral superimposed on a horizontally shaded centavo symbol, ¢—i.e., as a "monogram"— but described by collectors according to its metallic composition)

Type 2—Zapatista (like Type 1, but struck at the Mexico City mint while it was under the control of Emiliano Zapata's Revolutionary troops; distinguishable from Type 1 coins of 1915 by their smaller size)

Type 3—Bronze (like Type 1, but with less tin and more zinc in the composition)

Type 1 (Bronze). BW-506, KM-419.

Composition: 0.950 copper, 0.040 tin, 0.010 zinc. *Weight:* 6 g. *Obverse:* The national coat of arms with the eagle facing forward, head to the right, above a spray of oak and laurel; above, the legend **ESTADOS UNIDOS MEXICANOS**. *Reverse:* At the center, within an open wreath of laurel, a large number 2 superimposed on a horizontally shaded centavo symbol (¢). At the top, between the wreath tips, the date; below the wreath, the mintmark M̥. *Diameter:* 25 mm. *Edge:* Smooth.

	Mintage	F	VF	EF	UNC	BU
1905	50,000	$140.00	$285.00	$430.00	$1,045.00	$1,425.00
1906, Wide Date	9,998,400	4.25	9.50	22.00	80.75	95.00
1906, Narrow Date	*	5.75	12.50	25.00	85.00	105.00
1906, Inverted 6	*	32.00	55.00	165.00	380.00	475.00

* Included above.

Type 2 (Zapatista). BW-507, KM-420.

Composition: 0.950 copper, 0.025 tin, 0.025 zinc. *Weight:* 3 g. *Obverse:* The national coat of arms with the eagle facing forward, head to the right, above a spray of oak and laurel; above, the legend **ESTADOS UNIDOS MEXICANOS**. *Reverse:* At the center, within an open wreath of laurel, a large number 2 superimposed on a horizontally shaded centavo symbol (¢). At the top, between the wreath tips, the date; below the wreath, the mintmark M̥. *Diameter:* 20 mm. *Edge:* Smooth.

Note: These reduced-size 2-centavo coins were struck at the Mexico City mint while it was under the control of Zapata's troops, and are commonly referred to as "Zapatista" coins.

	Mintage	F	VF	EF	UNC	BU
1915	486,980	$6.75	$9.50	$24.00	$65.00	$95.00

Type 3 (Bronze). BW-506.1, KM-419.

Composition: 0.950 copper, 0.025 tin, 0.025 zinc. *Weight:* 6 g. *Obverse:* The national coat of arms with the eagle facing forward, head to the right, above a spray of oak and laurel; above, the legend **ESTADOS UNIDOS MEXICANOS**. *Reverse:* At the center, within an open wreath of laurel, a large number 2 superimposed on a horizontally shaded centavo symbol (¢). At the top, between the wreath tips, the date; below the wreath, the mintmark M̊. *Diameter:* 25 mm. *Edge:* Smooth.

	Mintage	F	VF	EF	UNC	BU
1920	1,325,000	$4.75	$19.00	$50.00	$165.00	$285.00
1921	4,275,000	2.85	7.25	19.00	55.00	85.00
1922	[dash]	310.00	710.00	1,660.00	4,000.00	5,000.00
1924	750,000		24.00	55.00	260.00	330.00
1925	3,650,000	2.15	3.80	10.50	32.00	35.00
1926	4,750,000	0.95	2.85	7.75	28.00	32.00
1926, Large 6 Over Small 6	*	4.75	9.50	28.00	70.00	95.00
1927	7,250,000	0.85	3.00	5.75	22.00	30.00
1928	3,250,000	0.85	1.20	4.25	24.00	32.00
1929	250,000	70.00	165.00	215.00	525.00	710.00
1935	1,250,000	0.45	12.50	28.00	70.00	95.00
1939	5,000,000	0.45	0.95	3.80	20.00	28.00
1941	3,550,000	0.40	0.45	1.90	17.00	25.00

* Included above.

5 CENTAVOS

The Mexican 5 centavos under the Reform of 1905 were made in seven basic types:

Type 1—Nickel (with the value depicted as 5 CENTAVOS and surrounded by a historic Aztec border)

Type 2—Monogram (with the value depicted as a numeral superimposed on a horizontally shaded centavo symbol, ¢—i.e., as a "monogram")

Type 3—Aztec Calendar (with the border on the reverse depicting the ancient Aztec Calendar Stone, discussed in detail in appendix B)

Type 4—Josefa Grande (with a bust of Josefa Ortiz de Domínguez, insurgent supporter during the War of Independence)

Type 5—White Josefa (with a different bust of Josefa Ortiz de Domínguez, and with more nickel in the composition, yielding a whitish appearance)

Type 6—Brass (similar to Type 5, but in brass)

Type 7—Brass, Reduced (similar to Type 6, but 2.5 mm smaller in diameter)

Type 1 (Nickel). BW-508, KM-421.

Composition: 1.00 nickel. *Weight:* 5 g. *Obverse:* The national coat of arms with the eagle facing forward, head to the right, above a spray of oak and laurel; above, the legend **ESTADOS UNIDOS MEXICANOS**. *Reverse:* At the center, a large, horizontally shaded number 5 with **CENTAVOS** below and the date above. Between the date and the 5, the mintmark **M**. Surrounding all, a geometric border of quincunxes and points (after the Aztec Calendar Stone), with an inner ring of beads. *Diameter:* 20 mm. *Edge:* Smooth.

	Mintage	F	VF	EF	UNC	BU
1905	1,420,000	$4.75	$14.00	$38.00	$190.00	$260.00
1906, 6 Over 5	**	9.50	24.00	50.00	165.00	235.00
1906, Small Mintmark	10,614,000	0.95	1.90	5.75	55.00	70.00
1906, Large Mintmark	*	0.95	1.90	5.75	55.00	70.00
1907	4,000,000	1.90	4.75	19.00	285.00	355.00
1909	2,051,600	4.75	19.00	50.00	235.00	310.00
1910	6,181,200	1.90	4.75	14.00	80.75	120.00
1911, Narrow Date	4,486,925	0.95	2.85	5.75	55.00	70.00
1911, Wide Date	Inc. in above	1.90	4.75	11.50	70.00	95.00
1912, Small Mintmark	420,000	55.00	70.00	165.00	430.00	620.00
1912, Large Mintmark	*	42.00	60.00	140.00	355.00	570.00
1913, Narrow Date	2,035,000	1.65	3.80	9.50	95.00	165.00
1913, Wide Date	*	1.65	3.80	9.50	95.00	165.00
1914, Narrow Date	2,000,000	0.95	2.85	5.75	55.00	70.00
1914, Wide Date	*	1.90	4.75	11.50	70.00	95.00

* Included above. ** Included below.

Type 2 (Monogram). BW-509, KM-422.

Composition: 0.950 copper, 0.025 tin, 0.025 zinc. *Weight:* 9 g. *Obverse:* The national coat of arms with the eagle facing forward, head to the right, above a spray of oak and laurel; above, the legend **ESTADOS UNIDOS MEXICANOS**. *Reverse:* At the center, within an open wreath of laurel, a large number 5 superimposed on a horizontally shaded centavo symbol (¢). At the top, between the wreath tips, the date; below the wreath, the mintmark M̊. *Diameter:* 28 mm. *Edge:* Smooth.

The Coinage Reform of 1905 • 19

	Mintage	F	VF	EF	UNC	BU
1914	2,500,000	$7.75	$19.00	$50.00	$190.00	$235.00
1915	11,423,940	2.85	9.50	32.00	70.00	140.00
1916	2,860,000	14.00	32.00	120.00	475.00	570.00
1917	800,000	60.00	140.00	310.00	620.00	710.00
1918	1,332,000	19.00	50.00	120.00	475.00	570.00
1919	400,000	95.00	165.00	330.00	950.00	1,140.00
1920	5,920,000	4.75	19.00	38.00	140.00	285.00
1921	2,080,000	9.50	24.00	60.00	215.00	310.00
1924	780,000	28.00	50.00	120.00	475.00	570.00
1925	4,040,000	4.75	19.00	50.00	190.00	235.00
1926	3,160,000	4.75	19.00	50.00	190.00	235.00
1927	3,600,000	3.80	9.50	28.00	140.00	190.00
1928, Large Date	1,740,000	9.50	14.00	50.00	190.00	235.00
1928, Small Date	*	19.00	28.00	70.00	235.00	285.00
1929	2,400,000	3.80	9.50	32.00	70.00	140.00
1929, Large 29 Over Small 29	*	7.75	14.00	60.00	190.00	235.00
1930, Large Oval 0	2,600,000	4.75	14.00	32.00	165.00	215.00
1930, Small Square 0	*	19.00	50.00	120.00	310.00	400.00
1931		475.00	950.00	1,900.00	2,850.00	4,275.00
1933	8,000,000	0.95	1.90	2.85	24.00	32.00
1934	10,000,000	1.90	2.85	4.75	28.00	38.00
1935	21,980,000	0.95	1.90	2.85	24.00	32.00

* Included above.

Type 3 (Aztec Calendar). BW-510, KM-423.

Composition: 0.800 copper, 0.200 nickel. *Weight:* 4 g. *Obverse:* Above a spray of oak and laurel, the national coat of arms depicting the eagle in profile to the left, with thick, detailed, evenly spaced feathers and large, fleshy feet. Above, the legend **ESTADOS UNIDOS MEXICANOS**. *Reverse:* At the center, a large number 5 shaded in a basket-weave pattern, with **CENTAVOS** below and the date above. Between the date and the 5, the mintmark **M**. Surrounding all, a broad, elaborate border depicting the Ring of Splendor on the Aztec Calendar Stone. *Diameter:* 20.5 mm. *Edge:* Smooth.

	Mintage	F	VF	EF	UNC	BU
1936	46,700,000	$0.95	$1.90	$4.75	$11.50	$17.00
1937	49,060,000	0.95	1.90	4.75	11.50	17.00
1938	33,400,000	3.80	7.75	19.00	95.00	165.00
1940	22,800,000	0.45	0.95	1.20	10.50	12.50
1942	7,100,000	1.90	3.80	7.75	25.00	32.00

Type 4 (Josefa Grande). BW-511, KM-424.

Composition: 0.950 copper, 010 tin, 0.040 zinc. *Weight:* 6.5 g. *Obverse:* Above a spray of oak and laurel, the national coat of arms depicting the eagle in profile to the left, with stylized, blade-like feathers and large feet. Above, the legend ESTADOS UNIDOS MEXICANOS. *Reverse:* A left-facing head of Josefa Ortiz de Domínguez, with CINCO CENTAVOS and · [date] · surrounding and the mintmark M̊ in the field to the right of the head. *Diameter:* 25.5 mm. *Edge:* Smooth.

	Mintage	F	VF	EF	UNC	BU
1942	900,000	$6.75	$14.00	$70.00	$140.00	$260.00
1943	54,660,000	0.45	0.70	0.95	2.85	4.75
1944	53,463,120	0.25	0.45	0.70	1.90	2.85
1945	44,262,000	0.25	0.45	0.70	1.90	2.85
1946	49,054,000	0.25	0.45	0.70	1.90	2.85
1951	50,758,000	0.45	0.70	1.90	3.80	5.75
1952	17,674,000	1.40	2.85	4.75	9.50	13.00
1953	31,568,000	0.95	1.90	3.80	7.75	10.50
1954	58,680,000	0.45	0.70	0.95	2.85	4.75
1955	31,114,000	0.95	1.90	3.80	9.50	12.50

Type 5 (White Josefa). BW-512, KM-425.

Composition: 0.750 copper, 0.250 nickel. *Weight:* 4 g. *Obverse:* Above a spray of oak and laurel, the national coat of arms depicting the eagle in profile to the left, with stylized, leaf-like feathers and very large feet. Above, the legend ESTADOS UNIDOS MEXICANOS. *Reverse:* A right-facing bust of Josefa Ortiz de Domínguez. To left of the bust, 1950 above the mintmark M̊; to right of the bust, the number 5 above Cˢ (centavos) with a dot below. *Diameter:* 20.5 mm. *Edge:* Smooth.

	Mintage	F	VF	EF	UNC	BU
1950	5,700,000	$0.55	$0.95	$1.90	$5.75	$7.75

Josefa Ortiz de Domínguez

Josefa Ortiz was born to Spanish parents in Valladolid, Mexico, on April 19, 1773. Her parents died when she was a small child and she was cared for by an older sister. Because she was a Creole (of Spanish descent) she was accepted into a good school. She met her future husband, Miguel Domínguez, while in college. Married in 1791, they had 14 children.

Miguel Domínguez moved the family to Querétaro in 1802 when he was appointed a magistrate there. Josefa became committed to the independence movement and attended secret meetings with such revolutionaries as Father Miguel Hidalgo y Costilla and Ignacio Allende.

The revolt was planned to begin on December 8, 1810. In September of that year, the chief magistrate ordered his subordinate, Josefa's husband, to conduct a house-to-house raid looking for insurgents who might be stockpiling weapons in their homes. Miguel Domínguez locked his wife in her bedroom, both for her own protection and to prevent her from alerting her friends. The latter had prearranged a signal, however, and by stamping on her bedroom floor she was able to alert a conspirator who in turn warned the other rebels.

Father Hidalgo moved up the date of the revolution and issued what came to be known as the *grito de Dolores* (see page 131), a call to arms for a just and fair Mexican government, effectively declaring war on the Spanish authorities.

Josefa was arrested for treason and taken to Mexico City, where she was tried and convicted. She was imprisoned in a series of convents until her husband secured her release in 1817. The Mexican emperor, Agustín de Iturbide, offered Josefa a role at his court, but she declined, citing her republican ideals.

Josefa died in Mexico City on March 2, 1829. A plaza there is named for her. She is revered for her heroism in the War of Independence, her hatred of oppression, and her championing of indigenous peoples. While she remained proud of her Spanish blood, she opposed the caste system imposed by Spanish priests and identified herself as Mexican.

Type 6 (Brass). BW-513, KM-426.

Without dot at the back of the head.

With dot at the back of the head.

Composition: 0.850 copper, 0.150 zinc. *Weight:* 4 g. *Obverse:* Above a spray of oak and laurel, the national coat of arms depicting the eagle in profile to the left, with stylized, leaf-like feathers and very large feet. Above, the legend **ESTADOS UNIDOS MEXICANOS**. *Reverse:* A right-facing bust of Josefa Ortiz de Domínguez, with **CINCO CENTAVOS** above. In the field to the right of the bust, the mintmark M̥ above the date. *Diameter:* 20.5 mm. *Edge:* Smooth.

	Mintage	F	VF	EF	UNC	BU
1954, Dot		$4.75	$14.00	$50.00	$190.00	$235.00
1954, No Dot		2.85	6.75	28.00	140.00	190.00
1955	12,136,000	0.45	0.95	1.90	8.50	12.50
1956	60,216,000	0.25	0.45	0.95	1.90	2.85
1957	55,288,000	0.25	0.45	0.95	1.90	2.85
1958	104,624,000	0.15	0.35	0.70	1.20	1.90
1959	106,000,000	0.15	0.35	0.70	1.20	1.90
1960	99,144,000	0.15	0.35	0.70	1.20	1.90
1960, Copper-Nickel					310.00	330.00
1961	61,136,000	0.10	0.10	0.15	0.70	1.20
1962	47,232,000	0.10	0.10	0.15	0.70	1.20
1962, Copper-Nickel					310.00	330.00
1963	156,680,000	0.10	0.10	0.15	0.45	0.95
1963, Copper-Nickel					310.00	330.00
1964	71,168,000	0.10	0.10	0.15	0.45	0.95
1965	155,720,000	0.10	0.10	0.15	0.45	0.95
1965, Copper-Nickel					330.00	355.00
1966	124,944,000	0.10	0.10	0.15	0.45	0.95
1967	118,819,000	0.10	0.10	0.15	0.45	0.95
1968	189,588,000	0.10	0.10	0.15	0.45	0.95
1969	210,492,000	0.10	0.10	0.15	0.45	0.95

Type 7 (Brass, Reduced). BW-514, KM-427.

The 1973 varieties with Flat-Top 3 (left) and Round-Top 3.

Composition: 0.850 copper, 0.150 zinc. *Weight:* 2.75 g. *Obverse:* Above a spray of oak and laurel, the national coat of arms depicting the eagle in profile to the left, with the feathers and other elements drawn as outlines instead of in full relief. Above, the legend **ESTADOS UNIDOS MEXICANOS**. *Reverse:* A right-facing bust of Josefa Ortiz de Domínguez, with **CINCO CENTAVOS M̥ [date]** surrounding. *Diameter:* 18 mm. *Edge:* Smooth.

	Mintage	F	VF	EF	UNC	BU
1970	163,368,000	$0.10	$0.10	$0.15	$0.40	$0.45
1971	198,844,000	0.10	0.10	0.15	0.40	0.45
1972	225,000,00	0.10	0.10	0.15	0.40	0.45
1973, Flat-Top 3	595,070,000	0.10	0.10	0.15	0.40	0.45
1973, Round-Top 3	*	0.10	0.10	0.15	0.40	0.45
1974	401,584,000	0.10	0.10	0.15	0.40	0.45
1975	342,308,000	0.10	0.10	0.15	0.40	0.45
1976	367,524,000	0.10	0.10	0.15	0.40	0.45

* Included above.

10 CENTAVOS

The 10 centavos under the Reform of 1905 were made in seven basic types:

Type 1—.800 (with small radiant liberty cap on the reverse)

Type 2—Little .800 (like Type 1, but 3 mm smaller in diameter, and with slightly different composition)

Type 3—Large Bronze (with the value depicted as a numeral superimposed on a horizontally shaded centavo symbol, ¢—i.e., as a "monogram"—but described by its size and composition)

Type 4—.720, Monogram (same as Type 2, but with reduced silver content)

Type 5—Aztec Calendar (with the border on the reverse depicting the ancient Aztec Calendar Stone, discussed in detail in appendix B)

Type 6—Juárez (depicting Revolutionary president Benito Juárez García)

Type 7—Ear of Corn (depicting an ear of corn or *maize*, an agricultural staple)

Type 1 (.800). BW-515, KM-428.

Composition: 0.800 silver, 0.200 copper. *Weight:* 2.5 g. *Obverse:* The national coat of arms with the eagle facing forward, head to the right, above a spray of oak and laurel; above, the legend **ESTADOS UNIDOS MEXICANOS**. *Reverse:* At the top, above an open wreath of oak and laurel, a small radiant liberty cap. On the radiance below the cap, a large, horizontally shaded number 10 with **CENTAVOS / [date]** below. The mintmark **M** is below and slightly between the digits of the denomination. *Diameter:* 18 mm. *Edge:* Reeded.

	Mintage	F	VF	EF	UNC	BU
1905	3,920,000	$5.75	$6.75	$9.50	$32.00	$42.00
1906	8,410,000	4.75	5.75	7.75	26.00	32.00
1906, Low 6	*	5.75	6.75	9.50	32.00	42.00
1907, Straight 7	5,950,000	4.75	5.75	7.75	24.00	32.00
1907, Curved 7	*	5.75	6.75	9.50	32.00	42.00
1907, 7 Over 6	*	42.00	70.00	215.00	330.00	430.00
1909	2,620,000	6.75	8.50	14.00	70.00	95.00
1910	3,450,000	5.75	6.75	9.50	24.00	28.00
1910, 10 Over 00	*	9.50	14.00	50.00	90.00	120.00
1911, Narrow Date	25,950,000	6.75	8.50	14.00	70.00	95.00
1911, Wide Date	*	4.75	6.75	9.50	38.00	60.00
1912	1,350,000	6.75	8.50	16.00	70.00	95.00
1912, Low 2	*	9.50	14.00	50.00	90.00	120.00
1913	1,990,000	4.75	6.75	9.50	32.00	50.00
1913, 3 Over 2		6.75	9.50	19.00	70.00	95.00
1914, Narrow Date	2,119,000	2.85	4.75	5.75	14.00	19.00
1914, Wide Date	*	2.85	4.75	5.75	11.50	14.00

* Included above.

Type 2 (Little .800). BW-516, KM-429.

Composition: 0.800 silver, 0.200 copper. *Weight:* 1.8125 g. *Obverse:* The national coat of arms with the eagle facing forward, head to the right, above a spray of oak and laurel; above, the legend **ESTADOS UNIDOS MEXICANOS**. *Reverse:* At the top, above an open wreath of oak and laurel, a small radiant liberty cap. On the radiance below the cap, a large, horizontally shaded number 10 with **CENTAVOS / 1919** below. The mintmark **M** is below and slightly between the digits of the denomination. *Diameter:* 15 mm. *Edge:* Reeded.

	Mintage	F	VF	EF	UNC	BU
1919	8,360,000	$7.75	$9.50	$19.00	$70.00	$95.00

Type 3 (Large Bronze). BW-517, KM-430.

Composition: 0.950 copper, 0.025 tin, 0.025 zinc. *Weight:* 12 g. *Obverse:* The national coat of arms with the eagle facing forward, head to the right, above a spray of oak and laurel; above, the legend **ESTADOS UNIDOS MEXICANOS**. *Reverse:* At the center, within an open wreath of laurel, a large number 10 superimposed on a horizontally shaded centavo symbol (¢). At the top, between the wreath tips, the date; below the wreath, the mintmark M̊. *Diameter:* 30.5 mm. *Edge:* Plain.

	Mintage	F	VF	EF	UNC	BU
1919	1,232,000	$19.00	$28.00	$70.00	$260.00	$310.00
1920	6,612,000	24.00	32.00	120.00	330.00	430.00
1921	2,255,000	24.00	32.00	140.00	400.00	500.00
1935	5,970,000	14.00	19.00	42.00	120.00	215.00

Type 4 (.720, Monogram). BW-518, KM-431.

Composition: 0.720 silver, 0.280 copper. *Weight:* 1.666 g. *Obverse:* The national coat of arms with the eagle facing forward, head to the right, above a spray of oak and laurel; above, the legend **ESTADOS UNIDOS MEXICANOS**. *Reverse:* At the top, above an open wreath of oak and laurel, a small radiant liberty cap. On the radiance below the cap, a large, horizontally shaded number 10 with **CENTAVOS** / [date] below. The mintmark M is below and slightly between the digits of the denomination. *Diameter:* 15 mm. *Edge:* Reeded.

	Mintage	F	VF	EF	UNC	BU
1925	5,350,000	$1.90	$2.85	$3.80	$32.00	$42.00
1925, 25 Over 15	*	14.00	24.00	42.00	110.00	140.00
1925, 5 Over 3	*	14.00	24.00	42.00	110.00	140.00
1926	2,650,000	4.75	8.50	19.00	55.00	80.75
1926, 26 Over 16	*	19.00	32.00	70.00	120.00	165.00
1927	2,810,000	1.90	2.85	3.80	17.00	20.00
1927, 27 Over 17	*	7.75	14.00	28.00	55.00	80.75

* Included above.

Type 4 (.720, Monogram). BW-518, *continued*

	Mintage	F	VF	EF	UNC	BU
1928	5,270,000	1.90	2.85	4.75	9.50	11.50
1930	2,000,000	2.85	3.80	7.75	17.00	24.00
1933 (a)	5,000,000	1.90	2.85	4.75	9.50	11.50
1934	8,000,000	0.95	1.90	2.85	7.75	9.50
1935	3,500,000	2.85	3.80	7.75	14.00	19.00

a. Varieties with low/high 33 exist; they are valued the same as the normal-date variety.

Type 5 (Aztec Calendar). BW-519, KM-432.

Composition: 0.800 copper, 0.200 nickel. *Weight:* 5.5 g. *Obverse:* Above a spray of oak and laurel, the national coat of arms depicting the eagle in profile to the left, with thick, detailed, evenly spaced feathers and large, fleshy feet. Above, the legend **ESTADOS UNIDOS MEXICANOS**. *Reverse:* At the center, a large number 10 shaded in a basket-weave pattern, with **CENTAVOS** below and the date above. Between the date and the 10, the mintmark **M**. Surrounding all, a broad, elaborate border depicting the Ring of Splendor on the Aztec Calendar Stone. *Diameter:* 23.5 mm. *Edge:* Plain.

	Mintage	F	VF	EF	UNC	BU
1936	33,030,000	$0.95	$1.90	$4.75	$11.50	$16.00
1937	3,000,000	9.50	14.00	55.00	150.00	190.00
1938	3,650,000	2.85	4.75	14.00	55.00	85.00
1939	6,920,000	0.95	1.90	6.75	30.00	42.00
1940	12,300,000	0.25	0.45	1.90	4.75	6.75
1942	14,380,000	0.95	1.90	3.80	7.75	9.50
1945	9,557,500	0.25	0.45	1.90	4.75	6.75
1946	46,230,000	0.25	0.45	1.90	4.75	6.75

Type 6 (Juárez). BW-520, KM-433.

Composition: 0.950 copper, 0.050 zinc. *Weight:* 5.5 g. *Obverse:* Above a spray of oak and laurel, the national coat of arms depicting the eagle in profile to the left, with stylized, leaf-like feathers and very large feet. Above, the legend **ESTADOS UNIDOS MEXICANOS**. *Reverse:* A left-facing bust of Benito Juárez García, with **DIEZ CENTAVOS Mo [date]** surrounding. *Diameter:* 23.5 mm. *Edge:* Plain.

	Mintage	F	VF	EF	UNC	BU
1955	1,817,500	$0.95	$1.90	$5.75	$19.00	$24.00
1956	5,255,000	0.95	1.90	3.80	14.00	19.00
1957	11,925,000	0.25	0.45	0.95	2.85	4.75
1959	26,140,000	0.25	0.45	0.70	1.90	2.85
1966	5,872,500	0.25	0.45	0.70	1.90	2.85
1967	32,317,500	0.25	0.45	0.70	0.95	1.90

Benito Juárez García

Benito Pablo Juárez García was born on March 21, 1806, to Zapoteco Indian parents in the village of San Pablo Guelatao, Oaxaca. When he was three years old his parents died, and he was sent to live with his grandparents and later an uncle. As a child, he worked both in the cornfields and as a shepherd, until he joined his older sister in Oaxaca de Juárez when he was 12. He enrolled in school and was a determined student despite knowing little or no Spanish.

As an adult he entered the seminary but left to study law. Shortly after attaining his law degree, he began his political career as a city alderman, later becoming a judge. Juárez married Margarita Maza Parada in 1843 and served as governor of Oaxaca from 1847 until 1852. As governor, he improved the state's finances, doubled the number of schools, and built roads and ports.

In December 1853 Juárez was exiled to Cuba by Mexico's dictator, Antonio Lopéz de Santa Anna, along with a number of prominent liberals. After being transferred to New Orleans, he spent two years planning his return to Mexico and developing ideas for reform. Juárez's opportunity came when the liberals returned to power in 1855 and he became minister of justice. In 1857 he was chosen to be lead justice of the Supreme Court, and in the same year he and fellow liberals promulgated a new constitution.

A Freemason and eventually an effective, five-time president of Mexico, Benito Juárez is one of Mexico's most beloved national heroes. He is credited with fighting French occupation, lessening the power of the Catholic Church, and establishing Mexico as a constitutional democracy and federal republic. He fought to raise rural Mexicans out of poverty, while facing discrimination through his entire career due to his indigenous origins. His period of leadership is known as *La Reforma del Norte* (The Reform of the North). He died in office in 1872.

Type 7 (Ear of Corn). BW-521, KM-434.

Composition: 0.750 copper, 0.250 zinc. *Weight:* 1.485 g. *Obverse:* Above a spray of oak and laurel, the national coat of arms depicting the eagle in profile to the left, with the feathers and other elements drawn as outlines instead of in full relief. Above, the legend **ESTADOS UNIDOS MEXICANOS**. *Reverse:* At the center, a partially shucked ear of corn on a plain field. In the upper part of the field, divided by the ear, 10 / Cs. In the lower part of the field, divided by the stem, the date and mintmark M̥. *Diameter:* 15 mm. *Edge:* Paired reeding.

	Mintage	F	VF	EF	UNC	BU
1974, 6 Rows, Sharp	6,000,000	$0.10	$0.10	$0.25	$0.70	$0.95
1975, 5 Rows, Sharp	5,550,000	0.10	0.10	0.25	0.70	0.95
1976, 5 Rows, Sharp	7,680,000	0.10	0.10	0.25	0.70	0.95
1977, 5 Rows, Thin	144,650,000	0.10	0.45	0.95	1.40	1.90
1977, 6 Rows, Blunt/Thick	*	0.10	0.15	0.25	0.70	0.95
1978, 6 Rows, Blunt/Thick	271,870,000	0.10	0.45	0.95	1.40	1.90
1978, 5 Rows, Long/Thin	*	0.10	0.45	0.95	1.40	1.90
1978, Doubled Die	*	120.00	165.00	190.00	215.00	260.00
1979, 5 Rows, Long/Thin	375,660,000	0.10	0.25	0.45	0.95	1.40
1979, 6 Rows, Long/Thin	*	0.10	0.15	0.25	0.70	0.95
1980, 6 Rows, Long/Blunt	21,290,000	0.10	0.15	0.25	0.70	0.95
1980, 80 Over 79, 6 Rows, Long/Blunt	*	1.90	2.85	4.75	6.75	9.50

Note: "Rows" refers to rows of corn. The words "Sharp," "Thin," etc., refer to stem styles. * Included above.

Type 7: Row and Stem Varieties

Variety collectors have a wide range of choices when it comes to the Ear of Corn reverse. The corn can have five or six rows of kernels, and the stem style can vary in length, thickness, and sharpness. Four of the common style combinations are illustrated here.

5 rows of corn; stem long and thin.

6 rows of corn; stem sharp.

6 rows of corn; stem blunt and thick.

6 rows of corn; stem long and thin.

20 CENTAVOS

The 20 centavos under the Reform of 1905 were made in nine basic types:

Type 1—.800 (with small radiant liberty cap on the reverse)

Type 2—Little .800 (like Type 1, but 3 mm smaller in diameter)

Type 3—Monogram (with the value depicted as a numeral superimposed on a horizontally shaded centavo symbol, ¢—i.e., as a "monogram")

Type 4—.720 (same as Type 2, but with reduced silver content)

Type 5—Pyramid (depicting the Aztec Pyramid of the Sun at Teotihuacán)

Type 6—New Eagle (like Type 5, but with the eagle redesigned to have stylized, leaf-like feathers and very large feet)

Type 7—Restyled Eagle (like Type 6, but with the obverse further redesigned such that all the devices are depicted as raised outlines on a flat surface, rather than as fully contoured shapes)

Type 8—Madero (depicting Francisco Madero, first president of the Revolutionary government)

Type 9—Olmec (honoring the ancient Mesoamerican culture with a depiction of an Olmec "colossal head" statue)

Type 1 (.800). BW-522, KM-435.

Composition: 0.800 silver, 0.200 copper. *Weight:* 5 g. *Obverse:* The national coat of arms with the eagle facing forward, head to the right, above a spray of oak and laurel; above, the legend **ESTADOS UNIDOS MEXICANOS**. *Reverse:* At the top, above an open wreath of oak and laurel, a small radiant liberty cap. On the radiance below the cap, a horizontally shaded number **20** with **CENTAVOS / [date]** below. The mintmark **M** is below and slightly between the digits of the denomination. *Diameter:* 22 mm. *Edge:* Reeded.

	Mintage	F	VF	EF	UNC	BU
1905	2,565,000	$6.75	$9.50	$28.00	$85.00	$120.00
1906	6,860,000	5.75	7.75	14.00	38.00	60.00
1907, Straight 7	9,434,699	6.75	8.50	19.00	55.00	110.00
1907, Curved 7	*	6.75	9.50	28.00	85.00	120.00
1908	350,000	38.00	70.00	215.00	1,520.00	2,150.00
1910	1,135,000	8.50	9.50	28.00	85.00	120.00
1910, Second 1 Over Inverted 1	*	8.50	9.50	19.00	75.00	95.00

* Included above.

Type 1 (.800). BW-522, continued

	Mintage	F	VF	EF	UNC	BU
1911	1,150,000	11.50	14.00	32.00	95.00	125.00
1912	625,000	19.00	38.00	95.00	215.00	285.00
1913	1,000,000	12.50	14.00	28.00	95.00	120.00
1914, Narrow Date	1,500,000	12.50	14.00	28.00	95.00	120.00
1914, Wide Date	*	12.50	14.00	28.00	95.00	120.00

* Included above.

Type 2 (Little .800). BW-523, KM-436.

Composition: 0.800 silver, 0.200 copper. *Weight:* 3.525 g. *Obverse:* The national coat of arms with the eagle facing forward, head to the right, above a spray of oak and laurel; above, the legend **ESTADOS UNIDOS MEXICANOS**. *Reverse:* At the top, above an open wreath of oak and laurel, a small radiant liberty cap. On the radiance below the cap, a horizontally shaded number **20** with **CENTAVOS / 1919** below. The mintmark **M** is below and slightly between the digits of the denomination. *Diameter:* 19 mm. *Edge:* Reeded.

	Mintage	F	VF	EF	UNC	BU
1919	4,155,000	$9.50	$28.00	$70.00	$165.00	$215.00

Type 3 (Monogram). BW-524, KM-437.

Composition: 0.950 copper, 025 tin, 0.025 zinc. *Weight:* 15 g. *Obverse:* The national coat of arms with the eagle facing forward, head to the right, above a spray of oak and laurel; above, the legend **ESTADOS UNIDOS MEXICANOS**. *Reverse:* At the center, within an open wreath of laurel, a large number **20** superimposed on a horizontally shaded centavo symbol (¢). At the top, between the wreath tips, the date; below the wreath, the mintmark M̊. *Diameter:* 32.5 mm. *Edge:* Plain.

	Mintage	F	VF	EF	UNC	BU
1920	4,835,450	$24.00	$70.00	$190.00	$450.00	$570.00
1935	20,000,000	4.75	14.00	32.00	70.00	95.00

Type 4 (.720). BW-525, KM-438.

Composition: 0.720 silver, 0.280 copper. *Weight:* 3.333 g. *Obverse:* The national coat of arms with the eagle facing forward, head to the right, above a spray of oak and laurel; above, the legend **ESTADOS UNIDOS MEXICANOS**. *Reverse:* At the top, above an open wreath of oak and laurel, a small radiant liberty cap. On the radiance below the cap, a horizontally shaded number **20** with **CENTAVOS / [date]** below. The mintmark **M** is below and slightly between the digits of the 20. *Diameter:* 19 mm. *Edge:* Reeded.

	Mintage	F	VF	EF	UNC	BU
1920	3,710,000	$9.50	$14.00	$28.00	$140.00	$190.00
1921	6,160,000	9.50	14.00	19.00	110.00	140.00
1925	1,450,000	9.50	14.00	28.00	120.00	165.00
1926, 6 Over 5	*	19.00	32.00	70.00	310.00	380.00
1926	1,465,000	7.75	14.00	28.00	95.00	165.00
1927	1,405,000	7.75	14.00	28.00	95.00	165.00
1928	3,630,000	3.80	4.75	7.75	12.50	19.00
1930 (a)	1,000,000	6.75	9.50	24.00	38.00	70.00
1933 (b)	2,500,000	3.80	5.75	6.75	9.50	14.00
1934	2,500,000	3.80	5.75	6.75	9.50	14.00
1935	2,460,000	3.80	5.75	6.75	9.50	14.00
1937	10,000,000	3.80	4.75	5.75	6.75	7.75
1939	8,800,000	3.80	4.75	5.75	6.75	7.75
1940	3,000,000	3.80	4.75	5.75	6.75	7.75
1941	5,740,000	3.80	4.75	5.75	6.75	7.75
1942	12,460,000	3.80	4.75	5.75	6.75	7.75
1943	3,955,000	3.80	4.75	5.75	6.75	7.75

* Included above. **a.** Varieties with low/high 0 exist; they are valued the same as the normal-date variety. **b.** A variety with high second 3 exists; it is valued the same as the normal-date variety.

Type 5 (Pyramid). BW-526, KM-439.

Composition: 0.950 copper, 0.040 zinc, 0.010 tin. *Weight:* 10 g. *Obverse:* Above a spray of oak and laurel, the national coat of arms depicting the eagle in profile to the left, with stylized, blade-like feathers and large, fleshy feet. Above, the legend **ESTADOS UNIDOS MEXICANOS**. *Reverse:* At the center, the Pyramid of the Sun, with the location **TEOTIHUACAN** engraved at the base and, in the background, the volcanoes Ixtaccíhuatl and Popocatépetl. At the top, a small radiant liberty cap; on the radiance, divided by the cap, an outlined number **20**. Below the radiance, the mintmark M̊. At the bottom, in two lines and flanked by a saguaro cactus (left) and a nopal cactus (right), **CENTAVOS** and the date. *Diameter:* 28.5 mm. *Edge:* Plain.

	Mintage	F	VF	EF	UNC	BU
1943	46,350,000	$0.95	$1.90	$2.85	$9.50	$19.00
1944	83,650,000	0.95	1.90	2.85	11.50	24.00
1945	26,800,500	0.95	1.90	2.85	9.50	19.00
1946	25,695,000	0.45	0.95	1.90	5.75	7.75
1951 (a)	11,385,000	2.85	4.75	19.00	80.75	95.00
1952	6,559,500	2.85	4.75	14.00	55.00	70.00
1953	26,947,500	0.45	0.95	1.90	7.75	12.50
1954	40,108,000	0.45	0.95	1.90	7.75	12.50
1955	16,950,000	2.85	4.75	14.00	55.00	70.00

a. Composition: 0.950 copper, 0.050 zinc

Type 6 (New Eagle). BW-527, KM-440.

Composition: 0.950 copper, 0.050 zinc. *Weight:* 10 g. *Obverse:* Above a spray of oak and laurel, the national coat of arms depicting the eagle in profile to the left, with stylized, leaf-like feathers and very large feet. Above, the legend **ESTADOS UNIDOS MEXICANOS**. *Reverse:* At the center, the Pyramid of the Sun, with the location **TEOTIHUACAN** engraved at the base and, in the background, the volcanoes Ixtaccíhuatl and Popocatépetl. At the top, a small radiant liberty cap; on the radiance, divided by the cap, an outlined number **20**. Below the radiance, the mintmark M̊. At the bottom, in two lines and flanked by a saguaro cactus (left) and a nopal cactus (right), **CENTAVOS** and the date. *Diameter:* 28.5 mm. *Edge:* Plain.

	Mintage	F	VF	EF	UNC	BU
1955	(a)	$0.95	$1.90	$2.85	$11.50	$24.00
1956	22,431,000	0.25	0.45	0.95	3.80	5.75
1957	13,455,000	0.70	1.90	3.80	6.75	9.50
1959	6,016,500	1.90	4.75	14.00	60.00	75.00
1960	39,756,000	0.25	0.45	0.95	1.90	2.85
1963	14,869,000	0.25	0.45	0.95	1.90	2.85
1964	28,653,500	0.25	0.45	0.95	1.90	2.85

a. Included in mintage for 1955, Type 5.

	Mintage	F	VF	EF	UNC	BU
1965	74,161,500	0.25	0.45	0.95	1.90	2.85
1966	43,744,500	0.25	0.45	0.95	1.90	2.85
1967	46,486,500	0.25	0.45	0.95	1.90	2.85
1968	15,477,000	0.25	0.45	0.95	1.90	2.85
1969	63,646,500	0.25	0.45	0.95	1.90	2.85
1970	76,287,000	0.25	0.45	0.95	1.90	2.85
1971	49,891,500	0.25	0.45	0.95	1.90	2.85

Pyramid of the Sun

Located in the city of Teotihuacán along the broad Avenue of the Dead, the famous Pyramid of the Sun—more than 200 feet tall and 700 feet wide—is one of Mexico's largest structures from ancient civilization. At its height, Teotihuacán was a major metropolis with a population of more than 100,000. The city was built long before the Nahuatl-speaking Mexica (Aztecs) migrated into the area, and was filled with pyramidal temple buildings as large as those found in Egypt.

The Pyramid of the Sun is situated over a large, clover-shaped underground cave, which appears to have served as a place of ancient fire and water rituals. It was possibly a "place of emergence"—a womb-like cave resembling those found in universal creation myths and stories about the underworld. The pyramid on top was constructed in phases. The first made it nearly the size it is now. The second phase saw the addition of more ritualistic elements, such as an altar on top. The surface of the temple was finished with lime plaster, then covered with vivid murals featuring the jaguar, snake, and star motifs seen on other, similarly aged structures. Thanks to centuries of looting and intentional destruction of the ritual areas, the temple's purpose (including whether it was dedicated to a particular deity), along with the purpose of the cave below, is unknown.

In recent years, scientists from the National Autonomous University (UNAM) imaged the building to look for hidden tunnels in the earth-filled interior. They discovered that the 3-million-ton volcanic-stone structure may eventually be in danger of collapse, due—ironically—to exposure to the sun and consequent drying-out of the supporting soil.

Type 7 (Restyled Eagle). BW-528, KM-441.

Composition: 0.950 copper, 0.050 zinc. *Weight:* 9.8 g. *Obverse:* Above a spray of oak and laurel, the national coat of arms depicting the eagle in profile to the left, with the feathers and other elements drawn as outlines instead of in full relief. Above, the legend **ESTADOS UNIDOS MEXICANOS**. *Reverse:* At the center, the Pyramid of the Sun, with the location **TEOTIHUACAN** engraved at the base and, in the background, the volcanoes Ixtaccíhuatl and Popocatépetl. At the top, a small radiant liberty cap; on the radiance, divided by the cap, an outlined number **20**. Below the radiance, the mintmark M̥. At the bottom, in two lines and flanked by a saguaro cactus (left) and a nopal cactus (right), **CENTAVOS** and the date. *Diameter:* 28.5 mm. *Edge:* Plain.

	Mintage	F	VF	EF	UNC	BU
1971	(a)	$0.25	$0.45	$0.95	$1.90	$2.85
1973	78,398,000	0.25	0.45	0.95	1.90	2.85
1974	34,200,000	0.25	0.45	0.95	1.90	2.85

a. Included in mintage for 1971, Type 6.

Type 8 (Madero). BW-529, KM-442.

The date of the 1981, 81 Over 82, variety.

Composition: 0.750 copper, 0.250 nickel. *Weight:* 3 g. *Obverse:* Above a spray of oak and laurel, the national coat of arms depicting the eagle in profile to the left, with the feathers and other elements drawn as outlines instead of in full relief. Above, the legend **ESTADOS UNIDOS MEXICANOS**. *Reverse:* On a plain field, a bust of Francisco Madero in semi-profile to the right. To the left of the bust, the mintmark M̥ and the date; to the right of the bust, **20$^{c.}$**. *Diameter:* 20 mm. *Edge:* Paired reeding.

	Mintage	F	VF	EF	UNC	BU	PF
1974	112,000,000	$0.10	$0.10	$0.15	$0.35	$0.45	
1975	611,000,000	0.10	0.10	0.15	0.35	0.45	
1976	394,000,000	0.10	0.10	0.15	0.35	0.45	
1977	394,350,000	0.10	0.10	0.15	0.35	0.45	
1977, Doubled-Die Reverse	*	95.00	140.00	190.00	260.00	310.00	
1978	527,950,000	0.10	0.10	0.15	0.35	0.45	
1978, Doubled-Die Reverse	*	50.00	70.00	120.00	165.00	235.00	
1979	4,615,000	0.10	0.10	0.15	0.35	0.45	
1979, Doubled-Die Reverse	*	50.00	70.00	120.00	165.00	235.00	
1980	326,500,000	0.10	0.10	0.15	0.35	0.45	
1980, 80 Over 79	*	3.80	5.75	9.50	14.00	19.00	
1981, Open 8	248,500,000	0.25	0.45	0.70	1.20	1.90	
1981, Closed 8, High Date	*	0.25	0.45	0.70	1.20	1.90	
1981, Closed 8, Low Date	*	0.45	0.95	1.90	3.80	4.75	
1981, 1 Over 2	*	19.00	38.00	75.00	150.00	175.00	
1982, Short Lapel	**	0.25	0.45	0.70	0.95	1.40	
1982, Long Lapel	286,855,000	0.25	0.45	0.70	0.95	1.40	
1983, Round-Top 3	100,930,000	0.25	0.45	0.70	1.20	1.90	
1983, Flat-Top 3	*	0.25	0.45	0.70	1.20	1.90	
1983, Proof	1,048						$38.00

* Included above. ** Included below.

Type 9 (Olmec). BW-530, KM-491.

Composition: 0.950 copper, 0.050 zinc. *Weight:* 3.04 g. *Obverse:* Above a spray of oak and laurel, the national coat of arms depicting the eagle in profile to the left, with feathers resembling plates of armor. Above, the legend **ESTADOS UNIDOS MEXICANOS**. *Reverse:* Slightly above center, an Olmec colossal-head statue; to the left, placed vertically, the words **culturo olmeco**. From the end of "olmeco," a slender, chainlike design wraps fully around the head and returns to the field at far left. To the right of the head, the date is superimposed over the chain; below the head, a large **20¢**. The mintmark M̊ is at far left, at the end of the chain. *Diameter:* 20 mm. *Edge:* Reeded.

	Mintage	F	VF	EF	UNC	BU	PF
1983	200,000,000	$0.10	$0.20	$0.25	$1.30	$2.50	
1983, Proof	50						$165.00
1984	180,320,000	0.10	0.20	0.25	1.30	2.50	

Francisco Madero

Francisco Madero was born on October 30, 1873, in the northern state of Coahuila, to one of the wealthiest families in Mexico. Madero is credited with starting the Mexican Revolution, which ousted dictator Porfirio Díaz. Madero served as president from 1911 until his assassination in 1913 by Victoriano Huerta, one of Díaz's former generals.

After studying business and agriculture in the United States and Europe, Madero returned to Mexico to run some of his family's businesses. When his early attempts at running for public office failed, he funded several newspapers in order to advance his reformist ideas.

A Spiritualist, Madero idolized Benito Juárez García and his democratic ideals. In 1908 Madero wrote a book that he said was at the direction of the spirits, including that of Juárez himself. Titled *The Presidential Succession of 1910,* the book insisted that the dictatorial reign of Díaz must end. When Díaz promised the Mexican people free elections in 1910, Madero decided to run for president.

Díaz had initially vowed not to run for reelection, but he reneged; and when Madero's campaign proved popular, Díaz had Madero arrested. After escaping prison Madero fled to San Antonio and called for an armed revolution. The revolt was supported by Emiliano Zapata, Pascual Orozco, and Francisco ("Pancho") Villa, who raised armies in support of the cause.

When he realized his forces were beaten, Díaz surrendered and was allowed to leave the country. Madero was elected president but was unprepared for the political realities he was up against. To some of his former supporters in the revolution, he was not radical enough. He did little to dismantle the power structure that favored wealthy families like his own.

In 1912, Orozco rebelled against Madero but was defeated by Victoriano Huerta. General Huerta later turned against Madero when the latter refused to punish Pancho Villa for not following Huerta's orders. The U.S. ambassador to Mexico, concerned about foreign business investments there, conspired with Huerta and Díaz's nephew to stage a coup in which Madero was overthrown and assassinated.

25 CENTAVOS

The 25 centavos under the Reform of 1905 fall into two basic types:

Types 1—Scales (with the classic Balance Scale design on the reverse)

Type 2—Madero (depicting Francisco Madero, first president of the Revolutionary government)

Type 1 (Scales). BW-531, KM-443.

Composition: 0.500 copper, 0.300 silver, 0.100 nickel, 0.100 zinc. *Weight:* 3.333 g. *Obverse:* Above a spray of oak and laurel, the national coat of arms depicting the eagle in profile to the left, with stylized, leaf-like feathers and very large feet. Above, the legend **ESTADOS UNIDOS MEXICANOS**. *Reverse:* Below a small radiant liberty cap, a crossed sword and balance scale; between the pans of the scale, a scroll bearing the word **LEY**. In the field near the top, divided by the liberty cap, 25 / **Cs**. At the bottom, **Mo · [date]**. *Diameter:* 21.5 mm. *Edge:* Reeded.

	Mintage	F	VF	EF	UNC	BU
1950	77,060,000	$0.25	$0.45	$0.95	$1.40	$1.90
1951	41,172,000	0.25	0.45	0.95	1.40	1.90
1952	29,264,000	0.25	0.70	1.20	1.90	2.85
1953	38,144,000	0.25	0.45	0.95	1.40	1.90

Type 2 (Madero). BW-532, KM-444.

1966 Closed Beak (left) and Open Beak varieties.

Composition: 0.750 copper, 0.250 nickel. *Weight:* 5.5 g. *Obverse:* Above a spray of oak and laurel, the national coat of arms depicting the eagle in profile to the left, with stylized, scale-like feathers and large feet. Above, the legend **ESTADOS UNIDOS MEXICANOS**. *Reverse:* A bust of Francisco Madero in three-quarter profile to the right, with **VEINTICINCO CENTAVOS [date]** surrounding. Mintmark M̊ to the right of the bust, near the date. *Diameter:* 23 mm. *Edge:* Reeded.

	Mintage	F	VF	EF	UNC	BU
1964	20,686,000	$0.15	$0.25	$0.45	$0.70	$0.95
1966, Closed Beak	180,000	0.45	0.95	1.90	2.85	4.75
1966, Open Beak	*	1.90	3.80	5.75	10.50	14.00

* Included above.

50 CENTAVOS

The 50 centavos under the Reform of 1905 were made in nine basic types:

Type 1—.800 (with small radiant liberty cap on the reverse)

Type 2—.800, Reduced (like Type 1, but 3 mm smaller in diameter)

Type 3—.720 (like Type 2, but with reduced silver content)

Type 4—.420 (like Type 3, but with further reduced silver content)

Type 5—Cuauhtémoc (depicting the famed Aztec leader of that name)

Type 6—Big Cuauhtémoc (with Aztec-style profile bust of the leader, and 7 mm larger in diameter than Type 5)

Type 7—Copper-nickel (like Type 6, but with a copper-nickel composition, and 8 mm smaller in diameter)

Type 8—Stylized Eagle (like Type 7, but with the obverse redesigned such that all the devices are depicted as raised outlines on a flat surface, rather than as fully contoured shapes)

Type 9—Palenque (honoring ancient Mesoamerican culture with a depiction of Pakal the Great, leader of the Mayan city of Palenque)

Type 1 (.800). BW-533, KM-445.

Composition: 0.800 silver, 0.200 copper. *Weight:* 12.5 g. *Obverse:* The national coat of arms with the eagle facing forward, head to the right, above a spray of oak and laurel; above, the legend ESTADOS UNIDOS MEXICANOS. *Reverse:* At the top, above an open wreath of oak and laurel, a small radiant liberty cap. On the radiance below the cap, a horizontally shaded number 50 with CENTAVOS / [date] below. The mintmark M is below and slightly between the digits of the denomination. *Diameter:* 30 mm. *Edge:* Lettered INDEPENDENCIA Y LIBERTAD.

	Mintage	F	VF	EF	UNC	BU
1905	2,446,000	$11.50	$17.00	$40.00	$120.00	$165.00
1906, Open 9	16,966,000	BV+5%	BV+5%	11.50	28.00	55.00

The Coinage Reform of 1905 • 39

	Mintage	F	VF	EF	UNC	BU
1906, Closed 9	*	14.00	20.00	40.00	60.00	95.00
1907, Curved 7	33,761,239	BV+5%	BV+5%	10.50	20.00	28.00
1907, Straight 7	*	BV+5%	BV+5%	11.50	22.00	32.00
1908	488,000	50.00	80.75	190.00	525.00	850.00
1912	3,736,000	BV+5%	BV+5%	19.00	32.00	50.00
1913	10,510,000	BV+5%	BV+5%	11.50	22.00	25.00
1913, 13 Over 07	*	45.00	80.00	135.00	400.00	500.00
1913, 3 Over 2	*	14.00	20.00	40.00	70.00	120.00
1914 (a)	7,710,000	BV+5%	BV+5%	11.50	28.00	42.00
1916	480,000	42.00	55.00	95.00	165.00	215.00
1916, First 1 Over Inverted 1	*	42.00	55.00	95.00	165.00	215.00
1917	37,112,000	BV+5%	BV+5%	11.50	22.00	25.00
1918	1,320,000	55.00	65.00	120.00	190.00	260.00

* Included above. **a.** The 1914 strikes exist with either narrow or wide date; no particular premium is attached to either variety.

Type 2 (.800, Reduced). BW-534, KM-446.

Composition: 0.800 silver, 0.200 copper. *Weight:* 9.06 g. *Obverse:* The national coat of arms with the eagle facing forward, head to the right, above a spray of oak and laurel; above, the legend **ESTADOS UNIDOS MEXICANOS**. *Reverse:* At the top, above an open wreath of oak and laurel, a small radiant liberty cap. On the radiance below the cap, a horizontally shaded number **50** with **CENTAVOS** / [date] below. The mintmark **M** is below and slightly between the digits of the denomination. *Diameter:* 27 mm. *Edge:* Lettered **INDEPENDENCIA Y LIBERTAD**.

	Mintage	F	VF	EF	UNC	BU
1918	2,760,000	$24.00	$32.00	$60.00	$95.00	$235.00
1918, 8 Over 7	*	330.00	475.00	665.00	1,140.00	1,425.00
1919	29,670,000	24.00	30.00	55.00	80.75	140.00

* Included above.

Type 3 (.720). BW-535, KM-447.

Composition: 0.720 silver, 0.280 copper. *Weight:* 8.33 g. *Obverse:* The national coat of arms with the eagle facing forward, head to the right, above a spray of oak and laurel; above, the legend ESTADOS UNIDOS MEXICANOS. *Reverse:* At the top, above an open wreath of oak and laurel, a small radiant liberty cap. On the radiance below the cap, a horizontally shaded number 50 with CENTAVOS / [date] below. The mintmark M is below and slightly between the digits of the denomination. *Diameter:* 27 mm. *Edge:* Lettered INDEPENDENCIA Y LIBERTAD.

	Mintage	F	VF	EF	UNC	BU
1919	10,200,000	$24.00	$38.00	$55.00	$85.00	$120.00
1920	27,166,000	19.00	28.00	42.00	70.00	95.00
1921	21,864,000	19.00	28.00	42.00	70.00	95.00
1925	3,280,000	24.00	38.00	65.00	115.00	165.00
1937	20,000,000	BV+5%	BV+5%	8.50	12.50	17.00
1938	100,000	50.00	70.00	120.00	215.00	285.00
1939	10,440,000	BV+5%	BV+5%	8.50	12.50	17.00
1942	800,000	BV+5%	BV+5%	8.50	12.50	17.00
1943	41,512,000	BV+5%	BV+5%	BV+5%	6.75	8.50
1944	55,806,000	BV+5%	BV+5%	BV+5%	6.75	8.50
1945	56,766,000	BV+5%	BV+5%	BV+5%	6.75	8.50

Type 4 (.420). BW-536, KM-448.

Composition: 0.580 copper, 0.420 silver. *Weight:* 7.973 g. *Obverse:* The national coat of arms with the eagle facing forward, head to the right, above a spray of oak and laurel; above, the legend ESTADOS UNIDOS MEXICANOS. *Reverse:* At the top, above an open wreath of oak and laurel, a small radiant liberty cap. On the radiance below the cap, a horizontally shaded number 50 with CENTAVOS / 1935 below. The mintmark M is below and slightly between the digits of the denomination. *Diameter:* 27 mm. *Edge:* Lettered INDEPENDENCIA Y LIBERTAD.

	Mintage	F	VF	EF	UNC	BU
1935	70,800,000	BV+5%	BV+5%	BV+5%	$4.75	$6.75

Type 5 (Cuauhtémoc). BW-537, KM-449.

Composition: 0.500 copper, 0.300 silver, 0.100 nickel, 0.100 zinc. *Weight:* 6.666 g. *Obverse:* Above a spray of oak and laurel, the national coat of arms depicting the eagle in profile to the left, with stylized, leaf-like feathers and very large feet. Above, the legend **ESTADOS UNIDOS MEXICANOS**. *Reverse:* Slightly to left of center, a bust of Cuauhtémoc in three-quarter profile to the right on a plain field, with the date placed vertically at the left. At upper right, the mintmark M̊, above a small Aztec eagle diving toward the denomination, **50 / CS**. *Diameter:* 26 mm. *Edge:* Reeded.

	Mintage	F	VF	EF	UNC	BU
1950	13,570,000	$1.90	$2.50	$2.85	$3.80	$5.75
1951	3,650,000	2.85	3.35	3.80	4.75	6.75

Type 6 (Big Cuauhtémoc). BW-538, KM-450.

Composition: 0.950 copper, 0.025 tin, 0.025 zinc. *Weight:* 14 g. *Obverse:* Above a spray of oak and laurel, the national coat of arms depicting the eagle in profile to the left, with stylized, leaf-like feathers and very large feet. Above, the legend **ESTADOS UNIDOS MEXICANOS**. *Reverse:* The head of Cuauhtémoc wearing an Aztec-style headdress, in profile to the left, with a tiny M̊ in the medallion above the forehead; · **CINCUENTA CENTAVOS** · and **Mo [date]** surrounds. *Diameter:* 33 mm. *Edge:* Reeded.

	Mintage	F	VF	EF	UNC	BU
1955	3,502,000	$1.90	$2.85	$7.75	$24.00	$30.00
1956	34,643,000	0.45	0.95	1.90	3.80	5.75
1957	9,675,000	0.95	1.90	3.35	5.75	8.50
1959	4,540,000	0.70	1.90	2.85	4.75	6.75

Cuauhtémoc

The last Mexica (Aztec) emperor was a nephew of the emperor Moctezuma II, who ruled from Tenochtitlán at the time the Spanish arrived. Moctezuma died soon after they took the city. His brother, Cuitláhuac, ascended to the throne and drove the invaders out; but he had ruled for scarcely 80 days when he died of the smallpox virus the invaders had unknowingly brought to the New World.

Cuauhtémoc, whose father had ruled the Aztecs before Moctezuma, was a trained, experienced warrior of noble blood. He was selected by vote to take the throne and lead the people against the Spanish.

The Spanish, meanwhile, were assembling their troops outside the city of Tenochtitlán. They were joined by many of the Aztecs' enemies—warriors from defeated cities that had been forced to pay regular tribute to Moctezuma. With their aid, Hernán Cortés soon took the Valley of Mexico; Cuauhtémoc's forces, with the city's women fighting alongside the men, were able to hold Tenochtitlán for a time, but eventually the Spaniards seized control of the markets and threatened to starve the Aztecs out. Cuauhtémoc attempted to escape across the water to rally forces from the countryside, but he was captured and the resistance came to an end.

One of many statues in Mexico City commemorating the last Aztec emperor, Cuauhtémoc. He is depicted, in differing styles, on the Type 5 and Type 6 fifty centavos and the Type 1 five pesos.

Cortés treated Cuauhtémoc kindly at first, but when the young Aztec ruler refused to reveal the location of the vast treasure Cortés was certain existed, the Spaniard had him tortured. Cuauhtémoc was allowed to continue as a puppet ruler for a short time, but Cortés eventually had him executed, for fear that he would mount a rebellion if he were released.

Cuauhtémoc is remembered with pride in Mexico, and his likeness has been rendered in many different styles in public art, depending on the artistic traditions of the time. The name *Cuauhtémoc* means "he who descends like an eagle"; hence the small, diving eagle that appears on the Type 5 fifty centavos.

Type 7 (Copper-nickel). BW-539, KM-451.

Composition: 0.750 copper, 0.250 nickel. *Weight:* 6.5 g. *Obverse:* Above a spray of oak and laurel, the national coat of arms depicting the eagle in profile to the left, with stylized, leaf-like feathers and very large feet. Above, the legend ESTADOS UNIDOS MEXICANOS. *Reverse:* The head of Cuauhtémoc wearing an Aztec-style headdress in profile to the left, with a tiny M̊ in the medallion above the forehead; · CINCUENTA CENTAVOS · and Mo [date] surrounds. *Diameter:* 25 mm. *Edge:* Reeded.

	Mintage	F	VF	EF	UNC	BU
1964	43,806,000	$0.15	$0.25	$0.45	$0.70	$1.20
1965	14,326,000	0.15	0.25	0.45	0.70	1.20
1966	1,726,000	0.25	0.45	0.95	1.90	2.85
1967	55,244,000	0.15	0.25	0.45	0.70	1.20
1968	80,438,000	0.15	0.25	0.45	0.70	1.20
1969	87,640,000	0.15	0.25	0.45	0.70	1.20

Type 8 (Stylized Eagle). BW-540, KM-452.

Composition: 0.750 copper, 0.250 nickel. *Weight:* 6.5 g. *Obverse:* Above a spray of oak and laurel, the national coat of arms depicting the eagle in profile to the left, with the feathers and other elements drawn as outlines instead of in full relief. Above, the legend ESTADOS UNIDOS MEXICANOS. *Reverse:* The head of Cuauhtémoc wearing an Aztec-style headdress in profile to the left, with a tiny M̊ in the medallion above the forehead; · CINCUENTA CENTAVOS · and Mo [date] surrounds. *Diameter:* 25 mm. *Edge:* Reeded.

	Mintage	F	VF	EF	UNC	BU	PF
1970	76,236,000	$0.15	$0.25	$0.45	$0.95	$1.40	
1971	125,288,000	0.15	0.25	0.45	0.95	1.40	
1972	16,000,000	0.70	1.20	1.80	3.00	4.75	
1975, Dots	177,958,000	0.50	0.85	1.40	3.50	7.75	
1975, No Dots	*	0.15	0.25	0.45	0.70	1.90	
1976, Dots	37,480,000	0.20	0.45	0.95	4.25	5.75	

* Included above.

Palenque

Ancient Palenque was once ruled by Pakal the Great, depicted in this museum bust.

A Mayan city-state lost deep in the heart of Mexico, Palenque was rediscovered by the Spanish in the late 1700s. The city is nested among dark, jungle-forested hills and overlooks a broad coastal plain. The ruins are often cloaked in heavy mist, and streams wind their way through the center of the city. Even the name of the city was lost to time, so the Spaniards named it for a nearby village, Santo Domingo de Palenque.

Relics recovered from the site indicate that it had been inhabited since the third century, and was at its height between the fifth and seventh centuries, when most of the temples, towers, and pyramids were constructed. An estimated 1,400 structures remain in the city, but only a few dozen have been excavated. Palenque has a planned urban layout that meshes with the landscape, and a very sophisticated building style that skillfully reduced the thickness of the walls. This lightness of the structures and ornamentation makes the city very elegant, and the interior spaces and galleries feel spacious in comparison to those of other, larger ancient cities. All of Palenque appears to have been richly decorated in its heyday.

Records have been found of most of the kings and queens of Palenque, including its most famous ruler, Pakal the Great. One body has even been discovered: the Red Queen of Palenque, a female skeleton covered in cinnabar and placed in a richly adorned tomb in Temple XIII.

Once the city was abandoned, the jungle grew quickly to cover the structures; this appears to be what prevented Palenque from being looted. It became a quiet sanctuary cocooned with ancient secrets. It is still unknown what caused the people of Palenque to abandon the city to nature.

In addition to being remembered on the Type 9 fifty centavos, the Palenque site appears on a new 5 pesos in the Mayan group of the Pre-Columbian Collections.

Type 8 (Stylized Eagle). BW-540, continued

	Mintage	F	VF	EF	UNC	BU	PF
1976, No Dots	**	0.15	0.25	0.45	0.70	1.20	
1977	12,410,000	4.75	7.75	11.50	26.00	30.00	
1978	85,400,000	0.15	0.25	0.45	0.70	1.20	
1979, Round 9	229,000,000	0.15	0.25	0.45	0.70	1.20	
1979, Square 9	*	0.15	0.25	0.45	1.40	1.90	
1980, Rnd 9, Wide Dt	89,978,000	0.15	0.25	0.45	1.40	1.90	
1980, Squ 9, Narr Dt	*	0.25	0.45	0.95	1.65	2.50	
1981, Rectangular 9, Narrow Date	142,212,000	0.45	0.95	1.90	3.35	4.75	
1981, Rnd 9, Wide Dt	*	0.25	0.45	0.95	1.65	2.50	
1982	45,474,000	0.15	0.25	0.45	1.40	1.90	
1983	90,318,000	0.15	0.25	0.45	1.40	1.90	
1983, Proof							$165.00

** Included in 1976, Dots. * Included above.

Type 9 (Palenque). BW-541, KM-492.

Composition: Stainless steel. *Weight:* 4.2 g. *Obverse:* Above a spray of oak and laurel, the national coat of arms depicting the eagle in profile to the left, with feathers resembling plates of armor. Above, the legend **ESTADOS UNIDOS MEXICANOS**. *Reverse:* Slightly to the right of center, the head of a Mayan of ancient Palenque, possibly Pakal the Great, in semi-profile to the left. To left of the head, 50¢ **PALENQUE** is placed vertically atop the date, which is placed horizontally. At far right, the mintmark M̊. *Diameter:* 21.9 mm. *Edge:* Plain.

	Mintage	F	VF	EF	UNC	BU	PF
1983, Thick Snake	99,540,000	$0.95	$1.40	$2.50	$3.80	$5.75	
1983, Thin Snake	*	0.25	0.45	0.70	1.65	2.50	
1983, Proof							$175.00

* Included above.

1 PESO

Pesos under the Reform of 1905 were made in nine basic types:

Type 1—Caballito (with an effigy of Liberty on horseback)

Type 2—.800 (with small radiant liberty cap and wreath)

Type 3—.720 (like Type 2, but with reduced silver content)

Type 4—Little Morelos (with head of War of Independence hero José María Morelos)

Type 5—General Morelos (with bust of Morelos in three-quarter profile to left)

Type 6—Constitution (circulating commemorative of the Constitution of 1857, with head of former president Benito Juárez García facing left)

Type 7—.100 (with bust of Morelos in profile, facing right)

Type 8—Copper-nickel (with head of Morelos in profile, facing left)

Type 9—Steel (with bust of Morelos in three-quarter profile to right)

Type 1 (Caballito). BW-542, KM-453.

Composition: 0.9027 silver, 0.0973 copper. *Weight:* 27.07 g. *Obverse:* The national coat of arms with the eagle facing forward, head to the right, above a spray of oak and laurel; above, the legend **ESTADOS UNIDOS MEXICANOS**. Below, divided by the base of the cactus, **UN / PESO**. *Reverse:* A horse galloping to the left, ridden by Liberty in a flowing gown; she looks over her shoulder to the right, holding a torch aloft in her left hand and a branch of laurel in her right, which rests slightly on the horse's neck. In the background is a rising sun with long, single-line rays; in the exergue at the bottom, the date with a dot to each side. *Diameter:* 39 mm. *Edge:* Lettered **INDEPENDENCIA Y LIBERTAD**.

Note: Without mintmark.

	Mintage	F	VF	EF	UNC	BU
1910	3,814,000	$50.00	$55.00	$70.00	$235.00	$380.00
1911	1,227,000	50.00	55.00	70.00	285.00	430.00
1911, Short Ray	*	95.00	115.00	140.00	1,425.00	3,325.00
1912	322,000	42.00	65.00	80.75	355.00	475.00
1913	2,880,000	50.00	55.00	70.00	285.00	430.00
1913, 3 Over 2	*	55.00	70.00	95.00	430.00	950.00
1914	120,000	430.00	665.00	950.00	2,850.00	4,750.00

* Included above.

The Little Horse

As the 100th anniversary of Independence approached, the mint considered how best to commemorate the event. The decision was made to hire the celebrated French engraver Charles Pillet, who agreed to take the job.

According to noted Mexican numismatic researcher Alberto F. Pradeau, Pillet submitted three 50-centavo coins, 30 mm in diameter, all alike except for the edges: one plain, one with raised letters, and one with incused letters. The lettering on the latter two read INDEPENDENCIA Y LIBERTAD. The mint purchased the designs and dies but opted not to produce the 50-centavo denomination. Instead, Pillet was asked to produce patterns for a 1-peso coin, 39 mm in diameter. He provided two, with the edges lettered as on the 50-centavo patterns (raised on one, incused on the other).

The design was approved and the coinage authorized on December 27, 1909. Striking began in January 1910, but mint personnel noticed certain shortcomings of the dies. In some places (like the horse's hooves), the relief was too shallow; in others (like Liberty's left arm and hand), it was too high. Francisco Valdes, the head of the coining department, was dispatched to Europe in April with instructions to have Pillet correct the dies.

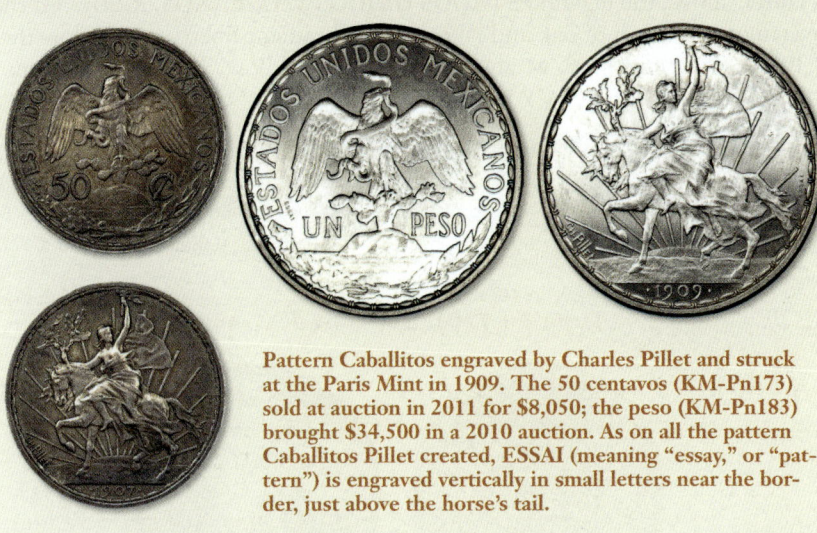

Pattern Caballitos engraved by Charles Pillet and struck at the Paris Mint in 1909. The 50 centavos (KM-Pn173) sold at auction in 2011 for $8,050; the peso (KM-Pn183) brought $34,500 in a 2010 auction. As on all the pattern Caballitos Pillet created, ESSAI (meaning "essay," or "pattern") is engraved vertically in small letters near the border, just above the horse's tail.

Valdes had previously spent six months in the U.S. mints in Philadelphia and Denver, and had worked with the engraver Charles Barber. After conferring with Pillet, who was willing to do the work, Valdes felt sure Barber would serve better. Although Pillet protested, Barber was hired for the job, and the master dies were shipped to him in November 1910. He returned them the following February, ready for use.

The Caballito was among the iconic Mexican coins chosen to be reproduced in the commemorative Numismatic Heritage of Mexico Series (see page 281).

Type 2 (.800). BW-543, KM-454.

1 peso, Type 2, 1913, 3 Over 2 overdate.

Composition: 0.800 silver, 0.200 copper. *Weight:* 18.125 g. *Obverse:* The national coat of arms with the eagle facing forward, head to the right, above a spray of oak and laurel; above, the legend **ESTADOS UNIDOS MEXICANOS**. *Reverse:* At the top, above an open wreath of oak and laurel, a small radiant liberty cap. Below the rays, **UN PESO**, with mintmark **M** above and the date below. *Diameter:* 34 mm. *Edge:* Lettered **INDEPENDENCIA Y LIBERTAD**.

	Mintage	F	VF	EF	UNC	BU
1918	3,050,000	$55.00	$95.00	$190.00	$665.00	$950.00
1918, 8 Over 7	*	165.00	330.00	665.00	1,235.00	1,660.00
1919	6,151,000	55.00	90.00	165.00	380.00	710.00

* Included above.

Type 3 (.720). BW-544, KM-455.

Composition: 0.720 silver, 0.280 copper. *Weight:* 16.66 g. *Obverse:* The national coat of arms with the eagle facing forward, head to the right, above a spray of oak and laurel; above, the legend **ESTADOS UNIDOS MEXICANOS**. Near the top, divided by the eagle's head, **0.7 / 20** ("0.720," denoting the reduced fineness). *Reverse:* At the top, above an open wreath of oak and laurel, a small radiant liberty cap. Below the rays, **UN PESO**, with mintmark **M** above and the date below. *Diameter:* 34 mm. *Edge:* Lettered **INDEPENDENCIA Y LIBERTAD**.

The Coinage Reform of 1905 • 49

	Mintage	F	VF	EF	UNC	BU
1920	8,830,000	$42.00	$60.00	$95.00	$230.00	$330.00
1920, 20 Over 10	*	50.00	80.75	140.00	285.00	430.00
1921	5,480,000	32.00	50.00	70.00	190.00	235.00
1921, 9 Over Inv. 9	*	50.0	70.00	120.00	235.00	330.00
1922	33,620,000	BV+5%	BV+5%	BV+5%	26.00	32.00
1923	35,280,000	BV+5%	BV+5%	BV+5%	26.00	32.00
1924	33,060,000	BV+5%	BV+5%	BV+5%	26.00	32.00
1925	9,160,000	BV+5%	BV+5%	70.00	120.00	235.00
1926	28,840,000	BV+5%	BV+5%	BV+5%	26.00	32.00
1927	5,060,000	BV+5%	BV+5%	38.00	70.00	95.00
1932	50,770,000	BV+5%	BV+5%	BV+5%	18.00	22.00
1933	43,920,000	BV+5%	BV+5%	BV+5%	18.00	22.00
1933, 3 Over 2	*	50.00	70.00	120.00	235.00	330.00
1933, 1 Over Inv. 1	*	BV+5%	BV+5%	BV+5%	22.00	26.00
1934	22,070,000	BV+5%	BV+5%	BV+5%	18.00	22.00
1934, 4 Over 3	*	50.00	70.00	120.00	235.00	330.00
1935	8,050,000	BV+5%	BV+5%	BV+5%	18.00	22.00
1938	30,000,000	BV+5%	BV+5%	BV+5%	13.00	18.00
1940	20,000,000	BV+5%	BV+5%	BV+5%	13.00	18.00
1943	47,622,000	BV+5%	BV+5%	BV+5%	13.00	18.00
1944	39,522,000	BV+5%	BV+5%	BV+5%	13.00	18.00
1945	37,300,000	BV+5%	BV+5%	BV+5%	13.00	18.00

* Included above.

Type 4 (Little Morelos). BW-545, KM-456.

Composition: 0.500 silver, 0.400 copper, 0.060 nickel, 0.040 zinc. *Weight:* 14 g. *Obverse:* Above a spray of oak and laurel, the national coat of arms depicting the eagle in profile to the left, with thick, detailed, evenly spaced feathers and large, fleshy feet. Above, the legend **ESTADOS UNIDOS MEXICANOS**. *Reverse:* The head of José María Morelos in profile to the right, with **MORELOS** in small letters along the base of the neck. Around the border below, ·**UN PESO [date] Mo. 14 Gr. 0.500**· (with "14 Gr." indicating the weight, 14 grams; and "0.500" indicating the fineness). *Diameter:* 32 mm. *Edge:* Reeded.

	Mintage	F	VF	EF	UNC	BU	PF
1947	61,460,000	BV+5%	BV+5%	BV+5%	$8.50	$10.50	
1948	22,915,000	BV+5%	BV+5%	BV+5%	8.50	10.50	
1949	40,000,000	$380.00	$620.00	$850.00	1,800.00	2,750.00	
1949, Proof							$3,575.00

José María Morelos

José María Morelos was born on September 30, 1765, in Valladolid, Mexico. Born into poverty, Morelos was a farm worker before entering the seminary. He was ordained in 1797 and served as a priest in Churumuco and Carácuaro until 1810, when he joined the War of Independence.

When Morelos met with his former school president, Father Miguel Hidalgo y Costilla, to volunteer, Hidalgo made him a lieutenant and sent him to round up troops. Hidalgo charged Morelos with capturing the port of Acapulco, which was enormously profitable to the Spanish. On the march west, Morelos gathered soldiers and achieved victory after victory over Spanish forces. By the time he reached Acapulco, he had built an army of thousands, including many Spanish deserters.

Along the way, Morelos used some of the Church's fortunes to fund his army. He also had coinage struck to pay his troops—in silver if possible, but often with copper coins, with the understanding that they could be exchanged for silver and gold once the war was over. The SUD ("south") coinage issued under Morelos is among the most iconic in Mexican numismatics, and has been reproduced as part of the Numismatic Heritage of Mexico Series (see page 279).

In 1813, Morelos called to order a national constituent congress of representatives from the territories he controlled. To those present, he outlined his "Sentimientos de la Nacion" (Sentiments of the Nation); similar to the U.S. Declaration of Independence, Morelos's document not only declared independence from Spain, but abolished slavery and instituted the title *American* for all native-born people, eliminating ethnic distinctions. The congress embraced his document, endorsed a declaration of independence from Spain, and drew up a constitution establishing executive, legislative, and judicial branches of government.

Morelos was captured by Spanish troops in late 1815 and was put on trial in Mexico City for treason and other crimes. He was convicted and executed by firing squad on December 22.

In honor of Morelos, his native city, Valladolid, was renamed Morelia in 1828. In

A 2 reales of the famous SUD design, issued at the behest of José María Morelos during the War of Independence.

1869, President Benito Juárez named the state of Morelos for him. During World War II, the United States named a battleship, the SS *José M. Morelos*, in his honor. His portrait appears on the Type 4, 5, 7, 8, and 9 one pesos; the 200 and 1,000 pesos commemorating the 175th anniversary of the War of Independence; and the 5 pesos commemorating the 200th anniversary of the War of Independence.

Type 5 (General Morelos). BW-546, KM-457.

Composition: 0.500 copper, 0.300 silver, 0.100 nickel, 0.100 zinc. *Weight:* 13.33 g. *Obverse:* Above a spray of oak and laurel, the national coat of arms depicting the eagle in profile to the left, with stylized, leaf-like feathers and very large feet. Above, the legend **ESTADOS UNIDOS MEXICANOS**. *Reverse:* On a plain field, a bust of José María Morelos in three-quarter profile to the left, in a general's uniform. To left of the bust, 1 / PESO / 1950 / M̊. *Diameter:* 32 mm. *Edge:* Reeded.

Note: Morelos's coat was unlike those of the other generals in that it had a distinctively large, high collar and no epaulets.

	Mintage	F	VF	EF	UNC	BU
1950	3,287,000	BV+5%	BV+5%	$7.75	$11.50	$14.00

Type 6 (Constitution). BW-547, KM-458.

Composition: 0.700 copper, 0.100 silver, 0.100 nickel, 0.100 zinc. *Weight:* 16 g. *Obverse:* At the center, a small national coat of arms depicting the eagle in profile to the left, with stylized, leaf-like feathers and very large feet, all within an open wreath of oak and laurel. The legend • **ESTADOS UNIDOS MEXICANOS** • and **UN PESO 1957** surrounds. *Reverse:* A head of Benito Juárez García facing left with legend · CENTENARIO DE LA CONSTITUCION DE MEXICO · and 1857·1957. *Diameter:* 34.5 mm. *Edge:* Lettered INDEPENDENCIA Y LIBERTAD.

	Mintage	F	VF	EF	UNC	BU
1957	500,000	$2.85	$4.75	$6.75	$11.50	$14.00

Type 7 (.100). BW-548, KM-459.

Composition: 0.700 copper, 0.100 silver, 0.100 nickel, 0.100 zinc. *Weight:* 16 g. *Obverse:* At the center, a small national coat of arms depicting the eagle in profile to the left, with stylized, leaf-like feathers and very large feet, all within an open wreath of oak and laurel. The legend · ESTADOS UNIDOS MEXICANOS · and UN PESO [date]. *Reverse:* Within an open wreath of oak and laurel, a right-facing profile bust of José María Morelos in a general's uniform. To left of the bust, the mintmark M̥. *Diameter:* 34.5 mm. *Edge:* Lettered INDEPENDENCIA Y LIBERTAD.

	Mintage	F	VF	EF	UNC	BU
1957	28,273,000	BV+5%	BV+5%	BV+5%	$4.75	$5.75
1958	41,899,000	BV+5%	BV+5%	BV+5%	1.90	2.85
1959	27,369,000	BV+5%	BV+5%	BV+5%	5.75	6.75
1960	26,259,000	BV+5%	BV+5%	BV+5%	4.75	5.75
1961	52,601,000	BV+5%	BV+5%	BV+5%	2.85	3.80
1962	61,094,000	BV+5%	BV+5%	BV+5%	2.85	3.80
1963	26,394,000	BV+5%	BV+5%	BV+5%	1.90	2.85
1964	15,615,000	BV+5%	BV+5%	BV+5%	1.90	2.85
1965	5,004,000	BV+5%	BV+5%	BV+5%	1.90	2.85
1966	30,998,000	BV+5%	BV+5%	BV+5%	1.90	2.85
1967	9,308,000	BV+5%	BV+5%	BV+5%	2.85	3.80

Type 8 (Copper-nickel). BW-549, KM-460.

Composition: 0.750 copper, 0.250 nickel. *Weight:* 9 g. *Obverse:* Above a spray of oak and laurel, the national coat of arms depicting the eagle in profile to the left, with the feathers and other elements drawn as outlines instead of in full relief. Above, the legend **ESTADOS UNIDOS MEXICANOS**. *Reverse:* On a plain field, a left-facing head of José María Morelos in a general's uniform. To left of the head, **UN PESO**; below, the date. *Diameter:* 29 mm. *Edge:* Reeded.

	Mintage	F	VF	EF	UNC	BU	PF
1970, Narrow Date	102,715,000	$0.15	$0.25	$0.45	$0.95	$1.20	
1970, Wide Date	*	0.45	1.40	2.50	4.75	6.75	
1971	426,222,000	0.15	0.20	0.25	0.70	0.95	
1972	120,000,000	0.15	0.20	0.25	0.70	0.95	
1974	63,700,000	0.15	0.20	0.25	0.70	0.95	
1975, Wide Date	205,979,000	0.20	0.30	0.45	1.40	1.90	
1975, Narrow Date	*	0.20	0.30	0.45	1.40	1.90	
1976	94,489,000	0.15	0.25	0.45	0.95	1.20	
1977, Thick Date	94,364,000	0.20	0.30	0.45	1.40	1.90	
1977, Thin Date	*	0.70	1.90	3.80	7.75	14.00	
1978, Open 8	55,140,000	0.70	1.90	3.80	7.75	14.00	
1978, Closed 8	208,300,000	0.15	0.25	0.45	1.40	1.65	
1979, Thin Date	117,884,000	0.15	0.25	0.45	1.40	1.65	
1979, Thick Date	*	0.15	0.25	0.45	1.40	1.65	
1980, Closed 8, Wide Date	318,800,000	0.15	0.25	0.45	1.40	1.65	
1980, Closed 8, Narrow Date	23,865,000	0.35	0.45	1.20	10.50	13.00	
1980, Open 8	*	0.35	0.45	1.20	10.50	13.00	
1981, Closed 8, Narrow Date	**	0.15	0.25	0.45	1.40	1.65	
1981, Open 8, Wide Date	58,616,000	0.45	0.95	2.50	7.75	9.50	
1981, Closed 8, Open 9	*	0.20	0.40	0.95	2.85	3.80	
1981, Closed 8 and 9	*	0.45	0.70	1.65	4.75	6.75	
1982	235,000,000	0.25	0.45	0.95	2.50	2.85	
1982, 8 Open at the Base	*	0.95	2.85	4.75	6.75	8.50	
1983, Wide Date	100,000,000	0.25	0.45	0.95	2.85	3.80	
1983, Narrow Date	*	0.25	0.45	0.95	2.85	3.80	
1983, Open 8	*	0.65	1.00	3.80	7.25	12.50	
1983, Proof	1,048						$32.00
1983, 8 Open at the Base, Proof	*						50.00

* Included above. ** Included below.

Type 9 (Steel). BW-550, KM-496.

Composition: stainless steel. *Weight:* 6.07 g. *Obverse:* Above a spray of oak and laurel, the national coat of arms depicting the eagle in profile to the left, with feathers resembling plates of armor. Above, the legend ESTADOS UNIDOS MEXICANOS. *Reverse:* On a plain field, a bust of José Morelos in three-quarter profile to the right, in a general's uniform. To the left of the bust, the mintmark M̥; to the right, 1$ and the date. At upper right, **josé m⁰ morelos** (in lowercase letters). *Diameter:* 24.5 mm. *Edge:* Plain.

	Mintage	F	VF	EF	UNC	BU	PF
1984, No Initials	722,802,000	$0.10	$0.15	$0.35	$0.95	$1.40	
1984, Engraver Initials "ra"	*	0.10	0.15	0.35	0.95	1.40	
1985	985,000,000	0.10	0.15	0.35	0.95	1.40	
1986	740,000,000	0.10	0.15	0.35	0.95	1.40	
1987	250,000,000	0.10	0.15	0.35	0.95	1.40	
1987, Proof	2 known						$1,330.00

* Included above.

2 PESOS

The 2 pesos under the Reform of 1905 were made both in gold and in silver:

Type 1—Victoria (depicting Mexico City's *Monumento a la Independencia*, or Monument of Independence, a statue based on Nike, the Greek goddess of victory)

Type 2—2-peso gold (with a wreath on the reverse)

Type 2 (2-peso gold). BW-651, KM-461.

Composition: 0.900 gold, 0.100 copper. *Weight:* 1.666 g. *Obverse:* The national coat of arms with the eagle facing forward, head to the right, above a spray of oak and laurel; above, the legend ESTADOS UNIDOS MEXICANOS. *Reverse:* Within an open wreath of laurel, DOS / PESOS. At the top, between the wreath tips, the date; at the bottom, below the bow on the wreath, the mintmark M̥. *Diameter:* 13 mm. *Edge:* Reeded.

	Mintage	F	VF	EF	UNC	BU
1919	1,670,000	BV+3%	BV+3%	$60.00	$80.75	$100.00
1920	4,282,428	BV+3%	BV+3%	60.00	80.75	100.00
1920, 20 Over 10	*	BV+3%	BV+3%	60.00	80.75	105.00
1944	10,000	BV+3%	$100.00	145.00	170.00	200.00
1945, Restrike	4,590,493	BV	BV	BV	BV+10%	BV+15%
1946	167,500	BV+3%	BV+3%	60.00	80.75	100.00
1947	25,000	BV+3%	BV+3%	60.00	80.75	105.00

* Included above.

El Ángel del la Independencia

The *Monumento a la Independencia,* popularly known as the *Angel of Independence* or *El Ángel,* is a columnar monument located in a circular *zócalo,* or plaza, in Mexico City. The 118-foot column is crowned by a gold-plated bronze statue of Nike, the Greek goddess of victory, which stands 22 feet high. The finished monument was inaugurated in 1910 to commemorate the centennial of the beginning of the War of Independence.

Originally ordered by the dictator Santa Anna's administration, to be constructed in the Plaza de la Constitución, the project fell through. President Porfirio Díaz revived the project, and the first stone was placed in 1902. Statues representing Peace, Law, Justice, and War stand at the corners of the column's base, inside which the remains of 14 heroes of the War of Independence were interred until 2010 (when they were moved to a different location as part of the War of Independence bicentennial celebrations). Four of these heroes—Miguel Hidalgo y Costilla, José María Morelos, Javier Mina, and Vicente Guerrero—are represented by marble statues in front of the monument. Above them, Victory leans slightly forward, holding a laurel wreath high above Hidalgo's head. In her left hand she holds a broken chain, representing freedom.

In 1929 an eternal flame was added to the monument site. In 1957, as a result of a major earthquake, the Victory statue fell to the ground and broke into several pieces. After a year of restoration, the statue was returned to the top and the site was reopened.

One of the most beloved spots in Mexico City, the monument is often the scene of celebrations, sports gatherings, and political rallies. A popular tourist destination as well, the *Monumento a la Independencia* is free to visit. If one is willing to brave the narrow, 12-story staircase inside the column, the view from the balcony is said to be extraordinary. Among the sights it affords is the Castillo de Chapultepec, where the 14 heroes of the War of Independence are now interred.

In addition to her appearance on the Type 1 two pesos, El Ángel has graced the reverses of the 1981 Gold Coins of Mexico Program bullion issues, and nearly all the gold, silver, and platinum coins in the Libertad bullion series.

Type 1 (Victoria). BW-551, KM-462.

Composition: 0.900 silver, 0.100 copper. *Weight:* 26.666 g. *Obverse:* Within a wreath of oak and laurel, the national coat of arms depicting the eagle in profile to the left, with stylized, blade-like feathers, exceptionally long tail and wing feathers, and a prominently arched neck with large beak. The legend ·ESTADOS·UNIDOS ·MEXICANOS· and MDCCCXXI✠MCMXXI (1821–1921) surrounds. *Reverse:* The Victory statue from the *Monumento de la Independencia*, facing forward, with volcanoes in the background. To the left of the statue, **DOS / PESOS**. To the right, the coin's silver weight in grams: **24 Gr. / PLATA / PURA**. *Diameter:* 39 mm. *Edge:* Reeded.

Note: A coin with full feathers visible on the eagle's left knee will command a premium.

	Mintage	F	VF	EF	UNC	BU
1921	1,277,500	38.00	55.00	75.00	285.00	400.00
1921, Feathers on Knee	*				400.00	570.00

* Included above.

2-1/2 PESOS

The 2-1/2-peso gold coin under the Reform of 1905 was made in one design; collectors describe it by its denomination.

Type 1 (2-1/2-peso gold). BW-652, KM-463.

Composition: 0.900 gold, 0.100 copper. *Weight:* 2.0833 g. *Obverse:* The national coat of arms with the eagle facing forward, head to the right, above a spray of oak and laurel; above, the legend **ESTADOS UNIDOS MEXICANOS**. *Reverse:* The head of Father Miguel Hidalgo y Costilla in profile to the left. Surrounding the profile counterclockwise from the left, and divided by the truncation of the neck, **DOS Y MEDIO** and **PESOS** ★ **[date]**. *Diameter:* 15.5 mm. *Edge:* Reeded.

	Mintage	F	VF	EF	UNC	BU
1918	1,704,000	BV+3%	BV+3%	BV+3%	$105.00	$130.00
1919	984,000	BV+3%	BV+3%	BV+3%	105.00	130.00
1920	607,060	BV+3%	BV+3%	BV+3%	100.00	125.00
1920, 20 Over 10	*	BV+3%	BV+3%	$165.00	185.00	225.00
1944	20,000	BV+3%	BV+3%	125.00	145.00	170.00
1945, Restrike	5,025,087	BV	BV	BV	BV+10%	BV+15%
1946	163,000	BV+3%	BV+3%	85.00	95.00	120.00
1947	24,000	$310.00	$355.00	400.00	450.00	550.00
1948	63,000	BV+3%	BV+3%	BV+3%	100.00	125.00

* Included above.

5 PESOS

The 5 pesos under the Reform of 1905 were made in both gold and silver, and, later, in base metal. The gold version, made in one design, is called *5 peso gold*. The non-gold 5 pesos was produced in 10 basic types, as follows:

> Type 1—Cuauhtémoc (depicting the famous Aztec leader of that name)
>
> Type 2—Railroad (commemorating the opening of the Southeastern Railroad, with a depiction of a locomotive passing a plantation)
>
> Type 3—Hidalgo (honoring the birth-bicentennial of War of Independence hero Father Miguel Hidalgo y Costilla, with his portrait in front of the church where he famously delivered the *grito de Dolores*)
>
> Type 4—Hidalgo/Wreath (depicting Hidalgo within a wreath of oak and laurel)
>
> Type 5—Hidalgo/Chico (like type 4, but with legend instead of wreath)
>
> Type 6—Constitution (commemorating the Constitution of 1857, with a portrait of former president Benito Juárez García)
>
> Type 7—Carranza (commemorating the centennial of the birth of Revolutionary hero Venustiano Carranza)
>
> Type 8—Guerrero (with bust of War of Independence hero Vicente Guerrero)
>
> Type 9—Quetzalcóatl (honoring Mesoamerican culture with a depiction of the "Feathered Serpent" god Quetzalcóatl)
>
> Type 10—Reduced (smaller size and new aluminum-bronze composition, with simple $5 design)

5-peso gold. BW-653, KM-464.

Composition: 0.900 gold, 0.100 copper. *Weight:* 4.1666 g. *Obverse:* The national coat of arms with the eagle facing forward, head to the right, above a spray of oak and laurel; above, the legend **ESTADOS UNIDOS MEXICANOS**. *Reverse:* The head of Miguel Hidalgo y Costilla in profile to the left. Surrounding the profile and divided by the truncation of the neck, **CINCO PESOS** at left, with mintmark **M**, a star, and the date at right. *Diameter:* 19 mm. *Edge:* lettered **INDEPENDENCIA Y LIBERTAD**.

	Mintage	F	VF	EF	UNC	BU
1905	18,076	$330.00	$525.00	$620.00	$710.00	$850.00
1906	4,638,000	BV+3%	BV+3%	BV+3%	170.00	225.00
1907	1,088,000	BV+3%	BV+3%	BV+3%	170.00	225.00
1907, 7 Over 6	*	BV+3%	BV+3%	215.00	245.00	270.00
1910	100,000	BV+3%	BV+3%	BV+3%	195.00	255.00
1918	609,000	BV+3%	BV+3%	BV+3%	170.00	225.00
1918, 8 Over 7	*	BV+3%	BV+3%	BV+3%	195.00	255.00
1919	506,000	BV+3%	BV+3%	BV+3%	170.00	225.00
1920	2,384,598	BV+3%	BV+3%	BV+3%	170.00	225.00
1955, Restrike	1,764,643	BV+3%	BV+3%	BV+3%	BV+10%	BV+15%

* Included above.

Type 1 (Cuauhtémoc). BW-552, KM-465.

Composition: 0.900 silver, 0.100 copper. *Weight:* 30 g. *Obverse:* Above a spray of oak and laurel, the national coat of arms with the eagle in profile to the left, with stylized, blade-like feathers and large feet. Above, the legend **ESTADOS UNIDOS MEXICANOS**. *Reverse:* The head of Cuauhtémoc in Aztec-style headdress, facing left, with **CUAUHTEMOC** in small letters below the bust. Surrounding the portrait, · **CINCO PESOS** · and **30 GRAMOS** · **LEY 0.900** · **Mo [date]**, with GRAMOS referencing the weight and LEY the fineness. *Diameter:* 40 mm. *Edge:* Reeded.

	Mintage	F	VF	EF	UNC	BU
1947	5,110,000	BV+3%	BV+3%	BV+3%	$37.00	$40.00
1948	26,740,000	BV+3%	BV+3%	BV+3%	35.00	38.00

Type 2 (Railroad, 1950). BW-553, KM-466.

Composition: 0.900 silver, 0.100 copper. *Weight:* 27.777 g. *Obverse:* Slightly above center, above a spray of oak and laurel, a small national coat of arms depicting the eagle in profile to the left, with stylized, leaf-like feathers and very large feet. The legend **ESTADOS UNIDOS MEXICANOS** surrounds, with **CINCO PESOS** below the spray. To the left of the spray, fineness **LEY / 0.720**; to the right of the spray, **PESO** above the coin's weight (in grams), 27 $^7/_9$ 6. At the bottom, the mintmark **Mo** and the date. *Reverse:* A complex scene with a locomotive in the foreground and, in the background, a plantation scene with a forest, fields, and two palm trees. Behind all, a rising sun with blade-shaped rays, and with **1950** inscribed on the half-circle. Surrounding all, the legend **INAUGURACION DEL FERROCARRIL DEL SURESTE ·** ("Inauguration of the Southeastern Railway"). *Diameter:* 40 mm. *Edge:* Lettered **AGRICULTURA-INDUSTRIA-COMERCIO**.

	Mintage	F	VF	EF	UNC	BU
1950	200,000	$26.00	$30.00	$40.00	$50.00	$65.00

Type 3 (Hidalgo). BW-554, KM-468.

Composition: 0.720 silver, 0.280 copper. *Weight:* 27.777 g. *Obverse:* Slightly above center, above a spray of oak and laurel, a small national coat of arms depicting the eagle in profile to the left, with stylized, leaf-like feathers and very large feet. The legend **ESTADOS UNIDOS MEXICANOS** surrounds, with **CINCO PESOS** below the spray. To the left of the spray, **PESO** above the coin's weight (in grams), 27 $\frac{7}{9}$ 6; to the right of the spray, fineness **LEY / 0.720**. At the bottom, the mintmark **Mo** and **1953**. *Reverse:* Slightly to right of center, a bust of Miguel Hidalgo y

Costilla in three-quarter profile; in the background to the left, the Parroquia de Nuestra Señora de Dolores ("Parish Church of Our Lady of Sorrows"). At the top, AÑO DE HIDALGO ("Year of Hidalgo"); above the church, 1753 / 1953. *Diameter:* 40 mm. *Edge:* Lettered **AGRICULTURA INDUSTRIA COMERCIO**.

	Mintage	F	VF	EF	UNC	BU
1953	1,000,000	BV+3%	BV+3%	BV+3%	$26.00	$30.00

El Ferrocarril del Sureste

Close-up of the locomotive on the Railroad 5 pesos. With the rising sun in the east, the engine is traveling south, indicating the new route from Mexico City all the way to the peninsula. The palm trees and plantation represent Yucatán. The crops are likely corn; the forest in the middle may be Yucatán's ceiba trees, which have unusually tall, bare trunks and small, high leaf canopies.

In the early 20th century, the railways *(ferrocarriles)* in Yucatán were used mainly to carry freight from the plantations to the ports on the peninsula, and were not connected to the lines in the rest of the country. In the 1930s, under the Lázaro Cárdenas administration, a huge infrastructure project was initiated to link the nation's railways to the isolated Ferrocarriles Unidos de Yucatán. The result, the Ferrocarril del Sureste (Southeast Railroad) was completed in 1950 and inaugurated by then-president Miguel Alemán. The event was commemorated on a 5-peso coin of 1950, which today is a favorite among collectors for its beauty as much as its historic significance. The type is so highly regarded it is included in the Numismatic Heritage Series, and it is considered essential to a complete modern type set of Mexican coins.

A 1901 steam engine similar in type to the engine depicted on the coin. Steam engines, when placed into service, lasted many decades.

Type 4 (Hidalgo/Wreath). BW-555, KM-467.

Composition: 0.720 silver, 0.280 copper. *Weight:* 27.777 g. *Obverse:* Slightly above center, above a spray of oak and laurel, a small national coat of arms depicting the eagle in profile to the left, with stylized, leaf-like feathers and very large feet. The legend ESTADOS UNIDOS MEXICANOS surrounds, with CINCO PESOS below the spray. To the left of the spray, PESO above the coin's weight (in grams), $27\frac{7}{9}$ 6; to the right of the spray, fineness LEY / 0.720. At the bottom, the mintmark Mo and the date. *Reverse:* Within an open wreath of laurel, the head of Miguel Hidalgo y Costilla in profile to the left, with HIDALGO below the neck and mintmark M̊ to the right of the head. *Diameter:* 40 mm. *Edge:* Lettered AGRICULTURA INDUSTRIA COMERCIO.

	Mintage	F	VF	EF	UNC	BU
1951 (a)	4,985,000	BV+3%	BV+3%	BV+3%	$26.00	$32.00
1952 (a)	9,595,000	BV+3%	BV+3%	BV+3%	26.00	32.00
1953 (a)	20,376,000	BV+3%	BV+3%	BV+3%	26.00	32.00
1954	30,000	$32.00	$38.00	$55.00	75.00	90.00

a. The snake on the 1951, 1952, and 1953 coins is struck either with or without a tongue. No particular premium is attached to either variety.

The Parish Church of Dolores Hidalgo

The Church of Our Lady of Sorrows today, in the town of Dolores Hidalgo, named in honor of Father Miguel and the *grito de Dolores*.

When Father Miguel Hidalgo y Costilla delivered his famous plea, the *grito de Dolores* that ignited the Mexican War of Independence (see the sidebar on page 131–132), he was speaking to his flock in Our Lady of Sorrows, a parish church built around 1710. The bell rung by Hidalgo to raise the countryside has been moved to the National Palace, in Mexico City, where it is rung each year on September 16 in memory of the event. In addition to appearing on the Type 3 circulating 5 pesos, Our Lady of Sorrows is featured on the reverse of a 20-peso Proof coin commemorating the bicentennial of the start of the War of Independence.

Type 5 (Hidalgo/Chico). BW-556, KM-469.

Composition: 0.720 silver, 0.280 copper. *Weight:* 18.055 g. *Obverse:* At the center, a small national coat of arms depicting the eagle in profile to the left, with stylized, leaf-like feathers and very large feet; the arms are enclosed in a circle formed by a spray of oak and laurel below and the legend ESTADOS UNIDOS MEXICANOS above. Surrounding all, · CINCO PESOS · with weight 18.055 G ·, the date, and fineness · LEY .720. *Reverse:* On a plain field, the head of Miguel Hidalgo y Costilla in profile to the left, with the legend · INDEPENDENCIA Y LIBERTAD · and HIDALGO surrounding, and the mintmark M̥ to the right of the head. *Diameter:* 36 mm. *Edge:* Reeded.

	Mintage	F	VF	EF	UNC	BU
1955	4,271,000	BV+3%	BV+3%	BV+3%	$15.00	$17.00
1956	4,596,000	BV+3%	BV+3%	BV+3%	15.00	17.00
1957	3,464,000	BV+3%	BV+3%	BV+3%	15.00	17.00

Type 6 (Constitution). BW-557, KM-470.

Composition: 0.720 silver, 0.280 copper. *Weight:* 18.05 g. *Obverse:* At the center, a small national coat of arms depicting the eagle in profile to the left, with stylized, leaf-like feathers and very large feet; the arms are enclosed in a circle formed by a spray of oak and laurel below and the legend ESTADOS UNIDOS MEXICANOS above. Surrounding all, · CINCO PESOS · and the weight, date, and fineness: 18.055 G · 1957 · LEY .720. *Reverse:* The head of Benito Juárez García in profile to the left, with the legend · CENTENARIO DE LA CONSTITUCION DE MEXICO · and 1857·1957. To the right of the head, the mintmark M̥. *Diameter:* 36 mm. *Edge:* Reeded.

	Mintage	F	VF	EF	UNC	BU
1957	200,000	BV+5%	BV+5%	$13.00	$15.00	$18.00

Type 7 (Carranza). BW-558, KM-471.

Composition: 0.720 silver, 0.280 copper. *Weight:* 18.055 g. *Obverse:* At the center, a small national coat of arms depicting the eagle in profile to the left, with stylized, leaf-like feathers and very large feet; the arms are enclosed in a circle formed by a spray of oak and laurel below and the legend **ESTADOS UNIDOS MEXICANOS** above. Surrounding all, · **CINCO PESOS** · and the weight, date, and fineness: **18.055 G · 1959 · LEY .720**. *Reverse:* The head of Venustiano Carranza in profile to the left, surrounded by the legend · **AÑO DE CARRANZA** · and **1859·1959** (with curling ornaments in place of the dots). To the right of the neck, the mintmark M̥. *Diameter:* 36 mm. *Edge:* Plain.

	Mintage	F	VF	EF	UNC	BU
1959	1,000,000	BV+3%	BV+3%	BV+3%	$22.00	$26.00

Type 8 (Guerrero). BW-559, KM-472.

Composition: 0.750 copper, 0.250 nickel. *Weight:* 15 g. *Obverse:* Above a spray of oak and laurel, the national coat of arms with the eagle in profile to the left, the feathers and other elements drawn as outlines instead of in full relief. Legend **ESTADOS UNIDOS MEXICANOS**. *Reverse:* On a plain field, a bust of Vicente Guerrero in profile to the right below the denomination **CINCO PESOS**. To the left of the bust, the date; to the right, the mintmark M̥. *Diameter:* 33 mm. *Edge:* Lettered **INDEPENDENCIA Y LIBERTAD**.

	Mintage	F	VF	EF	UNC	BU
1971	28,457,000	$0.25	$0.45	$0.95	$2.50	$3.80
1972	75,000,000	0.25	0.45	0.95	2.15	2.60
1973	19,405,000	0.25	0.95	1.65	3.80	5.75
1974	34,500,000	0.25	0.45	0.70	1.40	2.15
1976, SmDt, Open 9 and 6	26,121,000	0.25	0.45	1.20	4.00	5.25
1976, LgDt, Closed 9 and 6	121,550,000	0.25	0.45	0.70	1.40	2.15
1977	102,000,000	0.25	0.45	0.70	1.40	2.15
1978	25,700,000	0.25	0.95	1.90	4.75	8.00

Type 9 (Quetzalcóatl). BW-560, KM-485.

Composition: 0.750 copper, 0.250 nickel. *Weight:* 10.36 g. *Obverse:* On a heptagonal field, the national coat of arms above a spray of oak and laurel, with the eagle in profile to the left, its feathers resembling plates of armor. Above, the legend ESTA-DOS UNIDOS MEXICANOS. *Reverse:* To the right of center on a heptagonal field, the head of the feathered-serpent god Quetzalcóatl facing left, with the mintmark M̥ above and **QUETZALCOATL** in small letters below. To the left of the head, stacked vertically, the denomination 5 / $. At the bottom, the date. *Diameter:* 27.1 mm. *Edge:* Lettered **INDEPENDENCIA Y LIBERTAD**.

	Mintage	F	VF	EF	UNC	BU	PF	ChPF
1980	266,900,000	$0.25	$0.45	$0.60	$1.65	$2.15		
1981	30,500,000	0.25	0.45	0.60	1.90	3.00		
1982	20,000,000	0.45	0.95	1.65	4.75	5.75		
1982, Pf	1,048						$55.00	
1983, Pf	7 known						1,250.00	1,425.00
1983, Proof, Bronze							710.00	
1984	16,300,000	0.45	0.95	1.65	4.75	5.75		
1985	76,900,000	0.45	0.95	1.65	4.75	5.75		

Type 10 (Reduced). BW-561, KM-502.

Composition: 0.920 copper, 0.060 aluminum, 0.020 nickel. *Weight:* 3.12 g. *Obverse:* Above a spray of oak and laurel, the national coat of arms with the eagle facing left, its feathers resembling plates of armor. Above, the legend **ESTADOS UNIDOS**

MEXICANOS. *Reverse:* The denomination $5, with a large number 5 shaded with a screen-like pattern and placed to the right of the field. To the left of the number, above the peso symbol ($), the date; below the peso symbol, the mintmark M̥. *Diameter:* 17 mm. *Edge:* Reeded.

	Mintage	F	VF	EF	UNC	BU	PF
1985	30,000,000	$0.05	$0.10	$0.25	$0.45	$0.95	
1987	81,900,000	3.80	6.75	8.50	11.50	14.00	
1988	76,600,000	0.05	0.10	0.25	0.45	0.95	
1988, Proof	2 known						$570.00

Quetzalcóatl

Quetzalcóatl is the Nahuatl name for an ancient Mesoamerican god who is often depicted as a dragonlike creature with feathers. The Mayans called him Kukulcán; although he has many names, they all mean *feathered serpent*. He was considered a creator god, and was said to have created mankind from his own bones, blood, and tissues, after the previous worlds were destroyed by fire and flood. Sometimes he is depicted as a man, a white god with light hair and eyes very different from those of the indigenous people who worshipped him. When Hernán Cortés appeared in Mexico—pale of skin, his face fringed with a beard—the emperor Moctezuma II believed him to be the earthly incarnation of Quetzalcóatl, and received him peacefully.

Quetzalcóatl was one of several important gods in the Mesoamerican pantheon. He was a patron god of the priesthood and knowledge; the giver of the calendar; a god of wind, rain, water, and the planet Venus; and the giver of maize (corn) to the people. He connected the earth and the sky and thereby united the people, and sometimes was a symbol of death and resurrection.

Quetzalcóatl/Kukulcán is one of the most popular and enduring myths of the ancient people of Mexico, and, in addition to appearing on the Type 9 five pesos, the effigy is depicted on two Pre-Columbian Collections issues: the Proof gold one-ounce coin in the Teotihuacán Collection, and a Proof five-ounce silver coin in the Toltec Collection. The silver five-ounce coin in the Mayan Collection features the pyramid dedicated to Kukulán.

A sculpture of Quetzalcóatl at the entrance to the Teotihuacán ruins.

10 PESOS

The 10 pesos under the Reform of 1905 were made in seven basic types. The gold 10 pesos is described by its denomination; the other six types are as follows:

Type 1—Hidalgo Grande (large diameter, with head of Father Miguel Hidalgo y Costilla in profile to the left)

Type 2—Constitution (commemorating the Constitution of 1857, with a profile portrait of former president Benito Juárez García)

Type 3—Hidalgo/Madero (commemorating the 150th anniversary of independence and the 50th anniversary of federation with a pair of portraits: Miguel Hidalgo y Costilla, hero of the War of Independence; and Francisco Madero, hero of the Revolution)

Type 4—Hidalgo, Thin (a heptagonal coin with the head of Hidalgo in profile to the left, on a thin flan)

Type 5—Hidalgo, Thick (like Type 4, on a thicker flan)

Type 6—Hidalgo, Steel (with new metallic composition and a forward-facing head of Hidalgo)

Type 1a (10-peso gold). BW-654, KM-473.

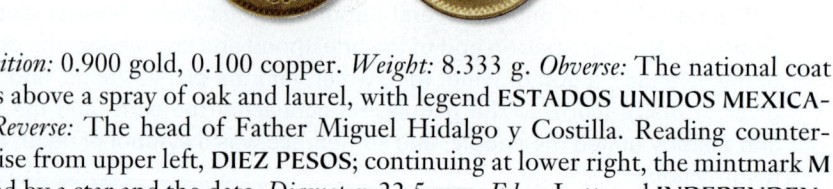

Composition: 0.900 gold, 0.100 copper. *Weight:* 8.333 g. *Obverse:* The national coat of arms above a spray of oak and laurel, with legend **ESTADOS UNIDOS MEXICANOS**. *Reverse:* The head of Father Miguel Hidalgo y Costilla. Reading counterclockwise from upper left, **DIEZ PESOS**; continuing at lower right, the mintmark **M** followed by a star and the date. *Diameter:* 22.5 mm. *Edge:* Lettered **INDEPENDENCIA Y LIBERTAD**.

	Mintage	F	VF	EF	UNC	BU
1905	38,612	BV+3%	$310.00	$355.00	$500.00	$640.00
1906	2,949,000	BV+3%	BV+3%	BV+3%	355.00	450.00
1907	1,589,000	BV+3%	BV+3%	BV+3%	355.00	450.00
1908	890,000	BV+3%	BV+3%	BV+3%	355.00	450.00
1910	451,000	BV+3%	BV+3%	BV+3%	355.00	450.00
1916	26,000	BV+3%	310.00	355.00	500.00	640.00
1917	1,966,500	BV+3%	BV+3%	BV+3%	355.00	450.00
1919	266,000	BV+3%	BV+3%	BV+3%	355.00	450.00
1920	22,603,000	$525.00	680.00	900.00	1,280.00	1,615.00
1959, Restrike	954,983	BV	BV	BV	BV+10%	BV+12%

Type 1 (Hidalgo Grande). BW-562, KM-474.

Composition: 0.900 silver, 0.100 copper. *Weight:* 28.888 g. *Obverse:* At the center, a small national coat of arms depicting the eagle in profile to the left, with stylized, leaf-like feathers and very large feet; the arms are enclosed in a circle formed by a spray of oak and laurel below and the legend ESTADOS UNIDOS MEXICANOS above. Surrounding all, · DIEZ PESOS · with weight 28.888 G ·, the date, and fineness · LEY .900. *Reverse:* On a plain field, the head of Miguel Hidalgo y Costilla in profile to the left, with the legend · INDEPENDENCIA Y LIBERTAD · and HIDALGO surrounding and the mintmark M̥ to the right of the head. *Diameter:* 40 mm. *Edge:* Reeded.

	Mintage	F	VF	EF	UNC	BU
1955	584,500	BV	BV	$32.00	$38.00	$40.00
1956	3,535,000	BV	BV	30.00	32.00	38.00

Type 2 (Constitution). BW-563, KM-475.

Composition: 0.900 silver, 0.100 copper. *Weight:* 28.888 g. *Obverse:* At the center, a small national coat of arms depicting the eagle in profile to the left, with stylized, leaf-like feathers and very large feet; the arms are enclosed in a circle formed by a spray of oak and laurel below and the legend ESTADOS UNIDOS MEXICANOS above. Surrounding all, · DIEZ PESOS · and the weight, date, and fineness: 28.888 G · 1957 · LEY .900. *Reverse:* The head of Benito Juárez García in profile to the left with the legend · CENTENARIO DE LA CONSTITUCION DE MEXICO · and 1857·1957. To the right of the head, the mintmark M̥. *Diameter:* 40 mm. *Edge:* Lettered INDEPENDENCIA Y LIBERTAD.

	Mintage	F	VF	EF	UNC	BU
1957	100,000	BV	BV	$32.00	$38.00	$40.00

Type 3 (Hidalgo/Madero). BW-564, KM-476.

Composition: 0.900 silver, 0.100 copper. *Weight:* 28.888 g. *Obverse:* At the center, a small national coat of arms depicting the eagle in profile to the left, with stylized, leaf-like feathers and very large feet; the arms are enclosed in a circle formed by a spray of oak and laurel below and the legend **ESTADOS UNIDOS MEXICANOS** above. Surrounding all, · **DIEZ PESOS** · and the weight, date, and fineness: **28.888 G · 1960 · LEY .900**. The mintmark M̥ is to the left of the snake in the coat of arms. *Reverse:* Busts of Miguel Hidalgo y Costilla and Francisco Madero, with **HIDALGO** and **MADERO**, respectively, in small letters below the busts. Legend · **INDEPENDENCIA Y LIBERTAD** · and **SUFRAGIO EFECTIVO NO REELECCION**. Above the portraits, the date; to the left of the portraits, 1810; to the right, 1910. *Diameter:* 40 mm. *Edge:* Reeded.

	Mintage	F	VF	EF	UNC	BU
1960	1,000,000	BV	BV	$32.00	$38.00	$40.00

Type 4 (Hidalgo/Thin). BW-565, KM-477.1.

Composition: 0.750 copper, 0.250 nickel. *Weight:* 10 g. *Obverse:* Above a half-wreath of oak and laurel, the national coat of arms depicting the eagle in profile to the left, with the feathers and other elements drawn as outlines instead of in full relief. Above, the legend **ESTADOS UNIDOS MEXICANOS**. *Reverse:* The head of Miguel Hidalgo y Costilla in profile to the left. Above, **DIEZ PESOS**; at lower right, the date; at lower left, the mintmark M̥. *Diameter:* Heptagonal; 30.4 mm. *Edge:* Plain.

Note: Minted on a thin flan.

	Mintage	F	VF	EF	UNC	BU	PF
1974	3,900,000	$0.45	$0.85	$1.40	$3.00	$3.80	
1974, Proof							$570.00
1975	1,000,000	1.90	2.85	4.75	7.75	9.50	
1976	74,500,000	0.15	0.25	0.45	1.65	2.50	
1976, Open 6	*	0.45	0.85	1.40	3.00	3.80	
1976, Proof							570.00
1977	79,620,000	0.15	0.25	0.45	1.65	2.50	

* Included above.

Type 5 (Hidalgo, Thick). BW-566, KM-477.2.

Composition: 0.750 copper, 0.250 nickel. *Weight:* 14 g. *Obverse:* Above a half-wreath of oak and laurel, the national coat of arms depicting the eagle in profile to the left, with the feathers and other elements drawn as outlines instead of in full relief. Above, the legend **ESTADOS UNIDOS MEXICANOS**. *Reverse:* The head of Miguel Hidalgo y Costilla in profile to the left. Above, **DIEZ PESOS**; at lower right, the date; at lower left, the mintmark M̥. *Diameter:* Heptagonal; 30.4 mm. *Edge:* Plain.

Note: Minted on a thick flan.

	Mintage	F	VF	EF	Unc.	BU	PF
1978	124,850,000	$0.25	$0.70	$1.20	$2.50	$2.85	
1979	57,200,000	0.25	0.95	1.40	2.85	3.80	
1980	55,200,000	0.25	0.95	1.40	2.85	3.80	
1981	222,767,990	0.25	0.70	1.20	2.50	2.85	
1982	151,770,000	0.25	0.70	1.20	2.50	2.85	
1982, Proof							$50.00
1983, Proof	3 known						1,800.00
1985	58,000,000	0.70	1.40	2.85	5.75	6.75	

Type 6 (Hidalgo, Steel). BW-567, KM-512.

Composition: stainless steel. *Weight:* 3.84 g. *Obverse:* Above a spray of oak and laurel, the national coat of arms depicting the eagle in profile to the left, with feathers resembling plates of armor. Above, the legend **ESTADOS UNIDOS MEXICANOS**. *Reverse:* To the right, on a plain field, a forward-facing head of Miguel Hidalgo y

Costilla, with **HIDALGO** below and four dots (the number 10 in Braille) above. To the left of the portrait, a large **$10** placed vertically atop the date, which is placed horizontally; to the right, the mintmark M̊. *Diameter:* 19 mm. *Edge:* Plain.

	Mintage	F	VF	EF	Unc.	BU	PF
1985	257,000,000	$0.10	$0.20	$0.35	$0.70	$0.95	
1986	392,000,000	0.10	0.20	0.35	0.70	0.95	
1987	305,000,000	0.10	0.15	0.20	0.45	0.60	
1988	500,300,000	0.10	0.15	0.20	0.35	0.50	
1989		0.10	0.25	0.45	0.85	1.20	
1990		0.10	0.25	0.45	0.85	1.20	
1990, Proof	2 known						$550.00

20 PESOS

The 20 pesos under the Reform of 1905 were made in three basic types. The gold 20 pesos is described by its denomination; the other two types are as follows:

Type 1—Mayan Culture type (honoring the ancient Mesoamerican culture with a design from the traditional Mayan ball game)

Type 2—Victoria (with bust of former president Guadalupe Victoria)

20-Peso Gold. BW-655, KM-478.

Composition: 0.900 gold, 0.100 copper. *Weight:* 16.666 g. *Obverse:* Above a spray of oak and laurel, the national coat of arms with the eagle facing left; set at an angle below the wing, the date. Legend **ESTADOS UNIDOS MEXICANOS**. *Reverse:* Above center, the Aztec Calendar Stone, with **VEINTE PESOS** around the lower edge. At the bottom, the gold weight: ★ **15 Gr. ORO PURO** ★. *Diameter:* 27.5 mm. *Edge:* Lettered **INDEPENDENCIA Y LIBERTAD**.

Note: Without mintmark.

	Mintage	F	VF	EF	Unc.	BU
1917	852,000	BV+3%	BV+3%	BV+3%	$680.00	$850.00
1918	2,830,500	BV+3%	BV+3%	BV+3%	710.00	850.00
1919	1,093,500	BV+3%	BV+3%	BV+3%	710.00	850.00
1920	462,198	BV+3%	BV+3%	BV+3%	710.00	850.00
1920, 20 Over 10	*	BV+3%	BV+3%	BV+3%	710.00	850.00
1921	921,500	BV+3%	BV+3%	BV+3%	710.00	850.00
1921, 21 Over 11	*	BV+3%	BV+3%	BV+3%	710.00	850.00
1959, Restrike	1,158,414	BV+3%	BV+3%	BV+3%	BV+8%	BV+10%

* Included above.

Type 1 (Mayan Culture). BW-568, KM-486.

Composition: 0.750 copper, 0.250 nickel. *Weight:* 15.14 g. *Obverse:* Above a spray of oak and laurel, the national coat of arms with the eagle facing left, its feathers resembling plates of armor. Above, the legend **ESTADOS UNIDOS MEXICANOS**. *Reverse:* To right of center, a simplified rendering of the round ball-court marker from the ancient Mayan ritual ball game; **$20** is superimposed on the left side of the marker. Above the peso symbol ($), **CULTURA MAYA**; below the symbol, the date. At the bottom, the mintmark M̥. *Diameter:* 32 mm. *Edge:* Lettered **INDEPENDENCIA Y LIBERTAD**.

Note: The sidebar on pages 388 and 389 discusses the ball game and marker.

	Mintage	F	VF	EF	Unc.	BU	PF
1980	84,900,000	$0.25	$0.45	$0.80	$2.60	$3.35	
1981	250,573,396	0.25	0.45	0.80	2.60	3.35	
1982	236,892,000	0.40	0.80	1.40	2.85	3.80	
1982, Proof	1,048						$55.00
1983, Proof	3 known						1,615.00
1984	55,000,000	0.70	0.95	1.90	3.80	4.75	

Type 2 (Victoria). BW-569, KM-508.

Composition: 0.920 copper, 0.060 aluminum, 0.020 nickel. *Weight:* 5.86 g. *Obverse:* Above a spray of oak and laurel, the national coat of arms with the eagle facing left, its feathers resembling plates of armor. Legend **ESTADOS UNIDOS MEXICANOS**. *Reverse:* To the right of center, a bust of Guadalupe Victoria in three-quarter profile toward the left. To the left of the bust, a large **$20** placed vertically atop the date, which is placed horizontally. Below the bust, in small letters, **G VICTORIA**; to right of the bust, the mintmark M̥. Near the top, five dots in the Braille configuration for "20." *Diameter:* 21 mm. *Edge:* Reeded.

	Mintage	F	VF	EF	Unc.	BU	PF
1985, Wide Date, Open 5	25,000,000	$0.10	$0.10	$0.20	$1.15	$1.30	
1985, Narrow Date, Open 5	*	0.10	0.15	0.25	1.65	2.15	
1985, Wide Date, Closed 5	*	0.20	0.25	0.40	1.90	2.50	
1986	10,000,000	0.45	1.20	2.85	4.75	6.75	
1988, Closed 8	355,200,000	0.10	0.10	0.25	0.70	0.95	
1988, Open 8	*	0.25	0.45	1.00	2.00	3.00	
1989	289,100,000	0.10	0.15	0.30	1.65	2.15	
1990	126,550,000	0.20	0.25	0.40	1.90	2.50	
1990, Doubled-Die Reverse	*	0.25	0.45	1.00	2.00	3.00	
1990, Proof	3 known						$610.00

* Included above.

25 PESOS

Circulating 25 pesos under the Reform of 1905 were made in two basic types:

Type 1—Olympics (commemorating the 1968 Summer Olympic Games in Mexico City)

Type 2—Juárez (commemorating the 100th anniversary of the death of former president Benito Juárez García)

See chapter 4 for commemorative 25-peso coinage.

Type 1 (Olympics). BW-570, KM-479.

Composition: 0.720 silver, 0.280 copper. *Weight:* 22 g. *Obverse:* Above a sprig of oak and laurel, the national coat of arms depicting a left-facing eagle with somewhat stylized, leaf-like feathers and large feet. Above, the legend **ESTADOS UNIDOS MEXICANOS**. To the eagle's left, **25 / PESOS**, with PESOS in the shape of a three-sided shield. To the eagle's right, fineness **LEY / 0.720** with mintmark M̊ below. *Reverse:* At center, Aztec ball player superimposed over an outline of a ball court, with the five Olympic rings at the bottom. Legend **JUEGOS DE LA XIX OLIMPIADA MEXICO 1968**. *Diameter:* 38 mm. *Edge:* Lettered **INDEPENDENCIA Y LIBERTAD**.

Note: On Variety 1 (BW-570.1, KM-479.1), the Olympic rings are aligned. On Variety 2 (BW-570.2, KM-479.2), the center ring is low. On Variety 3 (BW 570.3, KM-479.3), the center ring is low and the snake's tongue is curved. See the sidebar on pages 388 and 389 for information on the Mesoamerican ball game.

	Mintage	F	VF	EF	Unc.	BU
1968, Variety 1	27,181,500	BV	BV	BV	$15.00	$18.00
1968, Variety 2	*	BV	BV	BV	19.00	22.00
1968, Variety 3	*	BV	BV	BV	19.00	22.00

* Included above.

Mexico 1968 Olympics

A Mexican medal commemorating the 1968 Olympics (G-1017), combining the modern era with the ancient cultures of Mexico. Shown at actual size (40 mm).

In 1968 Mexico hosted the 19th Summer Olympic Games—the first Olympics to be held in a Latin American country. It was a tumultuous time in world affairs, with the war in Vietnam, the Robert Kennedy and Martin Luther King Jr. assassinations, the Civil Rights movement, and other areas of unrest. In Mexico City, the army fired on participants of a student protest march just days before the games were scheduled to begin. The students, largely from the UNAM (see the sidebar on pages 267 and 268) were protesting the spending of funds on the Games instead of on social programs.

Adding to the politically charged atmosphere of the Games, African American athletes Tommie Smith (gold) and John Carlos (silver) mounted the medal platform for the 200 meters and raised their fists in a Black Power salute instead of saluting the American flag. The International Olympic Committee sent them home for the civil-rights protest gesture, citing their violation of the Olympics' principle of being nonpolitical.

Most of the athletes, however, were simply there to compete in their chosen sports. Mexico City's high elevation (7,350 feet) took a toll on the performance of many athletes and influenced numerous events for good or ill. On the plus side, the thin air helped participants set records in short (up to 400-meter) races as well as in jumps, vaults, throws, and leaps.

For high-jumpers, the 1968 Games will be remembered as the ones in which American Dick Fosbury introduced his new high-jumping technique, the Fosbury flop, later adopted by others in the sport. Drug testing debuted at the 1968 Games; the first doping disqualification was for alcohol use by a Swedish pentathlete. The 1968 Games were the first to be telecast to the world in color; and for the first time, a woman, Norma Enriqueta Basilio, lit the Olympic cauldron.

Mexico had beaten bids by Detroit, Buenos Aires, and Lyon to host the Games, which were the first to be held in a Spanish-speaking country. The primary venue was the UNAM's Estadio Olimpico Universitario, which is depicted on a 2010 commemorative 10 pesos.

Type 2 (Juárez). BW-571, KM-480.

Composition: 0.720 silver, 0.280 copper. *Weight:* 22 g. *Obverse:* Above a spray of oak and laurel, the national coat of arms depicting the eagle in profile to the left, with the feathers and other elements drawn as outlines instead of in full relief. Above, the legend **ESTADOS UNIDOS MEXICANOS**. *Reverse:* A bust of Benito Juárez García in three-quarter profile angled to the left. Legend · **VEINTICINCO PESOS** · with fineness **LEY 0.720**, the mintmark M°, and **1972**. *Diameter:* 38 mm. *Edge:* Lettered **INDEPENDENCIA Y LIBERTAD**.

	Mintage	F	VF	EF	Unc.	BU
1972	2,000,000	BV	BV	BV	$19.00	$22.00

50 PESOS

Circulating 50 pesos under the Reform of 1905 were made in four basic types. The gold 50 pesos, which commemorates the 100th anniversary of independence from Spain, is known as the *Centenario*. The other three types are as follows:

Type 1—Coyolxauhqui (honoring ancient Mesoamerican culture with images from the Aztec myth of Coyolxauhqui, as depicted in the Templo Mayor in Mexico City)

Types 2—Juárez, Copper-Nickel (commemorating the 100th anniversary of the death of former president Benito Juárez García)

Type 3—Juárez, Steel (like Type 2, but in steel composition)

See chapter 4 for commemorative 50-peso coinage.

50-Peso Gold (Centenario). BW-656, KM-481.

Composition: 0.900 gold, 0.100 copper. *Weight:* 41.6666 g. *Obverse:* The national coat of arms with the eagle facing forward, head to the right, above a spray of oak and laurel; above, the legend **ESTADOS UNIDOS MEXICANOS**. *Reverse:* The statue atop the *Independence Monument*, known as *El Ángel* (based on Nike, the Greek goddess of victory), with volcanoes in the background. To the left of the statue, **50 / PESOS**. To the right, the coin's gold weight, **37.5Gr. / ORO / PURO**. At lower right, the date; at lower left, **1821**. *Diameter:* 37 mm. *Edge:* Lettered **INDEPENDENCIA Y LIBERTAD**.

Note: Without mintmark. See the sidebar on page 56 for more information on the monument.

	Mintage	F	VF	EF	Unc.	BU
1921	180,400	BV+3%	BV+3%	BV+3%	$2,150.00	$2,500.00
1922	462,600	BV+3%	BV+3%	BV+3%	1,750.00	1,950.00
1923	431,800	BV+3%	BV+3%	BV+3%	1,750.00	1,950.00
1924	439,400	BV+3%	BV+3%	BV+3%	1,750.00	1,950.00
1925	716,000	BV+3%	BV+3%	BV+3%	1,750.00	1,950.00
1926	600,000	BV+3%	BV+3%	BV+3%	1,750.00	1,950.00
1927	606,000	BV+3%	BV+3%	BV+3%	1,750.00	1,950.00
1928	538,000	BV+3%	BV+3%	BV+3%	1,750.00	1,950.00
1929	458,000	BV+3%	BV+3%	BV+3%	1,750.00	1,950.00
1930	371,600	BV+3%	BV+3%	BV+3%	1,750.00	1,950.00
1931	136,860	BV+3%	BV+3%	BV+3%	2,150.00	2,500.00
1931, 1 Over 0		BV+3%	BV+3%	BV+3%	2,150.00	2,500.00
1944	592,900	BV+3%	BV+3%	BV+3%	1,750.00	1,950.00
1945	1,012,000	BV+3%	BV+3%	BV+3%	1,750.00	1,950.00
1946	1,588,000	BV+3%	BV+3%	BV+3%	1,750.00	1,950.00
1947, Restrike (a)	3,975,654	BV	BV	BV	BV+4%	BV+6%

a. Some 309,000 coins were originally struck in 1947, followed by 3,975,654 restrikes the same year. The originals and the 1947 restrikes are indistinguishable. The mint produced restrikes again in the 1990s and 2000s; these can be distinguished from the 1947 strikes by their prooflike and matte finishes (respectively).

50-Peso Gold (Centenario). BW-656.1, KM-482.

Composition: 0.900 gold, 0.100 copper. *Weight:* 41.6666 g. *Obverse:* The national coat of arms with the eagle facing forward, head to the right, above a spray of oak and laurel; above, the legend **ESTADOS UNIDOS MEXICANOS**. *Reverse:* The statue atop the *Independence Monument*, known as *El Ángel* (based on Nike, the Greek goddess of victory), with volcanoes in the background. On both the left and the right sides of the statue, the coin's gold weight, 37.5Gr. / **ORO** / **PURO**. At the bottom, divided by the base of the statue, 1821 / 1943. *Diameter:* 37 mm. *Edge:* Lettered **INDEPENDENCIA Y LIBERTAD**.

Note: Without mintmark.

	Mintage	F	VF	EF	Unc.	BU
1943, No Denomination	89,400	BV+3%	BV+3%	BV+3%	$1,650.00	$1,850.00

The Metcalf Restrike

Shown at actual size (37 mm).

In the 1950s, collector Edward H. Metcalf commissioned five restrikes, in platinum, of the 1947 Centenario. Although they were struck from the original dies, and in a heavier metal, they weigh slightly less than the gold Centenarios (41.666 g. for the gold vs. 41.3 g. for the platinum). Unlike the originals, they have plain edges. The restrikes are well known to Centenario enthusiasts for both their pristine beauty and their great rarity. Past auction prices have ranged from $9,000 to $11,500.

Type 1 (Coyolxauhqui). BW-577, KM-490.

Composition: 0.750 copper, 0.250 nickel. *Weight:* 19.63 g. *Obverse:* Above a spray of oak and laurel, the national coat of arms depicting the eagle in profile to the left, with feathers resembling plates of armor. Above, the legend **ESTADOS UNIDOS MEXICANOS**. *Reverse:* Slightly left of center, the dismembered Aztec goddess Coyolxauhqui, as carved on a stone in Mexico City. To the right, the denomination $ / 50, with the peso symbol ($) placed above the zero. Below the zero, the date; below the date, the mintmark M̥. A border of points and beads in the style of the Aztec Calendar Stone extends from the figure's left foot around the field to the left, and back to the figure's left hand. Inside this border, the legend **templo mayor de méxico** and · **coyolxauhqui** ·. *Diameter:* 36 mm. *Edge:* Reeded.

	Mintage	F	VF	EF	UNC	BU	PF
1982	222,890,000	$1.20	$1.90	$3.35	$5.75	$6.75	
1983	45,000,000	1.20	2.50	4.25	6.75	7.75	
1983, Proof	1,048						$60.00
1984	73,537,000	0.95	1.65	2.85	3.80	4.75	
1984, Proof	4 known						710.00

Coyolxauhqui

A celestial Nahuatl goddess of Aztec mythology, Coyolxauhqui, whose name means "face painted with bells" or "golden bells," was a powerful magician and the leader of the southern star gods. She was the daughter of the earth goddess Coatlicue, who gave birth to 400 children.

Coyolxauhqui became angry and embarrassed because her mother had become magically impregnated by a ball of feathers that fell on her in a temple. Coyolxauhqui rallied her siblings to kill their mother—but the instant Coatlicue was killed, the god Huitzilopochtli sprang from her womb fully armed for battle. He killed

The stone disk depicting the death of Coyolxauhqui, unearthed in Mexico City in 1978. The disk measures about 7.5 feet across at its widest point and is about a foot thick. Made of volcanic stone, it weighs approximately 8 tons.

many of his siblings, including Coyolxauhqui, then cut off her limbs and head with a fire serpent. In a moment of softness, he tossed the head into the sky to become the moon, so that everyone would be comforted by it. The depiction of Coyolxauhqui appears only on the Type 1 fifty pesos.

Type 2 (Juárez, Copper-nickel). BW-578, KM-495.

Composition: 0.750 copper, 0.250 nickel. *Weight:* 8.55 g. *Obverse:* Above a spray of oak and laurel, the national coat of arms with the eagle facing left, its feathers resembling plates of armor. Above, the legend **ESTADOS UNIDOS MEXICANOS**. *Reverse:* To the right of center, a bust of Benito Juárez García in three-quarter profile toward the left. Below the bust, in small letters, **JUAREZ**; to right of the bust, the mintmark M̊. To the left of the bust, a large **$50** placed vertically atop the date, which is placed horizontally. Near the top, five dots in the Braille configuration for "50." *Diameter:* 23.6 mm. *Edge:* Reeded.

	Mintage	F	VF	EF	Unc.	BU
1984	94,216,000	$0.25	$0.95	$1.90	$2.85	$3.80
1985	296,000,000	0.10	0.20	0.35	1.40	1.90
1986	50,000,000	2.60	5.50	7.75	10.50	11.50
1987	210,000,000	0.10	0.20	0.35	1.40	1.90
1988	80,200,000	2.15	4.75	7.75	12.50	14.00

Type 3 (Juárez, Steel). BW-579, KM-495a.

Composition: stainless steel. *Weight:* 7.17 g. *Obverse:* Above a spray of oak and laurel, the national coat of arms with the eagle facing left, its feathers resembling plates of armor. Above, the legend **ESTADOS UNIDOS MEXICANOS**. *Reverse:* To the right of center, a bust of Benito Juárez García in three-quarter profile toward the left. Below the bust, in small letters, **JUAREZ**; to right of the bust, the mintmark M̊. To the left of the bust, a large **$50** placed vertically atop the date, which is placed horizontally. Near the top, five dots in the Braille configuration for "50." *Diameter:* 23.6 mm. *Edge:* Plain.

	Mintage	F	VF	EF	Unc.	BU
1988	353,300,000	$0.10	$0.20	$0.55	$1.40	$1.90
1990	180,000,000	0.10	0.20	0.55	1.40	1.90
1992	84,520,000	0.10	0.20	0.55	1.20	1.40

100 PESOS

Circulating 100 pesos under the Reform of 1905 were made in two basic types:

Type 1—Morelos (depicting War of Independence hero José María Morelos)

Type 2—Carranza (depicting Revolutionary hero Venustiano Carranza)

See chapter 4 for commemorative 100-peso coinage.

Type 1 (Morelos). BW-586, KM-483.1.

Composition: 0.720 silver, 0.280 copper. *Weight:* 27.77 g. *Obverse:* Above a spray of oak and laurel, the national coat of arms depicting the eagle in profile to the left, with the feathers and other elements drawn as outlines instead of in full relief. Above, the legend **ESTADOS UNIDOS MEXICANOS**. *Reverse:* A forward-facing bust of José María Morelos on a plain field. To left of the bust, **CIEN / PESOS**; to right, the mintmark M̊ above the date. Below, silver weight **PLATA PURA 20 G^r.** and fineness **LEY .720**. *Diameter:* 39 mm. *Edge:* Reeded.

	Mintage	F	VF	EF	Unc.	BU	PF
1977, Low 7s	5,225,000	BV	BV	BV	$19.00	$22.00	
1977, High 7s (a)	*	BV	BV	BV	19.00	22.00	
1977, Level 7s	*	BV	BV	BV	19.00	22.00	
1978	9,879,000	BV	BV	BV	19.00	22.00	
1979	783,500	BV	BV	BV	19.00	22.00	
1979, Proof							$525.00

* Included above. **a.** BW-586.1.

Type 2 (Carranza). BW-587, KM-493.

Composition: 0.920 copper, 0.060 aluminum, 0.020 nickel. *Weight:* 11.97 g. *Obverse:* Above a spray of oak and laurel, the national coat of arms with the eagle facing left, its feathers resembling plates of armor. Above, the legend **ESTADOS UNIDOS MEXICANOS**. *Reverse:* To the left of center, a bust of Venustiano Carranza in three-quarter profile toward the right. Below the bust, in small letters, **V. CARRANZA**; to left of the bust, the mintmark M̊. To the right of the bust, a large **$100** placed vertically atop the date, which is placed horizontally. Near the top, seven dots in the Braille configuration for "100." *Diameter:* 26.5 mm. *Edge:* Paired reeding.

	Mintage	F	VF	EF	UNC	BU	PF
1984	277,809,000	$0.25	$0.45	$0.95	$2.15	$2.85	
1984 Over 1984	*	19.00	28.00	32.00	55.00	65.00	
1985 (a)	377,423,000	0.25	0.45	0.95	2.15	2.85	
1986	43,000,000	0.35	0.85	2.15	4.75	5.75	
1987	165,000,000	0.25	0.45	0.95	2.15	2.85	
1987, Doubled Eyeglasses	*	60.00	105.00	155.00	215.00	260.00	
1988	433,100,000	0.25	0.45	0.95	2.15	2.85	
1989	135,630,000	0.70	1.40	2.85	5.25	6.75	
1990	248,350,000	0.10	0.15	0.70	1.65	2.50	
1990, Proof							$1,330.00
1991		0.25	0.45	0.70	1.65	2.50	
1992		0.25	0.45	0.70	1.65	2.50	

* Included above. **a.** The 1985 coins are struck with either a curved-top or a flat-top 5. No particular premium is attached to either variety.

Venustiano Carranza

Venustiano Carranza Garza, president of Mexico from 1917 to 1920, was one of the four major leaders of the Mexican Revolution. Of those four, the other three—Emiliano Zapata, Francisco "Pancho" Villa, and Francisco Madero—are more widely remembered and celebrated today, due largely to their broader embrace of Revolutionary reforms and their general popularity with the Mexican public.

A tall, humorless man who was utterly lacking in charisma, Carranza was nonetheless well educated and ambitious. With his family's financial backing he entered local and regional politics during the rule of Porfirio Díaz, whom he deeply disliked. Carranza supported Francisco Madero in the latter's successful bid to oust Díaz, and despite doing little to actually assist Madero, he was made minister of war.

He took a dim view of Madero's presidential conduct, believing the latter ought to be tougher and less concerned with humanitarian ideals. He felt Madero's weakness, as he saw it, would bring his downfall, and he began forming political alliances just in case. Not long after Victoriano Huerta had Madero overthrown and executed, Carranza began to raise an army and a rebellion.

In the interest of defeating Huerta, Carranza forged an alliance with Pancho Villa, Emiliano Zapata, and Álvaro Obregón. With the first two, especially, the alliance was uncomfortable. Villa was a wild card who often disobeyed orders, creating diplomatic messes for Carranza to handle. Both Villa and Zapata sought farther-reaching reforms than Carranza, a centrist, wanted. Huerta had scarcely surrendered when Villa and Zapata broke with Carranza. Only Obregón remained loyal, and with his help Carranza was ultimately elected president.

In addition to resisting popular constitutional reforms that he considered too radical, Carranza was instrumental in the assassination of the beloved Revolutionary hero Zapata. He was unable to defeat Pancho Villa, however, and when the latter raided Columbus, New Mexico, Carranza gave the U.S. government his blessing to enter Mexico to hunt him down. This move was not warmly received by the public; Villa was popular in the countryside, and the United States was badly out of favor.

The U.S. government never captured Villa, and Obregón split with Carranza when the latter refused to support his bid for the presidency. Fearing Mexico had another dictator at the helm, Obregón attempted to assassinate Carranza; he failed, but Carranza was killed in an ambush not long afterward.

Although he never supported the sweeping reforms his compatriots sought, and his presidency left much to be desired, Carranza is still remembered as a major force in the Mexican Revolution. In addition to appearing on the Type 2 100 pesos, he is remembered on the Type 7 "Year of Carranza" 5 pesos; a Centennial of the Revolution Series circulating 5 pesos (Type A25); and the 1985 Revolution commemoratives: 200 pesos (circulating, Type 2) and 500 pesos (Proof, Type 1).

200 PESOS

Circulating 200 pesos under the Reform of 1905 were made in three basic types:

Type 1—Independence (commemorating the 175th anniversary of independence from Spain)

Type 2—Revolution (commemorating the 75th anniversary of the Mexican Revolution)

Type 3—World Cup Futbol (a limited-mintage circulating coin struck in conjunction with the commemorative series discussed in the "250 Pesos" section.)

See chapter 4 for commemorative 200-peso coinage.

Type 1 (Independence). BW-598, KM-509.

Composition: 0.750 copper, 0.250 nickel. *Weight:* 17.19 g. *Obverse:* Above a spray of oak and laurel, the national coat of arms with the eagle facing left, its feathers resembling plates of armor. Above, the legend **ESTADOS UNIDOS MEXICANOS**. *Reverse:* At the left, Mexico City's *Monumento de la Independencia*. In left-facing profile at the right, four quadragate busts (Ignacio Allende, Father Miguel Hidalgo y Costilla, José Morelos, and Vicente Guerrero), each with his surname beneath in small letters. Above the busts, **$200** and a partial border consisting of a broken chain, signifying freedom; below, **175 ANIVERSARIO DE / LA INDEPENDENCIA / DE MEXICO**. To the far left of the monument, **1985**; The mintmark M̥ is at the bottom. *Diameter:* 29.6 mm. *Edge:* lettered **INDEPENDENCIA Y LIBERTAD**.

	Mintage	F	VF	EF	Unc.	BU
1985	75,000,000	$0.45	$0.70	$2.50	$4.25	$5.00

Type 2 (Revolution). BW-599, KM-510.

Composition: 0.750 copper, 0.250 nickel. *Weight:* 17.19 g. *Obverse:* Above a spray of oak and laurel, the national coat of arms with the eagle facing left, its feathers resembling plates of armor. Above, the legend ESTADOS UNIDOS MEXICANOS. *Reverse:* In left-facing profile at the right, four quadragate busts (Emiliano Zapata, Francisco Madero, Venustiano Carranza, and Francisco "Pancho" Villa), each with his surname beneath in small letters. Behind the portraits, the dome of the *Monumento de la Revolucion.* The legend 75 ANIVERSARIO DE LA REVOLUCION MEXICANA surrounds, with 75 ANIVERSARIO placed vertically in the field at the left, in the location occupied by the *Monumento de la Independencia* on Type 1. Below the busts, $200 / 1985; at far left, the mintmark M̥. *Diameter:* 29.6 mm. *Edge:* Lettered INDEPENDENCIA Y LIBERTAD.

	Mintage	F	VF	EF	Unc.	BU
1985	98,590,000	$0.45	$0.70	$2.50	$4.25	$5.00

Type 3 (World Cup Futbol). BW-600, KM-525.

Composition: 0.750 copper, 0.250 nickel. *Weight:* 17.19 g. *Obverse:* Above a spray of oak and laurel, the national coat of arms with the eagle facing left, its feathers resembling plates of armor. Legend ESTADOS UNIDOS MEXICANOS. *Reverse:* Three futbol (soccer) players chasing a ball. Vertically at left, $200; at far right, the mintmark M̥. Above the players, COPA MUNDIAL DE FUTBOL. At the bottom, Mexico 86 / 1986. *Diameter:* 29.5 mm. *Edge:* Reeded.

	Mintage	F	VF	EF	Unc.	BU
1986	50,000,000	$0.45	$0.70	$2.15	$4.00	$4.75

250 PESOS

Reform of 1905 coins in the 250-peso denomination were struck only as commemoratives in honor of the 1986 World Cup Soccer ("futbol") Games, held in Mexico City. Other denominations were struck for this commemorative series, as well; all are discussed in chapter 4.

500 PESOS

The 500 pesos under the Reform of 1905 were made in seven basic types. Types 1 through 4 were commemoratives struck for the 1986 World Cup Soccer Games (see the previous section, "250 Pesos"). Types 5 and 7 were also commemoratives, honoring the anniversaries of the Revolution and of the nationalization of the oil industry, respectively. All are discussed in chapter 4. Only Type 6, the "Madero" type, was struck for circulation and is listed here.

Type 6 (Madero). BW-611, KM-529.

Composition: .750 copper, 0.250 nickel. *Weight:* 12.7 g. *Obverse:* Above a spray of oak and laurel, the national coat of arms with the eagle facing left, its feathers resembling plates of armor. Legend **ESTADOS UNIDOS MEXICANOS**. *Reverse:* Slightly to left of center, a bust of Francisco Madero in three-quarter profile to the right. Below the bust, **$500**; to left of the bust, the date (behind the head) and **Madero** (behind the shoulder); to right of the bust, the mintmark M̥. *Diameter:* 28.6 mm. *Edge:* Reeded.

	Mintage	F	VF	EF	Unc.	BU	PF
1986	20,000,000	$0.40	$0.45	$0.85	$3.25	$3.50	
1987	180,000,000	0.40	0.45	0.70	2.15	2.85	
1988	230,000,000	0.25	0.25	0.45	2.50	2.85	
1988, Proof	2 known						$620.00
1989	40,000,000	0.45	0.45	0.70	2.15	2.85	
1992	20,000,000	0.45	0.70	1.40	10.50	13.00	

1,000 PESOS

The 1,000 pesos under the Reform of 1905 were made in five basic types. Type 1 (World Cup Football Games), Type 2 (175th anniversary of independence), and Type 3 (50th anniversary of the nationalization of the oil industry), are commemoratives and are discussed in chapter 4. The other two types, which will be discussed here, are as follows:

Type 4—Juana (depicting 17th-century scholar, nun, and poet Juana de Asbaje)

Type 5—Atlan (with the Aztec glyph representing the ancient tribute-town Atlan)

Type 4 (Juana). BW-616, KM-536.

Composition: 0.920 copper, 0.060 aluminum, 0.020 nickel. *Weight:* 14.85 g. *Obverse:* Above a spray of oak and laurel, the national coat of arms with the eagle facing left, its feathers resembling plates of armor. Legend ESTADOS UNIDOS MEXICANOS. *Reverse:* A bust of Juana de Asbaje in three-quarter profile toward the left, with JUANA DE ASBAJE below. To the left of the bust, a large $1000 placed vertically atop the date, which is placed horizontally. To right of the bust, the mintmark M̊. *Diameter:* 30.9 mm. *Edge:* Reeded.

	Mintage	F	VF	EF	Unc.	BU	PF
1988	229,300,000	$0.70	$1.90	$3.35	$3.80	$4.25	
1989	215,716,000	0.70	1.90	3.35	3.80	4.25	
1990	41,291,000	0.80	2.60	3.00	4.25	4.75	
1990, Proof	2 known						$525.00
1991	42,468,000	0.95	1.90	3.00	3.50	5.50	
1992	84,725,000	0.95	1.90	3.00	3.50	5.50	

Juana Inés de Asbaje

Juana Inés de Asbaje was born November 12, 1651, in Amecameca. The illegitimate daughter of a Spanish captain and a Criollo woman, she was an extremely precocious child, learning to read by age three and mastering Greek logic by adolescence. She defied cultural taboos in order to educate herself, and at age 19 joined a convent so she could dedicate her life to study and writing. Her plays and poems questioned the role of women in society and defended their right to an education, attracting anger from the Church but admiration from the nobility. She died of bubonic plague in 1695.

The portrait on the 1,000 pesos depicts Juana in three-quarter profile. Below her chin is the upper part of an ornament that appears in all portraits of her from the time she entered the convent: an oval disk about 10 to 12 inches tall, apparently worn around the neck or pinned high on her habit. The object is an *escudo de monja*—literally, "nun's shield." In New Spain, nuns were prohibited from wearing gold crosses or any other devotional jewelry made of precious metals or stones. They chose to wear shields painted with religious scenes, in obedience to the rule, or perhaps even in defiance of it. In Juana's portraits, her shield depicts the Anunciation, in which the angel Gabriel tells the Virgin Mary she will conceive.

Atlan

The Atlan glyph, as it appears on the coin and rendered as a drawing. The Nahuatl word *Atlan* means *place of much water*. The bowl-shaped base of the glyph represents a riverbed; the horizontal lines represent water; and the two teeth mean "more" or "many."

The 100-peso Huitzilapan pattern (KM-Pn246), struck in aluminum and weighing 0.8 g. Diameter: 15 mm.

The 2,000-peso Monumento a la Revolución pattern (KM-Pn250), bimetallic, 3.96 g. Diameter: 20.5 mm.

In 1991, under the pressures of hyperinflation, the mint produced a series of large-denomination pattern coins in different metals, denominations, and reverse motifs: aluminum 100 pesos (Huitzilapan, KM-Pn246) and 200 pesos (Xochimilco, KM-Pn247); aluminum-bronze 500 pesos (Atenango, KM-Pn248) and 1,000 pesos (Atlan, KM-Pn249); and a bimetallic 2,000 pesos (Monument of the Revolution, KM-Pn250). The 1994 legislation authorizing the currency reform made the denominations moot and the coins were never issued, but somehow a number of the Atlan 1,000 pesos (and a few of the Monument 2,000 pesos) found their way into circulation.

Atlan is thought to have been a province that was defeated by Moctezuma II and included on the tribute rolls of the Codex Mendoza. Atlan's tribute was paid in raw cotton and cotton cloth. The province's original location was probably just northwest of Tenochtitlán (Mexico City), where the name Atlan survives in the modern town name Pahuatlán. In addition to paying tribute to Moctezuma, Atlan served as a military outpost for the Mexica—a place to stop nearby enemies before they could draw too close to Tenochtitlán.

Neither Atlan nor any of the other motifs mentioned here appear on other Mexican coins to date, with the exception of the *Monument of the Revolution.* In addition to its pattern usage, it appears on the 1985 Revolution commemoratives: 200 pesos (circulating, Type 2) and 500 pesos (Proof, Type 1).

Type 5 (Atlan). BW-617, KM-643.

Composition: 0.750 copper, 0.250 aluminum, nickel. *Weight:* 14.85 g. *Obverse:* Above a spray of oak and laurel, the national coat of arms with the eagle facing left, its feathers resembling plates of armor. Legend **ESTADOS UNIDOS MEXICANOS**. *Reverse:* At the center, a large **$1000**, with mintmark M̊ below and **1988** at the bottom. At the top, an Aztec glyph, with **ATLAN** directly below. *Diameter:* 22 mm.

Note: Although it can be found in circulation, this coin was never officially issued.

	Mintage	F	VF	EF	Unc.	BU
1991		$2.85	$4.75	$6.75	$7.75	$9.50

2,000 PESOS

Reform of 1905 coins in the 2,000-peso denomination were struck only as commemoratives, in honor of the 1986 World Cup Soccer Games held in Mexico City; see chapter 4.

5,000 PESOS

Reform of 1905 coins in the 5,000-peso denomination were struck in one design only: Type 1, Oil Industry (in honor of the 50-year anniversary of the nationalization of the oil industry).

Type 1 (Oil Industry). BW-619, KM-531.

Composition: 0.750 copper, 0.250 nickel. *Weight:* 17.37 g. *Obverse:* Above a spray of oak and laurel, the national coat of arms with the eagle facing left, its feathers resembling plates of armor. Above, the legend **ESTADOS UNIDOS MEXICANOS**. *Reverse:* At center, the *Fuente de Petróleos* (*Monument to the Oil Industry*). At the top, **CINCUENTENARIO**; at the bottom, **EXPROPIACION PETROLERA**. In the field to the left, $5000 placed vertically; to the right, 1988. Below the monument, 1938–1988 / M̊. *Diameter:* 33.4 mm. *Edge:* Reeded.

	Mintage	F	VF	EF	Unc.	BU
1988	50,000,000	$2.85	$3.80	$4.75	$6.75	$8.50

Fuente de Petróleos

The *Fuente de Petróleos,* also known as the *Oil Monument,* towers over Paseo de la Reforma in Mexico City. The 14-ton bronze statue depicts an Indian woman leading a group of toiling oil workers, and commemorates the nationalization of the oil industry by President Lázaro Cárdenas. Inscribed on the monument's 59-foot obelisk are the years 1810 (marking the beginning of the War of Independence), 1821 (the year Mexico won its independence), and 1938 (the year oil reserves and companies were nationalized).

The Coinage Reform of 1992

Approaching the latter part of 1992, the inflation rate had reached new heights within Mexico. The country had issued circulating coinage in the 1,000-peso denomination, including the bronze-aluminum Juana de Asbaje (1988–1992), as well as a copper-nickel 5,000 pesos released in 1988 to commemorate the 50th anniversary of the nationalization of the oil industry. Paper money was issued in values up to 20,000 pesos to accommodate business transactions. Speculators began to hoard and melt the copper-nickel coinage as the value of its metallic content exceeded its face value.

In early 1992, in order to stabilize the complex economy of Mexico and to better control inflation and the rate of exchange, President Carlos Salinas de Gortari requested the director general of the Casa de Moneda de México, Lic. Alfredo Lelo de Larrea y Robles, to devise a new coinage system with a newly designated monetary unit: the *nuevo peso* (new peso). In the new system the decimal was moved by three digits to eliminate the last three zeros of the current denominations (e.g., 1 new peso was the equivalent of 1,000 "old" pesos). This enabled Mexico to make use of the national currency and coinage still circulating at the time.

The commission for the new monetary system included representatives of the Casa de Moneda de México and the Banco de México, and brought together engineers, metallurgists, and artists to work on the new monetary units. Some of the items they took into consideration were portability, efficiency in the minting process, the face value as opposed to the value of the metal content (to deter hoarding), and difficulty of counterfeiting.

The decree authorizing the new monetary system was published June 22, 1992, in the *Diario Oficial de la Federación*, and became effective January 1, 1993. It covered the denominations of 5, 10, 20, and 50 centavos; and 1, 2, 5, and 10 pesos. The decree modified Article 2 and Article 5 of the monetary laws of the United States of Mexico, published in the *Diario Oficial de la Federación*, July 23, 1990.

Due to its importance to Mexican history and culture, the Aztec Calendar Stone (Piedra del Sol) was selected as the theme for the new coinage. The designs used for the reverses of the coins are from the various rings of the Calendar Stone (see appendix B).

On January 1, 1996, the term *nuevo* was deleted from the name of the denominations on the 1 peso and larger coins. The *nuevos pesos* continued to circulate, but the coinage struck after January 1, 1996, had only the peso symbol ($) in front of the denomination. The *nuevos pesos*, which corresponded to the monetary unit that was in effect until December 31, 1992, remained legal tender until December 31, 1995.

After that date they were exchangeable at commercial banks at an equivalent of 1,000 to 1 for bank notes and coins corresponding to the new monetary unit in pesos. All the coinage of the *nuevos pesos* denomination remained the same in design, except for the dropping of the N.

The government also made an effort to withdraw the silver-centered bimetallic coins because they were being hoarded for their silver content. There is confusion as to the final outcome of this endeavor, since some reports indicate that the government lifted the withdrawal. Circulating N$20 and N$50 coins were reported as late as 2004 in Mexico City.

In 2003, the Mexico Mint began two consecutive commemorative series in honor of the 180th anniversary of the Mexican Federation. Each series consisted of one coin for each state in the federation, with an additional coin for the Distrito Federal. In both series, the denominations were 10 pesos (silver Proofs only) and 100 pesos (bimetallic: circulating coins in silver and bronze-aluminum, and Proofs in silver and gold). The first, or *heraldic*, series commenced in 2003. Each reverse featured a different state's coat of arms, and the coins were issued in descending alphabetical order, from Zacatecas through Aguascalientes.

The second, or *emblematic*, series began in 2005. Each state's reverse featured images "related to architecture, art, science, fauna, flora, typical dresses or dances or geographical areas of interest peculiar to each state" (Banco de México, "The History of Coins and Banknotes in Mexico," www.banxico.org). The coins were released in normal alphabetical order, from Aguascalientes through Zacatecas. For both series in the program, the obverses bore the national coat of arms.

Numerous other circulating commemoratives were released from 2005 onward. These included the 400th anniversary of the first edition of *El Ingenioso Hidalgo Don Quijote de la Mancha*, by Miguel de Cervantes; the 470th anniversary of the Casa de Moneda de México; the 80th anniversary of the creation of the Banco de México; and the 100th anniversary of the 1905 Monetary Reform. Non-circulating commemoratives, including the Proof-only designs, are discussed in chapter 4.

5 CENTAVOS
Type A1. BW-671, KM-546.

Composition: stainless steel. *Weight:* 1.58 g. *Obverse:* At center, above a half wreath of oak and laurel, the national coat of arms with the eagle facing left, its feathers resembling plates of armor. Above, the legend **ESTADOS UNIDOS MEXICANOS**. *Reverse:* At center of a pentagonal (five-sided) field, a large 5¢, with the date above the 5 and the mintmark M̊ above the centavo symbol (¢). To the left and below, a partial border of stylized sun-rays from the Anillo de los Quincunces (Ring of Quincunxes) on the Aztec Calendar Stone. *Diameter:* 15.5 mm. *Edge:* Plain.

	Mintage	F	VF	EF	Unc	BU	PF	ChPF
1992	136,800,000	$0.10	$0.10	$0.20	$0.25	$1.35		
1993	234,000,000	0.10	0.10	0.20	0.25	1.35		
1994	125,000,000	0.10	0.10	0.20	0.25	1.35		
1995	195,000,000	0.10	0.10	0.20	0.25	1.35		
1995, Proof	(6,981)						$0.45	$3.50
1996	104,831,000	0.10	0.10	0.20	0.25	1.35		
1997	153,675,000	0.10	0.10	0.20	0.25	1.35		
1998	64,417,000	0.10	0.10	0.20	0.25	1.35		
1999	9,949,000	0.10	0.10	0.20	0.25	1.35		
2000	10,871,000	0.90	1.80	4.50	9.00	22.50		
2001	34,811,000	0.10	0.10	0.20	0.25	1.35		
2002	14,901,000	0.10	0.10	0.20	0.25	1.35		

10 CENTAVOS
Type A1. BW-672, KM-547.

Composition: stainless steel. *Weight:* 2.08 g. *Obverse:* At center, above a half wreath of oak and laurel, the national coat of arms with the eagle facing left, its feathers resembling plates of armor. Above, the legend **ESTADOS UNIDOS MEXICANOS**. *Reverse:* At center of a hexagonal (six-sided) field, a large 10¢, with the date and the mintmark M̊ above and below the 0, respectively. To the right and below, a partial border of points and beads, representing blood and jade, from the Anillo del Sacrificio (Ring of Sacrifice) on the Aztec Calendar Stone. *Diameter:* 17 mm. *Edge:* Plain.

	Mintage	F	VF	EF	Unc	BU	PF	ChPF
1992	121,250,000	$0.10	$0.10	$0.20	$0.25	$1.35		
1993	755,000,000	0.10	0.10	0.20	0.25	1.35		
1994	557,000,000	0.10	0.10	0.20	0.25	1.35		
1995	560,000,000	0.10	0.10	0.20	0.25	1.35		
1995, Proof	(6,981)						$0.45	$3.50
1996	594,216,000	0.10	0.10	0.20	0.25	1.35		
1997	581,622,000	0.10	0.10	0.20	0.25	1.35		
1998	602,667,000	0.10	0.10	0.20	0.25	1.35		
1999	488,346,000	0.10	0.10	0.20	0.25	1.35		
2000	577,546,000	0.10	0.10	0.20	0.25	1.35		
2001	618,061,000	0.10	0.10	0.20	0.25	1.35		
2002	463,968,000	0.10	0.10	0.20	0.25	1.35		
2003	378,938,000	0.10	0.10	0.20	0.25	1.35		
2004	393,705,000	0.10	0.10	0.20	0.25	1.35		
2005	488,594,000	0.10	0.10	0.20	0.25	1.35		
2006	473,261,000	0.10	0.10	0.20	0.25	1.35		

Type A1. BW-672, continued

	Mintage	F	VF	EF	Unc	BU	PF	ChPF
2007	498,735,000	0.10	0.10	0.20	0.25	1.35		
2008	433,951,000	0.10	0.10	0.20	0.25	1.35		
2009	90,968,000	0.25	0.45	0.90	1.80	2.25		

Type A2. BW-672.1, KM-934.

Composition: stainless steel. *Weight:* 2.08 g. *Obverse:* At center, above a half wreath of oak and laurel, the national coat of arms with the eagle facing left, its feathers resembling plates of armor. Above, the legend ESTADOS UNIDOS MEXICANOS. *Reverse:* At the center of (and nearly filling) a circular field, a very large 10¢, with the date and the mintmark M̥ above and below the 0, respectively. To the right and below, a partial border of points and beads, representing blood and jade, from the Anillo del Sacrificio (Ring of Sacrifice) on the Aztec Calendar Stone. The border is angled as on the hexagonal field of the previous type. *Diameter:* 14.5 mm. *Edge:* Plain.

	Mintage	F	VF	EF	Unc	BU
2009	343,772,000	$0.10	$0.10	$0.15	$0.20	$0.25
2010	453,849,000	0.10	0.10	0.15	0.20	0.25
2011	463,960,000	0.10	0.10	0.15	0.20	0.25
2012	419,017,000	0.10	0.10	0.15	0.20	0.25
2013	*399,143,000*	0.10	0.10	0.15	0.20	0.25
2014		0.10	0.10	0.15	0.20	0.25

20 CENTAVOS
Type A1. BW-673, KM-548.

Composition: 0.92 copper, 0.06 aluminum, 0.02 nickel. *Weight:* 3.04 g. *Obverse:* At center, above a half wreath of oak and laurel, the national coat of arms with the eagle facing left, its feathers resembling plates of armor. Above, the legend ESTADOS UNIDOS MEXICANOS. *Reverse:* At center of a dodecagonal (12-sided) field, a large 20¢ with the date above and the mintmark M̥ below. From upper left to lower right, a partial border of repeated Reed (Acatl) glyphs, representing the 13th-day glyph on the Aztec Calendar Stone. *Diameter:* 19.5 mm. *Edge:* Plain.

	Mintage	F	VF	EF	Unc	BU	PF	ChPF
1992	95,000,000	$0.10	$0.15	$0.25	$0.35	$1.25		
1993	95,000,000	0.10	0.15	0.25	0.35	1.25		
1994	105,000,000	0.10	0.15	0.25	0.35	1.25		
1995	180,000,000	0.10	0.15	0.25	0.35	1.25		
1995, Proof	(6,981)						$0.75	$5.50
1996	54,896,000	0.10	0.15	0.25	0.35	1.25		
1997	178,807,000	0.10	0.15	0.25	0.35	1.25		
1998	223,847,000	0.10	0.15	0.25	0.35	1.25		
1999	233,753,000	0.10	0.15	0.25	0.35	1.25		
2000	223,973,000	0.10	0.15	0.25	0.35	1.25		
2001	234,360,000	0.10	0.15	0.25	0.35	1.25		
2002	229,256,000	0.10	0.15	0.25	0.35	1.25		
2003	149,518,000	0.10	0.15	0.25	0.35	1.25		
2004	174,351,000	0.10	0.15	0.25	0.35	1.25		
2005	204,426,000	0.10	0.15	0.25	0.35	1.25		
2006	234,263,000	0.10	0.15	0.25	0.35	1.25		
2007	234,301,000	0.10	0.15	0.25	0.35	1.25		
2008	214,313,000	0.10	0.15	0.25	0.35	1.25		
2009	41,167,000	0.45	0.90	1.80	2.75	4.50		

Type A2. BW-673.1, KM-935.

Composition: 0.92 copper, 0.06 aluminum, 0.02 nickel. *Weight:* 2.258 g. *Obverse:* At center, above a half wreath of oak and laurel, the national coat of arms with the eagle facing left, its feathers resembling plates of armor. Above, the legend ESTADOS UNIDOS MEXICANOS. *Reverse:* At the center of a circular field, a large 20¢ with the date above and the mintmark M̥ below. From upper left to lower right, a partial border of stylized designs from Reed (Acatl), the 13th-day glyph on the Aztec Calendar Stone. *Diameter:* 15.3 mm, round planchet. *Edge:* Non-continuous grooved.

	Mintage	F	VF	EF	Unc	BU
2009	164,362,000	$0.10	$0.10	$0.15	$0.20	$0.25
2010	224,359,000	0.10	0.10	0.15	0.20	0.25
2011	239,362,000	0.10	0.10	0.15	0.20	0.25
2012	209,434,000	0.10	0.10	0.15	0.20	0.25
2013	*194,429,000*	0.10	0.10	0.15	0.20	0.25
2014		0.10	0.10	0.15	0.20	0.25

50 CENTAVOS
Type A1. BW-674, KM-549.

Composition: 0.92 copper 0.06 aluminum, 0.02 nickel. *Weight:* 4.39 g. *Obverse:* At center of a dodecagonal (12-sided) field, above a half wreath of oak and laurel, the national coat of arms with the eagle facing left, its feathers resembling plates of armor. Above, the legend **ESTADOS UNIDOS MEXICANOS**. *Reverse:* At center of a dodecagonal field, a large **50¢** with the date above and the mintmark M̊ below. From upper left, around the bottom, to upper right, a border of stylized feathers and blade-handles from the Anillo del Sacrificio (Ring of Sacrifice) on the Aztec Calendar Stone. *Diameter:* 22 mm, dodecagonal planchet. *Edge:* Plain.

	Mintage	F	VF	EF	Unc	BU	PF	ChPF
1992	120,150,000	$0.10	$0.20	$0.45	$0.70	$1.60		
1993	330,000,000	0.10	0.20	0.45	0.70	1.60		
1994	100,000,000	0.10	0.20	0.45	0.70	1.60		
1995	60,000,000	0.10	0.20	0.45	0.70	1.60		
1995, Proof	(6,981)						$0.90	$6.50
1996	69,956,000	0.10	0.20	0.45	0.70	1.60		
1997	129,029,000	0.10	0.20	0.45	0.70	1.60		
1998	223,605,000	0.10	0.20	0.45	0.70	1.60		
1999	89,516,000	0.10	0.20	0.45	0.70	1.60		
2000	135,112,000	0.10	0.20	0.45	0.70	1.60		
2001	199,006,000	0.10	0.20	0.45	0.70	1.60		
2002	94,552,000	0.10	0.20	0.45	0.70	1.60		
2003	124,522,000	0.10	0.20	0.45	0.70	1.60		
2004	154,434,000	0.10	0.20	0.45	0.70	1.60		
2005	179,296,000	0.10	0.20	0.45	0.70	1.60		
2006	234,142,000	0.10	0.20	0.45	0.70	1.60		
2007	253,634,000	0.10	0.20	0.45	0.70	1.60		
2008	249,279,000	0.10	0.20	0.45	0.70	1.60		
2009	90,602,000	0.10	0.20	0.45	0.70	1.60		

Type A2. BW-674.1, KM-936.

Composition: stainless steel. *Weight:* 3.103 g. *Obverse:* At center of a circular field, above a half wreath of oak and laurel, the national coat of arms with the eagle facing left, its feathers resembling plates of armor. Above, the legend **ESTADOS UNIDOS MEXICANOS**. *Reverse:* At center of a circular field, a large 50¢ with the date above and the mintmark M̥ below. From upper left, around the bottom, to upper right, a border of stylized feathers and blade-handles from the Anillo del Sacrificio (Ring of Sacrifice) on the Aztec Calendar Stone. *Diameter:* 17 mm, round planchet. *Edge:* Grooved.

	Mintage	F	VF	EF	Unc	BU
2009	19,910,000	$0.20	$0.25	$0.55	$0.75	$1.80
2010	114,567,000	0.20	0.25	0.55	0.75	1.80
2011	194,480,000	0.20	0.25	0.55	0.75	1.80
2012	359,183,000	0.20	0.25	0.55	0.75	1.80
2013	*359,338,000*	0.20	0.25	0.55	0.75	1.80
2014		0.20	0.25	0.55	0.75	1.80

NEW 1 PESO
Type A1. BW-675, KM-550.

Composition: bimetallic (center, 0.92 copper, 0.06 aluminum, 0.02 nickel; outer ring, stainless steel). *Weight:* 3.95 g. *Obverse:* On the bronze-aluminum center, the national coat of arms with the eagle facing left, its feathers resembling plates of armor. On the stainless-steel outer ring, the legend **ESTADOS UNIDOS MEXICANOS** above, with a half-wreath of oak and laurel below. *Reverse:* On the bronze-aluminum center, the denomination N$1 with large 1; above, the date; to the right, the mintmark M̥. On the outer ring, a simplified depiction of the Anillo del Resplandor (Ring of Splendor) on the Aztec Calendar Stone. *Diameter:* 21 mm. *Edge:* Plain.

	Mintage	F	VF	EF	Unc	BU	PF	ChPF
1992	144,000,000	$0.10	$0.20	$0.70	$1.35	$2.50		
1993	329,860,000	0.10	0.20	0.70	1.35	2.50		
1994	221,000,000	0.10	0.20	0.70	1.35	2.50		
1995	125,000,000	0.10	0.20	0.70	1.35	2.50		
1995, Proof	(6,981)						$2.50	$6.50

1 PESO
Type A2. BW-675.1, KM-603.

Composition: bimetallic (center, 0.92 copper, 0.06 aluminum, 0.02 nickel; outer ring, stainless steel). *Weight:* 3.95 g. *Obverse:* On the bronze-aluminum center, the national coat of arms with the eagle facing left, its feathers resembling plates of armor. On the stainless-steel outer ring, the legend ESTADOS UNIDOS MEXICANOS above, with a half-wreath of oak and laurel below. *Reverse:* On the bronze-aluminum center, a large $1 with the date above and the mintmark M̥ to the right. On the outer ring, a simplified depiction of the Anillo del Resplandor (Ring of Splendor) on the Aztec Calendar Stone. *Diameter:* 21 mm. *Edge:* Plain.

	Mintage	F	VF	EF	Unc	BU
1996	169,510,000	$0.10	$0.20	$0.70	$1.35	$2.50
1997	222,870,000	0.10	0.20	0.70	1.35	2.50
1998	261,942,000	0.10	0.20	0.70	1.35	2.50
1999	99,168,000	0.10	0.20	0.70	1.35	2.50
2000	158,379,000	0.10	0.20	0.70	1.35	2.50
2001	208,576,000	0.10	0.20	0.70	1.35	2.50
2002	119,514,000	0.10	0.20	0.70	1.35	2.50
2003	169,320,000	0.10	0.20	0.70	1.35	2.50
2004	208,611,000	0.10	0.20	0.70	1.35	2.50
2005	253,923,000	0.10	0.20	0.70	1.35	2.50
2006	289,834,000	0.10	0.20	0.70	1.35	2.50
2007	368,408,000	0.10	0.20	0.70	1.35	2.50
2008	363,878,000	0.10	0.20	0.70	1.35	2.50
2009	239,229,000	0.10	0.20	0.70	1.35	2.50
2010	209,313,000	0.10	0.20	0.70	1.35	2.50
2011	199,283,000	0.10	0.20	0.70	1.35	2.50
2012	383,908,000	0.10	0.20	0.70	1.35	2.50
2013	*264,288,000*	0.10	0.20	0.70	1.35	2.50
2014		0.10	0.20	0.70	1.35	2.50

NEW 2 PESOS
Type A1. BW-676, KM-551.

Composition: bimetallic (center, 0.92 copper, 0.06 aluminum, 0.02 nickel; outer ring, stainless steel). *Weight:* 5.19 g. *Obverse:* On the bronze-aluminum center, the national coat of arms with the eagle facing left, its feathers resembling plates of armor. On the stainless-steel outer ring, the legend **ESTADOS UNIDOS MEXICANOS** above, with a half-wreath of oak and laurel below. *Reverse:* On the bronze-aluminum center, the denomination **N$2** with large 2; to the left of the top of the 2, the date; to the right, the mintmark M̥. On the outer ring, selected glyphs from the Anillo de los Días (Ring of Days) on the Aztec Calendar Stone. *Diameter:* 23 mm. *Edge:* Plain.

	Mintage	F	VF	EF	Unc	BU	PF	ChPF
1992	60,000,000	$0.15	$0.25	$0.90	$2.25	$3.60		
1993	77,000,000	0.15	0.25	0.90	2.25	3.60		
1994	44,000,000	0.15	0.25	0.90	2.25	3.60		
1995	20,000,000	0.15	0.25	0.90	2.25	3.60		
1995, Proof	(6,981)						$4.50	$8.00

2 PESOS

Type A2. BW-676.1, KM-604.

Composition: bimetallic (center 0.92 copper, 0.06 aluminum, 0.02 nickel; outer ring, stainless steel). *Weight:* 7.07 g. *Obverse:* On the bronze-aluminum center, the national coat of arms with the eagle facing left, its feathers resembling plates of armor. On the stainless-steel ring, the legend **ESTADOS UNIDOS MEXICANOS** above, with a half-wreath of oak and laurel below. *Reverse:* On the bronze-aluminum center, a large **$2**; to the left side of the top of the 2, the date; to the right, the mintmark M̥. On the outer ring, selected glyphs from the Anillo de los Días (Ring of Days), the outer ring on the Aztec Calendar Stone. *Diameter:* 23 mm. *Edge:* Plain.

	Mintage	F	VF	EF	Unc	BU
1996	24,902,000	$0.15	$0.25	$0.90	$2.25	$3.60
1997	34,560,000	0.15	0.25	0.90	2.25	3.60
1998	104,138,000	0.15	0.25	0.90	2.25	3.60
1999	34,713,000	0.15	0.25	0.90	2.25	3.60
2000	69,322,000	0.15	0.25	0.90	2.25	3.60
2001	74,563,000	0.15	0.25	0.90	2.25	3.60
2002	74,547,000	0.15	0.25	0.90	2.25	3.60
2003	39,814,000	0.15	0.25	0.90	2.25	3.60
2004	89,496,000	0.15	0.25	0.90	2.25	3.60
2005	94,532,000	0.15	0.25	0.90	2.25	3.60
2006	144,123,000	0.15	0.25	0.90	2.25	3.60
2007	129,422,000	0.15	0.25	0.90	2.25	3.60

Type A2. BW-676.1, continued

	Mintage	F	VF	EF	Unc	BU
2008	134,235,000	0.15	0.25	0.90	2.25	3.60
2009	64,650,000	0.15	0.25	0.90	2.25	3.60
2010	34,878,000	0.15	0.25	0.90	2.25	3.60
2011	114,522,000	0.15	0.25	0.90	2.25	3.60
2012	134,445,000	0.15	0.25	0.90	2.25	3.60
2013	*104,596,000*	0.15	0.25	0.90	2.25	3.60
2014		0.15	0.25	0.90	2.25	3.60

NEW 5 PESOS
Type A1. BW-679, KM-552.

Composition: bimetallic (center, 0.92 copper, 0.06 aluminum, 0.02 nickel; outer ring, stainless steel). *Weight:* 7.07 g. *Obverse:* On the bronze-aluminum center, the national coat of arms with the eagle facing left, its feathers resembling plates of armor. On the stainless-steel ring, the legend ESTADOS UNIDOS MEXICANOS above, with a half-wreath of oak and laurel below. *Reverse:* On the bronze-aluminum center, the denomination N$5 with large 5; to the left of the top of the 5, the date; to the right, the mintmark M̥. On the outer ring, a depiction of the Anillo de las Serpientes (Ring of Serpents) on the Aztec Calendar Stone. *Diameter:* 25.5 mm. *Edge:* Plain.

	Mintage	F	VF	EF	Unc	BU	PF
1992	70,000,000	$0.25	$0.70	$1.80	$3.85	$7.65	
1993	168,240,000	0.25	0.70	1.80	3.85	7.65	
1994	58,000,000	0.25	0.70	1.80	3.85	7.65	
1995, Proof	(6,981)						$40.00

5 PESOS
Type A2. BW-680, KM-605.

Composition: bimetallic (center 0.92 copper, 0.06 aluminum, 0.02 nickel; outer ring, stainless steel). *Weight:* 7.07 g. *Obverse:* On the bronze-aluminum center, the national coat of arms with the eagle facing left, its feathers resembling plates of armor. On the stainless-steel ring, the legend **ESTADOS UNIDOS MEXICANOS** above, with a half-wreath of oak and laurel below. *Reverse:* At the center, a large $5; to the left of the top of the 5, the date; to the right, the mintmark M̊. On the outer ring, a depiction of the Anillo de las Serpientes (Ring of Serpents) on the Aztec Calendar Stone. *Diameter:* 25.5 mm. *Edge:* Plain.

	Mintage	F	VF	EF	Unc	BU
1997	39,468,000	$0.45	$0.70	$1.80	$2.75	$4.75
1998	103,729,000	0.45	0.70	1.80	2.75	4.75
1999	59,427,000	0.45	0.70	1.80	2.75	4.75
2000	20,869,000	0.45	0.70	1.80	2.75	4.75
2001	79,169,000	0.45	0.70	1.80	2.75	4.75
2002	34,754,000	0.45	0.70	1.80	2.75	4.75
2003	54,676,000	0.45	0.45	1.80	2.75	4.75
2004	89,518,000	0.45	0.45	1.80	2.75	4.75
2005	94,482,000	0.45	0.45	1.80	2.75	4.75
2006	89,447,000	0.45	0.45	1.80	2.75	4.75
2007	123,382,000	0.45	0.45	1.80	2.75	4.75
2008	9,939,000	0.45	0.45	1.80	2.75	4.75
2009	9,898,000	0.90	2.75	3.60	5.40	8.00
2010	6,929,000	0.90	2.75	3.60	5.40	8.00
2011	209,214,000	0.25	0.35	0.90	1.60	2.25
2012	159,398,000	0.25	0.35	0.90	1.60	2.25
2013	*129,464,000*	0.25	0.35	0.90	1.60	2.25
2014		0.25	0.35	0.90	1.60	2.25

THE BICENTENNIAL OF INDEPENDENCE AND THE CENTENNIAL OF THE REVOLUTION

Two very important series, authorized by decree on October 23, 2007, were released to commemorate important figures of the War of Independence (which commenced in 1810) and the Mexican Revolution (which began in 1910). The first issues of the two series were released in November 2008, with the remainder released through the centennial and bicentennial year, 2010.

Type A24 (Bicentennial of the War of Independence, BW-680)
Ignacio López Rayón. BW-680.1, KM-894.

A lawyer in Mexico City, Ignacio López Rayón became heavily involved in the military under Miguel Hidalgo y Costilla. In addition to leading an army, he served as secretary of state of the provisional government and presided over the Supreme National Congress of America. After the war he was treasurer of San Luis Potosí until his death in 1832.

Composition: bimetallic (center: 0.92 copper, 0.06 aluminum, 0.02 nickel; outer ring: stainless steel). *Weight:* 7.07 g. *Obverse:* On the bronze-aluminum center, the national coat of arms with the eagle in profile to the left, its feathers resembling plates of armor. On the stainless-steel outer ring, the legend **ESTADOS UNIDOS MEXICANOS** above, with a half-wreath of oak and laurel below. *Reverse:* On the bronze-aluminum center, a bust of López Rayón in profile to the right; to the left of the bust, $5; to the right, M̥ / 2008; below, **IGNACIO LÓPEZ RAYÓN**. On the outer ring, **BICENTENARIO DE LA INDEPENDENCIA** at the top, with • **MÉXICO 2010** • below. *Diameter:* 25.5 mm. *Edge:* Plain.

	Mintage	F	VF	EF	Unc	BU	PL
2008	9,934,397	$0.25	$0.35	$0.45	$0.90	$1.35	
2008, Prooflike	(4,267)						$7.20

Carlos María de Bustamante. BW-680.3, KM-896.

A strong supporter of independence from Spain and founder of the Mexican newspaper *Diario de México*, Carlos María de Bustamante was jailed a great many times for his openness in expressing liberal ideals. His autobiography, *Lo Que Se Dice, y Lo Que Se Hace*, is considered a frank depiction of contemporary history.

Composition: bimetallic (center: 0.92 copper, 0.06 aluminum, 0.02 nickel; outer ring: stainless steel). *Weight:* 7.07 g. *Obverse:* On the bronze-aluminum center, the national coat of arms with the eagle in profile to the left, its feathers resembling plates of armor. On the stainless-steel outer ring, the legend **ESTADOS UNIDOS MEXICANOS** above, with a half-wreath of oak and laurel below. *Reverse:* On the bronze-aluminum center, a bust of María de Bustamante in profile to the left; to the left of the bust, $5; to the right, M̥ / 2008; below, **CARLOS MARÍA DE BUSTAMANTE**. On the outer ring, **BICENTENARIO DE LA INDEPENDENCIA** at the top, with • **MÉXICO 2010** • below. *Diameter:* 25.5 mm. *Edge:* Plain.

	Mintage	F	VF	EF	Unc	BU	PL
2008	9,941,302	$0.25	$0.35	$0.45	$0.90	$1.35	
2008, Prooflike	(4,852)						$7.20

Francisco Xavier Mina. BW-680.5, KM-898.

Unlike the other major leaders of the War of Independence, who were mainly Mexican-born Creoles, Francisco Xavier Mina was born in Spain, and became a lawyer and a successful military officer there. While in England he met insurgent Servando Teresa de Mier, who persuaded him of the colonists' cause. He traveled to Mexico and joined the war with about 300 soldiers at his command. A year later, he was captured and executed. He was 27 years old.

Composition: bimetallic (center: 0.92 copper, 0.06 aluminum, 0.02 nickel; outer ring: stainless steel). *Weight:* 7.07 g. *Obverse:* On the bronze-aluminum center, the national coat of arms with the eagle in profile to the left, its feathers resembling plates of armor. On the stainless-steel outer ring, the legend **ESTADOS UNIDOS MEXICANOS** above, with a half-wreath of oak and laurel below. *Reverse:* On the bronze-aluminum center, a forward-facing bust of Xavier Mina with the face turned slightly to the left; to the right of the bust, **$5**; to the left, **M̊ / 2008**; below, **FRANCISCO XAVIER MINA**. On the outer ring, **BICENTENARIO DE LA INDEPENDENCIA** at the top, with • **MÉXICO 2010** • below. *Diameter:* 25.5 mm. *Edge:* Plain.

	Mintage	F	VF	EF	Unc	BU	PL
2008	9,914,938	$0.25	$0.35	$0.45	$0.90	$1.35	
2008, Prooflike	(4,523)						$7.20

Francisco Primo de Verdad y Ramos. BW-680.7, KM-900.1.

A Mexican-born lawyer and a politician of New Spain, Francisco Primo de Verdad y Ramos was jailed numerous times for advocating freedom from Spain. He eventually died in prison, and became a martyr to the independence movement.

Brilliant Uncirculated; error, without dots in the legend (BW-680.7a, KM-900.2).

Prooflike reverse, with dots correctly included in the legend.

Composition: bimetallic (center: 0.92 copper, 0.06 aluminum, 0.02 nickel; outer ring: stainless steel). *Weight:* 7.07 g. *Obverse:* On the bronze-aluminum center, the national coat of arms with the eagle in profile to the left, its feathers resembling plates of armor. On the stainless-steel outer ring, the legend **ESTADOS UNIDOS MEXICANOS** above, with a half-wreath of oak and laurel below. *Reverse:* On the bronze-aluminum center, a bust of Primo de Verdad in three-quarter profile to the right; to the left of the bust, **$5**; to the right, M̊ / **2008**; below, **FRANCISCO PRIMO DE VERDAD Y RAMOS**. On the outer ring, **BICENTENARIO DE LA INDEPENDENCIA** at the top, with • **MÉXICO 2010** • below. *Diameter:* 25.5 mm. *Edge:* Plain.

	Mintage	F	VF	EF	Unc	BU	PL
2008, Dot	9,937,000	$0.25	$0.35	$0.45	$0.90	$1.35	
2008, Dot, Prooflike	(4,279)						$7.20
2008, No Dot		2.75	5.40	9.00	15.00	18.00	

Mariano Matamoros. BW-680.9, KM-902.

A rebel priest of the War of Independence, Mariano Matamoros was elevated to the rank of lieutenant general by Jose María Morelos, making him effectively second in command of the army. He was captured during a battle with Augustín de Iturbide's forces; negotiations for an exchange were refused, and he was executed by firing squad.

Composition: bimetallic (center: 0.92 copper, 0.06 aluminum, 0.02 nickel; outer ring: stainless steel). *Weight:* 7.07 g. *Obverse:* On the bronze-aluminum center, the national coat of arms with the eagle in profile to the left, its feathers resembling plates of armor. On the stainless-steel outer ring, the legend **ESTADOS UNIDOS MEXICANOS** above, with a half-wreath of oak and laurel below. *Reverse:* On the bronze-aluminum center, a bust of Matamoros in three-quarter profile to the left, his head turned somewhat to the right; to the left of the bust, **$5**; to the right, M̊ / **2008**; below, **MARIANO MATAMOROS**. On the outer ring, **BICENTENARIO DE LA INDEPENDENCIA** at the top, with • **MÉXICO 2010** • below. *Diameter:* 25.5 mm. *Edge:* Plain.

	Mintage	F	VF	EF	Unc	BU	PL
2008	9,947,802	$0.25	$0.35	$0.45	$0.90	$1.35	
2008, Prooflike	(4,820)						$7.20

Miguel Ramos Arizpe. BW-680.11, KM-904.

Miguel Ramos Arizpe was a Catholic priest who was elected deputy for Coahuila in 1810. A promoter of independence, he was arrested for treason and was imprisoned until the War of Independence was over. He returned home and helped draft the Constitution of 1824, then went on to serve as minister of justice under several presidents. Ramos Arizpe is often called the Father of Mexican Federalism.

Composition: bimetallic (center: 0.92 copper, 0.06 aluminum, 0.02 nickel; outer ring: stainless steel). *Weight:* 7.07 g. *Obverse:* On the bronze-aluminum center, the national coat of arms with the eagle in profile to the left, its feathers resembling plates of armor. On the stainless-steel outer ring, the legend ESTADOS UNIDOS MEXICANOS above, with a half-wreath of oak and laurel below. *Reverse:* On the bronze-aluminum center, a bust of Ramos Arizpe in profile to the right; to the left of the bust, $5; to the right, M̊ / 2008; below, MIGUEL RAMOS ARIZPE. On the outer ring, BICENTENARIO DE LA INDEPENDENCIA at the top, with • MÉXICO 2010 • below. *Diameter:* 25.5 mm. *Edge:* Plain.

	Mintage	F	VF	EF	Unc	BU	PL
2008	9,927,433	$0.25	$0.35	$0.45	$0.90	$1.35	
2008, Prooflike	(4,683)						$7.20

Hermenegildo Galeana. BW-680.13, KM-906.

Born into a plantation-owning family, Hermenegildo Galeana never learned to read or write. His military talents were evident, however, and he became one of José María Morelos's closest and longest-term collaborators. He was killed in battle in 1814 and his head cut off and put on display by the Spanish. Locations in Chihuahua, Puebla, Nuevo León, and Guerrero were named in his honor, along with two Mexican Navy vessels.

Composition: bimetallic (center: 0.92 copper, 0.06 aluminum, 0.02 nickel; outer ring: stainless steel). *Weight:* 7.07 g. *Obverse:* On the bronze-aluminum center, the national coat of arms with the eagle in profile to the left, its feathers resembling plates of armor. On the stainless-steel outer ring, the legend ESTADOS UNIDOS MEXICANOS above, with a half-wreath of oak and laurel below. *Reverse:* On the bronze-aluminum center, a bust of Galeana in three-quarter profile to the left; to the left of the bust, $5; to the right, M̊ / 2008; below, HERMENEGILDO GALEANA. On the outer ring, BICENTENARIO DE LA INDEPENDENCIA at the top, with • MÉXICO 2010 • below. *Diameter:* 25.5 mm. *Edge:* Plain.

	Mintage	F	VF	EF	Unc	BU	PL
2008	9,935,901	$0.25	$0.35	$0.45	$0.90	$1.35	
2008, Prooflike	(4,966)						$7.20

José María Cos. BW-680.15, KM-908.

Born in Zacatecas, this doctor of theology participated in the War of Independence through the power of the press. The violence of war greatly disturbed José María Cos; he edited several pro-independence newspapers, advocated minimal bloodshed, and participated in the drafting of the 1815 Constitution of Apatzingán.

Composition: bimetallic (center: 0.92 copper, 0.06 aluminum, 0.02 nickel; outer ring: stainless steel). *Weight:* 7.07 g. *Obverse:* On the bronze-aluminum center, the national coat of arms with the eagle in profile to the left, its feathers resembling plates of armor. On the stainless-steel outer ring, the legend **ESTADOS UNIDOS MEXICANOS** above, with a half-wreath of oak and laurel below. *Reverse:* On the bronze-aluminum center, a bust of María Cos in three-quarter profile to the right; to the left of the bust, $5; to the right, M̊ / 2009; below, **JOSÉ MARÍA COS**. On the outer ring, **BICENTENARIO DE LA INDEPENDENCIA** at the top, with • **MÉXICO 2010** • below. *Diameter:* 25.5 mm. *Edge:* Plain.

	Mintage	F	VF	EF	Unc	BU	PL
2009	9,935,040	$0.25	$0.35	$0.45	$0.90	$1.35	
2009, Prooflike	(4,950)						$7.20

Pedro Moreno. BW-680.17, KM-910.

Pedro Moreno was a trader who organized guerrillas from among the peasants of his hacienda. He was joined in battle by Francisco Xavier Mina, with whom he fought many successful battles before being caught and executed by the Royalists.

Composition: bimetallic (center: 0.92 copper, 0.06 aluminum, 0.02 nickel; outer ring: stainless steel). *Weight:* 7.07 g. *Obverse:* On the bronze-aluminum center, the national coat of arms with the eagle in profile to the left, its feathers resembling plates of armor. On the stainless-steel outer ring, the legend **ESTADOS UNIDOS MEXICANOS** above, with a half-wreath of oak and laurel below. *Reverse:* On the bronze-aluminum center, a forward-facing bust of Pedro Moreno with head head turned partway to the right; to the left of the bust, $5; to the right, M̊ / 2009; below, **PEDRO MORENO**. On the outer ring, **BICENTENARIO DE LA INDEPENDENCIA** at the top, with • **MÉXICO 2010** • below. *Diameter:* 25.5 mm. *Edge:* Plain.

	Mintage	F	VF	EF	Unc	BU	PL
2009	6,942,480	$0.25	$0.35	$0.45	$0.90	$1.35	
2009, Prooflike	(4,940)						$7.20

Agustín de Iturbide. BW-680.19, KM-912.

Agustín de Iturbide was a Mexican born of Spanish descent (i.e., a Criollo), and as such was welcomed into the Royalist army, where for 10 years he fought the rebel uprising. When events in Spain constricted the powers of Ferdinand VII, Iturbide feared Mexico might succeed in becoming a republic. He offered an olive branch to the Insurgents, with whom he and his former Royalist soldiers finally won independence from Spain. Iturbide was made constitutional emperor, but abdicated after less than a year and was sent into exile. He later returned to Mexico, with good intentions but without having secured release from the terms of his exile, and was executed. (See volumes 1 and 3 for chapters on the coinage of Emperor Augustín I.)

Composition: bimetallic (center: 0.92 copper, 0.06 aluminum, 0.02 nickel; outer ring: stainless steel). *Weight:* 7.07 g. *Obverse:* On the bronze-aluminum center, the national coat of arms with the eagle in profile to the left, its feathers resembling plates of armor. On the stainless-steel outer ring, the legend **ESTADOS UNIDOS MEXICANOS** above, with a half-wreath of oak and laurel below. *Reverse:* On the bronze-aluminum center, a bust of Iturbide in profile to the left; to the right of the bust, **$5**; to the left, M̥ / 2009; below, **AGUSTÍN DE ITURBIDE**. On the outer ring, **BICENTENARIO DE LA INDEPENDENCIA** at the top, with • **MÉXICO 2010** • below. *Diameter:* 25.5 mm. *Edge:* Plain.

	Mintage	F	VF	EF	Unc	BU	PL
2009	6,944,222	$0.25	$0.35	$0.45	$0.90	$1.35	
2009, Prooflike	(4,838)						$7.20

Nicolás Bravo. BW-680.21, KM-914.

A Mexican general and politician who had no love for the Spanish, Nicolás Bravo and his family were among the first Criollos to support the rebellion. He fought alongside Hermenegildo Galeana and José María Morelos, and was with Iturbide and the Army of the Three Guarantees when they entered Mexico City in triumph. He served as president on three occasions, and had a reputation as a good leader, a tough fighter, and an extremely honorable man.

Composition: bimetallic (center: 0.92 copper, 0.06 aluminum, 0.02 nickel; outer ring: stainless steel). *Weight:* 7.07 g. *Obverse:* On the bronze-aluminum center, the national coat of arms with the eagle in profile to the left, its feathers resembling plates of armor. On the stainless-steel outer ring, the legend ESTADOS UNIDOS MEXICANOS above, with a half-wreath of oak and laurel below. *Reverse:* On the bronze-aluminum center, a bust of Bravo in three-quarter profile to the left; to the right of the bust, $5; to the left, M̥ / 2009; below, NICOLÁS BRAVO. On the outer ring, BICENTENARIO DE LA INDEPENDENCIA at the top, with • MÉXICO 2010 • below. *Diameter:* 25.5 mm. *Edge:* Plain.

	Mintage	F	VF	EF	Unc	BU	PL
2009	6,930,174	$0.25	$0.35	$0.45	$0.90	$1.35	
2009, Prooflike	(4,780)						$7.20

Servando Teresa de Mier. BW-680.23, KM-916.

A Dominican friar, Servando Teresa de Mier was punished for delivering a sermon that contradicted the accepted stories of the Virgin of Guadalupe. He was stripped of his credentials and exiled to Spain, then found his way to Rome, where he left the Dominican order and became a secular priest. He was imprisoned repeatedly for the satire and "disrespect" in his writings, including a humorous piece in support of Mexican independence. Over the course of more than 20 years he made his way back to Mexico, where he opposed the Iturbide regime and earned great respect from his compatriots.

Composition: bimetallic (center: 0.92 copper, 0.06 aluminum, 0.02 nickel; outer ring: stainless steel). *Weight:* 7.07 g. *Obverse:* On the bronze-aluminum center, the national coat of arms with the eagle in profile to the left, its feathers resembling plates of armor. On the stainless-steel outer ring, the legend ESTADOS UNIDOS MEXICANOS above, with a half-wreath of oak and laurel below. *Reverse:* On the bronze-aluminum center, a bust of Mier in nearly full profile to the left; to the right of the bust, $5; to the left, M̥ / 2009; below, SERVANDO TERESA DE MIER. On the outer ring, BICENTENARIO DE LA INDEPENDENCIA at the top, with • MÉXICO 2010 • below. *Diameter:* 25.5 mm. *Edge:* Plain.

	Mintage	F	VF	EF	Unc	BU	PL
2009	6,937,421	$0.25	$0.35	$0.45	$0.90	$1.35	
2009, Prooflike	(4,675)						$7.20

Leona Vicario. BW-680.25, KM-919.

Leona Vicario was a supporter of Mexican independence, and provided the rebels with as much information, money, medicine, and other forms of assistance as she could. She was jailed twice for her activities, but survived the War of Independence. She is the only civilian woman to have received a State funeral in Mexico.

Composition: bimetallic (center: 0.92 copper, 0.06 aluminum, 0.02 nickel; outer ring: stainless steel). *Weight:* 7.07 g. *Obverse:* On the bronze-aluminum center, the national coat of arms with the eagle in profile to the left, its feathers resembling plates of armor. On the stainless-steel outer ring, the legend **ESTADOS UNIDOS MEXICANOS** above, with a half-wreath of oak and laurel below. *Reverse:* On the bronze-aluminum center, a bust of Vicario in profile to the left; to the right of the bust, **$5**; to the left, M̊ / **2009**; below, **LEONA VICARIO**. On the outer ring, **BICENTENARIO DE LA INDEPENDENCIA** at the top, with • **MÉXICO 2010** • below. *Diameter:* 25.5 mm. *Edge:* Plain.

	Mintage	F	VF	EF	Unc	BU	PL
2009	6,937,872	$0.25	$0.35	$0.45	$0.90	$1.35	
2009, Prooflike	(4,730)						$7.20

Miguel Hidalgo y Costilla. BW-680.27, KM-UL.

A Mexican Catholic priest and folk hero of the War of Independence, Miguel Hidalgo y Costilla is one of the most revered historic figures in Mexico. He not only issued the call to freedom (the *grito de Dolores* that ignited the uprising), he rallied the indigenous peasants to battle and brought important military figures (e.g., Ignacio López Ráyon and José María Morelos) to the rebel side. (See also the sidebar on pages 132–134.)

Composition: bimetallic (center: 0.92 copper, 0.06 aluminum, 0.02 nickel; outer ring: stainless steel). *Weight:* 7.07 g. *Obverse:* On the bronze-aluminum center, the national coat of arms with the eagle in profile to the left, its feathers resembling plates of armor. On the stainless-steel outer ring, the legend **ESTADOS UNIDOS MEXICANOS** above, with a half-wreath of oak and laurel below. *Reverse:* On the bronze-aluminum center, a bust of Hidalgo in three-quarter profile to the left; to the left of the bust, $5; to the right, M̊ / 2010; below, **MIGUEL HIDALGO Y COSTILLA**. On the outer ring, **BICENTENARIO DE LA INDEPENDENCIA** at the top, with • **MÉXICO 2010** • below. *Diameter:* 25.5 mm. *Edge:* Plain.

	Mintage	F	VF	EF	Unc	BU	PL
2010	6,932,486	$0.25	$0.35	$0.45	$0.90	$1.35	
2010, Prooflike	(4,763)						$7.20

José María Morelos y Pavón. BW-680.29, KM-UL.

Born into a working-class family of mixed indigenous, Spanish, and African blood, José María Morelos was a priest and a friend of Miguel Hidalgo y Costilla. The latter persuaded him to join the cause, and he quickly proved to be one of the greatest rebel commanders of the war. He was eventually captured by Spanish authorities and executed for treason. (See also the sidebar on pages 50 and 51.)

Composition: bimetallic (center: 0.92 copper, 0.06 aluminum, 0.02 nickel; outer ring: stainless steel). *Weight:* 7.07 g. *Obverse:* On the bronze-aluminum center, the national coat of arms with the eagle in profile to the left, its feathers resembling plates of armor. On the stainless-steel outer ring, the legend **ESTADOS UNIDOS MEXICANOS** above, with a half-wreath of oak and laurel below. *Reverse:* On the bronze-aluminum center, a bust of Morelos in three-quarter profile to the right; to the left of the bust, $5; to the right, M̊ / 2010; below, **JOSÉ MARÍA MORELOS Y PAVÓN**. On the outer ring, **BICENTENARIO DE LA INDEPENDENCIA** at the top, with • **MÉXICO 2010** • below. *Diameter:* 25.5 mm. *Edge:* Plain.

	Mintage	F	VF	EF	Unc	BU	PL
2010	6,927,961	$0.25	$0.35	$0.45	$0.90	$1.35	
2010, Prooflike	(4,725)						$7.20

Vicente Guerrero

Vicente Guerrero was born August 10, 1782, to a Criollo father and an African mother in Tixtla, near Acapulco. Although his mother's race relegated her to the lowest social class in 18th-century Mexico, the wealth and influence of his father's relations secured Vicente's registration as a Criollo. His family supported Spanish rule, despite the personal difficulties that had been imposed upon them by the rigid class system. Vicente, however, became a firm anti-colonialist.

A mule driver who could neither read nor write, Guerrero joined the War of Independence in 1810, fighting under José María Morelos. He distinguished himself in battle and rose to the rank of lieutenant colonel. After Morelos's execution, Guerrero and his small army employed guerilla warfare against the Spanish, winning nearly 500 battles. He eventually joined forces with Augustín de Iturbide, viewing the latter's ambitions as Mexico's best chance for independence from Spain. Iturbide set forth his Plan of Iguala, with its now-famous "three guarantees": independence as a constitutional monarchy; establishment of Roman Catholicism as the sole religion; and the abolition of social classes, with equal rights extended to all. Guerrero ensured that African Mexicans were included in this provision.

In 1829 Guerrero was defeated in a bid for the second presidency of Mexico by Manuel Gómez Pedraza, who, like Iturbide, had entered the War of Independence on the Spanish side. Guerrero's supporters organized a widespread revolt. Gómez Pedraza renounced the presidency and fled the country, and Guerrero was made president.

Within months, the political turmoil of the newly independent country brought Guerrero's presidency down. Stripped of his powers by Congress after being betrayed by his vice president, Anastasio Bustamante, Guerrero returned to his home in southern Mexico to gather supporters and mount a rebellion. While he was in Acapulco, friends of Bustamante tricked Guerrero into boarding a ship, where he was subsequently captured. A trumped-up court martial was staged, and Guerrero was executed on February 14, 1831. Guerrero loyalists revolted in turn, forcing Bustamante to flee for his life.

Mexicans revere Vicente Guerrero as a hero in the fight for independence and the first man of color to serve as president of Mexico. In addition to his appearance on the commemorative five pesos, he is depicted on the Type 8 five pesos of the Coinage Reform of 1905.

Vicente Guerrero. BW-680.31, KM-UL.

The first black and indigenous president of Mexico, Vicente Guerrero made huge policy changes that ultimately helped the working classes and indigenous people (see sidebar).

Composition: bimetallic (center: 0.92 copper, 0.06 aluminum, 0.02 nickel; outer ring: stainless steel). *Weight:* 7.07 g. *Obverse:* On the bronze-aluminum center, the national coat of arms with the eagle in profile to the left, its feathers resembling plates of armor. On the stainless-steel outer ring, the legend **ESTADOS UNIDOS MEXICANOS** above, with a half-wreath of oak and laurel below. *Reverse:* On the bronze-aluminum center, a bust of Guerrero in three-quarter profile to the left; to the left of the bust, $5; to the right, M̥ / 2010; below, **VICENTE GUERRERO**. On the outer ring, **BICENTENARIO DE LA INDEPENDENCIA** at the top, with • MÉXICO 2010 • below. *Diameter:* 25.5 mm. *Edge:* Plain.

	Mintage	F	VF	EF	Unc	BU	PL
2010	6,929,709	$0.25	$0.35	$0.45	$0.90	$1.35	
2010, Prooflike	(4,716)						$7.20

Ignacio Allende. BW-680.33, KM-UL.

Ignacio Allende was born a privileged man in one of the highest social classes, and became a captain of the Spanish army in Mexico. He joined Miguel Hidalgo y Costilla and others in secret meetings to plan a rebellion; when the plan was discovered early and Hidalgo was forced to launch the rebellion ahead of schedule, Allende openly joined in and was made lieutenant general, second only to Hidalgo. While making their way toward the United States, where they hoped to raise more money for their army, they were ambushed and defeated by the Royalists. Both Allende and Hidalgo were captured, tried, and executed.

Composition: bimetallic (center: 0.92 copper, 0.06 aluminum, 0.02 nickel; outer ring: stainless steel). *Weight:* 7.07 g. *Obverse:* On the bronze-aluminum center, the national coat of arms with the eagle in profile to the left, its feathers resembling plates of armor. On the stainless-steel outer ring, the legend **ESTADOS UNIDOS MEXICANOS** above, with a half-wreath of oak and laurel below. *Reverse:* On the bronze-aluminum center, a bust of Allende in three-quarter profile to the right, his head turned back to the left; to the left of the bust, $5; to the right, M̥ / 2010; below, **IGNACIO ALLENDE**. On the outer ring, **BICENTENARIO DE LA INDEPENDENCIA** at the top, with • **MÉXICO 2010** • below. *Diameter:* 25.5 mm. *Edge:* Plain.

	Mintage	F	VF	EF	Unc	BU	PL
2010	6,939,957	$0.25	$0.35	$0.45	$0.90	$1.35	
2010, Prooflike	(4,752)						$7.20

Guadalupe Victoria. BW-680.35, KM-UL.

After fighting alongside José María Morelos, Hermenegildo Galeana, and Nicolás Bravo, Guadalupe Victoria became Mexico's first president after independence was won. He would be the only president in the first 30 years of the republic to serve a full term in office. Among other accomplishments, Victoria established a national treasury, promoted educational reform, and stabilized the border between the United States and Mexico. He also issued a decree formally abolishing slavery during the first annual reenactment of the *grito de Dolores* on September 16, 1825. (See also the sidebar on page 112.)

Composition: bimetallic (center: 0.92 copper, 0.06 aluminum, 0.02 nickel; outer ring: stainless steel). *Weight:* 7.07 g. *Obverse:* On the bronze-aluminum center, the national coat of arms with the eagle in profile to the left, its feathers resembling plates of armor. On the stainless-steel outer ring, the legend **ESTADOS UNIDOS MEXICANOS** above, with a half-wreath of oak and laurel below. *Reverse:* On the bronze-aluminum center, a forward-facing bust of Victoria with the head turned slightly to the left; to the left of the bust, $5; to the right, M̥ / 2010; below, **GUADALUPE VICTORIA**. On the outer ring, **BICENTENARIO DE LA INDEPENDENCIA** at the top, with • **MÉXICO 2010** • below. *Diameter:* 25.5 mm. *Edge:* Plain.

	Mintage	F	VF	EF	Unc	BU	PL
2010	6,934,638	$0.25	$0.35	$0.45	$0.90	$1.35	
2010, Prooflike	(4,767)						$7.20

Guadalupe Victoria

Guadalupe Victoria, born on September 29, 1786, in Tamazula, Durango, served as the first president of Mexico. He was christened José Miguel Ramón Adaucto Fernandez y Félix but changed his name in honor of Mexico's patron saint (the Virgin of Guadalupe) and as a symbol of the struggle again Spanish domination.

Orphaned at an early age, Victoria was cared for by an uncle. He studied at the seminary in Durango before going on to obtain a law degree in Mexico City. In 1812 he became a soldier in the battle for independence from Spain; within two years he'd become a rebel leader and military hero. After a series of major defeats at the hands of the Royalists, however, his men turned against him, and he was forced to hide in the jungles of Veracrúz for nearly four years.

Rumors of the Plan of Iguala, which called for a constitutional monarchy, inspired Victoria to come out of hiding in 1821. For contending that Mexico must become a republic led by a president rather than a king, he was jailed by the imperialist forces. He escaped and fled back to Veracrúz, where he and other leaders signed an act demanding that the Mexican congress, previously dissolved by the imperialists, be reinstated.

Emperor Agustín de Iturbide was ousted in March 1823, and shortly after, Spanish forces at the Fort of San Juan de Ulúa fired on the port in Veracrúz Harbor. Victoria negotiated peace with Spain and helped maintain executive power until a presidential election could be held. He won the election in 1824 and served as president until 1829. His presidency survived a revolt by his vice president (Nicolás Bravo) and conflicts with European business interests.

Though Victoria was successful in establishing diplomatic relations with major countries like the United States and Great Britain, his time in office was hampered by Mexico's financial problems. With the help of a British diplomat, Victoria negotiated foreign loans, which eased Mexico's fiscal woes and allowed Victoria to claim some small social progress.

Guadalupe Victoria died from epilepsy in 1843 at the age of 56. Officially declared a national hero in 1925, he is credited for helping abolish slavery and promote religious tolerance in Mexico. He is depicted on the Independence-bicentennial 5 pesos, as well as on the Type 2 twenty pesos.

Josefa Ortiz de Domínguez. BW-680.37, KM-UL.

Josefa Ortiz de Domínguez was deeply sympathetic with the communities and indigenous people who were being oppressed by the Spanish colonial government. She began to conspire with the rebels, for which she and her husband were both imprisoned. Today she is one of the heroes of independence who are called out by name in the annual *grito de Dolores*. (See also the sidebar on page 21.)

Composition: bimetallic (center: 0.92 copper, 0.06 aluminum, 0.02 nickel; outer ring: stainless steel). *Weight:* 7.07 g. *Obverse:* On the bronze-aluminum center, the national coat of arms with the eagle in profile to the left, its feathers resembling plates of armor. On the stainless-steel outer ring, the legend **ESTADOS UNIDOS MEXICANOS** above, with a half-wreath of oak and laurel below. *Reverse:* On the bronze-aluminum center, a bust of Ortiz de Domínguez in profile to the right; to the left of the bust, $5; to the right, M̊ / 2010; below, **JOSEFA ORTIZ DE DOMÍNGUEZ**. On the outer ring, **BICENTENARIO DE LA INDEPENDENCIA** at the top, with • **MÉXICO 2010** • below. *Diameter:* 25.5 mm. *Edge:* Plain.

	Mintage	F	VF	EF	Unc	BU	PL
2010	6,936,400	$0.25	$0.35	$0.45	$0.90	$1.35	
2010, Prooflike	(4,743)						$7.20

Type A25 (Centennial of the Mexican Revolution, BW-680)

Álvaro Obregón. BW-680.2, KM-895.

Álvaro Obregón Salido, president of Mexico from 1920 to 1924, was a brilliant strategist and politician. He participated first-hand in the Revolution and survived the brutal chaos and political intrigues that came in its wake. His was the first stable presidency since the Revolution had begun. He enabled badly needed educational, land, and labor-law reforms and was elected to a second term in 1928; he was assassinated before the term began.

Composition: bimetallic (center, 0.92 copper, 0.06 aluminum, 0.02 nickel; outer ring, stainless steel). *Weight:* 7.07 g. *Obverse:* On the bronze-aluminum center, the national coat of arms with the eagle in profile to the left, its feathers resembling plates of armor; on the stainless-steel outer ring, the legend **ESTADOS UNIDOS**

MEXICANOS above, with a half-wreath of oak and laurel below. *Reverse:* On the bronze-aluminum center, a bust of Obregón in three-quarter profile to the left. To the left of the bust, $5; to the right of the bust, M̊ / 2008; below, ÁLVARO OBREGÓN. On the outer ring, CENTENARIO DE LA REVOLUCIÓN at the top, with • MÉXICO 2010 • below. *Diameter:* 25.5 mm. *Edge:* Plain.

	Mintage	F	VF	EF	Unc	BU	PL
2008	9,948,722	$0.25	$0.35	$0.45	$0.90	$1.35	
2008, Prooflike	(4,727)						$7.20

José Vasconcelos. BW-680.4, KM-897.

A Mexican writer and philosopher, José Vasconcelos Calderón wrote several books that profoundly affected other writers, poets, anthropologists, and philosophers. After organizing a movement to oust Victoriano Huerta he was forced into exile in Paris for a time. He made many contributions to the Revolutionary effort and was an intellectual force in Mexico for years afterward. His support enabled the development of the Mexican mural movement and was a significant influence on the poet Octavio Paz (discussed in the sidebar on pages 135 and 136).

Composition: bimetallic (center, 0.92 copper, 0.06 aluminum, 0.02 nickel; outer ring, stainless steel). *Weight:* 7.07 g. *Obverse:* On the bronze-aluminum center, the national coat of arms with the eagle in profile to the left, its feathers resembling plates of armor; on the stainless-steel outer ring, the legend ESTADOS UNIDOS MEXICANOS above, with a half-wreath of oak and laurel below. *Reverse:* On the bronze-aluminum center, a bust of Vasconcelos Calderón in three-quarter profile to the left. To the left of the bust, $5; to the right of the bust, M̊ / 2008. On the outer ring, CENTENARIO DE LA REVOLUCIÓN at the top, with • MÉXICO 2010 • below. *Diameter:* 25.5 mm. *Edge:* Plain.

	Mintage	F	VF	EF	Unc	BU	PL
2008	9,939,839	$0.25	$0.35	$0.45	$0.90	$1.35	
2008, Prooflike	(4,767)						$7.20

Francisco Villa. BW-680.6, KM-899.

Born to poor peasants in Durango, José Doroteo Arango Arámbula spent his youth roving with a band of outlaws. After stealing a horse and killing an army officer, he took the name Francisco "Pancho" Villa. The Revolution channeled his roguish behavior into the service of the rebels, and he became a successful general. A charismatic figure, Villa was popular with his soldiers and a hero of the peasants of northern Mexico; but he was a political and military rival of his co-revolutionaries, one of whom had him assassinated after the Revolution.

Composition: bimetallic (center, 0.92 copper, 0.06 aluminum, 0.02 nickel; outer ring, stainless steel). *Weight:* 7.07 g. *Obverse:* On the bronze-aluminum center, the national coat of arms with the eagle in profile to the left, its feathers resembling plates of armor; on the stainless-steel outer ring, the legend **ESTADOS UNIDOS MEXICANOS** above, with a half-wreath of oak and laurel below. *Reverse:* On the bronze-aluminum center, a half-length figure of Francisco Villa on horseback, in three-quarter profile to the left. Above the portrait, **$5 / 2008**; at lower left, below the horse's reins, the mintmark **Ṁ**; below the portrait, **FRANCISCO VILLA**. On the outer ring, **CENTENARIO DE LA REVOLUCIÓN** at the top, with • **MÉXICO 2010** • below. *Diameter:* 25.5 mm. *Edge:* Plain.

	Mintage	F	VF	EF	Unc	BU	PL
2008	9,917,084	$0.25	$0.35	$0.45	$0.90	$1.35	
2008, Prooflike	(4,866)						$7.20

Heriberto Jara Corona. BW-680.8, KM-901.

A handsome soldier and politician who was also an important Mexican revolutionary, Heriberto Jara Corona served in congress several times, and was ambassador to Cuba, governor of Tabasco, and governor of Veracruz. He was among those who drafted the Constitution of 1917, and received numerous awards and honors over the course of his illustrious career.

Composition: bimetallic (center, 0.92 copper, 0.06 aluminum, 0.02 nickel; outer ring, stainless steel). *Weight:* 7.07 g. *Obverse:* On the bronze-aluminum center, the national coat of arms with the eagle in profile to the left, its feathers resembling plates of armor; on the stainless-steel outer ring, the legend **ESTADOS UNIDOS MEXICANOS** above, with a half-wreath of oak and laurel below. *Reverse:* On the bronze-aluminum center, a bust of Jara Corona in three-quarter profile to the left. To the left of the bust, **$5**; to the right of the bust, **Ṁ / 2008**; below, **HERIBERTO JARA**. On the outer ring, **CENTENARIO DE LA REVOLUCIÓN** at the top, with • **MÉXICO 2010** • below. *Diameter:* 25.5 mm. *Edge:* Plain.

	Mintage	F	VF	EF	Unc	BU	PL
2008	9,936,333	$0.25	$0.35	$0.45	$0.90	$1.35	
2008, Prooflike	(4,870)						$7.20

Ricardo Flores Magón. BW-680.10, KM-903.

A Mexican anarchist, Ricardo Flores Magón ran the radical newspaper *Regeneración*, which opposed the regime of dictator Porfirio Díaz. In 1904 Flores Magón's writings, which would help pave the way for the Revolution of 1910, were banned in Mexico, and he fled to the United States. He remained there for the rest of his life. Jailed several times for organizing workers and fomenting unrest against the Mexican government, he eventually died in prison in Leavenworth, Kansas.

Composition: bimetallic (center, 0.92 copper, 0.06 aluminum, 0.02 nickel; outer ring, stainless steel). *Weight:* 7.07 g. *Obverse:* On the bronze-aluminum center, the national coat of arms with the eagle in profile to the left, its feathers resembling plates of armor; on the stainless-steel outer ring, the legend **ESTADOS UNIDOS MEXICANOS** above, with a half-wreath of oak and laurel below. *Reverse:* On the bronze-aluminum center, a bust of Flores Magón in nearly full profile to the right. To the left of the bust, **$5**; to the right of the bust, **M̊ / 2008**; below, **RICARDO FLORES MAGÓN**. On the outer ring, **CENTENARIO DE LA REVOLUCIÓN** at the top, with • **MÉXICO 2010** • below. *Diameter:* 25.5 mm. *Edge:* Plain.

	Mintage	F	VF	EF	Unc	BU	PL
2008	9,940,278	$0.25	$0.35	$0.45	$0.90	$1.35	
2008, Prooflike	(4,690)						$7.20

Francisco J. Múgica. BW-680.12, KM-905.

A journalist and political revolutionary, Francisco J. Múgica led rebel forces in Michoacán during the Mexican Revolution, serving at times with Pascual Orozco, Venustiano Carranza, and Alvar Obregón (the latter of whom would later attempt to have him assassinated). After participating in the 1917 Constituent Congress, he went on to serve in many governmental positions, including the governorships of Baja California Sur, Michoacán, and Tabasco.

Composition: bimetallic (center, 0.92 copper, 0.06 aluminum, 0.02 nickel; outer ring, stainless steel). *Weight:* 7.07 g. *Obverse:* On the bronze-aluminum center, the national coat of arms with the eagle in profile to the left, its feathers resembling plates of armor; on the stainless-steel outer ring, the legend **ESTADOS UNIDOS MEXICANOS** above, with a half-wreath of oak and laurel below. *Reverse:* On the bronze-aluminum center, a bust of Múgica in three-quarter profile to the left. To the left of the bust, $5; to the right of the bust, M̥ / 2008; below, **FRANCISCO J. MÚGICA**. On the outer ring, **CENTENARIO DE LA REVOLUCIÓN** at the top, with • **MÉXICO 2010** • below. *Diameter:* 25.5 mm. *Edge:* Plain.

	Mintage	F	VF	EF	Unc	BU	PL
2008	9,926,537	$0.25	$0.35	$0.45	$0.90	$1.35	
2008, Prooflike	(4,588)						$7.20

Filomeno Mata. BW-680.14, KM-907.

Filomeno Mata, a highly successful Mexican journalist, founded several newspapers over the course of his career. Initially a proponent of Porfirio Díaz, he was appointed director of the Government Printing Office by the dictator. Eventually he had a change of heart, and he founded the *Diario del Hogar*, a newspaper that blatantly opposed Díaz. Between criticizing the dictator and founding a liberal reformist group, Mata often found himself in prison. He died of natural causes early in the Revolution, after supporting Francisco Madero in the latter's presidential campaign. A municipality in Veracrúz was later named in Mata's honor.

Composition: bimetallic (center, 0.92 copper, 0.06 aluminum, 0.02 nickel; outer ring, stainless steel). *Weight:* 7.07 g. *Obverse:* On the bronze-aluminum center, the national coat of arms with the eagle in profile to the left, its feathers resembling plates of armor; on the stainless-steel outer ring, the legend **ESTADOS UNIDOS MEXICANOS** above, with a half-wreath of oak and laurel below. *Reverse:* On the bronze-aluminum center, a forward-facing bust of Mata angled slightly to the left. To the right of the bust, $5; to the left of the bust, M̥ / 2009; below, **FILOMENA MATA**. On the outer ring, **CENTENARIO DE LA REVOLUCIÓN** at the top, with • **MÉXICO 2010** • below. *Diameter:* 25.5 mm. *Edge:* Plain.

	Mintage	F	VF	EF	Unc	BU	PL
2009	9,935,689	$0.25	$0.35	$0.45	$0.90	$1.35	
2009, Prooflike	(4,920)						$7.20

Carmen Serdán. BW-680.16, KM-909.

An ardent supporter of Francisco Madero, organizing the clandestine purchase of weapons and the distribution of revolutionary propaganda, Carmen Serdán is said to have fired the first shot of the Revolution. The police had learned that her family's home held a stockpile of weapons intended for use against the Díaz government. When the police chief entered the house Serdán shot at him; the shot set off not only a heated battle between the 21 Maderistas in the house and some 500 soldiers and policemen outside, but the Revolution itself. Serdán was wounded, captured, and sent to jail. After her release she worked as a nurse in various hospitals until her death in 1948.

Composition: bimetallic (center, 0.92 copper, 0.06 aluminum, 0.02 nickel; outer ring, stainless steel). *Weight:* 7.07 g. *Obverse:* On the bronze-aluminum center, the national coat of arms with the eagle in profile to the left, its feathers resembling plates of armor; on the stainless-steel outer ring, the legend **ESTADOS UNIDOS MEXICANOS** above, with a half-wreath of oak and laurel below. *Reverse:* On the bronze-aluminum center, a forward-facing bust of Serdán with her face turned partway to the right. To the left of the bust, $5; to the right of the bust, M̊ / 2009; below, **CARMEN SERDÁN**. On the outer ring, **CENTENARIO DE LA REVOLUCIÓN** at the top, with • **MÉXICO 2010** • below. *Diameter:* 25.5 mm. *Edge:* Plain.

	Mintage	F	VF	EF	Unc	BU	PL
2009	7,160,841	$0.25	$0.35	$0.45	$0.90	$1.35	
2009, Prooflike	(4,787)						$7.20

Andrés Molina Enríquez. BW-680.18, KM-911.

A sociologist and amateur anthropologist, as well as a justice of the peace, Andrés Molina Enríquez is best known for his book *Los Grandes Problemas Nacionales* (The Great National Problems), which focused on land reform and the rights and place in society of indigenous people. The book was deeply critical of the regime of Porfirio Díaz, and is considered one of the paving stones on the road to the Revolution.

Composition: bimetallic (center, 0.92 copper, 0.06 aluminum, 0.02 nickel; outer ring, stainless steel). *Weight:* 7.07 g. *Obverse:* On the bronze-aluminum center, the national coat of arms with the eagle in profile to the left, its feathers resembling plates of armor; on the stainless-steel outer ring, the legend **ESTADOS UNIDOS MEXICANOS** above, with a half-wreath of oak and laurel below. *Reverse:* On the bronze-aluminum center, a bust of Molina Enríquez in three-quarter profile to the right. To the left of the bust, **$5**; to the right of the bust, **M̊ / 2009**; below, **ANDRÉS MOLINA ENRÍQUEZ**. On the outer ring, **CENTENARIO DE LA REVOLUCIÓN** at the top, with • **MÉXICO 2010** • below. *Diameter:* 25.5 mm. *Edge:* Plain.

	Mintage	F	VF	EF	Unc	BU	PL
2009	6,942,763	$0.25	$0.35	$0.45	$0.90	$1.35	
2009, Prooflike	(4,666)						$7.20

Luis Cabrera. BW-680.20, KM-913.

A teacher, lawyer, writer, and politician who penned articles against Porfirio Díaz, Luis Vicente Cabrera Lobato went on to serve in various civil positions under Venustiano Carranza. In later years he was deported to Guatemala by a political opponent; after his return he was offered a candidacy for president on two different occasions, both of which he declined. He spent the remainder of his life as an attorney and a presidential adviser.

Composition: bimetallic (center, 0.92 copper, 0.06 aluminum, 0.02 nickel; outer ring, stainless steel). *Weight:* 7.07 g. *Obverse:* On the bronze-aluminum center, the national coat of arms with the eagle in profile to the left, its feathers resembling plates of armor; on the stainless-steel outer ring, the legend **ESTADOS UNIDOS MEXICANOS** above, with a half-wreath of oak and laurel below. *Reverse:* On the bronze-aluminum center, a bust of Cabrera in three-quarter profile to the left. To the right of the bust, **$5**; to the left of the bust, **M̊ / 2009**; below, **LUIS CABRERA**. On the outer ring, **CENTENARIO DE LA REVOLUCIÓN** at the top, with • **MÉXICO 2010** • below. *Diameter:* 25.5 mm. *Edge:* Plain.

	Mintage	F	VF	EF	Unc	BU	PL
2009	6,902,593	$0.25	$0.35	$0.45	$0.90	$1.35	
2009, Prooflike	(4,656)						$7.20

Eulalio Gutiérrez. BW-680.22, KM-915.

Eulalio Gutiérrez Ortiz played many roles during the Mexican Revolution. He participated in Francisco Madero's Anti-reelectionist Party, fought on the side of the rebels, and returned home to serve as mayor of Ramos Arizpe. He rejoined the military, in the army of Venustiano Carranza, and went on to serve as provisional president of Mexico for a few months between 1914 and 1915. A month after he took office, Francisco Villa and Emiliano Zapata took Mexico City; Gutiérrez resigned the presidency and exiled himself temporarily to the United States, returning later to Mexico under amnesty.

Composition: bimetallic (center, 0.92 copper, 0.06 aluminum, 0.02 nickel; outer ring, stainless steel). *Weight:* 7.07 g. *Obverse:* On the bronze-aluminum center, the national coat of arms with the eagle in profile to the left, its feathers resembling plates of armor; on the stainless-steel outer ring, the legend **ESTADOS UNIDOS MEXICANOS** above, with a half-wreath of oak and laurel below. *Reverse:* On the bronze-aluminum center, a bust of Gutiérrez in three-quarter profile to the right. To the left of the bust, $5; to the right of the bust, M̥ / 2009; below, **EULALIO GUTIÉRREZ**. On the outer ring, **CENTENARIO DE LA REVOLUCIÓN** at the top, with • MÉXICO 2010 • below. *Diameter:* 25.5 mm. *Edge:* Plain.

	Mintage	F	VF	EF	Unc	BU	PL
2009	6,908,760	$0.25	$0.35	$0.45	$0.90	$1.35	
2009, Prooflike	(4,862)						$7.20

Otilio Montaño. BW-680.24, KM-917.

A Morelos schoolteacher, Otilio Montaño Sánchez was a supporter of Francisco Madero in the latter's struggle against Porfirio Díaz. He eventually joined Emiliano Zapata's army as a general and introduced the latter to the philosophy of anarchism. When Madero failed to live up to his promises, Montaño assisted Zapata in drafting the famous Plan of Ayala, which called for extensive land reform, declared Madero a traitor to the Revolution, and named Pascual Orozco the Revolution's new leader.

Composition: bimetallic (center, 0.92 copper, 0.06 aluminum, 0.02 nickel; outer ring, stainless steel). *Weight:* 7.07 g. *Obverse:* On the bronze-aluminum center, the national coat of arms with the eagle in profile to the left, its feathers resembling plates of armor; on the stainless-steel outer ring, the legend **ESTADOS UNIDOS MEXICANOS** above, with a half-wreath of oak and laurel below. *Reverse:* On the bronze-aluminum center, a forward-facing bust of Montaño with the head turned slightly to the left. To the right of the bust, $5; to the left of the bust, M̥ / 2009; below, **OTILIO MONTAÑO**. On the outer ring, **CENTENARIO DE LA REVOLUCIÓN** at the top, with • MÉXICO 2010 • below. *Diameter:* 25.5 mm. *Edge:* Plain.

	Mintage	F	VF	EF	Unc	BU	PL
2009	6,890,052	$0.25	$0.35	$0.45	$0.90	$1.35	
2009, Prooflike	(4,923)						$7.20

Belisario Domínguez. BW-680.26, KM-918.

An early martyr to the Revolution, Belisario Domínguez Palencia was a physician and a politician. He briefly served as a liberal senator, delivering a memorable speech in 1913 against dictator Victoriano Huerta. Domínguez was murdered as a consequence, and his tongue cut out. A medal of honor, a dam, and his hometown are named after him.

Composition: bimetallic (center, 0.92 copper, 0.06 aluminum, 0.02 nickel; outer ring, stainless steel). *Weight:* 7.07 g. *Obverse:* On the bronze-aluminum center, the national coat of arms with the eagle in profile to the left, its feathers resembling plates of armor; on the stainless-steel outer ring, the legend **ESTADOS UNIDOS MEXICANOS** above, with a half-wreath of oak and laurel below. *Reverse:* On the bronze-aluminum center, a forward-facing bust of Domínguez with the head turned partway to the left. To the right of the bust, **$5**; to the left of the bust, **M̊ / 2009**; below, **BELISARIO DOMÍNGUEZ**. On the outer ring, **CENTENARIO DE LA REVOLUCIÓN** at the top, with • **MÉXICO 2010** • below. *Diameter:* 25.5 mm. *Edge:* Plain.

	Mintage	F	VF	EF	Unc	BU	PL
2009	6,926,606	$0.25	$0.35	$0.45	$0.90	$1.35	
2009, Prooflike	(4,773)						$7.20

Francisco I. Madero. BW-680.28, KM-UL.

Although he was born into a very privileged family, Francisco Madero had great compassion for the common people of Mexico. He was a major catalyst of the Revolution, and ultimately took office as Mexico's 33rd president. He was assassinated two years later. (See also the sidebar on pages 36.)

Composition: bimetallic (center, 0.92 copper, 0.06 aluminum, 0.02 nickel; outer ring, stainless steel). *Weight:* 7.07 g. *Obverse:* On the bronze-aluminum center, the national coat of arms with the eagle in profile to the left, its feathers resembling plates of armor; on the stainless-steel outer ring, the legend **ESTADOS UNIDOS MEXICANOS** above, with a half-wreath of oak and laurel below. *Reverse:* On the bronze-aluminum center, a forward-facing bust of Madero with the head turned slightly to the left. To the left of the bust, $5; to the right of the bust, M̥ / 2010; below, **FRANCISCO I. MADERO**. On the outer ring, **CENTENARIO DE LA REVOLUCIÓN** at the top, with • **MÉXICO 2010** • below. *Diameter:* 25.5 mm. *Edge:* Plain.

	Mintage	F	VF	EF	Unc	BU	PL
2010	6,930,998	$0.25	$0.35	$0.45	$0.90	$1.35	
2010, Prooflike	(4,750)						$7.20

Emiliano Zapata. BW-680.30, KM-UL.

Of all those at the forefront of the Revolution—Venustiano Carranza, Emiliano Zapata, Francisco Villa, Francisco Madero, and Alvaro Obregón—Zapata was the passionate idealist; and aside from Villa, he may be the best remembered today. A Nahuatl-speaking son of a farmer, Zapata was deeply respected among the peasantry, who made him their leader in 1909. He led his intensely loyal army through the gains and reversals of the Revolution, never wavering in his devotion to the rights of the common people or in his responsibility to his troops. In addition to his military successes, he founded the agrarian movement that came to be known as *Zapatismo;* it combined Mayan practices with Marxism, anarchism, and libertarian socialism, and was dedicated to social justice. He was ultimately cornered and killed by the *federales* in 1919.

Composition: bimetallic (center, 0.92 copper, 0.06 aluminum, 0.02 nickel; outer ring, stainless steel). *Weight:* 7.07 g. *Obverse:* On the bronze-aluminum center, the national coat of arms with the eagle in profile to the left, its feathers resembling plates of armor; on the stainless-steel outer ring, the legend **ESTADOS UNIDOS MEXICANOS** above, with a half-wreath of oak and laurel below. *Reverse:* On the bronze-aluminum center, a bust of Zapata angled three-quarters to the left with the head facing forward. To the right of the bust, $5; to the left of the bust, M̥ / 2010; below, **EMILIANO ZAPATA**. On the outer ring, **CENTENARIO DE LA REVOLUCIÓN** at the top, with • **MÉXICO 2010** • below. *Diameter:* 25.5 mm. *Edge:* Plain.

	Mintage	F	VF	EF	Unc	BU	PL
2010	6,921,306	$0.25	$0.35	$0.45	$0.90	$1.35	
2010, Prooflike	(4,810)						$7.20

Venustiano Carranza. BW-680.32, KM-UL.

A well-educated and wealthy man, Venustiano Carranza was one of the "Big Four" of the Revolution (see the sidebar on pages 80 and 81). He was elected president after the execution of Francisco Madero and the subsequent defeat of the dictator who had ordered the execution, Victoriano Huerta. Carranza was later killed by his enemies in an ambush.

Composition: bimetallic (center, 0.92 copper, 0.06 aluminum, 0.02 nickel; outer ring, stainless steel). *Weight:* 7.07 g. *Obverse:* On the bronze-aluminum center, the national coat of arms with the eagle in profile to the left, its feathers resembling plates of armor; on the stainless-steel outer ring, the legend **ESTADOS UNIDOS MEXICANOS** above, with a half-wreath of oak and laurel below. *Reverse:* On the bronze-aluminum center, a forward-facing bust of Venustiano Carranza with the head turned slightly to the left. To the right of the bust, **$5**; to the left of the bust, M̊ / 2010; below, **VENUSTIANO CARRANZA**. On the outer ring, **CENTENARIO DE LA REVOLUCIÓN** at the top, with • **MÉXICO 2010** • below. *Diameter:* 25.5 mm. *Edge:* Plain.

	Mintage	F	VF	EF	Unc	BU	PL
2010	6,936,993	$0.25	$0.35	$0.45	$0.90	$1.35	
2010, Prooflike	(4,837)						$7.20

La Soldadera. BW-680.34, KM-UL.

Soldaderas often were military camp-followers—not always voluntarily—who cooked and cleaned for the soldiers and were often their concubines. These activities continued during the Revolution; by then, however, women also went into combat side-by-side with the men, and the *soldaderas* lived, fought, and often died as revolutionaries for their country. (See the sidebar on pages 275 and 276.)

Composition: bimetallic (center, 0.92 copper, 0.06 aluminum, 0.02 nickel; outer ring, stainless steel). *Weight:* 7.07 g. *Obverse:* On the bronze-aluminum center, the national coat of arms with the eagle in profile to the left, its feathers resembling plates of armor; on the stainless-steel outer ring, the legend **ESTADOS UNIDOS**

MEXICANOS above, with a half-wreath of oak and laurel below. *Reverse:* On the bronze-aluminum center, a forward-facing bust of a young *soldadera*, wearing braids and crossed bandoliers. To the right of the bust, **$5**; to the left of the bust, M̊ / 2010; below, **SOLDADERA**. On the outer ring, **CENTENARIO DE LA REVOLUCIÓN** at the top, with • MÉXICO 2010 • below. *Diameter:* 25.5 mm. *Edge:* Plain.

	Mintage	F	VF	EF	Unc	BU	PL
2010	6,936,336	$0.25	$0.35	$0.45	$0.90	$1.35	
2010, Prooflike	(4,730)						$7.20

José María Pino Suárez. BW-680.36, KM-UL.

A poetry-writing lawyer, journalist, and revolutionary, José María Pino Suárez dedicated his adult life to the fight for Mexico's democracy. He served briefly as governor of Yucatán, was sworn into Congress, and was later appointed the secretary of public education under President Francisco Madero. When encouraged to flee with his family, he chose to stay at the president's side. For his loyalty, he was executed along with Madero by Victoriano Huerta.

Composition: bimetallic (center, 0.92 copper, 0.06 aluminum, 0.02 nickel; outer ring, stainless steel). *Weight:* 7.07 g. *Obverse:* On the bronze-aluminum center, the national coat of arms with the eagle in profile to the left, its feathers resembling plates of armor; on the stainless-steel outer ring, the legend **ESTADOS UNIDOS MEXICANOS** above, with a half-wreath of oak and laurel below. *Reverse:* On the bronze-aluminum center, a forward-facing bust of Pino Suárez with the head turned slightly to the right. To the right of the bust, **$5**; to the left of the bust, M̊ / 2010; below, **JOSÉ MARÍA PINO SUÁREZ**. On the outer ring, **CENTENARIO DE LA REVOLUCIÓN** at the top, with • MÉXICO 2010 • below. *Diameter:* 25.5 mm. *Edge:* Plain.

	Mintage	F	VF	EF	Unc	BU	PL
2010	6,930,255	$0.25	$0.35	$0.45	$0.90	$1.35	
2010, Prooflike	(4,752)						$7.20

NEW 10 PESOS
Type A1. BW-681, KM-553.

Composition: bimetallic (center, 0.925 silver, 0.075 copper; outer ring, 0.92 copper, 0.06 aluminum, 0.02 nickel). *Weight:* 11.138 g. *Obverse:* On the silver center, the national coat of arms with the eagle facing left, its feathers resembling plates of armor. On the bronze-aluminum outer ring, the legend **ESTADOS UNIDOS MEXICANOS** above, with a half-wreath of oak and laurel below. *Reverse:* On the silver center, the innermost design on the Aztec Calendar Stone, with the god Tonatiuh in the middle. On the outer ring, the denomination **N$10** at the top and **DIEZ NUEVOS PESOS** at the bottom, with the date at upper left and the mintmark M̥ at upper right. *Diameter:* 28 mm. *Edge:* Reeded.

	Mintage	F	VF	EF	Unc	BU	PF	ChPF
1992	20,000,000	$6.50	$6.50	$7.00	$8.00	$14.00		
1993	47,981,000	6.50	6.50	7.00	8.00	14.00		
1994	15,000,000	6.50	6.50	7.00	8.00	14.00		
1995	15,000,000	6.50	6.50	7.00	8.00	14.00		
1995, Proof	(6,981)						$14.50	$18.00

10 PESOS
Type A2. BW-681.1, KM-616.

Composition: bimetallic (center, silver-plated alpaca, 0.65 copper, 0.10 nickel, 0.25 zinc; outer ring, 0.92 copper, 0.06 aluminum, 0.02 nickel). *Weight:* 10.329 g. *Obverse:* On the alpaca (also known as German silver) center, the national coat of arms with the eagle facing left, its feathers resembling plates of armor. On the bronze-aluminum outer ring, the legend **ESTADOS UNIDOS MEXICANOS** above, with a half-wreath of oak and laurel below. *Reverse:* On the alpaca center, the innermost design on the Aztec Calendar Stone, with the god Tonatiuh in the middle. On the outer ring, the denomination **$10** at the top and **DIEZ PESOS** at the bottom, with the date at upper left and the mintmark M̥ at upper right. *Diameter:* 28 mm. *Edge:* Reeded.

	Mintage	F	VF	EF	Unc	BU
1997	44,837,000	$0.90	$1.15	$2.25	$4.75	$10.75
1998, Small Date	203,735,000	0.90	1.15	2.25	4.75	10.75
1999	29,842,000	0.90	1.15	2.25	4.75	10.75

Tonatiuh and Ollin

At the center of the Aztec Calendar Stone, Tonatiuh appears within the Ollin symbol (outlined in magenta). To the left and right, his clawed hands appear to hold human hearts. (See appendix B for more detail.)

At first glance, some of the many known Ollin depictions seem to be unrelated, but closer study reveals a common theme: two lines crossing at the center, with a twist suggesting a change in direction. The first and last of those shown here have the added element of a sacrificial knife.

The Aztecs believed that time was divided into five ages, called *suns:* 4 Jaguar, 4 Wind, 4 Rain, 4 Water, and the present age, 4 Movement. In each of the previous ages mankind was created anew, only to perish at the end of the age. Tonatiuh, who appears at the center of the Aztec Calendar Stone, was the god of the fifth age, and of the sun itself. He is depicted with a flint knife for a tongue and with two clawed hands, each holding a human heart.

The Aztecs, believing the sun would refuse to move through the sky unless fed with human blood, ritually sacrificed thousands of people every year to Tonatiuh (and to the other gods as well). Among other roles, Tonatiuh was the patron of warriors, especially those who captured war victims to be used for sacrifice.

On the Calendar Stone, his face and claws are placed within the "Ollin" symbol, which represents movement—the defining theme of his era. (It is foretold that this world, the fifth sun, will end as the result of a massive earthquake.) Ollin was rendered in several styles by the Aztecs. On the Calendar Stone, the emblem is large enough to include multiple other symbols (see appendix B); this form is the main element on the reverse of all 10 pesos of the 1992 Currency Reform. Elsewhere, it is rendered more simply, rather like an X with a twist at the center. These simpler versions have also appeared on several Mexican coins, often as a border or as a dividing element between phrases (see, for example, the 10 pesos, Type A3).

Type A3. BW-681.2, KM-636.

Edge lettering.

Composition: bimetallic (center, silver-plated alpaca, 0.65 copper, 0.10 nickel, 0.25 zinc; outer ring, 0.92 copper, 0.06 aluminum, 0.02 nickel). *Weight:* 10.329 g. *Obverse:* On the alpaca (also known as German silver) center, the national coat of arms with the eagle facing left, its feathers resembling plates of armor. On the bronze-aluminum outer ring, the legend ESTADOS UNIDOS MEXICANOS above, with a half-wreath of oak and laurel below. *Reverse:* On the alpaca center, the innermost design on the Aztec Calendar Stone, with the god Tonatiuh in the middle. On the outer ring, the denomination $10 at the top and AÑO [date] at the bottom, with the mintmark M̊ at far left. At 2, 4, 8, and 10 o'clock, the Ollin glyph. *Diameter:* 28 mm. *Edge:* Lettered with AÑO and the date three times.

	Mintage	F	VF	EF	Unc	BU
2000	24,839,000	$0.90	$1.15	$2.25	$4.75	$10.75
2001	44,768,000	0.90	1.15	2.25	4.75	10.75

Type A4. BW-681.3, KM-UL.

Composition: bimetallic (center, silver-plated alpaca, 0.65 copper, 0.10 nickel, 0.25 zinc; outer ring, 0.92 copper, 0.06 aluminum, 0.02 nickel). *Weight:* 10.329 g. *Obverse:* On the alpaca (also known as German silver) center, the national coat of arms with the eagle facing left, its feathers resembling plates of armor. On the bronze-aluminum outer ring, the legend ESTADOS UNIDOS MEXICANOS above, with a half-wreath of oak and laurel below. *Reverse:* On the alpaca center, the innermost design on the Aztec Calendar Stone, with Tonatiuh in the middle. On the outer ring, the denomination $10 at the top and DIEZ PESOS at the bottom, with the year at upper left and the mintmark M̊ at upper right. *Diameter:* 28 mm. *Edge:* Reeded.

	Mintage	F	VF	EF	Unc	BU
2002	44,721,000	$0.90	$1.15	$2.25	$4.75	$10.75
2004	74,739,000	0.90	1.15	2.25	4.75	10.75
2005	64,616,000	0.90	1.15	2.25	4.75	10.75
2006	84,575,000	0.90	1.15	2.25	4.75	10.75
2007	89,678,000	0.90	1.15	2.25	4.75	10.75
2008	64,744,000	0.90	1.15	2.25	4.75	10.75
2009	54,812,000	0.90	1.15	2.25	4.75	10.75
2010	54,822,000	0.90	1.15	2.25	4.75	10.75
2011	69,731,000	0.90	1.15	2.25	4.75	10.75
2012	89,732,000	0.90	1.15	2.25	4.75	10.75
2013	*44,769,000*	0.90	1.15	2.25	4.75	10.75
2014		0.90	1.15	2.25	4.75	10.75

150TH ANNIVERSARY OF THE BATTLE OF PUEBLA AND THE DEATH OF GENERAL IGNACIO ZARAGOZA

Type 1. BW-720, KM-UL.

This 10-peso coin was released to commemorate the victory of 4,500 Mexican troops over a well-equipped French force of 8,000 in Puebla on May 5, 1862, at Fort Loreto and Fort Guadalupe. (See the sidebar).

Composition: bimetallic (center, silver-plated alpaca, 0.65 copper, 0.10 nickel, 0.25 zinc; outer ring, 0.92 copper, 0.06 aluminum, 0.02 nickel). *Weight:* 10.329 g. *Obverse:* On the alpaca (also known as German silver) center, the national coat of arms with the eagle facing left, its feathers resembling plates of armor. On the bronze-aluminum outer ring, the legend ESTADOS UNIDOS MEXICANOS above, with a half-wreath of oak and laurel below. *Reverse:* On the outer ring, the denomination $10 at the bottom, flanked by the dates 1862 and 2012; around the top, · 150 ANIVERSARIO DE LA BATALLA DE PUEBLA · with 5 DE MAYO just below. At center, a bust of General Ignacio Zaragoza in three-quarter profile to the left, with GRAL. I. ZARAGOZA in tiny letters above. In the background to the left of the bust, a battle scene (French invaders and Mexican troops, with the forts of Oreto and Guadalupe in the distance); to the right of the bust, the mintmark M̥. *Diameter:* 28 mm. *Edge:* Alternating plain and reeded.

	Mintage	F	VF	EF	Unc	BU
2012	29,871,000	$1.00	$1.00	$2.25	$5.00	$10.75

The Battle of Puebla

In 1962, Mexico issued medals in gold and silver to commemorate the centennial of the Battle of Puebla. The common design shows General Ignacio Zaragoza on horseback, riding between enemy mortars in the foreground and the forts in the background.

In 1862 Mexico was deeply in debt to the governments of Britain, France, and Spain. Economic troubles at home were such that President Benito Juárez García was forced to suspend payment on these debts. The three European creditors came together and sent troops across the ocean with the intention of forcing Mexico to resume payment—or at least, that was the intention of Britain and Spain. Once the ships arrived and the Spanish had captured the port at Veracrúz, they learned, along with the British, that Napoleon III had intended all along to conquer Mexico outright, and they withdrew. With the United States embroiled in a civil war, France was almost guaranteed success in establishing a puppet state in Mexico, laying claim to Latin American trade as well as to Mexico's rich silver mines.

The first few military encounters were successes for the French. In one of these encounters, Mexican general Ignacio Zaragoza and his troops were badly beaten in the field; Zaragoza withdrew his men to Puebla and its stout, well-supplied forts of Loreto and Guadalupe, which stood on two opposite hilltops.

The French launched a badly planned assault on the forts; when their artillery ran out of ammunition, their entire reserves had to join the fight. General Zaragoza sent his cavalry out to attack the weakened force from both flanks, and sent more men to attack them as they retreated. By the time the French withdrew, they had lost more than 450 troops to approximately 80 of Zaragoza's.

It was a comparatively small loss for the French, however, as they subdued Mexican forces elsewhere, took Mexico City, and established a puppet empire with Maximilian at its head. In spite of Napoleon III's success—or perhaps even because of it—Mexicans were intensely proud of the victory at Puebla. Shortly before the capital fell and President Juárez was forced to flee with his government to northern Mexico, he declared May 5 would henceforth be a national holiday. Today it is popularly known as Cinco de Mayo.

General Ignacio Zaragoza

Ignacio Zaragoza Seguín was originally a student of the seminary, but he was drawn to the military during the repressive rule of Antonio López de Santa Anna. Zaragoza proved to be an excellent strategist, and under his command, the volunteer army capably ousted the dictator.

Under President Benito Juárez García, Zaragoza served for a few short months as secretary of war. His military brilliance was soon needed on the field, however, and he resigned his post in order to lead the defense against Napoleon III's invasion. Having successfully repelled the French from Acultzingo and then Forts Loreto and Guadalupe in Puebla, he wrote to the president, *"Las armas nacionales se han cubierto de gloria"* (The national arms have been covered with glory), a quote that would later appear on 500-peso banknotes from 1995 to 2010.

Zaragoza died of typhoid fever soon after his heroic May 5 victory; he was 33 years old.

NEW 20 PESOS
Type A1. BW-682, KM-561.

Composition: bimetallic (center, 0.925 silver, 0.075 copper; outer ring, 0.92 copper, 0.06 aluminum, 0.02 nickel). *Weight:* 15.945 g. *Obverse:* On the silver center, the national coat of arms with the eagle facing left, its feathers resembling plates of armor. On the bronze-aluminum outer ring, the legend **ESTADOS UNIDOS MEXICANOS** above, with a half-wreath of oak and laurel below. *Reverse:* On the outer ring, the denomination **N$20** at the top with an open wreath of laurel below. At the center, the head of Miguel Hidalgo y Costilla in profile to the left. To the right of the portrait, the mintmark M̊ above the date; below the neck of the portrait, **HIDALGO**. *Diameter:* 32 mm. *Edge:* Reeded.

	Mintage	F	VF	EF	Unc	BU
1993	25,000,000	$9.00	$10.00	$11.00	$12.00	$16.00
1994	5,000,000	9.00	10.00	11.00	12.00	16.00
1995	5,000,000	9.00	10.00	11.00	12.00	16.00

Miguel Hidalgo y Costilla

Miguel Hidalgo y Costilla was born to Criollo parents on May 8, 1753, in what is now Guanajuato. He was educated in a seminary and entered the Catholic priesthood. An enormously intelligent student, he studied the works of the Enlightenment in French and spoke the indigenous languages of the laborers on the hacienda of which his father had been a manager. In the early years of priesthood he taught at the seminary where he'd been a student, rising through the levels as an administrator until his liberal ideas—including questioning the Pope and the Crown—and his poor management of school funds led to his dismissal.

Hidalgo was able to secure position at the parish church in Dolores, where he found the parishioners in terrible, and even dire, circumstances. Colonial laws protected the wealth of the colonists and the Crown at the expense of the laborers, particularly the indigenous people. Hidalgo continued his studies, which included forms of trade and agriculture that could help his flock improve their lot in life: beekeeping, brick-making, the tanning of leather goods, and many other skills. As he stood a good chance of achieving his goal—making his parishioners capable of sustaining themselves independently of the Spanish—he was ordered to stop.

Hidalgo began to attend secret meetings with like-minded community leaders, including Ignacio Allende, Josefa Ortiz de Domínguez, Juan Aldama, and others. They formulated a plan to start a revolution and overthrow the colonial government. Their plot, which was intended to unfold in December 1810, is now known as the Conspiracy of Querétaro. Somehow their plans were discovered by the authorities, who began to round up suspected conspirators. Fearing his imminent arrest, Hidalgo decided to go forward with the plan ahead of schedule, and around 6 a.m. on September 16, he ordered the bells of the church to be rung, calling together his congregation. He stood before them with Allende and Aldama and called upon the parishioners to revolt. His exact words, which became known as the *grito* (cry) *de Dolores,* are unknown, but in essence, he said, "Long live religion! Long live our Lady of Guadalupe! Long live the Americas, and death to corrupt government!"

Hidalgo and Allende led the parishioners, armed with little other than their farming implements, into battle. The army—in reality a furious, untrained mob—swelled as it moved through the countryside, from 800 people to 90,000 or more. What they lacked in discipline and weaponry the insurgents made up for in numbers and passion, and they won many early victories.

Eventually, however, Hidalgo's lack of military expertise and the insurgents' lack of training began to take their toll. Between heavy casualties and desertions the army began to shrink, and Allende took over as military commander. The force headed toward the United States with the aim of gaining support and badly needed money, but their leadership was betrayed and captured in March 1811. Hidalgo, Allende, and two others were executed by firing squad and their heads mounted on the four corners of the public granary in the city of Guanajuato, where they remained for ten years as a warning to potential rebels—but it was too late for even this grisly Spanish response. The War of Independence was underway.

Today the remains of Hidalgo, Allende, and 12 other heroes of the War of Independence are interred at the Castle of Chapultepec. The spirit of Hidalgo's *grito de Dolores* lives on in the modern El Grito, which takes place in the *zocalo* in front of the National Palace—and in similar locations in each of the state capitals—at on the eve of Mexican Independence Day each year. El Grito is a call-and-response between the president (or governor) and the assembled citizens. At 11 p.m., the president calls out the following lines, each of which the crowd answers with *"¡Viva!"* (or *"Vivan,"* as appropriate). Some of the lines differ, depending on the location of El Grito, but in essence they are:

> *¡Mexicanos!*
> *¡Vivan los heroes que nos dieron patria!**
> *¡Viva Hidalgo!*
> *¡Viva Morelos!*
> *¡Viva Josefa Ortiz de Domínguez!*
> *¡Viva Allende!*
> *¡Vivan Aldama y Matamoros!*
> *¡Viva nuestra independencia!***
> *¡Viva Mexico!*
> *¡Viva Mexico!*
> *¡Viva Mexico!*

In addition to his appearance on the Independence-bicentennial 5 pesos, Hidalgo has appeared on a number of Mexican coins over the years. On circulating coins, he is depicted on the 5 pesos, Types 3–5; the 10 pesos, Types 1 and 3–6; the 20 pesos, Type A1; and the 200 pesos, Type 1. He also appears on the Bicentennial of the War of Independence commemorative 20 pesos and on two gold medallic coins issued in honor of his birth bicentennial, not to mention on scores of paper-money issues and medals.

---

* *"Los heroes que nos dieron patria"*—The heroes who gave us the Fatherland.
** *"Nuestra independencia"*—Our independence.

20 PESOS
Type A2. BW-682.1, KM-637.

Composition: bimetallic (center, 0.65 copper, 0.10 nickel, 0.25 zinc; outer ring, 0.92 copper, 0.06 aluminum, 0.02 nickel). *Weight:* 15.945 g. *Obverse:* On the alpaca (German silver) center, the national coat of arms with the eagle facing left, its feathers resembling plates of armor. On the bronze-aluminum outer ring, the legend ESTADOS UNIDOS MEXICANOS above, with a half-wreath of oak and laurel below. *Reverse:* At the center, a left-facing figure of the god Xiuhtecuhtli. Above the figure, FUEGO NUEVO (New Fire); to the right of the figure, $20 and the mintmark M̥; at lower right, XIUHTECUHTLI. Surrounding the center on the outer ring, a pattern of stylized sun-rays from the Aztec Calendar Stone. At the bottom of the ring, divided by the lowermost ray, AÑO / [date]. *Diameter:* 32 mm. *Edge:* Alternating plain and reeded.

	Mintage	F	VF	EF	Unc	BU
2000	14,850,000	$1.80	$2.25	$4.50	$10.00	$12.00
2001	2,478,000	1.80	2.25	4.50	10.00	12.00

Xiuhtecuhtli

In Aztec mythology, Xiuhtecuhtli—whose name means "Turquoise Lord"—was the god of fire and the owner of time. He was the parent of all the gods, and ruled over volcanoes, daylight, and warmth; among other important roles, he was believed to carry souls into the afterlife. A young and vigorous god, he is thought to have a dual nature, with his other aspect being Huehueteotl, the "Old God," who was also associated with fire.

At the end of each 52-year cycle, the cosmos was thought to become dangerous and unstable; the Aztecs protected the world during this time with the New Fire ceremony.

Xiuhtecuhtli with an offering of rubber balls, as depicted in the Codex Mendoza. Rubber was sacred to the Aztecs, representing fertility (among other things). The figure on the 20 pesos is similar but carries a torch, representing the god's relationship with fire.

Preparations and rituals were carried out for days in every household and temple. At the culmination of the ceremony, every fire in the land was extinguished, from the homes to the temples. The fire in the temple of Huehueteotl was kindled anew in the body of a sacrificial victim. Torches were lit from the fire and carried to the other temples to relight their braziers, and from those braziers, all the other fires in each city were relit from those in the temples. Xiuhtecuhtli / Huehueteotl was appeased, and order was temporarily restored to the world.

Type A3. BW-682.2, KM-638.

Composition: bimetallic (center, 0.65 copper, 0.10 nickel, 0.25 zinc; outer ring, 0.92 copper, 0.06 aluminum, 0.02 nickel). *Weight:* 15.996 g. *Obverse:* On the alpaca (German silver) center, the national coat of arms with the eagle facing left, its feathers resembling plates of armor. On the bronze-aluminum outer ring, the legend **ESTADOS UNIDOS MEXICANOS** above, with a half-wreath of oak and laurel below. *Reverse:* To the left of center, a forward-facing bust of Mexican poet and Nobel Laureate Octavio Paz, the head turned partway to the right. In the field to the right of the bust, extending onto the outer ring, a famous verse by the poet: **Todo es presencia, / todos los siglos son / esta Presente** ("Everything is presence, / all the centuries are / this Presence"). Below the verse, a reproduction of Paz's signature. At the top of the outer ring, **$20**, with **AÑO [date]** below and the mintmark M̥ at far left. *Diameter:* 32 mm. *Edge:* Alternating plain and reeded.

	Mintage	F	VF	EF	Unc	BU
2000	14,943,000	$1.80	$2.25	$4.50	$10.00	$12.00
2001	2,515,000	1.80	2.25	4.50	10.00	10.00

Type A4. BW-682.4, KM-UL.

Composition: bimetallic (center, 0.65 copper, 0.10 nickel, 0.25 zinc; outer ring, 0.92 copper, 0.06 aluminum, 0.02 nickel). *Weight:* 15.996 g. *Obverse:* On the alpaca (German silver) center, the national coat of arms with the eagle facing left, its feathers resembling plates of armor. On the bronze-aluminum outer ring, the legend **ESTADOS UNIDOS MEXICANOS** above, with a half-wreath of oak and laurel below. *Reverse:* To the left of center, a bust of Mexican poet and Nobel Laureate Octavio Paz in three-quarter profile to the right, with hand to chin. In the field to the right of the bust, **Premio Nobel de / Literatura / 1990**. At the top of the outer ring, $20 with **OCTAVIO PAZ** immediately below; at the bottom, near the inner edge and reading counterclockwise, a famous verse by the poet: **Todo es presencia, todos los siglos son esta Presente** ("Everything is presence, all the centuries are this Presence"). Below the verse, **VEINTE PESOS**. At upper left, *2010*; at upper right, the mintmark M̊. *Diameter:* 32 mm. *Edge:* Alternating plain and reeded.

	Mintage	F	VF	EF	Unc	BU
2010	4,954,000	$1.80	$2.25	$4.50	$10.00	$12.00

Octavio Paz

The prolific Mexican author and diplomat Octavio Paz Lozano was born in 1914 into a highly educated family who would influence him throughout his life and career. His father and grandfather were political journalists, and his grandfather was the first Mexican to write a novel with an overtly Indian theme. They routinely kept company with other progressive intellectuals, including Emiliano Zapata.

Paz began his writing career early, and traveled abroad. In 1938, riding the crest of the wave of a new generation of Mexican writers, he began the publication *Taller* (meaning "workshop"). Several years later, he entered diplomatic service and traveled to France, where he was influenced by the surrealists, and wrote *The Labyrinth of Solitude,* his definitive work on Mexican national identity. He traveled to Asia, Japan, Germany, Switzerland, and India, where he wrote *The Grammarian Monkey* and *East Slope.* His travels brought the influences of Buddhism, surrealism, Hinduism, and Marxism to his work. He resigned from diplomatic service in 1968 in protest over the government's bloody slaughter of protesting students during the Olympic Games in Mexico. He continued his work as an editor for several years and published the magazines *Plural* (which was ultimately shut down by the Mexican government) and, later, *Vuelta.* In the course of his life, Paz wrote a prolific quantity of essays on poetry, literary and art criticism, economics, sexuality, anthropology, Mexican politics, culture, and history. His well-respected and influential works have been translated into numerous languages.

> The list of awards, fellowships, and prizes received by Octavio Paz is lengthy. They include, among many others, an honorary doctorate at Harvard in 1980; the 1981 Miguel de Cervantes Award (the most important literary award in the Spanish-speaking world); and the 1982 American Neustadt Prize. In 1990 he was awarded the Nobel Prize for Literature, for his "impassioned writing with wide horizons, characterized by sensuous intelligence and humanistic integrity."
>
> Octavio Paz died in Mexico in 1998, at the age of 84.

100TH ANNIVERSARY OF THE DEATH OF BELISARIO DOMÍNGUEZ PALENCIA

Type 9. BW-720.1, KM-UL.

This 20-peso coin marks the centenary of the execution of Senator Belisario Domínguez Palencia on October 7, 1913. The distinguished senator was one of several who had spoken out against dictator Victoriano Huerta, after the latter mounted a coup against the legally elected government and murdered its president, Francisco Madero, and vice president, José María Pino Suárez.

Composition: bimetallic (center, silver-plated alpaca, 0.65 copper, 0.10 nickel, 0.25 zinc; outer ring, 0.92 copper, 0.06 aluminum, 0.02 nickel). *Weight:* 15.945 g. *Obverse:* On the alpaca (German silver) center, the national coat of arms with the eagle facing left, its feathers resembling plates of armor. On the bronze-aluminum outer ring, the legend ESTADOS UNIDOS MEXICANOS above, with a half-wreath of oak and laurel below. *Reverse:* On the outer ring, the denomination $20 at the bottom; at the left, 100 ANIVERSARIO / LUCTUOSO (100th Anniversary / of His Death); at the right, 150 ANIVERSARIO / DE SU NACIMIENTO (150th Anniversary / of His Birth). At the center, a forward-facing bust of Domínguez with the head turned partway to the right, with the mintmark M̊ in the upper right field and the dates 1863–2013 at lower right, along the edge. At the top of the coin, in three lines (beginning on the outer ring and continuing on the silver center), BELISARIO / DOMÍNGUEZ / ENNOBLECIÓ A LA PATRIA (Belisario / Domínguez / Dignified Our Fatherland). *Diameter:* 32 mm. *Edge:* Alternating plain and reeded.

	Mintage	F	VF	EF	Unc	BU
2013	985,000	$1.80	$1.80	$2.50	$10.00	$12.00

Belisario Domínguez Palencia

Belisario Domínguez Palencia was a senator who, while serving in Mexico's Congress, memorably spoke out against dictator Victoriano Huerta. This act of defiance would cost the liberal politician his life.

Born in 1863 in Comitán, Chiapas, Domínguez moved to Paris in 1879 to continue his studies, focusing on education and medicine. He lived in France for ten years, in 1889 returning to Mexico and in 1890 marrying Delina Zebadúa Palencia, with whom he would have four children. The physician's political activity began in the decades leading up to the Revolution. He was well known in the Liberal Party, published political columns, and encouraged citizens to monitor the government. He was elected mayor of Comitán in 1909, beginning his service on the first day of 1910, and in 1913 replaced his friend Senator Leopoldo Gout when the latter died in office. While serving in Congress Domínguez was openly critical of the coup d'état and subsequent regime of Victoriano Huerta. In September 1913 he publicized two proclamations accusing Huerta of lying to Congress, weakening the Republic, and leading a treacherous and illegitimate government. In no uncertain terms he condemned Huerta as a traitor and a murderer.

On the night of October 7, 1913, Domínguez was seized by pro-Huerta conspirators and taken to a cemetery where he was murdered. Huerta's minister of the interior, a surgeon, reportedly cut out Domínguez's tongue and sent it to the dictator as a trophy of the assassination. The murder of the outspoken senator contributed to the public outrage that would force Huerta from power a few months later.

In 1915 the martyr's hometown was renamed Comitán de Domínguez in his memory. Since 1953, Mexico's Senate has bestowed the Belisario Domínguez Medal of Honor, the nation's highest actively presented award. It is granted to eminent Mexicans with a distinguished lifetime career of contribution toward the welfare of Mexico and of mankind. The Senate declared 2013 would be celebrated as the Year of Belisario Domínguez. He has been honored on a circulating 5 pesos in the Bicentennial of Independence (2009) in addition to the 2013 commemorative of the 100th anniversary of his death.

100TH ANNIVERSARY OF MEXICO'S ARMED FORCES
Type I. BW-720.2, KM-UL.

Composition: bimetallic (center, silver-plated alpaca, 0.65 copper, 0.10 nickel, 0.25 zinc; outer ring, 0.92 copper, 0.06 aluminum, 0.02 nickel). *Weight:* 15.945 g. *Obverse:* On the alpaca (German silver) center, the national coat of arms with the eagle facing left, its feathers resembling plates of armor. On the bronze-aluminum outer ring, the legend ESTADOS UNIDOS MEXICANOS above, with a half-wreath of oak and laurel below. *Reverse:* At the center, a stylized profile of a soldier flanked by the dates 1913 and 2013 and surrounded by a pattern of concentric circles. Above, the legend 100 Años del Ejército Mexicano (100 Years of Mexico's Armed Forces); below, 100 Años de LEALTAD (100 Years of Loyalty). On the outer ring,

Mexico's Armed Forces

The armed forces of Mexico are organized under two main branches: the National Defense Army and the Armada de Mexico (i.e., the Navy). The Mexican Air Force is part of the Army.

The Mexican Navy includes a naval aviation branch (FAN) and an amphibious naval infantry force (the Marines). Mexico's coast guard, the Mexican Maritime Search and Rescue unit, is also part of the Navy. The Special Forces, military police, and presidential guard are nominally part of the Army but have their own command structures.

Operating separately from the Army and Navy is a corps made up of two mechanized infantry brigades stationed in Mexico City. Outside of the regular military, a kind of volunteer militia called the Rural Defense Corps works with law enforcement and helps out during natural disasters and with other special needs.

The Mexican armed forces are professionals. While Mexico does require national service for young men, draftees are not integrated into the Army and Navy. They mostly serve on weekends, undergoing military training and performing social-service work.

the denomination **$20** at the bottom, with **VEINTE PESOS** at the top; at the left, **2013**; at the right, the mintmark M̥. *Diameter:* 32 mm. *Edge:* Alternating plain and reeded.

	Mintage	F	VF	EF	Unc	BU
2013	4,956,000	$1.80	$1.80	$2.50	$10.00	$12.00

100TH ANNIVERSARY OF THE HEROIC DEED OF THE PORT OF VERACRUZ

In the spring of 1914, a U.S. gunboat was stationed in the Port of Veracruz to protect the city's U.S. citizens and economic interests from the approaching forces of Venustiano Carranza. A misunderstanding between the Mexican forces and a few American sailors who had gone ashore aggravated the existing tension between the two governments. On April 21, U.S. ships took the port, ostensibly to block a shipment of foreign arms from reaching dictator Victoriano Huerta, whose forces were engaged elsewhere. Defense of the city fell to its citizens and the cadets and officers at the Veracruz Naval Academy. Two particularly heroic cadets, Virgilio Uribe and Lieutenant José Azueta Abad, died during the conflict and are honored on this 20-peso circulating commemorative.

Type 2. BW-720.3, KM-UL.

Composition: bimetallic (center, silver-plated alpaca, 0.65 copper, 0.10 nickel, 0.25 zinc; outer ring, 0.92 copper, 0.06 aluminum, 0.02 nickel). *Weight:* 15.945 g. *Obverse:* On the alpaca (German silver) center, the national coat of arms with the eagle facing left, its feathers resembling plates of armor. On the bronze-aluminum outer ring, the legend **ESTADOS UNIDOS MEXICANOS** above, with a half-wreath of oak and laurel below. *Reverse:* Around the outer ring, the legend **CENTENARIO DE LA GESTA HEROICA DE VERACRUZ**, with the dates **1914–2014** on a banner at the bottom. On the alpaca center, in the upper background, the busts of two young men angled slightly to the left, with the names **JOSÉ AZUETA** and **VIRGILIO URIBE** above them on the ring, and the mintmark M̥ to the left in the field. In the lower foreground, extending the full width of the coin, the Naval Academy building and, at left, the figures of several armed citizens; at right, a large anchor is superimposed over all. To the right of the anchor, **$20**; below the building, **ESCUELA NAVAL**. *Diameter:* 32 mm. *Edge:* Alternating plain and reeded.

	Mintage	F	VF	EF	Unc	BU
2014		$1.80	$2.00	$2.50	$10.00	$12.00

100TH ANNIVERSARY OF THE TAKING OF ZACATECAS

This 20-peso coin marks the centennial of the bloody Battle of Zacatecas, in which the Revolutionaries wrested control of the city and its critical railway junction from the control of Victoriano Huerta. Pancho Villa and his ablest general, Felipe Ángeles Ramirez, brought Villa's Division of the North to join forces with General Panfilo Natera García's troops. Together they annihilated the federal army in a victory that marked the beginning of the end for the dictator.

Type 3. BW-720.4, KM-UL.

Composition: bimetallic (center, silver-plated alpaca, 0.65 copper, 0.10 nickel, 0.25 zinc; outer ring, 0.92 copper, 0.06 aluminum, 0.02 nickel). *Weight:* 15.945 g. *Obverse:* On the alpaca (German silver) center, the national coat of arms with the eagle facing left, its feathers resembling plates of armor. On the bronze-aluminum outer ring, the legend **ESTADOS UNIDOS MEXICANOS** above, with a half-wreath of oak and laurel below. *Reverse:* Around the outer ring, the legend **CENTENARIO DE LA TOMA DE ZACATECAS**; at the bottom, the denomination **$20**, flanked by the dates **1914–2014** at the left and the mintmark M̥ at the right. On the alpaca center, in the background, a forward-facing figure of Francisco "Pancho Villa" on horseback, with **Fro. Villa** above. In the foreground, at lower left, a bust of General Felipe Ángeles Ramirez in three-quarter profile toward the center, with **Felipe / Ángeles** incused on the chest; at lower right, a bust of General Panfilo Natera García angled slightly to the left, with **Panfilo / Natera** incused on the chest. At the bottom, the top of the strategic mountaintop of La Bufa surmounted by a cross. *Diameter:* 32 mm. *Edge:* Alternating plain and reeded.

	Mintage	F	VF	EF	Unc	BU
2014		$1.80	$2.00	$2.50	$10.00	$12.00

NEW 50 PESOS
Type A1. BW-683, KM-571.

Composition: bimetallic (center, 0.925 silver, 0.075 copper; outer ring, 0.92 copper, 0.06 aluminum, 0.02 nickel). *Weight:* 33.967 g. *Obverse:* On the silver center, the national coat of arms with the eagle facing left, its feathers resembling plates of armor. On the bronze-aluminum outer ring, the legend **ESTADOS UNIDOS MEXICANOS** above, with a half-wreath of oak and laurel below. *Reverse:* On the center, in front of the Mexican flag, the busts of six young men—the "Boy Heroes," military cadets from the school in Chapultepec Castle, Mexico City, who were killed defending the castle against the Americans during the Mexican–American War in 1847. Below the central design, **NIÑOS HÉROES**; above left, the mintmark M̥; above right, the date. On the outer ring, the denomination **N$50** at the top with a half-wreath of laurel below. *Diameter:* 39 mm. *Edge:* Reeded.

	Mintage	F	VF	EF	Unc	BU
1993	2,000,000	$16.00	$18.00	$20.00	$25.00	$30.00
1994	1,500,000	16.00	18.00	20.00	25.00	30.00
1995	1,500,000	16.00	18.00	20.00	25.00	30.00

100 PESOS
MEXICAN STATE FEDERATION SERIES

Following the abdication of Iturbide, the Constitution of 1824 declared Mexico a federal representative republic. Mexico at the time consisted of 19 states, as follows (in order of admission to the Federation; modern spellings):

Chiapas	Jalisco	Oaxaca	Tabasco
Chihuahua	México (Estado de)	Puebla	Tamaulipas
Coahuila y Tejas		Querétaro	Veracruz
Durango	Michoacán	San Luis Potosí	Yucatán
Guanajuato	Nuevo León	Sonora y Sinaloa	Zacatecas

In addition to the states, Mexico held five federal territories: Alta California, Baja California, Colima, Tlaxcala, and Santa Fe de Nuevo México. The Constitution noted that "a constitutional law will fix the character of Tlaxcala."

Los Niños Héroes

The Niños Héroes (Boy Heroes) were six young military cadets who were killed while fighting for their country in the Mexican-American war. Ranging in age from 13 to 19, they died defending their military academy at Chapultepec Castle, on a hill in Mexico City.

On September 13, 1847, General Antonio López de Santa Anna held control of Mexico City. General Nicolás Bravo commanded Chapultepec Hill, an important defensive vantage point on Mexico City's west side, with fewer than 1,000 soldiers—including the 200 cadets of the military academy.

The American forces greatly outnumbered the cadet defenders, who nonetheless fought back for two hours. Bravo eventually ordered the cadets to retreat, but Juan de la Barrera, Juan Escutia, Francisco Márquez, Agustín Melgar, Fernando Montes de Oca, and Vicente Suárez refused to surrender. All six were killed in battle; Escutia is said to have wrapped himself in the Mexican flag and jumped from the roof of the castle to keep the flag from being captured. The boys' bodies are interred at the Monument to the Heroic Cadets in Chapultepec.

Few in the United States are aware of Los Niños Héroes today, but their memory does reverberate now and again. American presidents Harry Truman and Bill Clinton have paid their respects at the historic battle site. The U.S. Marines' "Battle Hymn" begins, "From the halls of Montezuma"—a lyric that refers to the battle for Chapultepec Castle. Civil War buffs may know the battle as the only one in which Robert E. Lee and Ulysses S. Grant fought side by side.

In Mexico, however, the six cadets are among the most beloved national heroes. They are honored by *Los Niños Héroes* monument in Chapultepec Park in Mexico City. Their images appear on Mexican currency, and streets, schools, and public parks are named for them. A transit station in Mexico City—Metro Niños Héroes—is named in their honor, and a national holiday on September 13 is dedicated to their memory.

A lithograph depicting the onslaught of soldiers the cadets stayed to face, with the castle in the background. Today Chapultepec Castle is home of the National History Museum.

Two Mexican State Federation Series commemorate the federation. All 31 of the modern states and the Distrito Federal participated in both series, each of which consists of 10-peso silver Proofs and 100-peso bimetallic Proofs, along with 100-peso bimetallic circulating coins (listed here). The Proofs from this series are cataloged in chapter 4.

Issued during an era of hyperinflation, the bimetallic circulating coins were immediately hoarded, due to the 92.5% silver content of their center discs. It is unknown how many of the coins were destroyed due to the removal and subsequent melting of their silver centers, or how many survive today.

Type A1 (Series 1: Heraldic; BW-684)

Series 1, the heraldic series, features each state's coat of arms. It commenced in 2003; the state coins were issued in descending alphabetical order, with the final coins, representing Aguascalientes, issued in 2005.

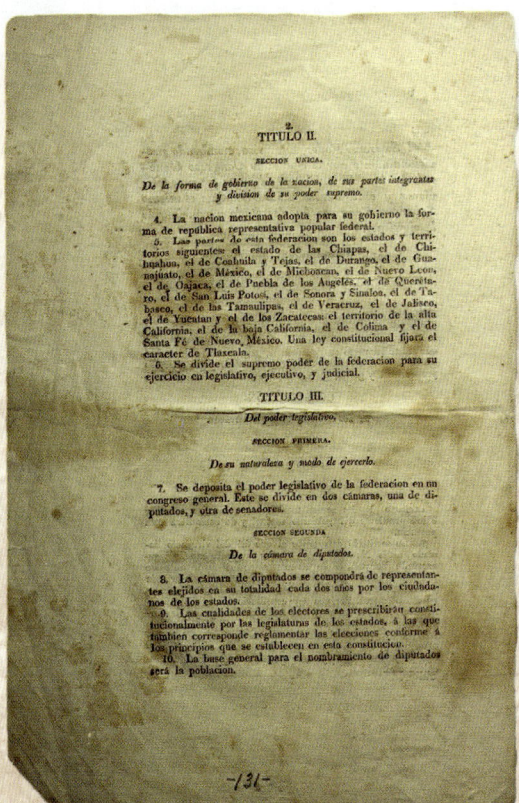

The states of the newly formed federation were listed in Title II, Article 5, of the Federal Constitution of the United Mexican States, October 4, 1824. The illustration is the related page from the document as disseminated by the newly formed Mexican government shortly afterward.

The common obverse for 100-peso circulating coins in Mexican State Federation Series 1.

Zacatecas   Yucatán   Veracrúz

Composition: bimetallic (center, 0.925 silver, 0.075 copper; outer ring, 0.92 copper, 0.06 aluminum, 0.02 nickel). *Weight:* 33.967 g. *Obverse:* On the silver center, the national coat of arms with the eagle facing left, its feathers resembling plates of armor; on the bronze-aluminum outer ring, the legend **ESTADOS UNIDOS MEXICANOS** above, with a half-wreath of oak and laurel below. *Diameter:* 39 mm. *Edge:* Alternating plain and reeded.

Zacatecas Reverse Design
On the silver center, the coat of arms of Zacatecas, with **2003** above. On the bronze-aluminum outer ring, **ESTADO DE ZACATECAS** at the top, with **$100** at the bottom and the mintmark M̊ at far left.

Yucatán Reverse Design
On the silver center, the coat of arms of Yucatán, with **2003** above. On the bronze-aluminum outer ring, **ESTADO DE YUCATAN** at the top, with **$100** at the bottom and the mintmark M̊ at far left.

Veracrúz Reverse Design
On the silver center, the coat of arms of Veracrúz, with **2003** to the right. On the bronze-aluminum outer ring, **ESTADO DE VERACRUZ-LLAVE** at the top, with **$100** at the bottom and the mintmark M̊ at far left.

	Mintage	F	VF	EF	Unc	BU
2003, Zacatecas. BW-684.1, KM-688	244,900	$16.00	$20.00	$22.50	$27.00	32.00
2003, Yucatán. BW-684.2, KM-689	235,763	16.00	20.00	22.50	27.00	32.00
2003, Veracrúz. BW-684.3, KM-690	248,810	16.00	20.00	22.50	27.00	32.00

The Coinage Reform of 1992 • 145

      Tlaxcala   Tamaulipas   Tabasco

Composition: bimetallic (center, 0.925 silver, 0.075 copper; outer ring, 0.92 copper, 0.06 aluminum, 0.02 nickel). *Weight:* 33.967 g. *Obverse:* On the silver center, the national coat of arms with the eagle facing left, its feathers resembling plates of armor; on the bronze-aluminum outer ring, the legend **ESTADOS UNIDOS MEXICANOS** above, with a half-wreath of oak and laurel below. *Diameter:* 39 mm. *Edge:* Alternating plain and reeded.

Tlaxcala Reverse Design
On the silver center, the coat of arms of Tlaxcala, with **2003** above. On the bronze-aluminum outer ring, **ESTADO DE TLAXCALA** at the top, with **$100** at the bottom and the mintmark M̥ at far left.

Tamaulipas Reverse Design
On the silver center, the coat of arms of Tamaulipas, with **2004** above. On the bronze-aluminum outer ring, **ESTADO DE TAMAULIPAS** at the top, with **$100** at the bottom and the mintmark M̥ at far left.

Tabasco Reverse Design
On the silver center, the coat of arms of Tabasco, with **2004** to the right. On the bronze-aluminum outer ring, **ESTADO DE TABASCO** at the top, with **$100** at the bottom and the mintmark M̥ at far left.

	Mintage	**F**	**VF**	**EF**	**Unc**	**BU**
2003, Tlaxcala. BW-684.4, KM-691	248,976	$16.00	$20.00	$22.50	$27.00	$32.00
2004, Tamaulipas. BW-684.5, KM-692	249,398	16.00	20.00	22.50	27.00	32.00
2004, Tabasco. BW-684.6, KM-693	249,318	16.00	20.00	22.50	27.00	32.00

   Sonora   Sinaloa   San Luis Potosí

Composition: bimetallic (center, 0.925 silver, 0.075 copper; outer ring, 0.92 copper, 0.06 aluminum, 0.02 nickel). *Weight:* 33.967 g. *Obverse:* On the silver center, the national coat of arms with the eagle facing left, its feathers resembling plates of armor; on the bronze-aluminum outer ring, the legend **ESTADOS UNIDOS MEXICANOS** above, with a half-wreath of oak and laurel below. *Diameter:* 39 mm. *Edge:* Alternating plain and reeded.

Sonora Reverse Design
On the silver center, the coat of arms of Sonora, with **2004** above. On the bronze-aluminum outer ring, **ESTADO DE SONORA** at the top, with **$100** at the bottom and the mintmark M̊ at far left.

Sinaloa Reverse Design
On the silver center, the coat of arms of Sinaloa, with **2004** to the right. On the bronze-aluminum outer ring, **ESTADO DE SINALOA** at the top, with **$100** at the bottom and the mintmark M̊ at far left.

San Luis Potosí Reverse Design
On the silver center, the coat of arms of San Luis Potosí, with **2004** below. On the bronze-aluminum outer ring, **ESTADO DE SAN LUIS POTOSI** at the top, with **$100** at the bottom and the mintmark M̊ at far left.

	Mintage	F	VF	EF	Unc	BU
2004, Sonora. BW-684.7, KM-694	249,300	$16.00	$20.00	$22.50	$27.00	$32.00
2004, Sinaloa. BW-684.8, KM-695	244,722	16.00	20.00	22.50	27.00	32.00
2004, San Luis Potosí. BW-684.9, KM-803	249,662	16.00	20.00	22.50	27.00	32.00

| Quintana Roo | Querétaro | Puebla |

Composition: bimetallic (center, 0.925 silver, 0.075 copper; outer ring, 0.92 copper, 0.06 aluminum, 0.02 nickel). *Weight:* 33.967 g. *Obverse:* On the silver center, the national coat of arms with the eagle facing left, its feathers resembling plates of armor; on the bronze-aluminum outer ring, the legend **ESTADOS UNIDOS MEXICANOS** above, with a half-wreath of oak and laurel below. *Diameter:* 39 mm. *Edge:* Alternating plain and reeded.

Quintana Roo Reverse Design
On the silver center, the coat of arms of Quintana Roo, with **2004** below. On the bronze-aluminum outer ring, **ESTADO DE QUINTANA ROO** at the top, with **$100** at the bottom and the mintmark M̊ at far left.

Querétaro Reverse Design
On the silver center, the coat of arms of Querétaro, with **2004** to the right. On the bronze-aluminum outer ring, **ESTADO DE QUERETARO ARTEAGA** at the top, with **$100** at the bottom and the mintmark M̊ at far left.

Puebla Reverse Design
On the silver center, the coat of arms of Puebla, with **2004** to the right. On the bronze-aluminum outer ring, **ESTADO DE PUEBLA** at the top, with **$100** at the bottom and the mintmark M̊ at far left.

	Mintage	F	VF	EF	Unc	BU
2004, Quintana Roo. BW-684.11, KM-736	249,134	$16.00	$20.00	$22.50	$27.00	$32.00
2004, Querétaro. BW-684.10, KM-734	249,263	16.00	20.00	22.50	27.00	32.00
2004, Puebla. BW-684.12, KM-738	248,850	16.00	20.00	22.50	27.00	32.00

      Oaxaca   Nuevo León   Nayarit

Composition: bimetallic (center, 0.925 silver, 0.075 copper; outer ring, 0.92 copper, 0.06 aluminum, 0.02 nickel). *Weight:* 33.967 g. *Obverse:* On the silver center, the national coat of arms with the eagle facing left, its feathers resembling plates of armor; on the bronze-aluminum outer ring, the legend **ESTADOS UNIDOS MEXICANOS** above, with a half-wreath of oak and laurel below. *Diameter:* 39 mm. *Edge:* Alternating plain and reeded.

Oaxaca Reverse Design
On the silver center, the coat of arms of Oaxaca, with **2004** to the right. On the bronze-aluminum outer ring, **ESTADO DE OAXACA** at the top, with **$100** at the bottom and the mintmark M̥ at far left.

Nuevo León Reverse Design
On the silver center, the coat of arms of Nuevo León, with **2004** to the right. On the bronze-aluminum outer ring, **ESTADO DE NUEVO LEON** at the top, with **$100** at the bottom and the mintmark M̥ at far left.

Nayarit Reverse Design
On the silver center, the coat of arms of Nayarit, with **2004** above. On the bronze-aluminum outer ring, **ESTADO DE NAYARIT** at the top, with **$100** at the bottom and the mintmark M̥ at far left.

	Mintage	F	VF	EF	Unc	BU
2004, Oaxaca. BW-684.13, KM-740	249,589	$16.00	$20.00	$22.50	$27.00	$32.00
2004, Nuevo León. BW-684.14, KM-742	249,199	16.00	20.00	22.50	27.00	32.00
2004, Nayarit. BW-684.15, KM-744	248,305	16.00	20.00	22.50	27.00	32.00

      Morelos   Michoacán   Estado de México

Composition: bimetallic (center, 0.925 silver, 0.075 copper; outer ring, 0.92 copper, 0.06 aluminum, 0.02 nickel). *Weight:* 33.967 g. *Obverse:* On the silver center, the national coat of arms with the eagle facing left, its feathers resembling plates of armor; on the bronze-aluminum outer ring, the legend **ESTADOS UNIDOS MEXICANOS** above, with a half-wreath of oak and laurel below. *Diameter:* 39 mm. *Edge:* Alternating plain and reeded.

Morelos Reverse Design
On the silver center, the coat of arms of Morelos, with **2004** above. On the bronze-aluminum outer ring, **ESTADO DE MORELOS** at the top, with **$100** at the bottom and the mintmark M̥ at far left.

Michoacán Reverse Design
On the silver center, the coat of arms of Michoacán, with **2004** to the right. On the bronze-aluminum outer ring, **ESTADO DE MICHOACAN DE OCAMPO** at the top, with **$100** at the bottom and the mintmark M̥ at far left.

Estado de México Reverse Design
On the silver center, the coat of arms of the State of Mexico, with **2004** to the right. On the bronze-aluminum outer ring, **ESTADO DE MEXICO** at the top, with **$100** at the bottom and the mintmark M̥ at far left.

	Mintage	F	VF	EF	Unc	BU
2004, Morelos. BW-684.16, KM-746	249,260	$16.00	$20.00	$22.50	$27.00	$32.00
2004, Michoacán. BW-684.17, KM-804	249,492	16.00	20.00	22.50	27.00	32.00
2004, Estado de México. BW-684.18, KM-748	249,800	16.00	20.00	22.50	27.00	32.00

| Jalisco | Hidalgo | Guerrero |

Composition: bimetallic (center, 0.925 silver, 0.075 copper; outer ring, 0.92 copper, 0.06 aluminum, 0.02 nickel). *Weight:* 33.967 g. *Obverse:* On the silver center, the national coat of arms with the eagle facing left, its feathers resembling plates of armor; on the bronze-aluminum outer ring, the legend **ESTADOS UNIDOS MEXICANOS** above, with a half-wreath of oak and laurel below. *Diameter:* 39 mm. *Edge:* Alternating plain and reeded.

Jalisco Reverse Design
On the silver center, the coat of arms of Jalisco, with **2004** at upper left. On the bronze-aluminum outer ring, **ESTADO DE JALISCO** at the top, with **$100** at the bottom and the mintmark M̥ at far left.

Hidalgo Reverse Design
On the silver center, the coat of arms of Hidalgo, with **2005** above. On the bronze-aluminum outer ring, **ESTADO DE HIDALGO** at the top, with **$100** at the bottom and the mintmark M̥ at far left.

Guerrero Reverse Design
On the silver center, the coat of arms of Guerrero, with **2005** to the right. On the bronze-aluminum outer ring, **GUERRERO** at the top, with **$100** at the bottom and the mintmark M̥ at far left.

	Mintage	F	VF	EF	Unc	BU
2004, Jalisco. BW-684.19, KM-750	249,115	$16.00	$20.00	$22.50	$27.00	$32.00
2005, Hidalgo. BW-684.20, KM-717	249,820	16.00	20.00	22.50	27.00	32.00
2005, Guerrero. BW-684.21, KM-716	248,850	16.00	20.00	22.50	27.00	32.00

The Coinage Reform of 1992

Guanajuato

Durango

Distrito Federal

Composition: bimetallic (center, 0.925 silver, 0.075 copper; outer ring, 0.92 copper, 0.06 aluminum, 0.02 nickel). *Weight:* 33.967 g. *Obverse:* On the silver center, the national coat of arms with the eagle facing left, its feathers resembling plates of armor; on the bronze-aluminum outer ring, the legend **ESTADOS UNIDOS MEXICANOS** above, with a half-wreath of oak and laurel below. *Diameter:* 39 mm. *Edge:* Alternating plain and reeded.

Guanajuato Reverse Design
On the silver center, the coat of arms of Guanajuato, with **2005** below. On the bronze-aluminum outer ring, **ESTADO DE GUANAJUATO** at the top, with **$100** at the bottom and the mintmark M̥ at far left.

Durango Reverse Design
On the silver center, the coat of arms of Durango, with **2005** below. On the bronze-aluminum outer ring, **ESTADO DE DURANGO** at the top, with **$100** at the bottom and the mintmark M̥ at far left.

Distrito Federal Reverse Design
On the silver center, the coat of arms of the Federal District, with **2005** above. On the bronze-aluminum outer ring, **DISTRITO FEDERAL** at the top, with **$100** at the bottom and the mintmark M̥ at far left.

	Mintage	F	VF	EF	Unc	BU
2005, Guanajuato. BW-684.22, KM-715	249,489	$16.00	$20.00	$22.50	$27.00	$32.00
2005, Durango. BW-684.24, KM-714	249,774	16.00	20.00	22.50	27.00	32.00
2005, Distrito Federal. BW-684.23, KM-713	249,461	16.00	20.00	22.50	27.00	32.00

| Colima | Coahuila | Chihuahua |

Composition: bimetallic (center, 0.925 silver, 0.075 copper; outer ring, 0.92 copper, 0.06 aluminum, 0.02 nickel). *Weight:* 33.967 g. *Obverse:* On the silver center, the national coat of arms with the eagle facing left, its feathers resembling plates of armor; on the bronze-aluminum outer ring, the legend **ESTADOS UNIDOS MEXICANOS** above, with a half-wreath of oak and laurel below. *Diameter:* 39 mm. *Edge:* Alternating plain and reeded.

Colima Reverse Design
On the silver center, the coat of arms of Colima, with **2005** to the right. On the bronze-aluminum outer ring, **ESTADO DE COLIMA** at the top, with **$100** at the bottom and the mintmark M̥ at far left.

Coahuila Reverse Design
On the silver center, the coat of arms of Coahuila, with **2005** above. On the bronze-aluminum outer ring, **ESTADO DE COAHUILA DE ZARAGOZA** at the top, with **$100** at the bottom and the mintmark M̥ at lower left.

Chihuahua Reverse Design
On the silver center, the coat of arms of Chihuahua, with **2005** above. On the bronze-aluminum outer ring, **ESTADO DE CHIHUAHUA** at the top, with **$100** at the bottom and the mintmark M̥ at far left.

	Mintage	**F**	**VF**	**EF**	**Unc**	**BU**
2005, Colima. BW-684.27, KM-729	248,850	$16.00	$20.00	$22.50	$27.00	$32.00
2005, Coahuila. BW-684.28, KM-752	247,991	16.00	20.00	22.50	27.00	32.00
2005, Chihuahua. BW-684.25, KM-754	249,102	16.00	20.00	22.50	27.00	32.00

The Coinage Reform of 1992 • 153

Chiapas

Campeche

Baja California Sur

Composition: bimetallic (center, 0.925 silver, 0.075 copper; outer ring, 0.92 copper, 0.06 aluminum, 0.02 nickel). *Weight:* 33.967 g. *Obverse:* On the silver center, the national coat of arms with the eagle facing left, its feathers resembling plates of armor; on the bronze-aluminum outer ring, the legend **ESTADOS UNIDOS MEXICANOS** above, with a half-wreath of oak and laurel below. *Diameter:* 39 mm. *Edge:* Alternating plain and reeded.

Chiapas Reverse Design
On the silver center, the coat of arms of Chiapas, with **2005** to the right. On the bronze-aluminum outer ring, **ESTADO DE CHIAPAS** at the top, with **$100** at the bottom and the mintmark M̊ at far left.

Campeche Reverse Design
On the silver center, the coat of arms of Campeche, with **2005** to the right. On the bronze-aluminum outer ring, **ESTADO DE CAMPECHE** at the top, with **$100** at the bottom and the mintmark M̊ at far left.

Baja California Sur Reverse Design
On the silver center, the coat of arms of Baja California Sur, with **2005** above. On the bronze-aluminum outer ring, **ESTADO DE BAJA CALIFORNIA SUR** at the top, with **$100** at the bottom and the mintmark M̊ at lower left.

	Mintage	F	VF	EF	Unc	BU
2005, Chiapas. BW-684.26, KM-712	249,417	$16.00	$20.00	$22.50	$27.00	$32.00
2005, Campeche. BW-684.29, KM-727	249,040	16.00	20.00	22.50	27.00	32.00
2005, Baja California Sur. BW-684.30, KM-723	249,585	16.00	20.00	22.50	27.00	32.00

| Baja California | Aguascalientes |

Composition: bimetallic (center, 0.925 silver, 0.075 copper; outer ring, 0.92 copper, 0.06 aluminum, 0.02 nickel). *Weight:* 33.967 g. *Obverse:* On the silver center, the national coat of arms with the eagle facing left, its feathers resembling plates of armor; on the bronze-aluminum outer ring, the legend ESTADOS UNIDOS MEXICANOS above, with a half-wreath of oak and laurel below. *Diameter:* 39 mm. *Edge:* Alternating plain and reeded.

Baja California Reverse Design
On the silver center, the coat of arms of Baja California, with 2005 to the right. On the bronze-aluminum outer ring, ESTADO DE BAJA CALIFORNIA at the top, with $100 at the bottom and the mintmark M̥ at far left.

Aguascalientes Reverse Design
On the silver center, the coat of arms of Aguascalientes, with 2005 below. On the bronze-aluminum outer ring, ESTADO DE AGUASCALIENTES at the top, with $100 at the bottom and the mintmark M̥ at far left.

	Mintage	F	VF	EF	Unc	BU
2005, Baja California. BW-684.31, KM-725	249,263	$16.00	$20.00	$22.50	$27.00	$32.00
2005, Aguascalientes. BW-684.32, KM-721	248,410	16.00	20.00	22.50	27.00	32.00

Type A3 (Series 2: Emblematic; BW-685)
Series 2, the emblematic series, features emblems representing each state's history or character. It commenced in 2005; the state coins were issued in ascending alphabetical order, with the final coins (representing Zacatecas) issued in 2007.

The common obverse for 100-peso circulating coins in Mexican State Federation Series 2.

| Aguascalientes | Baja California | Baja California Sur |

Composition: bimetallic (center, 0.925 silver, 0.075 copper; outer ring, 0.92 copper, 0.06 aluminum, 0.02 nickel). *Weight:* 33.967 g. *Obverse:* On the silver center, the national coat of arms with the eagle facing left, its wings resembling plates of armor. On the bronze-aluminum outer ring, the legend **ESTADOS UNIDOS MEXICANOS** above, with a half-wreath of oak and laurel below. *Diameter:* 39 mm. *Edge:* Alternating plain and reeded.

Aguascalientes Reverse Design
Slightly to the right on the silver center and extending into the bronze-aluminum ring, the Templo de San Antonio. To the left of the church, in the background, the entrance gate of the Jardín de San Marcos; to the left in the foreground, the eagle and ionic capital of the *Exedra* monument. At the top of the silver center, $100. At the top of the outer ring, **AGUASCALIENTES 2005**, with the mintmark M̥ at the left. Below the mintmark, reading counterclockwise, **MÉXICO**.

Baja California Reverse Design
On the silver center, the head of a bighorn sheep, with $100 above. Two outlined "roads," one to the left and one to the right, extend from the outer ring onto the silver center and appear to converge somewhere behind the sheep. Above the roads are curved lines resembling mountains. On the outer ring, at the top, **BAJA CALIFORNIA**; below, **GOBIERNO DEL ESTADO**; at the left, the mintmark M̥; at the right, 2005.

Baja California Sur Reverse Design
Bisecting the silver center, an outline map of Baja California Sur. To the left of the map, a deer as depicted in regional cave paintings; to the right, a saguaro cactus. On the bronze-aluminum outer ring, **ESTADO DE BAJA CALIFORNIA SUR** surrounding, with $100 at the bottom. To the left of the denomination, the mintmark M̥; to the right, 2006.

	Mintage	F	VF	EF	Unc	BU
2005, Aguascalientes. BW-685.1, KM-719	149,705	$17.00	$20.00	$22.00	$25.00	$32.00
2005, Baja California. BW-685.2, KM-758	149,771	17.00	20.00	22.00	25.00	32.00
2006, Baja California Sur. BW-685.3, KM-762	149,152	17.00	20.00	22.00	25.00	32.00

Campeche　　　　　Chiapas　　　　　Chihuahua

Composition: bimetallic (center, 0.925 silver, 0.075 copper; outer ring, 0.92 copper, 0.06 aluminum, 0.02 nickel). *Weight:* 33.967 g. *Obverse:* On the silver center, the national coat of arms with the eagle facing left, its wings resembling plates of armor. On the bronze-aluminum outer ring, the legend ESTADOS UNIDOS MEXICANOS above, with a half-wreath of oak and laurel below. *Diameter:* 39 mm. *Edge:* Alternating plain and reeded.

Campeche Reverse Design
On the silver center, a jade mask, with $100 at upper left, the mintmark M̊ at lower left, and 2006 at upper right. On the bronze-aluminum outer ring, ESTADO DE CAMPECHE and MÁSCARA DE JADE · CALAKMUL, CAMPECHE.

Chiapas Reverse Design
On the silver center, the head of Palenque ruler Pakal in three-quarter profile to the left, with M̊ / 2006 at upper left and $100 at lower right. On the bronze-aluminum outer ring, CHIAPAS and CABEZA MAYA DEL REY PAKAL, PALENQUE.

Chihuahua Reverse Design
On the silver center and extending above and below onto the outer ring, the Angel of Freedom monument. Above the angel's left wing, the mintmark M̊; below it, 2006. Below the angel's right wing, $100. Around the top of the outer ring, an ornamental half-border. Reading counterclockwise, MÉXICO at lower left and ANGEL DE LA LIBERTAD, CHIHUAHUA at lower right

	Mintage	F	VF	EF	Unc	BU
2006, Campeche. BW-685.4, KM-760	149,803	$17.00	$20.00	$22.00	$25.00	$32.00
2006, Chiapas. BW-685.7, KM-773	149,491	17.00	20.00	22.00	25.00	32.00
2006, Chihuahua. BW-685.8, KM-775	149,557	17.00	20.00	22.00	25.00	32.00

| Coahuila | Colima | Distrito Federal |

Composition: bimetallic (center, 0.925 silver, 0.075 copper; outer ring, 0.92 copper, 0.06 aluminum, 0.02 nickel). *Weight:* 33.967 g. *Obverse:* On the silver center, the national coat of arms with the eagle facing left, its wings resembling plates of armor. On the bronze-aluminum outer ring, the legend **ESTADOS UNIDOS MEXICANOS** above, with a half-wreath of oak and laurel below. *Diameter:* 39 mm. *Edge:* Alternating plain and reeded.

Coahuila Reverse Design
Extending across the outer ring and the silver center, an outline map of Coahuila with an array of emblems both inside and outside. Outside the map, clockwise from upper right, chimneys of the Nava Power Plant, a steel beam, the belfry of the Catedral de Santiago del Saltillo, the statue *Christ of the Noas*, and the Amistad Dam. Inside the map, an endangered box turtle, a mining cart in a mineshaft, and a bundle of grapes. At the top of the silver center, **2006 / $100**, with the mintmark M̊ above on the outer ring. At the bottom of the outer ring, a banner reading **COAHUILA DE ZARAGOZA**.

Colima Reverse Design
Extending across the outer ring and the silver center, two volcanoes, with a small coat of arms of Colima in the foreground and palm fronds to the right of the arms. At the top of the silver center, the word **Generoso**, with **2006** below left and **$100** below right. At the top of the outer ring, in an italic typeface, **Colima**, with the mintmark M̊ at far left.

Distrito Federal Reverse Design
Extending across the outer ring and the silver center, the Federal District Building. On the silver center, at the top, **$100**; at the bottom, **2006**; below and to the left of the denomination, the mintmark M̊. On the outer ring, at the top, **DISTRITO FEDERAL**, with **ANTIGUO AYUNTAMIENTO** at the bottom.

	Mintage	F	VF	EF	Unc	BU
2006, Coahuila. BW-685.5, KM-781	149,560	$17.00	$20.00	$22.00	$25.00	$32.00
2006, Colima. BW-685.6, KM-777	149,041	17.00	20.00	22.00	25.00	32.00
2006, Distrito Federal. BW-685.9, KM-779	149,522	17.00	20.00	22.00	25.00	32.00

      Durango   Guanajuato   Guerrero

Composition: bimetallic (center, 0.925 silver, 0.075 copper; outer ring, 0.92 copper, 0.06 aluminum, 0.02 nickel). *Weight:* 33.967 g. *Obverse:* On the silver center, the national coat of arms with the eagle facing left, its wings resembling plates of armor. On the bronze-aluminum outer ring, the legend **ESTADOS UNIDOS MEXICANOS** above, with a half-wreath of oak and laurel below. *Diameter:* 39 mm. *Edge:* Alternating plain and reeded.

Durango Reverse Design
On the silver center, a Durango Pine tree, with **$100** to the left, **2006** to the right, and the mintmark M̥ below. On the outer ring, **PRIMERA RESERVA NACIONAL FORESTAL** and **DURANGO**.

Guanajuato Reverse Design
Extending across the outer ring and the silver center, a montage of emblems: slightly above center, a small coat of arms of Guanajuato; in the left foreground, a statue of Miguel Hidalgo y Costilla; filling the background, the Teatro Juárez; at lower right, the monument *El Pípila*; at upper right, an Inca dove. At center, in a script typeface, **Guanajuato**. At right, between the dove and *El Pípila*, 2006 / $100. At upper left, the mintmark M̥.

Guerrero Reverse Design
Extending across the outer ring and the silver center, a montage of emblems: at left, a large, stylized portrait of Vicente Guerrero in three-quarter profile to the right, merging into a jaguar mask at the bottom. At center, the Catedral de Santa Prisca; at far right, the La Quebrada Cliff and a cliff diver; below the cliff, a poinsettia. At the top of the silver center, **$100**; at far right, extending into the ring, the mintmark M̥ and **2006**. At the top of the outer ring, **GUERRERO**.

	Mintage	F	VF	EF	Unc	BU
2006, Durango. BW-685.10, KM-787	149,034	$17.00	$20.00	$22.00	$25.00	$32.00
2006, Guanajuato. BW-685.11, KM-789	149,921	17.00	20.00	22.00	25.00	32.00
2006, Guerrero. BW-685.12, KM-791	149,675	17.00	20.00	22.00	25.00	32.00

| Hidalgo | Jalisco | Estado de México |

Composition: bimetallic (center, 0.925 silver, 0.075 copper; outer ring, 0.92 copper, 0.06 aluminum, 0.02 nickel). *Weight:* 33.967 g. *Obverse:* On the silver center, the national coat of arms with the eagle facing left, its wings resembling plates of armor. On the bronze-aluminum outer ring, the legend **ESTADOS UNIDOS MEXICANOS** above, with a half-wreath of oak and laurel below. *Diameter:* 39 mm. *Edge:* Alternating plain and reeded.

Hidalgo Reverse Design
Extending across the outer ring and the silver center, the Pachuca Monumental Clock. To the left of the clock, **RELOJ / MONUMENTAL / DE / PACHUCA / HIDALGO** and, in a script typeface, **La / Bella / Airosa / 2006**. To the right, the mintmark M̥; at the top, **$100**.

Jalisco Reverse Design
Extending across the outer ring and the silver center, the Cabañas Hospice. On the silver center, **M̥ / 2006** to the left and **$100** to the right. On the outer ring, **ESTADO DE JALISCO** at the top and **HOSPICIO CABAÑAS** at the bottom.

Estado de México Reverse Design
On the silver center, the Pyramid of the Moon, with three volcanoes—Ixtaccihuatl, Popocatépetl, and Xinantecatl—in the background, and **2006** at the top. On the outer ring, **ESTADO DE MÉXICO** at the top, **$100** at the bottom, and the mintmark M̥ at lower left.

	Mintage	F	VF	EF	Unc	BU
2006, Hidalgo. BW-685.13, KM-793	149,272	$17.00	$20.00	$22.00	$25.00	$32.00
2006, Jalisco. BW-685.14, KM-795	149,749	17.00	20.00	22.00	25.00	32.00
2006, Estado de México. BW-685.15, KM-802	149,377	17.00	20.00	22.00	25.00	32.00

| Michoacán | Morelos | Nayarit |

Composition: bimetallic (center, 0.925 silver, 0.075 copper; outer ring, 0.92 copper, 0.06 aluminum, 0.02 nickel). *Weight:* 33.967 g. *Obverse:* On the silver center, the national coat of arms with the eagle facing left, its wings resembling plates of armor. On the bronze-aluminum outer ring, the legend **ESTADOS UNIDOS MEXICANOS** above, with a half-wreath of oak and laurel below. *Diameter:* 39 mm. *Edge:* Alternating plain and reeded.

Michoacán Reverse Design
On the silver center, four Monarch butterflies in varying sizes, with **2006** to the right. On the outer ring **ESTADO DE MICHOACAN** at the top, $100 at the bottom, and the mintmark M̊ at lower left.

Morelos Reverse Design
Extending across the outer ring and the silver center, the Palace of Cortés in the background with a costumed Chinelo character in the right foreground. Above the palace, **ESTADO DE / MORELOS**; below, **PALACIO DE CORTÉS**. On the outer ring, $100 at the top, the mintmark M̊ at far right, and **2006** at the bottom.

Nayarit Reverse Design
On the silver center, an aerial view of the ancient manmade island Mexcaltitlán de Uribe, with **2007** above and **Isla de Mexcaltitlán** below. On the outer ring, **ESTADO DE NAYARIT** at the top, with $100 at the bottom and the mintmark M̊ at far left.

	Mintage	F	VF	EF	Unc	BU
2006, Michoacán. BW-685.16, KM-785	149,730	$17.00	$20.00	$22.00	$25.00	$32.00
2006, Morelos. BW-685.17, KM-800	149,648	17.00	20.00	22.00	25.00	32.00
2007, Nayarit. BW-685.18, KM-798	149,058	17.00	20.00	22.00	25.00	32.00

The Coinage Reform of 1992 • 161

      Nuevo León   Oaxaca   Puebla

Composition: bimetallic (center, 0.925 silver, 0.075 copper; outer ring, 0.92 copper, 0.06 aluminum, 0.02 nickel). *Weight:* 33.967 g. *Obverse:* On the silver center, the national coat of arms with the eagle facing left, its wings resembling plates of armor. On the bronze-aluminum outer ring, the legend **ESTADOS UNIDOS MEXICANOS** above, with a half-wreath of oak and laurel below. *Diameter:* 39 mm. *Edge:* Alternating plain and reeded.

Nuevo León Reverse Design
Extending across the outer ring and the silver center, a panoramic view of Cerro de la Silla (Saddle Hill) in the background, with the ironworks of the Parque Fundidora in the right foreground. On the silver center above the hills, $100 / 2007. On the outer ring, **ESTADO DE NUEVO LEÓN** at the top, with the mintmark M̥ at far right.

Oaxaca Reverse Design
On the silver center, the Macedonio Alcalá Theater, with the mintmark M̥ to the right of the dome. On the outer ring, in a fanciful, Art Nouveau–style typeface, **$100 OAXACA 2007** at the top, with **Teatro Macedonio Alcalá** at the bottom.

Puebla Reverse Design
On the silver center, an emblem similar to the Nahuatl glyph Ollin ("movement"); above the emblem, **2007** and **$100** at left and right, respectively; to the left of the emblem, the mintmark M̥; below, **ESTADO DE PUEBLA**. On the outer ring, patterns from an 18th-century Talavera ceramic plate.

	Mintage	F	VF	EF	Unc	BU
2007, Nuevo León. BW-685.19, KM-848	149,425	$17.00	$20.00	$22.00	$25.00	$32.00
2007, Oaxaca. BW-685.20, KM-849	149,892	17.00	20.00	22.00	25.00	32.00
2007, Puebla. BW-685.21, KM-850	149,474	17.00	20.00	22.00	25.00	32.00

| Querétaro | Quintana Roo | San Luis Potosí |

Composition: bimetallic (center, 0.925 silver, 0.075 copper; outer ring, 0.92 copper, 0.06 aluminum, 0.02 nickel). *Weight:* 33.967 g. *Obverse:* On the silver center, the national coat of arms with the eagle facing left, its wings resembling plates of armor. On the bronze-aluminum outer ring, the legend **ESTADOS UNIDOS MEXICANOS** above, with a half-wreath of oak and laurel below. *Diameter:* 39 mm. *Edge:* Alternating plain and reeded.

Querétaro Reverse Design
On the silver center, part of the Querétaro aqueduct at left, with the Iglesia de Santa Rosa at right. On the outer ring, **ESTADO DE QUERÉTARO ARTEAGA** at the top, and **Acueducto** ⊕ **Santa Rosa de Viterbo** at the bottom; at left, **2007**; at right, the mintmark M̥.

Quintana Roo Reverse Design
On the silver center, the ancient ruins of Tulum at the right, with a figure from the Temple of Masks at the left; between them, stylized rays representing the sun, with **2007** at their center; at lower right, the mintmark M̥. On the outer ring, **QUINTANA ROO** at the top, with **$100** at the bottom.

San Luis Potosí Reverse Design
On the silver center, the Old Royal Treasury Building with the mintmark M̥ at upper left. On the outer ring, · **SAN LUIS POTOSÍ** · at the top; around the bottom, separated by curling ornaments, **$100, CAJA REAL,** and **2007**.

	Mintage	F	VF	EF	Unc	BU
2007, Querétaro. BW-685.22, KM-852	149,127	$17.00	$20.00	$22.00	$25.00	$32.00
2007, Quintana Roo. BW-685.23, KM-851	149,582	17.00	20.00	22.00	25.00	32.00
2007, San Luis Potosí. BW-685.24, KM-853	148,750	17.00	20.00	22.00	25.00	32.00

| | Sinaloa | Sonora | Tabasco |

Composition: bimetallic (center, 0.925 silver, 0.075 copper; outer ring, 0.92 copper, 0.06 aluminum, 0.02 nickel). *Weight:* 33.967 g. *Obverse:* On the silver center, the national coat of arms with the eagle facing left, its wings resembling plates of armor. On the bronze-aluminum outer ring, the legend **ESTADOS UNIDOS MEXICANOS** above, with a half-wreath of oak and laurel below. *Diameter:* 39 mm. *Edge:* Alternating plain and reeded.

Sinaloa Reverse Design
On the silver center, a sliced-open pitahaya (dragonfruit) upon a pile of uncut fruits; at the left, M̥ / **2007**; at the right, **$100**; below, **LUGAR DE PITAHAYAS**. At the top of the outer ring, **ESTADO DE SINALOA**.

Sonora Reverse Design
On the silver center, a silhouette of a Yaqui deer-dancer in the left foreground, with silhouetted landscape features—desert, saguaro cactus, mountains, and the sun—in the background. On the outer ring, **ESTADO DE SONORA** at the top, with **$100** at the bottom; at left, reading counterclockwise, **2007**; at right, the mintmark M̥.

Tabasco Reverse Design
Extending across the outer ring and the silver center, the Tabasco Planetarium and the Fishermen Fountain, with an Olmec giant stone head in the foreground at the right and **2007** above. On the outer ring, **TABASCO** at the top with **$100** at the bottom; at upper left, the mintmark M̥.

	Mintage	F	VF	EF	Unc	BU
2007, Sinaloa. BW-685.25, KM-854	149,032	$17.00	$20.00	$22.00	$25.00	$32.00
2007, Sonora. BW-685.26, KM-855	149,891	17.00	20.00	22.00	25.00	32.00
2007, Tabasco. BW-685.27, KM-856	149,715	17.00	20.00	22.00	25.00	32.00

| Tamaulipas | Tlaxcala | Veracrúz |

Composition: bimetallic (center, 0.925 silver, 0.075 copper; outer ring, 0.92 copper, 0.06 aluminum, 0.02 nickel). *Weight:* 33.967 g. *Obverse:* On the silver center, the national coat of arms with the eagle facing left, its wings resembling plates of armor. On the bronze-aluminum outer ring, the legend **ESTADOS UNIDOS MEXICANOS** above, with a half-wreath of oak and laurel below. *Diameter:* 39 mm. *Edge:* Alternating plain and reeded.

Tamaulipas Reverse Design
On the silver center, the landscape feature known as Bernal's Hill, with **$100** at the top and the mintmark M̊ at upper right; below, **CERRO DEL BERNAL / GONZÁLEZ, TAMAULIPAS / 2007**. On the outer ring, at the top, **TAMAULIPAS**.

Tlaxcala Reverse Design
Extending across the outer ring and the silver center, from left to right: the Ocotlán Church, the Open Chapel, and the tower of the former Convent of San Francisco behind the Ranchero Aguilar Bullring. Below these, the Government Palace, with **$100** just above it. Surmounting all, the coat of arms of Tlaxcala, with the mintmark M̊ to the right. On the outer ring, at the top, **ESTADO DE TLAXCALA**; at the bottom, **2007**.

Veracrúz Reverse Design
On the silver center, the Tajín Pyramid, with **TAJÍN** above and **$100** below. On the outer ring, **· 2007 · VERACRUZ ·** and **DE IGNACIO DE LA LLAVE ·**, with the mintmark M̊ at far right.

	Mintage	F	VF	EF	Unc	BU
2007, Tamaulipas. BW-685.28, KM-857	149,776	$17.00	$20.00	$22.00	$25.00	$32.00
2007, Tlaxcala. BW-685.29, KM-858	149,465	17.00	20.00	22.00	25.00	32.00
2007, Veracrúz. BW-685.30, KM-859	149,703	17.00	20.00	22.00	25.00	32.00

Yucatán   Zacatecas

Composition: bimetallic (center, 0.925 silver, 0.075 copper; outer ring, 0.92 copper, 0.06 aluminum, 0.02 nickel). *Weight:* 33.967 g. *Obverse:* On the silver center, the national coat of arms with the eagle facing left, its wings resembling plates of armor. On the bronze-aluminum outer ring, the legend **ESTADOS UNIDOS MEXICANOS** above, with a half-wreath of oak and laurel below. *Diameter:* 39 mm. *Edge:* Alternating plain and reeded.

Yucatán Reverse Design
At left on the silver center, a modernized rendering of Chichén Itzá's El Castillo, with ribbon-like flourishes in the field to the right. At the top of the silver center, **Yucatán** (underscored) / **2007**; at lower right, the mintmark M̥. On the outer ring, **$100** at the top, with **Castillo de Chichén Itzá** at the bottom.

Zacatecas Reverse Design
Extending across the outer ring and the silver center, the Zacatecas Cable Car at far left with the Mining Monument below it; filling the center, the Zacatecas Cathedral, with **$100** above. On the outer ring, **Zacatecas** at the top, with **2007** at far right and the mintmark M̥ at far left.

	Mintage	F	VF	EF	Unc	BU
2007, Yucatán. BW-685.31, KM-860	149,579	$17.00	$20.00	$22.00	$25.00	$32.00
2007, Zacatecas. BW-685.32, KM-861	148,833	17.00	20.00	22.00	25.00	32.00

Other Mexican Anniversaries

The year 2005 also saw the release of circulating commemoratives in smaller series (compared to the 32 federation coins). The first of these commemorated the 400th anniversary of Miguel de Cervantes' *El Ingenioso Hidalgo Don Quijote de la Mancha* ("Don Quixote"). Three others honored events of national importance in Mexico's monetary history: the 470th anniversary of the Casa de Moneda de México; the 80th anniversary of the Banco de México; and the 100th anniversary of the 1905 Monetary Reform. (The Proof issuances of this series are listed in chapter 4.)

These issues were followed in 2006 by a 100-peso coin honoring the bicentennial of the birth of President Benito Juárez García.

All of these coins suffered the same fate as the bimetallic, circulating 100 pesos of the Mexican State Federation Series: namely, hoarding by the public, due to their 92.5% silver centers. Since the last State Federation coins were issued in 2007, Mexico has not released circulating coins with significant silver content.

400th Anniversary of "Don Quijote de la Mancha"
Type A7. BW-690, KM-705.

Composition: bimetallic (center, 0.925 silver, 0.075 copper; outer ring, 0.92 copper, 0.06 aluminum, 0.02 nickel). *Weight:* 3.967 g. *Obverse:* On the silver center, the national coat of arms with the eagle facing left, its feathers resembling plates of armor. On the bronze-aluminum outer ring, the legend **ESTADOS UNIDOS MEXICANOS** above, with a half-wreath of oak and laurel below. *Reverse:* At the center, a reproduction of the famous engraving *Calavera Quijotesca* (a skeletal horse and rider with spear, galloping to the right and scattering smaller skeletons in their wake); above, the Mexican artist's name, **J.G. POSADA** and the mintmark M̥. The denomination **$100** is below. Around the outer ring, • **DON QUIJOTE DE LA MANCHA** • above, with the dates **1605–** / **2005** (divided by **400 ANIVERSARIO**) below. *Diameter:* 39 mm. *Edge:* Alternating plain and reeded.

Note: The Don Quixote commemorative was issued in two denominations: a silver Proof 20 pesos and a bimetallic 100 pesos, which was produced as a circulating coin and as prooflike non-circulating legal tender. Although the 100 pesos were struck in both 2005 and 2006, all have the 2005 date. Those struck in 2005—namely, the circulation strike and some with the prooflike strike—were produced with thinner, stylized lettering on the reverse outer ring and are now referenced as Variety 1. Those struck in 2006—the remaining prooflike coins—have a thicker typeface on the reverse outer ring and have a diamond inside each of the initials D,

O, and Q. These are now known as Variety 2. The silver Proof and the bimetallic prooflike issues are listed in chapter 4.

See pages 263 and 264 for more information on Cervantes and *Don Quijote*.

	Mintage	F	VF	EF	Unc	BU
2005, Variety 1, Thin Letters	726,833				$30.00	$35.00

Title page of the first edition of *Don Quijote*.

100th Anniversary of the 1905 Monetary Reform
Type A3. BW-686, KM-730.

Composition: bimetallic (center, 0.925 silver, 0.075 copper; outer ring, 0.92 copper, 0.06 aluminum, 0.02 nickel). *Weight:* 3.967 g. *Obverse:* On the silver center, the national coat of arms with the eagle facing left, its feathers resembling plates of armor. On the bronze-aluminum outer ring, the legend ESTADOS UNIDOS MEXICANOS above, with a half-wreath of oak and laurel below. *Reverse:* At the center, a small radiant liberty cap above the denomination $100. To the left and right, the dates 1905 and 2005, respectively, with the mintmark M̊ above the date. At the top of the outer ring, REFORMA MONETARIA (Monetary Reform), above a half-wreath of oak and laurel. *Diameter:* 39 mm. *Edge:* Alternating plain and reeded.

	Mintage	F	VF	EF	Unc	BU
2005	49,716	$18.00	$20.00	$27.00	$32.00	$40.00

470th Anniversary of the Casa de Moneda de México
Type A4. BW-687, KM-731.

Composition: bimetallic (center, 0.925 silver, 0.075 copper; outer ring, 0.92 copper, 0.06 aluminum, 0.02 nickel). *Weight:* 3.967 g. *Obverse:* On the silver center, the national coat of arms with the eagle facing left, its feathers resembling plates of armor. On the bronze-aluminum outer ring, the legend ESTADOS UNIDOS MEXICANOS above, with a half-wreath of oak and laurel below. *Reverse:* On the silver center, off-center to the right, a screw-style coin press, with the denomination $100 to the left. Above and below the press, the dates 1535 and 2005, respectively, with the mintmark M̊ to the right. At the top of the outer ring, CASA DE MONEDA DE MÉXICO; at the bottom, • 470 ANIVERSARIO •. *Diameter:* 39 mm. *Edge:* Alternating plain and reeded.

	Mintage	F	VF	EF	Unc	BU
2005	49,895	$18.00	$20.00	$27.00	$30.00	$40.00

80th Anniversary of the Banco de México
Type A5. BW-688, KM-732.

Composition: bimetallic (center, 0.925 silver, 0.075 copper; outer ring, 0.92 copper, 0.06 aluminum, 0.02 nickel). *Weight:* 3.967 g. *Obverse:* On the silver center, the national coat of arms with the eagle facing left, its feathers resembling plates of armor. On the bronze-aluminum outer ring, the legend **ESTADOS UNIDOS MEXICANOS** above, with a half-wreath of oak and laurel below. *Reverse:* At center and extending through the outer ring, the rare 1925 one-hundred-peso note of the Banco de México. Above the note, the denomination **$100**. At the top, the dates **1925** and **2005**, separated by the logo of the Banco de México; to the left of this text, the mintmark M̥. At the bottom, **LXXX / ANIVERSARIO** (80th Anniversary). *Diameter:* 39 mm. *Edge:* Alternating plain and reeded.

	Mintage	F	VF	EF	Unc	BU
2005	49,712	$18.00	$20.00	$27.00	$30.00	$40.00

Bicentennial of the Birth of Benito Juárez García
Type A4. BW-689, KM-764.

Composition: bimetallic (center, 0.925 silver, 0.075 copper; outer ring, 0.92 copper, 0.06 aluminum, 0.02 nickel). *Weight:* 3.967 g. *Obverse:* On the silver center, the national coat of arms with the eagle facing left, its feathers resembling plates of armor. On the bronze-aluminum outer ring, the legend **ESTADOS UNIDOS MEXICANOS** above, with a half-wreath of oak and laurel below. *Reverse:* At center, a forward-facing bust of Benito Juárez García with the head turned partway to the left. Below, a facsimile of his signature; to the left, the mintmark M̥; to the right, **2006**. Around the outer ring, **BICENTENARIO DEL NATALICIO DE BENITO JUÁREZ GARCÍA** and **$100**. *Diameter:* 39 mm. *Edge:* Alternating plain and reeded.

Note: Silver Proofs were not issued for this event. See also page 27 for more information about President Juárez.

	Mintage	F	VF	EF	Unc	BU
2006	49,913	$18.00	$20.00	$27.00	$30.00	$40.00

Commemorative Coinage

Mexico has issued numerous commemorative, non-circulating legal tender (NCLT) coins, both in bimetallic composition and in the precious metals silver, gold, and platinum. In most cases, both Uncirculated and Proof commemoratives are struck in precious metals, and in low mintages. Some series have circulating counterparts (listed in chapter 3), while others do not. The type numbers used by collectors and referenced herein are organized by denomination, not by series. Thus, type numbers that appear to be missing are actually listed with circulating coinage in the previous chapters, and may or may not refer to designs in the same series. (For example, in the 25-peso denomination, Type 1 is a circulating commemorative that celebrates the 1968 Summer Olympic Games in Mexico City, and Type 2 is a circulating commemorative honoring 100th anniversary of the death of Benito Juárez García. Types 3 through 7 are Proof and Brilliant Uncirculated NCLT coins commemorating the 1986 World Cup Soccer games, and are listed in the current chapter.)

The NCLT classification makes it easier to navigate import regulations through customs. Non-circulating legal tender coins are subject to customs duties, but other legal-tender coins are not. Some purists within the hobby believe that NCLT coinage should not be viewed as or collected as coins because they do not circulate freely. Other numismatists hold the contrasting view that since they were issued by an official decree of a legitimate government, have a valid denomination, and have legal tender status, they *are* coins and are therefore collectible.

The Libertad series (which does not have a denomination but does have legal tender status, by official decree) is listed in chapter 9.

1986 WORLD CUP FUTBOL GAMES

In 1986 Mexico was the host country for the FIFA World Cup Football (Soccer) Games, also called the Copa Mundial de Fútbol. A major earthquake the previous year had cast doubt on Mexico's ability to host, but the games were able to proceed as planned, taking place in Mexico City from May 31 to June 29. This was the second tournament to feature 24 teams, and the format had been changed so that the second round was played on a knockout basis. In the final match Argentina defeated Germany 3–2. Meanwhile, up in the stands, a phenomenon called the Mexican wave was developing; it would become popular among fans at sporting events world-wide.

To commemorate the honor of hosting the World Cup, Mexico issued both circulating and NCLT coins in 1985 and 1986. Among the non-circulating coins, those in the Brilliant Uncirculated format have a high-quality, uniform finish on the field and devices, and display the silver fineness. Proofs have a mirrored field and frosted devices, and lack the indication of fineness.

25 pesos, Type 3, 1985 ("Mexico86" on Ball). BW-572, KM-497. Brilliant Uncirculated.

Composition: 0.720 silver. *Weight:* 7.776 g. *Obverse:* The national coat of arms with the eagle facing left, its feathers resembling plates of armor. Above, the legend **ESTADOS UNIDOS MEXICANOS**; below, a half-wreath of oak and laurel. *Reverse:* Slightly below center, a futbol in motion to the right with horizontal streaks to the left, suggesting speed. Below the streaks and crossing the futbol, **Mexico86**, with **1985** and fineness **PLATA 720** (in two lines) below. Above the main design, **$25**; at the top, **COPA MUNDIAL DE FUTBOL**; at the bottom, the mintmark **M̥**. *Diameter:* 26 mm. *Edge:* Plain.

Note: Unlike on other silver coins in the series, the "México86" logo on the Type 3, Brilliant Uncirculated 25 pesos lacks the accent over the é and the dot over the i. Examples with the accent and dot have been observed on the market, but their rarity and value have not been established.

	Mintage	BU
1985	473,605	$15.00

25 pesos, Type 4, 1985 ("México86" and Three Ornaments). BW-573, KM-503. Proof.

Composition: 0.925 silver. *Weight:* 8.406 g. *Obverse:* The national coat of arms with the eagle facing left, its feathers resembling plates of armor. Above, the legend **ESTADOS UNIDOS MEXICANOS**; below, a half-wreath of oak and laurel. *Reverse:* Placed diagonally across the center, three overlapping devices—a pre-Hispanic emblem, a Spanish *ojo de buey* (or "bullseye," a type of window often seen in Spanish colonial architecture), and a modern futbol—with horizontal streaks to the left, suggesting speed. Below the emblems, **México86**; above the emblems, **$25 / 1985**. Beginning at the top and continuing clockwise to the right, the legend **COPA**

MUNDIAL DE FUTBOL; at the bottom, the mintmark M̥. *Diameter:* 26 mm. *Edge:* Plain.

	Mintage	PF
1985	52,002	$18.00

25 pesos, Type 5, 1985 ("México86" Below Futbol). BW-574, KM-514. Proof.

Composition: 0.925 silver. *Weight:* 8.406 g. *Obverse:* The national coat of arms with the eagle facing left, its feathers resembling plates of armor. Above, the legend **ESTADOS UNIDOS MEXICANOS**; below, a half-wreath of oak and laurel. *Reverse:* A futbol in motion to the right with horizontal streaks to the left, suggesting speed. Below the streaks and futbol, **México86**, with the mintmark M̥ to the right. Above the futbol, **$25**; at the top, **COPA MUNDIAL DE FUTBOL**; at the bottom, **1985**. *Diameter:* 26 mm. *Edge:* Plain.

	Mintage	PF
1985	21,260	$18.00

25 pesos, Type 6, 1986 ("México86" on Ball). BW-575, KM-497a. Proof.

Composition: 0.925 silver. *Weight:* 8.406 g. *Obverse:* The national coat of arms with the eagle facing left, its feathers resembling plates of armor. Above, the legend **ESTADOS UNIDOS MEXICANOS**; below, a half-wreath of oak and laurel. *Reverse:* Slightly below center, a futbol in motion to the right with horizontal streaks to the left, suggesting speed. Below the streaks and crossing the futbol, **México86**, with **1986** below. Above the main design, **$25**; at the top, **COPA MUNDIAL DE FUTBOL**; at the bottom, the mintmark M̥. *Diameter:* 26 mm. *Edge:* Plain.

	Mintage	PF
1986	22,552	$18.00

25 pesos, Type 7, 1986 ("México86" Below Ball in Net).
BW-576, KM-519. Proof.

Composition: 0.925 silver. *Weight:* 8.406 g. *Obverse:* The national coat of arms with the eagle facing left, its feathers resembling plates of armor. Above, the legend **ESTADOS UNIDOS MEXICANOS**; below, a half-wreath of oak and laurel. *Reverse:* Filling the right half of the field, a net with a futbol in its upper section. To the left of the futbol, **1986 / $ / 25**, with **COPA MUNDIAL DE FUTBOL** and **México86** below. At the bottom, the mintmark M̊. *Diameter:* 26 mm. *Edge:* Plain.

	Mintage	PF
1986	20,172	$18.00

50 pesos, Type 4, 1985 (Feet Chasing Ball).
BW-580, KM-498. Brilliant Uncirculated.

Composition: 0.720 silver. *Weight:* 15.552 g. *Obverse:* The national coat of arms with the eagle facing left, its feathers resembling plates of armor. Above, the legend **ESTADOS UNIDOS MEXICANOS**; below, a half-wreath of oak and laurel. *Reverse:* The lower legs and feet of a futbol player, chasing a ball to the left. Just above the ball, **$50**; below the player's left foot (which is placed on the ground), **México86**, with the mintmark M̊ and fineness **PLATA 720** to the right of the foot in two lines. Above the player's raised right foot, **1985**. Beginning at the top and continuing clockwise to the right, the legend **COPA MUNDIAL DE FUTBOL**. *Diameter:* 32 mm. *Edge:* Plain.

	Mintage	BU
1985	439,763	$22.00

50 pesos, Type 5, 1985 (Mayan Ball Player). BW-581, KM-504. Proof.

Composition: 0.925 silver. *Weight:* 16.831 g. *Obverse:* The national coat of arms with the eagle facing left, its feathers resembling plates of armor. Above, the legend **ESTADOS UNIDOS MEXICANOS**; below, a half-wreath of oak and laurel. *Reverse:* In the left half of the field, a Mayan ball player chasing a small, flying rubber ball to the right; streaks to the left of the player indicate speed. Above the rubber ball, the mintmark M̥; to the right of the ball, a Mayan ball marker with **1985** above and a modern futbol below. Placed vertically at far right, $50. At the top, **COPA MUNDIAL DE FUTBOL**; at the bottom, **México86**. *Diameter:* 32 mm. *Edge:* Plain.

	Mintage	PF
1985	41,255	$28.00

50 pesos, Type 6, 1985 (Modern Ball Player). BW-582, KM-515. Proof.

Composition: 0.925 silver. *Weight:* 16.831 g. *Obverse:* The national coat of arms with the eagle facing left, its feathers resembling plates of armor. Above, the legend **ESTADOS UNIDOS MEXICANOS**; below, a half-wreath of oak and laurel. *Reverse:* In the left half of the field, a modern futbol player chasing a ball along the ground to the right; streaks to the left of the player indicate speed. At the right, below the player's raised left arm, $50, with **1985** M̥ below. Beneath all, **México86 / COPA MUNDIAL DE FUTBOL**. *Diameter:* 32 mm. *Edge:* Plain.

	Mintage	PF
1985	24,907	$28.00

50 pesos, Type 7, 1985 (Feet Chasing Ball). BW-583, KM-498a. Proof.

Composition: 0.925 silver. *Weight:* 16.831 g. *Obverse:* The national coat of arms with the eagle facing left, its feathers resembling plates of armor. Above, the legend **ESTADOS UNIDOS MEXICANOS**; below, a half-wreath of oak and laurel. *Reverse:* The lower legs and feet of a futbol player, chasing a ball to the left. Just above the ball, **$50**; below the player's left foot (which is placed on the ground), **México86**, with the mintmark M̥ to the right of the foot. Above the player's raised right foot, **1985**. Beginning at the top and continuing clockwise to the right, the legend **COPA MUNDIAL DE FUTBOL**. *Diameter:* 32 mm. *Edge:* Plain.

	Mintage	PF
1986	19,564	$28.00

50 pesos, Type 8, 1986 (Three Balls). BW-584, KM-523. Proof.

Composition: 0.925 silver. *Weight:* 16.831 g. *Obverse:* The national coat of arms with the eagle facing left, its feathers resembling plates of armor. Above, the legend **ESTADOS UNIDOS MEXICANOS**; below, a half-wreath of oak and laurel. *Reverse:* In the upper right field, three overlapping futbols in graduating sizes, placed diagonally. To the left of the balls, **$ / 50**; to the right and slightly below the balls, the mintmark M̥. Centered beneath all, **COPA MUNDIAL DE FUTBOL / México86 / 1986**. *Diameter:* 32 mm. *Edge:* Plain.

	Mintage	PF
1986	18,653	$28.00

100 pesos, Type 3, 1985 (Ball With Stylized Ornaments). BW-588, KM-499. Brilliant Uncirculated.

Composition: 0.720 silver. *Weight:* 31.103 g. *Obverse:* The national coat of arms with the eagle facing left, its feathers resembling plates of armor. Above, the legend **ESTADOS UNIDOS MEXICANOS**; below, a half-wreath of oak and laurel. *Reverse:* Across the center, a futbol traveling to the right, with streaks to the left indicating speed. At far left, superimposed over the streaks, a pre-Columbian deity figure facing left; complex flourishes at its back embrace the ball. To the right of the central motif, **PLATA / 720**; above it, **$100**; below it, **México86**. At the top, **COPA MUNDIAL DE FUTBOL**, with **1985** at the bottom. To the right of the lower right flourish, the mintmark M̥. *Diameter:* 38 mm. *Edge:* Plain.

	Mintage	BU
1985	449,247	$30.00

100 pesos, Type 4, 1985 (Ball With Stylized Ornaments). BW-589, KM-499a. Proof.

Composition: 0.925 silver. *Weight:* 32.625 g. *Obverse:* The national coat of arms with the eagle facing left, its feathers resembling plates of armor. Above, the legend **ESTADOS UNIDOS MEXICANOS**; below, a half-wreath of oak and laurel. *Reverse:* Across the center, a futbol traveling to the right, with streaks to the left indicating speed. At far left, superimposed over the streaks, a pre-Columbian deity figure facing left; complex flourishes at its back embrace the ball. Above the central motif, **$100**; below it, **México86**. At the top, **COPA MUNDIAL DE FUTBOL**, with **1985** at the bottom. To the right of the lower right flourish, the mintmark M̥. *Diameter:* 38 mm. *Edge:* Plain.

	Mintage	PF
1985	26,964	$45.00

100 pesos, Type 5, 1985 (Goalie and Ball in Net). BW-590, KM-505. Proof.

Composition: 0.925 silver. *Weight:* 32.625 g. *Obverse:* The national coat of arms with the eagle facing left, its feathers resembling plates of armor. Above, the legend **ESTADOS UNIDOS MEXICANOS**; below, a half-wreath of oak and laurel. *Reverse:* Filling the right half of the field, the head and shoulders of a goalie in profile, heading a ball upward behind a net. In the lower left part of the field, placed vertically along the edge of the net, **1985 / México86 / COPA MUNDIAL DE FUTBOL**. In the upper left part of the field, **$ / 100**, with the mintmark M̊ somewhat below. *Diameter:* 38 mm. *Edge:* Plain.

	Mintage	PF
1985	71,718	$45.00

100 pesos, Type 6, 1986 (Goalie Holding Ball). BW-591, KM-521. Proof.

Composition: 0.925 silver. *Weight:* 32.625 g. *Obverse:* The national coat of arms with the eagle facing left, its feathers resembling plates of armor. Above, the legend **ESTADOS UNIDOS MEXICANOS**; below, a half-wreath of oak and laurel. *Reverse:* At center, a forward-facing, stylized figure of a goalie diving toward the right with a ball in his hands. Streaks to the left of the figure indicate speed. Above the goalie's head, **1986**; below the head, the mintmark M̊. At the top, **$500**; at the bottom, **México86 / COPA MUNDIAL DE FUTBOL**. *Diameter:* 38 mm. *Edge:* Plain.

	Mintage	PF
1986	19,279	$45.00

100 pesos, Type 7, 1986 (Ball and Globe). BW-592, KM-524. Proof.

Composition: 0.925 silver. *Weight:* 32.625 g. *Obverse:* The national coat of arms with the eagle facing left, its feathers resembling plates of armor. Above, the legend **ESTADOS UNIDOS MEXICANOS**; below, a half-wreath of oak and laurel. *Reverse:* At upper left, a futbol shape suggested by the presence of alternating patches; at lower right, slightly behind the futbol, a globe. Below the futbol and extending across the globe, **México86**, with the mintmark M̥ above left and **1986** below left. At upper right, partly overlapping the futbol, **$100**. Beginning near the top and continuing clockwise to the right, **COPA MUNDIAL DE FUTBOL**. *Diameter:* 38 mm. *Edge:* Plain.

	Mintage	PF
1986	18,510	$45.00

200 pesos, Type 4, 1986 (Ball With Two Globes). BW-601, KM-526. Brilliant Uncirculated.

Composition: 0.999 silver. *Weight:* 62.206 g. *Obverse:* The national coat of arms with the eagle facing left, its feathers resembling plates of armor. Above, the legend **ESTADOS UNIDOS MEXICANOS**; below, a half-wreath of oak and laurel. *Reverse:* At the center, a small futbol flanked by and slightly overlapping globes of the Western Hemisphere (at left) and the Eastern Hemisphere (at right). Above, **$200 / LEY 999**; below, **MEXICO86 / 1986**; to the right, the mintmark M̥. Surrounding all, the legend · **COPA MUNDIAL DE FUTBOL** · and **2 ONZAS PLATA PURA**. *Diameter:* 48 mm. *Edge:* Plain.

	Mintage	BU
1986	23,489	$80.00

250 pesos, Type 1, 1985 (Ball With Ornamented Background). BW-602a, KM-500.1. Brilliant Uncirculated.

Composition: 0.900 gold. *Weight:* 8.640 g. *Obverse:* The national coat of arms with the eagle facing left, its feathers resembling plates of armor. Above, the legend **ESTADOS UNIDOS MEXICANOS**; below, a half-wreath of oak and laurel. *Reverse:* Filling the upper half of the field, a wall of emblems in a Mayan design; at center, in front of the wall, a futbol with M̊ / **1985** to the left and **$** / **250** to the right. Centered below, in three lines, **COPA MUNDIAL DE FUTBOL, México86**, and fineness **ORO 900**. *Diameter:* 22 mm. *Edge:* Plain.

Note: Some catalogs also list this design and format with the date 1986, but the existence of such a coin has never been confirmed.

	Mintage	BU
1985	100,000	$450.00

250 pesos, Type 2, 1986 (Ball With Ornamented Background). BW-603a, KM-500.2. Proof.

Composition: 0.900 gold. *Weight:* 8.640 g. *Obverse:* The national coat of arms with the eagle facing left, its feathers resembling plates of armor. Above, the legend **ESTADOS UNIDOS MEXICANOS**; below, a half-wreath of oak and laurel. *Reverse:* Filling the upper half of the field, a wall of emblems in a Mayan design; at center, in front of the wall, a futbol with M̊ / **1986** to the left and **$** / **250** to the right. Centered below, **COPA MUNDIAL DE FUTBOL / México86**. *Diameter:* 22 mm. *Edge:* Plain.

Note: Some catalogs also list this design in BU format with the date 1985, but the existence of such a coin has never been confirmed.

	Mintage	PF
1986	4,506	$500.00

250 pesos, Type 4, 1985 (Mounted Victory With Ball).
BW-605a, KM-506.2. Proof.

Composition: 0.900 gold. *Weight:* 8.640 g. *Obverse:* The national coat of arms with the eagle facing left, its feathers resembling plates of armor. Above, the legend **ESTADOS UNIDOS MEXICANOS**; below, a half-wreath of oak and laurel. *Reverse:* The Mounted Victory emblem from the Caballito peso, with a large futbol in the background. On the futbol just to the right of Victory, **$ / 250**, with the mintmark **M̊** at far right in the field. Above, **1985 450 años de la casa de moneda**. Below, **México86 / COPA MUNDIAL DE FUTBOL**. *Diameter:* 22 mm. *Edge:* Plain.

Note: (1) As the legend above the central device indicates, Type 4 honors the 450th anniversary of the Casa de Monéda in addition to the 1986 World Cup. (2) Some catalogs also list this design in BU format with the date 1986, but the existence of such a coin has never been confirmed.

	Mintage	PF
1985	80,000	$500.00

500 pesos, Type 1, 1985 (Ball Player and Aztec Calendar).
BW-606a, KM-501.1. Brilliant Uncirculated.

Composition: 0.900 gold. *Weight:* 17.280 g. *Obverse:* The national coat of arms with the eagle facing left, its feathers resembling plates of armor. Above, the legend **ESTADOS UNIDOS MEXICANOS**; below, a half-wreath of oak and laurel. *Reverse:* In the background, slightly to the left of center, the Aztec Calendar Stone, with a running futbol player and ball in front of the Stone to the right. At the bottom in two lines, **México86** and fineness **ORO 900**, with **1985** in the far left field and, in the far right field, **$ / 500 / M̊**. Beginning at the top and continuing clockwise, **COPA MUNDIAL DE FUTBOL**. *Diameter:* 28 mm. *Edge:* Plain.

Note: Some catalogs also list this design and format with the date 1986, but the existence of such a coin has never been confirmed.

	Mintage	BU
1985	51,776	$900.00

500 pesos, Type 2, 1986 (Ball Player and Aztec Calendar). BW-607.1a, KM-501.2. Proof.

Composition: 0.900 gold. *Weight:* 17.280 g. *Obverse:* The national coat of arms with the eagle facing left, its feathers resembling plates of armor. Above, the legend **ESTADOS UNIDOS MEXICANOS**; below, a half-wreath of oak and laurel. *Reverse:* In the background, slightly to the left of center, the Aztec Calendar Stone, with a running futbol player and ball in front of the Stone to the right. At the bottom, **México86**, with **1986** in the far left field and, in the far right field, **$ / 500 / M̊**. Beginning at the top and continuing clockwise, **COPA MUNDIAL DE FUTBOL**. *Diameter:* 28 mm. *Edge:* Plain.

Note: Some catalogs also list this design and format with the date 1985, but the existence of such a coin has never been confirmed.

	Mintage	PF
1986	unknown	$975.00

500 pesos, Type 3, 1985 (Ball and Coin). BW-609a, KM-507.2. Proof.

Composition: 0.900 gold. *Weight:* 17.280 g. *Obverse:* The national coat of arms with the eagle facing left, its feathers resembling plates of armor. Above, the legend **ESTADOS UNIDOS MEXICANOS**; below, a half-wreath of oak and laurel. *Reverse:* Above center, a depiction of a Carlos and Johanna real, with a futbol in front of it to the right. At far left, **$ / 500**; at far right, **M̊ / 1985**. Above, **450 años de la casa de moneda**; below, **México86 / COPA MUNDIAL DE FUTBOL**. *Diameter:* 28 mm. *Edge:* Plain.

Note: (1) As the legend above the central device indicates, Type 3 honors the 450th anniversary of the Casa de Moneda in addition to the 1986 World Cup. (2) Some catalogs also list this design in a BU format, but the existence of such a coin has never been confirmed.

	Mintage	PF
1985	unknown	$1,800.00

1,000 pesos, Type 2, 1986 (Ball With Globes).
BW-614a, KM-527. Brilliant Uncirculated.

Composition: 0.999 gold. *Weight:* 31.050 g. *Obverse:* The national coat of arms with the eagle facing left, its feathers resembling plates of armor. Above, the legend **ESTADOS UNIDOS MEXICANOS**; below, a half-wreath of oak and laurel. *Reverse:* At the center, a small futbol flanked by and slightly overlapping globes of the Western Hemisphere (at left) and the Eastern Hemisphere (at right). Above, **$1000 / LEY 999**; below, **MEXICO86 / 1986**; to the right, the mintmark M̊. Surrounding all, the legend • **COPA MUNDIAL DE FUTBOL** • and **1 ONZA ORO PURO**. *Diameter:* 30 mm. *Edge:* Plain.

	Mintage	BU
1986	1,279	$1,800.00

2,000 pesos, Type 1, 1986 (Ball With Globes).
BW-618a, KM-528. Brilliant Uncirculated.

Composition: 0.999 gold. *Weight:* 62.200 g. *Obverse:* The national coat of arms with the eagle facing left, its feathers resembling plates of armor. Above, the legend **ESTADOS UNIDOS MEXICANOS**; below, a half-wreath of oak and laurel. *Reverse:* At the center, a small futbol flanked by and slightly overlapping globes of the Western Hemisphere (at left) and the Eastern Hemisphere (at right). Above, **$2000 / LEY 999**; below, **MEXICO86 / 1986**; to the right, the mintmark M̊. Surrounding all, the legend • **COPA MUNDIAL DE FUTBOL** • and **2 ONZAS ORO PURO**. *Diameter:* 36 mm. *Edge:* Plain.

	Mintage	BU
1986	964	$3,250.00

175TH ANNIVERSARY OF INDEPENDENCE

In 1985 two coins were issued to commemorate the 175th anniversary of the beginning of the War of Independence: a 200-peso circulating issue in copper-nickel (see chapter 2), and a 1,000-peso NCLT issue in 0.900 gold.

1,000 pesos, Type 1, 1985. BW-613a, KM-513. Proof.

Composition: 0.900 gold. *Weight:* 17.280 g. *Obverse:* The national coat of arms with the eagle facing left, its feathers resembling plates of armor. Above, the legend **ESTADOS UNIDOS MEXICANOS**; below, a half-wreath of oak and laurel. *Reverse:* At the left, Mexico City's *Monumento de la Independencia* (see also page 55). To the right, in left-facing profile, four jugate busts (Ignacio Allende, Miguel Hidalgo y Costilla, José María Morelos, and Vicente Guerrero), each with his surname beneath in small letters. Above the busts, **$1000** and a partial border consisting of a broken chain, signifying freedom; below, **175 ANIVERSARIO DE / LA INDEPENDENCIA / DE MEXICO**. To the far left of the monument, **1985**; the mintmark **M̊** is at the bottom. *Diameter:* 38 mm. *Edge:* Plain.

	Mintage	PF
1985	3,721	$825

75TH ANNIVERSARY OF THE REVOLUTION

In 1985, in honor of the 75th anniversary of the start of the Mexican Revolution, two commemorative coins were issued: a 200-peso copper-nickel circulating coin (see chapter 2) and a Proof 500 pesos in 0.925 silver.

500 pesos, Type 1, 1985. BW-610b, KM-511. Proof.

Composition: 0.9250 silver. *Weight:* 33.450 g. *Obverse:* The national coat of arms with the eagle facing left, its feathers resembling plates of armor. Above, the legend **ESTADOS UNIDOS MEXICANOS**; below, a half-wreath of oak and laurel. *Reverse:* To the right, in left-facing profile, four jugate busts (Emiliano Zapata, Francisco Madero, Venustiano Carranza, and Francisco "Pancho" Villa), each with his surname beneath in small letters. Behind the portraits, the dome of the *Monumento de la Revolucion*. The legend 75 ANIVERSARIO DE LA REVOLUCION MEXICANA surrounds, with 75 ANIVERSARIO placed vertically in the field at the left. Below the busts, $500 / 1985; at far left, the mintmark M̥. *Diameter:* 40 mm. *Edge:* Plain.

	Mintage	PF
1985	40,002	$50.00

Monumento de la Revolucion

When the dictator Porfirio Díaz laid the first stone of a new legislative palace, in September 1910, he was unaware of the destiny of either his "presidency" or the structure. The building was intended to be one of the grandest in Mexico City, but the Revolution put constraints on the available resources, and the work was suspended.

After the Revolution, the structure was scheduled to be demolished. Architect Carlos Obregón Santacilia proposed that the cupola be saved and redesigned as a monument. The finished structure stood 220 feet high, making it the tallest triumphal arch in the world (the *Arc de Triomphe,* in Paris, is 164 feet; Berlin's *Brandenburg Gate,* 85 feet). The Art Deco style of the era is apparent in the design of the sculptural figures at the four corners of the roof, representing Worker Laws, Agricultural Laws, Reformation Laws, and Independence.

In subsequent years, the Monumento de la Revolucion became a mausoleum for the remains of several major Revolutionary figures, including Francisco Madero and Venustiano Carranza.

WORLD WIDE FUND FOR NATURE

The World Wide Fund for Nature is one of the largest nongovernmental conservation groups in the world. The WWF was founded in 1961; its mission is "to stop the degradation of the planet's natural environment and to build a future in which humans live in harmony with nature."

In 1987, Mexico took part in a WWF project to protect the monarch butterfly *(Danaus plexippus)*. Well known for its distinctive yellow-and-black markings and its large annual migration, which covers thousands of miles, the monarch butterfly typically overwinters along the Gulf Coast, including in Mexico. Environmentalists are seeking to have it classified internationally as endangered—herbicides are eliminating the butterfly's preferred food (the milkweed plant), and its prime overwintering habitat, the oyamel tree *(Abies religiosa)*, is in decline. In addition to establishing habitat protections, Mexico commemorated the species with a 100-peso Proof coin in 0.720 silver, with a reverse that features the monarch butterfly.

In 1998 Mexico participated in a joint effort to commemorate the WWF's 35th anniversary, issuing a Proof 5 pesos honoring the *lobo* (the Mexican wolf, or *Canis lupus*). The Mexican wolf is the smallest of North America's gray wolves and is also the most endangered. It was considered a symbol of war and the sun in pre-Columbian Mexico. In 1979, a recovery plan was begun to release captive-bred wolves into the wild in the hopes of reestablishing them in their historical range in western Mexico. The first birth of a wild wolf litter in Mexico was reported in 2014.

5 pesos, Type A4, 1998 (Lobo). BW-593.2, KM-627. Proof.

Composition: 0.999 silver. *Weight:* 31.1035 g. *Obverse:* The national coat of arms with the eagle facing left, its feathers resembling plates of armor. Above, the legend **ESTADOS UNIDOS MEXICANOS**; below, a half-wreath of oak and laurel. *Reverse:* At the center, a wolf and cub, with **LOBO** above and **CANIS LUPUS** below. At far left, **1998** above the mintmark M̊; at far right, the circular logo of the WWF above $5. *Diameter:* 40 mm. *Edge:* Reeded.

Note: The image released by the mint and frequently reproduced elsewhere is of a coin dated 1997, a date not seen in the marketplace. It is likely the image is of a pattern coin; all regular issues are dated 1998.

	Mintage	PF
1998	13,004	$100.00

100 pesos, Type 8, 1987 (Monarch). BW-593.1, KM-537. Proof.

Composition: 0.720 silver. *Weight:* 32.6250 g. *Obverse:* The national coat of arms with the eagle facing left, its feathers resembling plates of armor. Above, the legend **ESTADOS UNIDOS MEXICANOS**; below, a half-wreath of oak and laurel. *Reverse:* Encircling the field in a counterclockwise direction, 10 monarch butterflies in graduating sizes. At upper right, in three lines, **1987**, **$100**, and the mintmark M̥. At the center of the field, fineness **plata / .720** above **mariposa / monarca**. *Diameter:* 38 mm. *Edge:* Plain.

	Mintage	PF
1987	28,500	$70.00

50TH ANNIVERSARY OF THE NATIONALIZATION OF THE OIL INDUSTRY

In 1988 Mexico issued circulating and commemorative coins in honor of the 50th anniversary of the nationalization of the oil industry, which took place during the presidency of Lázaro Cárdenas. The Brilliant Uncirculated NCLT coins were issued in denominations of 50, 100, 500, and 1,000 pesos. A copper-nickel circulating 5,000 pesos was also released; see chapter 2.

50 pesos, Type 9, 1988 (Monument). BW-585, KM-532. Brilliant Uncirculated.

Composition: 0.999 silver. *Weight:* 15.550 g. *Obverse:* The national coat of arms with the eagle facing left, its feathers resembling plates of armor. Above, the legend **ESTADOS UNIDOS MEXICANOS**; below, a half-wreath of oak and laurel. *Reverse:* At center, the *Fuente de Petróleos (Monument to the Oil Industry)*. At the top, **CIN-**

CUENTENARIO; at the bottom, **EXPROPIACION PETROLERA**. In the field to the left, **50 / PESOS** placed vertically; to the right, fineness **LEY / 0.999**. Below the monument, 1938–1988 above the mintmark M̊. *Diameter:* 31 mm. *Edge:* Reeded.

	Mintage	BU
(1988)	20,000	$45.00

100 pesos, Type 9, 1988 (Cárdenas).
BW-594, KM-533. Brilliant Uncirculated.

Composition: 0.999 silver. *Weight:* 31.103 g. *Obverse:* The national coat of arms with the eagle facing left, its feathers resembling plates of armor. Above, the legend **ESTADOS UNIDOS MEXICANOS**; below, a half-wreath of oak and laurel. *Reverse:* At the center, above a spray of laurel, a forward-facing bust of Lázaro Cárdenas, his face turned slightly to the left; below the bust, **L. CARDENAS**. At the top, **EXPROPACION / PETROLERA**; at the bottom, below the spray, **50 / ANIVERSARIO / 1938-1988**. To the left of the bust, **$100**; to the right, the mintmark M̊ above the fineness, **Ley 0.999**. *Diameter:* 38 mm. *Edge:* Plain.

	Mintage	BU
1988	20,000	$50.00

500 pesos, Type 2, 1988 (Monument).
BW-612, KM-534. Brilliant Uncirculated.

Composition: 0.900 gold. *Weight:* 17.280 g. *Obverse:* The national coat of arms with the eagle facing left, its feathers resembling plates of armor. Above, the legend **ESTADOS UNIDOS MEXICANOS**; below, a half-wreath of oak and laurel. *Reverse:* At center, the *Fuente de Petróleos (Monument to the Oil Industry)*. At the top, **CINCUENTENARIO**; at the bottom, **EXPROPIACION PETROLERA**. In the field to the left, **500 / PESOS** placed vertically; to the right, fineness **LEY / 0.999**. Below the monument, **1938–1988** above the mintmark M̥. *Diameter:* 28 mm. *Edge:* Plain.

	Mintage	BU
1988	611	$850.00

1,000 pesos, Type 2, 1988 (Cárdenas).
BW-615, KM-535. Brilliant Uncirculated.

Composition: 0.900 gold. *Weight:* 34.559 g. *Obverse:* The national coat of arms with the eagle facing left, its feathers resembling plates of armor. Above, the legend **ESTADOS UNIDOS MEXICANOS**; below, a half-wreath of oak and laurel. *Reverse:* At the center, above a spray of laurel, a forward-facing bust of Lázaro Cárdenas, his face turned slightly to the left; below the bust, **L. CARDENAS**. At the top, **EXPROPACION / PETROLERA**; at the bottom, below the spray, **50 / ANIVERSARIO / 1938-1988**. To the left of the bust, **$1000**; to the right, the mintmark M̥ above the fineness, **Ley 0.900**. *Diameter:* 34.5 mm. *Edge:* Plain.

	Mintage	BU
1988	657	$1,800.00

Lázaro Cárdenas

Lázaro Cárdenas, president of Mexico from 1934 to 1940, was responsible for nationalizing the country's oil industry on March 18, 1938. Foreign companies had controlled Mexico's oil reserves since the days of the dictator Porfirio Díaz. The expropriation, which Cárdenas announced to the nation via radio broadcast, was seen as an expression of national sovereignty and was very popular with the Mexican people. On the Paseo de la Reforma in Mexico City, a monument to the nationalization, the *Fuente de Petroleos* (literally "Fountain of Oil"), portrays oil workers in a heroic manner (see page 88).

Mexico compensated the ousted oil companies for their losses, taking on significant national debt during the Great Depression to do so. Mexico's state oil company is called Pemex.

Cárdenas is credited, more so than any other president, with implementing the reforms set out in Mexico's 1917 constitution, including land and agriculture reform. He is also remembered for supporting the Spanish Republic and welcoming refugees from the Spanish Civil War.

SAVE THE CHILDREN FUND

Since its creation in London in 1919, Save the Children International has worked with the children of the poor in 120 countries. In addition to fighting hunger and poverty, the nonprofit organization also works to uphold children's rights as spelled out in the "Declaration of the Rights of the Child"—10 principles adopted by the U.N. General Assembly in 1959. The declaration did not become international law until 1990.

Mexico, in conjunction with several other countries, issued coins to commemorate the 70th anniversary of the founding of the Save the Children Fund, with each coin featuring children in an activity characteristic of the issuing country. Mexico's 100-peso issue depicts three children playing *piñata*, a game popular with Mexican children on festive occasions.

100 pesos, Type 10, 1991. BW-595, KM-539. Proof.

Composition: 0.925 silver. *Weight:* 33.625 g. *Obverse:* Above a spray of oak and laurel, the national coat of arms with the eagle facing left, its feathers resembling plates of armor. Above, the legend **ESTADOS UNIDOS MEXICANOS**. *Reverse:* At center, a standing, blindfolded girl swings a stick at a piñata above, while a seated boy and girl gather the falling treats. At the left, **1 ONZA / DE PLATA** above fineness **LEY .925**; at the right, **$10 / 1991** above the mintmark M̥. At the bottom, **SALVE A LOS NIÑOS** (Save the Children). *Diameter:* 40 mm. *Edge:* Plain.

	Mintage	PF
1991	11,000	$50.00

UNITED NATIONS ENVIRONMENT PROGRAMME

The United Nations Environment Programme (UNEP) is dedicated to helping developing countries implement effective environmental policies. Established by the United Nations in 1972 and headquartered in Nairobi, Kenya, UNEP disseminates a wide variety of information on the environment for policymakers and the public. UNEP works on a variety of issues, including climate change, disasters and conflicts, ecosystem management, environmental governance, chemicals and waste, and resource efficiency. UNEP helps Mexico's Ministry of Environment and Natural Resources with green-energy initiatives.

In 1992, to commemorate the 20th anniversary of UNEP, Mexico issued a Proof 100 pesos featuring the vaquita marina *(Phocoena sinus)*—a species of porpoise discovered in 1958 when three skulls were found on the shores of the Gulf of California. The smallest of the porpoises, the vaquita is not social like a dolphin; it surfaces quickly to breathe and avoids interaction with people and boats. The vaquita is considered one of the most endangered marine mammals in the world. Because of its elusive nature, little is known about its longevity and breeding habits. Mexico is leading the vaquita conservation efforts by banning the use of gillnets in its habitat, creating a nature reserve where the vaquitas are known to exist, and educating and compensating fisherman who actively aid in the recovery of this species.

100 pesos, Type 12, 1992. BW-597, KM-566. Proof.

Composition: 0.999 silver. *Weight:* 31.1035 g. *Obverse:* The national coat of arms with the eagle facing left, its feathers resembling plates of armor. Above, the legend **ESTADOS UNIDOS MEXICANOS**; below, a half-wreath of oak and laurel. *Reverse:* Filling the right half of the coin, a vaquita swimming in a clockwise direction amid horizontal streamers of kelp. From the left, a school of small fish swim toward the vaquita. At the top, **$100**; to the left of the vaquita's tail, **1992**; at far right, the mintmark M̥. *Diameter:* 40 mm. *Edge:* Plain.

	Mintage	PF
1992	28,007	$60.00

IBEROAMERICANA SERIES

In 1991, Mexico and 15 other countries embarked on an ongoing program of coins and medals struck for the Iberoamericana Series, which celebrates the cultures of Spain, Portugal, and the numerous countries that were at one time their colonies. Eight series were issued from 1991 through 2010, with various countries participating.

In every series, each participant nation contributes a silver 40-mm coin, the obverse of which bears the coat of arms of the issuing country at center, surrounded by the coats of arms of the other participating countries. Each series' set includes a 40-mm medal; the series concluded in 2012 with the issuance of medals from each of 10 countries. (See the sidebar on pages 197–199.) The series' themes, and the designs Mexico has contributed to each series (all in Proof format), are as follows.

QUINCENTENNIAL OF THE DISCOVERY OF THE AMERICAS

The first Iberoamericana Series, issued in 1991 and 1992, commemorated the historic voyages of Christopher Columbus (Cristoforo Colombo in his native Italian). In the employ of the Spanish monarchs Columbus made four expeditions across the Atlantic; at first, the objective was to reach the East Indies, but Columbus found Hispaniola instead. His subsequent voyages were the beginning of Spain's colonization of the New World.

Mexico's contribution to the first series was the historic *Columnaria* (Pillars) design, with globes of the Western and Eastern Hemispheres between the Pillars of Hercules, and the ships of Christopher Columbus below. This is the only coin in the series denominated 100 pesos; later Iberoamericana coins are denominated 5 pesos.

**100 pesos, Type A2, 1991 and 1992.
BW-596.1 and 596.2, KM-540. Proof.**

Composition: 0.925 silver. *Weight:* 27.00 g. *Obverse:* At the center, a small national coat of arms with the eagle facing left, its feathers resembling plates of armor, encircled by a spray of oak and laurel (below) and the legend **ESTADOS UNIDOS MEXICANOS** (above). Surrounding the coat of arms, the emblems of the other nations participating in the series (see the sidebar). *Reverse:* At the center, the Western and Eastern Hemispheres, slightly overlapping, flanked by the crowned Pillars of Hercules, which emerge from the sea below. The pillars are wrapped in banners reading **PLUS** (at left) and **VLTR** (at right); in the water between them sail the three galleons of Columbus. Above the hemispheres, in two lines, $100 and the date; at far right, the mintmark M̥. At the top, the legend **ENCUENTRO DE DOS MUNDOS** (Meeting of Two Worlds); at the bottom, ∴ 1492–1992 ∴. *Diameter:* 40 mm. *Edge:* Reeded.

	Mintage	PF
1991	30,000	$75
1992	20,000	70

ENDANGERED NATIVE ANIMAL SPECIES

The second Iberoamericana series was issued in 1994. Mexico's contribution, with the denomination N$5 to accommodate the coinage reform of 1992, depicts the olive ridley sea turtle *(Lepidochelys olivacea)*, known in Mexico as the golfina turtle, on the reverse. The species is relatively small, with adults rarely exceeding two feet in length and about 100 pounds. Although the golfina is the most abundant sea turtle in the world, populations have declined by half since the 1960s. Mexico is one of only five places in the world to host an *arribada*, or "arrival by sea," whereby thousands of golfina turtles gather in the water before coming ashore en masse to lay their heart-shaped eggs.

New 5 pesos, Type A3, 1994. BW-596.3, KM-588. Proof.

Composition: 0.925 silver. *Weight:* 27.00 g. *Obverse:* At the center, a small national coat of arms with the eagle facing left, its feathers resembling plates of armor, encircled by a spray of oak and laurel (below) and the legend **ESTADOS UNIDOS MEXICANOS** (above). Surrounding the coat of arms, the emblems of the other nations participating in the series (see the sidebar). *Reverse:* Filling the center, a golfina sea turtle swimming to the right, amid four horizontal lines of stylized waves. At the top, **ENCUENTRO DE DOS MUNDOS** at far right, N$5 / 1994 / M̥. *Diameter:* 40 mm. *Edge:* Reeded.

	Mintage	PF
1994	11,005	$80.00

IBEROAMERICAN DANCES AND COSTUMES

Mexico's contribution to the third series, which commenced in 1996, depicts the Jarabe Tapatío, a traditional Mexican dance that dates from the 15th century in Spain. The Jarabe Tapatío (Mexican Hat Dance) represents the courtship of a man and woman, with the woman rejecting and then accepting the man's advances. The sexual connotations of the dance and its challenge to Spanish rule caused it to be banned by the church in the 19th century. The woman wears a colorful dress costume called the *china poblana*, while the man wears a heavily decorated *charro* outfit. The dance was declared the national folk dance of Mexico when Russian ballerina Anna Pavlova fell in love with it.

**5 pesos, Type A5, 1997 and 1998.
BW-596.4 and 596.5, KM-629. Proof.**

Composition: 0.925 silver. *Weight:* 27.00 g. *Obverse:* At the center, a small national coat of arms with the eagle facing left, its feathers resembling plates of armor, encircled by a spray of oak and laurel (below) and the legend **ESTADOS UNIDOS MEXICANOS** (above). Surrounding the coat of arms, the emblems of the other nations participating in the series (see the sidebar). *Reverse:* At the center, a man (left) and woman (right) in traditional costume, performing the Jarabe Tapatío. At lower left, $5; at lower right, the mintmark M̊ and the date. At the top, JARABE TAPATIO; at the bottom, **MEXICO**. *Diameter:* 40 mm. *Edge:* Reeded.

	Mintage	PF
1997	8,011	$280.00
1998	3,000	300.00

MAN AND THE HORSE

For the fourth series, Mexico's contribution, dated 2000 but released in 2001, depicts the Paso de la Muerte, or "Ride of Death." The Spanish brought horses to Mexico, along with an event called the *charreada*—a kind of rough, competitive rodeo. In the Paso de la Muerte event, a *charro* (cowboy) attempts to leap from his galloping horse to the back of an unbroken horse with no saddle or bridle. The goal is to remain on the wild horse until it stops bucking, and if this is not possible, to avoid falling under the other galloping horses and their *charros*.

5 pesos, Type A21, 2000. BW-596.6, KM-670. Proof.

Composition: 0.925 silver. *Weight:* 27.00 g. *Obverse:* At the center, a small national coat of arms with the eagle facing left, its feathers resembling plates of armor, encircled by a spray of oak and laurel (below) and the legend **ESTADOS UNIDOS MEXICANOS** (above). Surrounding the coat of arms, the emblems of the other nations participating in the series (see the sidebar). *Reverse:* Two horses galloping from right to left against a background of a board fence. A *charro* is in midair above the horse near the fence, about to land on its bare back. The head of a third horse (saddled) is visible just behind the others. At far left, $5; at lower right, M̊. At the top, **EL HOMBRE Y SU CABALLO**; at the bottom, **2000 / PASO DE LA MUERTE**. *Diameter:* 40 mm. *Edge:* Reeded.

	Mintage	PF
2000	9,000	$80.00

THE NAUTICAL TRADITION

In the fifth series, the central figure of Mexico's coin, the *Galeón de Acapulco*, commemorates the galleons (Spanish sailing ships) that made trade possible between the Far East and Mexico during the Hernán Cortes era of the early 1500s. The galleons brought silks and spices from China and works of art from Japan. Returning to Manila, in the Philippines, the ships took millions of pesos in silver to pay for the Asian goods. The ships were vulnerable to storms, fires, pirates, and shipwrecks. The final *Galeón de Acapulco* voyage took place in 1815, during Mexico's struggle for independence from Spain.

5 pesos, Type A22, 2003. BW-596.7, KM-678. Proof.

Composition: 0.925 silver. *Weight:* 27.00 g. *Obverse:* At the center, a small national coat of arms with the eagle facing left, its feathers resembling plates of armor, encircled by a spray of oak and laurel (below) and the legend **ESTADOS UNIDOS MEXICANOS** (above). Surrounding the coat of arms, the emblems of the other nations participating in the series (see the sidebar). *Reverse:* At the center, the *Galeón de Acapulco* sailing on choppy water, flanked by the Pacific coastlines of the Eastern and Western Hemispheres. Dotted lines connect the routes between the Philippines (labeled **PILIPINAS**) and the city labeled **ACAPULCO**. In the foreground at the bottom, the small figures of a Spaniard and a native man (possibly Cortes and Moctezuma) exchange goods. In the right-hand field, above the waves, $5 / 2003; below the waves, the mintmark M̥. Surrounding all, **ENCUENTRO DE DOS MUNDOS** at the top and **GALEÓN DE ACAPULCO** at the bottom, joined by a border of rope. *Diameter:* 40 mm. *Edge:* Reeded.

	Mintage	PF
2003	17,105	$80.00

Architecture and Monuments

The reverse of Mexico's contribution to the sixth series features the Palacio de Bellas Artes (Palace of Fine Arts), which is located next to the Alameda Central Park in Mexico City. It is home to Mexico's national theater, ballet, and symphony orchestra. President Porfirio Díaz commissioned the palace to replace the old national theater building. Italian architect Adamo Boari was awarded the project, which was delayed by political strife and construction problems. Finally completed in 1934, the palace blends Art Nouveau, Art Deco, and Baroque architectural styles.

5 pesos, Type A23, 2005. BW-596.8, KM-765. Proof.

Composition: 0.925 silver. *Weight:* 27.00 g. *Obverse:* At the center, a small national coat of arms with the eagle facing left, its feathers resembling plates of armor, encircled by a spray of oak and laurel (below) and the legend **ESTADOS UNIDOS MEXICANOS** (above). Surrounding the coat of arms, the emblems of the other nations participating in the series (see the sidebar). *Reverse:* At the center, the Palacio de Bellas Artes, with $5 placed at upper left, the mintmark M̥ at upper right, and **2005** below. At the top, **ENCUENTRO DE DOS MUNDOS**; at the bottom, **PALACIO DE BELLAS ARTES – MÉXICO**. *Diameter:* 40 mm. *Edge:* Reeded.

	Mintage	PF
2005	8,005	$90.00

IBEROAMERICAN COUNTRIES IN THE OLYMPIC SPORTS

Each country in the seventh series depicted the sports that historically have represented their Olympic spirit. Mexico's contribution celebrates Disciplinas de Oro Olimpico Mexicano (Mexican Gold-Medal Disciplines): at the left is a Mayan ball player in the game of *pelota*; on a panel at the right, symbols depict the six Olympic sports in which Mexican participants have won gold medals.

Equestrian Humberto Mariles has the most Mexican individual gold medals with two, both won at the London games of 1948. Mexico's greatest victory in recent years was the national soccer team's gold-medal upset of Brazil in the 2012 London games. The 2–1 victory was the Mexican soccer team's first international trophy of any kind.

5 pesos, Type A24, 2008. BW-596.9, KM-805. Proof.

Composition: 0.925 silver. *Weight:* 27.00 g. *Obverse:* At the center, a small national coat of arms with the eagle facing left, its feathers resembling plates of armor, encircled by a spray of oak and laurel (below) and the legend **ESTADOS UNIDOS MEXICANOS** (above). Surrounding the coat of arms, the emblems of the other nations participating in the series (see the sidebar). *Reverse:* In the left two-thirds of the field, on a plain background, the figure of a Mayan ball player leaping up and to the right, with a ball in the air near his left hip. In the rightmost third of the field, on a vertically striped background, small silhouettes of athletes in six Olympic sports (clockwise from the top): equestrian, race-walking, swimming, weight lifting, boxing, and diving. At the top of the plain area of the field, **DISCIPLINAS DE / ORO OLIMPICO / MEXICANO**, with the mintmark M̊ near the bottom center. At far left, 2008 / $5; reading clockwise from lower left, **ENCUENTRO DE DOS MUNDOS**. *Diameter:* 40 mm. *Edge:* Reeded.

	Mintage	PF
2008	8,013	$90.00

Historical Iberoamerican Coins

In the eighth series, Mexico's coin (dated 2010 and released in 2011) carries the series name, "Monedas Historicas Iberoamericanas." In the background is a portion of a 1562 map, the "Carta Marina Nuova Tavola," by Girolamo Ruscelli; it depicts one of the earliest cartographic depictions of California's peninsula (just visible above the denomination on the coin). Superimposed over the map is Mexico's chosen historical coin, the 1 peso of 1910, known as the "Caballito." It was designed by French engraver Charles Pillet and commemorated the 100th anniversary of the start of the War of Independence. An extremely beautiful coin, it is one of the most highly regarded Mexican issues of all time. (See also the sidebar on pages 47.)

5 pesos, Type A25, 2010. BW-596.10, KM-UL. Proof.

Composition: 0.925 silver. *Weight:* 27.00 g. *Obverse:* At the center, a small national coat of arms with the eagle facing left, its feathers resembling plates of armor, encircled by a spray of oak and laurel (below) and the legend **ESTADOS UNIDOS MEXICANOS** (above). Surrounding the coat of arms, the emblems of the other nations participating in the series (see the sidebar). *Reverse:* Filling the entire field, a fragment of the "Carta Marina Nuova Tavola," with a web of lines connecting seaports on the map. In the foreground, slightly to the right and overlapping one another, the reverse and obverse of a Caballito peso. At upper left, the mintmark M̥; at lower left, $5 / 2010. Surrounding all, ❖ **MONEDAS HISTORICAS IBEROAMERICANAS** ❖ (above) and **MEXICO** (below). *Diameter:* 40 mm. *Edge:* Reeded.

	Mintage	PF
2010	8,000	$90.00

Iberoamerican Cooperation

The Iberoamericana Series lasted more than 20 years, from the first coin issuance in 1991 through the conclusion of the series in 2012. In all, 16 countries participated—14 from Latin America, plus Portugal and Spain. Of those countries, seven participated in all of the themes: Argentina, Cuba, Mexico, Nicaragua, Peru, Portugal, and Spain.

For the ninth and final issuance, the countries that had participated most throughout the series—the main seven plus Guatemala and Paraguay—produced 40-mm commemorative medals (Mexico's mintage was 2,000). The reverse of Mexico's contribution displays miniature versions of each of its eight Iberoamericana issues, along with the fleet of Columbus between the outlined continents of Europe and North and South America. The legend at the center reads ENCUENTRO DE DOS MUNDOS 2012. For the obverse, Mexico chose the historic coat of arms of the Republic, with the legend REPUBLICA MEXICANA.

Mexico's contribution to the final, medal-only series; the medals, like the coins, are 40 mm in diameter.

The Participants and Their Coats of Arms

Argentina (Series I–IX) **Bolivia** (Series I, III) **Brazil** (Series I) **Chile** (Series I)

Colombia (Series I) **Cuba** (Series I–IX) **Ecuador** (Series I–VII) **Guatemala** (Series II–IV, VI–IX)

PRE-COLUMBIAN SERIES

In 1992 Mexico launched its Pre-Columbian Series: six collections commemorating six cultures of Mexico's Pre-Columbian era. There are many varieties, denominations, and metal finishes in the Pre-Columbian series; these are covered in depth in chapter 10.

In 1992 the first collection issued honored the Aztecs. Designs featured the Piedra de Tizoc (Tizoc Stone), Guerrero Águila (Eagle Warrior), Xochipilli (God of Flowers), Brasero Efigie (Brazier Effigy), Huehueteotl (God of Fire), and Jaguar / Piedra de los Soles (Jaguar / Stone of the Suns).

The Central Veracruz Collection, issued in 1993, featured the the Pirámide de El Tajín (Tajín Pyramid), Bajorrelieve de El Tajín (Bas-relief of The Tajín), Palma con Cocodrilo (Palm With Crocodile), Anciano con Brasero (Elderly Man With Brazier), Carita Sonriente (Smiling Face), and Hacha Ceremonial (Ceremonial Hatchet).

In 1994 the Mayan Collection featured the Pirámide del Castillo (Pyramid of the Castle), Chaac-Mool (a reclining ceremonial figure), Mascarón del Dios Chaac (Mask of God Chaac), Lápida Tumba de Palenque (Gravestone of a Palenque Tomb), Dintel 26 (Lintel 26), and Personaje de Jaina (Personage of Jaina).

The next collection, issued in 1996, honored the Olmec culture, featuring the Cabeza Olmeca (Olmec Head), Señor de las Limas (Master of the Limes), Hombre Jaguar (Jaguar Man), El Luchador (The Wrestler), Hacha Ceremonial (Cermonial Ax), and Sacerdote (Priest).

The 1997 Teotihuacán Collection featured the Pirámide del Sol (Pyramid of the Sun), Disco de la Muerte (Disc of Death), Mascara (Mask), Vasija (Vessel), Jugador de Pelota (Ball Player), and Serpiente Eplumada (Feathered Serpent).

The final collection, issued in 1998, honored the Toltecs and featured the Atlantes (statues of Toltec warriors), Quetzalcóatl (Feathered Serpent), Jaguar, Sacerdote (Priest), Serpiente con Cráneo (Serpent With Skull), and Águila (Eagle).

UNICEF / FOR THE CHILDREN OF THE WORLD

UNICEF is the acronym for the United Nations International Children's Emergency Fund. Governments and private donors fund UNICEF's work to help children in developing countries. Among other projects in Mexico, UNICEF supports community centers where indigenous children unable to attend traditional schools can get an education. The United National General Assembly established UNICEF in 1946 to help feed children in countries battered by World War II. UNICEF won the Nobel Peace Prize in 1965.

In 1999, Mexico participated in a UNICEF program by issuing two commemorative coins, one silver, one gold, with the legend **PARA LOS NIÑOS DEL MUNDO** (For the Children of the World).

5 pesos, Type A6, 1999. BW-601.1, KM-640. Proof.

Composition: 0.999 silver. *Weight:* 31.103 g. *Obverse:* The national coat of arms with the eagle facing left, its feathers resembling plates of armor. Above, the legend **ESTADOS UNIDOS MEXICANOS**; below, a half-wreath of oak and laurel. *Reverse:* In the lower half of the coin, a boy (left) and girl (center) stand in a sandy area flying a kite, with a hilly or mountainous horizon behind them. Above the girl, the UNICEF logo; above the boy, $5; at far left, the mintmark M̥. At the top, **PARA LOS NIÑOS DEL MUNDO**; at the bottom, incused into the sandy background, 1999. *Diameter:* 40 mm. *Edge:* Reeded.

	Mintage	PF
1999	4,010	$50.00

20 pesos, Type A4, 1999. BW-803, KM-641. Proof.

Composition: 0.999 gold. *Weight:* 6.221 g. *Obverse:* The national coat of arms with the eagle facing left, its feathers resembling plates of armor. Above, the legend **ESTADOS UNIDOS MEXICANOS**; below, a half-wreath of oak and laurel. *Reverse:* Against a desert background with a butte at the left and a fence at the right, a *charrito* (little cowboy) dances in the loop of his whirling lasso. Above the butte, **$20**; above the fence, the UNICEF logo; at the top, **PARA LOS NIÑOS DEL MUNDO**. At the bottom, incused into the sandy background, **1999**; at lower left, below the lasso, the mintmark M̥ (also incused). *Diameter:* 22 mm. *Edge:* Reeded.

	Mintage	PF
1999	1,510	$475.00

HISTORY OF NAVIGATION

In 1999, a Proof 5 pesos commemorated Mexico's naval history and the centennial of Mexico's Heroica Escuela Naval Militar—the training academy of the Armada de México (Mexican Navy). The reverse of the coin depicts the 1,800-ton, 297-foot sailing ship *Cuauhtémoc*, which is used to train officers and fourth-year cadets.

5 pesos, Type A16, 1999. BW-602, KM-635. Proof.

Composition: 0.999 silver. *Weight:* 19.60 g. *Obverse:* The national coat of arms with the eagle facing left, its feathers resembling plates of armor. Above, the legend **ESTADOS UNIDOS MEXICANOS**; below, a half-wreath of oak and laurel. *Reverse:* To the right of center, the naval training ship *Cuauhtémoc* sailing to the left, toward small silhouettes of the Western and Eastern Hemispheres. Above the hemispheres, **$5 / 1999**. At the top, **BUQUE ESCUELA CUAUHTEMOC** (Training Ship Cuauhtémoc) / **CENTENARIO DE LA H. ESCUELA NAVAL MILITAR** (Centennial of the Heroic Military Navy School). At far right, the mintmark M̥. *Diameter:* 34 mm. *Edge:* Reeded.

	Mintage	PF
1999	15,504	$50.00

MILLENNIUM COLLECTION

In 1999 and 2000, to commemorate the arrival of the third millennium, Mexico released its Millennium Coin Collection, which consisted of four Proofs: three 5 pesos designed by Mexican artists in a national competition, and one 10 pesos designed by the Mexico Mint. The themes for the three 5-peso coins, and the designs that won the right to represent each theme, are as follows:

Mexican History During the Second Millennium—The winning reverse design, by Olga María Vega de Ochoa, depicts a pre-Hispanic emblem from the Mixtec-Zapotec culture: the head of an eagle with three coiled serpents around it.

Man's Role in the Conservation of Nature in the New Millennium—Francisco Ortega Romero designed the reverse emblem: a butterfly shape formed from several different creatures, including a fish and birds. Below the butterfly, two human hands spread apart, cradling the elements above.

World Peace in the Third Millennium—The third reverse, designed by Omar Jiménez Torres, combines the shape of a hand with the profile of a dove, carrying an olive branch in its beak.

The fourth theme in the series, "Mexico During the Second Millennium," is represented by a 10-peso coin designed by a Mexico Mint artist. It depicts three architectural masterpieces of Mexico: the library at the National University of Mexico (UNAM), the aqueduct of Querétaro, and the Mayan Observatory.

5 pesos, Type A7, 1999/2000 (Eagle and Serpents). BW-603.1, KM-632. Proof.

Composition: 0.999 silver. *Weight:* 31.18 g. *Obverse:* The national coat of arms with the eagle facing left, its feathers resembling plates of armor. Above, the legend **ESTADOS UNIDOS MEXICANOS**; below, a half-wreath of oak and laurel. Surrounding the central devices, 10 different national coats of arms used throughout Mexico's history. *Reverse:* To the left of center, a circular motif composed of an eagle's head surrounded by three coiled serpents, with the mintmark M̥ at far left. To the right, the denomination, represented by a small peso symbol, $, above the eagle's head and a large 5 in the right field, slightly overlapping the eagle and disappearing off the edge of the coin. Below the eagle, a raised horizontal zone, with the dates **1999 / 2000** incused. *Diameter:* 40 mm. *Edge:* Reeded.

Note: The design is sometimes referenced as the "fisherman's jewel," although this terminology is not used in mint documentation.

	Mintage	PF
1999 / 2000	48,080	$75.00

5 pesos, Type A8, 1999/2000 (Butterfly). BW-603.2, KM-630. Proof.

Composition: 0.999 silver. *Weight:* 31.18 g. *Obverse:* The national coat of arms with the eagle facing left, its feathers resembling plates of armor. Above, the legend **ESTADOS UNIDOS MEXICANOS**; below, a half-wreath of oak and laurel. Surrounding the central devices, 10 different national coats of arms used throughout Mexico's history. *Reverse:* At the center, a large butterfly; disguised in the design of its spread wings, a parrot and flower (upper left), a fish (lower left), and a hummingbird (upper and lower right). Disguised in the antennae, two small dolphins. Below the butterfly, two spread hands with a seed pod between them; emerging from each hand, a bare branch forming a partial border around the field. To the left of the butterfly, M̊ / $5, with **1999 · 2000** at upper right. *Diameter:* 40 mm. *Edge:* Reeded.

	Mintage	PF
1999 / 2000	47,435	$75.00

5 pesos, Type A9, 1999/2000 (Dove). BW-603.3, KM-631. Proof.

Composition: 0.999 silver. *Weight:* 31.18 g. *Obverse:* The national coat of arms with the eagle facing left, its feathers resembling plates of armor. Above, the legend **ESTADOS UNIDOS MEXICANOS**; below, a half-wreath of oak and laurel. Surrounding the central devices, 10 different national coats of arms used throughout Mexico's history. *Reverse:* At the center, an open palm in a shape resembling a dove; from the dove's "beak" (the thumb) at left protrudes a stylized olive branch. At upper left, $5; at lower right, the mintmark M̊. Below, the conjoined dates **1999** and **2000**, with the final digit in the first date designed to serve as both a 9 and a 2. *Diameter:* 40 mm. *Edge:* Reeded.

	Mintage	PF
1999 / 2000	47,389	$75.00

10 pesos, Type A10, 1999/2000 (Second Millennium). BW-603.4, KM-633. Proof.

Composition: 0.999 silver. *Weight:* 62.03 g. *Obverse:* The national coat of arms with the eagle facing left, its feathers resembling plates of armor. Above, the legend **ESTADOS UNIDOS MEXICANOS**; below, a half-wreath of oak and laurel. Surrounding the central devices, 10 different national coats of arms used throughout Mexico's history. *Reverse:* At center, enclosed within a circle, a montage of three structures: at upper left, in the background the UNAM library; crossing the middle ground from lower left to upper right, the aqueduct of Querétaro; in the lower foreground, the Mayan Observatory. To the left within the circle, the mintmark M̊; at upper right, **1999 – 2000**; at far right, **$10**. Outside the circle, reading clockwise from far left, **SEGUNDO MILENIO**, with the remaining border filled by a pre-Columbian serpent motif. *Diameter:* 48 mm. *Edge:* Reeded.

	Mintage	PF
1999 / 2000	47,641	$95.00

The Mexican Eagle

No one knows for certain what kind of bird was intended in the Codex Mendoza, but in general it's thought to be a golden eagle—*Aquila chrysaetos,* which is the national bird of Mexico and was quite common when the Codex was written in the 1540s. It has been speculated, however, that the bird in the Codex is in fact a caracara (either *Caracara cheriway* or another subspecies), also common in Mexico, based on similarities between the two birds, primarily the ruffled feathers that each has at the back of the head.

The eagle from the Codex Mendoza; note the shortness of the fleshy part of the leg.

Golden eagles, however—like many bird species—ruffle the feathers on their heads and necks when provoked (see the photos). Moreover, the golden eagle's feathers can rise from the top of the head down the neck, as is the case on the Codex eagle. The feathers atop the caracara's head are flat, with the raised feathers stopping in a peak at the back of the head.

Another pro-caracara argument is that the lower half of its legs is featherless, like those of the Codex eagle, whereas the golden eagle's legs are mostly feathered. Golden eagles are, indeed, feathered all the way to the feet, but their ankles have a zone of semi-bare skin with only a thin, pale scrim of feathers. Much like the gap between a pants-leg and a shoe, this area is most visible when the legs are fully extended, as when the eagle is diving for prey. (This is difficult to see in photos of captive birds, whose ankles are covered with tethers.) The small bit of bare leg on the Codex eagle seems to resemble this gap on the golden eagle more closely than the one on the leggy caracara.

An additional argument in favor of the golden eagle is simply the rest of the codex. The cactus is green; its fruits are red. The water is blue-green, and the canals are drawn with a rippled edge to suggest water. The people have tan to dark-brown skin. In other words, the scribes were depicting their world, including their myths, with great care. Their eagle is made solidly brown, from one end to the other, unlike the caracara, which has distinctive white areas on the neck, chest, and tail. The Codex eagle's beak is short and hooked; it is black at the tip, but yellow at the corner of the mouth and at the top, between the eyes—all features of the golden eagle's beak. The caracara's beak is longer and straighter, and is yellow to yellow-orange for half or more of its length; its tip is light gray.

The identity of the bird in the Codex may seem like useless trivia, but the study of history, like the study of coins, is in large part the study of details. Something as small as a bone fragment in a vast desert can reveal a previously hidden link between events or cultures. With respect to the Codex Mendoza, it would be a strange choice for the warlike Aztecs to represent themselves with a slow-moving carrion-eater (the caracara) rather than the powerful, predatory eagle. And if that *did* turn out to be the case, it would open an unexpected lines of inquiry for future researchers.

A golden eagle with head and neck feathers bristled in warning.

A golden eagle with the area of thin feathers at the ankle (visible on the unbanded leg).

A caracara in flight. Note the distinctive coloration and long legs, as well as the color and shape of the beak.

ENDANGERED SPECIES IN MEXICO COLLECTION

In 2001 the Endangered Species in Mexico (Animales en Peligro de Extinción en México) Collection was issued. The collection consists of 10 coins denominated 5 pesos in a satin BU finish; four are dated 2000, with the remaining six dated 2001. These coins were sold as a complete collection, with an informative album titled *Monedas y Especies (Coins and Species)*. A portion of the proceeds of the sale of the collection went to protecting the endangered species.

5 Pesos, Type A11, 2000 (Royal Eagle). BW-604.1, KM-652. Brilliant Uncirculated.

The golden eagle *(Aquila chrysaetos)* is the most widely distributed eagle species, and is the national bird of Mexico. The golden eagle is very large, with a wingspan that measures about six feet. Golden eagles are thought to mate for life; the pair may reuse their old nests or alternate among several nests each breeding season. Often referred to as "royal eagles," their use in falconry was generally reserved for emperors and kings.

Composition: 0.999 silver. *Weight:* 31.103 g. *Obverse:* The national coat of arms with the eagle facing left, its feathers resembling plates of armor. Above, the legend **ESTADOS UNIDOS MEXICANOS**; below, a half-wreath of oak and laurel. Surrounding the central devices, 10 different national coats of arms used throughout Mexico's history. *Reverse:* At the center of a diamond-shaped area, a golden eagle on a branch, facing toward the right. Below the eagle, the mintmark M̊; to the right, **2000**; along the upper left side of the diamond, *(Aquila chrysaetos)*. Outside the diamond, to the left on the vertically shaded half of the field, **$5**; above the upper right edge, **AGUILA REAL**; below the lower right edge, **ANIMALES EN PELIGRO DE EXTINCION / EN MEXICO**. *Diameter:* 40 mm. *Edge:* Reeded.

	Mintage	BU
2000	30,000	$90.00

5 Pesos, Type A12, 2000 (Pronghorn).
BW-604.2, KM-657. Brilliant Uncirculated.

The pronghorn *(Antilocapra americana)* resembles an antelope; able to sustain a speed of 35 miles per hour for three to four miles, it is the fastest land animal in the Western Hemisphere. Males have antlers that range from 5 to about 15 inches, while females have very short antlers that are sometimes barely visible. Adults are brown, with white fur on the sides, rump, chest, and throat; the males have a stripe of black fur along the cheekbone. The pronghorn can be found from Canada through the west-central United States to northern Mexico. The Mexican subspecies, *Antilocapra americana Mexicana*, is endangered.

Composition: 0.999 silver. *Weight:* 31.103 g. *Obverse:* The national coat of arms with the eagle facing left, its feathers resembling plates of armor. Above, the legend **ESTADOS UNIDOS MEXICANOS**; below, a half-wreath of oak and laurel. Surrounding the central devices, 10 different national coats of arms used throughout Mexico's history. *Reverse:* At the center of a diamond-shaped area, a pronghorn trotting toward the right against a background of sand and cacti. Below the pronghorn, **2000**; above, the mintmark M̊; along the upper left side of the diamond, **(Antilocapra americana)**. Outside the diamond, to the left on the vertically shaded half of the field, **$5**; above the upper right edge, **BERRENDO**; below the lower right edge, **ANIMALES EN PELIGRO DE EXTINCION / EN MEXICO**. *Diameter:* 40 mm. *Edge:* Reeded.

	Mintage	BU
2000	30,000	$55.00

5 Pesos, Type A13, 2000 (River Crocodile).
BW-604.3, KM-655. Brilliant Uncirculated.

The American crocodile *(Crocodylus acutus)*, Mexico's largest reptile, lives primarily in coastal areas of southern Mexico. Measuring 12 to 15 feet in length, it eats mostly fish, reptiles, birds, small mammals, and occasionally larger animals such as deer. Considered an endangered species in Mexico and other parts of its range, the American crocodile can be distinguished from the non-endangered American alligator by its longer, sharper snout and the lower teeth that are visible when its mouth is closed.

Composition: 0.999 silver. *Weight:* 31.103 g. *Obverse:* The national coat of arms with the eagle facing left, its feathers resembling plates of armor. Above, the legend **ESTADOS UNIDOS MEXICANOS**; below, a half-wreath of oak and laurel. Surrounding the central devices, 10 different national coats of arms used throughout Mexico's history. *Reverse:* At the center of a diamond-shaped area, a crocodile facing right, its mouth open, against a background of grasses. Below the crocodile, the mintmark M̥; above, **2000**; along the upper left side of the diamond, *(Crocodylus acutus)*. Outside the diamond, to the left on the vertically shaded half of the field, **$5**; above the upper right edge, **COCODRILO DEL RIO**; below the lower right edge, **ANIMALES EN PELIGRO DE EXTINCION / EN MEXICO**. *Diameter:* 40 mm. *Edge:* Reeded.

	Mintage	BU
2000	30,000	$55.00

5 Pesos, Type A14, 2000 (River Otter).
BW-604.4, KM-656. Brilliant Uncirculated.

The river otter *(Lontra longicaudis)*, also known as a "water dog," belongs to the same family that includes skunks, badgers, and weasels. It spends most of the day swimming in rivers, lakes, and lagoons, mainly near coastlands, although some populate the large rivers and lakes of mountain areas. It feeds mainly on fish and crustaceans. The river otter has a long, wide tail and webbed toes, and weighs 10 to 30 pounds. Its populations have declined radically due to hunting (for its beautiful pelt) and habitat destruction. It is considered endangered in Mexico and throughout much of its habitat in the Americas.

Composition: 0.999 silver. *Weight:* 31.103 g. *Obverse:* The national coat of arms with the eagle facing left, its feathers resembling plates of armor. Above, the legend

ESTADOS UNIDOS MEXICANOS; below, a half-wreath of oak and laurel. Surrounding the central devices, 10 different national coats of arms used throughout Mexico's history. *Reverse:* At the center of a diamond-shaped area, an otter facing left on a muddy bank. Below the otter, the mintmark M̥; to the left, **2000**; along the upper right side of the diamond, *(Lontra longicaudis)*. Outside the diamond, to the right on the vertically shaded half of the field, $5; above the upper left edge, **NUTRIA DEL RIO**; below the lower left edge, **ANIMALES EN PELIGRO DE EXTINCION / EN MEXICO**. *Diameter:* 40 mm. *Edge:* Reeded.

	Mintage	BU
2000	30,000	$55.00

5 Pesos, Type A15, 2001 (Black Bear).
BW-604.5, KM-654. Brilliant Uncirculated.

The American black bear *(Ursus americanus)* prefers sparsely settled, forested areas, and is the smallest of the bear species in North America. Measuring between 4 and 6 feet long and weighing 200 to 500 pounds or more, it has a large head and ears and a very small tail. Seventy percent of black bears are, indeed, black; the remainder range from dark brown to cinnamon to cream. Eyesight and hearing in a black bear is generally better than in human beings, and its sense of smell is seven times better than that of a dog. The Mexican black bear *(Ursus americanus eremicus)*, a subspecies of *Ursus americanus*, is considered very endangered.

Composition: 0.999 silver. *Weight:* 31.103 g. *Obverse:* The national coat of arms with the eagle facing left, its feathers resembling plates of armor. Above, the legend **ESTADOS UNIDOS MEXICANOS**; below, a half-wreath of oak and laurel. Surrounding the central devices, 10 different national coats of arms used throughout Mexico's history. *Reverse:* At the center of a diamond-shaped area, a black bear facing left in a patch of grass. Below the bear, the mintmark M̥; above, **2001**; along the upper right side of the diamond, *(Ursus americanus)*. Outside the diamond, to the right on the vertically shaded half of the field, $5; above the upper left edge, **OSO NEGRO**; below the lower left edge, **ANIMALES EN PELIGRO DE EXTINCION / EN MEXICO**. *Diameter:* 40 mm. *Edge:* Reeded.

	Mintage	BU
2000	30,000	$55.00

5 Pesos, Type A16, 2001 (Manatee).
BW-604.6, KM-651. Brilliant Uncirculated.

The manatee *(Trichechus manatus)*, or sea cow, is a gentle creature that prefers warm, shallow water in rivers, estuaries, and coastal areas, primarily along the Gulf of Mexico and the Caribbean. Measuring about 8 to 11 feet long and weighing between 400 and 1,200 pounds, a typical manatee consumes up to 10% of its body weight each day, mostly in vegetation but occasionally in fish and small invertebrates. It is considered in danger of extinction, and the Mexican government has outlawed hunting of the creature.

Composition: 0.999 silver. *Weight:* 31.103 g. *Obverse:* The national coat of arms with the eagle facing left, its feathers resembling plates of armor. Above, the legend **ESTADOS UNIDOS MEXICANOS**; below, a half-wreath of oak and laurel. Surrounding the central devices, 10 different national coats of arms used throughout Mexico's history. *Reverse:* At the center of a diamond-shaped area, a manatee facing left amid a few wavy lines suggesting water. Below the manatee, **2001**; to the left, the mintmark M̊; along the upper right side of the diamond, *(Trichechus manatus)*. Outside the diamond, to the right on the vertically shaded half of the field, **$5**; above the upper left edge, **MANATI**; below the lower left edge, **ANIMALES EN PELIGRO DE EXTINCION / EN MEXICO**. *Diameter:* 40 mm. *Edge:* Reeded.

	Mintage	BU
2000	30,000	$55.00

5 Pesos, Type A17, 2001 (Jaguar).
BW-604.7, KM-658. Brilliant Uncirculated.

The jaguar *(Panthera onca)* is North America's largest cat. Adults weigh up to 325 pounds and measure approximately 6 feet long, not including the two- to three-foot tail. The jaguar has a stout body and short fur, usually yellow-ochre in color, covered in large black spots on its back with black-and-yellow rosettes at its sides. Jaguars prefer to live in densely forested areas adjacent to water, as they are strong swimmers. In Mayan culture, the jaguar was thought to facilitate communication between the living and the dead, and was thought to provide protection for the royal family. The jaguar is all but extinct in the United States; Mexico's subspecies, *Panthera onca hernandesii*, is threatened and its numbers are declining. Hunting in Mexico is solely limited to "problem animals."

Composition: 0.999 silver. *Weight:* 31.103 g. *Obverse:* The national coat of arms with the eagle facing left, its feathers resembling plates of armor. Above, the legend **ESTADOS UNIDOS MEXICANOS**; below, a half-wreath of oak and laurel. Surrounding the central devices, 10 different national coats of arms used throughout Mexico's history. *Reverse:* At the center of a diamond-shaped area, a reclining jaguar facing forward and to the right against a background of tall grasses. Below the jaguar, **2001**; to the right, the mintmark M̥; along the upper left side of the diamond, **(Panthera onca)**. Outside the diamond, to the left on the vertically shaded half of the field, **$5**; above the upper right edge, **JAGUAR**; below the lower right edge, **ANIMALES EN PELIGRO DE EXTINCION / EN MEXICO**. *Diameter:* 40 mm. *Edge:* Reeded.

	Mintage	BU
2000	30,000	$55.00

5 Pesos, Type A18, 2001 (Harpy Eagle). BW-604.8, KM-653. Brilliant Uncirculated.

The largest and strongest eagle in the world, the harpy eagle *(Harpia harpyja)* has a wing span of about six feet, while its body is about three feet long. Its distinctive features include its large size, a crest of long black feathers on its head, and the color of its plumage, which is pale gray on its head and white on its underside; a black band separates the head from the chest while its wings are black. Its beak is strong and hooked, and it has very powerful talons and claws that are as long as a man's fingers. The harpy eagle is almost extinct in Mexico. Its habitat ranges from Mexico through Central and South America to Argentina.

Composition: 0.999 silver. *Weight:* 31.103 g. *Obverse:* The national coat of arms with the eagle facing left, its feathers resembling plates of armor. Above, the legend ESTADOS UNIDOS MEXICANOS; below, a half-wreath of oak and laurel. Surrounding the central devices, 10 different national coats of arms used throughout Mexico's history. *Reverse:* At the center of a diamond-shaped area, a harpy eagle on a branch, facing toward the right. Below the eagle, the mintmark M̊; to the right, 2001; along the upper left side of the diamond, *(Harpia harpyja)*. Outside the diamond, to the left on the vertically shaded half of the field, $5; above the upper right edge, AGUILA ARPIA; below the lower right edge, ANIMALES EN PELIGRO DE EXTINCION / EN MEXICO. *Diameter:* 40 mm. *Edge:* Reeded.

	Mintage	BU
2000	30,000	$55.00

5 Pesos, Type A19, 2001 (Volcano Rabbit). BW-604.9, KM-660. Brilliant Uncirculated.

Also known as the *teporingo* or *zacatuche*, the volcano rabbit *(Romerolagus diazi)* is native to four volcanoes located south of Mexico City. It is the smallest of the Mexican rabbits, and the second-smallest rabbit in the world. Besides its small size, it is also known for the color of its fur, which is a dark dove-grey; its small, round ears; and its small tail, which is hardly visible. Adults can measure up to 11 inches long and weigh approximately one pound. Unlike most rabbits, which thump their feet to warn other rabbits of danger, the volcano rabbit emits high-pitched sounds and whistles. The volcano rabbit is considered endangered, and it is illegal to hunt them.

Composition: 0.999 silver. *Weight:* 31.103 g. *Obverse:* The national coat of arms with the eagle facing left, its feathers resembling plates of armor. Above, the legend ESTADOS UNIDOS MEXICANOS; below, a half-wreath of oak and laurel. Surrounding the central devices, 10 different national coats of arms used throughout Mexico's history. *Reverse:* At the center of a diamond-shaped area, a volcano rabbit facing right from a cluster of grass. Below the rabbit, the mintmark M̊; above, 2001; along the upper left side of the diamond, *(Romerolagus diazi)*. Outside the diamond, to the left on the vertically shaded half of the field, $5; above the upper right edge, ZACATUCHE; below the lower right edge, ANIMALES EN PELIGRO DE EXTINCION / EN MEXICO. *Diameter:* 40 mm. *Edge:* Reeded.

	Mintage	BU
2000	30,000	$55.00

5 Pesos, Type A20, 2001 (Prairie Dog). BW-604.10, KM-659. Brilliant Uncirculated.

The black-tipped prairie dog *(Cynomys ludovicianus)* is a highly social, burrowing rodent. It can be found from southern Canada to northwest Mexico, although members of the endangered Mexican subspecies, *Cynomys mexicanus*, are found only in the grasslands in the San Luis Potosí / Coahuila / Nuevo León area. They can weigh up to two pounds, and resemble large squirrels. Prairie dogs live in colonies, or "towns," that can consist of five to thousands of animals, although the Mexican prairie dog prefers smaller colonies. Considered a pest to farmers and ranchers, it was poisoned nearly to extinction; it now occupies less than 5% of its former territory.

Composition: 0.999 silver. *Weight:* 31.103 g. *Obverse:* The national coat of arms with the eagle facing left, its feathers resembling plates of armor. Above, the legend **ESTADOS UNIDOS MEXICANOS**; below, a half-wreath of oak and laurel. Surrounding the central devices, 10 different national coats of arms used throughout Mexico's history. *Reverse:* At the center of a diamond-shaped area, a prairie dog sitting upright in a patch of grass and facing left. Below the prairie dog, the mintmark M̥; to the left, **2001**; along the upper right side of the diamond, *(Cynomys ludovicianus)*. Outside the diamond, to the right on the vertically shaded half of the field, **$5**; above the upper left edge, **PERRITO DE LAS PRADERAS**; below the lower left edge, **ANIMALES EN PELIGRO DE EXTINCION / EN MEXICO**. *Diameter:* 40 mm. *Edge:* Reeded.

	Mintage	BU
2000	30,000	$55.00

MEXICAN STATE CONFEDERATION SERIES

In 2003 Mexico joined the United States and Canada in releasing state commemorative series. Mexico's two series of commemoratives honored the 180th anniversary of the union of the states of the Mexican Republic into a federation. Each series consisted of one design for each of the 31 states in the federation, with an additional design for the Distrito Federal. The denominations for each series were 10 pesos (silver Proofs only) and 100 pesos (bimetallic circulating coins in silver and bronze-aluminum, and bimetallic Proofs in silver and gold).

The first, or "heraldic," series commenced in 2003. Each reverse featured a different state's coat of arms, and the coins were issued in descending alphabetical order, from Zacatecas through Aguascalientes. The mintage for circulating coins in the first series was 250,000 for each state; half of the mintage was issued within the coin's own state, and the other half around the other states of Mexico. The silver Proofs each had a mintage of 10,000 per state, with the bimetallic gold-and-silver Proofs at 1,000 per state.

The second, or "emblematic," series began in 2005. Each state's reverse featured images "related to architecture, art, science, fauna, flora, typical dresses or dances or geographical areas of interest peculiar to each state" (Banco de México, "The History of Coins and Banknotes in Mexico," www.banxico.org). The coins were released in ascending alphabetical order, from Aguascalientes through Zacatecas. The mintages varied slightly, but all were approximately 150,000 per state for the Brilliant Uncirculated; 6,000 per state in Proof silver; and 600 per state in Proof bimetallic gold and silver.

The 100-peso BU issues in bimetallic silver and bronze-aluminum were struck for circulation. Although very few actually circulated, they are listed in chapter 3 with normal circulating coins, in the interest of consistency. In early 2007, when silver was US$19 to US$20 an ounce, the silver centers were popped out of a large number of the 100-peso BUs and melted, because the silver value of the center exceeded the face value of the coin.

TYPE A5 (SERIES 1: HERALDIC; BW-606)
10 Pesos, Silver

The common obverse design for all Series 1 Proof 10 pesos.

Zacatecas

Veracruz

Yucatán

Composition: 0.999 silver. *Weight:* 31.1035 g. *Obverse:* The national coat of arms with the eagle facing left, its feathers resembling plates of armor. Above, the legend **ESTADOS UNIDOS MEXICANOS**; below, a half-wreath of oak and laurel. *Diameter:* 40 mm. *Edge:* Reeded.

Zacatecas Reverse Design
At center, the coat of arms of Zacatecas, with **2003** above and the mintmark M̊ to the left. At the top, **ESTADO DE ZACATECAS**; at the bottom, **$10**.

Yucatán Reverse Design
At center, the coat of arms of Yucatán, with **2003** above and the mintmark M̊ to the left. At the top, **ESTADO DE YUCATAN**; at the bottom, **$10**.

Veracruz Reverse Design
At center, the coat of arms of Veracruz, with **2003** to the right and the mintmark M̊ to the left. At the top, **ESTADO DE VERACRUZ-LLAVE**; at the bottom, **$10**.

	Mintage	PF
2003, Zacatecas. BW-606.1, KM-679	10,000	$70.00
2003, Yucatán. BW-606.2, KM-680	10,000	70.00
2003, Veracruz. BW-606.3, KM-681	10,000	70.00

Commemorative Coinage • 217

Tlaxcala

Tamaulipas

Tabasco

Composition: 0.999 silver. *Weight:* 31.1035 g. *Obverse:* The national coat of arms with the eagle facing left, its feathers resembling plates of armor. Above, the legend **ESTADOS UNIDOS MEXICANOS**; below, a half-wreath of oak and laurel. *Diameter:* 40 mm. *Edge:* Reeded.

Tlaxcala Reverse Design
At center, the coat of arms of Tlaxcala, with **2003** above and the mintmark M̥ to the left. At the top, **ESTADO DE TLAXCALA**; at the bottom, **$10**.

Tamaulipas Reverse Design
At center, the coat of arms of Tamaulipas, with **2004** above and the mintmark M̥ to the left. At the top, **ESTADO DE TAMAULIPAS**; at the bottom, **$10**.

Tabasco Reverse Design
At center, the coat of arms of Tabasco, with **2004** to the right and the mintmark M̥ to the left. At the top, **ESTADO DE TABASCO**; at the bottom, **$10**.

	Mintage	PF
2003, Tlaxcala. BW-606.4, KM-682	10,000	$70.00
2004, Tamaulipas. BW-606.5, KM-683	10,000	70.00
2004, Tabasco. BW-606.6, KM-684	10,000	70.00

Sonora

Sinaloa

San Luis Potosí

Composition: 0.999 silver. *Weight:* 31.1035 g. *Obverse:* The national coat of arms with the eagle facing left, its feathers resembling plates of armor. Above, the legend **ESTADOS UNIDOS MEXICANOS**; below, a half-wreath of oak and laurel. *Diameter:* 40 mm. *Edge:* Reeded.

Sonora Reverse Design
At center, the coat of arms of Sonora, with 2004 above and the mintmark M̥ to the left. At the top, **ESTADO DE SONORA**; at the bottom, $10.

Sinaloa Reverse Design
At center, the coat of arms of Sinaloa, with 2004 to the right and the mintmark M̥ to the left. At the top, **ESTADO DE SINALOA**; at the bottom, $10.

San Luis Potosí Reverse Design
At center, the coat of arms of San Luis Potosí, with 2004 below and the mintmark M̥ to the left. At the top, **ESTADO DE SAN LUIS POTOSI**; at the bottom, $10.

	Mintage	PF
2004, Sonora. BW-606.7, KM-685	10,000	$70.00
2004, Sinaloa. BW-606.8, KM-686	10,000	70.00
2004, San Luis Potosí. BW-606.9, KM-687	10,000	70.00

Commemorative Coinage • 219

Quintana Roo

Querétaro

Puebla

Composition: 0.999 silver. *Weight:* 31.1035 g. *Obverse:* The national coat of arms with the eagle facing left, its feathers resembling plates of armor. Above, the legend **ESTADOS UNIDOS MEXICANOS**; below, a half-wreath of oak and laurel. *Diameter:* 40 mm. *Edge:* Reeded.

Quintana Roo Reverse Design
At center, the coat of arms of Quintana Roo, with **2004** below and the mintmark M̊ to the left. At the top, **ESTADO DE QUINTANA ROO**; at the bottom, **$10**.

Querétaro Reverse Design
At center, the coat of arms of Querétaro, with **2004** to the right and the mintmark M̊ to the left. At the top, **ESTADO DE QUERETARO ARTEAGA**; at the bottom, **$10**.

Puebla Reverse Design
At center, the coat of arms of Puebla, with **2004** to the right and the mintmark M̊ to the left. At the top, **ESTADO DE PUEBLA**; at the bottom, **$10**.

	Mintage	PF
2004, Quintana Roo. BW-606.10, KM-735	10,000	$70.00
2004, Querétaro. BW-606.11, KM-733	10,000	70.00
2004, Puebla. BW-606.12, KM-737	10,000	70.00

Oaxaca

Nuevo León

Nayarit

Composition: 0.999 silver. *Weight:* 31.1035 g. *Obverse:* The national coat of arms with the eagle facing left, its feathers resembling plates of armor. Above, the legend **ESTADOS UNIDOS MEXICANOS**; below, a half-wreath of oak and laurel. *Diameter:* 40 mm. *Edge:* Reeded.

Oaxaca Reverse Design
At center, the coat of arms of Oaxaca, with **2004** to the right and the mintmark $\overset{o}{M}$ to the left. At the top, **ESTADO DE OAXACA**; at the bottom, $10.

Nuevo León Reverse Design
At center, the coat of arms of Nuevo León, with **2004** to the right and the mintmark $\overset{o}{M}$ to the left. At the top, **ESTADO DE NUEVO LEON**; at the bottom, $10.

Nayarit Reverse Design
At center, the coat of arms of Nayarit, with **2004** above and the mintmark $\overset{o}{M}$ to the left. At the top, **ESTADO DE NAYARIT**; at the bottom, $10.

	Mintage	PF
2004, Oaxaca. BW-606.13, KM-739	10,000	$70.00
2004, Nuevo León. BW-606.14, KM-741	10,000	70.00
2004, Nayarit. BW-606.15, KM-743	10,000	70.00

Morelos

Michoacán

Estado de México

Composition: 0.999 silver. *Weight:* 31.1035 g. *Obverse:* The national coat of arms with the eagle facing left, its feathers resembling plates of armor. Above, the legend ESTADOS UNIDOS MEXICANOS; below, a half-wreath of oak and laurel. *Diameter:* 40 mm. *Edge:* Reeded.

Morelos Reverse Design
At center, the coat of arms of Morelos, with 2004 above and the mintmark M̥ to the left. At the top, ESTADO DE MORELOS; at the bottom, $10.

Michoacán Reverse Design
At center, the coat of arms of Michoacán, with 2004 to the right and the mintmark M̥ at lower left. At the top, ESTADO DE MICHOACAN DE OCAMPO; at the bottom, $10.

Estado de México Reverse Design
At center, the coat of arms of México, with 2004 below and the mintmark M̥ to the left. At the top, ESTADO DE MEXICO; at the bottom, $10.

	Mintage	PF
2004, Morelos. BW-606.16, KM-745	10,000	$70.00
2004, Michoacán. BW-606.17, KM-796	10,000	70.00
2004, Estado de México. BW-606.18, KM-747	10,000	70.00

Jalisco
Hidalgo
Guerrero

Composition: 0.999 silver. *Weight:* 31.1035 g. *Obverse:* The national coat of arms with the eagle facing left, its feathers resembling plates of armor. Above, the legend **ESTADOS UNIDOS MEXICANOS**; below, a half-wreath of oak and laurel. *Diameter:* 40 mm. *Edge:* Reeded.

Jalisco Reverse Design
At center, the coat of arms of Jalisco, with **2004** above left and the mintmark M̊ at far left. At the top, **ESTADO DE JALISCO**; at the bottom, **$10**.

Hidalgo Reverse Design
At center, the coat of arms of Hidalgo, with **2005** below and the mintmark M̊ to the left. At the top, **ESTADO DE HIDALGO**; at the bottom, **$10**.

Guerrero Reverse Design
At center, the coat of arms of Guerrero, with **2005** to the right and the mintmark M̊ to the left. At the top, **ESTADO DE GUERRERO**; at the bottom, **$10**.

	Mintage	PF
2004, Jalisco. BW-606.19, K M-749	10,000	$70.00
2005, Hidalgo. BW-606.20, KM-711	10,000	70.00
2005, Guerrero. BW-606.21, KM-710	10,000	70.00

Commemorative Coinage • 223

Guanajuato

Distrito Federal

Durango

Composition: 0.999 silver. *Weight:* 31.1035 g. *Obverse:* The national coat of arms with the eagle facing left, its feathers resembling plates of armor. Above, the legend **ESTADOS UNIDOS MEXICANOS**; below, a half-wreath of oak and laurel. *Diameter:* 40 mm. *Edge:* Reeded.

Guanajuato Reverse Design
At center, the coat of arms of Guanajuato, with **2005** below and the mintmark M̥ to the left. At the top, **ESTADO DE GUANAJUATO**; at the bottom, **$10**.

Durango Reverse Design
At center, the coat of arms of Durango, with **2005** below and the mintmark M̥ to the left. At the top, **ESTADO DE DURANGO**; at the bottom, **$10**.

Distrito Federal Reverse Design
At center, the coat of arms of the Distrito Federal, with **2005** above and the mintmark M̥ to the left. At the top, **DISTRITO FEDERAL**; at the bottom, **$10**.

	Mintage	PF
2005, Guanajuato. BW-606.22, KM-709	10,000	$70.00
2005, Durango. BW-606.23, KM-708	10,000	70.00
2005, Distrito Federal. BW-606.24, KM-707	10,000	70.00

Colima

Chihuahua

Coahuila

Composition: 0.999 silver. *Weight:* 31.1035 g. *Obverse:* The national coat of arms with the eagle facing left, its feathers resembling plates of armor. Above, the legend **ESTADOS UNIDOS MEXICANOS**; below, a half-wreath of oak and laurel. *Diameter:* 40 mm. *Edge:* Reeded.

Colima Reverse Design
At center, the coat of arms of Colima, with **2005** to the right and the mintmark M̥ to the left. At the top, **ESTADO DE COLIMA**; at the bottom, $10.

Coahuila Reverse Design
At center, the coat of arms of Coahuila, with **2005** above and the mintmark M̥ to the left. At the top, **ESTADO DE COAHUILA DE ZARAGOZA**; at the bottom, $10.

Chihuahua Reverse Design
At center, the coat of arms of Chihuahua, with **2005** above and the mintmark M̥ to the left. At the top, **ESTADO DE CHIHUAHUA**; at the bottom, $10.

	Mintage	PF
2005, Colima. BW-606.25, KM-728	10,000	$70.00
2005, Coahuila. BW-606.26, KM-751	10,000	70.00
2005, Chihuahua. BW-606.27, KM-753	10,000	70.00

Chiapas

Campeche

Baja California Sur

Composition: 0.999 silver. *Weight:* 31.1035 g. *Obverse:* The national coat of arms with the eagle facing left, its feathers resembling plates of armor. Above, the legend **ESTADOS UNIDOS MEXICANOS**; below, a half-wreath of oak and laurel. *Diameter:* 40 mm. *Edge:* Reeded.

Chiapas Reverse Design
At center, the coat of arms of Chiapas, with **2005** to the right and the mintmark M̥ to the left. At the top, **ESTADO DE CHIAPAS**; at the bottom, **$10**.

Campeche Reverse Design
At center, the coat of arms of Campeche, with **2005** to the right and the mintmark M̥ to the left. At the top, **ESTADO DE CAMPECHE**; at the bottom, **$10**.

Baja California Sur Reverse Design
At center, the coat of arms of Baja California Sur, with **2005** to the right and the mintmark M̥ to the left. At the top, **ESTADO DE BAJA CALIFORNIA SUR**; at the bottom, **$10**.

	Mintage	PF
2005, Chiapas. BW-606.28, KM-706	10,000	$70.00
2005, Campeche. BW-606.29, KM-726	10,000	70.00
2005, Baja California Sur. BW-606.30, KM-724	10,000	70.00

Baja California   Aguascalientes

Composition: 0.999 silver. *Weight:* 31.1035 g. *Obverse:* The national coat of arms with the eagle facing left, its feathers resembling plates of armor. Above, the legend **ESTADOS UNIDOS MEXICANOS**; below, a half-wreath of oak and laurel. *Diameter:* 40 mm. *Edge:* Reeded.

Baja California Reverse Design
At center, the coat of arms of Baja California, with **2005** to the right and the mintmark M̥ to the left. At the top, **ESTADO DE BAJA CALIFORNIA**; at the bottom, **$10**.

Aguascalientes Reverse Design
At center, the coat of arms of Aguascalientes, with **2005** above and the mintmark M̥ to the left. At the top, **ESTADO DE AGUASCALIENTES**; at the bottom, **$10**.

	Mintage	PF
2005, Baja California. BW-606.31, KM-722	10,000	$70.00
2005, Aguascalientes. BW-606.32, KM-720	10,000	70.00

TYPE A2 (SERIES 1: HERALDIC; BW-684)
100 Pesos, Bimetallic

The common obverse design for all Series 1 Proof 100 pesos.

Zacatecas Yucatán Veracruz

Composition: bimetallic (center, 0.999 gold; outer ring, 0.999 silver). *Weight:* 29.169 g. *Obverse:* On the gold center, the national coat of arms with the eagle facing left, its feathers resembling plates of armor; on the silver outer ring, the legend **ESTADOS UNIDOS MEXICANOS** above, with a half-wreath of oak and laurel below. *Diameter:* 34.5 mm. *Edge:* Paired plain and reeded.

Zacatecas Reverse Design
On the gold center, the coat of arms of Zacatecas, with **2003** above. On the silver outer ring, **ESTADO DE ZACATECAS** at the top, with **$100** at the bottom and the mintmark M̥ at far left.

Yucatán Reverse Design
On the gold center, the coat of arms of Yucatán, with **2003** above. On the silver outer ring, **ESTADO DE YUCATAN** at the top, with **$100** at the bottom and the mintmark M̥ at far left.

Veracruz Reverse Design
On the gold center, the coat of arms of Veracruz, with **2003** to the right. On the silver outer ring, **ESTADO DE VERACRUZ-LLAVE** at the top, with **$100** at the bottom and the mintmark M̥ at far left.

	Mintage	PL
2003, Zacatecas. BW-684.1, KM-696	1,000	$900.00
2003, Yucatán. BW-684.2, KM-697	1,000	900.00
2003, Veracruz. BW-684.3, KM-698	1,000	900.00

Tlaxcala   Tamaulipas   Tabasco

Composition: bimetallic (center, 0.999 gold; outer ring, 0.999 silver). *Weight:* 29.169 g. *Obverse:* On the gold center, the national coat of arms with the eagle facing left, its feathers resembling plates of armor; on the silver outer ring, the legend **ESTADOS UNIDOS MEXICANOS** above, with a half-wreath of oak and laurel below. *Diameter:* 34.5 mm. *Edge:* Paired plain and reeded.

Tlaxcala Reverse Design
On the gold center, the coat of arms of Tlaxcala, with **2003** above. On the silver outer ring, **ESTADO DE TLAXCALA** at the top, with **$100** at the bottom and the mintmark M̊ at far left.

Tamaulipas Reverse Design
On the gold center, the coat of arms of Tamaulipas, with **2004** above. On the silver outer ring, **ESTADO DE TAMAULIPAS** at the top, with **$100** at the bottom and the mintmark M̊ at far left.

Tabasco Reverse Design
On the gold center, the coat of arms of Tabasco, with **2004** to the right. On the silver outer ring, **ESTADO DE TABASCO** at the top, with **$100** at the bottom and the mintmark M̊ at far left.

	Mintage	PL
2003, Tlaxcala. BW-684.4, KM-699	1,000	$900.00
2004, Tamaulipas. BW-684.5, KM-700	1,000	900.00
2004, Tabasco. BW-684.6, KM-701	1,000	900.00

| Sonora | Sinaloa | San Luis Potosí |

Composition: bimetallic (center, 0.999 gold; outer ring, 0.999 silver). *Weight:* 29.169 g. *Obverse:* On the gold center, the national coat of arms with the eagle facing left, its feathers resembling plates of armor; on the silver outer ring, the legend ESTADOS UNIDOS MEXICANOS above, with a half-wreath of oak and laurel below. *Diameter:* 34.5 mm. *Edge:* Paired plain and reeded.

Sonora Reverse Design
On the gold center, the coat of arms of Sonora, with **2004** above. On the silver outer ring, **ESTADO DE SONORA** at the top, with **$100** at the bottom and the mintmark M̥ at far left.

Sinaloa Reverse Design
On the gold center, the coat of arms of Sinaloa, with **2004** to the right. On the silver outer ring, **ESTADO DE SINALOA** at the top, with **$100** at the bottom and the mintmark M̥ at far left.

San Luis Potosí Reverse Design
On the gold center, the coat of arms of san Luis Potosí, with **2004** below. On the silver outer ring, **ESTADO DE SAN LUIS POTOSI** at the top, with **$100** at the bottom and the mintmark M̥ at far left.

	Mintage	PL
2004, Sonora. BW-684.7, KM-702	1,000	$900.00
2004, Sinaloa. BW-684.8, KM-703	1,000	900.00
2004, San Luis Potosí. BW-684.9, KM-806	1,000	900.00

      Quintana Roo   Querétaro   Puebla

Composition: bimetallic (center, 0.999 gold; outer ring, 0.999 silver). *Weight:* 29.169 g. *Obverse:* On the gold center, the national coat of arms with the eagle facing left, its feathers resembling plates of armor; on the silver outer ring, the legend **ESTADOS UNIDOS MEXICANOS** above, with a half-wreath of oak and laurel below. *Diameter:* 34.5 mm. *Edge:* Paired plain and reeded.

Quintana Roo Reverse Design
On the gold center, the coat of arms of Quintana Roo, with **2004** below. On the silver outer ring, **ESTADO DE QUINTANA ROO** at the top, with **$100** at the bottom and the mintmark M̥ at far left.

Querétaro Reverse Design
On the gold center, the coat of arms of Querétaro, with **2004** to the right. On the silver outer ring, **ESTADO DE QUERETARO ARTEAGA** at the top, with **$100** at the bottom and the mintmark M̥ at lower left.

Puebla Reverse Design
On the gold center, the coat of arms of Puebla, with **2004** to the right. On the silver outer ring, **ESTADO DE PUEBLA** at the top, with **$100** at the bottom and the mintmark M̥ at far left.

	Mintage	PL
2004, Quintana Roo. BW-684.10, KM-807	1,000	$900.00
2004, Querétaro. BW-684.11, KM-808	1,000	900.00
2004, Puebla. BW-684.12, KM-809	1,000	900.00

Oaxaca

Nuevo León

Nayarit

Composition: bimetallic (center, 0.999 gold; outer ring, 0.999 silver). *Weight:* 29.169 g. *Obverse:* On the gold center, the national coat of arms with the eagle facing left, its feathers resembling plates of armor; on the silver outer ring, the legend ESTADOS UNIDOS MEXICANOS above, with a half-wreath of oak and laurel below. *Diameter:* 34.5 mm. *Edge:* Paired plain and reeded.

Oaxaca Reverse Design
On the gold center, the coat of arms of Oaxaca, with **2004** to the right. On the silver outer ring, **ESTADO DE OAXACA** at the top, with **$100** at the bottom and the mintmark M̊ at far left.

Nuevo León Reverse Design
On the gold center, the coat of arms of Nuevo León, with **2004** to the right. On the silver outer ring, **ESTADO DE NUEVO LEON** at the top, with **$100** at the bottom and the mintmark M̊ at far left.

Nayarit Reverse Design
On the gold center, the coat of arms of Nayarit, with **2004** above. On the silver outer ring, **ESTADO DE NAYARIT** at the top, with **$100** at the bottom and the mintmark M̊ at far left.

	Mintage	PL
2004, Oaxaca. BW-684.13, KM-810	1,000	$900.00
2004, Nuevo León. BW-684.14, KM-811	1,000	900.00
2004, Nayarit. BW-684.15, KM-812	1,000	900.00

Morelos   Michoacán   Estado de México

Composition: bimetallic (center, 0.999 gold; outer ring, 0.999 silver). *Weight:* 29.169 g. *Obverse:* On the gold center, the national coat of arms with the eagle facing left, its feathers resembling plates of armor; on the silver outer ring, the legend **ESTADOS UNIDOS MEXICANOS** above, with a half-wreath of oak and laurel below. *Diameter:* 34.5 mm. *Edge:* Paired plain and reeded.

Morelos Reverse Design
On the gold center, the coat of arms of Morelos, with **2004** above. On the silver outer ring, **ESTADO DE MORELOS** at the top, with **$100** at the bottom and the mintmark M̊ at far left.

Michoacán Reverse Design
On the gold center, the coat of arms of Michoacán, with **2004** to the right. On the silver outer ring, **ESTADO DE MICHOACAN DE OCAMPO** at the top, with **$100** at the bottom and the mintmark M̊ at lower left.

Estado de México Reverse Design
On the gold center, the coat of arms of México, with **2004** below. On the silver outer ring, **ESTADO DE MEXICO** at the top, with **$100** at the bottom and the mintmark M̊ at far left.

	Mintage	PL
2004, Morelos. BW-684.16, KM-813	1,000	$900.00
2004, Michoacán. BW-684.17, KM-814	1,000	900.00
2004, México, Estado de. BW-684.18, KM-815	1,000	900.00

Jalisco   Hidalgo   Guerrero

Composition: bimetallic (center, 0.999 gold; outer ring, 0.999 silver). *Weight:* 29.169 g. *Obverse:* On the gold center, the national coat of arms with the eagle facing left, its feathers resembling plates of armor; on the silver outer ring, the legend ESTADOS UNIDOS MEXICANOS above, with a half-wreath of oak and laurel below. *Diameter:* 34.5 mm. *Edge:* Paired plain and reeded.

Jalisco Reverse Design
On the gold center, the coat of arms of Jalisco, with **2004** at upper left. On the silver outer ring, **ESTADO DE JALISCO** at the top, with **$100** at the bottom and the mintmark M̥ at far left.

Hidalgo Reverse Design
On the gold center, the coat of arms of Hidalgo, with **2005** above. On the silver outer ring, **ESTADO DE HIDALGO** at the top, with **$100** at the bottom and the mintmark M̥ at far left.

Guerrero Reverse Design
On the gold center, the coat of arms of Guerrero, with **2005** to the right. On the silver outer ring, **ESTADO DE GUERRERO** at the top, with **$100** at the bottom and the mintmark M̥ at far left.

	Mintage	PL
2004, Jalisco. BW-684.19, KM-816	1,000	$900.00
2005, Hidalgo. BW-684.20, KM-817	1,000	900.00
2005, Guerrero. BW-684.21, KM-818	1,000	900.00

Guanajuato

Durango

Distrito Federal

Composition: bimetallic (center, 0.999 gold; outer ring, 0.999 silver). *Weight:* 29.169 g. *Obverse:* On the gold center, the national coat of arms with the eagle facing left, its feathers resembling plates of armor; on the silver outer ring, the legend **ESTADOS UNIDOS MEXICANOS** above, with a half-wreath of oak and laurel below. *Diameter:* 34.5 mm. *Edge:* Paired plain and reeded.

Guanajuato Reverse Design
On the gold center, the coat of arms of Guanajuato, with **2005** below. On the silver outer ring, **ESTADO DE GUANAJUATO** at the top, with **$100** at the bottom and the mintmark M̥ at far left.

Durango Reverse Design
On the gold center, the coat of arms of Durango, with **2005** below. On the silver outer ring, **ESTADO DE DURANGO** at the top, with **$100** at the bottom and the mintmark M̥ at far left.

Distrito Federal Reverse Design
On the gold center, the coat of arms of the Distrito Federal, with **2005** above. On the silver outer ring, **DISTRITO FEDERAL** at the top, with **$100** at the bottom and the mintmark M̥ at far left.

	Mintage	PL
2005, Guanajuato. BW-684.22, KM-819	1,000	$900.00
2005, Durango. BW-684.23, KM-820	1,000	900.00
2005, Distrito Federal. BW-684.24, KM-821	1,000	900.00

| Colima | Coahuila | Chihuahua |

Composition: bimetallic (center, 0.999 gold; outer ring, 0.999 silver). *Weight:* 29.169 g. *Obverse:* On the gold center, the national coat of arms with the eagle facing left, its feathers resembling plates of armor; on the silver outer ring, the legend ESTADOS UNIDOS MEXICANOS above, with a half-wreath of oak and laurel below. *Diameter:* 34.5 mm. *Edge:* Paired plain and reeded.

Colima Reverse Design
On the gold center, the coat of arms of Colima, with **2005** to the right. On the silver outer ring, ESTADO DE COLIMA at the top, with **$100** at the bottom and the mintmark M̥ at far left.

Coahuila Reverse Design
On the gold center, the coat of arms of Coahuila, with **2005** above. On the silver outer ring, ESTADO DE COAHUILA DE ZARAGOZA at the top, with **$100** at the bottom and the mintmark M̥ at lower left.

Chihuahua Reverse Design
On the gold center, the coat of arms of Chihuahua, with **2005** above. On the silver outer ring, ESTADO DE CHIHUAHUA at the top, with **$100** at the bottom and the mintmark M̥ at far left.

	Mintage	PL
2005, Colima. BW-684.25, KM-824	1,000	$900.00
2005, Coahuila. BW-684.26, KM-825	1,000	900.00
2005, Chihuahua. BW-684.27, KM-822	1,000	900.00

| Chiapas | Campeche | Baja California Sur |

Composition: bimetallic (center, 0.999 gold; outer ring, 0.999 silver). *Weight:* 29.169 g. *Obverse:* On the gold center, the national coat of arms with the eagle facing left, its feathers resembling plates of armor; on the silver outer ring, the legend **ESTADOS UNIDOS MEXICANOS** above, with a half-wreath of oak and laurel below. *Diameter:* 34.5 mm. *Edge:* Paired plain and reeded.

Chiapas Reverse Design
On the gold center, the coat of arms of Chiapas, with **2005** to the right. On the silver outer ring, **ESTADO DE CHIAPAS** at the top, with **$100** at the bottom and the mintmark M̥ at far left.

Campeche Reverse Design
On the gold center, the coat of arms of Campeche, with **2005** to the right. On the silver outer ring, **ESTADO DE CAMPECHE** at the top, with **$100** at the bottom and the mintmark M̥ at far left.

Baja California Sur Reverse Design
On the gold center, the coat of arms of Baja California Sur, with **2005** above. On the silver outer ring, **ESTADO DE BAJA CALIFORNIA SUR** at the top, with **$100** at the bottom and the mintmark M̥ at far left.

	Mintage	PL
2005, Chiapas. BW-684.28, KM-823	1,000	$900.00
2005, Campeche. BW-684.29, KM-826	1,000	900.00
2005, Baja California Sur. BW-684.30, KM-827	1,000	900.00

      Baja California   Aguascalientes

Composition: bimetallic (center, 0.999 gold; outer ring, 0.999 silver). *Weight:* 29.169 g. *Obverse:* On the gold center, the national coat of arms with the eagle facing left, its feathers resembling plates of armor; on the silver outer ring, the legend **ESTADOS UNIDOS MEXICANOS** above, with a half-wreath of oak and laurel below. *Diameter:* 34.5 mm. *Edge:* Paired plain and reeded.

Baja California Reverse Design
On the gold center, the coat of arms of Baja California, with 2005 to the right. On the silver outer ring, **ESTADO DE BAJA CALIFORNIA** at the top, with **$100** at the bottom and the mintmark M̥ at far left.

Aguascalientes Reverse Design
On the gold center, the coat of arms of Aguascalientes, with 2005 below. On the silver outer ring, **ESTADO DE AGUASCALIENTES** at the top, with **$100** at the bottom and the mintmark M̥ at lower left.

	Mintage	PL
2005, Baja California. BW-684.31, KM-828	1,000	$900.00
2005, Aguascalientes. BW-684.32, KM-829	1,000	900.00

Type A6 (Series 2: Emblematic; BW-609)
10 Pesos, Silver

The common obverse design for all Series 2 Proof 10 pesos.

Aguascalientes

Baja California

Baja California Sur

Composition: 0.999 silver. *Weight:* 31.1035 g. *Obverse:* The national coat of arms with the eagle facing left, its feathers resembling plates of armor. Above, the legend **ESTADOS UNIDOS MEXICANOS**; below, a half-wreath of oak and laurel. *Diameter:* 40 mm. *Edge:* Reeded.

Aguascalientes Reverse Design
Slightly to the right of center, the Templo de San Antonio. To the left of the church, in the background, the entrance gate of the Jardín de San Marcos; to the left in the foreground, the eagle and ionic capital of the *Exedra* monument. Above the architecture, **$10**; to the left, the mintmark M̊; at lower left, aligned with the edge and reading clockwise, **MEXICO**. At the top, **AGUASCALIENTES 2005**.

Baja California Reverse Design
At center, the head of a bighorn sheep, with **$10** above. Two outlined "roads," one to the left and one to the right, extend from the outer ring onto the silver center and appear to converge somewhere behind the sheep. Above the roads are curved lines resembling mountains. At the top, **BAJA CALIFORNIA**; at the bottom, **GOBIERNO DEL ESTADO**; at the left **2005**; at the right, the mintmark M̊.

Baja California Sur Reverse Design
Bisecting the center, an outline map of Baja California Sur. To the left of the map, a deer as depicted in regional cave paintings; to the right, a saguaro cactus. **ESTADO DE BAJA CALIFORNIA SUR** surrounds, with **$10** at the bottom. To the left of the denomination, the mintmark M̊; to the right, **2006**.

	Mintage	PF
2005, Aguascalientes. BW-609.1, KM-718	6,000	$70.00
2005, Baja California. BW-609.2, KM-757	6,000	70.00
2006, Baja California Sur. BW-609.3, KM-761	6,000	70.00

Campeche

Chiapas

Chihuahua

Composition: 0.999 silver. *Weight:* 31.1035 g. *Obverse:* The national coat of arms with the eagle facing left, its feathers resembling plates of armor. Above, the legend **ESTADOS UNIDOS MEXICANOS**; below, a half-wreath of oak and laurel. *Diameter:* 40 mm. *Edge:* Reeded.

Campeche Reverse Design

At center, a jade mask, with **$10** at upper left, the mintmark M̥ at lower left, and **2006** at upper right. At the top, **ESTADO DE CAMPECHE**; at the bottom, **MÁSCARA DE JADE · CALAKMUL, CAMPECHE**.

Chiapas Reverse Design

At center, the head of Palenque ruler Pakal in three-quarter profile to the left, with M̥ / **2006** at upper left and **$10** at lower right. At the top, **ESTADO DE CHIAPAS**; at the bottom, **CABEZA MAYA DEL REY PAKAL, PALENQUE**.

Chihuahua Reverse Design

At center, the Angel of Freedom monument. Above the left wing, the mintmark M̥; below it, **2006**. Below the right wing, **$10**. Around the top of the outer ring, an ornamental half-border. Reading counterclockwise, **MÉXICO** at lower left and **ANGEL DE LA LIBERTAD, CHIHUAHUA** at lower right.

	Mintage	PF
2006, Campeche. BW-609.4, KM-759	6,000	$70.00
2006, Chiapas. BW-609.5, KM-772	6,000	70.00
2006, Chihuahua. BW-609.6, KM-774	6,000	70.00

Coahuila

Distrito Federal

Colima

Composition: 0.999 silver. *Weight:* 31.1035 g. *Obverse:* The national coat of arms with the eagle facing left, its feathers resembling plates of armor. Above, the legend **ESTADOS UNIDOS MEXICANOS**; below, a half-wreath of oak and laurel. *Diameter:* 40 mm. *Edge:* Reeded.

Coahuila Reverse Design
At center, an outline map of Coahuila with an array of emblems both inside and outside. Outside the map, clockwise from upper right, chimneys of the Nava Power Plant, a steel beam, the belfry of the Catedral de Santiago del Saltillo, the statue *Christ of the Noas*, and the Amistad Dam. Inside the map, clockwise from upper left, an endangered box turtle, a mining cart in a mineshaft, and a bundle of grapes. Also inside the map, at the top, M̥ / 2006 / $10. At the bottom, a banner reading **COAHUILA DE ZARAGOZA**.

Colima Reverse Design
Filling the background of the lower half of the field, two volcanoes; in the foreground, with a small coat of arms of Colima with palm fronds to the right of the arms. Above the volcanoes, the word **Generoso**, with **2006** below left and **$10** below right. At the top, in an italic typeface, **Colima**, with the mintmark M̥ at far left.

Distrito Federal Reverse Design
Across the center, the Federal District Building, with $10 above and 2006 below. To the left of the denomination and slightly lower, the mintmark M̥. At the top, **DISTRITO FEDERAL**, with **ANTIGUO AYUNTAMIENTO** at the bottom.

	Mintage	PF
2006, Coahuila. BW-609.7, KM-780	6,000	$70.00
2006, Colima. BW-609.8, KM-776	6,000	70.00
2006, Distrito Federal. BW-609.9, KM-778	6,000	70.00

Durango

Guerrero

Guanajuato

Composition: 0.999 silver. *Weight:* 31.1035 g. *Obverse:* The national coat of arms with the eagle facing left, its feathers resembling plates of armor. Above, the legend **ESTADOS UNIDOS MEXICANOS**; below, a half-wreath of oak and laurel. *Diameter:* 40 mm. *Edge:* Reeded.

Durango Reverse Design
At center, a Durango Pine tree, with **$10** to the left, **2006** to the right, and the mintmark M̊ below. The legend **PRIMERA RESERVA NACIONAL FORESTAL** surrounds, with **DURANGO** at the bottom.

Guanajuato Reverse Design
A montage of emblems. In the left foreground, a statue of Miguel Hidalgo y Costilla; filling the background, the Teatro Juárez; at lower right, the monument *El Pipíla*; at upper right, an Inca dove. Slightly above center, superimposed over the theater, a small coat of arms of Guanajuato; below it, in a script typeface, **Guanajuato**. In the field to the right, between the dove and *El Pipíla*, 2006 / $10. At upper left, the mintmark M̊.

Guerrero Reverse Design
A montage of emblems in a flat, cut-out style. At left, a large portrait of Vicente Guerrero in three-quarter profile to the right, merging into a jaguar mask at the bottom. At center, the Catedral de Santa Prisca; at far right, La Quebrada Cliff and a cliff diver; below the cliff, a poinsettia. At the top, **GUERRERO / $10**; at far right, incused into the silhouette of the cliff, the mintmark M̊ and 2006.

	Mintage	PF
2006, Durango. BW-609.10, KM-786	6,000	$70.00
2006, Guanajuato. BW-609.11, KM-788	6,000	70.00
2006, Guerrero. BW-609.12, KM-790	6,000	70.00

Hidalgo

Jalisco

Estado de México

Composition: 0.999 silver. *Weight:* 31.1035 g. *Obverse:* The national coat of arms with the eagle facing left, its feathers resembling plates of armor. Above, the legend **ESTADOS UNIDOS MEXICANOS**; below, a half-wreath of oak and laurel. *Diameter:* 40 mm. *Edge:* Reeded.

Hidalgo Reverse Design
To right of center, the Pachuca Monumental Clock. To the left of the clock, **RELOJ / MONUMENTAL / DE / PACHUCA / HIDALGO** and, in a script typeface, **La / Bella / Airosa / 2006**. To the right, the mintmark M̊; at the top, **$10**.

Jalisco Reverse Design
Across the center, the Cabañas Hospice, with M̊ / **2006** above it to the left and **$10** above to the right. At the top, **ESTADO DE JALISCO**; at the bottom, **HOSPICIO CABAÑAS**.

Estado de México Reverse Design
Filling a circular area at center, the Pyramid of the Moon with three volcanoes—Ixtaccihuatl, Popocatépetl, and Xinantecatl—in the background, and **2006** above. At the top, **ESTADO DE MÉXICO**; at the bottom, **$10**; and at lower left, the mintmark M̊.

	Mintage	PF
2006, Hidalgo. BW-609.13, KM-792	6,000	$70.00
2006, Jalisco. BW-609.14, KM-794	6,000	70.00
2006, Estado de México. BW-609.15, KM-830	6,000	70.00

Michoacán

Nayarit

Morelos

Composition: 0.999 silver. *Weight:* 31.1035 g. *Obverse:* The national coat of arms with the eagle facing left, its feathers resembling plates of armor. Above, the legend **ESTADOS UNIDOS MEXICANOS**; below, a half-wreath of oak and laurel. *Diameter:* 40 mm. *Edge:* Reeded.

Michoacán Reverse Design
At center, four monarch butterflies in varying sizes, with **2006** to the right and the mintmark M̥ at lower left. At the top, **ESTADO DE MICHOACAN**; at the bottom, **$10**.

Morelos Reverse Design
Across the center from the left, the Palace of Cortés in the background; in the right foreground, a costumed Chinelo character. Above the palace, **ESTADO DE / MORELOS**; below, **PALACIO DE CORTÉS**. At the top, **$10**; at far right, the mintmark M̥; at the bottom, **2006**.

Nayarit Reverse Design
At center, an aerial view of the ancient manmade island Mexcaltitlán de Uribe, with **2007** above and **Isla de Mexcaltitlán** below. At the top, **ESTADO DE NAYARIT**; at the bottom, **$10**; at far left, the mintmark M̥.

	Mintage	PF
2006, Michoacán. BW-609.16, KM-831	6,000	$70.00
2006, Morelos. BW-609.17, KM-832	6,000	70.00
2007, Nayarit. BW-609.18, KM-833	6,000	70.00

Nuevo León

Oaxaca

Puebla

Composition: 0.999 silver. *Weight:* 31.1035 g. *Obverse:* The national coat of arms with the eagle facing left, its feathers resembling plates of armor. Above, the legend **ESTADOS UNIDOS MEXICANOS**; below, a half-wreath of oak and laurel. *Diameter:* 40 mm. *Edge:* Reeded.

Nuevo León Reverse Design
Filling the lower half of the field, a panoramic view of Cerro de la Silla (Saddle Hill) in the background, with the ironworks of the Parque Fundidora in the right foreground. Centered above the hills, **$10 / 2007**. At the top, **ESTADO DE NUEVO LEÓN**, with the mintmark M̥ at far right.

Oaxaca Reverse Design
In a circular area at center, the Macedonio Alcalá Theater, with the mintmark M̥ to the right of the dome. Surrounding, in a fanciful, Art Nouveau–style typeface, **$10 OAXACA 2007** at the top, with **Teatro Macedonio Alcalá** at the bottom.

Puebla Reverse Design
At center, an emblem similar to the Nahuatl glyph Ollin ("movement"); above the emblem, **2007** and **$10** at left and right, respectively; to the left of the emblem, the mintmark M̥; below, **ESTADO DE PUEBLA**. Surrounding all, a border of patterns from an 18th-century Talavera ceramic plate.

	Mintage	PF
2007, Nuevo León. BW-609.19, KM-834	6,000	$70.00
2007, Oaxaca. BW-609.20, KM-835	6,000	70.00
2007, Puebla. BW-609.21, KM-836	6,000	70.00

Querétaro

San Luis Potosí

Quintana Roo

Composition: 0.999 silver. *Weight:* 31.1035 g. *Obverse:* The national coat of arms with the eagle facing left, its feathers resembling plates of armor. Above, the legend **ESTADOS UNIDOS MEXICANOS**; below, a half-wreath of oak and laurel. *Diameter:* 40 mm. *Edge:* Reeded.

Querétaro Reverse Design
At center, part of the Querétaro aqueduct at left, with the Iglesia de Santa Rosa at right and $10 below. At the top, **ESTADO DE QUERÉTARO ARTEAGA**; at the bottom, **Acueducto ✠ Santa Rosa de Viterbo**. At far left, 2007; at far right, the mintmark M̥.

Quintana Roo Reverse Design
In a circular area at center, the ancient ruins of Tulum at the right, with a figure from the Temple of Masks at the left; between them, stylized rays representing the sun, with 2007 at their center; at lower right, the mintmark M̥. At the top, **QUINTANA ROO**; at the bottom, $10.

San Luis Potosí Reverse Design
In a circular area at center, the Old Royal Treasury Building with the mintmark M̥ above and to the left. At the top, **· SAN LUIS POTOSÍ ·**; around the bottom, $10 **CAJA REAL** 2007.

	Mintage	PF
2007, Querétaro. BW-609.23, KM-838	6,000	$70.00
2007, Quintana Roo. BW-609.22, KM-837	6,000	70.00
2007, San Luis Potosí. BW-609.24, KM-839	6,000	70.00

Sinaloa

Tabasco

Sonora

Composition: 0.999 silver. *Weight:* 31.1035 g. *Obverse:* The national coat of arms with the eagle facing left, its feathers resembling plates of armor. Above, the legend **ESTADOS UNIDOS MEXICANOS**; below, a half-wreath of oak and laurel. *Diameter:* 40 mm. *Edge:* Reeded.

Sinaloa Reverse Design
At center, a sliced-open pitahaya (dragonfruit) upon a pile of uncut fruits; at the left, M̊ / 2007; at the right, $10; below, **LUGAR DE PITAHAYAS**. At the top, **ESTADO DE SINALOA**.

Sonora Reverse Design
In a circular area at center, a silhouette of a Yaqui deer-dancer in the left foreground, with silhouetted landscape features—desert, saguaro cactus, mountains, and the sun—in the background. At the top, **ESTADO DE SONORA**, with $10 at the bottom; at far left, reading counterclockwise, 2007; at far right, the mintmark M̊.

Tabasco Reverse Design
Across the background from the left, the Tabasco Planetarium, with the Fishermen Fountain in the middle ground at center and an Olmec giant stone head in the foreground at the right. At the top, **TABASCO / 2007**; at the bottom, $10; at upper left, the mintmark M̊.

	Mintage	PF
2007, Sinaloa. BW-609.25, KM-840	6,000	$70.00
2007, Sonora. BW-609.26, KM-841	6,000	70.00
2007, Tabasco. BW-609.27, KM-842	6,000	70.00

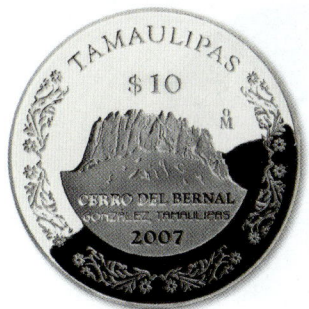
Tamaulipas

Tlaxcala

Veracruz

Composition: 0.999 silver. *Weight:* 31.1035 g. *Obverse:* The national coat of arms with the eagle facing left, its feathers resembling plates of armor. Above, the legend **ESTADOS UNIDOS MEXICANOS**; below, a half-wreath of oak and laurel. *Diameter:* 40 mm. *Edge:* Reeded.

Tamaulipas Reverse Design
In a circular area at center, the landscape feature known as Bernal's Hill, with **$10** above it and the mintmark M̥ at upper right. Incused into the landscape below the hill, **CERRO DEL BERNAL / GONZÁLEZ, TAMAULIPAS / 2007**. At the top, **TAMAULIPAS**.

Tlaxcala Reverse Design
A montage of architectural features. From left to right, the Ocotlán Church, the Open Chapel, and the tower of the former Convent of San Francisco behind the Ranchero Aguilar Bullring. Below these, the Government Palace, with **$10** just above it and **2007** below. Surmounting all, the coat of arms of Tlaxcala, with the mintmark M̥ to its right. At the top, **ESTADO DE TLAXCALA**.

Veracruz Reverse Design
At center, the Tajín Pyramid, with **TAJÍN** above, **$10** below, and the mintmark M̥ at upper right. Surrounding, **· 2007 · VERACRUZ ·** at the top and **DE IGNACIO DE LA LLAVE ·** at the bottom.

	Mintage	PF
2007, Tamaulipas. BW-609.28, KM-843	6,000	$70.00
2007, Tlaxcala. BW-609.29, KM-844	6,000	70.00
2007, Veracruz. BW-609.30, KM-845	6,000	70.00

Yucatán   Zacatecas

Composition: 0.999 silver. *Weight:* 31.1035 g. *Obverse:* The national coat of arms with the eagle facing left, its feathers resembling plates of armor. Above, the legend **ESTADOS UNIDOS MEXICANOS**; below, a half-wreath of oak and laurel. *Diameter:* 40 mm. *Edge:* Reeded.

Yucatán Reverse Design
Somewhat to the left of and below center, a modernized rendering of Chichén Itzá's El Castillo, with ribbon-like flourishes in the field above and to the right. Above the steps, **Yucatán** (underscored) / **2007**; at lower right, the mintmark M̊. At the top, **$10**; at the bottom, **Castillo de Chichén Itzá**.

Zacatecas Reverse Design
At upper left, the Zacatecas Cable Car, with the Mining Monument below it; filling the center, the Zacatecas Cathedral, with **$10** above. At the top, **Zacatecas**; at far right, **2007**; at far left, touching the cable, the mintmark M̊.

	Mintage	PF
2007, Yucatán. BW-609.31, KM-846	6,000	$70.00
2007, Zacatecas. BW-609.32, KM-847	6,000	70.00

Type A4 (Series 2: Emblematic; BW-685)
100 Pesos, Bimetallic

The common obverse design for all Series 2 Proof 100 pesos.

      Aguascalientes   **Baja California**   **Baja California Sur**

Composition: bimetallic (center, 0.999 gold; outer ring, 0.999 silver). *Weight:* 29.169 g. *Obverse:* On the gold center, the national coat of arms with the eagle facing left, its feathers resembling plates of armor; on the silver outer ring, the legend **ESTADOS UNIDOS MEXICANOS** above, with a half-wreath of oak and laurel below. *Diameter:* 34.5 mm. *Edge:* Paired plain and reeded.

Aguascalientes Reverse Design
Slightly to the right on the gold center and extending into the silver ring, the Templo de San Antonio. To the left of the church, in the background, the entrance gate of the Jardín de San Marcos; to the left in the foreground, the eagle and ionic capital of the *Exedra* monument. At the top of the gold center, $100. At the top of the outer ring, **AGUASCALIENTES 2005**, with the mintmark M̥ at the left. Below the mintmark, reading counterclockwise, **MÉXICO**.

Baja California Reverse Design
On the gold center, the head of a bighorn sheep, with $100 above. Two outlined "roads," one to the left and one to the right, extend from the outer ring onto the gold center and appear to converge somewhere behind the sheep. Above the roads are curved lines resembling mountains. On the outer ring, at the top, **BAJA CALIFORNIA**; below, **GOBIERNO DEL ESTADO**; at the left, **2005**; at the right, the mintmark M̥.

Baja California Sur Reverse Design
Bisecting the gold center, an outline map of Baja California Sur. To the left of the map, a deer as depicted in regional cave paintings; to the right, a saguaro cactus. On the silver outer ring, **ESTADO DE BAJA CALIFORNIA SUR** surrounds, with $100 at the bottom. To the left of the denomination, the mintmark M̥; to the right, **2006**.

	Mintage	PL
2005, Aguascalientes. BW-685.1, KM-862	600	$900.00
2005, Baja California. BW-685.2, KM-863	600	900.00
2006, Baja California Sur. BW-685.3, KM-864	600	900.00

| Campeche | Chiapas | Chihuahua |

Composition: bimetallic (center, 0.999 gold; outer ring, 0.999 silver). *Weight:* 29.169 g. *Obverse:* On the gold center, the national coat of arms with the eagle facing left, its feathers resembling plates of armor; on the silver outer ring, the legend **ESTADOS UNIDOS MEXICANOS** above, with a half-wreath of oak and laurel below. *Diameter:* 34.5 mm. *Edge:* Paired plain and reeded.

Campeche Reverse Design
On the gold center, a jade mask, with **$100** at upper left, the mintmark M̥ at lower left, and **2006** at upper right. On the silver outer ring, **ESTADO DE CAMPECHE** and **MÁSCARA DE JADE · CALAKMUL, CAMPECHE**.

Chiapas Reverse Design
On the gold center, the head of Palenque ruler Pakal in three-quarter profile to the left, with M̥ / **2006** at upper left and **$100** at lower right. On the silver outer ring, **CHIAPAS** and **CABEZA MAYA DEL REY PAKAL, PALENQUE**.

Chihuahua Reverse Design
On the gold center and extending above and below onto the outer ring, the Angel of Freedom monument. Above the left wing, the mintmark M̥; below the it, **2006**. Below the right wing, **$100**. Around the top of the outer ring, an ornamental half-border. Reading counterclockwise, **MÉXICO** at lower left and **ANGEL DE LA LIBERTAD, CHIHUAHUA** at lower right.

	Mintage	PL
2006, Campeche. BW-685.4, KM-865	600	$900.00
2006, Chiapas. BW-685.7, KM-866	600	900.00
2006, Chihuahua. BW-685.8, KM-867	600	900.00

Coahuila   Colima   Distrito Federal

Composition: bimetallic (center, 0.999 gold; outer ring, 0.999 silver). *Weight:* 29.169 g. *Obverse:* On the gold center, the national coat of arms with the eagle facing left, its feathers resembling plates of armor; on the silver outer ring, the legend **ESTADOS UNIDOS MEXICANOS** above, with a half-wreath of oak and laurel below. *Diameter:* 34.5 mm. *Edge:* Paired plain and reeded.

Coahuila Reverse Design
Extending across the outer ring and the gold center, an outline map of Coahuila with an array of emblems both inside and outside. Outside the map, clockwise from upper right, chimneys of the Nava Power Plant, a steel beam, the belfry of the Catedral de Santiago del Saltillo, the statue *Christ of the Noas*, and the Amistad Dam. Inside the map, clockwise from upper left, an endangered box turtle, a mining cart in a mineshaft, and a bundle of grapes. At the top of the gold center, **2006 / $100**, with the mintmark M̥ above on the outer ring. At the bottom of the outer ring, a banner reading **COAHUILA DE ZARAGOZA**.

Colima Reverse Design
Extending across the outer ring and the gold center, two volcanoes, with a small coat of arms of Colima in the foreground and palm fronds to the right of the arms. At the top of the gold center, the word **Generoso**, with **2006** below left and **$100** below right. At the top of the outer ring, in an italic typeface, **Colima**, with the mintmark M̥ at far left.

Distrito Federal Reverse Design
Extending across the outer ring and the gold center, the Federal District Building. On the gold center, at the top, **$100**; at the bottom, **2006**; below and to the left of the denomination, the mintmark M̥. On the outer ring, at the top, **DISTRITO FEDERAL**, with **ANTIGUO AYUNTAMIENTO** at the bottom.

	Mintage	PL
2006, Coahuila. BW-685.5, KM-868	600	$900.00
2006, Colima. BW-685.6, KM-869	600	900.00
2006, Distrito Federal. BW-685.9, KM-870	600	900.00

Durango   Guanajuato   Guerrero

Composition: bimetallic (center, 0.999 gold; outer ring, 0.999 silver). *Weight:* 29.169 g. *Obverse:* On the gold center, the national coat of arms with the eagle facing left, its feathers resembling plates of armor; on the silver outer ring, the legend **ESTADOS UNIDOS MEXICANOS** above, with a half-wreath of oak and laurel below. *Diameter:* 34.5 mm. *Edge:* Paired plain and reeded.

Durango Reverse Design
On the gold center, a Durango Pine tree, with **$100** to the left, **2006** to the right, and the mintmark M̥ below. On the outer ring, **PRIMERA RESERVA NACIONAL FORESTAL** and **DURANGO**.

Guanajuato Reverse Design
Extending across the outer ring and the gold center, a montage of emblems. Slightly above center, a small coat of arms of Guanajuato; in the left foreground, a statue of Miguel Hidalgo y Costilla; filling the background, the Teatro Juárez; at lower right, the monument *El Pipíla*; at upper right, an Inca dove. At center, in a script typeface, **Guanajuato**. At right, between the dove and *El Pipíla*, **2006 / $100**. At upper left, the mintmark M̥.

Guerrero Reverse Design
Extending across the outer ring and the gold center, a montage of emblems in a flat, cut-out style. At left, a large, stylized portrait of Vicente Guerrero in three-quarter profile to the right, merging into a jaguar mask at the bottom. At center, the Catedral de Santa Prisca; at far right, the La Quebrada Cliff and a cliff diver; below the cliff, a poinsettia. At the top of the gold center, **$100**; at far right, extending into the ring, the mintmark M̥ and **2006**. At the top of the outer ring, **GUERRERO**.

	Mintage	PL
2006, Durango. BW-685.10, KM-871	600	$900.00
2006, Guanajuato. BW-685.11, KM-872	600	900.00
2006, Guerrero. BW-685.12, KM-873	600	900.00

Hidalgo　　　　　　　　Jalisco　　　　　　　　Estado de México

Composition: bimetallic (center, 0.999 gold; outer ring, 0.999 silver). *Weight:* 29.169 g. *Obverse:* On the gold center, the national coat of arms with the eagle facing left, its feathers resembling plates of armor; on the silver outer ring, the legend ESTADOS UNIDOS MEXICANOS above, with a half-wreath of oak and laurel below. *Diameter:* 34.5 mm. *Edge:* Paired plain and reeded.

Hidalgo Reverse Design
Extending across the outer ring and the gold center, the Pachuca Monumental Clock. To the left of the clock, **RELOJ / MONUMENTAL / DE / PACHUCA / HIDALGO** and, in a script typeface, **La / Bella / Airosa / 2006**. To the right, the mintmark M̥; at the top, $100.

Jalisco Reverse Design
Extending across the outer ring and the gold center, the Cabañas Hospice. On the gold center, M̥ / 2006 to the left and $100 to the right. On the outer ring, **ESTADO DE JALISCO** at the top and **HOSPICIO CABAÑAS** at the bottom.

Estado de México Reverse Design
On the gold center, the Pyramid of the Moon, with three volcanoes—Ixtaccihuatl, Popocatépetl, and Xinantecatl—in the background, and 2006 at the top. On the outer ring, **ESTADO DE MÉXICO** at the top, $100 at the bottom, and the mintmark M̥ at lower left.

	Mintage	PL
2006, Hidalgo. BW-685.13, KM-874	600	$900.00
2006, Jalisco. BW-685.14, KM-875	600	900.00
2006, Estado de México. BW-685.15, KM-876	600	900.00

Michoacán	Morelos	Nayarit

Composition: bimetallic (center, 0.999 gold; outer ring, 0.999 silver). *Weight:* 29.169 g. *Obverse:* On the gold center, the national coat of arms with the eagle facing left, its feathers resembling plates of armor; on the silver outer ring, the legend **ESTADOS UNIDOS MEXICANOS** above, with a half-wreath of oak and laurel below. *Diameter:* 34.5 mm. *Edge:* Paired plain and reeded.

Michoacán Reverse Design
On the gold center, four monarch butterflies in varying sizes, with **2006** to the right. On the outer ring **ESTADO DE MICHOACAN** at the top, **$100** at the bottom, and the mintmark M̥ at lower left.

Morelos Reverse Design
Extending across the outer ring and the gold center, the Palace of Cortés in the background with a costumed Chinelo character in the right foreground. Above the palace, **ESTADO DE / MORELOS**; below, **PALACIO DE CORTÉS**. On the outer ring, **$100** at the top, the mintmark M̥ at far right, and **2006** at the bottom.

Nayarit Reverse Design
On the gold center, an aerial view of the ancient manmade island Mexcaltitlán de Uribe, with **2007** above and **Isla de Mexcaltitlán** below. On the outer ring, **ESTADO DE NAYARIT** at the top, with **$100** at the bottom and the mintmark M̥ at far left.

	Mintage	PL
2006, Michoacán. BW-685.16, KM-877	600	$900.00
2006, Morelos. BW-685.17, KM-878	600	900.00
2007, Nayarit. BW-685.18, KM-879	600	900.00

| Nuevo León | Oaxaca | Puebla |

Mexico Mint artist renderings; not actual coins.

Composition: bimetallic (center, 0.999 gold; outer ring, 0.999 silver). *Weight:* 29.169 g. *Obverse:* On the gold center, the national coat of arms with the eagle facing left, its feathers resembling plates of armor; on the silver outer ring, the legend **ESTADOS UNIDOS MEXICANOS** above, with a half-wreath of oak and laurel below. *Diameter:* 34.5 mm. *Edge:* Paired plain and reeded.

Nuevo León Reverse Design
Extending across the outer ring and the gold center, a panoramic view of Cerro de la Silla (Saddle Hill) in the background, with the ironworks of the Parque Fundidora in the right foreground. On the gold center above the hills, $100 / 2007. On the outer ring, **ESTADO DE NUEVO LEÓN** at the top, with the mintmark M̥ at far right.

Oaxaca Reverse Design
On the gold center, the Macedonio Alcalá Theater, with the mintmark M̥ to the right of the dome. On the outer ring, in a fanciful, Art Nouveau–style typeface, $100 OAXACA 2007 at the top, with **Teatro Macedonio Alcalá** at the bottom.

Puebla Reverse Design
On the gold center, an emblem similar to the Nahuatl glyph Ollin ("movement"); above the emblem, 2007 and $100 at left and right, respectively; to the left of the emblem, the mintmark M̥; below, **ESTADO DE PUEBLA**. On the outer ring, a border of patterns from an 18th-century Talavera ceramic plate.

	Mintage	PL
2007, Nuevo León. BW-685.19, KM-880	600	$900.00
2007, Oaxaca. BW-685.20, KM-881	600	900.00
2007, Puebla. BW-685.21, KM-882	600	900.00

| Querétaro | Quintana Roo | San Luis Potosí |

Mexico Mint artist renderings; not actual coins.

Composition: bimetallic (center, 0.999 gold; outer ring, 0.999 silver). *Weight:* 29.169 g. *Obverse:* On the gold center, the national coat of arms with the eagle facing left, its feathers resembling plates of armor; on the silver outer ring, the legend **ESTADOS UNIDOS MEXICANOS** above, with a half-wreath of oak and laurel below. *Diameter:* 34.5 mm. *Edge:* Paired plain and reeded.

Querétaro Reverse Design
On the gold center, part of the Querétaro aqueduct at left, with the Iglesia de Santa Rosa at right. On the outer ring, **ESTADO DE QUERÉTARO ARTEAGA** at the top, and **Acueducto** ✣ **Santa Rosa de Viterbo** at the bottom; at left, 2007; at right, the mintmark M̥.

Quintana Roo Reverse Design
On the gold center, the ancient ruins of Tulum at the right, with a figure from the Temple of Masks at the left; between them, stylized rays representing the sun, with 2007 at their center; at lower right, the mintmark M̥. On the outer ring, **QUINTANA ROO** at the top, with **$100** at the bottom.

San Luis Potosí Reverse Design
On the gold center, the Old Royal Treasury Building with the mintmark M̥ at upper left. On the outer ring, **· SAN LUIS POTOSÍ ·** at the top; around the bottom, **$100** ⚜ **CAJA REAL** ✤ **2007**.

	Mintage	PL
2007, Querétaro. BW-685.23, KM-884	600	$900.00
2007, Quintana Roo. BW-685.22, KM-883	600	900.00
2007, San Luis Potosí. BW-685.24, KM-885	600	900.00

Sinaloa   Sonora   Tabasco

Mexico Mint artist renderings; not actual coins.

Composition: bimetallic (center, 0.999 gold; outer ring, 0.999 silver). *Weight:* 29.169 g. *Obverse:* On the gold center, the national coat of arms with the eagle facing left, its feathers resembling plates of armor; on the silver outer ring, the legend **ESTADOS UNIDOS MEXICANOS** above, with a half-wreath of oak and laurel below. *Diameter:* 34.5 mm. *Edge:* Paired plain and reeded.

Sinaloa Reverse Design
On the gold center, a sliced-open pitahaya (dragonfruit) upon a pile of uncut fruits; at the left, M̊ / 2007; at the right, $100; below, **LUGAR DE PITAHAYAS**. At the top of the outer ring, **ESTADO DE SINALOA**.

Sonora Reverse Design
On the gold center, a silhouette of a Yaqui deer-dancer in the left foreground, with silhouetted landscape features—desert, saguaro cactus, mountains, and the sun—in the background. On the outer ring, **ESTADO DE SONORA** at the top, with **$100** at the bottom; at left, reading counterclockwise, 2007; at right, the mintmark M̊.

Tabasco Reverse Design
Extending across the outer ring and the gold center, the Tabasco Planetarium and the Fishermen Fountain, with an Olmec giant stone head in the foreground at the right and 2007 above. On the outer ring, **TABASCO** at the top with **$100** at the bottom; at upper left, the mintmark M̊.

	Mintage	PL
2007, Sinaloa. BW-685.25, KM-886	600	$900.00
2007, Sonora. BW-685.26, KM-887	600	900.00
2007, Tabasco. BW-685.27, KM-888	600	900.00

| Tamaulipas | Tlaxcala | Veracruz |

Mexico Mint artist renderings; not actual coins.

Composition: bimetallic (center, 0.999 gold; outer ring, 0.999 silver). *Weight:* 29.169 g. *Obverse:* On the gold center, the national coat of arms with the eagle facing left, its feathers resembling plates of armor; on the silver outer ring, the legend **ESTADOS UNIDOS MEXICANOS** above, with a half-wreath of oak and laurel below. *Diameter:* 34.5 mm. *Edge:* Paired plain and reeded.

Tamaulipas Reverse Design
On the gold center, the landscape feature known as Bernal's Hill, with **$100** at the top and the mintmark M̊ at upper right; below, **CERRO DEL BERNAL / GONZÁLEZ, TAMAULIPAS / 2007**. On the outer ring, at the top, **TAMAULIPAS**.

Tlaxcala Reverse Design
Extending across the outer ring and the gold center, from left to right: the Ocotlán Church, the Open Chapel, and the tower of the former Convent of San Francisco behind the Ranchero Aguilar Bullring. Below these, the Government Palace, with **$100** just above it. Surmounting all, the coat of arms of Tlaxcala, with the mintmark M̊ to the right. On the outer ring, at the top, **ESTADO DE TLAXCALA**; at the bottom, **2007**.

Veracruz Reverse Design
On the gold center, the Tajín Pyramid, with **TAJÍN** above and **$100** below. On the outer ring, **· 2007 · VERACRUZ ·** and **DE IGNACIO DE LA LLAVE ·**, with the mintmark M̊ at far right.

	Mintage	PL
2007, Tamaulipas. BW-685.28, KM-889	600	$900.00
2007, Tlaxcala. BW-685.29, KM-890	600	900.00
2007, Veracruz. BW-685.30, KM-891	600	900.00

Yucatán   Zacatecas

Mexico Mint artist renderings; not actual coins.

Composition: bimetallic (center, 0.999 gold; outer ring, 0.999 silver). *Weight:* 29.169 g. *Obverse:* On the gold center, the national coat of arms with the eagle facing left, its feathers resembling plates of armor; on the silver outer ring, the legend **ESTADOS UNIDOS MEXICANOS** above, with a half-wreath of oak and laurel below. *Diameter:* 34.5 mm. *Edge:* Paired plain and reeded.

Yucatán Reverse Design
At left on the gold center, a modernized rendering of Chichén Itzá's El Castillo, with ribbon-like flourishes in the field to the right. At the top of the gold center, **Yucatán** (underscored) / **2007**; at lower right, the mintmark M̊. On the outer ring, **$100** at the top, with **Castillo de Chichén Itzá** at the bottom.

Zacatecas Reverse Design
Extending across the outer ring and the gold center, the Zacatecas Cable Car at left with the Mining Monument below it; filling the center, the Zacatecas Cathedral, with **$100** above. On the outer ring, **Zacatecas** at the top, with **2007** at far right and the mintmark M̊ at far left.

	Mintage	PL
2007, Yucatán. BW-685.31, KM-892	600	$900.00
2007, Zacatecas. BW-685.32, KM-893	600	900.00

33RD INTERNATIONAL CERVANTINO FESTIVAL

The 33rd Festival Internacional Cervantino took place in October 2005 in Guanajuato. This multifaceted cultural festival, named in honor of Spanish writer Miguel de Cervantes Saavedra and held annually since 1972, celebrates theater, dance, music, and other art forms. A Brilliant Uncirculated 10-peso coin commemorated the 33rd renewal of the festival. All were sold exclusively at the festival, and none reached the general numismatic market. A special session was held at the festival in honor of the 400th anniversary of the publication of Cervantes's *Don Quijote de la Mancha*; commemorative coins were issued for that as well (see the next listing).

10 pesos, Type A7, 2005. BW-757, KM-766. Brilliant Uncirculated.

Composition: 0.999 silver. *Weight:* 30.500 g. *Obverse:* The national coat of arms with the eagle facing left, its feathers resembling plates of armor. Above, the legend **ESTADOS UNIDOS MEXICANOS**; below, a half-wreath of oak and laurel. *Reverse:* At center, a stylized representation of Don Quixote on his horse, galloping from right to left. Above the front of the horse, **$10**; above the back, M̊ / **2005**. Below the horse, the circular emblem of the festival (at its center, a ruffled collar represents Cervantes; around its border, **IV CENTENARIO** and **DON QUIJOTE**). Reading clockwise from lower left and divided by Don Quixote's lance, **33 FESTIVAL INTER / NACIONAL CERVANTINO**. *Diameter:* 40 mm. *Edge:* Reeded.

	Mintage	BU
2005	1,205	$285.00

400TH ANNIVERSARY OF DON QUIJOTE DE LA MANCHA

On June 21, 2005, Mexico issued a decree authorizing a new 20-peso coin, "El Ingenioso Hidalgo Don Quijote de la Mancha," to commemorate the 400th anniversary of publication of *Don Quijote de la Mancha*, written by Miguel de Cervantes Saavedra. (See the sidebar on pages 263 and 264. Part 1 of the book was published in 1605, the anniversary commemorated by the coin; part 2 was published in 1615.)

From *Calavera Quijotesca*, a 19th-century engraving by J.G. Posada.

The reverse design, a skeletal horse and rider galloping through a crowd of other skeletons and scattering their bones in the air, is based on an engraving titled *Calavera Quijotesca*, by Mexican illustrator José Guadalupe Posada (1851–1913). Posada's *calaveras*—satirical skeletal figures that poked fun at dictator Porfirio Díaz and Mexico's bourgeoisie—were very popular with the underclass, and later influenced the imagery around the Día de los Muertos (Day of the Dead) celebrations. Despite his popularity, the artist died in poverty and was buried in an unmarked grave.

The Don Quixote commemorative was issued in two denominations: a silver 20 pesos (Proof only) and a bimetallic 100 pesos, which was produced as a circulating coin and as prooflike non-circulating legal tender. Although the 100 pesos were struck in both 2005 and 2006, all are dated 2005. Those that were actually struck in 2005—namely, the circulation strike and some with the prooflike strike—were produced with thinner, sans-serif lettering on the reverse outer ring and are now referenced as Variety 1. Those struck in 2006—the remaining prooflike coins—have a thicker, serif typeface on the reverse outer ring and have a diamond inside each of the initials D, O, and Q. These are now known as Variety 2.

20 pesos, Type A4, 2005. BW-804, KM-704. Proof.

Composition: 0.999 silver. *Weight:* 61.30 g. *Obverse:* The national coat of arms with the eagle facing left, its feathers resembling plates of armor. Above, the legend **ESTADOS UNIDOS MEXICANOS**; below, a half-wreath of oak and laurel. *Reverse:* Filling the center, a skeletal horse and rider galloping from left to right, scattering smaller human skeletons in their wake. Above, **J.G. POSADA** and the mintmark M̊; below, $20. Around the top, • **DON QUIJOTE DE LA MANCHA** •. Around the bottom, **400 ANIVERSARIO**, flanked by the dates 1605- (left) and -2005 (right). *Diameter:* 48 mm. *Edge:* Plain.

	Mintage	PF
2005	3,605	$145.00

100 pesos, Type A5, 2005 (Variety 1). BW-854.1, KM-705. Prooflike.

Composition: bimetallic (center: 0.925 silver; outer ring: bronze-aluminum). *Weight:* 33.30 g. *Obverse:* On the silver center, the national coat of arms with the eagle in profile to the left, the feathers resembling plates of armor. On the bronze-aluminum outer ring, the legend **ESTADOS UNIDOS MEXICANOS** above, with a half-wreath of oak and laurel below. *Reverse:* On the silver center, a skeletal horse and rider galloping from left to right, scattering smaller human skeletons in their wake. Above, **J.G. POSADA** and the mintmark M̊; below, $100. On the outer ring, in thin, sans-serif letters, the following legends: around the top, • **DON QUIJOTE DE LA MANCHA** •, and around the bottom, **400 ANIVERSARIO**, flanked by the dates 1605- (left) and -2005 (right). *Diameter:* 39 mm. *Edge:* Paired plain and reeded.

	Mintage	PL
2005	3,761	$50.00

100 pesos, Type A5, 2005 (2006; Variety 2). BW-854.2, KM-705. Prooflike.

Composition: bimetallic (center: 0.925 silver; outer ring: bronze-aluminum). *Weight:* 33.30 g. *Obverse:* On the silver center, the national coat of arms with the eagle in profile to the left, the feathers resembling plates of armor. On the bronze-aluminum outer ring, the legend **ESTADOS UNIDOS MEXICANOS** above, with a half-wreath of oak and laurel below. *Reverse:* On the silver center, a skeletal horse and rider galloping from left to right, scattering smaller human skeletons in their wake. Above, J.G. POSADA and the mintmark M̥; below, $100. On the outer ring, in thicker letters with serifs, the following legends: around the top, · **DON QUIJOTE DE LA MANCHA** ·, and around the bottom, **400 ANIVERSARIO**, flanked by the dates **1605**- (left) and -**2005** (right). *Diameter:* 39 mm. *Edge:* Paired plain and reeded.

	Mintage	PL
2005 (2006)	5,201	$70.00

Cervantes and Don Quixote

Miguel de Cervantes Saavedra is one of Spain's most celebrated writers. Born near Madrid in 1547, Cervantes enjoys a reputation in Spain similar to that of William Shakespeare in England. He is best known for his satirical fictional work *Don Quijote,* which was a popular success in its day and is often regarded as the first European novel.

Don Quijote was published in two parts over ten years. The first part, *El Ingenioso Hidalgo Don Quijote de la Mancha* (The Ingenious Gentleman Don Quijote of La Mancha), was published while he was in debtors' prison. It was an instant hit with the public, who appreciated its satire on popular ideas of romantic chivalry, its unexpected use of everyday language, and its pointed social commentary. Although the book did not make its author rich, it did allow him to start making a living as a writer, and elevated him from poverty for the first time in his life.

The story, which wraps a moral quest in humor and cynicism, centers around an old man who has read so many books on chivalry they have affected his perception of reality. He decides to become a knight, and, mounting his old horse, sets off on many amusing and fantastical adventures—much to the puzzlement of the people he encounters. Like the country of Spain, the character of Don Quijote was trapped somewhere between the Middle Ages and the modern world, unable to fully embrace or let go of either one.

The second part of the story, *Ocho Comedias y Ocho Entremeses* (Eight New Comedies and Eight New Interludes), was published nine years later, while Cervantes was living in Madrid. *Ocho Comedias* is more introspective than *El Ingenioso Hidalgo,* and considerable realism is evident in the more well-developed character's actions.

The combined work is by turns powerful, tragic, farcical, serious, and philosophical; one of the most influential books from the Spanish Golden Age, it has been translated into almost every modern language.

Miguel de Cervantes died of diabetes on April 22, 1616, one day before the death of William Shakespeare.

MEXICAN MONETARY ANNIVERSARIES

The year 2005 brought the anniversaries of three important events in Mexico's financial history: the 80th anniversary of the founding of the Banco de México; the 470th anniversary of the establishment of the Casa de Moneda de México; and the 100th anniversary of the Coinage Reform of 1905. These events were commemorated by a new series; all three commemoratives were produced as silver Proofs (Banco de México, 20 pesos; Casa de Moneda, 10 pesos; 1905 Reform, 5 pesos) and as 100-peso circulating coins (which are listed in chapter 3).

80TH ANNIVERSARY OF THE BANCO DE MÉXICO

The first coin in the series marked the 80th anniversary of the establishment of the Banco de México, the country's central bank and its only banknote-issuing institution. In honor of this fact, the reverse design features the Banco de México's 100-peso note of 1925 (BKM-2673). The American Bank Note Company produced this very rare note.

A specimen version of the rare 100-peso note depicted on the coin.

20 pesos, Type A4, 2005. BW-805, KM-767. Proof.

Composition: 0.999 silver. *Weight:* 61.500 g. *Obverse:* The national coat of arms with the eagle facing left, its feathers resembling plates of armor. Above, the legend **ESTADOS UNIDOS MEXICANOS**; below, a half-wreath of oak and laurel. *Reverse:* Across the center, a reproduction of a 100-peso banknote of 1925, with **$20** centered above it and the mintmark M̥ at upper left. Around the top, the dates **1925** and **2005** placed to the left and right, respectively, of the logo of the Banco de México. At the bottom, **LXXX / ANIVERSARIO**. *Diameter:* 48 mm. *Edge:* Plain.

	Mintage	PF
2005	3,005	$70.00

470TH ANNIVERSARY OF THE CASA DE MONEDA DE MÉXICO

The second issue in the series commemorates the 470th anniversary of the Casa de Moneda de México (the Mexico Mint). The oldest operating mint in the Americas, the Casa de Moneda was established by royal decree of May 11, 1535, issued by Queen Jane of Castilla. The coinage of Mexico circulated around the world and was legal tender in the United States until 1857.

10 pesos, Type A7, 2005. BW-856, KM-768. Proof.

Composition: 0.999 silver. *Weight:* 30.60 g. *Obverse:* The national coat of arms with the eagle facing left, its feathers resembling plates of armor. Above, the legend **ESTADOS UNIDOS MEXICANOS**; below, a half-wreath of oak and laurel. *Reverse:* Slightly to the right of center, an antique screw press with the dates **1535** above and **2005** below; to the left, **$10**; to the right, the mintmark M̥. Around the top, · **CASA DE MONEDA DE MÉXICO** ·, with **470 ANIVERSARIO** around the bottom. *Diameter:* 40 mm. *Edge:* Plain.

	Mintage	PF
2005	2,005	$100.00

100TH ANNIVERSARY OF THE COINAGE REFORM OF 1905

The third issue honors the 1905 Reform that standardized Mexico's coinage and centralized its production. The reverse features the small radiant liberty cap depicted on the 50 centavos and the 1 peso of the 1905 Reform.

5 pesos, Type A2, 2005. BW-859, KM-769. Proof.

Composition: 0.999 silver. *Weight:* 15.40 g. *Obverse:* The national coat of arms with the eagle facing left, its feathers resembling plates of armor. Above, the legend **ESTADOS UNIDOS MEXICANOS**; below, a half-wreath of oak and laurel. *Reverse:* At the center, a small radiant liberty cap, with **REFORMA MONETARIA** above and the denomination $5 below. To the left, **1905**; to the right, **2005**, with the mintmark M̥ slightly above. Below all, a half-wreath of oak and laurel. *Diameter:* 33 mm. *Edge:* Plain.

	Mintage	PF
2005	1,505	$70.00

100TH ANNIVERSARY OF THE UNAM

This 10-peso silver prooflike coin commemorates the 100th anniversary of the National Autonomous University (Universidad Nacional Autónoma de México, or UNAM; see the sidebar). The fields of the coin are heavily frosted, with contrasting mirrored devices. This unusual coin was approved in (and is dated) 2010, but it was not released until September 29, 2011.

10 pesos, Type 1, 2010. BW-862, KM-UL. Prooflike.

Composition: .0.999 silver. *Weight:* 30.7 g. *Obverse:* The national coat of arms with the eagle facing left, its feathers resembling plates of armor. Above, the legend **ESTADOS UNIDOS MEXICANOS**; below, a half-wreath of oak and laurel. The letters and devices are mirrored on a frosted field. *Reverse:* On a fully frosted field and slightly above center, raised and mirrored depictions of the UNAM's Central Library (left) and the Rectory Tower (right), with the Olympic Stadium behind them. Below the architecture, the human figures from the sculptural mural *People to University, University to People*, also raised and mirrored. All letters and numbers are incused, smoothly but without full mirrored finish, as follows: centered directly above the buildings, **100 / AÑOS**, with **$10** to the near right; below the mural figures, **2010**; at far left, the mintmark **M̥**. Around the top, **UNIVERSIDAD NACIONAL AUTÓNOMA DE MÉXICO**; around the bottom, *"POR MI RAZA HABLARÁ EL ESPÍRITU"* ("Through my race the spirit will speak"). *Diameter:* 40 mm. *Edge:* Reeded.

	Mintage	PL
2006	5,000	$70.00

The National Autonomous University (UNAM)

The National Autonomous University of Mexico is the oldest institution of higher education in the Americas and the largest in Latin America. The government-financed public university grew out of the Royal and Pontifical University of Mexico, which was established in 1551 by the viceroy of what was then New Spain. The modern university was officially founded in 1910 and was granted autonomy from government control in 1929, with the university's rector being made the final authority in all matters. The UNAM's stated aim is "to serve both the country and humanity, train professionals, organize and carry out research, mainly on national problems and conditions, and offer cultural benefits in the broadest sense possible."

For many in Mexico, and in Latin America in general, the UNAM is a symbol of independent thought and social activism. Its independence from government control of its financial and academic affairs is fiercely protected. The university's professors and its more than 300,000 students are among the most politically active in the world, and the campus has frequently been the site of major student strikes and demonstrations. The 1968 Olympic Games, the opening and closing ceremonies of which were held at the university's stadium, were particular targets of the Mexican student movement of the 1960s.

The UNAM has produced scores of politicians, artists, writers, diplomats, and other cultural leaders, along with three Nobel laureates (including Octavio Paz, who appears on two circulating commemorative Mexican coins; see pages 134 and 135). Its historic main campus is the site of murals by some of Mexico's most famous artists, including Diego Rivera.

The coin commemorating the university's 100th anniversary depicts three iconic campus structures and one of its famous murals: *People to University, University to People,* by David Alfaro Siqueiros. The large mural, located on the south wall of the Rectory Tower, is an *escultopintura* (sculpture-painting), and depicts several students in bas-relief. The student at top left of the mural points forward with a pencil with one arm, and back at the university with the other arm. The other students carry symbols of education and knowledge: a book, a model of a tower building, and a compass. In the background at top left is a group demonstration, representing the link between knowledge and social issues.

People to University, University to People, by David Alfaro Siqueiros.

The Rectory Tower, at left. Visible at the right is the Central Library.

The Central Library, covered in a mosaic by Juan O'Gorman.

Also depicted on the coin are three famous campus structures: the Rectory Tower, the Olympic Stadium, and the Central Library. The latter holds one of the largest collections in Mexico, and is decorated on all four sides with a tiled mural by artist Juan O'Gorman. The north, south, east, and west walls, respectively, depict Mexico's pre-Columbian history, its colonial history, the contemporaneous world, and the UNAM and modern Mexico.

At the bottom of the coin are the university's motto, written by philosopher and former UNAM president José Vasconcelos: *"Por mi raza hablará el espíritu"* ("Through my race the spirit will speak")—that is, the spirit of the Mexican people will be expressed in a uniquely Mexican, non-European society.

BENITO JUÁREZ GARCÍA BIRTH BICENTENNIAL

In 2006, a Brilliant Uncirculated, bimetallic 100 pesos was issued to honor the birth bicentennial of Benito Juárez García, born on March 21, 1806, in San Pablo Guelatao, Oaxaca. A native Zapotec in a country that ranked indigenous people in the lowest possible social class, Juárez García obtained an education and became a lawyer and, later, a judge. As a progressive reformer, he went on to become a strong president of Mexico during five different but vitally important terms of office. He is remembered for his role in expelling the French occupation, and revered for his dedication to democracy and to the rights and well-being of Mexico's indigenous people. (See also page 27.)

100 pesos, Type A9, 2006. BW-860.1, KM-764. Prooflike.

Composition: bimetallic (center: 0.925 silver; outer ring: bronze-aluminum). *Weight:* 33.967 g. *Obverse:* On the silver center, the national coat of arms with the eagle in profile to the left, the feathers resembling plates of armor. On the bronze-aluminum outer ring, the legend ESTADOS UNIDOS MEXICANOS above, with a half-wreath of oak and laurel below. *Reverse:* On the silver center, a bust of Benito Juárez García in three-quarter profile to the right, his head turned somewhat to the left. To the right of the bust, 2006; to the left, the mintmark M̥; below, a facsimile of Juárez García's signature. On the outer ring, BICENTENARIO DEL NATALICIO DE BENITO JUÁREZ GARCÍA, with $100 at the bottom. *Diameter:* 39 mm. *Edge:* Paired plain and reeded.

	Mintage	BU
2006	49,913	$35.00

2006 FIFA WORLD CUP, GERMANY

In 2006, Mexico participated in the quadrennial Fédération Internationale de Football Association (FIFA) World Cup. The vote to choose hosts for the 2006 renewal, back in 2000, had been highly controversial; one of the delegates even abstained on the eve of the vote, which resulted in Germany's being picked over South Africa to host the 2006 Cup.

Two commemorative Proof coins were issued in honor of the event: a silver 5 pesos and a gold 25 pesos.

The Mexican team played hard but was unable to make it past the Argentinian team to get to the quarter-finals. Argentina won 2–1; Mexico's goal was scored by Rafael Márquez, who is widely regarded as Mexico's best player of all time.

5 pesos, Type A3, 2006. BW-861, KM-770. Proof.

Composition: 0.999 silver. *Weight:* 33.30 g. *Obverse:* The national coat of arms with the eagle facing left, its feathers resembling plates of armor. Above, the legend **ESTADOS UNIDOS MEXICANOS**; below, a half-wreath of oak and laurel. *Reverse:* To the left of center, a figure of a Mayan ball player with an airborne rubber ball near his hip; at far right, a Mayan goal marker above a modern-day futbol. In the background, connecting the player, goal marker, and ball, an outline of a modern futbol. Beginning at lower left and reading clockwise around the field, the legend **COPA MUNDIAL DE LA FIFA ALEMANIA 2006**; at the bottom, **$5 MEXICO M̥**. *Diameter:* 40 mm. *Edge:* Plain.

	Mintage	PF
2006	40,005	$85.00

25 pesos, Type A1, 2006. BW-862, KM-UL. Proof.

Composition: 0.999 gold. *Weight:* 15.55 g. *Obverse:* The national coat of arms with the eagle facing left, its feathers resembling plates of armor. Above, the legend **ESTADOS UNIDOS MEXICANOS**; below, a half-wreath of oak and laurel. *Reverse:* At the center, a kneeling Mayan ball player with his feet to the left, his face to the right. At far right, a Mayan goal marker above and slightly overlapping a modern-day futbol. Beginning at lower left and reading clockwise around the field, the legend **COPA MUNDIAL DE LA FIFA ALEMANIA 2006**; at the bottom, **$25 MEXICO M̥**. *Diameter:* 23 mm. *Edge:* Plain.

	Mintage	PF
2006	9,505	$675

BICENTENNIAL OF THE WAR OF INDEPENDENCE

In 2010, to commemorate the bicentennial of the War of Independence, Mexico issued two silver 20-peso Proofs, along with two gold 200 pesos, one in Brilliant Uncirculated and one in Proof. The 20-peso coins were produced with two different reverse designs. The first depicts the Parroquia de Dolores, the parish church where Father Miguel Hidalgo y Costilla gave the call to the populace to rise up on September 16, 1810 (see also the sidebar on page 61). The second depicts the standing figures of Hidalgo y Costilla and General José María Morelos, another hero of the War of Independence.

20 pesos, Type A5, 2010 (Church). BW-805.1, KM-UL. Proof.

Composition: 0.999 silver. *Weight:* 62.0 g. *Obverse:* The national coat of arms with the eagle facing left, its feathers resembling plates of armor. Above, the legend **ESTADOS UNIDOS MEXICANOS**; below, a half-wreath of oak and laurel. *Reverse:* To the right of center, the front of Dolores Parish Church, angled toward the left. Shown separately at upper left, the church bell swinging to the right as it strikes the clapper. Directly above the church, **$20**; to its left, below the bell, **1810 / 2010**; on the church itself, incused at lower right, the mintmark **M̥**. Reading clockwise from lower left, divided by the bell, the legend **Bicentenario de la / Independencia de México**. *Diameter:* 48 mm. *Edge:* Reeded.

	Mintage	PF
2010	15,000	$135.00

20 pesos, Type A6, 2010 (Hidalgo and Morelos).
BW-805.2, KM-UL. Proof.

Composition: 0.999 silver. *Weight:* 62.0 g. *Obverse:* The national coat of arms with the eagle facing left, its feathers resembling plates of armor. Above, the legend **ESTADOS UNIDOS MEXICANOS**; below, a half-wreath of oak and laurel. *Reverse:* At center, the standing figures of José María Morelos (left) and Miguel Hidalgo y Costilla (right), both in three-quarter profile toward the center. Morelos holds a sword in his right hand and his historic "Sentimientos de la Nación" (Sentiments of the Nation) document in his left. Between the heads of the two figures, **$20**; at far left, the mintmark M̥. The legend **1810 - BICENTENARIO DE LA INDEPENDENCIA - 2010** surrounds. *Diameter:* 48 mm. *Edge:* Reeded.

	Mintage	PF
2010	15,000	$135.00

200 pesos, Type A1, 2010 (Winged Victory).
BW-859 and 589.1, KM-UL. Brilliant Uncirculated and Proof.

Brilliant Uncirculated and Proof finishes.

Composition: 0.900 gold. *Weight:* 41.67 g. *Obverse:* The national coat of arms with the eagle facing left, its feathers resembling plates of armor. Above, the legend **ESTADOS UNIDOS MEXICANOS**; below, a half-wreath of oak and laurel. *Reverse:* At center, the Winged Victory figure from the top of the Independence Monument, in three-quarter profile to the right, one wing extending to the upper left edge. Directly above, **BICENTENARIO** and, below the word, **1810 / - / 2010**. At far right, 200 / PESOS, with the mintmark M̊ below. Reading clockwise from lower left, 37.5 g ORO PURO. *Diameter:* 37 mm. *Edge:* Reeded.

	Mintage	BU	PF
2010	50,000	$2,275.00	
2010	5,000		3,300.00

CENTENNIAL OF THE MEXICAN REVOLUTION

In conjunction with the Bicentennial of the War of Independence, the Centennial of the Mexican Revolution was commemorated with the issue of two Proof 10 pesos in two designs, each taken from an iconic photograph of the Revolution.

Women who went with the men into combat, whether to attend to the needs of the men or to fight, were called *soldaderas* (see the sidebar on pages 275 and 276). The reverse of the first 10-peso coin depicts a *soldadera* as she stands on the steps of a railway car, looking cautiously at her surroundings. The second reverse design shows four Revolutionary soldiers seated in front of a locomotive. The photos are illustrated alongside the coins for comparison.

10 pesos, Type A8, 2010 (Soldadera). BW-860.2, KM-UL. Proof.

A *soldadera* photographed in the courtyards of Buenavista Station, Mexico City, in 1912 by Mexican photojournalist Gerónimo Hernández.

Composition: 0.999 silver. *Weight:* 62.0 g. *Obverse:* The national coat of arms with the eagle facing left, its feathers resembling plates of armor. Above, the legend **ESTADOS UNIDOS MEXICANOS**; below, a half-wreath of oak and laurel. *Reverse:* Filling a circular area at the center, a reproduction of the iconic Gerónimo Hernández photo in which a woman is seen stepping from a train while glancing anxiously to her left. On the surrounding ring, at the top, 1910 ~ REVOLUCIÓN MEXICANA ~ 2010; at the bottom, $10; at lower right, the mintmark M̥. *Diameter:* 48 mm. *Edge:* Reeded.

	Mintage	PF
2010	20,000	$135.00

10 pesos, Type A9, 2010 (Railroad). BW-860.3, KM-UL. Proof.

Revolutionaries photographed by German photojournalist Hugo Brehme, who came to Mexico in 1908 for a visit but remained until his death in 1954.

Composition: 0.999 silver. *Weight:* 62.0 g. *Obverse:* The national coat of arms with the eagle facing left, its feathers resembling plates of armor. Above, the legend **ESTADOS UNIDOS MEXICANOS**; below, a half-wreath of oak and laurel. *Reverse:* Filling the left and center, a reproduction iof the iconic Hugo Brehme photo depicting four armed rebels seated in front of a steam engine. At near right, **$10**; at upper right, reading clockwise, **REVOLUCIÓN MEXICANA / 1910-2010**; at lower right, the mintmark M̥. *Diameter:* 48 mm. *Edge:* Reeded.

	Mintage	PF
2010	20,000	$135.00

Las Soldaderas

A *soldadera* was a woman who went into the field during the Mexican Revolution, or who otherwise contributed to the rebel cause at great danger to herself and her family. The term originally referred to camp followers and prostitutes, but grew to include serving-women, nurses, wives who wanted to keep their families together, mothers, and any other women who traveled with the soldiers. Eventually, it included female insurgents who fought alongside men.

The Mexican tradition of women on the battlefield began with indigenous women who followed their warrior mates into war, often taking up arms and fighting to the death. The most legendary of these women were thought of as goddesses of war, and their exploits were documented in Aztec codices. The conquistadors later used women as quartermasters, charging them with distributing supplies and provisions to soldiers.

During the Revolution, wives and mothers who chose to follow their men to war usually travelled in the rear of the battalions with their children and belongings. They were in charge of cooking, cleaning, nursing the sick, and making camp, and most of them were unpaid. Some became spies and joined the camp followers of the enemy armies to gain information.

Some Revolutionary leaders actively recruited women to fight, and several women rose to prominence—particularly in Emilio Zapata's army. Margarita Neri, a brutal guerilla fighter, terrorized Tabasco and Chiapas with a large force of soldiers. Margarita Ortega and her daughter, Rosaura, were couriers and spies who ultimately died in service to the cause. Petra

Herrera, who used the pseudonym Pedro Herrera, dressed as a man to go into combat and distinguished herself as a fierce fighter and responsible leader. After establishing her reputation, she revealed herself as a female and achieved the rank of colonel. She was shot and killed on assignment as a spy while disguised as a bartender. María de la Luz Espinoza Barrera was also a highly accomplished soldier; unlike Herrera, she survived the Revolution, and actually received a veteran's pension.

Many female social reformers, women interested in causes like women's suffrage and fair wages, served the cause outside the military, and often suffered imprisonment and even execution. Flores de Andrade led a secret group that plotted the overthrow of Porfirio Díaz; caught, tried, and sentence to death, she managed to survive long enough for U.S. president William Howard Taft to intervene on her behalf. Dolores Jiménez y Muro and Juana Gutiérrez de Mendoza, both Maderistas, were the editors of liberal publications that championed social reform; both spent time in jail, and both ultimately joined Zapata after Francisco Madero's assassination.

The *soldaderas* named here are only a handful of the thousands who fought, wrote, nursed, served, and led on behalf of the Revolutionaries. They are commemorated on the Proof 10 pesos mentioned in this chapter, and on the circulating 5 pesos in the Centennial of the Revolution Series, discussed in chapter 3.

NUMISMATIC HERITAGE OF MEXICO SERIES

The common obverse for all Numismatic Heritage of Mexico Series coins.

In 2011, the Casa de Moneda initiated a new series presenting the historical coinage of Mexico from Spanish colonial times through the modern era. A few members of the series commemorate not only the coin's design type but its role in trade (e.g., coins chopmarked during use in China). The bimetallic coins were issued with a Brilliant Uncirculated finish. Each reverse bears a reproduction of a different historical coin, and each coin contains 1/2 ounce of sterling silver.

The designs of each series are described using the terminology found in this encyclopedia (rather than English translations of the Casa de Moneda's terminology), to make it easier to find information about the historical originals in volumes 1 and 3.

Series I

100 pesos, Type A10.1, 2011 (Pillars). BW-861.1, KM-UL. Prooflike.

During the second reign of King Philip V, Mexico began to produce coinage with a screw press, yielding a vast upgrade in quality over the previous, hammered coins. The new "milled" coins were perfectly round and their surfaces were evenly struck. Unlike their hammered counterparts, they had designs impressed in the edges to prevent illegal clipping of the silver or gold from the coins. Their reverse design—the Pillars of Hercules flanking two globes above a stretch of water—lends the coins their U.S. name, *Pillar coinage*. In Mexico, the name for these issues is *coins of worlds and seas*.

Series 1, BW-861.1.

Milled coinage, Pillar type (8 reales, Philip V, 1732); BW-28.1.

Composition: Bimetallic (center: 0.925 sterling silver; outer ring: bronze-aluminum-nickel alloy). *Weight:* 33.967 g. *Obverse:* On the silver center, the national coat of arms with the eagle in profile to the left, the feathers resembling plates of armor. On the stainless-steel outer ring, the legend **ESTADOS UNIDOS MEXICANOS** above, with a half-wreath of oak and laurel below. *Reverse:* On the outer ring, · **HERENCIA NUMISMÁTICA DE MÉXICO** · on the upper half, with **$100** at the bottom; at left and right, respectively, M̥ and **2011**. On the silver center, a reproduction of a 1732-M̥ Pillar-style 8 reales (BW-28.1, original diameter 40 mm). *Diameter:* 39 mm. *Edge:* Smooth reeding.

	Mintage	PL
2011	8,000	$55.00

100 pesos, Type A10.2, 2011 (Bust). BW-861.2, KM-UL. Prooflike.

Under King Charles III, Spanish milled coinage underwent a major design change. Formerly, the Spanish coat of arms had graced the obverse, while the reverse bore two globes flanked by the Pillars of Hercules. Now, the arms moved to the reverse, in place of the globes; a bust of the king appeared on the obverse. This would remain the design standard for the rest of the colonial era. Charles III, in the robe and laurel wreath of a Roman emperor, appears on the first Portrait 8 reales.

Series 1, BW-861.2.

Milled coinage, Bust or Portrait type (8 reales, Charles III, 1783); BW-28.6.

Composition: Bimetallic (center: 0.925 sterling silver; outer ring: bronze-aluminum-nickel alloy). *Weight:* 33.967 g. *Obverse:* On the silver center, the national coat of arms with the eagle in profile to the left, the feathers resembling plates of armor. On the stainless-steel outer ring, the legend **ESTADOS UNIDOS MEXICANOS** above, with a half-wreath of oak and laurel below. *Reverse:* On the outer ring, **· HERENCIA NUMISMÁTICA DE MÉXICO ·** on the upper half, with **$100** at the bottom; at left and right, respectively, M̊ and 2011. On the silver center, a reproduction of a 1783-M̊ Portrait- (or Bust-) style 8 reales (BW-28.6, original diameter 38 mm). *Diameter:* 39 mm. *Edge:* Smooth reeding.

	Mintage	PL
2011	8,000	$55.00

100 pesos, Type A10.3, 2011 (SUD). BW-861.3, KM-UL. Prooflike.

During the War of Independence, insurgent general José María Morelos y Pavón had his own coins minted to pay his troops. These copper coins, with a bow-and-arrow motif and the word SUD ("south"), were given out with the expectation that they would be redeemable in silver and gold when such coins became available. The Banco de México describes them as "Mexico's first fiduciary coins and . . . the first real Mexican coins."

Series 1, BW-861.3.

War of Independence, Insurgent coinage, SUD (8 reales, Oaxaca, 1914); BW-93.1.

Composition: Bimetallic (center: 0.925 sterling silver; outer ring: bronze-aluminum-nickel alloy). *Weight:* 33.967 g. *Obverse:* On the silver center, the national coat of arms with the eagle in profile to the left, the feathers resembling plates of armor. On the stainless-steel outer ring, the legend **ESTADOS UNIDOS MEXICANOS** above, with a half-wreath of oak and laurel below. *Reverse:* On the outer ring, • **HERENCIA NUMISMÁTICA DE MÉXICO** • on the upper half, with **$100** at the bottom; at left and right, respectively, M̊ and **2011**. On the silver center, a reproduction of a SUD 8 reales (BW-93.1, original diameter 38 mm) minted in 1914. *Diameter:* 39 mm. *Edge:* Smooth reeding.

	Mintage	PL
2011	8,000	$55.00

100 pesos, Type A10.4, 2011 (Cap and Rays).
BW-861.4, KM-UL. Prooflike.

In 1823 the new republic minted its first coinage, denominated in reales and escudos. The obverse design is the Profile Eagle; the reverse design for silver coins is a large, radiant liberty cap (hence the expression still used in Mexico during a coin toss: "Eagle or Sun?"). Cap and Rays coins with the Profile Eagle obverse were produced from 1823 to 1825, at three mints and in four denominations.

Series 1, BW-861.4.

Republic reales coinage, Cap and Rays (8 reales, Durango, 1824); BW-206.5.

Composition: Bimetallic (center: 0.925 sterling silver; outer ring: bronze-aluminum-nickel alloy). *Weight:* 33.967 g. *Obverse:* On the silver center, the national coat of arms with the eagle in profile to the left, the feathers resembling plates of armor. On the stainless-steel outer ring, the legend **ESTADOS UNIDOS MEXICANOS** above, with a half-wreath of oak and laurel below. *Reverse:* On the outer ring, • **HERENCIA NUMISMÁTICA DE MÉXICO** • on the upper half, with **$100** at the bottom; at left and right, respectively, M̊ and **2011**. On the silver center, a reproduction of an 1824-D₀ Cap and Rays 8 reales (BW-206.5, original diameter 38 mm). *Diameter:* 39 mm. *Edge:* Smooth reeding.

	Mintage	PL
2011	8,000	$55.00

100 pesos, Type A10.5, 2011 (Caballito). BW-861.5, KM-UL. Prooflike.

One of the most beautiful Mexican coins ever designed, the 1 peso of 1914 was both the first peso of the 1905 Currency Reform and a circulating commemorative of the centennial of the War of Independence. On its reverse, against a dramatic sunrise background, a bridle-less horse gallops toward the left, ridden by Liberty in a flowing gown. She is looking back over her shoulder to the right; in her left hand, she holds a torch above her head, while in her right, near the horse's neck, she holds a branch of laurel. The coin is affectionately known as the Caballito ("little horse").

Series 1, BW-861.5.

1905 Currency Reform coinage, Caballito (1 peso, 1914); BW-542.

Composition: Bimetallic (center: 0.925 sterling silver; outer ring: bronze-aluminum-nickel alloy). *Weight:* 33.967 g. *Obverse:* On the silver center, the national coat of arms with the eagle in profile to the left, the feathers resembling plates of armor. On the stainless-steel outer ring, the legend **ESTADOS UNIDOS MEXICANOS** above, with a half-wreath of oak and laurel below. *Reverse:* On the outer ring, • **HERENCIA NUMISMÁTICA DE MÉXICO** • on the upper half, with **$100** at the bottom; at left and right, respectively, M̊ and **2011**. On the silver center, a reproduction of a 1914 Caballito peso (BW-542, original diameter 39 mm). *Diameter:* 39 mm. *Edge:* Smooth reeding.

	Mintage	PL
2011	8,000	$55.00

100 pesos, Type A10.6, 2011 (Bolita). BW-861.6, KM-UL. Prooflike.

An iconic coin of the Revolution, the Bolita peso was minted in Hidalgo del Parral in the state of Chihuahua. Although the origins of Parral coinage are a bit murky, it may have been authorized by Francisco (Pancho) Villa through General Maclovia Herrera Cano. The coin gets its nickname for the *bolita* (little ball) over which the denomination is superimposed. It is quite rare; versions without the ball are somewhat more common on the market.

Series 1, BW-861.6.

Mexican Revolution coinage, Bolita (1 peso, Hidalgo del Parral, 1913); BW-286.

Composition: Bimetallic (center: 0.925 sterling silver; outer ring: bronze-aluminum-nickel alloy). *Weight:* 33.967 g. *Obverse:* On the silver center, the national coat of arms with the eagle in profile to the left, the feathers resembling plates of armor. On the stainless-steel outer ring, the legend **ESTADOS UNIDOS MEXICANOS** above, with a half-wreath of oak and laurel below. *Reverse:* On the outer ring, • HERENCIA NUMISMÁTICA DE MÉXICO • on the upper half, with $100 at the bottom; at left and right, respectively, M̊ and 2011. On the silver center, a reproduction of a 1913 Bolita peso (BW-286, original diameter 38.8mm). *Diameter:* 39 mm. *Edge:* Smooth reeding.

	Mintage	PL
2011	8,000	$55.00

Series II

100 pesos, Type A11.1, 2012 (Milled: Chopmarked and Counterstamped). BW-862.1, KM-UL. Prooflike.

The first coin in Series II demonstrates both the historic prestige of the Mexican 8 reales and the reach of imperial Spain. The underlying coin was issued under King Charles IV (written "IIII" on the coin). It bears Chinese chopmarks on both sides, and a Spanish counterstamp on the portrait bust. China was both a ready consumer and a determined counterfeiter of the 8 reales, so each time a silver coin passed through the hands of a Chinese bank or money-changer, it would be stamped with the handler's unique mark, or *chop*, to guarantee its silver content. Coins circulating in the Philippines, as this one did, were counterstamped by the Spanish colonial government to guarantee their legality. The counterstamp F.7° indicates the authority of King Ferdinand VII.

Series 2, BW-862.1.

Milled coinage, Bust or Portrait type, counterstamped (8 reales, Charles IV, 1804); BW-28.10.

Composition: Bimetallic (center: 0.925 sterling silver; outer ring: bronze-aluminum-nickel alloy). *Weight:* 33.967 g. *Obverse:* On the silver center, the national coat of arms with the eagle in profile to the left, the feathers resembling plates of armor. On the stainless-steel outer ring, the legend ESTADOS UNIDOS MEXICANOS above, with a half-wreath of oak and laurel below. *Reverse:* On the outer ring, • HERENCIA NUMISMÁTICA DE MÉXICO • on the upper half, with $100 at the bottom; at left and right, respectively, M̊ and 2012. On the silver center, a reproduction of an 1804-M̊ 8 reales of Charles IV (BW-28.10, original diameter 40 mm). *Diameter:* 39 mm. *Edge:* Smooth reeding.

	Mintage	PL
2012	8,000	$55.00

100 pesos, Type A11.2, 2012 (Cob). BW-862.2, KM-UL. Prooflike.

Cob coins were struck with a hammer on somewhat irregular planchets. Despite their ragged edges and lumpy surfaces, the coins were widely accepted by the public, due to the purity of their silver content (0.931 fine). The coin chosen to commemorate the cob era is an 8 reales struck during the reign of King Philip III.

Series 2, BW-862.2.

Cob coinage (8 reales, Philip III, 1608); BW-15.1.

Composition: Bimetallic (center: 0.925 sterling silver; outer ring: bronze-aluminum-nickel alloy). *Weight:* 33.967 g. *Obverse:* On the silver center, the national coat of arms with the eagle in profile to the left, the feathers resembling plates of armor. On the stainless-steel outer ring, the legend **ESTADOS UNIDOS MEXICANOS** above, with a half-wreath of oak and laurel below. *Reverse:* On the outer ring, • **HERENCIA NUMISMÁTICA DE MÉXICO** • on the upper half, with **$100** at the bottom; at left and right, respectively, M̊ and **2012**. On the silver center, a reproduction of a Philip III 8 reales, 1608-M̊ (BW-15.1, original diameter about 30 mm). *Diameter:* 39 mm. *Edge:* Smooth reeding.

	Mintage	PL
2012	8,000	$55.00

100 pesos, Type A11.3, 2012 (Royalist L.V.O.).
BW-862.3, KM-UL. Prooflike.

The War of Independence disrupted coinage for the Royalists, leading to the establishment of provisional mints. In 1810 and 1811, before the Insurgents captured the city, the Royalists produced silver coins displaying the hill of La Bufa and, on its shoulder to the right, the rock formation called El Grillo. Atop La Bufa is the cross of the chapel of Nuestra Señora del Patrocinio (Our Lady of the Patronage, a colonial convent). Below the hills is the abbreviation L.V.O. (*labor vincit omnia*, Latin for "labor conquers all"). The provisional coins were struck in the Ferdinand VII Bust style in denominations of 1/2 real, 1 real, 2 reales, and 8 reales.

Series 2, BW-862.3.

War of Independence, Royalist provisional coinage, L.V.O.
(8 reales, Zacatecas, 1811); BW-73.1.

Composition: Bimetallic (center: 0.925 sterling silver; outer ring: bronze-aluminum-nickel alloy). *Weight:* 33.967 g. *Obverse:* On the silver center, the national coat of arms with the eagle in profile to the left, the feathers resembling plates of armor. On the stainless-steel outer ring, the legend ESTADOS UNIDOS MEXICANOS above, with a half-wreath of oak and laurel below. *Reverse:* On the outer ring, • HERENCIA NUMISMÁTICA DE MÉXICO • on the upper half, with $100 at the bottom; at left and right, respectively, M̥ and 2012. On the silver center, a reproduction of a Royalist provisional L.V.O. 8 reales (BW-73.1, original diameter 41 mm). *Diameter:* 39 mm. *Edge:* Smooth reeding.

	Mintage	PL
2012	8,000	$55.00

100 pesos, Type A11.4, 2012 (Maximilian).
BW-862.4, KM-UL. Prooflike.

Near the end of the First Republic, the Mexican government attempted to convert the reales system of coinage to the decimal system. By the time of the French Intervention, however, only the 1-, 5-, and 10-centavo denominations had been produced. The French Regency decreed the minting of 5 and 10 centavos in April 1863; two years later, Emperor Maximilian decreed coins of 1/2, 1, 5, 10, 25, and 50 centavos, and 1, 5, 10, and 20 pesos, all bearing his effigy.

Series 2, BW-862.4.

Maximilian coinage (1 peso, Mexico City, 1866); BW-231.

Composition: Bimetallic (center: 0.925 sterling silver; outer ring: bronze-aluminum-nickel alloy). *Weight:* 33.967 g. *Obverse:* On the silver center, the national coat of arms with the eagle in profile to the left, the feathers resembling plates of armor. On the stainless-steel outer ring, the legend **ESTADOS UNIDOS MEXICANOS** above, with a half-wreath of oak and laurel below. *Reverse:* On the outer ring, • HERENCIA NUMISMÁTICA DE MÉXICO • on the upper half, with $100 at the bottom; at left and right, respectively, M̊ and 2012. On the silver center, a reproduction of an 1866-M̊ gold 20 pesos (BW-231, original diameter 35 mm). *Diameter:* 39 mm. *Edge:* Smooth reeding.

	Mintage	PL
2012	8,000	$55.00

100 pesos, Type A11.5, 2012 (Hand on Book).
BW-862.5, KM-UL. Prooflike.

The official reverse design chosen for gold coins of the First Republic came to be known as the Hand on Book motif. At the center of the design lies an open book inscribed with the word LEY ("law"). Over the book, a hand holds a short staff on the end of which hangs a liberty cap. The hand is pointing toward the book, linking the concepts of liberty (the cap) and the rule of law (LEY).

Series 2, BW-862.5.

Republic reales coinage, Hand on Book (8 escudos, Mexico City, 1828); BW-212.9.

Composition: Bimetallic (center: 0.925 sterling silver; outer ring: bronze-aluminum-nickel alloy). *Weight:* 33.967 g. *Obverse:* On the silver center, the national coat of arms with the eagle in profile to the left, the feathers resembling plates of armor. On the stainless-steel outer ring, the legend ESTADOS UNIDOS MEXICANOS above, with a half-wreath of oak and laurel below. *Reverse:* On the outer ring, • HERENCIA NUMISMÁTICA DE MÉXICO • on the upper half, with $100 at the bottom; at left and right, respectively, $\overset{\circ}{M}$ and 2012. On the silver center, a reproduction of an 1828-$\overset{\circ}{M}$ gold 8 escudos, assayed by J.M. (BW-212.9, original diameter 37 mm). *Diameter:* 39 mm. *Edge:* Smooth reeding.

	Mintage	PL
2012	8,000	$55.00

100 pesos, Type A11.6, 2012 (Railroad). BW-862.6, KM-UL. Prooflike.
In 1950, after two decades of planning and construction, the Ferrocarril del Sureste (Southeastern Railway) was opened (see the sidebar on pages 60). It connected the isolated Ferrocarriles Unidos de Yucatán with the larger national system, thus opening a rail line between Mexico City and the peninsula. The coin commemorating the event depicts a steam engine and tracks in front of a lushly planted hacienda, with palm trees signifying the link to Yucatán. A rising sun with bladelike rays, incused with the date 1950, fills the background.

Series 2, BW-862.6.

1905 Currency Reform coinage, Railroad (5 pesos, Mexico City, 1950); BW-553.

Composition: Bimetallic (center: 0.925 sterling silver; outer ring: bronze-aluminum-nickel alloy). *Weight:* 33.967 g. *Obverse:* On the silver center, the national coat of arms with the eagle in profile to the left, the feathers resembling plates of armor. On the stainless-steel outer ring, the legend **ESTADOS UNIDOS MEXICANOS** above, with a half-wreath of oak and laurel below. *Reverse:* On the outer ring, • **HERENCIA NUMISMÁTICA DE MÉXICO** • on the upper half, with $100 at the bottom; at left and right, respectively, M̥ and **2012**. On the silver center, a reproduction of a 1950 Railroad 5 pesos (BW-553, original diameter 40 mm). *Diameter:* 39 mm. *Edge:* Smooth reeding.

	Mintage	PL
2012	8,000	$55.00

Series III

100 pesos, Type A12.1, 2013 (Campo Morado).
BW-863.1, KM-UL. Prooflike.

During the Revolution, Guerrero was the base of operations of Emiliano Zapata, under whose authority coins were struck in seven temporary locations. The mines of Campo Morado, in particular, provided enough silver and copper to make it one of Zapata's better mints. The 2-peso design of the region is one of the most recognizable among Revolutionary coinage: a sun with a face above a smoking volcano flanked by mountains. The design appears on the only coin produced by the nearby mining camp of Suriana, which is a great rarity today.

Series 3, BW-863.1.

Mexican Revolution coinage, Campo Morado (2 pesos, Suriana, Guerrero, 1915); BW-312.

Composition: Bimetallic (center: 0.925 sterling silver; outer ring: bronze-aluminum-nickel alloy). *Weight:* 33.967 g. *Obverse:* On the silver center, the national coat of arms with the eagle in profile to the left, the feathers resembling plates of armor. On the stainless-steel outer ring, the legend **ESTADOS UNIDOS MEXICANOS** above, with a half-wreath of oak and laurel below. *Reverse:* On the outer ring, • **HERENCIA NUMISMÁTICA DE MÉXICO** • on the upper half, with $100 at the bottom; at left and right, respectively, M̊ and 2013. On the silver center, a reproduction of a Campo Morado / Suriana 2 pesos of 1915 (BW-312, original diameter 39 mm). *Diameter:* 39 mm. *Edge:* Smooth reeding.

	Mintage	PL
2013	8,000	$55.00

100 pesos, Type A12.2, 2013 (Carlos and Johanna). BW-863.2, KM-UL. Prooflike.

The first coins minted at the first mint in the New World were the coins of Carlos and Johanna (King Charles I of Spain and Queen Johanna I of Castile). A 3-reales example with mintmark ₥ and assayer mark R was chosen for the commemorative series; the denomination is represented by three dots. On the reverse are the Pillars of Hercules and the legend **PLVS VLTRA** (Plus Ultra), meaning "more beyond" or "further beyond"—referring to the notion that Christopher Columbus had proven there was more to the world beyond the limits placed by Hercules.

Series 3, BW-863.2.

Carlos and Johanna coinage, Early Series (3 reales); BW-7.

Composition: Bimetallic (center: 0.925 sterling silver; outer ring: bronze-aluminum-nickel alloy). *Weight:* 33.967 g. *Obverse:* On the silver center, the national coat of arms with the eagle in profile to the left, the feathers resembling plates of armor. On the stainless-steel outer ring, the legend **ESTADOS UNIDOS MEXICANOS** above, with a half-wreath of oak and laurel below. *Reverse:* On the outer ring, • **HERENCIA NUMISMÁTICA DE MÉXICO** • on the upper half, with **$100** at the bottom; at left and right, respectively, ₥ and **2013**. On the silver center, a reproduction of an Early Series Carlos and Johanna 3 reales (BW-7, original diameter 31 mm). *Diameter:* 39 mm. *Edge:* Smooth reeding.

	Mintage	PL
2013	8,000	$55.00

100 pesos, Type A12.3, 2013 (Balance Scale). BW-863.3, KM-UL. Prooflike.

The Balance Scale peso was intended to replace the 8 reales as a trade dollar. Its three motifs—a sword, a two-pan scale, and a scroll with the word LEY—represented the executive, judicial, and legislative branches, respectively, of Mexico's government. It was struck from 1869 through 1873, but was never widely embraced. In 1874 the government gave up on the idea of a decimal trade dollar and restored the familiar and popular Liberty Cap 8 reales for that purpose.

Series 3, BW-863.3.

Republic decimal coinage, Balance Scale (1 peso, Zacatecas, 1872); BW-258.9.

Composition: Bimetallic (center: 0.925 sterling silver; outer ring: bronze-aluminum-nickel alloy). *Weight:* 33.967 g. *Obverse:* On the silver center, the national coat of arms with the eagle in profile to the left, the feathers resembling plates of armor. On the stainless-steel outer ring, the legend ESTADOS UNIDOS MEXICANOS above, with a half-wreath of oak and laurel below. *Reverse:* On the outer ring, • HERENCIA NUMISMÁTICA DE MÉXICO • on the upper half, with $100 at the bottom; at left and right, respectively, M̥ and 2013. On the silver center, a reproduction of an 1872-Zₛ, H Balance Scale peso (BW-258.9, original diameter 37 mm). *Diameter:* 39 mm. *Edge:* Smooth reeding.

	Mintage	PL
2013	8,000	$55.00

100 pesos, Type A12.4, 2013 (Cap and Rays: Chopmarked). BW-863.4, KM-UL. Prooflike.

In the 19th century, the Mexican 8 reales was the world's most popular trade dollar, and China was eager for silver coins. On the streets of China the coins were valued by weight rather than denomination, and counterfeiting was common. Thus, each time an authentic silver coin passed through the hands of a local bank or money-changer, the handler would imprint a unique mark, or *chop*, as a guarantee of the coin's silver content.

Series 3, BW-863.4.

Republic reales coinage, Cap and Rays, chopmarked (8 reales, Chihuahua, 1887); BW-206.3.

Composition: Bimetallic (center: 0.925 sterling silver; outer ring: bronze-aluminum-nickel alloy). *Weight:* 33.967 g. *Obverse:* On the silver center, the national coat of arms with the eagle in profile to the left, the feathers resembling plates of armor. On the stainless-steel outer ring, the legend **ESTADOS UNIDOS MEXICANOS** above, with a half-wreath of oak and laurel below. *Reverse:* On the outer ring, • **HERENCIA NUMISMÁTICA DE MÉXICO** • on the upper half, with **$100** at the bottom; at left and right, respectively, M̊ and **2013**. On the silver center, a reproduction of an 1887-CA 8 reales, assayed by M.M. (BW-206.3, original diameter 39 mm). *Diameter:* 39 mm. *Edge:* Smooth reeding.

	Mintage	PL
2013	8,000	$55.00

100 pesos, Type A12.5, 2013 (Supreme National Congress of America). BW-863.5, KM-UL. Prooflike.

On August 19, 1811, in the village of Zitácuaro, Michoacán, Ignacio López Rayón announced the first independent government of Mexico: the Suprema Junta de América (Supreme National Congress of America). The coinage features an eagle standing on a nopal cactus that is growing atop a brick bridge with three arches (possibly one of the local aqueducts). This is the first appearance on coinage of the eagle and cactus that are now ingrained in Mexico's national identity. The coins were minted only in 1811 and 1812, as the junta was supplanted by a new congress in Chilpancingo in 1813.

Series 3, BW-863.5.

War of Independence, Insurgent coinage, Supreme National Congress of America (8 reales, 1811); BW-153.1.

Composition: Bimetallic (center: 0.925 sterling silver; outer ring: bronze-aluminum-nickel alloy). *Weight:* 33.967 g. *Obverse:* On the silver center, the national coat of arms with the eagle in profile to the left, the feathers resembling plates of armor. On the stainless-steel outer ring, the legend **ESTADOS UNIDOS MEXICANOS** above, with a half-wreath of oak and laurel below. *Reverse:* On the outer ring, • **HERENCIA NUMISMÁTICA DE MÉXICO** • on the upper half, with $100 at the bottom; at left and right, respectively, M̥ and 2013. On the silver center, a reproduction of an 1811-dated Supreme National Congress of America silver 8 reales (BW-153.1, original diameter 35 mm). *Diameter:* 39 mm. *Edge:* Smooth reeding.

	Mintage	PL
2013	8,000	$55.00

100 pesos, Type A12.6, 2013 (Iturbide). BW-863.6, KM-UL. Prooflike.

The coinage of the short rule of Augustín de Iturbide consists largely of issues from the mint in Mexico City. These coins depict a right-facing bust of Emperor Augustín I on the obverse, and a crowned Mexican eagle on a nopal cactus growing from a rock on the reverse. The Supreme National Congress of America coinage was the first to display the eagle-and-cactus motif (see the previous entry); Iturbide's coins were the first to depict the emblem in something like its modern form.

Series 3, BW-863.6.

Iturbide coinage (8 escudos, Mexico City, 1822); BW-168.1.

Composition: Bimetallic (center: 0.925 sterling silver; outer ring: bronze-aluminum-nickel alloy). *Weight:* 33.967 g. *Obverse:* On the silver center, the national coat of arms with the eagle in profile to the left, the feathers resembling plates of armor. On the stainless-steel outer ring, the legend ESTADOS UNIDOS MEXICANOS above, with a half-wreath of oak and laurel below. *Reverse:* On the outer ring, · HERENCIA NUMISMÁTICA DE MÉXICO · on the upper half, with $100 at the bottom; at left and right, respectively, M̊ and 2013. On the silver center, a reproduction of an 1822-M̊, JM gold 8 escudos (BW-168.1, original diameter 37 mm). *Diameter:* 39 mm. *Edge:* Smooth reeding.

	Mintage	PL
2013	8,000	$55.00

Series IV

100 pesos, Type A13.1, 2014 (Muera Huerta).
BW-864.1, KM-UL. Prooflike.

In 1914 two of Pancho Villa's generals, Severino Ceniceros and Calixto Contreras, ordered the minting of the now-famous Muera Huerta ("Death to [President Victoriano] Huerta") pesos. It was an act of supreme contempt for the president, who had ordered Villa's death by firing squad. The type chosen to commemorate this iconic coin is one of the varieties also known as a Six Star peso, for the six stars on the reverse.

Series 4, BW-864.1.

Mexican Revolution coinage, Muera Huerta (1 peso, Six Stars, Durango, 1914); BW-288.2.

Composition: Bimetallic (center: 0.925 sterling silver; outer ring: bronze-aluminum-nickel alloy). *Weight:* 33.967 g. *Obverse:* On the silver center, the national coat of arms with the eagle in profile to the left, the feathers resembling plates of armor. On the stainless-steel outer ring, the legend ESTADOS UNIDOS MEXICANOS above, with a half-wreath of oak and laurel below. *Reverse:* On the outer ring, • HERENCIA NUMISMÁTICA DE MÉXICO • on the upper half, with $100 at the bottom; at left and right, respectively, M̥ and 2014. On the silver center, a reproduction of a 1914 Muera Huerta peso, Six Stars (BW-288.2, original diameter 38.9 mm). *Diameter:* 39 mm. *Edge:* Smooth reeding.

	Mintage	PL
2014		$55.00

100 pesos, Type A13.2, 2014 (Bust, *Pelucona*).
BW-864.2, KM-UL. Prooflike.

The gold Bust-style colonial coins of kings Philip V and Ferdinand VI are known as *peluconas*, thanks to the style of the portrait's wig (in English, a *peruke*; in Spanish, a *pelucona*).

Series 4, BW-864.2.

Milled coinage, *pelucona* (8 escudos, Ferdinand VI, 1748); BW-33.3.

Composition: Bimetallic (center: 0.925 sterling silver; outer ring: bronze-aluminum-nickel alloy). *Weight:* 33.967 g. *Obverse:* On the silver center, the national coat of arms with the eagle in profile to the left, the feathers resembling plates of armor. On the stainless-steel outer ring, the legend **ESTADOS UNIDOS MEXICANOS** above, with a half-wreath of oak and laurel below. *Reverse:* On the outer ring, · **HERENCIA NUMISMÁTICA DE MÉXICO** · on the upper half, with **$100** at the bottom; at left and right, respectively, M̊ and **2014**. On the silver center, a reproduction of a 1748-M̊ gold 8 escudos of Ferdinand VI, assayer mark M-F (BW-33.3, original diameter 38 mm). *Diameter:* 39 mm. *Edge:* Smooth reeding.

	Mintage	PL
2014		$55.00

100 pesos, Type A13.3, 2014 (L. Y S.). BW-864.3, KM-UL. Prooflike.

On June 3, 1915, in the midst of the revolutionary upheaval, the State of Oaxaca declared itself free and sovereign (*libre y soberano*, abbreviated L. Y S.). The governor, José Inés Dávila, opened the old Oaxaca mint to produce coins for the new sovereign state. The circumstances were short-lived, however, as the forces of Venustiano Carranza entered the city of Oaxaca in March 1916; Dávila was executed several weeks later.

Series 4, BW-864.3.

Mexican Revolution coinage, Estado de Oaxaca L. Y S. (60 pesos, 1916); BW-355.

Composition: Bimetallic (center: 0.925 sterling silver; outer ring: bronze-aluminum-nickel alloy). *Weight:* 33.967 g. *Obverse:* On the silver center, the national coat of arms with the eagle in profile to the left, the feathers resembling plates of armor. On the stainless-steel outer ring, the legend **ESTADOS UNIDOS MEXICANOS** above, with a half-wreath of oak and laurel below. *Reverse:* On the outer ring, • **HERENCIA NUMISMÁTICA DE MÉXICO** • on the upper half, with $100 at the bottom; at left and right, respectively, M̥ and **2014**. On the silver center, a reproduction of a 1916 gold L. Y S. 60 pesos (BW-355, original diameter 40 mm). *Diameter:* 39 mm. *Edge:* Smooth reeding.

	Mintage	PL
2014		$55.00

100 pesos, Type A13.4, 2014 (Royalist Provisional). BW-864.4, KM-UL. Prooflike.

In Oaxaca in 1812, Royalist forces under Lt. General Antonio Pío González-Saravia had a local blacksmith shop prepare provisional, cast-silver coinage to alleviate the shortage of money. The coins were minted for only a brief time before the Insurgents took the city. The variety chosen to illustrate the type is called *león grande* ("large lion"), with the lion on the reverse filling the shield. (A reverse with normal-sized lion is shown for comparison.)

Series 4, BW-864.4.

War of Independence, Royalist provisional coinage (8 reales, Oaxaca, 1812); BW-60. Reverse with large lion.

Reverse with normal-sized lion.

Composition: Bimetallic (center: 0.925 sterling silver; outer ring: bronze-aluminum-nickel alloy). *Weight:* 33.967 g. *Obverse:* On the silver center, the national coat of arms with the eagle in profile to the left, the feathers resembling plates of armor.

On the stainless-steel outer ring, the legend ESTADOS UNIDOS MEXICANOS above, with a half-wreath of oak and laurel below. *Reverse:* On the outer ring, • HERENCIA NUMISMÁTICA DE MÉXICO • on the upper half, with $100 at the bottom; at left and right, respectively, M̊ and 2014. On the silver center, a reproduction of an 1812 Royalist provisional 8 reales from Oaxaca (BW-60, original diameter 40 mm). *Diameter:* 39 mm. *Edge:* Smooth reeding.

	Mintage	PL
2014		$55.00

100 pesos, Type A13.5, 2014 (Milled: Counterstamped and Punched). BW-864.5, KM-UL. Prooflike.

Among the most widely accepted coins in the Caribbean during the colonial era were the Mexican 8 reales, which were counterstamped by colonial authorities to indicate their validity. The example representing these coins, an 1806-M̊ 8 reales, is counterstamped with **E&D** (for the towns Essequibo and Demerary) and a value of **3.G.L** (3 Dutch guilders). It has also been counterpunched in a starburst shape; the punched-out section was used to make a smaller-denomination coin (3 bits; see the illustrated example).

Series 4, BW-864.5.

Milled coinage, counterstamped and punched (8 reales, Charles IV, 1806); BW-28.10.

Punched-out 3 bits (from a different coin than the above).

Composition: Bimetallic (center: 0.925 sterling silver; outer ring: bronze-aluminum-nickel alloy). *Weight:* 33.967 g. *Obverse:* On the silver center, the national coat of arms with the eagle in profile to the left, the feathers resembling plates of armor. On the stainless-steel outer ring, the legend **ESTADOS UNIDOS MEXICANOS** above, with a half-wreath of oak and laurel below. *Reverse:* On the outer ring, • **HERENCIA NUMISMÁTICA DE MÉXICO** • on the upper half, with $100 at the bottom; at left and right, respectively, M̊ and 2014. On the silver center, a reproduction of a milled 8 reales of Charles IV, dated 1806-M̊ (BW-28.10, original diameter 40 mm), counterstamped and counterpunched. *Diameter:* 39 mm. *Edge:* Smooth reeding.

	Mintage	PL
2014		$55.00

100 pesos, Type A13.6, 2014 (Republic Copper). BW-864.6, KM-UL. Prooflike.

During the First Republic, the state and federal governments struck small-denomination copper coins for which the public could exchange their colonial coppers. Overproduction and rampant counterfeiting began to severely devalue the coins, and in 1935 the national congress revoked the rights of the states to establish mints.

Series 4, BW-864.6.

Republic reales coinage, Upright Eagle (1/4 real, 1834); BW-197.3.

Composition: Bimetallic (center: 0.925 sterling silver; outer ring: bronze-aluminum-nickel alloy). *Weight:* 33.967 g. *Obverse:* On the silver center, the national coat of arms with the eagle in profile to the left, the feathers resembling plates of armor. On the stainless-steel outer ring, the legend **ESTADOS UNIDOS MEXICANOS** above, with a half-wreath of oak and laurel below. *Reverse:* On the outer ring, • **HERENCIA NUMISMÁTICA DE MÉXICO** • on the upper half, with $100 at the bottom; at left and right, respectively, M̊ and **2014**. On the silver center, a reproduction of an Upright Eagle copper 1/4 real, 1834-M̊ (BW-197.3, original diameter 27 mm). *Diameter:* 39 mm. *Edge:* Smooth reeding.

	Mintage	PL
2014		$55.00

Celebrating Mexico's Historic Coinage

The Numismatic Heritage Series, though it may be novel to some collectors, is not the first collection to celebrate Mexico's rich numismatic history. The Sociedad Numismática de México initiated a Coins on Medals series in 1971, with the obverse and reverse of each medal depicting the obverse and reverse of a historic Mexican coin. The medals were issued intermittently up to the late 1990s, ending with a total of 20 medals, a handful of which are quite rare. Although there is not a perfect overlap of the subject coins in the Coins on Medals and Numismatic Heritage series, most types are found in both collections. In addition to legends pertaining to the subject coins, the medals all have CONMEMORATIVA DE LA MONEDA MEXICANA on one side and MEXICO 1536 PRIMUM NUMISMA AMERICÆ on the other, along with the date of issue, the name of the Sociedad Numismatica, and pertinent details about the subject coin.

An interesting collecting challenge would be to assemble a set of Numismatic Heritage coins alongside examples of the originals, and, availability and cost permitting, the corresponding Coins on Medals issues. Several of the latter are pictured here.

War of Independence, coinage of Gen. José María Morelos, issued 1975, 38 mm. (Compare to Numismatic Heritage Series I, BW-861.3.)

War of Independence, coinage of Zacatecas, 8 reales, issued 1974, 38 mm. (Compare to Numismatic Heritage Series 2, BW-862.3.)

First coinage of Charles and Johanna, 4 reales, issued 1971, 38 mm. (Compare to Numismatic Heritage Series 3, BW-863.2.)

Bust coinage, 8 reales, issued 1973, 38 mm. (Compare to Numismatic Heritage Series 1, BW-861.2.)

CHICHÉN ITZÁ "070707" SERIES

In the autumn of 2012, Banco de México released a historically important series of five coins commemorating the declaration of Chichén Itzá as one of the "New-7Wonders of the World," after a public poll conducted by the New7Wonders Foundation in Zurich, Switzerland. (The site had been declared a World Cultural Heritage Site by UNESCO in 1988.) The New7Wonders designation was issued on July 7, 2007; hence the numerals 070707, which appear below the Casa de Moneda's mintmark on the reverse of each coin. These undated coins, honoring a part of Mayan cultural history, are a continuing effort on the part of the Casa de Moneda and the Banco de México to disperse Mexico's cultural history throughout the nation's coinage.

5 pesos, Type A26, (2012) (Nunnery). BW-870.1, KM-UL. Proof.

The Nunnery is part of the area of Chichén Itzá known as the Central Group, which also includes the Observatory, the Church, and Akab Dzib (Temple of Dark Writing, a structure that was filled with mysterious glyphs and that overlooked a *cenote*, or sacred well). Collectively, these buildings formed a sort of governmental palace. Despite its name, the Nunnery was likely a residence for high-ranking individuals. At a distance, the shape of the building and its architectural elements cause the structure to resemble the Chaac masks that decorate its surface.

Composition: 0.999 silver. *Weight:* 31.10 g. *Obverse:* At the center, a small national coat of arms with the eagle facing left, its feathers resembling plates of armor, encircled by a spray of oak and laurel (below) and the legend **ESTADOS UNIDOS MEXICANOS** (above). Surrounding the modern coat of arms, 10 additional coats of arms used throughout Mexico's history. *Reverse:* At the center of a plain field, the Casa de las Monjas (Nunnery Building), with $5 to the left and M̊ / 070707 to the right. At the top, **CHICHÉN ITZÁ**; at the bottom, **CASA DE LAS MONJAS**. *Diameter:* 40 mm. *Edge:* Plain.

	Mintage	PL
2012	10,000	$90.00

5 pesos, Type A27, (2012) (Church). BW-870.2, KM-UL. Proof.

Located in the same group of buildings as the Nunnery, the Church is one of the most frequently photographed of the structures, thanks to a surface that is heavily decorated with carved masks. Motifs on the building include serpents, the god Chaac, and four animals—an armadillo, a turtle, a snail, and a crab. In Mayan mythology, four *bacabs*, or deities, hold up the sky; they are represented by these and other animal forms in art and architecture.

Composition: 0.999 silver. *Weight:* 31.10 g. *Obverse:* At the center, a small national coat of arms with the eagle facing left, its feathers resembling plates of armor, encircled by a spray of oak and laurel (below) and the legend **ESTADOS UNIDOS MEXICANOS** (above). Surrounding the modern coat of arms, 10 additional coats of arms used throughout Mexico's history. *Reverse:* At the center of a plain field, the building called La Iglesia (The Church), with $5 to the left and M̥ / 070707 to the right. At the top, **CHICHÉN ITZÁ**; at the bottom, **LA IGLESIA**. *Diameter:* 40 mm. *Edge:* Plain.

	Mintage	PL
2012	10,000	$90.00

5 pesos, Type A28, (2012) (Observatory). BW-870.3, KM-UL. Proof.

Placed atop a large, square, terraced base on a longer rectangular base, the building called the Observatory contains two circular galleries with a stone spiral staircase leading to an observation room at the top. (The rounded dome and the spiral staircase lend the building its other nickname: El Caracol, or The Snail). The windows in the building were oriented so that the movements of the sun, moon, stars, and other celestial bodies could be easily tracked. Evidence of rebuilding indicates it needed to be "recalibrated" periodically.

Composition: 0.999 silver. *Weight:* 31.10 g. *Obverse:* At the center, a small national coat of arms with the eagle facing left, its feathers resembling plates of armor, encircled by a spray of oak and laurel (below) and the legend **ESTADOS UNIDOS MEXICANOS** (above). Surrounding the modern coat of arms, 10 additional coats of arms used throughout Mexico's history. *Reverse:* At the center of a plain field, the Observatory (Observatorio), with $5 to the left and M̥ / 070707 to the right. At the top, **CHICHÉN ITZÁ**; at the bottom, **OBSERVATORIO**. *Diameter:* 40 mm. *Edge:* Plain.

	Mintage	PL
2012	10,000	$90.00

10 pesos, Type A10, (2012) (Temple of Warriors). BW-870.4, KM-UL. Proof.

The Temple of Warriors is a step-pyramid structure that was intended for large gatherings. It has four platforms, and is flanked on two sides by 200 columns, carved with Toltec warriors, that were once plastered and painted in bright colors. A wide stair rises up the front to a building on top, the Temple of Chaac, with serpent-shaped columns in the doorways. The serpents have basins in their heads that may have been used for oil lamps.

Composition: 0.999 silver. *Weight:* 62.20 g. *Obverse:* At the center, a small national coat of arms with the eagle facing left, its feathers resembling plates of armor, encircled by a spray of oak and laurel (below) and the legend **ESTADOS UNIDOS MEXICANOS** (above). Surrounding the modern coat of arms, 10 additional coats of arms used throughout Mexico's history. *Reverse:* Filling the center of the field to the right-hand and lower edges, the Temple of Warriors (Templo de los Guerreros), with **$10** and **M̊ / 070707** in the field to the left. At the top, slightly left of center, **CHICHÉN ITZÁ**; at the bottom (incused), **TEMPLO DE LOS GUERREROS**. *Diameter:* 48 mm. *Edge:* Plain.

	Mintage	PL
2012	3,000	$200.00

20 pesos, Type A5, (2012) (Kukulcán). BW-870.5, KM-UL. Proof.

Kukulcán Pyramid, located at the city center and decorated with serpent and jaguar motifs, was used as an astronomical observatory. The number of steps and panels correspond perfectly to the number of solar days, the number of years in a Toltec cycle, and the number of months in a Mayan calendar year. It is an architectural wonder of numbers and design, especially as a peculiar combination of light and shadow on the stairs during the vernal and autumnal equinoxes make it appear as if a large serpent were slithering down the pyramid. Its massive size, central location, and formal design lend it another nickname: El Castillo (The Castle).

Shown reduced, actual size 65 mm.

Composition: 0.999 silver. *Weight:* 155.51 g. *Obverse:* At the center, a small national coat of arms with the eagle facing left, its feathers resembling plates of armor, encircled by a spray of oak and laurel (below) and the legend **ESTADOS UNIDOS MEXICANOS** (above). Surrounding the modern coat of arms, 10 additional coats of arms used throughout Mexico's history. *Reverse:* At the center of a plain field, Kukulcán Pyramid, with $20 to the left and M̊ / 070707 to the right. At the top, **CHICHÉN ITZÁ**; at the bottom, **PIRÁMIDE / DE KUKULCÁN**. *Diameter:* 65 mm. *Edge:* Plain.

	Mintage	PL
2012	3,000	$200.00

Chichén Itzá

The name of the pre-Columbian city Chichén Itzá means "at the mouth of the well of Itza." It was one of the largest Mayan cities, and may have held a very diverse population due to migrations from all over Mexico. This might explain the multitude of architectural styles found there. The site contains mainly stone buildings, some of which have been restored in the past 100 years. The famous Kukulkán Pyramid (also known as El Castillo) is located in the center of the city.

When the Spanish first arrived in Mexico, Mayans were still living in Chichén Itzá, although it was no longer an active urban metropolis. The Spaniards tried to move in, and began greedily dividing up the buildings and lands, but the docile Mayans turned extremely hostile and drove the Spanish soldiers out. It was a relatively short-lived victory, however; although it took another 50 years, the Spaniards eventually triumphed.

Chichén Itzá is the second most frequently visited ancient site in Mexico, with more than one million visitors each year.

El Castillo and the Nunnery in the early 1900s—long before Chichén Itzá was a major visitors' site.

MINT AND PROOF SETS

MINT SETS

The Banco de México began issuing Mint sets in 1977 in soft plastic sheets and continued to do so until 1989. Today, the Casa de Moneda de México strikes the coins and the Banco de México assembles the sets and distributes them. Technically they are not Mint sets, but the bank, as well as the Mexican hobby community in general, refers to them as Mint sets rather than as year sets.

Earlier-dated sets are common in the marketplace, but whether they are official Banco de México products is unknown. They are often seen packaged with a contemporary stamp or Easter Seal.

EARLY SERIES

In the early series the soft plastic pages used were not acid free, and many coins from these sets have been contaminated by polyvinyl chloride, commonly called PVC—a particular plastic that reacts with metal to produce an unattractive green film and spotting.

	BU
1977, half page (9 coins). BW-MS 1, KM-BS6	$150
1977, full page (9 coins). BW-MS 2, KM-BS7	120
1978, half page (9 coins). BW-MS 3, KM-BS8	150
1978, full page (9 coins). BW-MS 4, KM-BS9	120
1979, half page (8 coins). BW-MS 5, KM-BS10	25
1979, full page (8 coins). BW-MS 6, KM-BS11	25
1980, full page (9 coins). BW-MS 7, KM-BS12	20
1981, full page (9 coins). BW-MS 8, KM-BS13	20
1982, full page (7 coins). BW-MS 9, KM-BS14	20
1983, full page (11 coins, Round-Top 3 twenty centavos). BW-MS 10, KM-BS15	20
1983, full page (11 coins, Flat-Top 3 twenty centavos). BW-MS 10.1, KM-BS16	18
1984, full page (8 coins). BW-MS 11, KM-BS17	20
1985, full page (12 coins). BW-MS 12, KM-BS18	25
1986, full page (7 coins). BW-MS 13, KM-BS20	20
1987, full page (9 coins). BW-MS 14, KM-BS21	20
1988, full page (8 coins). BW-MS 15, KM-BS22	25
1989, full page (10 coins). BW-MS 16, KM-BS23	25

The illustrated set has been removed from its original, corrosive PVC packaging and stored in an album page from the Banco de México.

Late Series

Around 1992 the Banco de México began issuing Mint sets in hard plastic cases to replace the soft plastic sheets used in the early series. The bank then re-packaged the early series (1970–1989) in the hard plastic cases and continued to use the hard cases until 2000. In some instances these sets did not have examples of all coins issued in that year.

1970 Late Series Mint Set.

	BU
1970 (7 coins). BW-MS 17, KM-BS UL	$20
1971 (6 coins). BW-MS 18, KM-BS UL	20
1972 (6 coins). BW-MS 19, KM-BS1	35
1973 (5 coins). BW-MS 20, KM-BS2	25
1974 (7 coins). BW-MS 21, KM-BS3	35
1975 (7 coins). BW-MS 22, KM-BS4	25
1976 (9 coins). BW-MS 23, KM-BS5	20
1977 (9 coins). BW-MS 24, KM-BS6	40
1978 (9 coins). BW-MS 25, KM-BS8	40
1979 (9 coins). BW-MS 26, KM-BS10	30
1980 (9 coins). BW-MS 27, KM-BS12	30
1981 (9 coins). BW-MS 28, KM-BS13	30
1982 (7 coins). BW-MS 29, KM-BS14	25
1983 (10 coins, Round-Top 3 twenty centavos). BW-MS 30, KM-BS15	25
1983 (10 coins, Flat-Top 3 twenty centavos). BW-MS 30.1, KM-BS16	22

	BU
1984 (8 coins). BW-MS 31, KM-BS17	$30
1985 (12 coins). BW-MS 32, KM-BS19	35
1986 (7 coins). BW-MS 33, KM-BS20	25
1987 (9 coins). BW-MS 34, KM-BS21	25
1988 (8 coins). BW-MS 35, KM-BS22	30
1989 (10 coins). BW-MS 36, KM-BS23	25
1990 (8 coins). BW-MS 37, KM-BS24	25
1991 (4 coins). BW-MS 38, KM-BS25	20
1992 (5 coins). BW-MS 39, KM-BS26	20
1992 (8 N$ coins). BW-MS 40, KM-BS27	35
1993A (7 N$ coins). BW-MS 41, KM-BS28	25
1993B (3 N$ coins). BW-MS 42, KM-BS29	40
1994A (7 N$ coins). BW-MS 43, KM-BS30	25
1994B (3 N$ coins). BW-MS 43.1, KM-BS31	35
1995 (9 N$ coins). BW-MS 44, KM-BS32	60
1996 (6 N$ coins). BW-MS 45, KM-BS33	35
1997 (8 coins). BW-MS 46, KM-BS34	35
1998 (8 coins). BW-MS 47, KM-BS35	35
1999 (8 coins). BW-MS 48, KM-BS36	35

CURRENT SERIES

In 2000 the Banco de México continued to issue annual Mint sets, but the designs of the lightweight cardboard packaging were changed each year.

2001 Current Series Mint Set.

BU	
2000 (7 coins). BW-MS 49, KM-BS37	$35
2000 (3 coins). BW-MS 50, KM-BS UL	35
2001 (10 coins). BW-MS 51, KM-BS38	35
2002 (8 coins). BW-MS 52, KM-BS39	35
2003 (6 coins). BW-MS 53, KM-BS40	35
2004 (7 coins). BW-MS 54, KM-BS UL	35
2005 (7 coins). BW-MS 55, KM-BS UL	35
2006 (7 coins). BW-MS 56, KM-BS UL	35
2007 (7 coins). BW-MS 57, KM-BS UL	35
2008 (7 coins). BW-MS 58, KM-BS UL	35
2009 (7 coins). BW-MS 59, KM-BS UL	35
2010 (7 coins). BW-MS 60, KM-BS UL	35
2011 (7 coins). BW-MS 61, KM-BS UL	35

BICENTENNIAL OF INDEPENDENCE AND CENTENNIAL OF THE REVOLUTION

In 2008, two 5-peso commemorative series were initiated to celebrate the Bicentennial of Independence and the Centennial of the Revolution. The lightweight cardboard packaging has designs appropriate to the area of interest. Details on the persons honored during each year of the two series are given in chapter 3. (See page 313 of this chapter for the Proof sets.)

2008 Bicentennial of Independence Mint Set.

	BU
Bicentennial of Independence, 2008 (7 coins). BW-MS 70, KM-BS UL	$45
Bicentennial of Independence, 2009 (6 coins). BW-MS 72, KM-BS UL	45
Bicentennial of Independence, 2010 (6 coins). BW-MS 74, KM-BS UL	45
Centennial of the Revolution, 2008 (6 coins). BW-MS 71, KM BS UL	45
Centennial of the Revolution, 2009 (7 coins). BW-MS 73, KM BS UL	45
Centennial of the Revolution, 2010 (5 coins). BW-MS 75, KM BS UL	45

Note: At the conclusion of these two series, the Banco de México issued a complete Mint set consisting of all 37 coins. The value of this set in its original packaging is approximately $270.

1992–1993 PRESENTATION MINT SETS

In 1993 several Presentation Mint Sets were assembled by the Casa de Moneda de México. The nine-piece sets were presented in a wooden case with CONO MONETARIO MEXICANO 1993 and M̥ CASA DE MONEDA DE MÉXICO M̥ laser-engraved on the wooden case.

The Reform coinage sets contain the following coins, dated 1992 (except where noted otherwise): 5 centavos, 10 centavos (1993), 20 centavos (1993), 50 centavos, and New 1, 2, 5, 10, and 20 pesos. The number of sets assembled is unknown.

1992–1993 Presentation Mint Set.

	BU
1992–1993 (9 coins), BW-PMS 1, KM-BS28	$225

PROOF SETS

PATTERN PROOF SETS

In 1983 the Casa de Moneda struck Proof sets with 1982 and 1983 coins in the sets. The first 50 assembled sets did not contain the Proof Libertads, but did include two coins that were not used in the 998 sets with Proof Libertads: the 20 centavos of 1983 (KM-491) and the 50 centavos of 1983 (KM-492).

The seven coins contained in the Pattern Proof Sets without Libertad are as follows:

20 centavos, 1983, Type 9. BW-530, KM-491

50 centavos, 1983, Type 9, BW-541, KM-492

1 peso, 1983, Type 8, BW-549, KM-460. PF. 5 pesos, 1982, Type 9. BW-560, KM-485

10 pesos, 1982, Type 5. BW-566, KM-477.2

20 pesos, 1982, Type 1. BW-568, KM-486

50 pesos, 1983, Type 1. BW-577, KM-490

The eight coins contained in the Pattern Proof Sets with Libertad:

20 centavos, 1983, Type 8. BW-529, KM-442

50 centavos, 1983, Type 8. BW-540, KM-452

1 peso, 1983, Type 8. BW-549, KM-460

5 pesos, 1982, Type 9. BW-560, KM-485

10 pesos, 1982, Type 5. BW-566, KM-477.2

20 pesos, 1982, Type 1. BW-568, KM-486

50 pesos, 1983, Type 1. BW-577, KM-490

Libertad, 1983. BW-880, KM-494.1

Reportedly, 998 Brilliant Uncirculated Libertads were withdrawn from inventory and melted to strike the Proof 1-ounce coins. The Proof sets were packaged in facilities other than the mint, and there are some variations in the packaging.

1982–1983 Proof Set With Libertad.

	Mintage	PF
1982–1983 "Pattern Proof Set" (8 coins). BW-PS 1, KM-PS 2	50 sets	$750
1982–1983 (7 coins, without Libertad). BW-PS 2, KM-PS 3		350
1982–1983 (8 coins, with Libertad). BW-PS 3, KM-PS 1	998 sets	500

Rainbow Proof Sets

In 1989 the Casa de Moneda, under contract with a private firm, struck Proof coins in 1/4-ounce platinum, 1/2-ounce gold, and 1-ounce silver. They were packaged in nondescript, dark-blue cases outside the mint. It was reported that 3,500 Proof 1/2-ounce gold pieces were also struck, but this report appears to be erroneous, as only a little more than 700 Rainbow Proof Sets were prepared.

Rainbow Proof Set.

Mintage		PF
1989 (3 coins). BW-PS 4, KM-PS12	738 sets	$1,700

1995 Proof Sets

In 1995, sets were prepared containing all circulating coinage in Proof, plus the 5 pesos, which was struck in Proof only. The sets were issued in two packaging styles but were priced the same.

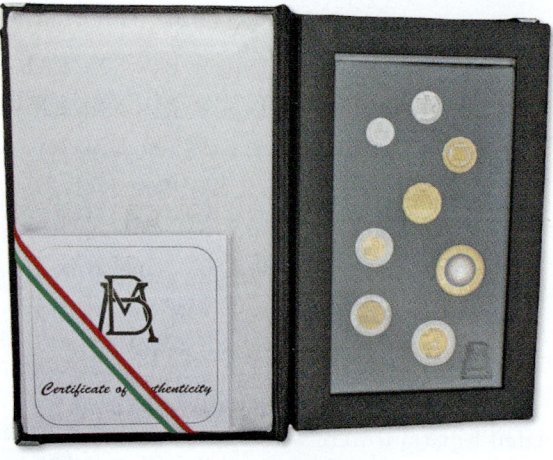

1995 Proof Set.

	Mintage	PF
1995 (8 coins). KM-UL, BW-PS 5	6,981 sets	$50

Bicentennial of Independence and Centennial of the Revolution

In 2010, Proof sets were issued for the Bicentennial of Independence and the Centennial of the Revolution commemorative series. Each set is packaged in a velvet case (Independence, green; Revolution, red) with a certificate. Details on the persons honored during each year of the two series are given in chapter 3. (See page 309 of this chapter for the Brilliant Uncirculated Mint Sets.)

Mint and Proof Sets • 315

2008 Bicentennial of
Independence Proof Set.

2008 Centennial of the
Revolution Proof Set.

	Mintage	PL
Bicentennial of Independence, 2008 (7 coins). BW-PS 6, KM-UL	1,000 sets	$50
Bicentennial of Independence, 2009 (6 coins). BW-PS 7, KM-UL	1,000 sets	45
Bicentennial of Independence, 2010 (6 coins). BW-PS 8, KM-UL	1,000 sets	45
Centennial of the Revolution, 2008 (6 coins). BW-PS 9, KM-UL	1,000 sets	45
Centennial of the Revolution, 2009 (7 coins). BW-PS 10, KM-UL	1,000 sets	50
Centennial of the Revolution, 2010 (5 coins). BW-PS 11, KM-UL	1,000 sets	40

Note: At the conclusion of these two series, the Banco de México issued three complete Proof sets. The values of these sets, in their original packaging, are as follows: the Bicentennial of Independence complete Proof set (19 coins), $140; the Centennial of the Revolution complete Proof set (18 coins), $135; and a combination Proof set consisting of all 37 coins, $275.

6

SILVER BULLION COINAGE
UNA ONZA

Over the centuries since it was first colonized by Spain and later won independence, Mexico has been one of the world's largest silver producers. It was always competitive in the silver trade-dollar market with the Liberty Cap 8 reales and Liberty Cap pesos, which were discontinued in 1909. In 1949, in an attempt to reestablish itself in world trade-dollar activities, Mexico issued the "Una Onza" (One Ounce) coin, following up with issues in 1978 through 1980. In 1982, Mexico instituted the silver Libertad program, which continues to the present day.

Onzas have no legal-tender status, and thus are subject to customs duties and regulations. All are 41 mm in diameter, with a reeded edge. The legends are in a sans-serif typeface. The obverse of the onza features the historic screw-press design (see the sidebar), while the reverse bears a balance scale.

The Screw Press

In the 1490s, while the Aztecs in Tenochtitlán were unknowingly enjoying the last decades before Spanish conquest and had no knowledge of (or interest in) coins, European populations were expanding. The need for coins was increasing; not only were the Europeans on the hunt for new sources of gold and silver, but their inventors were also looking for ways to make coins faster and to higher standards. The ancient method of coinage was to strike a disk of metal between two dies with a hammer. The resulting coins had unevenly impressed surfaces and rough edges, from which it was all too easy for unscrupulous people to snip or shave little bits of metal without detection. The problem was widely acknowledged: "All coins which do not have the rim complete, are not to be accepted as good," wrote Leonardo da Vinci. "[Thus,] all the coins should be a perfect circle. . . . Therefore have several plates of metal made of the same size and thickness, all drawn through the same gauge so as to come out in strips [from which] you will stamp the coins, . . . perfectly round and of the exact thickness, and weight." (Although da Vinci invented a drop-press device for punching out blanks from a strip of metal, no one knows whether it was actually used.)

The basic screw-press design: while one person fed blanks into the press, a team of men turned the weighted arm. Over time, the press was modified to replace human power with horse or hydraulic power, but the basic principles remain the same. The simple design is so effective that even today, smaller versions occupy basements and workshops the world over, allowing their users to craft designs in metal single-handedly and without the use of heat or electricity.

About a half-century later in Europe, the devices da Vinci envisioned had been created and refined: machines for producing the strips and punching out the blanks, and mechanical presses for stamping the designs. One of these presses was the *roller press,* in which the blanks were squeezed between heavy, rolling cylinders that impressed the blanks with designs. The other was the *screw press:* a large device with a horizontal arm, weighted at both ends, used to turn a screw that drove the upper coinage die downward onto the blank, which was held in place in the lower die. The utility of these methods was apparent from the first, and many countries attempted to use them—but most governments faced too much resistance from the established coin makers, who feared for their livelihoods. Thus, hammered coinage remained the standard (or at least the co-standard) in most of Europe until the mid-1600s.

Spain, an early adopter of mechanized minting, opted for the roller press, with which it produced its first milled coins in 1585. England and France eventually gravitated to the screw press, to which the Spanish mints switched in 1700. In 1732, Spain directed the mints in colonial Mexico to adopt the screw press, as well. Their first coinage, the Pillar dollar, was valued throughout the world for its metallic purity and the beauty of its design, and the historic screw press remains a symbol of the Casa de Moneda de México to this day.

1949. BW-875.1, KM-M49a.

Composition: 0.925 silver, .075 copper. *Weight:* 33.625 g. *Obverse:* A screw press at the center, with the legend CASA DE MONEDA DE MEXICO reading clockwise from upper left and 1949 reading counterclockwise at lower left. Above the press, the mintmark M̥. *Reverse:* At the center, a balance scale with PESO / 33.625 / GRAMOS above the left arm and LEY / 0.925 below the pillar. The legend UNA ONZA TROY = 480 GRANOS DE PLATA PURA ★ surrounds. *Diameter:* 41 mm. *Edge:* Reeded.

	Mintage	F	VF	EF	Unc.	BU
1949	1,000,000	BV	BV	BV	$40	$45

1978–1980. BW-875.2–875.8, KM-M49b.1–M49b.5.

1978, obverse, Variety 1.   1978, obverse, Variety 2.

1978, reverse.

Silver Bullion Coinage • 319

1979, obverse.

1979, reverse, Variety 3.

1979, reverse, Variety 4.

1980, Variety 5.1.

1980, Variety 5.

1980, Variety 5.2.

Composition: 0.925 silver, .075 copper. *Weight:* 33.625 g. *Obverse:* A screw press at the center, with the legend **CASA DE MONEDA DE MEXICO** reading clockwise from upper left, and the date reading counterclockwise at lower left. At the bottom, the mintmark M̊. *Reverse:* A balance scale at the center, surrounded by the legend **UNA ONZA TROY DE PLATA PURA**. Above the left arm of the scale, **LEY / .925**; below the pillar, **PESO / 33.625 / GRAMOS**. Mintmark M̊ at the bottom. *Diameter:* 41 mm. *Edge:* Reeded.

Varieties:

1978, Variety 1: Wide spacing (3 mm) between the words in DE MONEDA (BW-875.2, KM-M49b.1).

1978, Variety 2: Close spacing (2.75 mm) between the words in DE MONEDA (BW-875.3, KM-M49b.2).

1979, Variety 3: Left pan of scale points to U in UNA (BW-875.4, KM-M49b.3).

1979, Variety 4: Left pan of scale points between U and N in UNA (BW-875.5, KM-M49b.4).

1980, Variety 5: 1980 date with Variety 3 reverse (BW-875.6, KM-M49b.5).

1980, Variety 5.1: Obverse with 0/2 overdate (BW-875.7, KM-M49b.5).

1980, Variety 5.2: Obverse with 8/7 overdate (BW-875.8, KM-M49b.5).

	Mintage	F	VF	EF	Unc.	BU
1978, Variety 1	280,000	BV	BV	BV	$30	$35
1978, Variety 2	*	BV	BV	BV	30	35
1979, Variety 3	4,508,000	BV	BV	BV	30	35
1979, Variety 4	*	BV	BV	BV	30	35
1980, Variety 5	6,104,000	BV	BV	BV	30	35
1980, 0/2	*	BV	BV	BV	30	35
1980, 80/70	*	BV	BV	BV	30	35

* Included in number above.

1989, "El Capricho." BW-875.9, KM-UL.

Composition: 0.925 silver, .075 copper. *Weight:* 33.625 g. *Obverse:* A screw press at the center, with the legend **CASA DE MONEDA DE MEXICO** reading clockwise from upper left and **1989** reading counterclockwise at lower left. At the bottom, the mintmark M̥. *Reverse:* A balance scale at the center, surrounded by the legend **UNA ONZA TROY DE PLATA PURA**. Above the left arm of the scale, **LEY / .925**; below the pillar, **PESO / 33.625 / GRAMOS**. Mintmark M̥ at the bottom. *Diameter:* 41 mm. *Edge:* Reeded.

Note: *Capricho* is Spanish for "caprice," and indicates that this coin is something of an anomaly. Struck on the same dies as the 1978–1980 official issues, the 1989 Proof El Capricho does not appear in the official mintage reports; the unofficial estimate is that fewer than 50 were struck.

	Mintage	BU
1989, "El Capricho"	< 50	$2,500

BULLION COMMEMORATIVE SERIES

In 1987 and 1988, the Casa de Moneda de México produced the Bullion Commemorative Series: privately issued pieces struck under contract with a Texas coin dealer, with an obverse design slightly different than the design used on the official bullion pieces. Like the official onzas, the privately issued pieces are not legal tender and thus are subject to customs fees and regulations.

The obverse design for all has, as its central device, the Casa de Moneda's emblem—a 16th-century coining press—as used on the official issues. The legend **CASA DE MONEDA DE MEXICO** is placed essentially as it is on the official coins. The design differs from that of the official onza in that the date is directly above the press; the weight, metal, and fineness are to the left of the press; and the mintmark M̊ is to the right of the press. Moreover, on some of the issues the word **PROOF** appears in small type below the mintmark (it does not appear on the official onza).

200TH ANNIVERSARY OF THE U.S. CONSTITUTION

One of the Bullion Commemorative Series celebrated the 200th anniversary of the U.S. Constitution; this is the series most widely found in the secondary market. The coins were struck in 0.999 silver, in weights of 1, 5, and 12 ounces; in 0.900 gold, in weights of 1/4 ounce and 12 ounces (see chapter 7); and in 12-ounce, 0.999 fine platinum (see chapter 8).

1-oz. silver. BW-875.10, KM-MB37.

Composition: 0.999 silver. *Obverse:* At center, a large screw press, with the legend **CASA DE MONEDA DE MEXICO** reading clockwise from upper left. Directly above the press in small type, **1987 / LEY 999**. To the left of the press, **1 / ONZA / PLATA / PURA**; to the right of the press, the mintmark M̊. *Reverse:* Spanning the width of the field, a large desk or table; seated behind the table and facing forward are (from left to right), Benjamin Franklin, George Washington, and Thomas Jefferson. On the table between Washington's hands is a sheet of paper; with a quill in his right hand, Washington is writing the word "Constitution." An ink-bottle sits near his right wrist. Above the figures, the legend **THE CONSTITUTION OF THE U.S.A. 1787 ~ 1987**. Below the table, **200**TH **ANNIVERSARY**. *Diameter:* 40 mm. *Edge:* Reeded.

	Mintage	BU
1987		BV+5%

5-oz. silver. BW-882, KM-MB38.

Shown reduced; actual size 65 mm.

Composition: 0.999 silver. *Obverse:* At center, a large screw press, with the legend **CASA DE MONEDA DE MEXICO** reading clockwise from upper left. Directly above the press in small type, **1987 / LEY 999**. To the left of the press, **5 / ONZAS / PLATA / PURA**; to the right of the press, the mintmark M̊. *Reverse:* Spanning the width of the field, a large desk or table; seated behind the table and facing forward are (from left to right), Benjamin Franklin, George Washington, and Thomas Jefferson. On the table between Washington's hands is a sheet of paper; with a quill in his right hand, Washington is writing the word "Constitution." An ink-bottle sits near his right wrist. Above the figures, the legend **THE CONSTITUTION OF THE U.S.A. 1787~1987**. Below the table, **200ᵀᴴ ANNIVERSARY**. *Diameter:* 65 mm. *Edge:* Reeded.

	Mintage	BU
1987		BV+5%

12-oz. silver. BW-875.9.b, KM-MB39.

Shown reduced; actual size 80 mm.

Composition: 0.999 silver. *Obverse:* At center, a large screw press, with the legend **CASA DE MONEDA DE MEXICO** reading clockwise from upper left. Directly above the press in small type, **1987 / LEY 999**. To the left of the press, **5 / ONZAS / PLATA / PURA**; to the right of the press, the mintmark M̊. *Reverse:* Spanning the width of the field, a large desk or table; seated behind the table and facing forward are (from left to right), Benjamin Franklin, George Washington, and Thomas Jefferson. On the table between Washington's hands is a sheet of paper; with a quill in his right hand, Washington is writing the word "Constitution." An ink-bottle sits near his right wrist. Above the figures, the legend **THE CONSTITUTION OF THE U.S.A. 1787 ~ 1987**. Below the table, **200**TH **ANNIVERSARY**. *Diameter:* 80 mm. *Edge:* Reeded.

	Mintage	BU
1987		BV+5%

SAVE THE GIANT PANDA

Another issue of the 1987 Bullion Commemorative Series celebrated the fifth anniversary of the birth of Tohui, the famous offspring of pandas Pepe and Yin Yin. At that time Tohui was the only surviving Giant Panda ever born in captivity outside the Republic of China.

The silver Save the Giant Panda issues have a couple of additional design elements the other coins of the Bullion Commemorative Series do not have: a serial number on the edge, and an anniversary flame on the obverse marking the fifth year since the birth of Tohui in the Chapultepec Zoo. Bronze pattern coins were made for proposed gold 1/10-, 1/4-, 1/2-, 1-, and 5-ounce issues (they rarely appear on the market and are not listed individually here). A silver 12-ounce pattern was made, as well.

5-oz. silver. BW-896.c, KM-MB23.

Shown reduced; actual size 65 mm.

Composition: 0.999 silver. *Obverse:* At center, a large screw press, with the legend **CASA DE MONEDA DE MEXICO** reading clockwise from upper left. Directly above the press, **1987**. To the left of the press, **PLATA PURA / LEY .999**; to the right of the press, the mintmark **M̥**. *Reverse:* At center, a seated adult panda with cub, in semiprofile to the left. Reading clockwise from upper left, **aniversario del panda**. Below the pandas, **peso 5 onzas**; to the left of the pandas, the name **Tohui**, with a large **5º**, with a flame emerging from the top of the 5. *Diameter:* 65 mm. *Edge:* Reeded, with serial number.

Note: In some examples, the weight/denomination lacks the word "peso"; see the next listing for a similar example.

	Mintage	BU
1987		BV+10%
1987, silver pattern		BV+10%

12-oz. silver. BW-896.b, KM-MB24.

With "12 onzas."
With "peso 12 onzas."

All are shown reduced; actual size 80 mm.

Composition: 0.999 silver. *Obverse:* At center, a large screw press, with the legend **CASA DE MONEDA DE MEXICO** reading clockwise from upper left. Directly above the press, **1987**. To the left of the press, **PLATA PURA / LEY .999**; to the right of the press, the mintmark **M̥**. *Reverse:* At center, a seated adult panda with cub, in semiprofile to the left. Reading clockwise from upper left, **aniversario del panda**. Below the pandas, **peso 12 onzas**; to the left of the pandas, the name **Tohui**, with a large **5°**, with a flame emerging from the top of the 5. *Diameter*: 80 mm. *Edge*: Reeded, with serial number.

Note: In some examples, the weight/denomination lacks the word "peso."

	Mintage	PF
1987		BV+10%

The Greatest Moments in the History of the Games

This 1988 series features 12 great events of the Olympic Summer Games through the years, and honors the athletes for their achievements. The series was issued in 2-ounce and 12-ounce 0.999 silver medallions.

2-oz. silver. BW-897, KM-MB51.

Shown reduced; actual size 49 mm.

Composition: 0.999 silver. *Obverse:* At center, a large screw press, with the legend **CASA DE MONEDA DE MEXICO** reading clockwise from upper left. Directly above the press, **1988**. To the left of the press, **2** / **ONZAS** / **PLATA** / **PURA** / **.999**; to the right of the press, the mintmark **M̊** above the word **PROOF** (in small type). *Reverse:* At center, a reproduction of an ancient "wrestler stater" (a coin depicting two naked Olympic-style wrestlers); surrounding the stater, figures resembling 12 different Olympic sports, including equestrian, aquatic, track-and-field, gymnastic, and team-sport contests. *Diameter:* 49 mm. *Edge:* Plain.

	Mintage	BU
1988		BV+10%

12-oz. silver. BW-897.1, KM-MB52.

Illustration; not an actual coin. Shown reduced; actual size 80 mm.

Composition: 0.999 silver. *Obverse:* At center, a large screw press, with the legend **CASA DE MONEDA DE MEXICO** reading clockwise from upper left. Directly above the press, **1988**. To the left of the press, **12** / **ONZAS** / **PLATA** / **PURA** / **.999**; to the right of the press, the mintmark **M̊** above the word **PROOF** (in small type). *Reverse:* At center, a reproduction of an ancient "wrestler stater" (a coin depicting two naked Olympic-style wrestlers); surrounding the stater, figures resembling 12 different Olympic sports, including equestrian, aquatic, track-and-field, gymnastic, and team-sport contests. *Diameter:* 80 mm. *Edge:* Plain.

	Mintage	BU
1988		BV+10%

7

Gold Bullion Coinage
GOLD MEDALLIC COINAGE

On several occasions since the 1950s Mexico has issued gold medallic coinage, with no denomination, in honor of various anniversaries or concepts. The first such coins were issued in 1953, for the 200th anniversary of the birth of Father Miguel Hidalgo y Costilla. In 1957, a similar series commemorated the centennial of the 1857 Constitution. The year 1999 saw the issuance of a coin celebrating Mexico's numismatic History of Gold, and in 2011, the Cultural Fusion Series honored Mexico's rich cultural legacy.

Miguel Hidalgo y Costilla Birth Bicentennial

On May 8, 1753, Miguel Hidalgo y Costilla was born in New Spain to a *Criollo* (Creole) family. Brought up as a Catholic, well educated, and fluent in the languages of both the ruling class and the indigenous people, he became a Jesuit priest, and at age 50 located in the parish of Dolores. He was deeply devoted to the well being of the poor in his parish; largely indigenous, they were subjected to harsh treatment and economic restrictions by the Spanish colonial government. In 1810, Father Hidalgo joined a plot to overthrow the government, and on September 16, he summoned his congregation and called upon them to rebel. His rousing cry of independence became known as the *grito de Dolores*, and marked the beginning of the War of Independence.

In addition to the gold medallic coin listed here, a circulating silver 5 pesos with the same reverse design was issued for this occasion (see page 59).

**"10 pesos" (no denomination). 1953. BW-654.2, KM-M91a.
Brilliant Uncirculated.**

Composition: 0.900 gold. *Weight:* 8.333 g. *Obverse:* The national coat of arms with the eagle's breast to the fore, its body angling to the left and its head turned back to the right, with thin wings and naturalistic feathers. Above, the legend **REPUBLICA**

MEXICANA; below, a half-wreath of oak and laurel. *Reverse:* To the right of center, a bust of Hidalgo y Costilla in three-quarter profile to the left, with the legend AÑO DE HIDALGO reading clockwise at upper right. In the background to left of the bust, the Parroquia de Nuestra Señora de Dolores ("Parish Church of Our Lady of Sorrows"), with the dates 1753 / 1953 above. *Diameter:* 22.5 mm. *Edge:* Plain.

Note: No mintmark. This coin corresponds in weight and fineness to the previously issued gold 10 pesos, and is often cataloged as such.

	Mintage	F	VF	EF	Unc.	BU
1953		BV	BV	BV	BV+10%	BV+20%

"20 pesos" (no denomination). 1953. BW-655.3, KM-M92a.
Brilliant Uncirculated.

Composition: 0.900 gold. *Weight:* 16.666 g. *Obverse:* The national coat of arms with the eagle's breast to the fore, its body angling to the left and its head turned back to the right, with thin wings and naturalistic feathers. Above, the legend REPUBLICA MEXICANA; below, a half-wreath of oak and laurel. *Reverse:* A bust of Hidalgo y Costilla in three-quarter profile, with the legend AÑO DE HIDALGO above. The Dolores Parish Church is in the background to the left, with the dates 1753 / 1953 above. *Diameter:* 27.5 mm. *Edge:* Plain.

Note: No mintmark. This coin corresponds in weight and fineness to the previously issued gold 20 pesos, and is often cataloged as such.

	Mintage	F	VF	EF	Unc.	BU
1953		BV	BV	BV	BV+10%	BV+20%

CENTENNIAL OF THE MEXICAN CONSTITUTION OF 1857

On February 5, 1857, the Federal Constitution of United Mexican States established the individual rights of the Mexican people and curtailed the authority of the Church. Among the constitution's 128 articles were those abolishing slavery, granting freedom of speech and other rights, and removing religious dogma from public education. Conservatives were violently opposed to these terms, and subsequent decades in Mexico would see bloody struggles between secular and religious interests.

A circulating silver 1 peso with a bust of President Benito Juárez was also issued to honor this centennial (see pages 62 and 63).

"10 pesos" (no denomination). 1957. BW-654.3, KM-M123a.
Brilliant Uncirculated.

Composition: 0.900 gold. *Weight:* 8.333 g. *Obverse:* The national coat of arms with the eagle's breast to the fore, its body angling to the left and its head turned back to the right, with thin wings and naturalistic feathers. Above, the legend **REPUBLICA MEXICANA**; below, a half-wreath of oak and laurel. *Reverse:* At center, a bust of Benito Juárez in profile to the left, with the mintmark M̥ to the right of the head. Surrounding all, the legend **CENTENARIO DE LA CONSTITUCION DE MEXICO** and •1857-1957•. *Diameter:* 22.5 mm. *Edge:* Plain.

Note: This coin corresponds in weight and fineness to the previously issued gold 10 pesos, and is often cataloged as such.

	Mintage	F	VF	EF	Unc.	BU
1957		BV	BV	BV	BV+5%	BV+10%

"50 pesos" (no denomination). 1957. BW-656.2, KM-M122a.
Brilliant Uncirculated.

Composition: 0.900 gold. *Weight:* 41.666 g. *Obverse:* A female figure holding a book that bears the words **CONSTITUCION / 1857**, superimposed over an outline of Mexico against a background of a radiant sun. The legend **PRIMER / CENTENARIO / DE LA / CONSTITUCION / DE 1857** fills the upper-right quarter. *Reverse:* An interior scene of the Mexico's congress in session, with **CONGRESO / CONSTITUYENTE** above and the dates **1856–1857** in the exergue. *Diameter:* 37 mm. *Edge:* Plain.

Note: This coin corresponds in weight and fineness to the previously issued gold 50 pesos, and is often cataloged as such.

	Mintage	F	VF	EF	Unc.	BU
1957		BV	BV	BV	BV+5%	BV+10%

The Constitution of 1857

In 1857, the Federalists (or Liberals, as they came to be called) triumphed with the adoption of a new constitution that set forth sweeping reforms. The measures were seen as a bit inequitable and even a little extreme, but were meant to be a means to an end, enabling Mexico to become an independent nation and its citizens to learn peaceable democracy after so many years of war and strife.

The Constitution of 1857 was similar to the one written in 1824, and in fact was intended simply to restore the Constitution of 1824 with some minor changes. Congress, however, became divided between the moderate Liberals, who wanted only minor changes, and the pure Liberals, who wanted an entirely new document.

In the end, it was a radically new constitution. It introduced or reaffirmed such articles as the abolition of slavery; the provision of public education free from religious dogma; the right to freedom of speech, vocation, and religion; the right to bear arms; the elimination of special courts for the privileged; non-recognition of titles of nobility; and the abolition of cruel and unusual punishments (including the death penalty, except in certain instances). It prohibited both Church and State from profiting by acquiring and managing property not relevant to them, excluded clergy from public office, and divided the branches of government.

The constitution set off a reactionary conflict between Liberals and Conservatives that became known as the War of Reform—a political and military war that lasted for years and crippled the country financially. The Catholic Church objected to many of the articles in this new, Liberal ideology, and threatened excommunication of anyone who swore-in the new constitution.

A coup commenced and President Ignacio Comonfort resigned. Benito Juárez took office, but the Conservatives refused to acknowledge him. They started their own government in Mexico City, while Juárez governed from Guanajuato. Eventually the Liberals prevailed, but the struggle between the factions carried on until the beginning of the French Intervention.

HISTORY OF GOLD

In 1999, a medallic coin weighing 1/20th of an ounce was issued with a design honoring Mexico's rich tradition of artistic work in gold, which dates back to pre-Columbian times. The reverse of the coin depicts an Aztec man melting gold with the use of a muffle and a blow pipe; above the central figure is the word **TEOCUITLATL**, the Nahuatl word for "gold."

1/20-oz. gold. BW-657, KM-UL. Proof.

Composition: 0.999 gold. *Weight:* 1.417 g. *Obverse:* The national coat of arms with the eagle facing left, its feathers resembling plates of armor. Above, the legend ESTADOS UNIDOS MEXICANOS; below, a half-wreath of oak and laurel. *Reverse:* An Aztec goldsmith, with TEOCUITLATL above, 1999 LEY 0.999 below, mintmark M̊ at left, and 1/20 / DE ONZA / ORO PURO at right. *Diameter:* 13 mm. *Edge:* Plain.

	Mintage	PF
1999		$75.00

Cultural Fusion Series

In 2011, Mexico issued the Cultural Fusion Series of 0.750 fine gold coins. The series sought to promote Mexico's cultural legacy, in which the indigenous and Spanish worlds were fused in a new society with distinct aesthetic styles.

1/25-oz. gold. Type 1.1 (Spanish and Indigenous Cultures). 2011. BW-658.1, KM-UL. Proof.

The first coin in the series celebrates the coming-together of the Spanish and Mesoamerican peoples. It features busts of a Conquistador and the last Aztec emperor, Cuauhtémoc (see also page 42). Although the Spanish conquest and subsequent years of colonialism were devastating to the Mesoamericans, the two cultures became inextricably entwined, resulting in the modern nation of Mexico. The fusion of New and European Spain is further illustrated on the coin by an arrangement of Mexico's ubiquitous nopal cactus and the wheat introduced by the Spaniards.

Composition: 0.750 gold. *Weight:* 1.25 g. *Obverse:* The national coat of arms with the eagle facing left, its feathers resembling plates of armor. Above, the legend ESTADOS UNIDOS MEXICANOS; below, a half-wreath of oak and laurel. *Reverse:* To the left, a partial wreath of nopal cactus and wheat. Slightly off-center to the right, jugate busts of a Spanish conquistador and Emperor Cuauhtémoc, in profile to the left. At the top, FUSIÓN CULTURAL / 2011; at the bottom, the weight and fineness, 1.25 g DE ORO PURO LEY 0.750; at far left, the mintmark M̊. *Diameter:* 13 mm. *Edge:* Plain.

	Mintage	PF
2011	2,000	$150.00

1/25-oz. gold. Type 1.2 (Architecture). 2011. BW-658.2, KM-UL. Proof.

Before the arrival of the Spaniards, the Mesoamericans developed their own styles of architecture, including the Aztecs' and the Mayans' heavily decorated masterpieces of stone, adobe, and stucco. When Spanish architecture arrived, it emphasized classical order; the two styles intermixed and evolved together in a variety of ways, all of them uniquely Mexican. The coin celebrating "Architecture" also depicts elements of trade (Spanish coins) and agriculture (cacao and maguey, a tough, fibrous plant discussed under Type 1.4, Trade).

Composition: 0.750 gold. *Weight:* 1.25 g. *Obverse:* The national coat of arms with the eagle facing left, its feathers resembling plates of armor. Above, the legend ESTADOS UNIDOS MEXICANOS; below, a half-wreath of oak and laurel. *Reverse:* In the upper two-thirds of the field, an allegorical fusion of pyramid, church dome, and aqueduct, with three leaves of maguey sprouting from the base at the right. In the lower third, three overlapping, stylized Spanish coins at the left, with an opened pod of cacao at the right. At upper left, above the aqueduct, 2011; at center left, below the pyramid, **FUSIÓN CULTURAL**; around the bottom, the weight and fineness, **1.25 g DE ORO PURO LEY 0.750**. To the right of the cacao, the mintmark M̥. *Diameter:* 13 mm. *Edge:* Plain.

	Mintage	PF
2011	2,000	$150.00

1/25-oz. gold. Type 1.3 (Cacao). 2011. BW-658.3, KM-UL. Proof.

The Spaniards found New Spain to be rich in unusual new plants. One such plant was *cacahuatl*, a strange, brown bean that was used as a flavoring for food; a basis for a rich, sweet drink; and, fermented, as an alcoholic beverage. It was widely used as a medium of exchange among Mesoamericans. The Spaniards called the bean cacao, derived from its Nahuatl name; in time, it came to be known as cocoa. Cacao and the chocolate that is made from it were wildly popular in Europe. It was later introduced to other parts of the world by the Spanish and other colonial powers.

Composition: 0.750 gold. *Weight:* 1.25 g. *Obverse:* The national coat of arms with the eagle facing left, its feathers resembling plates of armor. Above, the legend ESTADOS UNIDOS MEXICANOS; below, a half-wreath of oak and laurel. *Reverse:* To the left, a stylized torso of an Aztec man in three-quarter profile to the right, carrying a large pod of cacao. In the field to the right, EL / CACAO, and below that, 2011 / M̥. Beginning at the top and reading clockwise, **XOCOLATL PARA EL MUNDO** ("Chocolate for the World"); beginning at far left and reading counterclockwise, the weight and fineness, **1.25 g DE ORO PURO LEY 0.750**. *Diameter:* 13 mm. *Edge:* Plain.

	Mintage	PF
2011	2,000	$150.00

1/25-oz. gold. Type 1.4 (Trade). 2011. BW-658.4, KM-UL. Proof.

The final coin in the series brings together a wealth of cultural and agricultural products from the Old World and the New. Spanish colonial trade brought, among other things, the horse, wheat, and Christianity to Mexico; the coinage of Carlos and Johanna, also depicted on the coin, was the first coinage in the New World. Among the many resources the Spaniards discovered in the new territory were cacao (discussed previously), maize, and maguey (agave)—an incredibly versatile Mesoamerican plant that could be made into paper, sugar, syrup, roof thatching, thread, pins, needles, rope, and alcoholic beverages. The latter two uses were of particular interest to the Spanish. Pulque, the alcoholic beverage made from the plant, was traditionally reserved for the upper classes in Mesoamerica; the Spanish decreed it should be available to everyone, and they made a great deal of money from the sale of it. They also exported the plant to another of their colonies, the Philippines, which became a major producer of maguey fiber for rope, fish nets, hammocks, and other uses.

Composition: 0.750 gold. *Weight:* 1.25 g. *Obverse:* The national coat of arms with the eagle facing left, its feathers resembling plates of armor. Above, the legend **ESTADOS UNIDOS MEXICANOS**; below, a half-wreath of oak and laurel. *Reverse:* A montage of images: in the background, a large cross and the head of a horse in profile to the left. In the foreground, at left, a wheat ear and an opened pod of cacao being poured into a rustic bowl; to the right of the bowl, a Spanish 2 reales; to the right of and behind the coin, an ear of maize rising from the leaves of a maguey plant. Reading clockwise at upper left of the cross, the legend **FUSIÓN CULTURAL**. Directly left of the cross and wheat, the weight and fineness **1.25 g / DE ORO PURO / LEY 0.750**, with **2011** below; at far right, the mintmark **M̥**. *Diameter:* 13 mm. *Edge:* Plain.

	Mintage	PF
2011	2,000	$150.00

"GOLD COINS OF MEXICO" PROGRAM

In 1981, Mexico initiated the Gold Coins of Mexico program to compete in the world market with the Canadian 1-ounce gold Maple Leaf and the South African 1-ounce gold Krugerrand. Mexico's coins were issued in weights of 1/4, 1/2, and 1 ounce, all in 0.999 gold and all bearing the same design. A small quantity of gold 1-ounce coins was issued for 1985 and 1988. The Gold Coins of Mexico program was supplanted by the Libertad program in 1991 (see chapter 9).

1/4-oz. gold. 1981. BW-G.1, KM-487. Brilliant Uncirculated.

Composition: 0.999 gold. *Weight:* 8.6396 g. *Obverse:* The national coat of arms with the eagle facing left, its feathers resembling plates of armor. Above, the legend **ESTADOS UNIDOS MEXICANOS**; below, a half-wreath of oak and laurel. *Reverse:* Winged Victory facing forward, a wreath of laurel in her raised right hand, a broken chain in her left; in the background, the mountains Ixtaccíhuatl and Popocatépetl. To Victory's left, **1/4 / onza / ORO / PURO**; to her right, **1981**; below the date, at the peak of the mountain, the mintmark **M̊**. At the bottom, **MEXICO**. *Diameter:* 22 mm. *Edge:* Plain.

	Mintage	F	VF	EF	Unc.	BU
1981	313,000	BV	BV	BV	BV+20%	$475.00

1/2-oz. gold. 1981. BW-G.2, KM-488. Brilliant Uncirculated.

Composition: 0.999 gold. *Weight:* 17.2792 g. *Obverse:* The national coat of arms with the eagle facing left, its feathers resembling plates of armor. Above, the legend **ESTADOS UNIDOS MEXICANOS**; below, a half-wreath of oak and laurel. *Reverse:* Winged Victory facing forward, a wreath of laurel in her raised right hand, a broken chain in her left; in the background, the mountains Ixtaccíhuatl and Popocatépetl. To Victory's left, **½ / onza / ORO / PURO**; to her right, **1981**; below the date, at the peak of the mountain, the mintmark **M̊**. At the bottom, **MEXICO**. *Diameter:* 28 mm. *Edge:* Plain.

	Mintage	F	VF	EF	Unc.	BU
1981	193,000	BV	BV	BV	BV+20%	$900.00

1-oz. gold. 1981, 1985, 1988. BW-G.3, KM-489. Brilliant Uncirculated.

Composition: 0.999 gold. *Weight:* 34.5585 g. *Obverse:* The national coat of arms with the eagle facing left, its feathers resembling plates of armor. Above, the legend **ESTADOS UNIDOS MEXICANOS**; below, a half-wreath of oak and laurel. *Reverse:* Winged Victory facing forward, a wreath of laurel in her raised right hand, a broken chain in her left; in the background, the mountains Ixtaccíhuatl and Popocatépetl. To Victory's left, **1 / onza / ORO / PURO**; to her right, the date; below the date, at the peak of the mountain, the mintmark M̥. At the bottom, **MEXICO**. *Diameter:* 32 mm. *Edge:* Plain.

	Mintage	F	VF	EF	Unc.	BU
1981	596,000	BV	BV	BV	BV+20%	$1,550.00
1985		BV	BV	BV	BV+20%	1,550.00
1988		BV	BV	BV	BV+20%	1,550.00

BULLION COMMEMORATIVE SERIES

200th Anniversary of the U.S. Constitution

In 1987 the Casa de Moneda de México released the Bullion Commemorative Series: privately issued pieces struck under contract with a Texas coin dealer, with an obverse design slightly different from the design used on the official bullion pieces. Like the official onzas, the privately issued pieces are not legal tender and thus are subject to customs fees and regulations. Three different series were produced; two were in silver only, while the 200th Anniversary of the U.S. Constitution series was struck in silver, gold, and platinum. This is the series most widely found in the secondary market. See chapter 6 for more information on the Bullion Commemorative Series and on the silver U.S. Constitution issues; see chapter 9 for the platinum U.S. Constitution issues.

1/4-oz. gold. 1987. BW-875.9.c, KM-MB40. Brilliant Uncirculated.

Composition: 0.999 gold. *Obverse:* At center, a large screw press, with the legend **CASA DE MONEDA DE MEXICO** reading clockwise from upper left. Directly above the press, in small type, **1987 / LEY 900**. To the left of the press, **1/4 / ONZA / ORO / PURO**; to the right of the press, the mintmark **M̊**. *Reverse:* Spanning the width of the field, a large desk or table; seated behind the table and facing forward are (from left to right), Benjamin Franklin, George Washington, and Thomas Jefferson. On the table between Washington's hands is a sheet of paper; with a quill in his right hand, Washington is writing the word "Constitution." An ink bottle sits near his right wrist. Above the figures, the legend **THE CONSTITUTION OF THE U.S.A. 1787 ~ 1987**. Below the table, **200ᵀᴴ ANNIVERSARY**. *Diameter:* 23 mm. *Edge:* Reeded.

	Mintage	BU
1987		BV+5%

12-oz. gold. 1987. BW-875.9.d, KM-UL. Brilliant Uncirculated.

Shown reduced; actual size 80 mm.

Composition: 0.999 gold. *Obverse:* At center, a large screw press, with the legend **CASA DE MONEDA DE MEXICO** reading clockwise from upper left. Directly above the press in small type, **1987 / LEY 999**. To the left of the press, **12 / ONZAS / ORO / PURO**; to the right of the press, the mintmark **M̊**. *Reverse:* Spanning the width of the field, a large desk or table; seated behind the table and facing forward are (from left to right), Benjamin Franklin, George Washington, and Thomas Jefferson. On the table between Washington's hands is a sheet of paper; with a quill in his right hand, Washington is writing the word "Constitution." An ink-bottle sits near his right wrist. Above the figures, the legend **THE CONSTITUTION OF THE U.S.A. 1787 ~ 1987**. Below the table, **200ᵀᴴ ANNIVERSARY**. *Diameter:* 80 mm. *Edge:* Reeded.

	Mintage	BU
1987		$16,250

8

PLATINUM BULLION COINAGE

In 1987, the Casa de Moneda struck 1-ounce platinum Proofs in the Republica Mexicana / Screw Press design. In addition, a very limited number of platinum specimens (five reported) were struck with 1947 fifty-peso Centenario dies; to date, no records have been found explaining these pieces.

In 1989, the Casa de Moneda struck 1/4-ounce platinum Proof Libertads under private contract. They were to be a part of the three-piece "Rainbow Proof Set" (see chapter 5 for the set; see chapter 9 for the Libertad coin).

PLATINUM MEDALLIC COINAGE

1-oz. platinum. 1987 (Screw Press). BW-898.5, KM-UL. Proof.

Composition: 0.9995 platinum. *Weight:* 31.103 g. *Obverse:* The national coat of arms with the eagle facing forward, wings spread, head to the right. Above, the legend **REPUBLICA MEXICANA**; below, a spray of oak and laurel. *Reverse:* At the center, a coinage screw press, with **ONE OUNCE / PLATINUM / 999.5** under the left arm of the press and **UNA ONZA / PLATINO / 999.5** under the right. Reading clockwise from upper left, the legend **CASA DE MONEDA DE MEXICO**, with **1987** reading counterclockwise at lower left. Centered above the press, the mintmark M̊; below, the letter **P**. *Diameter:* 38 mm. *Edge:* Reeded.

	Mintage	PF
1987	270	$1,400.00

50 pesos, platinum. 1947 (1987). BW-897, KM-UL. Proof.

Composition: 0.999 platinum. *Weight:* 41.300 g. *Obverse:* The national coat of arms with the eagle facing forward, wings spread, head to the right. Above, the legend **ESTADOS UNIDOS MEXICANOS**; below, a spray of oak and laurel. *Reverse:* Winged Victory facing forward, a wreath of laurel in her raised right hand, a broken chain in her left. In the background, the Valley of Mexico and, in the far distance, the mountains Ixtaccíhuatl and Popocatépetl. To Victory's left, **50 / PESOS**; to her right, **37.5Gr / ORO / PURO**; at the bottom, the date **1821** to the left of Victory's feet and **1947** to the right. *Diameter:* 38 mm. *Edge:* Plain.

	Mintage	PF
1947 (1987)	5	$9,500

BULLION COMMEMORATIVE SERIES

200TH ANNIVERSARY OF THE U.S. CONSTITUTION

In 1987 the Casa de Moneda de México released the Bullion Commemorative Series: privately issued pieces struck under contract with a Texas coin dealer, with an obverse design slightly different than the design used on the official bullion pieces. Like the official onzas, the privately issued pieces are not legal tender and thus are subject to customs fees and regulations. Three different series were produced; two were in silver only, while the 200th Anniversary of the U.S. Constitution series was struck in silver, gold, and platinum. This is the series most widely found in the secondary market. See chapter 6 for more information on the Bullion Commemorative Series and on the silver U.S. Constitution issues; see chapter 7 for the gold issues.

On the 12-ounce platinum coin, the English word "platinum" (rather than the Spanish *platino*) appears in the otherwise Spanish legend.

12-oz. platinum. 1987. BW-875.9.e, KM-UL. Proof.

Composite illustration; not an actual coin.

Composition: 0.999 platinum. *Weight:* Precise weight not available. *Obverse:* At center, a large screw press, with the legend **CASA DE MONEDA DE MEXICO** reading clockwise from upper left. Directly above the press in small type, **1987**. To the left of the press, **12 / ONZAS / PLATINUM / PURO**; to the right of the press, the mintmark M̊ above the word **PROOF** (in small type). *Reverse:* Spanning the width of the field, a large desk or table; seated behind the table and facing forward are (from left to right), Benjamin Franklin, George Washington, and Thomas Jefferson. On the table between Washington's hands is a sheet of paper; with a quill in his right hand, Washington is writing the word "Constitution." An ink-bottle sits near his right wrist. Above the figures, the legend **THE CONSTITUTION OF THE U.S.A. 1787 ~ 1987**. Below the table, **200ᵀᴴ ANNIVERSARY**. *Diameter:* Not available. *Edge:* Reeded.

	Mintage	PF
1987		$15,000

9

Libertads: Silver, Gold, and Platinum

LIBERTAD SILVER

By decree of December 28, 1981, Mexico expanded on the Gold Coins of Mexico program by authorizing 1-ounce silver Libertads. These followed the same designs as the gold coins: the national coat of arms on the obverse, with Winged Victory and the legendary mountains Ixtaccíhuatl and Popocatépetl on the reverse. The edges were lettered **INDEPENDENCIA Y LIBERTAD**.

In 1983 the Casa de Moneda de México issued Proof sets, each of which contained a Proof example of every circulating coin, plus the Libertad. To fill these sets, the Casa de Moneda withdrew 998 Brilliant Uncirculated Libertads from the market, melted them, and struck the planchets anew in Proof condition.

The Casa de Moneda didn't strike the 1-ounce Libertad in Proof again until 1986. In 1991, it issued fractional Libertads (1/20, 1/10, 1/4, and 1/2 ounce) in a Brilliant Uncirculated finish (sometimes described as a "Satin finish").

From 1993 to 1995, slight changes were made to the reverse design. Then, in 1996, the reverse was fully redesigned: Liberty was placed upon a pediment in three-quarter profile to the left with her arms outstretched. More of the valley of Mexico City was made visible behind her, and foliage details appeared in the foreground to either side of the pediment. The diameter was changed from 36 mm to 40 mm. Coins of this design are described as "New Libertads" by the mint.

In 1996, 2- and 5-ounce Brilliant Uncirculated and Proof Libertads were introduced, with the same reverse design as on the 1-ounce coin. The obverse, however, was redesigned to display 10 historic coats of arms of Mexico. In 2000, the 1-ounce Libertad's obverse was changed to the same design as that for the 2- and 5-ounce coins.

Although Libertads are struck with great care, varieties do exist in the series. During the years when lettered edges were used, there were occasional variations in the alignment of obverse and reverse dies during the minting process. This resulted in differing alignments between the edge lettering and the obverse and reverse designs. In addition, in the years 1982, 1983, and 1989, no decimal point was placed in the fineness.

Early Libertad Silver

1/20-oz. silver. BW-876, KM-542. Brilliant Uncirculated and Proof.

Composition: 0.999 silver. *Weight:* 1.5551 g. *Obverse:* The national coat of arms with the eagle facing left, its feathers resembling plates of armor. Above, the legend ESTADOS UNIDOS MEXICANOS; below, a half-wreath of oak and laurel. *Reverse:* Winged Victory facing forward, a wreath of laurel in her raised right hand, a broken chain in her left; in the background, the mountains Ixtaccíhuatl and Popocatépetl. To Victory's left, 1/20 / ONZA; to her right, PLATA / PuRA; below, [date] MEXICO LEY .999. To the right, the mintmark M̊ below Victory's hand. *Diameter:* 16 mm. *Edge:* Reeded.

	Mintage	BU	PF
1991	54,217 (a)	$10.50	
1992	295,783 (a)	10.50	
1992, Proof	5,000 (a)		$30.00
1993	100,000	10.50	
1993, Proof	5,002		30.00
1994	90,100	10.50	
1994, Proof	5,002		30.00
1995	50,000	10.50	
1995, Proof	2,000		35.00

a. Mint records are cumulative for the 1/20-oz. silver BU and Proof strikes of 1991 and 1992; individual mintages for these coins were not released. The figures here are based on the best available information.

The Legend of Ixtaccíhuatl and Popocatépetl

The two volcanoes that appear on the New Libertad, as well as on several other Mexican issues, are part of a larger mountain chain that shapes the Valley of Mexico. The volcano on the right, Popocatépetl (Nahuatl for "smoking mountain"), is the most active volcano in Mexico. The one on the left, Ixtaccíhuatl, has long been dormant; its name, which means "white woman" in Nahuatl, refers to its rounded, snow-covered peaks. In Spanish it is often called "Mujer Dormida," meaning "sleeping woman."

The volcanic mountains Ixtaccíhuatl and Popocatépetl, viewed across the Valley of Mexico.

An Aztec legend explains the two distinctive mountains, whose features dominate the landscape. When the ancient Aztecs lived in Tenochtitlán (now Mexico City), an emperor and his wife had a baby named Ixtaccíhuatl. Ixta grew up to be a great beauty, and fell in love with a tribal chief named Popoca. Before they could marry, a war broke out, and her father, the emperor, sent Popoca to bring back the head of the enemy chief. Only if he succeeded could he marry Ixta.

Popoca set out to kill the enemy, and was away for many months. While he was away, a jealous rival sent Ixta a false message that Popoca had been killed. She died of grief, not long before Popoca and his warriors returned. The heartbroken chief carried his love into the mountains, where he guarded her body until he, too, died of sorrow. The gods, impressed by their devotion, turned the bodies of the lovers into great volcanoes. To this day, smoke rises from Popocatépetl, who remains awake, watching over the sleeping Ixtaccíhuatl.

1/10-oz. silver. BW-877, KM-543. Brilliant Uncirculated and Proof.

Composition: 0.999 silver. *Weight:* 3.1103 g. *Obverse:* The national coat of arms with the eagle facing left, its feathers resembling plates of armor. Above, the legend **ESTADOS UNIDOS MEXICANOS**; below, a half-wreath of oak and laurel. *Reverse:* Winged Victory facing forward, a wreath of laurel in her raised right hand, a broken chain in her left; in the background, the mountains Ixtaccíhuatl and Popocatépetl. To Victory's left, 1/10 / ONZA; to the right, PLATA / PURA; below, [date] MEXICO LEY .999. To the right, the mintmark M̊ below Victory's hand. *Diameter:* 20 mm. *Edge:* Reeded.

	Mintage	BU	PF
1991	*50,017* (a)	$14.00	
1992	*299,983* (a)	14.00	
1992, Proof	*5,000* (a)		$28.00
1993	100,000	14.00	
1993, Proof	5,002		28.00
1994	90,100	14.00	
1994, Proof	5,002		28.00
1995	50,000	14.00	
1995, Proof	2,000		43.00

a. Mint records are cumulative for the 1/10-oz. silver BU and Proof strikes of 1991 and 1992; individual mintages for these coins were not released. The figures here are based on the best available information.

1/4-oz. silver. BW-878, KM-544. Brilliant Uncirculated and Proof.

Composition: 0.999 silver. *Weight:* 7.7758 g. *Obverse:* The national coat of arms with the eagle facing left, its feathers resembling plates of armor. Above, the legend **ESTADOS UNIDOS MEXICANOS**; below, a half-wreath of oak and laurel. *Reverse:* Winged Victory facing forward, a wreath of laurel in her raised right hand, a broken chain in her left; in the background, the mountains Ixtaccíhuatl and Popocatépetl. To Victory's left, 1/4 / ONZA; to the right, PLATA / PuRA; below, [date] MEXICO LEY .999. To the right, the mintmark M̥ below Victory's hand. *Diameter:* 25 mm. *Edge:* Reeded.

	Mintage	BU	PF
1991	46,017 (a)	$22.00	
1992	104,000 (a)	22.00	
1992, Proof	5,000 (a)		$36.00
1993	90,500	22.00	
1993, Proof	5,002		36.00
1994	90,100	22.00	
1994, Proof	5,002		36.00
1995	50,000	22.00	
1995, Proof	2,000		60.00

a. Mint records are cumulative for the 1/4-oz. silver BU and Proof strikes of 1991 and 1992; individual mintages for these coins were not released. The figures here are based on the best available information.

1/2-oz. silver. BW-879, KM-545. Brilliant Uncirculated and Proof.

Composition: 0.999 silver. *Weight:* 15.5517 g. *Obverse:* The national coat of arms with the eagle facing left, its feathers resembling plates of armor. Above, the legend **ESTADOS UNIDOS MEXICANOS**; below, a half-wreath of oak and laurel. *Reverse:* Winged Victory facing forward, a wreath of laurel in her raised right hand, a broken chain in her left; in the background, the mountains Ixtaccíhuatl and Popocatépetl. To Victory's left, 1/2 / ONZA; to the right, PLATA / PuRA; below, [date] MEXICO LEY .999. To the right, the mintmark M̥ below Victory's hand. *Diameter:* 30 mm. *Edge:* Reeded.

	Mintage	BU	PF
1991	50,618 (a)	$32.00	
1992	97,800 (a)	32.00	
1992, Proof	5,000 (a)		$43.00
1993	90,500	32.00	
1993, Proof	5,002		43.00
1994	90,100	32.00	
1994, Proof	5,002		43.00
1995	50,000	32.00	
1995, Proof	2,000		45.00

a. Mint records are cumulative for the 1/2-oz. silver BU and Proof strikes of 1991 and 1992; individual mintages for these coins were not released. The figures here are based on the best available information.

1-oz. silver. Type 1; Lettered Edge. BW-880, KM-494.1. Brilliant Uncirculated and Proof.

Without dot in fineness.

Composition: 0.999 silver. *Weight:* 31.1000 g. *Obverse:* The national coat of arms with the eagle facing left, its feathers resembling plates of armor. Above, the legend **ESTADOS UNIDOS MEXICANOS**; below, a half-wreath of oak and laurel. Eight dots on the cactus pad below the eagle's left claw. *Reverse:* Winged Victory facing forward, a wreath of laurel in her raised right hand, a broken chain in her left; in the background, the mountains Ixtaccíhuatl and Popocatépetl. To Victory's left (with legends in serif type), **1 / onza**; to the right, **PLATA / PURA**; below, **[date] MEXICO Ley .999**. To the right, the mintmark M̊ below Victory's hand. *Diameter:* 36 mm. *Edge:* Lettered **INDEPENDENCIA Y LIBERTAD**.

	Mintage	BU	PF
1982, No dot in fineness	1,049,680	$22.00	
1982, Pattern		—	
1983, No dot in fineness	1,001,768	23.00	
1983, Proof	998		$810.00
1984	1,014,000	22.00	
1985	2,017,000	23.00	

1-oz. silver. Type 1; Lettered Edge. BW-880, continued.

	Mintage	BU	PF
1986	1,699,426	$24.00	
1986, Proof	30,006		$45.00
1987	500,000	45.00	
1987, Doubled-die obverse	*	105.00	
1987, Proof	12,000		85.00
1988	1,500,500	60.00	
1989, No dot in fineness	1,396,500	50.00	
1989, No dot in fineness, Proof	10,000		190.00

* Included in the number above.

1-oz. silver. Type 1; Reeded Edge. BW 880.1, KM-494.2. Brilliant Uncirculated and Proof.

Composition: 0.999 silver. *Weight:* 31.1000 g. *Obverse:* The national coat of arms with the eagle facing left, its feathers resembling plates of armor. Above, the legend **ESTADOS UNIDOS MEXICANOS**; below, a half-wreath of oak and laurel. Eight dots on the cactus pad below the eagle's left claw. *Reverse:* Winged Victory facing forward, a wreath of laurel in her raised right hand, a broken chain in her left; in the background, the mountains Ixtaccíhuatl and Popocatépetl. To Victory's left (with legends in serif type), 1 / **onza**; to her right, **PLATA / PURA**; below, [date] MEXICO Ley .999. To the right, the mintmark M̊ below Victory's hand. *Diameter:* 36 mm. *Edge:* Reeded.

	Mintage	BU	PF
1988, Proof	10,000		$120.00
1990	1,200,002	$60.00	
1990, Proof	10,000		65.00
1991, Type 1	1,650,518	65.00	

1-oz. silver. Mule. BW-880.2, KM-494.5. Proof.

Composite illustration; not an actual coin.

Composition: 0.999 silver. *Weight:* 31.1000 g. *Obverse:* The national coat of arms with the eagle facing left, its feathers resembling plates of armor. Above, the legend **ESTADOS UNIDOS MEXICANOS**; below, a half-wreath of oak and laurel. Seven dots on the cactus pad below the eagle's left claw (Type 2). *Reverse:* Winged Victory facing forward, a wreath of laurel in her raised right hand, a broken chain in her left; in the background, the mountains Ixtaccíhuatl and Popocatépetl. To Victory's left (Type 1, with legends in serif type), 1 / **onza**; to her right, **PLATA / PURA**; below, **1991 MEXICO Ley .999**. To the right, the mintmark M̥ below Victory's hand. *Diameter:* 36 mm. *Edge:* Reeded.

	Mintage	PF
1991, Mule, Proof	10,000	$145.00

1-oz. silver. Type 2; First Reverse Restyling. BW-880.3, KM-494.3. Brilliant Uncirculated and Proof.

Composition: 0.999 silver. *Weight:* 31.1000 g. *Obverse:* The national coat of arms with the eagle facing left, its feathers resembling plates of armor. Above, the legend **ESTADOS UNIDOS MEXICANOS**; below, a half-wreath of oak and laurel. Seven dots on the cactus pad below the eagle's left claw. *Reverse:* Winged Victory facing forward, a wreath of laurel in her raised right hand, a broken chain in her left; in the background, the mountains Ixtaccíhuatl and Popocatépetl. To Victory's left (with legends in sans-serif type), 1 / **ONZA**; to her right, **PLATA / PuRA**; below, **[date] MEXICO LEY .999**. To the right, the mintmark M̥ below Victory's hand. *Diameter:* 36 mm. *Edge:* Reeded.

Note: "Type 2" describes changes to both the obverse and the reverse. On the obverse, there are seven dots on the cactus pad beneath the eagle's left claw (as opposed to eight on Type 1). On the reverse, the mint effected the first of two restylings, most evident in the change from serif to sans-serif typeface and an ornamental style of capitalization. The second reverse restyling, in 1996, placed Victory on a pediment in three-quarter profile to the left, with the Valley of Mexico in the background and the mountains in the far distance. The mint calls this second design the "New Libertad"; see the next section.

	Mintage	BU	PF
1991, Type 2	(a)	$65.00	
1992	2,458,000	38.00	
1992, Proof	10,000		$120.00
1993	1,000,000	38.00	
1993, Proof	5,002		120.00
1994	400,000	45.00	
1994, Proof	5,002		135.00
1995	500,000	34.00	
1995, Proof	2,000		340.00

a. Included in 1991, Type 1 mintage.

"New Libertad" Silver

1/20-oz. silver. BW-876.1, KM-609. Brilliant Uncirculated and Proof.

Composition: 0.999 silver. *Weight:* 1.5551 g. *Obverse:* The national coat of arms with the eagle facing left, its feathers resembling plates of armor. Above, the legend **ESTADOS UNIDOS MEXICANOS**; below, a half-wreath of oak and laurel. *Reverse:* Winged Victory on a pediment in three-quarter profile to the left, a wreath of laurel in her outstretched right hand, a broken chain in her left. In the background, the Valley of Mexico and, in the far distance, the mountains Ixtaccíhuatl and Popocatépetl. Reading clockwise from the left, the legend **1/20 ONZA / PLATA PURA / [date] LEY .999** (with the phrases divided by the wings). In the field to the right, the mintmark M̊. *Diameter:* 16 mm. *Edge:* Reeded.

	Mintage	BU	PF
1996	50,000	$10.50	
1996, Proof	1,000		$38.00
1997	20,000	20.00	
1997, Proof	800		38.00
1998	6,400	38.00	
1998, Proof	300		75.00
1999	8,001	38.00	
1999, Proof	600		65.00

	Mintage	BU	PF
2000	57,500	$10.50	
2000, Proof	900		$43.00
2001	25,000	10.50	
2001, Proof	1,500		28.00
2002	45,000	10.50	
2002, Proof	2,800		28.00
2003	50,000	10.50	
2003, Proof	4,400		26.00
2004	30,000	10.50	
2004, Proof	2,700		28.00
2005	15,000	10.50	
2005, Proof	2,600		28.00
2006	20,000	20.00	
2006, Proof	3,300		38.00
2007	3,500	14.00	
2007, Proof	4,000		30.00
2008	7,000	10.50	
2008, Proof	3,300		20.00
2009	10,000	10.50	
2009, Proof	5,000		17.00
2010	12,000	10.50	
2010, Proof	10,000		21.00
2011	15,000	10.50	
2011, Proof	10,000		17.00
2013	13,500	10.50	
2013, Proof	4,200		17.00
2014		10.50	
2014, Proof			17.00

1/10-oz. silver. BW-877.1, KM-610. Brilliant Uncirculated and Proof.

Composition: 0.999 silver. *Weight:* 3.1103 g. *Obverse:* The national coat of arms with the eagle facing left, its feathers resembling plates of armor. Above, the legend **ESTADOS UNIDOS MEXICANOS**; below, a half-wreath of oak and laurel. *Reverse:* Winged Victory on a pediment in three-quarter profile to the left, a wreath of laurel in her outstretched right hand, a broken chain in her left. In the background, the Valley of Mexico and, in the far distance, the mountains Ixtaccíhuatl and Popocatépetl. Reading clockwise from the left, the legend 1/10 ONZA / PLATA PURA / [date] LEY .999 (with the phrases divided by the wings). In the field to the right, the mintmark M̥. *Diameter:* 20 mm. *Edge:* Reeded.

	Mintage	BU	PF
1996	50,000	$14.00	
1996, Proof	1,000		$38.00
1997	20,000	30.00	
1997, Proof	800		43.00
1998	6,400	38.00	
1998, Proof	300		115.00
1999	8,000	28.00	
1999, Proof	600		95.00
2000	27,500	14.00	
2000, Proof	1,000		75.00
2001	25,000	14.00	
2001, Proof	1,500		45.00
2002	35,000	14.00	
2002, Proof	2,800		35.00
2003	20,000	14.00	
2003, Proof	4,900		35.00
2004	15,000	14.00	
2004, Proof	2,500		35.00
2005	9,277	14.00	
2005, Proof	3,000		35.00
2006	15,000	14.00	
2006, Proof	3,000		43.00
2007	3,500	14.00	
2007, Proof	4,000		35.00
2008	10,000	14.00	
2008, Proof	5,000		30.00
2009	10,000	14.00	
2009, Proof	5,000		21.00
2010	12,000	14.00	
2010, Proof	10,000		28.00
2011	15,000	14.00	
2011, Proof	10,000		23.00
2012	3,300	20.00	
2013	18,900	14.00	
2013, Proof	4,100		23.00
2014		11.50	
2014, Proof			20.00

1/4-oz. silver. BW-878.1, KM-611. Brilliant Uncirculated and Proof.

Proof.

Composition: 0.999 silver. *Weight:* 7.7758 g. *Obverse:* The national coat of arms with the eagle facing left, its feathers resembling plates of armor. Above, the legend **ESTADOS UNIDOS MEXICANOS**; below, a half-wreath of oak and laurel. *Reverse:* Winged Victory on a pediment in three-quarter profile to the left, a wreath of laurel in her outstretched right hand, a broken chain in her left. In the background, the Valley of Mexico and, in the far distance, the mountains Ixtaccíhuatl and Popocatépetl. Reading clockwise from the left, the legend **1/4 ONZA / PLATA PURA / [date] LEY .999** (with the phrases divided by the wings). In the field to the right, the mintmark M̥. *Diameter:* 27 mm. *Edge:* Reeded.

	Mintage	BU	PF
1996	50,000	$22.00	
1996, Proof	1,000		$40.00
1997	20,000	26.00	
1997, Proof	800		40.00
1998	6,400	52.00	
1998, Proof	300		135.00
1999	7,000	26.00	
1999, Proof	600		115.00
2000	21,000	22.00	
2000, Proof	700		75.00
2001	25,000	22.00	
2001, Proof	1,000		65.00
2002	35,000	22.00	
2002, Proof	2,800		42.00
2003	22,000	22.00	
2003, Proof	3,900		43.00
2004	15,000	25.00	
2004, Proof	2,500		42.00
2005	15,000	25.00	
2005, Proof	2,400		45.00
2006	15,000	25.00	
2006, Proof	2,900		45.00
2007	3,500	25.00	
2007, Proof	3,000		43.00
2008	9,000	35.00	
2008, Proof	2,900		45.00
2009	10,000	20.00	
2009, Proof	3,000		38.00
2010	15,500	21.00	
2010, Proof	5,000		38.00
2011	15,500	21.00	
2011, Proof	5,000		38.00
2012	16,700	23.00	
2013	9,600	17.00	
2013, Proof	3,200		38.00
2014		23.00	
2014, Proof			38.00

1/2-oz. silver. BW-879.1, KM-612. Brilliant Uncirculated and Proof.

Composition: 0.999 silver. *Weight:* 15.5517 g. *Obverse:* The national coat of arms with the eagle facing left, its feathers resembling plates of armor. Above, the legend **ESTADOS UNIDOS MEXICANOS**; below, a half-wreath of oak and laurel. *Reverse:* Winged Victory on a pediment in three-quarter profile to the left, a wreath of laurel in her outstretched right hand, a broken chain in her left. In the background, the Valley of Mexico and, in the far distance, the mountains Ixtaccíhuatl and Popocatépetl. Reading clockwise from the left, the legend **1/2 ONZA / PLATA PURA / [date] LEY .999** (with the phrases divided by the wings). In the field to the right, the mintmark M̥. *Diameter:* 33 mm. *Edge:* Reeded.

	Mintage	BU	PF
1996	50,000	$34.00	
1996, Proof	1,000		$45.00
1997	20,000	26.00	
1997, Proof	800		60.00
1998	6,400	80.00	
1998, Proof	2,500		285.00
1999	7,000	34.00	
1999, Proof	600		255.00
2000	20,000	34.00	
2000, Proof	700		115.00
2001	20,000	34.00	
2001, Proof	1,000		75.00
2002	35,000	34.00	
2002, Proof	2,800		43.00
2003	28,000	34.00	
2003, Proof	3,400		43.00
2004	20,000	34.00	
2004, Proof	2,500		43.00
2005	10,000	34.00	
2005, Proof	2,800		80.00
2006	15,000	34.00	
2006, Proof	2,900		60.00
2007	3,500	34.00	
2007, Proof	1,500		52.00
2008	9,000	32.00	
2008, Proof	2,500		40.00

	Mintage	BU	PF
2009	10,000	$26.00	
2009, Proof	3,000		$35.00
2010	20,000	26.00	
2010, Proof	5,000		35.00
2011	30,000	26.00	
2011, Proof	5,000		40.00
2012	17,000	28.00	
2013	24,500	26.00	
2013, Proof	3,000		42.00
2014		26.00	
2014, Proof			42.00

1-oz. silver. Second Reverse Restyling. BW-880.5, KM-613. Brilliant Uncirculated and Proof.

Composition: 0.999 silver. *Weight:* 31.1000 g. *Obverse:* The national coat of arms with the eagle facing left, its feathers resembling plates of armor. Above, the legend **ESTADOS UNIDOS MEXICANOS**; below, a half-wreath of oak and laurel. *Reverse:* Winged Victory on a pediment in three-quarter profile to the left, a wreath of laurel in her outstretched right hand, a broken chain in her left. In the background, the Valley of Mexico and, in the far distance, the mountains Ixtaccíhuatl and Popocatépetl. Reading clockwise from the left, the legend 1 ONZA / PLATA PURA / [date] LEY .999 (with the phrases divided by the wings). In the field to the right, the mintmark M̊. *Diameter:* 40 mm. *Edge:* Reeded.

Note: The "first reverse restyling" of the 1-ounce silver Libertad took place in 1991. Victory faced forward, as during previous years, but the typeface was changed from serif to sans-serif, and an ornamental style of capitalization was devised. The "second reverse restyling" was more comprehensive, and resulted in the New Libertad design.

	Mintage	BU	PF
1996	300,000	$100.00	
1996, Proof	2,000		$225.00
1997	100,000	100.00	
1997, Proof	1,500		245.00
1998	67,000	200.00	

1-oz. silver. Second Reverse Restyling. BW-880.5, continued.

	Mintage	BU	PF
1998, Proof	500		2,400.00
1999 (a)	95,000	105.00	
1999, Proof	600		1,700.00

a. In early 2015, a single mule (2000 obverse, 1999 reverse) was authenticated by NGC. No other examples have been observed; it is likely the mule was a test piece.

1-oz. silver. Obverse Restyled. BW-880.6, KM-639.
Brilliant Uncirculated and Proof.

Composition: 0.999 silver. *Weight:* 31.1000 g. *Obverse:* At center, the modern national coat of arms with the eagle facing left, its feathers resembling plates of armor, encircled by the legend **ESTADOS UNIDOS MEXICANOS** above and a half-wreath of oak and laurel below. Surrounding the central device, a ring of 10 historic Mexican coats of arms. *Reverse:* Winged Victory on a pediment in three-quarter profile to the left, a wreath of laurel in her outstretched right hand, a broken chain in her left. In the background, the Valley of Mexico and, in the far distance, the mountains Ixtaccíhuatl and Popocatépetl. Reading clockwise from the left, the legend **1 ONZA / PLATA PURA / [date] LEY .999** (with the phrases divided by the wings). In the field to the right, the mintmark M̥. *Diameter:* 40 mm. *Edge:* Reeded.

	Mintage	BU	PF
2000	340,000	$32.00	
2000, Proof	1,600		$725.00
2001	725,000	32.00	
2001, Proof	2,000		245.00
2002	850,000	38.00	
2002, Proof	3,800		225.00
2003	805,000	56.00	
2003, Proof	5,400		245.00
2004	450,000	38.00	
2004, Proof	3,000		225.00
2005	698,281	65.00	
2005, Proof	3,300		255.00
2006	300,000	75.00	
2006, Proof	4,000		270.00
2007	200,000	100.00	
2007, Proof	5,800		260.00
2008	950,000	60.00	

	Mintage	BU	PF
2008, Proof	11,000		$80.00
2009	1,650,000	$22.00	
2009, Proof	10,000		52.00
2010	1,000,000	24.00	
2010, Proof	10,000		52.00
2011	1,200,000	24.00	
2011, Proof	10,000		52.00
2012	746,400	24.00	
2012, Proof	4,200		75.00
2013	774,100	21.00	
2013, Proof	9,100		56.00
2014		20.00	
2014, Proof			52.00

2-oz. silver. BW-881, KM-614. Brilliant Uncirculated and Proof.

Composition: 0.999 silver. *Weight:* 62.2070 g. *Obverse:* At center, the modern national coat of arms with the eagle facing left, its feathers resembling plates of armor, encircled by the legend **ESTADOS UNIDOS MEXICANOS** above and a half-wreath of oak and laurel below. Surrounding the central device, a ring of 10 historic Mexican coats of arms. *Reverse:* Winged Victory on a pediment in three-quarter profile to the left, a wreath of laurel in her outstretched right hand, a broken chain in her left. In the background, the Valley of Mexico and, in the far distance, the mountains Ixtaccíhuatl and Popocatépetl. Reading clockwise from the left, the legend **2 ONZAS / PLATA PURA / [date] LEY .999** (with the phrases divided by the wings). In the field to the right, the mintmark M̥. *Diameter:* 48 mm. *Edge:* Reeded.

	Mintage	BU	PF
1996	50,000	$65.00	
1996, Proof	1,200		$200.00
1997	15,000	75.00	
1997, Proof	1,300		190.00
1998	7,000	85.00	
1998, Proof	400		725.00

2-oz. silver. BW-881, continued.

	Mintage	BU	PF
1999	5,000	$85.00	
1999, Proof	280		$1,400.00
2000	7,500	75.00	
2000, Proof	500		430.00
2001	6,700	75.00	
2001, Proof	500		300.00
2002	8,700	80.00	
2002, Proof	1,000		270.00
2003	9,500	85.00	
2003, Proof	800		245.00
2004	8,000	75.00	
2004, Proof	1,000		245.00
2005	3,549	80.00	
2005, Proof	600		360.00
2006	5,800	85.00	
2006, Proof	1,100		200.00
2007	8,000	85.00	
2007, Proof	500		330.00
2008	17,000	65.00	
2008, Proof	1,000		170.00
2009	46,000	45.00	
2009, Proof	6,200		85.00
2010	14,000	56.00	
2010, Proof	1,300		135.00
2011	14,000	56.00	
2011, Proof	1,000		125.00
2012	18,600	56.00	
2013	17,400	45.00	
2013, Proof	1,300		135.00
2014		52.00	
2014, Proof			235.00

5-oz. silver. BW-882, KM-615. Brilliant Uncirculated and Proof.

Shown reduced; actual size 65 mm.

Composition: 0.999 silver. *Weight:* 155.5100 g. At center, the modern national coat of arms with the eagle facing left, its feathers resembling plates of armor, encircled by the legend **ESTADOS UNIDOS MEXICANOS** above and a half-wreath of oak and laurel below. Surrounding the central device, a ring of 10 historic Mexican coats of arms. *Reverse:* Winged Victory on a pediment in three-quarter profile to the left, a wreath of laurel in her outstretched right hand, a broken chain in her left. In the background, the Valley of Mexico in the background and, in the far distance, the mountains Ixtaccíhuatl and Popocatépetl. Reading clockwise from the left, the legend **5 ONZAS / PLATA PURA / [date] LEY .999** (with the phrases divided by the wings). In the field to the right, the mintmark M̊. *Diameter:* 65 mm. *Edge:* Reeded.

	Mintage	BU	PF
1996	20,000	$145.00	
1996, Proof	1,200		$300.00
1997	10,000	145.00	
1997, Proof	1,300		340.00
1998	3,500	170.00	
1998, Proof	400		2,000.00
1999	2,800	160.00	
1999, Proof	100		5,700.00
2000	4,000	160.00	
2000, Proof	500		825.00
2001	4,000	135.00	
2001, Proof	600		430.00
2002	5,200	125.00	
2002, Proof	1,000		430.00
2003	6,000	135.00	
2003, Proof	1,500		340.00
2004	3,923	135.00	
2004, Proof	800		380.00
2005	2,401	170.00	
2005, Proof	1,000		440.00
2006	3,000	160.00	
2006, Proof	700		525.00
2007	3,000	160.00	
2007, Proof	500		525.00
2008	9,000	135.00	
2008, Proof	900		360.00
2009	21,000	115.00	
2009, Proof	5,000		225.00
2010	9,500	125.00	
2010, Proof	2,000		245.00
2011	10,000	105.00	
2011, Proof	2,000		235.00
2012	9,500	115.00	
2013	10,400	115.00	
2013, Proof	1,600		270.00
2014		115.00	
2014, Proof			340.00

1-Kilogram Silver

In 2002 Mexico issued a 1-kilogram Libertad coin in a Prooflike (PL) finish, with the same design as that of the 5-ounce Libertad. In contrast to the regular Proof coins, which have frosted devices on a mirrored field, the Libertad kilo has mirrored devices on a frosted field. In 2007, a totally new kilo reverse design was released; it featured, in relief, a large Aztec Calendar Stone within an incused border containing a raised legend and mintmark. The obverse has the same finish as the Libertad kilo obverse; on the reverse, however, it is the incused border that is mirrored and the devices that are frosted. Both of the kilos measure 110 mm in diameter and weigh 32.1178 ounces.

1-kg. silver. Libertad. BW-883, KM-677. Prooflike.

Shown reduced; actual size 110 mm.

Composition: 0.999 silver. *Weight:* 999.9775 g. *Obverse:* At center, the modern national coat of arms with the eagle facing left, its feathers resembling plates of armor, encircled by the legend **ESTADOS UNIDOS MEXICANOS** above and a half-wreath of oak and laurel below. Surrounding the central device, a ring of 10 historic Mexican coats of arms. *Reverse:* Winged Victory on a pediment in three-quarter profile to the left, a wreath of laurel in her outstretched right hand, a broken chain in her left. In the background, the Valley of Mexico and, in the far distance, the mountains Ixtaccíhuatl and Popocatépetl. Reading clockwise from the left, the legend **1 kg / PLATA PURA / [date] LEY .999** (with the phrases divided by the wings). In the field to the right, the mintmark M̥. *Diameter:* 110 mm. *Edge:* Reeded.

	Mintage	BU	PL
2002, Prooflike	1,820		$1,500.00
2003, Prooflike	1,514		1,400.00
2004, Prooflike	1,501		1,500.00
2005, Prooflike	500		1,550.00
2006, Prooflike	874		1,550.00
2007, Prooflike	700		1,600.00
2008 (a)	2,003	—	
2008, Prooflike	1,700		1,300.00

a. From 2008 through 2012, kilo Libertads in Brilliant Uncirculated were issued under an exclusive agreement and sold only in Germany.

	Mintage	BU	PL
2009 (a)	4,000	—	
2009, Prooflike	1,700		$1,150.00
2010 (a)	4,000	—	
2010, Prooflike	1,500		1,200.00
2011 (a)	6,000	—	
2011, Prooflike	1,000		1,300.00
2012 (a)	2,300	—	
2012, Prooflike	500		1,300.00
2013, Prooflike	400		1,475.00
2014, Prooflike			1,400.00

a. From 2008 through 2012, kilo Libertads in Brilliant Uncirculated were issued under an exclusive agreement and sold only in Germany.

1-kg. silver. Aztec Calendar. BW-884, KM-921. Prooflike.

Shown reduced; actual size 110 mm.

Composition: 0.999 silver. *Weight:* 999.9775 g. *Obverse:* At center, the modern national coat of arms with the eagle facing left, its feathers resembling plates of armor, encircled by the legend **ESTADOS UNIDOS MEXICANOS** above and a half-wreath of oak and laurel below. Surrounding the central device, a ring of 10 historic Mexican coats of arms. *Reverse:* At center, a large reproduction of the Aztec Calendar Stone; above, the legend **CALENDARIO AZTECA**; below, **$100 2011 1kg PLATA PURA LEY .999**. To the right of the stone, the mintmark M̊. *Diameter:* 110 mm. *Edge:* Reeded.

	Mintage	PL
2007, Prooflike	303	$2,100.00
2008, Prooflike	1,000	2,150.00
2009, Prooflike	1,500	1,700.00
2010, Prooflike	1,500	1,500.00
2011, Prooflike	1,500	1,500.00
2012, Prooflike	1,500	1,500.00
2013, Prooflike	500	1,500.00
2014, Prooflike		1,600.00

Libertad Gold

EARLY LIBERTAD GOLD
Mini Libertad Gold

In 1987 and 1988, gold 1/15- and 1/20-ounce coins were issued, with an Aztec calendar on the obverse and, on the reverse, Winged Victory. Where the word "peso" appears in the legend, it refers to the weight rather than the denomination. Between the two weights and several variations in the legends, seven distinct varieties were created.

The 1987 and 1988 fractional coins were produced under private contract between the Casa de Moneda de México and a Texas firm, and were shipped to Asia to be used in jewelry manufacturing. The mintages for the Brilliant Uncirculated and Proof versions are unknown, but are believed to be very low. Most of the unissued coins were melted in the late 1980s. Varieties 1 and 5 are rare; all others are extremely rare. These fractional gold issues can be found both cast and struck.

Fractional Libertad gold coins were not issued in the regular design (i.e., with the coat-of-arms obverse) until 1991.

1/20-oz. gold. Variety 1. BW-891, KM-530. Brilliant Uncirculated.

Composition: 0.900 gold. *Weight:* 1.70 g. *Obverse:* The Aztec Calendar Stone, placed just above center, with M̊ 1987 M̊ in the exergue below. *Reverse:* Winged Victory facing forward on a plain field, a wreath of laurel in her raised right hand, a broken chain in her left. Reading clockwise from the left, the legend **CASA DE MONEDA DE MEXICO** and, counterclockwise, **.ORO .900 PESO 1/20 oz.** *Diameter:* 13 mm. *Edge:* Reeded.

	Mintage	BU
1987, Variety 1		$380.00

1/20-oz. gold. Variety 2. BW-891.1, KM-UL. Prooflike.

Composition: 0.999 gold. *Weight:* 1.50 g. (inaccurate; actual weight 1.70 g.). *Obverse:* The Aztec Calendar Stone, placed just above center, with M̊ 1987 M̊ in the exergue below. *Reverse:* Winged Victory facing forward on a plain field, a wreath of laurel in her raised right hand, a broken chain in her left. Reading clockwise from the left, the legend **CASA DE MONEDA DE MEXICO** and, counterclockwise, **ORO PURO 1.500g.** *Diameter:* 13 mm. *Edge:* Plain.

	Mintage	PL
1987, Variety 2, Prooflike		$420.00

1/20-oz. gold. Variety 3. BW-891.2, KM-642. Proof.

Composition: 0.900 gold. *Weight:* 1.55 g. (inaccurate; actual weight 1.70 g.). *Obverse:* The Aztec Calendar Stone, placed just above center, with M̊ 1987 M̊ in the exergue below. *Reverse:* Winged Victory facing forward on a plain field, a wreath of laurel in her raised right hand, a broken chain in her left. Reading clockwise from the left, the legend **CASA DE MONEDA DE MEXICO** and, counterclockwise, **ORO 1.55g**. *Diameter:* 13 mm. *Edge:* Plain.

	Mintage	PF
1987, Variety 3, Proof		—

1/20-oz. gold. Variety 4. BW-891.3, KM-UL. Proof.

Composite illustration; not an actual coin.

Composition: 0.999 gold. *Weight:* 1.70 g. *Obverse:* The Aztec Calendar Stone, placed just above center, with M̊ 1988 M̊ in the exergue below. *Reverse:* Winged Victory facing forward on a plain field, a wreath of laurel in her raised right hand, a broken chain in her left. Reading clockwise from the left, the legend **CASA DE MONEDA DE MEXICO** and, counterclockwise, **.ORO .999 PESO 1/20 oz**. *Diameter:* 13 mm. *Edge:* Plain.

	Mintage	PF
1988, Variety 4, Proof		$380.00

1/20-oz. gold. Variety 4, Pattern. BW-890.3, KM-UL. Proof.

Composition: 0.999 gold. *Weight:* 1.70 g. *Obverse:* The Aztec Calendar Stone, placed just above center, with M̊ 1988 M̊ in the exergue below. *Reverse:* Winged Victory facing forward on a plain field, a wreath of laurel in her raised right hand, a broken chain in her left. Reading clockwise from the left, the legend **CASA DE MONEDA DE MEXICO** and, counterclockwise, **.ORO .999 PESO 1/20 oz**. In the field to the left, a large letter **P**. *Diameter:* 13 mm. *Edge:* Plain.

	Mintage	PF
1988, Variety 4, Proof, pattern		—

1/15-oz. gold. Variety 5. BW-890.1, KM-628. Brilliant Uncirculated.

Composition: 0.900 gold. *Weight:* 2.30 g. *Obverse:* The Aztec Calendar Stone, placed just above center, with M̊ 1987 M̊ in the exergue below. *Reverse:* Winged Victory facing forward on a plain field, a wreath of laurel in her raised right hand, a broken chain in her left. Reading clockwise from the left, the legend **CASA DE MONEDA DE MEXICO** and, counterclockwise, **.ORO .900 PESO 1/15 oz.** *Diameter:* 15.6 mm. *Edge:* Plain.

	Mintage	BU
1987, Variety 5		$430.00

1/15-oz. gold. Variety 6. BW-890.2, KM-UL. Proof.

Composition: 0.999 gold. *Weight:* 1.84 g. *Obverse:* The Aztec Calendar Stone, placed just above center, with M̊ 1987 M̊ in the exergue below. *Reverse:* Winged Victory facing forward on a plain field, a wreath of laurel in her raised right hand, a broken chain in her left. Reading clockwise from the left, the legend **CASA DE MONEDA DE MEXICO** and, counterclockwise, **ORO 1.84 g.** *Diameter:* 15.6 mm. *Edge:* Plain.

	Mintage	PF
1987, Variety 6, Proof		—

1/15-oz. gold. Variety 7. BW-890.3, KM-UL. Proof.

Composition: 0.999 gold. *Weight:* 1.94 g. *Obverse:* The Aztec Calendar Stone, placed just above center, with M̊ 1988 M̊ in the exergue below. *Reverse:* Winged Victory facing forward on a plain field, a wreath of laurel in her raised right hand, a broken chain in her left. Reading clockwise from the left, the legend **CASA DE MONEDA DE MEXICO** and, counterclockwise, **ORO .999 PESO 1/15 oz.** *Diameter:* 15.6 mm. *Edge:* Plain.

	Mintage	PF
1988, Variety 7, Proof		—

Original Libertad Gold

Libertad 0.999 fine gold coins in the regular design (coat-of-arms obverse, forward-facing Winged Victory reverse) were issued beginning in 1991, in weights of 1/20, 1/10, 1/4, 1/2, and 1 ounce. The gold Libertads were discontinued from 1995 through 1999. Starting in 2000, however, Brilliant Uncirculated 0.999 fine gold Libertads have been struck each year to date. Proof gold Libertads have been issued from 2004 to date.

1/20-oz. gold. BW-891.1a, KM-589. Brilliant Uncirculated.

Composition: 0.999 gold. *Weight:* 1.5551 g. *Obverse:* The national coat of arms with the eagle facing left, its feathers resembling plates of armor. Above, the legend **ESTADOS UNIDOS MEXICANOS**; below, a half-wreath of oak and laurel. *Reverse:* Winged Victory facing forward, a wreath of laurel in her raised right hand, a broken chain in her left; in the background, the mountains Ixtaccíhuatl and Popocatépetl. To Victory's left, 1/20 / ONZA; to her right, ORO / PURO; below, [date] MEXICO LEY .999. To the right, the mintmark M below Victory's hand. *Diameter:* 13 mm. *Edge:* Reeded.

	Mintage	BU
1991	10,000 (a)	$90.00
1992	63,858 (a)	90.00
1993	10,000	105.00
1994	10,000	105.00

a. Mint records are cumulative for the 1/20-oz. gold strikes of 1991 and 1992; individual mintages for these coins were not released. The figures here are based on the best available information.

1/10-oz. gold. BW-892, KM-541. Brilliant Uncirculated.

Composition: 0.999 gold. *Weight:* 3.1103 g. *Obverse:* The national coat of arms with the eagle facing left, its feathers resembling plates of armor. Above, the legend **ESTADOS UNIDOS MEXICANOS**; below, a half-wreath of oak and laurel. *Reverse:* Winged Victory facing forward, a wreath of laurel in her raised right hand, a broken chain in her left; in the background, the mountains Ixtaccíhuatl and Popocatépetl. To Victory's left, 1/10 / ONZA; to her right, ORO / PURO; below, [date] MEXICO LEY .999. To the right, the mintmark M below Victory's hand. *Diameter:* 16 mm. *Edge:* Reeded.

	Mintage	BU
1991	10,000 (a)	$160.00
1992	50,592 (a)	160.00
1993	10,000	180.00
1994	10,000	180.00

a. Mint records are cumulative for the 1/10-oz. gold strikes of 1991 and 1992; individual mintages for these coins were not released. The figures here are based on the best available information.

1/4-oz. gold. BW-893, KM-590. Brilliant Uncirculated.

Composition: 0.999 gold. *Weight:* 7.7758 g. *Obverse:* The national coat of arms with the eagle facing left, its feathers resembling plates of armor. Above, the legend **ESTADOS UNIDOS MEXICANOS**; below, a half-wreath of oak and laurel. *Reverse:* Winged Victory facing forward, a wreath of laurel in her raised right hand, a broken chain in her left; in the background, the mountains Ixtaccíhuatl and Popocatépetl. To Victory's left, 1/4 / ONZA; to her right, ORO / PURO; below, [date] MEXICO LEY .999. To the right, the mintmark M̐ below Victory's hand. *Diameter:* 23 mm. *Edge:* Reeded.

	Mintage	BU
1991	10,000 (a)	$340.00
1992	27,321 (a)	340.00
1993	2,500	360.00
1994	2,500	360.00

a. Mint records are cumulative for the 1/4-oz. gold strikes of 1991 and 1992; individual mintages for these coins were not released. The figures here are based on the best available information.

1/2-oz. gold. BW-894, KM-488. Proof.

In 1989, the Casa de Moneda struck Proof 1/2-ounce gold Libertads under private contract. They were to be a part of the three-piece "Rainbow Proof Set" (see chapter 5).

Composition: 0.900 gold. *Weight:* 17.2792 g. *Obverse:* The national coat of arms with the eagle facing left, its feathers resembling plates of armor. Above, the legend ESTADOS UNIDOS MEXICANOS; below, a half-wreath of oak and laurel. *Reverse:* Winged Victory facing forward, a wreath of laurel in her raised right hand, a broken chain in her left; in the background, the mountains Ixtaccíhuatl and Popocatépetl. To Victory's left, 1/2 / ONZA; to her right, ORO / PURO; below, [date] MEXICO LEY .900. To the right, the mintmark M̊ below Victory's hand. *Diameter:* 29 mm. *Edge:* Reeded.

	Mintage	PF
1989 (for Rainbow Proof Set)	704 (a)	$1,175.00

a. Mint records are cumulative for the 1/2-oz. gold strikes of 1989, 1991, and 1992; individual mintages for these coins were not released. The figures here are based on the best available information.

1/2-oz. gold. BW-895, KM-591. Brilliant Uncirculated.

Composition: 0.999 gold. *Weight:* 17.2792 g. *Obverse:* The national coat of arms with the eagle facing left, its feathers resembling plates of armor. Above, the legend ESTADOS UNIDOS MEXICANOS; below, a half-wreath of oak and laurel. *Reverse:* Winged Victory facing forward, a wreath of laurel in her raised right hand, a broken chain in her left; in the background, the mountains Ixtaccíhuatl and Popocatépetl. To Victory's left, 1/2 / ONZA; to her right, ORO / PURO; below, [date] MEXICO LEY .999. To the right, the mintmark M̊ below Victory's hand. *Diameter:* 29 mm. *Edge:* Reeded.

	Mintage	BU
1991	10,000 (a)	$625.00
1992	24,343 (a)	625.00
1993	2,500	665.00
1994	2,500	665.00

a. Mint records are cumulative for the 1/2-oz. gold strikes of 1989, 1991, and 1992; individual mintages for these coins were not released. The figures here are based on the best available information.

1-oz. gold. BW-896, KM-592. Brilliant Uncirculated.

Composition: 0.999 gold. *Weight:* 31.1035 g. *Obverse:* The national coat of arms with the eagle facing left, its feathers resembling plates of armor. Above, the legend ESTADOS UNIDOS MEXICANOS; below, a half-wreath of oak and laurel. *Reverse:* Winged Victory facing forward, a wreath of laurel in her raised right hand, a broken chain in her left; in the background, the mountains Ixtaccíhuatl and Popocatépetl. To Victory's left, 1 / ONZA; to her right, ORO / PURO; below, [date] MEXICO LEY .999. To the right, the mintmark M̥ below Victory's hand. *Diameter:* 34.5 mm. *Edge:* Reeded.

	Mintage	BU
1991	*109,193* (a)	$1,475.00
1992	*46,281* (a)	1,475.00
1993	73,881	1,475.00
1994	1,000	1,550.00

a. Mint records are cumulative for the 1-oz. gold strikes of 1991 and 1992; individual mintages for these coins were not released. The figures here are based on the best available information.

"NEW LIBERTAD" GOLD

1/20-oz. gold. BW-891.5, KM-671. Brilliant Uncirculated and Proof.

Proof.

Composition: 0.999 gold. *Weight:* 1.5551 g. *Obverse:* The national coat of arms with the eagle facing left, its feathers resembling plates of armor. Above, the legend ESTADOS UNIDOS MEXICANOS; below, a half-wreath of oak and laurel. *Reverse:* Winged Victory on a pediment in three-quarter profile to the left, a wreath of laurel in her outstretched right hand, a broken chain in her left. In the background, the Valley of Mexico and, in the far distance, the mountains Ixtaccíhuatl and Popocatépetl. Reading clockwise from the left, the legend 1/20 ONZA / ORO PURO / [date] LEY .999 (with the phrases divided by the wings). In the field to the right, the mintmark M̥. *Diameter:* 13 mm.

	Mintage	BU	PF
2000	5,300	$105.00	
2002	5,000	105.00	
2003	800	125.00	
2004	4,000	110.00	
2005	3,200	115.00	
2005, Proof	400		$135.00
2006	3,000	105.00	
2006, Proof	520		135.00
2007	1,200	105.00	
2007, Proof	500		135.00
2008	800	105.00	
2008, Proof	500		135.00
2009	2,000	95.00	

	Mintage	BU	PF
2009, Proof	600		$125.00
2010	1,500	$95.00	
2010, Proof	600		125.00
2011	2,500	95.00	
2011, Proof	1,100		125.00
2013	650	135.00	
2013, Proof	300		190.00
2014		95.00	
2014, Proof			170.00

1/10-oz. gold. BW-892.5, KM-672. Brilliant Uncirculated and Proof.

Proof.

Composition: 0.999 gold. *Weight:* 3.1103 g. *Obverse:* The national coat of arms with the eagle facing left, its feathers resembling plates of armor. Above, the legend **ESTADOS UNIDOS MEXICANOS**; below, a half-wreath of oak and laurel. *Reverse:* Winged Victory on a pediment in three-quarter profile to the left, a wreath of laurel in her outstretched right hand, a broken chain in her left. In the background, the Valley of Mexico and, in the far distance, the mountains Ixtaccíhuatl and Popocatépetl. Reading clockwise from the left, the legend **1/10 ONZA / ORO PURO / [date] LEY .999** (with the phrases divided by the wings). In the field to the right, the mintmark M̊. *Diameter:* 16 mm. *Edge:* Reeded.

	Mintage	BU	PF
2000	3,500	$190.00	
2002	5,000	155.00	
2003	300	220.00	
2004	2,000	155.00	
2005	500	155.00	
2005, Proof	400		$220.00
2006	4,000	155.00	
2006, Proof	520		200.00
2007	1,200	155.00	
2007, Proof	500		200.00
2008	2,500	155.00	
2008, Proof	500		200.00
2009	9,000	155.00	
2009, Proof	600		200.00
2010	4,500	155.00	
2010, Proof	600		200.00
2011	6,500	155.00	
2011, Proof	1,100		200.00
2013	2,150	190.00	

1/10-oz. gold. BW-892.5, continued.

	Mintage	BU	PF
2013, Proof	300		$340.00
2014		$155.00	
2014, Proof			345.00

1/4-oz. gold. BW-893.5, KM-673. Brilliant Uncirculated and Proof.

Proof.

Composition: 0.999 gold. *Weight:* 7.7758 g. *Obverse:* The national coat of arms with the eagle facing left, its feathers resembling plates of armor. Above, the legend **ESTADOS UNIDOS MEXICANOS**; below, a half-wreath of oak and laurel. *Reverse:* Winged Victory on a pediment in three-quarter profile to the left, a wreath of laurel in her outstretched right hand, a broken chain in her left. In the background, the Valley of Mexico and, in the far distance, the mountains Ixtaccíhuatl and Popocatépetl. Reading clockwise from the left, the legend **1/4 ONZA / ORO PURO / [date] LEY .999** (with the phrases divided by the wings). In the field to the right, the mintmark M̥. *Diameter:* 23 mm. *Edge:* Reeded.

	Mintage	BU	PF
2000	2,500	$360.00	
2002	5,000	360.00	
2003	300	575.00	
2004	1,500	360.00	
2004, Proof	1,000		$500.00
2005	500	345.00	
2005, Proof	2,600		500.00
2006	1,500	350.00	
2006, Proof	2,120		430.00
2007	500	350.00	
2007, Proof	1,500		500.00
2008	800	345.00	
2008, Proof	800		500.00
2009	3,000	345.00	
2009, Proof	1,700		490.00
2010	1,500	350.00	
2010, Proof	1,000		500.00
2011	1,500	350.00	
2011, Proof	2,000		500.00
2013	750	350.00	
2013, Proof	600		625.00
2014		350.00	
2014, Proof			525.00

1/2-oz. gold. BW-894.5, KM-674. Brilliant Uncirculated and Proof.

Proof.

Composition: 0.999 gold. *Weight:* 15.5517 g. *Obverse:* The national coat of arms with the eagle facing left, its feathers resembling plates of armor. Above, the legend **ESTADOS UNIDOS MEXICANOS**; below, a half-wreath of oak and laurel. *Reverse:* Winged Victory on a pediment in three-quarter profile to the left, a wreath of laurel in her outstretched right hand, a broken chain in her left. In the background, the Valley of Mexico and, in the far distance, the mountains Ixtaccíhuatl and Popocatépetl. Reading clockwise from the left, the legend **1/2 ONZA / ORO PURO / [date] LEY .999** (with the phrases divided by the wings). In the field to the right, the mintmark M̥. *Diameter:* 29 mm. *Edge:* Reeded.

	Mintage	BU	PF
2000	1,500	$725.00	
2002	5,000	645.00	
2003	300	850.00	
2004	500	645.00	
2005	500	665.00	
2005, Proof	400		$725.00
2006	500	645.00	
2006, Proof	520		725.00
2007	500	645.00	
2007, Proof	500		725.00
2008	300	725.00	
2008, Proof	500		700.00
2009	3,000	645.00	
2009, Proof	600		665.00
2010	1,500	645.00	
2010, Proof	600		700.00
2011	1,500	645.00	
2011, Proof	1,100		700.00
2013	500	645.00	
2013, Proof	300		850.00
2014		645.00	
2014, Proof			850.00

1-oz. gold. BW-895.5, KM-675. Brilliant Uncirculated and Proof.

Proof.

Composition: 0.999 gold. *Weight:* 31.1035 g. *Obverse:* At center, the modern national coat of arms with the eagle facing left, its feathers resembling plates of armor, encircled by the legend **ESTADOS UNIDOS MEXICANOS** above and a half-wreath of oak and laurel below. Surrounding the central device, a ring of 10 historic Mexican coats of arms. *Reverse:* Winged Victory on a pediment in three-quarter profile to the left, a wreath of laurel in her outstretched right hand, a broken chain in her left. In the background, the Valley of Mexico and, in the far distance, the mountains Ixtaccíhuatl and Popocatépetl. Reading clockwise from the left, the legend **1 ONZA / ORO PURO / [date] LEY .999** (with the phrases divided by the wings). In the field to the right, the mintmark M̥. *Diameter:* 34.5 mm. *Edge:* Reeded.

	Mintage	BU	PF
2000	2,370	$1,475.00	
2002	15,000	1,475.00	
2003	500	1,900.00	
2004	3,000	1,475.00	
2005	3,000	1,475.00	
2005, Proof	250		$1,800.00
2006	4,000	1,475.00	
2006, Proof	520		1,900.00
2007	2,500	1,475.00	
2007, Proof	500		1,600.00
2008	800	1,475.00	
2008, Proof	500		1,600.00
2009	6,200	1,400.00	
2009, Proof	600		1,475.00
2010	4,000	1,400.00	
2010, Proof	600		1,475.00
2011	3,000	1,400.00	
2011, Proof	1,100		1,475.00
2012	3,000	1,500.00	
2013	2,350	1,400.00	
2013, Proof	4,000		2,000.00
2014		1,300.00	
2014, Proof			1,700.00

1 Kilogram Gold

In 2012, the Banco de México released a 200-peso Proof 0.999 fine gold coin, the largest gold coin ever released by Mexico. It was part of a multi-coin program (including silver commemorative 20 pesos and gold commemorative 200 pesos) issued in honor of the 200th anniversary of the beginning of the War of Independence. A limited mintage of 200 of the 1-kilo coins was authorized.

1-kg. gold. 200 pesos, Bicentenario. BW-898, KM-UL. Proof.

Shown reduced; actual size 90 mm.

Composition: 0.999 gold. *Weight:* 1 kg. *Obverse:* At center, the modern national coat of arms with the eagle facing left, its feathers resembling plates of armor, encircled by the legend **ESTADOS UNIDOS MEXICANOS** above and a half-wreath of oak and laurel below. Surrounding the central device, a ring of 10 historic Mexican coats of arms. *Reverse:* At center, the Winged Victory figure from the Columna de la Independencia (Column of the Independence), with a wreath of laurel in her raised right hand and a broken chain in her left. Reading clockwise from the top, in large letters, **BICENTENARIO**; and in small letters, clockwise from lower left, **1kg ORO PURO** at the left. To the right of Victory's shoulder, **1810 / – / 2010**; below that, **200 / PESOS**. At lower right, the mintmark M̥. *Diameter:* 90 mm. *Edge:* Lettered **INDEPENDENCIA Y LIBERTAD**.

	Mintage	PF
2010 (2012), Proof	200	$43,000

LIBERTAD PLATINUM

Only one Libertad issue was produced in platinum: the 1/4-ounce Proof coins struck in 1989 by the Casa de Moneda under private contract. They were to be a part of the three-piece "Rainbow Proof Set" (see chapter 5).

1/4-oz. platinum. BW-898.1, KM-538. Proof.

Composition: 0.999 platinum. *Weight:* 7.7775 g. *Obverse:* The national coat of arms with the eagle facing left, its feathers resembling plates of armor. Above, the legend **ESTADOS UNIDOS MEXICANOS**; below, a half-wreath of oak and laurel. *Reverse:* Winged Victory facing forward, a wreath of laurel in her raised right hand, a broken chain in her left; in the background, the mountains Ixtaccíhuatl and Popocatépetl. To Victory's left, 1/4 / **onza**; to her right, **PLATINO / PURO**; around the bottom, **1989 MEXICO LEY** .999. In the field to the right, the mintmark M̥ below Victory's hand. *Diameter:* 27 mm. *Edge:* Plain.

	Mintage	PF
1989	704	$1,900.00

Pre-Columbian Collections

At the American Numismatic Association's convention in Baltimore, on July 28, 1993, the Banco de México held a press conference to announce the beginning of the Pre-Columbian Coin Program. Timed to coincide with celebrations of the 500th anniversary of Christopher Columbus's arrival in the New World in 1492, this series of commemorative coins honored six pre-Columbian civilizations: the Aztec, Central Veracruz, Maya, Olmec, Teotihuacán, and Toltec cultures. Each collection comprises the following:

- three silver coins of a single design, in weights of 1/4, 1/2, and 1 ounce (sold individually and in sets);
- three additional silver 1-ounce designs;
- one silver 5-ounce design; and
- three gold coins of a single design, in weights of 1/4, 1/2, and 1 ounce (sold individually and in sets).

Note that coins of the same weight and metallic content may have different denominations across the collections (and even within collections, due to the Coinage Reform of 1992). The program spanned the years 1992 through 1998; the only year during this time when none of the collections were issued was 1995.

In 1993, design changes were authorized on the Brilliant Uncirculated and Proof versions of three of the coins: the Brasero Efigie in the Aztec Collection, the Anciano con Brasero in the Central Veracruz Collection, and the Hombre Jaguar in the Olmec Collection. Previously the date and mintmark had been at the left and right, respectively, of the main image (Variety 1); the design change placed both the date and the mintmark side by side to the left of the main image (Variety 2). In addition, a change was made to the Proof format for the series. The 1992 Aztec Collection Proofs had featured frosted devices on a mirrored field, surrounded by a frosted border with raised, frosted devices and an incused, mirrored denomination. For Proofs from 1993 onward, the border area was mirrored like the field, with raised, frosted devices and a raised, frosted denomination. The 1-ounce silver Brazier Effigy Proofs, in the Aztec Collection, are the only coins that were made in both Proof formats.

The uniform specifications of this large and popular series make it easy to summarize the details as follows:

Ounces	Denominations	Weight	Diameter
Silver (0.999 fine)			
1/4 oz.	N$1, $1, $25	7.7700 g.	27 mm.
1/2 oz.	N$2, $2, $50	15.5517 g.	33 mm.
1 oz.	N$5, $5, $100	31.1030 g.	40 mm.
5 oz.	N$10, $10, $10,000	155.3100 g.	65 mm.
Gold (0.999 fine)			
1/4 oz.	N$25, $25, $250	7.7758 g.	23 mm.
1/2 oz.	N$50, $50, $500	15.5517 g.	29 mm.
1 oz.	N$100, $100, $1,000	31.1035 g.	35 mm.

THE AZTEC COLLECTION

The first series, released in 1992, honored the Aztecs, who ruled a mighty empire during the 1400s and early 1500s in an area reaching from central Mexico to Guatemala. The empire was forged in 1428 after the Tepanec War, when the city-states of Tenochtitlán, Texcoco, and Tlacopan united in the Mexica Triple Alliance. The Aztecs developed cities as large as any in Europe at that time; Tenochtitlán, the ruling city (and the largest), occupied an island in Lake Texcoco. The city called Texcoco lay to the northeast of the capital, and Tlacopan to the west. An innovative people, the Aztecs developed *chinampas*, often called "floating gardens"—plots of fertile land built on top of the lake to assist in agriculture and to expand the city. They constructed aqueducts to carry fresh water from the mountains, and dikes to prevent flooding and further expand their land. The Aztec used canoes to travel the canals that crisscrossed Tenochtitlán, and maintained roads linking the city to the mainland. Little remains of the former lake, and present-day Mexico City occupies the basin.

Tenochtitlán was a center for commerce, and merchants trekked between the city and the lowlands, trading in agricultural products and manufactured goods. Cacao beans and other valuable items were widely accepted as money. The Aztecs did not use beasts of burden, but planted their crops and carried their loads themselves. Although they were aware of the wheel, the rough, mountainous terrain made carts and other wheeled conveyances impractical; thus the merchants' goods were carried by human porters, in large backpacks called *tameme*, which were supported by straps on the porters' foreheads.

Like most other Mesoamerican cultures, the Aztecs worshipped numerous gods, many of which they appeased—often continuously—with blood. The patron god of Tenochtitlán, as well as the god of war and of the sun, was Huitzilopochtli, and it was to him that many of these sacrifices were made. Humans, usually slaves captured in war, were brought to the great temples and sacrificed by extraction of the heart. Non-fatal tributes, via self-bloodletting, were also offered on a regular basis. Much of the Aztecs' art was devoted to the gods and used in religious rituals, the most significant of which were performed in the twin pyramids of the Templo Mayor (Main Temple). This structure, situated in the center of Tenochtitlán, was dedicated to Huitzilopochtli and Tlaloc, the god of rain. The Aztecs observed a 260-day religious calendar and a 365-day solar calendar, which consisted of 18 months of 20 days each (plus five extra days).

Each of the Mexica Triple Alliance city-states had its own *tlatoani* (ruler); from the mid-1400s until 1520, Tenochtitlán's ruler was Moctezuma II. In 1519, the Spanish conquistador and explorer Hernán Cortés landed on the east coast of Mexico and marched inland to the Aztec capital. His forces were joined by Moctezuma's enemies—people who had been conquered by the Aztecs and forced to pay heavy tributes. (Among these new allies were the Totonacs, discussed in the Central Veracruz Collection section.) One myth holds that Moctezuma II initially believed Cortés was the feathered-serpent god Quetzalcóatl, who had vowed to return and destroy the Aztecs; but it is probable that this story was circulated by Cortés himself. Regardless, the Aztecs fought back and in 1520 drove the Spaniards from Tenochtitlán; but Cortés ultimately prevailed, Moctezuma II was killed, and the Aztec empire ceased to exist in 1521. (See page 42 for further discussion.)

SILVER ISSUES
Eagle Warrior (1/4, 1/2, and 1 oz.)

Eagle-warriors were the elites in the Aztec army. An eagle helmet was part of the uniform, and indicated the warriors' devotion to Huitzilopochtli—the god of war and of the sun, the hero-warrior, and the special guardian of Tenochtitlán.

The silver Guerrero Águila (Eagle Warrior) coin design is based on a terracotta sculpture in the Museo del Templo Mayor (Museum of the Great Temple) at Tenochtitlán. The coin's ornamental border is composed of repeated symbols resembling the Aztec glyph for "flint" or "knife," as depicted on the Stone of Moctezuma I—also called the *cuauhxicalli* ("sacrificial stone") of Moctezuma Ilhuicamina.

The Eagle Warrior design, in three weights, was first issued in 1992 in Proof only. Later in the year it was issued in Brilliant Uncirculated. The original 25-, 50-, and 100-peso denominations of the coins were demonetized by the Coinage Reform of 1992, so in 1993 the mint reissued the design in denominations of N$1, N$2, and N$5, in both Brilliant Uncirculated and Proof.

Guerrero Águila, or Eagle Warrior; Museum of the Great Temple, Tenochtitlán.

1/4-oz. silver, 25 pesos. 1992. BW-900, KM-554.
Brilliant Uncirculated and Proof.

Brilliant Uncirculated.

Composition: 0.999 silver. *Weight:* 7.7758 g. *Obverse:* On a semicircular, flat-bottomed field, the national coat of arms with the eagle facing left, its feathers resembling plates of armor. Above, the legend **ESTADOS UNIDOS MEXICANOS**; below, a half-wreath of oak and laurel. Surrounding the field, a border of Aztec glyphs for "knife"; below the border, 1/4 **ONZA DE PLATA / LEY 0.999**. *Reverse:* Filling the left and center portions of the field, an eagle-warrior in three-quarter profile to the right, with the mintmark M̊ to the left, 1992 to the right, and the legend **GUERRERO AGUILA** in the exergue below. Surrounding the field, a border of Aztec glyphs for "knife," with **$25** below. *Diameter:* 27 mm. *Edge:* Reeded.

	Mintage	BU	PF
1992	50,000	$19.00	
1992, Proof	1,600		$28.00

1/2-oz. silver, 50 pesos. 1992. BW-901, KM-555.
Brilliant Uncirculated and Proof.

Brilliant Uncirculated.

Composition: 0.999 silver. *Weight:* 15.5517 g. *Obverse:* On a semicircular, flat-bottomed field, the national coat of arms with the eagle facing left, its feathers resembling plates of armor. Above, the legend **ESTADOS UNIDOS MEXICANOS**; below, a half-wreath of oak and laurel. Surrounding the field, a border of Aztec glyphs for "knife"; below the border, 1/2 **ONZA DE PLATA / LEY 0.999**. *Reverse:* Filling the left and center portions of the field, an eagle-warrior in three-quarter profile to the right, with the mintmark M̊ to the left, 1992 to the right, and the legend **GUERRERO AGUILA** in the exergue below. Surrounding the field, a border of Aztec glyphs for "knife," with **$50** below. *Diameter:* 33 mm. *Edge:* Reeded.

	Mintage	BU	PF
1992	51,500	$28.00	
1992, Proof	4,300		$48.00

1-oz. silver, 100 pesos. 1992. BW-902, KM-556.
Brilliant Uncirculated and Proof.

Brilliant Uncirculated.

Composition: 0.999 silver. *Weight:* 31.1030 g. *Obverse:* On a semicircular, flat-bottomed field, the national coat of arms with the eagle facing left, its feathers resembling plates of armor. Above, the legend **ESTADOS UNIDOS MEXICANOS**; below, a half-wreath of oak and laurel. Surrounding the field, a border of Aztec glyphs for "knife"; below the border, **1 ONZA DE PLATA / LEY 0.999**. *Reverse:* Filling the left and center portions of the field, an eagle-warrior in three-quarter profile to the right, with the mintmark M̊ to the left, **1992** to the right, and the legend **GUERRERO AGUILA** in the exergue below. Surrounding the field, a border of Aztec glyphs for "knife," with **$100** below. *Diameter:* 40 mm. *Edge:* Reeded.

	Mintage	BU	PF
1992	205,000	$42.00	
1992, Proof	4,000		$75.00

1/4-oz. silver, New 1 peso. 1993. BW-907, KM-644.
Brilliant Uncirculated and Proof.

Brilliant Uncirculated.

Composition: 0.999 silver. *Weight:* 7.7700 g. *Obverse:* On a semicircular, flat-bottomed field, the national coat of arms with the eagle facing left, its feathers resembling plates of armor. Above, the legend **ESTADOS UNIDOS MEXICANOS**; below, a half-wreath of oak and laurel. Surrounding the field, a border of Aztec glyphs for "knife";

below the border, 1/4 **ONZA DE PLATA / LEY 0.999**. *Reverse:* At the center of the field, an eagle-warrior in three-quarter profile to the right, with the mintmark M̥ at left, **1993** at the right, and the legend **GUERRERO AGUILA** in the exergue below. Surrounding the field, a border of Aztec glyphs for "knife," with **N$1** below. *Diameter:* 27 mm. *Edge:* Reeded.

	Mintage	BU	PF
1993	3,505	$24.00	
1993, Proof	900		$62.00

1/2-oz. silver, New 2 pesos. 1993. BW-908, KM-645. Brilliant Uncirculated and Proof.

Brilliant Uncirculated.

Composition: 0.999 silver. *Weight:* 15.5517 g. *Obverse:* On a semicircular, flat-bottomed field, the national coat of arms with the eagle facing left, its feathers resembling plates of armor. Above, the legend **ESTADOS UNIDOS MEXICANOS**; below, a half-wreath of oak and laurel. Surrounding the field, a border of Aztec glyphs for "knife"; below the border, 1/2 **ONZA DE PLATA / LEY 0.999**. *Reverse:* At the center of the field, an eagle-warrior in three-quarter profile to the right, with the mintmark M̥ at left, **1993** at the right, and the legend **GUERRERO AGUILA** in the exergue below. Surrounding the field, a border of Aztec glyphs for "knife," with **N$2** below. *Diameter:* 33 mm. *Edge:* Reeded.

	Mintage	BU	PF
1993	1,500	$32.00	
1993, Proof	800		$95.00

1-oz. silver, New 5 pesos. 1993. BW-909, KM-646. Brilliant Uncirculated and Proof.

Brilliant Uncirculated.

Composition: 0.999 silver. *Weight:* 31.1030 g. *Obverse:* On a semicircular, flat-bottomed field, the national coat of arms with the eagle facing left, its feathers resembling plates of armor. Above, the legend **ESTADOS UNIDOS MEXICANOS**; below, a half-wreath of oak and laurel. Surrounding the field, a border of Aztec glyphs for "knife"; below the border, **1 ONZA DE PLATA / LEY 0.999**. *Reverse:* Filling the left and center portions of the field, an eagle-warrior in three-quarter profile to the right, with the mintmark **M̊** to the left, **1993** to the right, and the legend **GUERRERO AGUILA** in the exergue below. Surrounding the field, a border of Aztec glyphs for "knife," with **N$5** below. *Diameter:* 40 mm. *Edge:* Reeded.

	Mintage	BU	PF
1993	2,800	$70.00	
1993, Proof	2,300		$90.00

Brazier Effigy (1 oz.)

Effigy braziers depicted various gods and were used for incense and other fire-related rituals. The Brasero Efigie (Brazier Effigy) design depicts one such vessel, which is held in the Museum of the Great Temple at Tenochtitlán. The vessel honors Tlaloc, the god of rain and creation—one of the most important Aztec deities. The Aztecs believed that Tlaloc's tears flowed down his cheeks and regenerated the crops and fields. The repeated symbol in the coin's border is the Aztec glyph for "hand," as depicted on the Stone of Moctezuma I.

The 1-ounce silver Brazier Effigy design, denominated 100 pesos, was issued in 1992 in Proof only. As with the Eagle Warrior coins, the original denomination (in this case, 100 pesos only) was demonetized by the Coinage Reform of 1992. In 1993, the design was reissued in the new-5-pesos denomina-

Brazier effigy honoring Tlaloc; Museum of the Great Temple, Tenochtitlán.

tion in both Brilliant Uncirculated and Proof. Both formats that year were struck in Variety 1 (date to left, mintmark to right, mirrored border area, raised and frosted denomination) and Variety 2 (date and mintmark to left, frosted border area, incused and mirrored denomination). The Proofs were also struck in Variety 3 (date and mintmark to left, mirrored border area, raised and frosted denomination).

1-oz. silver, 100 pesos. 1992. BW-902.1, KM-563. Proof.

Proof.

Composition: 0.999 silver. *Weight:* 31.1030 g. *Obverse:* On a semicircular, flat-bottomed field, the national coat of arms with the eagle facing left, its feathers resembling plates of armor. Above, the legend **ESTADOS UNIDOS MEXICANOS**; below, a half-wreath of oak and laurel. Surrounding the field, a border of Aztec glyphs for "hand"; below the border, **1 ONZA DE PLATA / LEY 0.999**. *Reverse:* At the center of the field, a brazier effigy of the god Tlaloc, with **1992** at the left, the mintmark M̊ at the right, and **BRASERO EFIGIE** in the exergue below. Surrounding the field, a border of Aztec glyphs for "hand," with **$100** below. *Diameter:* 40 mm. *Edge:* Reeded.

	Mintage	BU	PF
1992, Proof	4,000		$85.00

1-oz. silver, New 5 pesos. 1993. BW-909.2, KM-648.
Brilliant Uncirculated and Proof.

Variety 1, Proof.

Variety 2, Proof.

Variety 3, Proof.

Composition: 0.999 silver. *Weight:* 31.1030 g. *Obverse:* On a semicircular, flat-bottomed field, the national coat of arms with the eagle facing left, its feathers resembling plates of armor. Above, the legend ESTADOS UNIDOS MEXICANOS; below, a half-wreath of oak and laurel. Surrounding the field, a border of Aztec glyphs for "hand"; below the border, 1 ONZA DE PLATA / LEY 0.999. *Reverse:* At the center of the field, a brazier effigy of the god Tlaloc, with 1993 at the left, the mintmark M̊ at the right, and BRASERO EFIGIE in the exergue below. Surrounding the field, a border of Aztec glyphs for "hand," with N$5 below. *Diameter:* 40 mm. *Edge:* Reeded.

	Mintage	BU	PF
1993, Variety 1 (a)	2,000	$65.00	
1993, Variety 1, Proof (a)	500		$120.00
1993, Variety 2 (b)	1,580	65.00	
1993, Variety 2, Proof (b)	1,300		140.00
1993, Variety 3, Proof (c)			95.00

a. Date to left, mintmark to right; Proof has mirrored border area with raised, frosted denomination. **b.** Date and mintmark to the left; Proof has frosted border area with incused, mirrored denomination. BW-909.2a, KM-UL.
c. Date and mintmark to the left; mirrored border area with raised, frosted denomination. BW-909.2b, KM-UL.

God of Fire (1 oz.)

The Cult of Fire was among the oldest in Mesoamerica. Its god, Huehuetéotl, was also known as the protector of the earth, the old deity, and the old god of fire. The Huehuetéotl sculpture depicted on the reverse of the coins, held in the Museum of the Great Temple at Tenochtitlán, represents the association between the gods of fire and the gods of water, who together governed the center of the universe and maintained the balance of the cosmos. The repeated symbol in the coin's border is the Aztec glyph for "bundle (of kindling)," as depicted on the Stone of Moctezuma I.

The old god of fire, Huehuetéotl; Museum of the Great Temple, Tenochtitlán.

The 1-ounce silver God of Fire design, denominated 100 pesos, was issued in 1992 in Proof only. The original denomination was made illegal by the Coinage Reform of 1992, so in 1993, the design was reissued in the new-5-pesos denomination, in both Brilliant Uncirculated and Proof.

1-oz. silver, 100 pesos. 1992. BW-902.2, KM-564. Proof.

Proof.

Composition: 0.999 silver. *Weight:* 31.1030 g. *Obverse:* On a semicircular, flat-bottomed field, the national coat of arms with the eagle facing left, its feathers resembling plates of armor. Above, the legend **ESTADOS UNIDOS MEXICANOS**; below, a half-wreath of oak and laurel. Surrounding the field, a border of Aztec glyphs for "bundle"; below the border, **1 ONZA DE PLATA / LEY 0.999**. *Reverse:* At the center of the field, a sculpture of Huehuetéotl, with **1992** at the left, the mintmark **M̊** at the right, and **HUEHUETEOTL** in the exergue below. Surrounding the field, a border of Aztec glyphs for "bundle," with **$100** below. *Diameter:* 40 mm. *Edge:* Reeded.

	Mintage	PF
1992, Proof	4,000	$85.00

1-oz. silver, New 5 pesos. 1993. BW-909.3, KM-649. Brilliant Uncirculated and Proof.

Proof.

Composition: 0.999 silver. *Weight:* 31.1030 g. *Obverse:* On a semicircular, flat-bottomed field, the national coat of arms with the eagle facing left, its feathers resembling plates of armor. Above, the legend **ESTADOS UNIDOS MEXICANOS**; below, a half-wreath of oak and laurel. Surrounding the field, a border of Aztec glyphs for "bundle"; below the border, **1 ONZA DE PLATA / LEY 0.999**. *Reverse:* At the center of the field, a sculpture of Huehuetéotl, with **1993** at the left, the mintmark **M̥** at the right, and **HUEHUETEOTL** in the exergue below. Surrounding the field, a border of Aztec glyphs for "bundle," with **N$5** below. *Diameter:* 40 mm. *Edge:* Reeded.

	Mintage	BU	PF
1993	5,405	$65.00	
1993, Proof	1,900		$95.00

God of Flowers (1 oz.)

Xochipilli, the god of flowers, symbolized the renovation of society and nature, and his body was tattooed all over with floral designs. The Aztecs performed intricate rites to dedicate their gardens to him. They even fought *guerras floridas* (flower wars)—covenants between neighboring rival communities that helped them obtain victims to sacrifice to Xochipilli. The sculpture on which the God of Flowers coin design is based is part of the collection of the Museo Nacional de Antropologia (National Museum of Anthropology) in Mexico City. The symbol repeated in the border is one of two simplified Aztec glyphs for "crocodile," as depicted on the Stone of Moctezuma I.

The 1-ounce silver God of Flowers design, denominated 100 pesos, was issued in 1992 in Proof only. The original denomination was demonetized by the Coinage Reform of 1992, so in 1993, the design was reissued in the new-5-pesos denomination, in both Brilliant Uncirculated and Proof.

Xochipilli, the god of flowers; National Museum of Anthropology, Mexico City.

1-oz. silver, 100 pesos. 1992. BW-902.3, KM-562. Proof.

Proof.

Composition: 0.999 silver. *Weight:* 31.1030 g. *Obverse:* On a semicircular, flat-bottomed field, the national coat of arms with the eagle facing left, its feathers resembling plates of armor. Above, the legend **ESTADOS UNIDOS MEXICANOS**; below, a half-wreath of oak and laurel. Surrounding the field, a border of Aztec glyphs for "crocodile"; below the border, **1 ONZA DE PLATA / LEY 0.999**. *Reverse:* At the center of the field, a sculpture of Xochipilli seated cross-legged on a pedestal, with **1992** at the left, the mintmark M̊ at the right, and **XOCHIPILLI** in the exergue below. Surrounding the field, a border of Aztec glyphs for "crocodile," with **$100** below. *Diameter:* 40 mm. *Edge:* Reeded.

	Mintage	PF
1992, Proof	4,000	$85.00

1-oz. silver, New 5 pesos. 1993. BW-909.4, KM-647.
Brilliant Uncirculated and Proof.

Proof.

Composition: 0.999 silver. *Weight:* 31.1030 g. *Obverse:* On a semicircular, flat-bottomed field, the national coat of arms with the eagle facing left, its feathers resembling plates of armor. Above, the legend **ESTADOS UNIDOS MEXICANOS**; below, a half-wreath of oak and laurel. Surrounding the field, a border of Aztec glyphs for "crocodile"; below the border, **1 ONZA DE PLATA / LEY 0.999**. *Reverse:* At the center of the field, a sculpture of Xochipilli seated cross-legged on a pedestal, with **1992** at the left, the mintmark M̊ at the right, and **XOCHIPILLI** in the exergue below. Surrounding the field, a border of Aztec glyphs for "crocodile," with **N$5** below. *Diameter:* 40 mm. *Edge:* Reeded.

	Mintage	BU	PF
1993	3,511	$65.00	
1993, Proof	1,900		$95.00

Tizoc Stone (5 oz.)

The Piedra de Tizoc, or Tizoc Stone, is a large monolith that was discovered in the Templo Mayor; it is currently housed in the National Museum of Anthropology in Mexico City. Its designs celebrated the victories of Tizoc (also known as "Wounded Leg"), who was the Aztec emperor from 1481 to 1486. It may also symbolize the ritual passing of the throne from Tizoc to his brother Ahuitzotl after Tizoc's untimely death.

The design on the Tizoc Stone coin is a motif that is repeated 14 times around the edge of the stone itself: two male warrior figures, the one on the left (possibly Tizoc) garbed as an Aztec god, holding the one on the right—a non-Aztec god—by the hair, a pose traditionally signifying defeat. The symbol repeated in the coin's border is one of two simplified Aztec glyphs for "crocodile," as depicted on the Stone of Moctezuma I.

Tizoc Stone motif; National Museum of Anthropology, Mexico City.

The 5-ounce silver Tizoc Stone design, denominated 10,000 pesos, was issued in 1992 in Brilliant Uncirculated and Proof. The original denomination was demonetized by the Coinage Reform of 1992, so in 1993, the design was reissued in the new-10-pesos denomination, in both Brilliant Uncirculated and Proof.

5-oz. silver, 10,000 pesos. 1992. BW-906, KM-557.
Brilliant Uncirculated and Proof.

Proof.

Shown reduced; actual size 65 mm.

Composition: 0.999 silver. *Weight:* 155.3100 g. *Obverse:* On a semicircular, flat-bottomed field, the national coat of arms with the eagle facing left, its feathers resembling plates of armor. Above, the legend **ESTADOS UNIDOS MEXICANOS**; below, a half-wreath of oak and laurel. Surrounding the field, a border of Aztec glyphs for "crocodile"; below the border, **5 ONZAS DE PLATA / LEY 0.999**. *Reverse:* At the center of the field, a bas-relief of two male warrior figures with the date at the left, the mintmark M̥ at the right, and **PIEDRA DE TIZOC** in the exergue below. Surrounding the field, a border of Aztec glyphs for "crocodile," with **$10000** below. *Diameter:* 65 mm. *Edge:* Reeded.

	Mintage	BU	PF
1992	51,900	$235.00	
1992, Proof	3,300		$335.00

5-oz. silver, New 10 pesos. 1993. BW-910, KM-650. Brilliant Uncirculated and Proof.

Brilliant Uncirculated.

Shown reduced; actual size 65 mm.

Composition: 0.999 silver. *Weight:* 155.3100 g. *Obverse:* On a semicircular, flat-bottomed field, the national coat of arms with the eagle facing left, its feathers resembling plates of armor. Above, the legend **ESTADOS UNIDOS MEXICANOS**; below, a half-wreath of oak and laurel. Surrounding the field, an Aztec-glyph border; below the border, **5 ONZAS DE PLATA / LEY 0.999**. *Reverse:* At the center of the field, a bas-relief of two male warrior figures with the date at the left, the mintmark M̊ at the right, and **PIEDRA DE TIZOC** in the exergue below. Surrounding the field, a stylized ornamental border with **N$10** below. *Diameter:* 65 mm. *Edge:* Reeded.

	Mintage	BU	PF
1992 (1993), Proof	(a)		$715.00
1993	1,905	$235.00	
1993, Proof	1,900		335.00

a. Only a very few pieces were released with this date error.

Gold Issues
Jaguar / Stone of the Suns (1/4, 1/2, and 1 oz.)

The Aztec creation myth held that, prior to the current epoch, the earth experienced four others, each with a new incarnation of the sun god. The first of these four prior ages was "Nahui Ocelotl," or 4-Jaguar, represented by the head of a jaguar and four large dots representing the number 4. The relief sculpture from which the design is taken, housed in the National Museum of Anthropology, is damaged at the upper left corner, such that only three

Nahui Ocelotl, or 4-Jaguar; National Museum of Anthropology.

of the four dots are visible. On the coin, as on the stone, only three of the dots are shown. The symbol repeated in the border is a circle enclosing a pair of crossed vertical and horizontal bands, as depicted on the Stone of Moctezuma I. (Archaeologists are unsure of the meaning of this symbol.)

Note that, although the legend on the coin references the Aztec Sun Stone (Piedra de los Soles), the image on the coin is based on a different artifact bearing the 4-Jaguar motif; see the photograph. On the Sun Stone, the dots around the jaguar are placed differently, and all are intact.

The Jaguar / Stone of the Suns design was issued in 1992 only, in Brilliant Uncirculated and Proof, in three weights: 1/4 ounce (denominated 250 pesos), 1/2 ounce (500 pesos), and 1 ounce (1,000 pesos).

1/4-oz. gold, 250 pesos. 1992. BW-903, KM-558.
Brilliant Uncirculated and Proof.

Brilliant Uncirculated.

Composition: 0.999 gold. *Weight:* 7.7758 g. *Obverse:* On a semicircular, flat-bottomed field, the national coat of arms with the eagle facing left, its feathers resembling plates of armor. Above, the legend **ESTADOS UNIDOS MEXICANOS**; below, a half-wreath of oak and laurel. Surrounding the field, a border of circular Aztec glyphs; below the border, **1/4 ONZA DE ORO / LEY 0.999**. *Reverse:* At the center of the field, a bas-relief depicting the head of a jaguar in profile to the left with three dots surrounding. To the left of the relief, the mintmark M̥; to the right, **1992**; in the exergue below, **JAGUAR / PIEDRA DE LOS SOLES**. Surrounding the field, a border of circular Aztec glyphs, with **$250** below. *Diameter:* 23 mm.

	Mintage	BU	PF
1992	12,000	$375.00	
1992, Proof	2,000		$715.00

1/2-oz. gold, 500 pesos. 1992. BW-904, KM-559.
Brilliant Uncirculated and Proof.

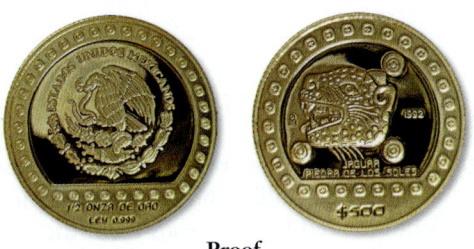

Proof.

Composition: 0.999 gold. *Weight:* 15.5517 g. *Obverse:* On a semicircular, flat-bottomed field, the national coat of arms with the eagle facing left, its feathers resembling plates of armor. Above, the legend ESTADOS UNIDOS MEXICANOS; below, a half-wreath of oak and laurel. Surrounding the field, a border of circular Aztec glyphs; below the border, 1/2 ONZA DE ORO / LEY 0.999. *Reverse:* At the center of the field, a bas-relief depicting the head of a jaguar in profile to the left with three dots surrounding. To the left of the relief, the mintmark M̊; to the right, 1992; in the exergue below, JAGUAR / PIEDRA DE LOS SOLES. Surrounding the field, a border of circular Aztec glyphs, with $500 below. *Diameter:* 29 mm. *Edge:* Reeded.

	Mintage	BU	PF
1992	12,000	$750.00	
1992, Proof	2,000		$1,400.00

1-oz. gold, 1,000 pesos. 1992. BW-905, KM-560.
Brilliant Uncirculated and Proof.

Proof.

Composition: 0.999 gold. *Weight:* 31.1035 g. *Obverse:* On a semicircular, flat-bottomed field, the national coat of arms with the eagle facing left, its feathers resembling plates of armor. Above, the legend ESTADOS UNIDOS MEXICANOS; below, a half-wreath of oak and laurel. Surrounding the field, a border of circular Aztec glyphs; below the border, 1 ONZA DE ORO / LEY 0.999. *Reverse:* At the center of the field, a bas-relief depicting the head of a jaguar in profile to the left with three dots surrounding. To the left of the relief, the mintmark M̊; to the right, 1992; in the exergue below, JAGUAR / PIEDRA DE LOS SOLES. Surrounding the field, a border of circular Aztec glyphs, with $1000 below. *Diameter:* 34.5 mm. *Edge:* Reeded.

	Mintage	BU	PF
1992	19,850	$1,500.00	
1992, Proof	2,000		$2,850.00

CENTRAL VERACRUZ COLLECTION

The Central Veracruz Collection, the second collection in the series, was issued in 1992, following the Aztec issues. Unlike the Aztec Collection issues, the Central Veracruz issues were denominated in new pesos from the outset, so there was no need to reissue them to conform with the Coinage Reform of 1992.

"Central Veracruz" is the name not of a single people, but of a geographic region and its broad collective culture—primarily the Totonac people, who built a complex civilization in the region of what is now the State of Veracruz. At the center of this region, in the southern hills of Mexico between the Cazones and Tecolutla rivers, stand the ruins of the Totonacs' largest city, El Tajín, which covered at least 2,600 acres in its prime.

El Tajín was known for its architecture, with its massive, pyramidal stone temples and palaces ranging around the open plazas of a mighty political center. The most dramatic structure was the Pirámide de los Nichos (Pyramid of the Niches), believed to have been the center of many religious rituals. Totonac priests led a complex religion in which numerous capricious gods, both good and evil, inhabited the sky, the earth, and the underworld; these gods were appeased with rituals, offerings, and sacrifices, frequently human, and often in the form of heart extraction or decapitation. The pyramid at the center of this religion is named for its 365 niches—one for each day of the solar calendar. Other significant monuments include 17 ball courts, more than at any other known site. The Mesoamerican ball-game was not only a significant sport for the people of El Tajín, it was a key element of their religious rituals, with the games often ending in human sacrifice (as depicted in some of the artwork that adorns the walls of the ball courts).

The economic backbone of Central Veracruz was agriculture, and the Totonacs' exports included feathers, pelts, hardwoods, and honey. The area was particularly noted for its cotton, vanilla, and maize, which reinforced the city's prominence as an agricultural center. As in other Mesoamerican cultures, cacao beans and other goods were commonly used for monetary exchange. The location of El Tajín made it an important stop along common trade routes from other regions of modern-day Mexico and Central America.

During the early 13th century El Tajín was attacked and burned, possibly by the Chichimecas; the Totonacs abandoned the city and resettled in the surrounding area. During the 15th century they were forcibly absorbed into the Aztec empire and required to pay tribute, in the form of both goods and humans (for slaves or sacrifice), to the Aztec capital, Tenochtitlán. The Totonacs were among those who joined the forces of Hernán Cortés in defeating the Aztecs (discussed in the previous section).

The abandoned city of El Tajín was overtaken by the jungle, and was unknown to Europeans until 1785 when Diego Ruiz, a colonial government official, was searching for illegal tobacco plants. It has been the subject of archaeological study since that time, and in 1992 was declared a UNESCO World Cultural Heritage Site. Today it attracts hundreds of thousands of visitors each year.

SILVER ISSUES
Bas-Relief of El Tajín (1/4, 1/2, and 1 oz.)

In the central section of El Tajín are the remains of 13 courts once used for the ritual ball-game, indicating the game's importance to the Totonacs. On the vertical walls of the south ball court is a bas-relief (the Bajorrelieve de El Tajín) depicting scenes of the ceremonial game interwoven with scrolls and bands. A section from this bas-relief is depicted on the silver three-coin group in the Central Veracruz

Collection. The borders on the coins are based on patterns in the bas-reliefs found in the El Tajín zone.

Silver 1-ounce coins in this design were issued in 1993 in both Brilliant Uncirculated and Proof, in three weights: 1/4 ounce (denominated new 1 peso), 1/2 ounce (new 2 pesos), and 1 ounce (new 5 pesos).

Figure from the walls of the south ball court at El Tajín.

The Mesoamerican Ball Game

The Mesoamerican ball game, called ōllamaliztli in Nahuatl, is the first known team sport in human history. Archaeologists have discovered stone-walled ball courts, varying widely in size but generally following a 4:1 length-to-width ratio, dating as far back as the 15th century BCE. The oldest courts are found in the tropical areas where the rubber tree, source of the heavy (about seven-pound) game ball, commonly grows. The game likely served different purposes across time and cultures. It was popular for informal recreation, and any upper-class citizen—man, woman, or child—could play. It often was an opportunity for gambling, and the ruling class used the games formally as a means to resolve conflicts without warfare. It was not until around 750 CE that ritual human sacrifice became a part of the game.

A modern-day *ulama* player in Sinaloa, dressed much as traditional *ōllamaliztli* players did for thousands of years.

Although the rules are unknown (and would have varied by location), the object of the game was likely similar to that of volleyball—namely, to keep the ball in play without letting it go out of bounds. Two teams, consisting of two to four members per team, would attempt to keep a large, heavy rubber ball in constant play by striking it with the hips until it was dropped or it flew out of the court. Points were gained by hitting the opposite end wall, and lost by either dropping the ball or failing to achieve a team goal. In the most widely known version of the game, only the hips were permitted to touch the ball, but other common versions allowed the use of wooden bats, stone hand-paddles, or padded forearms. The hip-ball version was particularly brutal, and despite the players' protective hip pads of leather and other materials, the Spaniards noted that they were heavily bruised and often badly injured. A flying seven-pound ball to the face, throat, or abdomen could even be fatal.

About 500 years ago, stone rings were added to the masonry walls of some of the ball courts. As they were placed about 15 to 20 feet from the ground, they were intended to make the game more exciting by adding the opportunity for bonus points.

Many of the rubber balls have been found, some dating back to about 1,500 BCE. Those that were offered ceremonially tend to be too large for practical use; actual game balls were a bit larger than a modern baseball. Ball players' clothing, being of more-perishable materials, has not been located and probably no longer exists; but the garments can be deduced from the ancient artwork on the ball-court walls and elsewhere. Generally, a player would have worn a loincloth with a leather hip guard, and possibly a girdle made of wood or wicker that was covered in leather or fabric (to help propel the ball further). Stone yokes have been found that also may have been worn, in addition to chest protectors, called *palmas*, on which animal mascots were often depicted. Kneepads, garters, and wrapped forearms were common; the elaborate helmets and headdresses often depicted in the artwork were probably used only in ceremonial contexts.

The Mesoamerican ball game largely disappeared during the colonial period, as the Spanish Catholics suppressed the game for religious reasons. It survived in places where the Spanish priests had less influence, and today still exists in Sinaloa as a game called *ulama*. It is played much as ordinary citizens once played it for recreation: on an open field or court with boundaries drawn on the ground. Players wear traditional clothing, and may either play the hip-only version of the game or use padded forearms or two-handed paddles.

1/4-oz. silver, New 1 peso. 1993. BW-911, KM-567. Brilliant Uncirculated and Proof.

Brilliant Uncirculated.

Composition: 0.999 silver. *Weight:* 7.7700 g. *Obverse:* On a rectangular field with rounded ends, the national coat of arms with the eagle facing left, its feathers resembling plates of armor. Above, the legend **ESTADOS UNIDOS MEXICANOS**; below, a half-wreath of oak and laurel. Surrounding the field, an ornamental border; below the border, 1/4 **ONZA DE PLATA / LEY 0.999**. *Reverse:* Nearly filling the field, a section of decorative bas-relief; incorporated into the relief, at upper left and right (respectively), 1993 and the mintmark M̊. In the exergue below the relief, **BAJORRELIEVE DE EL TAJIN**. Surrounding the field, an ornamental border, with N$1 below. *Diameter:* 27 mm. *Edge:* Reeded.

	Mintage	BU	PF
1993	100,005	$19.00	
1993, Proof	4,305		$28.00

1/2-oz. silver, New 2 pesos. 1993. BW-912, KM-568.
Brilliant Uncirculated and Proof.

Brilliant Uncirculated.

Composition: 0.999 silver. *Weight:* 15.5517 g. *Obverse:* On a rectangular field with rounded ends, the national coat of arms with the eagle facing left, its feathers resembling plates of armor. Above, the legend ESTADOS UNIDOS MEXICANOS; below, a half-wreath of oak and laurel. Surrounding the field, an ornamental border; below the border, 1/2 ONZA DE PLATA / LEY 0.999. *Reverse:* Nearly filling the field, a section of decorative bas-relief; incorporated into the relief, at upper left and right (respectively), 1993 and the mintmark M̊. In the exergue below the relief, BAJORRELIEVE DE EL TAJIN. Surrounding the field, an ornamental border, with N$2 below. *Diameter:* 33 mm. *Edge:* Reeded.

	Mintage	BU	PF
1993	100,005	$28.00	
1993, Proof	3,005		$48.00

1-oz. silver, New 5 pesos. 1993. BW-913, KM-569.
Brilliant Uncirculated and Proof.

Brilliant Uncirculated.

Composition: 0.999 silver. *Weight:* 31.1030 g. *Obverse:* On a rectangular field with rounded ends, the national coat of arms with the eagle facing left, its feathers resembling plates of armor. Above, the legend ESTADOS UNIDOS MEXICANOS; below, a half-wreath of oak and laurel. Surrounding the field, an ornamental border; below the border, 1 ONZA DE PLATA / LEY 0.999. *Reverse:* Nearly filling the field, a section of decorative bas-relief; incorporated into the relief, at upper left and right (respectively), 1993 and the mintmark M̊. In the exergue below the relief, **BAJORRELIEVE DE EL TAJIN**. Surrounding the field, an ornamental border, with **N$5** below. *Diameter:* 40 mm. *Edge:* Reeded.

	Mintage	BU	PF
1993	101,005	$42.00	
1993, Proof	4,405		$85.00

Palm With Crocodile (1 oz.)

The Palma con Cocodrilo (Palm With Crocodile) design is based on an artifact held in the National Museum of Anthropology. It reflects both the Gulf Coast landscape, where the Totonac civilization developed, and the Totonacs' fascination with the crocodile. The creature on the coin is viewed from above; its tail curls back around in imitation of a palm frond. The border is based on patterns in the bas-reliefs found in the El Tajín zone.

Illustration of a sculptural palm-and-crocodile motif similar to the one depicted on the coin.

Silver 1-ounce coins in this design, denominated new 5 pesos, were issued in 1993 in Brilliant Uncirculated and Proof.

1-oz. silver, New 5 pesos. 1993. BW-913.1, KM-582. Brilliant Uncirculated and Proof.

 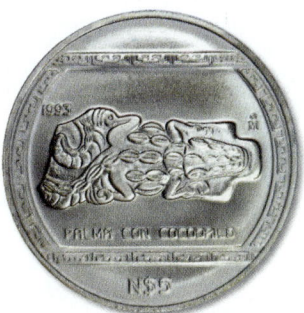

Brilliant Uncirculated.

Composition: 0.999 silver. *Weight:* 31.1030 g. *Obverse:* On a rectangular field with rounded ends, the national coat of arms with the eagle facing left, its feathers resembling plates of armor. Above, the legend **ESTADOS UNIDOS MEXICANOS**; below, a half-wreath of oak and laurel. Surrounding the field, an ornamental border; below the border, **1 ONZA DE PLATA / LEY 0.999**. *Reverse:* Horizontally placed on the field with its nose to the right, the figure of a crocodile with curled tale. In the field at upper left, **1993**; at upper right, the mintmark M̊; and in the exergue below, **PALMA CON COCODRILO**. Surrounding the field, an ornamental border, with **N$5** below. *Diameter:* Diameter 40 mm. *Edge:* Reeded.

	Mintage	BU	PF
1993	5,105	$52.00	
1993, Proof	3,855		$85.00

Smiling Face (1 oz.)

The Carita Sonriente (Smiling Face) is one of the most widely found art products of the Central Veracruz pre-Hispanic culture. These small, terra-cotta figurines, with their distinctive triangular heads and puffy, smiling faces, are often found in tombs. Explanations for their purpose vary: one is that they were thought to have magical powers that would aid the dead in the afterlife. Another suggests they represent drugged individuals (hence the puffy features) being prepared for sacrifice. The Smiling Face on which the coin design is based is held in the National Museum of Anthropology. The coin's border is based on patterns in the bas-reliefs found in the El Tajín zone.

Carita Sonriente, or Smiling Face; National Museum of Anthropology.

Silver 1-ounce coins in this design, denominated new 5 pesos, were issued in 1993 in Brilliant Uncirculated and Proof.

1-oz. silver, New 5 pesos. 1993. BW-913.2, KM-584. Brilliant Uncirculated and Proof.

Brilliant Uncirculated.

Composition: 0.999 silver. *Weight:* 31.1030 g. *Obverse:* On a rectangular field with rounded ends, the national coat of arms with the eagle facing left, its feathers resembling plates of armor. Above, the legend **ESTADOS UNIDOS MEXICANOS**; below, a half-wreath of oak and laurel. Surrounding the field, an ornamental border; below the border, **1 ONZA DE PLATA / LEY 0.999**. *Reverse:* At the center of the field, the head of a Smiling Face figurine. In the field to the left, **1993**; the mintmark M̊; and in the exergue below, **CARITA SONRIENTE**. Surrounding the field, an ornamental border with **N$5** below. *Diameter:* 40 mm. *Edge:* Reeded.

	Mintage	BU	PF
1993	5,105	$70.00	
1993, Proof	4,705		$85.00

Old Man With Brazier (1 oz.)

The Anciano con Brasero (Old Man With Brazier)—a seated elderly man with a brazier atop his head—represented the god of fire, who was worshipped across most pre-Columbian cultures. These sculptures, found in the Centro de las Mesas in the state of Veracruz, are made of terracotta, sometimes at life size. They have distinct elements of both Totonac and Teotihuacán styles, indicating the strong relationship between the two cultures. The one from which the coin design is taken is held in the National Museum of Anthropology. The border is based on patterns in the bas-reliefs found in the El Tajín zone.

Silver 1-ounce coins in this design, denominated new 5 pesos, were issued in 1993 in Brilliant Uncirculated and Proof. As with the silver coins in the Aztec Collection, the initial 1993 design placed the date to the left of the main device and the mintmark to the right (Variety 1); the coins were reissued later in the year with both the date and mintmark to the left (Variety 2).

Anciano con Brasero, or Old Man With Brazier; National Museum of Anthropology.

1-oz. silver, New 5 pesos. 1993. BW-913.3, KM-583. Brilliant Uncirculated and Proof.

Variety 1, Proof.

Variety 2 reverse, Proof.

Composition: 0.999 silver. *Weight:* 31.1030 g. *Obverse:* On a rectangular field with rounded ends, the national coat of arms with the eagle facing left, its feathers resembling plates of armor. Above, the legend ESTADOS UNIDOS MEXICANOS; below, a half-wreath of oak and laurel. Surrounding the field, an ornamental border; below the border, 1 ONZA DE PLATA / LEY 0.999. *Reverse:* At the center of the field, an old man sitting cross-legged in three-quarter profile to the right, balancing a large brazier on his head. In the field to the left, 1993; to the right, the mintmark M̊; and in the exergue below, ANCIANO CON BRASERO. Surrounding the field, an ornamental border, with N$5 below. *Diameter:* 40 mm. *Edge:* Reeded.

	Mintage	BU	PF
1993, Variety 1 (a)	1,500	$70.00	
1993, Variety 1, Proof (a)	1,500		$85.00
1993, Variety 2 (b)	1,700	70.00	
1993, Variety 2, Proof (b)	2,160		95.00

a. Date to left, mintmark to right. b. Date and mintmark to left; BW-913.3a, KM-UL.

Pyramid of the Niches (5 oz.)

The 5-ounce coin's design, called the Pirámide de El Tajín (Tajín Pyramid), depicts the Pyramid of the Niches, located in the Totonac city. The stepped pyramids of El Tajín are visually dramatic, a quality enhanced by the niches and jutting cornices on the tiers. The Pyramid of the Niches, in particular, has a total of 365 such niches, suggesting its use for calendar and ritual purposes. The coin's border is based on patterns in the bas-reliefs found in the El Tajín zone.

Pyramid of the Niches, El Tajín.

Silver 5-ounce coins in this design, denominated new 10 pesos, were issued in 1993 in Brilliant Uncirculated and Proof.

5-oz. silver, New 10 pesos. 1993. BW-914, KM-570.
Brilliant Uncirculated and Proof.

Proof.
Shown reduced; actual size 65 mm.

Composition: 0.999 silver. *Weight:* 155.515 g. *Obverse:* On a rectangular field with rounded ends, the national coat of arms with the eagle facing left, its feathers resembling plates of armor. Above, the legend ESTADOS UNIDOS MEXICANOS; below, a half-wreath of oak and laurel. Surrounding the field, an ornamental border; below the border, 5 ONZAS DE PLATA / LEY 0.999. *Reverse:* At the center of the field, the Pyramid of the Niches. In the field to the left, 1993; to the right, the mintmark M̥; and in the exergue below, PIRAMIDE DE EL TAJIN. Surrounding the field, an ornamental border, with N$10 below. *Diameter:* 65 mm. *Edge:* Reeded.

	Mintage	BU	PF
1993,	50,905	$235.00	
1993, Proof	4,148		$335.00

GOLD ISSUES
Ceremonial Hatchet (1/4, 1/2, and 1 oz.)

The three gold pieces in the collection depict a Hacha Ceremonial (Ceremonial Hatchet) held in the National Museum of Anthropology. The artifact is modeled after the head of a man, flattened in profile, and wearing a helmet that is probably associated with the *juego de pelota* (the Mesoamerican ball game). The fish shape of the helmet signifies the importance of the ocean in the Central Veracruz culture. The coins' border is based on patterns in the bas-reliefs found in the El Tajín zone.

Gold coins in this design were issued in 1993 in both Brilliant Uncirculated and Proof, in three weights: 1/4 ounce (denominated new 25 pesos), 1/2 ounce (new 50 pesos), and 1 ounce (new 100 pesos).

Illustration of the Hacha Ceremonial, or Ceremonial Hatchet; National Museum of Anthropology.

**1/4-oz. gold, New 25 pesos. 1993. BW-915, KM-585.
Brilliant Uncirculated and Proof.**

Proof.

Composition: 0.999 gold. *Weight:* 7.7758 g. *Obverse:* On a rectangular field with rounded ends, the national coat of arms with the eagle facing left, its feathers resembling plates of armor. Above, the legend ESTADOS UNIDOS MEXICANOS; below, a half-wreath of oak and laurel. Surrounding the field, an ornamental border; below the border, 1/4 ONZA DE ORO / LEY 0.999. *Reverse:* At the center of the field, an ax-head in the form of a man in profile wearing a fish-shaped helmet. In the field to the left, 1993; the mintmark M̊ to the right; and in the exergue below, HACHA CEREMONIAL. Surrounding the field, an ornamental border, with N$25 below. *Diameter:* 23 mm. *Edge:* Reeded.

	Mintage	BU	PF
1993	15,508	$450.00	
1993, Proof	802		$785.00

1/2-oz. gold, New 50 pesos. 1993. BW-916, KM-586.
Brilliant Uncirculated and Proof.

Proof.

Composition: 0.999 gold. *Weight:* 15.5517 g. *Obverse:* On a rectangular field with rounded ends, the national coat of arms with the eagle facing left, its feathers resembling plates of armor. Above, the legend ESTADOS UNIDOS MEXICANOS; below, a half-wreath of oak and laurel. Surrounding the field, an ornamental border; below the border, 1/2 ONZA DE ORO / LEY 0.999. *Reverse:* At the center of the field, an ax-head in the form of a man in profile wearing a fish-shaped helmet. In the field to the left, 1993; the mintmark M̊ to the right; and in the exergue below, HACHA CEREMONIAL. Surrounding the field, an ornamental border, with N$50 below. *Diameter:* 29 mm. *Edge:* Reeded.

	Mintage	BU	PF
1993	15,508	$875.00	
1993, Proof	802		$1,550.00

1-oz. gold, New 100 pesos. 1993. BW-917, KM-587.
Brilliant Uncirculated and Proof.

Proof.

Composition: 0.999 gold. *Weight:* 31.1030 g. *Obverse:* On a rectangular field with rounded ends, the national coat of arms with the eagle facing left, its feathers resembling plates of armor. Above, the legend **ESTADOS UNIDOS MEXICANOS**; below, a half-wreath of oak and laurel. Surrounding the field, an ornamental border; below the border, I **ONZA DE ORO / LEY 0.999**. *Reverse:* At the center of the field, an ax-head in the form of a man in profile wearing a fish-shaped helmet. In the field to the left, **1993**; the mintmark M̥ to the right; and in the exergue below, **HACHA CEREMONIAL**. Surrounding the field, an ornamental border, with **N$100** below. *Diameter:* 35 mm. *Edge:* Reeded.

	Mintage	BU	PF
1993	7,160	$1,750.00	
1993, Proof	500		$3,100.00

MAYAN COLLECTION

The third collection in the series honors the Mayan culture, one of the oldest of the Mesoamerican civilizations. Mayan history dates from circa 1800 BCE, with the most prosperous period beginning around 250 CE. The Maya occupied areas in modern-day southeast Mexico, the Yucatán Peninsula, Guatemala, Belize, El Salvador, and Honduras. The most prominent groups were the Yucatec (in present-day Yucatán) and the K'iche' (in present-day Guatemala). Distributed over a wide territory, the Maya are represented by multiple city-states—including Tikal, Chichén Itzá, and Palenque—rather than a single large city like Tenochtitlán. Within the cities, but also between a few of them, the Maya constructed *sacbeob*, or "white ways"—paved roads coated with limestone stucco. The most famous *sacbeob* are found in Yucatán, but many survive in other Mayan areas as well.

The Maya placed their ornate stone temples atop huge, step-sided pyramids. El Castillo (The Castle), located in Chichén Itzá, is the most widely recognized of these. The interiors of the temples were decorated with intricate murals and hieroglyphics, and in fact the Maya are noted for having the most fully developed written language known in the pre-Columbian Americas. They were also advanced in their studies of mathematics and astronomy and are particularly known for their sophisticated calendrical system.

The Mayan economy was largely agricultural, and evidence of their advances in this area can still be seen today, most notably in raised fields that were built in the swamps and flood plains. The society was hierarchical, with royalty at the top, followed by commoners, servants, and slaves. Only the nobility were allowed to serve as priests, who were responsible for ritual observances and maintaining the calendar, among other duties. (In the earlier centuries of Mayan history, priests were also rulers of their cities.) Like other Mesoamerican religions, Mayan rituals included human sacrifice, using methods of decapitation, heart removal, and disembowelment, which were depicted in their artwork.

When the Spanish arrived in the 16th century, the widespread Maya proved difficult to overthrow. In 1524, during the Spanish conquest of Guatemala, the K'iche' Maya were ultimately defeated by the conquistador Pedro de Alvarado and his forces. The Yucatec Maya were defeated by Francisco de Montejo some 20 years later. The resilient Maya endured, and their descendants still reside in the Yucatán Peninsula and Guatemala.

Silver Issues
Chaac-Mool (1/4, 1/2, and 1 oz.)

The three-piece silver group bears a characteristic emblem of Chichén Itzá: the Chaac-Mool (also spelled *chacmool*), which may have been associated with Mayan sacrificial rituals. The design, based on one such figure held in the National Museum of Anthropology, depicts a semi-reclining male figure. His knees are bent, his feet and elbows are on the ground, and his hands hold a tray or plate on his abdomen. His face is turned sharply to look over one shoulder (in the case of the coin design, toward the viewer). The border design is inspired by Mayan glyphs.

Chaac-Mool sacrificial altar from Chichén Itzá; National Museum of Anthropology.

Silver 1-ounce coins in this design were issued in 1994 in both Brilliant Uncirculated and Proof, in three weights: 1/4 ounce (denominated new 1 peso), 1/2 ounce (new 2 pesos), and 1 ounce (new 5 pesos).

1/4-oz. silver, New 1 peso. 1994. BW-918, KM-572.
Brilliant Uncirculated and Proof.

Brilliant Uncirculated.

Composition: 0.999 silver. *Weight:* 7.7700 g. *Obverse:* On a hexagonal field shifted above center, the national coat of arms with the eagle facing left, its feathers resembling plates of armor. Above, the legend **ESTADOS UNIDOS MEXICANOS**; below, a half-wreath of oak and laurel. An ornamental border surrounds the field on five sides, crossing into the field on the uppermost, sixth side; below the border, 1/4 **ONZA DE PLATA / LEY 0.999**. *Reverse:* At the center of the field, a Chaac-Mool figure, with **1994** to the left, the mintmark M̊ to the right, and **CHAAC-MOOL** in the exergue below. An ornamental border surrounds the field on five sides, crossing into the field on the uppermost, sixth side; below the border, **N$1**. *Diameter:* 27 mm. *Edge:* Reeded.

	Mintage	BU	PF
1994	53,505	$19.00	
1994, Proof	2,700		$28.00

1/2-oz. silver, New 2 pesos. 1994. BW-919, KM-573.
Brilliant Uncirculated and Proof.

Brilliant Uncirculated.

Composition: 0.999 silver. *Weight:* 15.5517 g. *Obverse:* On a hexagonal field shifted above center, the national coat of arms with the eagle facing left, its feathers resembling plates of armor. Above, the legend **ESTADOS UNIDOS MEXICANOS**; below, a half-wreath of oak and laurel. An ornamental border surrounds the field on five sides, crossing into the field on the uppermost, sixth side; below the border, **1/2 ONZA DE PLATA / LEY 0.999**. *Reverse:* At the center of the field, a Chaac-Mool figure, with **1994** to the left, the mintmark M̥ to the right, and **CHAAC-MOOL** in the exergue below. An ornamental border surrounds the field on five sides, crossing into the field on the uppermost, sixth side; below the border, **N$2**. *Diameter:* 33 mm. *Edge:* Reeded.

	Mintage	BU	PF
1994	51,500	$28.00	
1994, Proof	4,300		$48.00

1-oz. silver, New 5 pesos. 1994. BW-920, KM-574.
Brilliant Uncirculated and Proof.

Brilliant Uncirculated.

Composition: 0.999 silver. *Weight:* 31.1030 g. *Obverse:* On a hexagonal field shifted above center, the national coat of arms with the eagle facing left, its feathers resembling plates of armor. Above, the legend **ESTADOS UNIDOS MEXICANOS**; below, a half-wreath of oak and laurel. An ornamental border surrounds the field on five sides, crossing into the field on the uppermost, sixth side; below the border, **1 ONZA DE PLATA / LEY 0.999**. *Reverse:* At the center of the field, a Chaac-Mool figure, with **1994** to the left, the mintmark **M̊** to the right, and **CHAAC-MOOL** in the exergue below. An ornamental border surrounds the field on five sides, crossing into the field on the uppermost, sixth side; below the border, N$5. *Diameter:* 40 mm. *Edge:* Reeded.

	Mintage	BU	PF
1994	208,300	$42.00	
1994, Proof	6,700		$85.00

Lintel 26 (1 oz.)

The ruins of the ancient Mayan city Yaxchilán, in what is now the state of Chiapas, are famous for the sculpted lintels above the doorways. Archaeologists describe these important sculptures by number; the mint chose Dintel (Lintel) 26, now held in the National Museum of Anthropology, as the subject of this 1-ounce coin. The sculpture, which dates to about 726 A.D., depicts a ritual scene in which a woman gives the head (or a mask) of a jaguar to a dignitary or high priest. The coin's border design is inspired by Mayan glyphs.

Selection from Dintel (Lintel) 26 of Yaxchilán; National Museum of Anthropology.

Silver 1-ounce coins in this design, denominated new 5 pesos, were issued in 1994 in Brilliant Uncirculated and Proof.

**1-oz. silver, New 5 pesos. 1994. BW-920.1, KM-578.
Brilliant Uncirculated and Proof.**

Brilliant Uncirculated.

Composition: 0.999 silver. *Weight:* 31.1030 g. *Obverse:* On a hexagonal field shifted above center, the national coat of arms with the eagle facing left, its feathers resembling plates of armor. Above, the legend **ESTADOS UNIDOS MEXICANOS**; below, a half-wreath of oak and laurel. An ornamental border surrounds the field on five sides, crossing into the field on the uppermost, sixth side; below the border, **1 ONZA DE PLATA / LEY 0.999**. *Reverse:* At the center of the field, the upper half of

Lintel 26, with **1994** to the left, the mintmark M̊ to the right, and **DINTEL 26** in the exergue below. An ornamental border surrounds the field on five sides, crossing into the field on the uppermost, sixth side; below the border, **N$5**. *Diameter:* 40 mm. *Edge:* Reeded.

	Mintage	BU	PF
1994	4,080	$65.00	
1994, Proof	6,000		$85.00

Gravestone of a Palenque Tomb (1 oz.)

This 1-ounce coin's design, Lápida Tumba de Palenque (Gravestone of a Palenque Tomb), is taken from the bas-relief slab that covered the sarcophagus of the Mayan ruler Pakal in the ancient city of Palenque. The central figure of the design is the body of Pakal himself, who lies atop the monster of the sun at the base of the Tree of the World, as he prepares to journey to the afterlife. The coin's border design is inspired by Mayan glyphs.

Silver 1-ounce coins in this design, denominated new 5 pesos, were issued in 1994 in Brilliant Uncirculated and Proof.

Illustration depicting the sarcophagus cover of Pakal the Great.

**1-oz. silver, New 5 pesos. 1994. BW-920.2, KM-575.
Brilliant Uncirculated and Proof.**

Brilliant Uncirculated.

Composition: 0.999 silver. *Weight:* 31.1030 g. *Obverse:* On a hexagonal field shifted above center, the national coat of arms with the eagle facing left, its feathers resembling plates of armor. Above, the legend **ESTADOS UNIDOS MEXICANOS**; below, a half-wreath of oak and laurel. An ornamental border surrounds the field on five sides, crossing into the field on the uppermost, sixth side; below the border, **1 ONZA DE PLATA / LEY 0.999**. *Reverse:* At the center of the field, an ornamental segment of Pakal's tomb, with **1994** to the left, the mintmark M̊ to the right, and **LAPIDA TUMBA / DE PALENQUE** in the exergue below. An ornamental border surrounds the field on five sides, crossing into the field on the uppermost, sixth side; below the border, **N$5**. *Diameter:* 40 mm. *Edge:* Reeded.

	Mintage	BU	PF
1994	5,905	$65.00	
1994, Proof	6,300		$85.00

Mask of the God Chaac (1 oz.)

This design depicts the Mascarón del Dios Chaac (Mask of the God Chaac, the Mayan rain god), found on the façade of the Temple of Kabah in the Yucatán peninsula. The Mayan people made this their most persistent decorative element; indeed, it is repeated by the hundreds on the walls of the temple, which is also known as the Temple of the Masks. The example on the coin is located in the National Museum of Anthropology. The coin's border design is inspired by Mayan glyphs.

Mascarón del Dios Chaac (Mask of the God Chaac); National Museum of Anthropology.

Silver 1-ounce coins in this design, denominated new 5 pesos, were issued in 1994 in Brilliant Uncirculated and Proof.

1-oz. silver, New 5 pesos. 1994. BW-920.3, KM-577. Brilliant Uncirculated and Proof.

Brilliant Uncirculated.

Composition: 0.999 silver. *Weight:* 31.1030 g. *Obverse:* On a hexagonal field shifted above center, the national coat of arms with the eagle facing left, its feathers resembling plates of armor. Above, the legend **ESTADOS UNIDOS MEXICANOS**; below, a half-wreath of oak and laurel. An ornamental border surrounds the field on five sides, crossing into the field on the uppermost, sixth side; below the border, **1 ONZA DE PLATA / LEY 0.999.** *Reverse:* At the center of the field, a mask of the god Chaac, with 1994 to the left, the mintmark M̊ to the right, and **MASCARON / DEL DIOS CHAAC** in the exergue below. An ornamental border surrounds the field on five sides, crossing into the field on the uppermost, sixth side; below the border, N$5. *Diameter:* 40 mm. *Edge:* Reeded.

	Mintage	BU	PF
1994	3,011	$65.00	
1994, Proof	6,300		$85.00

Pyramid of the Castle (5 oz.)

The 5-ounce silver Mayan Collection coin depicts the stepped Pirámide del Castillo (Pyramid of the Castle), dedicated to the Mayan god Kukulcán. As the Mayan version of Quetzalcóatl, Kukulcán was the creator of the universe and was related to the four seasons. The name is also associated with the deified personality of a mythical king who restored the city of Chichén Itzá. The pyramid as depicted on the coin is illustrated on page 307. The border design is inspired by Mayan glyphs.

Silver 5-ounce coins in this design, denominated new 10 pesos, were issued in 1994 in Brilliant Uncirculated and Proof. Two varieties exist; the common variety is dated 1994, with the legend PIRAMIDE / DEL / CASTILLO. The rare variety is dated 1993 and has the legend PIRAMIDE / DEL CASTILLO / CHICHEN-ITZA. When it was originally released, it was cataloged as "extended legend," but it was soon found to be an error. All unsold specimens were melted; it is estimated that only about 25 to 30 survived.

**5-oz. silver, New 10 pesos. 1994. BW-921, KM-576.
Brilliant Uncirculated and Proof.**

Proof.

Error, "extended legend" reverse. Proof.

Shown reduced; actual size 65 mm.

Composition: 0.999 silver. *Weight:* 155.3100 g. *Obverse:* On a hexagonal field shifted above center, the national coat of arms with the eagle facing left, its feathers resembling plates of armor. Above, the legend **ESTADOS UNIDOS MEXICANOS**; below, a half-wreath of oak and laurel. An ornamental border surrounds the field on five sides, crossing into the field on the uppermost, sixth side; below the border, **1 ONZA DE PLATA / LEY 0.999**. *Reverse:* At the center of the field, the Pyramid of the Castle, with the date to the left, the mintmark M̥ to the right, and **PIRAMIDE / DEL / CASTILLO** in the exergue below. An ornamental border surrounds the field on five sides, crossing into the field on the uppermost, sixth side; below the border, **N$10**. *Diameter:* 65 mm. *Edge:* Reeded.

	Mintage	BU	PF
1993, Proof, So-called "extended legend" error (a)			$3,800.00
1994,	54,305	$235.00	
1994, Proof	5,500		335.00

a. Legend PIRAMIDE DEL CASTILLO / CHICHEN-ITZA (BW-921a; KM-UL); estimated 25 to 30 surviving.

Gold Issues
Personage of Jaina (1/4, 1/2, and 1 oz.)

The design on the three gold coins, called Personaje de Jaina, is based on the small, naturalistic, terracotta figurines sculpted by the Mayans. Thousands have been found on the small island of Jaina, which was used by the Mayans of Yucatán as a burial ground during the third and fourth centuries. Although many more have been found elsewhere, they are commonly known as Jaina figurines. The one reproduced on the coin depicts a civil dignitary sitting on a throne, and is part of the collection of the National Museum of Anthropology. The border design is inspired by Mayan glyphs.

Gold coins in this design were issued in 1994 in both Brilliant Uncirculated and Proof, in three weights: 1/4 ounce (denominated new 25 pesos), 1/2 ounce (new 50 pesos), and 1 ounce (new 100 pesos).

Jaina figurine; National Museum of Anthropology.

1/4-oz. gold, New 25 pesos. 1994. BW-922, KM-579.
Brilliant Uncirculated and Proof.

Proof.

Composition: 0.999 gold. *Weight:* 7.7758 g. *Obverse:* On a hexagonal field shifted above center, the national coat of arms with the eagle facing left, its feathers resembling plates of armor. Above, the legend **ESTADOS UNIDOS MEXICANOS**; below, a half-wreath of oak and laurel. An ornamental border surrounds the field on five sides, crossing into the field on the uppermost, sixth side; below the border, **1/4 ONZA DE ORO / LEY 0.999**. *Reverse:* At the center of the field, a Jaina figurine, with 1994 to the left, the mintmark M̥ to the right, and **PERSONAJE / DE JAINA** in the exergue below. An ornamental border surrounds the field on five sides, crossing into the field on the uppermost, sixth side; below the border, **N$25**. *Diameter:* 23 mm. *Edge:* Reeded.

	Mintage	BU	PF
1994	2,000	$475.00	
1994, Proof	501		$785.00

1/2-oz. gold, New 50 pesos. 1994. BW-923, KM-580.
Brilliant Uncirculated and Proof.

Proof.

Composition: 0.999 gold. *Weight:* 15.5517 g. *Obverse:* On a hexagonal field shifted above center, the national coat of arms with the eagle facing left, its feathers resembling plates of armor. Above, the legend **ESTADOS UNIDOS MEXICANOS**; below, a half-wreath of oak and laurel. An ornamental border surrounds the field on five sides, crossing into the field on the uppermost, sixth side; below the border, **1/2 ONZA DE ORO / LEY 0.999**. *Reverse:* At the center of the field, a Jaina figurine, with 1994 to the left, the mintmark M̥ to the right, and **PERSONAJE / DE JAINA** in the exergue below. An ornamental border surrounds the field on five sides, crossing into the field on the uppermost, sixth side; below the border, **N$50**. *Diameter:* 29 mm. *Edge:* Reeded.

	Mintage	BU	PF
1994	1,000	$950.00	
1994, Proof	501		$1,550.00

1-oz. gold, New 100 pesos. 1994. BW-924, KM-581. Brilliant Uncirculated and Proof.

Proof.

Composition: 0.999 gold. *Weight:* 31.1035 g. *Obverse:* On a hexagonal field shifted above center, the national coat of arms with the eagle facing left, its feathers resembling plates of armor. Above, the legend **ESTADOS UNIDOS MEXICANOS**; below, a half-wreath of oak and laurel. An ornamental border surrounds the field on five sides, crossing into the field on the uppermost, sixth side; below the border, **1 ONZA DE ORO / LEY 0.999**. *Reverse:* At the center of the field, a Jaina figurine, with 1994 to the left, the mintmark M̥ to the right, and **PERSONAJE / DE JAINA** in the exergue below. An ornamental border surrounds the field on five sides, crossing into the field on the uppermost, sixth side; below the border, N$100. *Diameter:* 35 mm. *Edge:* Reeded.

	Mintage	BU	PF
1994	1,000	$1,900.00	
1994, Proof	501		$3,100.00

OLMEC COLLECTION

The fourth collection in the program honors the Olmec culture, which flourished in central Mexico and parts of Guatemala, Honduras, and Costa Rica around 1200 to 400 BCE. The Olmec archaeological sites of San Lorenzo, La Venta, and Tres Zapotes are located in the tropical lowlands close to the Gulf of Mexico, in what are now the states of Veracruz and Tabasco.

The Olmecs created monumental basalt sculptures of heads, human figures, thrones, and supernatural creatures. The best known of these are called the Colossal Heads, which are believed to have represented individual rulers. Ranging in height from 5 to 11 feet, the Colossal Heads have been found in several of the Olmec cities; those found at San Lorenzo are the oldest. The basalt from which the sculptures were carved was brought down from the mountains some 60 miles to their final destinations in the lowlands.

Olmec society was hierarchical, with wealth and status determining social class. The higher class of rulers, priests, and skilled artisans lived in the cities; the lower class farmed the surrounding rural areas, producing cotton, maize, and squash. Through trade, they gained access to luxury items, including the precious jade from which they created jewelry, figurines, and various items for religious rituals. Mirrors of polished iron-ore have also been discovered; as seen in Olmec art, they were worn on the chests of the elite, including the priests, suggesting that mirrors may also have been used in rituals. Much speculation surrounds the Olmecs, but their artifacts suggest they were the first Mesoamerican culture to practice bloodletting, and that they created the Mesoamerican ball-game and invented the calendar that would later inspire the Mayan calendar.

The decline of the Olmec civilization came long before the Spanish arrived; its exact cause is unknown. Archeologists have suggested that a volcanic eruption may have forced their dispersal or that climate change may have devastated their crops. San Lorenzo was the first city to fall into decline, leading to the prominence of La Venta. When La Venta in turn declined and was abandoned, Tres Zapotes, located in what is now the Veracruz region, became the center of Olmec culture. The Olmec evolved into what is known as the Epi-Olmec culture, which gave rise to the Central Veracruz culture and the city of El Tajín (see the Central Veracruz section). It was not until the 1850s that what remains of the Olmec culture was discovered by Europeans.

Silver Issues

Master of the Limes (1/4, 1/2, and 1 oz.)

Señor de las Limas (Master of the Limes) is the central motif on the three-piece silver group of coins in this collection. It is modeled after the original Señor de las Limas, a greenstone sculpture of a seated priest with a baby jaguar-human in his arms. It was found in the Valley of the Limes in the region of Veracruz, and is held in the collection of the Museum of Anthropology in Xalapa. According to archaeologists, the sculpture is related to fertility and maternity rituals. The coin's border design is inspired by a pre-Columbian symbol for "fire."

Silver 1-ounce coins in this design were issued in 1996 in both Brilliant Uncirculated and Proof, in three weights: 1/4 ounce (denominated 1 peso), 1/2 ounce (2 pesos), and 1 ounce (5 pesos). These weights and denominations were issued again in 1998 in Brilliant Uncirculated only.

Señor de las Limas, or Master of the Limes; Museum of Anthropology, Xalapa.

1/4-oz. silver, 1 peso. 1996, 1998. BW-925, KM-593.
Brilliant Uncirculated and Proof.

Brilliant Uncirculated.

Composition: 0.999 silver. *Weight:* 7.7700 g. *Obverse:* On a square field with convex sides, the national coat of arms with the eagle facing left, its feathers resembling plates of armor. Above, the legend **ESTADOS UNIDOS MEXICANOS**; below, a half-wreath of oak and laurel. Surrounding the field, an ornamental border; below the border, **1/4 ONZA DE PLATA / LEY 0.999**. *Reverse:* At the center of the field, the Master of the Limes figure. To the left, **1996**; to the right, the mintmark M̊; in the exergue below, **SEÑOR DE LAS LIMAS**. Surrounding the field, an ornamental border, with **$1** below. *Diameter:* 27 mm. *Edge:* Reeded.

	Mintage	BU	PF
1996	6,400	$28.00	
1996, Proof	3,700		$38.00
1998	2,400	28.00	

1/2-oz. silver, 2 pesos. 1996, 1998. BW-926, M-594.
Brilliant Uncirculated and Proof.

Brilliant Uncirculated.

Composition: 0.999 silver. *Weight:* 15.5517 g. *Obverse:* On a square field with convex sides, the national coat of arms with the eagle facing left, its feathers resembling plates of armor. Above, the legend **ESTADOS UNIDOS MEXICANOS**; below, a half-wreath of oak and laurel. Surrounding the field, an ornamental border; below the border, **1/2 ONZA DE PLATA / LEY 0.999**. *Reverse:* At the center of the field, the Master of the Limes figure. To the left, **1996**; to the right, the mintmark M̊; in the exergue below, **SEÑOR DE LAS LIMAS**. Surrounding the field, an ornamental border, with **$2** below. *Diameter:* 33 mm. *Edge:* Reeded.

	Mintage	BU	PF
1996	6,500	$38.00	
1996, Proof	2,200		$48.00
1998	2,400	38.00	

**1-oz. silver, 5 pesos. 1996, 1998. BW-927, KM-595.
Brilliant Uncirculated and Proof.**

Brilliant Uncirculated.

Composition: 0.999 silver. *Weight:* 31.1030 g. *Obverse:* On a square field with convex sides, the national coat of arms with the eagle facing left, its feathers resembling plates of armor. Above, the legend **ESTADOS UNIDOS MEXICANOS**; below, a half-wreath of oak and laurel. Surrounding the field, an ornamental border; below the border, **1 ONZA DE PLATA / LEY 0.999**. *Reverse:* At the center of the field, the Master of the Limes figure. To the left, **1996**; to the right, the mintmark M̊; in the exergue below, **SEÑOR DE LAS LIMAS**. Surrounding the field, an ornamental border, with $5 below. *Diameter:* 40 mm. *Edge:* Reeded.

	Mintage	BU	PF
1996	9,200	$65.00	
1996, Proof	4,100		$85.00
1998	4,700	65.00	

Jaguar-Man (1 oz.)

These figures are some of the finest examples of Olmec sculpture and can be found in a number of poses. The most common, and the one used on the Hombre Jaguar (Jaguar-Man) coin, is a seated personage wearing a helmet; it is held in the collection of the National Museum of Anthropology. The facial features resemble those of a jaguar, which was the center of most Olmec rituals. The coin's border design is based on graphic elements on the Jaguar-Man's chest and headdress.

Silver 1-ounce coins in this design, denominated 5 pesos, were issued in 1996 in Brilliant Uncirculated and Proof. Both formats were struck in Variety 1 (date to the left, mintmark to the right) and Variety 2 (date and mintmark to the left). The design was issued again in 1998 in Brilliant Uncirculated, Variety 1 only.

Hombre Jaguar, or Jaguar-Man; National Museum of Anthropology.

1-oz. silver, 5 pesos. 1996, 1998. BW-927.3, KM-596. Brilliant Uncirculated and Proof.

Variety 1, Brilliant Uncirculated.

Variety 2 reverse, Brilliant Uncirculated.

Composition: 0.999 silver. *Weight:* 31.1030 g. *Obverse:* On a square field with convex sides, the national coat of arms with the eagle facing left, its feathers resembling plates of armor. Above, the legend **ESTADOS UNIDOS MEXICANOS**; below, a half-wreath of oak and laurel. Surrounding the field, an ornamental border; below the border, **1 ONZA DE PLATA / LEY 0.999**. *Reverse:* At the center of the field, the Jaguar-Man figure. To the left, **1996**; to the right, the mintmark M̊; in the exergue below, **HOMBRE JAGUAR**. Surrounding the field, an ornamental border, with **$5** below. *Diameter:* 40 mm. *Edge:* Reeded.

	Mintage	BU	PF
1996, Variety 1 (a)	1,500	$70.00	
1996, Variety 1, Proof (a)	2,800		$90.00
1996, Variety 2 (b)	1,500	70.00	
1996, Variety 2, Proof (b)	1,200		95.00
1998	2,300	70.00	

a. Date to left, mintmark to right. **b.** Date and mintmark to left; BW-927.3a, KM-UL.

The Wrestler (1 oz.)

The stone sculpture known as El Luchador (The Wrestler) was found in the state of Veracruz near the Rio Uxpanapa, and is housed in the National Museum of Anthropology. The sculpture is about 2 feet tall and represents a seated man with his arms at shoulder height, elbows bent, hands in fists—a dynamic attitude, as if he is playing some sort of sport or fighting. The coin's border is based on ornamental elements from a ceremonial Olmec vase.

Silver 1-ounce coins in this design, denominated 5 pesos, were issued in 1996 in Brilliant Uncirculated and Proof. The design was issued again in 1998 in Brilliant Uncirculated only.

El Luchador, or The Wrestler; National Museum of Anthropology.

1-oz. silver, 5 pesos. 1996, 1998. BW-927.1, KM-597.
Brilliant Uncirculated and Proof.

Brilliant Uncirculated.

Composition: 0.999 silver. *Weight:* 31.1030 g. *Obverse:* On a square field with convex sides, the national coat of arms with the eagle facing left, its feathers resembling plates of armor. Above, the legend **ESTADOS UNIDOS MEXICANOS**; below, a half-wreath of oak and laurel. Surrounding the field, an ornamental border; below the border, **1 ONZA DE PLATA / LEY 0.999**. *Reverse:* At the center of the field, the seated figure of the Wrestler. To the left, **1996**; to the right, the mintmark M̥; in the exergue below, **EL LUCHADOR**. Surrounding the field, an ornamental border, with **$5** below. *Diameter:* 40 mm. *Edge:* Reeded.

	Mintage	BU	PF
1996	7,100	$65.00	
1996, Proof	3,800		$85.00
1998	2,100	65.00	

Ceremonial Ax (1 oz.)

A Mesoamerican ceremonial ax or hachet was a piece of stone, often greenstone, carved into an ax-head shape and decorated with symbolic figures. A cleft was often carved into the back and top of the head. Ceremonial axes may have been used for rituals pertaining to agriculture. The humanlike figure on which the Olmec 1-ounce Hacha Ceremonial coin is based is from the National Museum of Anthropology. Its facial features resemble those of the Jaguar-Man; when the figure on which the design is based is viewed in profile, the body tapers at the bottom to a wedge. The coin's border design echoes the shape of the Jaguar-Man's eyebrows.

Silver 1-ounce coins in this design, denominated 5 pesos, were issued in 1996 in Brilliant Uncirculated and Proof. The design was issued again in 1998 in Brilliant Uncirculated only.

Illustration of a ceremonial ax of the type depicted on the Hacha Ceremonial coin.

1-oz. silver, 5 pesos. 1996, 1998. BW-927.2, KM-598. Brilliant Uncirculated and Proof.

Brilliant Uncirculated.

Composition: 0.999 silver. *Weight:* 31.1030 g. *Obverse:* On a square field with convex sides, the national coat of arms with the eagle facing left, its feathers resembling plates of armor. Above, the legend **ESTADOS UNIDOS MEXICANOS**; below, a half-wreath of oak and laurel. Surrounding the field, an ornamental border; below the border, **1 ONZA DE PLATA / LEY 0.999**. *Reverse:* At the center of the field, the Ceremonial Ax figure. To the left, **1996**; to the right, the mintmark M̊; in the exergue below, **HACHA CEREMONIAL**. Surrounding the field, an ornamental border with $5 below. *Diameter:* 40 mm. *Edge:* Reeded.

	Mintage	BU	PF
1996	7,500	$65.00	
1996, Proof	3,700		$85.00
1998	2,500	65.00	

Olmec Head (5 oz.)

The design on the 5-ounce coin depicts one of the most iconic sculptures of the Olmec culture: the Cabeza Olmeca, or Olmec Head. To date only 16 of these colossal heads have been found. Their weight ranges from 9 to 11 metric tons, and their height is from 5 to 11 feet. The head on which the coin's design is based is San Lorenzo Colossal Head 1, located at the Museum of Anthropology in Xalapa. Archaeologists are uncertain whether these heads represent gods, priest, or rulers, although the latter seems most likely. The emblem repeated in the coin's border design is based on the shape of the Jaguar-Man's mouth.

An Olmec colossal head, as depicted on the Cabeza Olmeca coin.

Silver 1-ounce coins in this design, denominated 10 pesos, were issued in 1996 in Brilliant Uncirculated and Proof. The design was issued again in 1998 in Brilliant Uncirculated only.

5-oz. silver, 10 pesos. 1996, 1998. BW-928, KM-599. Brilliant Uncirculated and Proof.

Proof.
Shown reduced; actual size 65 mm.

Composition: 0.999 silver. *Weight:* 155.3100 g. *Obverse:* On a square field with convex sides, the national coat of arms with the eagle facing left, its feathers resembling plates of armor. Above, the legend **ESTADOS UNIDOS MEXICANOS**; below, a half-wreath of oak and laurel. Surrounding the field, an ornamental border; below the border, **1 ONZA DE PLATA / LEY 0.999**. *Reverse:* At the center of the field, an Olmec Head. To the left, **1996**; to the right, the mintmark M̊; in the exergue below, **CABEZA OLMECA**. Surrounding the field, an ornamental border with **$10** below. *Diameter:* 65 mm. *Edge:* Reeded.

	Mintage	BU	PF
1996	5,560	$235.00	
1996, Proof	3,900		$310.00
1998	3,060	235.00	

GOLD ISSUES
Priest (1/4, 1/2, and 1 oz.)

The central motif on the gold coins in the Olmec Collection is the Sacerdote (Priest), a bas-relief figure found at the ancient ruins of La Venta and now located in the National Museum of Anthropology. In the sculpture, a priest or high dignitary is seated in profile, and is surrounded by a massive, undulating feathered serpent. The element repeated in the coin's border is based on a device in the headband of the Jaguar-Man.

Sacerdote, or Priest, from La Venta; National Museum of Anthropology.

Gold coins in this design were issued in 1996 in both Brilliant Uncirculated and Proof, in three weights: 1/4 ounce (denominated 25 pesos), 1/2 ounce (50 pesos), and 1 ounce (100 pesos). These weights and denominations were issued again in 1998, but in Brilliant Uncirculated only.

1/4-oz. gold, 25 pesos. 1996. BW-929, KM-600.
Brilliant Uncirculated and Proof.

Proof.

Composition: 0.999 gold. *Weight:* 7.7758 g. *Obverse:* On a square field with convex sides, the national coat of arms with the eagle facing left, its feathers resembling plates of armor. Above, the legend **ESTADOS UNIDOS MEXICANOS**; below, a half-wreath of oak and laurel. Surrounding the field, an ornamental border; below the border, **1/4 ONZA DE ORO / LEY 0.999**. *Reverse:* At the center of the field, a priest seated in profile and surrounded by a feathered serpent. To the left, **1996**; to the right, the mintmark M̊; in the exergue below, **SACERDOTE**. Surrounding the field, an ornamental border with **$25** below. *Diameter:* 23 mm. *Edge:* Reeded.

	Mintage	BU	PF
1996	500	$475.00	
1996, Proof	750		$785.00
1998		475.00	

1/2-oz. gold, 50 pesos. 1996. BW-930, KM-601.
Brilliant Uncirculated and Proof.

Proof.

Composition: 0.999 gold. *Weight:* 15.5517 g. *Obverse:* On a square field with convex sides, the national coat of arms with the eagle facing left, its feathers resembling plates of armor. Above, the legend **ESTADOS UNIDOS MEXICANOS**; below, a half-wreath of oak and laurel. Surrounding the field, an ornamental border; below the border, **1/2 ONZA DE ORO / LEY 0.999**. *Reverse:* At the center of the field, a Priest seated in profile and surrounded by a feathered serpent. To the left, **1996**; to the right, the mintmark M̊; in the exergue below, **SACERDOTE**. Surrounding the field, an ornamental border with **$50** below. *Diameter:* 29 mm. *Edge:* Reeded.

	Mintage	BU	PF
1996	500	$950.00	
1996, Proof	500		$1,550.00
1998		950.00	

1-oz. gold, 100 pesos. 1996. BW-931, KM-602.
Brilliant Uncirculated and Proof.

Proof.

Composition: 0.999 gold. *Weight:* 31.1035 g. *Obverse:* On a square field with convex sides, the national coat of arms with the eagle facing left, its feathers resembling plates of armor. Above, the legend **ESTADOS UNIDOS MEXICANOS**; below, a half-wreath of oak and laurel. Surrounding the field, an ornamental border; below the border, **1 ONZA DE ORO / LEY 0.999**. *Reverse:* At the center of the field, a Priest seated in profile and surrounded by a feathered serpent. To the left, **1996**; to the right, the mintmark M̊; in the exergue below, **SACERDOTE**. Surrounding the field, an ornamental border with **$100** below. *Diameter:* 35 mm. *Edge:* Reeded.

	Mintage	BU	PF
1996	500	$1,900.00	
1996, Proof	500		$3,100.00
1998		1,900.00	

THE TEOTIHUACÁN COLLECTION

Honored in the fifth collection, released in 1997, is the Teotihuacán culture. Around the second century BCE, in the valley of Mexico, several settlements joined to form a city. The city's name at the time is unknown; the Aztecs who discovered the remains of the city after its decline called it Teotihuacán, or "the city of the gods."

At its peak, Teotihuacán had more than 2,000 structures and a population of more than 100,000. Extending from modern-day Sinaloa in western Mexico to Guatemala in the southeast, it was the largest city in the world prior to the 1400s. Teotihuacán was a planned city, laid out on a complex grid. The primary street through the city was the Calle de los Muertos (Street of the Dead), with the Pyramid of the Moon at one end, the Pyramid of the Sun farther down the avenue, and the Ciudadela (a sunken, enclosed compound that may have been a marketplace) with the Temple of Quetzalcóatl still farther along. These pyramids are some of the most important of the pre-Columbian era. The Pyramid of the Sun is not only the largest pyramid in the city, but also one of the largest in the world. Underneath the pyramid is a tunnel that leads to a cave, which archeologists speculate either was a tomb or was thought to be an entrance to the underworld.

While the builders of the city are unknown, the society was a blend of many groups of people. The remaining architecture indicates that the majority of the housing consisted of multi-family apartment compounds, with the upper classes likely living in the compounds closer to the Avenue of the Dead and the rulers and priests living closer to the pyramids and temples. The staple export was obsidian, which may be what brought the city to its height of power and wealth. Ceramics were also a significant export. Teotihuacán was also a religious center, and people would travel from the surrounding areas to attend ceremonies and rituals. The religion featured several gods, the most important of which seems to have been the Great Goddess, whom scholars believe they have found depicted in murals. The Teotihuacanos practiced human sacrifice though methods of heart extraction, decapitation, bludgeoning of the head, and burying victims alive.

The city reached its greatest splendor from 350 CE to 650 CE, then suddenly declined. The final dissolution occurred about 700 CE. Some archaeologists hold that the city fell due to drought and famine. Others believe the city was laid low by a great fire, possibly from an internal uprising against the rulers (the burned buildings appear to have been government buildings). Despite its decline, the city was not abandoned until almost a century later.

In 1987, Teotihuacán was named a UNESCO World Heritage site.

Silver Issues

Disc of Death (1/4, 1/2, and 1 oz.)

The three-piece silver set in this collection features the Disco de la Muerte (Disc of Death): an extraordinary stone sculpture depicting a human skull at the center with rays radiating outward. At some point, the disc was broken around the edges, perhaps during a raid during the decline of the city. The sculpture is now located in the National Museum of Anthropology. The coin's border is inspired by a decorative element on a conical, three-legged Teotihuacán vessel, possibly also in the Museo Nacional.

Silver 1-ounce coins in this design were issued in 1997 and 1998 in both Brilliant Uncirculated and Proof, in three weights: 1/4 ounce (denominated 1 peso), 1/2 ounce (2 pesos), and 1 ounce (5 pesos).

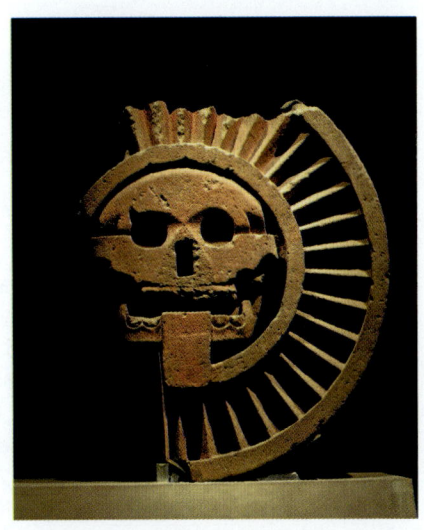

Disco de la Muerte, or Disc of Death; National Museum of Anthropology.

**1/4-oz. silver, 1 peso. 1997, 1998. BW-932, KM-617.
Brilliant Uncirculated and Proof.**

Brilliant Uncirculated.

Composition: 0.999 silver. *Weight:* 7.7700 g. *Obverse:* On a horizontal oval field, the national coat of arms with the eagle facing left, its feathers resembling plates of armor. Above, the legend **ESTADOS UNIDOS MEXICANOS**; below, a half-wreath of oak and laurel. Surrounding the field, an ornamental border; below the border, **1/4 ONZA DE PLATA / LEY 0.999**. *Reverse:* At the center of the field, the broken Disc of Death. To the left, the date; to the right, the mintmark M̥; in the exergue below, **DISCO DE LA MUERTE**. Surrounding the field, an ornamental border with $1 below. *Diameter:* 27 mm. *Edge:* Reeded.

	Mintage	BU	PF
1997	3,000	$28.00	
1997, Proof	1,600		$48.00
1998	2,400	28.00	
1998, Proof	506		95.00

1/2-oz. silver, 2 pesos. 1997, 1998. BW-933, KM-618.
Brilliant Uncirculated and Proof.

Brilliant Uncirculated.

Composition: 0.999 silver. *Weight:* 15.5517 g. *Obverse:* On a horizontal oval field, the national coat of arms with the eagle facing left, its feathers resembling plates of armor. Above, the legend **ESTADOS UNIDOS MEXICANOS**; below, a half-wreath of oak and laurel. Surrounding the field, an ornamental border; below the border, **1/2 ONZA DE PLATA / LEY 0.999**. *Reverse:* At the center of the field, the broken Disc of Death. To the left, the date; to the right, the mintmark M̥; in the exergue below, **DISCO DE LA MUERTE**. Surrounding the field, an ornamental border with $2 below. *Diameter:* 33 mm. *Edge:* Reeded.

	Mintage	BU	PF
1997	3,000	$38.00	
1997, Proof	1,600		$48.00
1998	2,400	38.00	
1998, Proof	506		120.00

1-oz. silver, 5 pesos. 1997, 1998. BW-934, KM-619.
Brilliant Uncirculated and Proof.

Brilliant Uncirculated.

Composition: 0.999 silver. *Weight:* 31.1030 g. *Obverse:* On a horizontal oval field, the national coat of arms with the eagle facing left, its feathers resembling plates of armor. Above, the legend **ESTADOS UNIDOS MEXICANOS**; below, a half-wreath of oak and laurel. Surrounding the field, an ornamental border; below the border, **1 ONZA DE PLATA / LEY 0.999**. *Reverse:* At the center of the field, the broken

Disc of Death. To the left, the date; to the right, the mintmark M̊; below, **DISCO DE LA MUERTE**. Surrounding the field, an ornamental border with $5 below. *Diameter:* 40 mm. *Edge:* Reeded.

Mask (1 oz.)

A magnificent stone *mascara* (mask) like the one depicted on the Mascara coin was part of the funerary dress for the high-ranking people of the Teotihuacán culture. The coin's border design is based on a decorative element found on another, turquoise-encrusted Teotihuacán mask.

Silver 1-ounce coins in this design, denominated 5 pesos, were issued in 1997 and 1998 in Brilliant Uncirculated and Proof.

Illustration of a mask of the type depicted on the 1-ounce Mascara (Mask) coin.

1-oz. silver, 5 pesos. 1997, 1998. BW-934.1, KM-620. Brilliant Uncirculated and Proof.

Brilliant Uncirculated.

Composition: 0.999 silver. *Weight:* 31.1030 g. *Obverse:* On a horizontal oval field, the national coat of arms with the eagle facing left, its feathers resembling plates of armor. Above, the legend **ESTADOS UNIDOS MEXICANOS**; below, a half-wreath of oak and laurel. Surrounding the field, an ornamental border; below the border, **1 ONZA DE PLATA / LEY 0.999**. *Reverse:* At the center of the field, a funeral mask. To the left, the date; to the right, the mintmark M̊; in the exergue below, **MASCARA**. Surrounding the field, an ornamental border with $5 below. *Diameter:* 40 mm. *Edge:* Reeded.

	Mintage	BU	PF
1997	4,500	$65.00	
1997, Proof	1,800		$90.00
1998	2,200	70.00	
1998, Proof	1,306		235.00

Vessel (1 oz.)

The design of this coin, called Vasija (Vessel), is based on a Teotihuacán vase or container shaped as a seated human figure. The vessel on the coin, currently housed in the National Museum of Anthropology, illustrates one of many types of human-shaped vessel-figurines. Their significance is unknown, although it is believed they represented gods or high-ranking individuals. The border of the coin is inspired by a design in the headdress of a Teotihuacán sculpture.

Silver 1-ounce coins in this design, denominated 5 pesos, were issued in 1997 and 1998 in Brilliant Uncirculated and Proof.

Illustration of a vessel of the type depicted on the 1-ounce Vasija (Vessel) coin.

1-oz. silver, 5 pesos. 1997, 1998. BW-934.2, KM-621.
Brilliant Uncirculated and Proof.

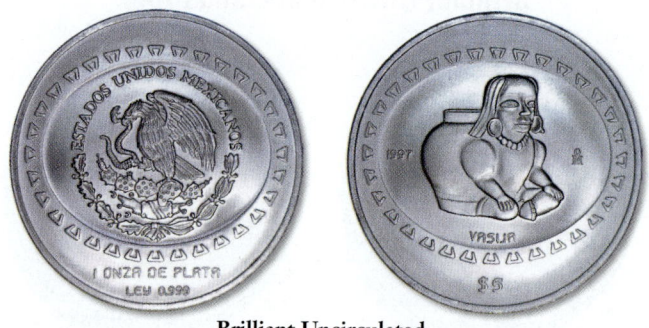

Brilliant Uncirculated.

Composition: 0.999 silver. *Weight:* 31.1030 g. *Obverse:* On a horizontal oval field, the national coat of arms with the eagle facing left, its feathers resembling plates of armor. Above, the legend **ESTADOS UNIDOS MEXICANOS**; below, a half-wreath of oak and laurel. Surrounding the field, an ornamental border; below the border, **1 ONZA DE PLATA / LEY 0.999**. *Reverse:* At the center of the field, a human-shaped vessel. To the left, the date; to the right, the mintmark M̊; in the exergue below, **VASIJA**. Surrounding the field, an ornamental border with $5 below. *Diameter:* 40 mm. *Edge:* Reeded.

	Mintage	BU	PF
1997	4,500	$65.00	
1997, Proof	1,800		$90.00
1998	2,300	70.00	
1998, Proof	1,406		235.00

Ball Player (1 oz.)

The reclining Jugador de Pelota (Ball Player) figure on this coin is based on a figurine molded in the orange ceramic clay that was common at a certain stage of the Teotihuacán culture; it is part of the collection of the National Museum of Anthropology. The figurines were important to the Teotihuacán commercial system, which extended to almost all of the Mesoamerican regions. The repeated element in the coin's border is based on a design found in an image of the goddess Chalchiuhtlicue.

Illustration of a figurine of the type depicted on the 1-ounce Jugador de Pelota (Ball Player) coin.

Silver 1-ounce coins in this design, denominated 5 pesos, were issued in 1997 and 1998 in Brilliant Uncirculated and Proof.

1-oz. silver, 5 pesos. 1997, 1998. BW-934.3, KM-622. Brilliant Uncirculated and Proof.

Brilliant Uncirculated.

Composition: 0.999 silver. *Weight:* 31.1030 g. *Obverse:* On a horizontal oval field, the national coat of arms with the eagle facing left, its feathers resembling plates of armor. Above, the legend **ESTADOS UNIDOS MEXICANOS**; below, a half-wreath of oak and laurel. Surrounding the field, an ornamental border; below the border, **1 ONZA DE PLATA / LEY 0.999**. *Reverse:* At the center of the field, the figure of a reclining ball player. To the left, the date; to the right, the mintmark M̥; in the exergue below, **JUGADOR DE PELOTA**. Surrounding the field, an ornamental border with $5 below. *Diameter:* 40 mm. *Edge:* Reeded.

	Mintage	BU	PF
1997	4,500	$65.00	
1997, Proof	1,800		$90.00
1998	2,400	70.00	
1998, Proof	1,606		235.00

Pyramid of the Sun (5 oz.)

The 5-ounce coin for this collection features the Pirámide del Sol (Pyramid of the Sun), an ambitious monument dedicated to the sun and important to the citizens of Teotihuacán. Its orientation is based on astronomical considerations, and deviates slightly on the north side. The repeated shape in the border is often found on ceremonial braziers honoring the fire-god Huehuetéotl.

Pyramid of the Sun, Teotihuacán.

Silver 5-ounce coins in this design, denominated 10 pesos, were issued in 1997 in Brilliant Uncirculated and Proof, and in 1998 in Brilliant Uncirculated only.

5-oz. silver, 10 pesos. 1997, 1998. BW-935, KM-623. Brilliant Uncirculated and Proof.

Proof.
Shown reduced; actual size 65 mm.

Composition: 0.999 silver. *Weight:* 155.3100 g. *Obverse:* On a horizontal oval field, the national coat of arms with the eagle facing left, its feathers resembling plates of armor. Above, the legend **ESTADOS UNIDOS MEXICANOS**; below, a half-wreath of oak and laurel. Surrounding the field, an ornamental border; below the border, **5 ONZAS DE PLATA / LEY 0.999**. *Reverse:* At the center of the field, the Pyramid of the Sun. At upper left, the date; at upper right, the mintmark M̊; in the exergue below, **PIRAMIDE DEL SOL**. Surrounding the field, an ornamental border with **$5** below. *Diameter:* 65 mm. *Edge:* Reeded.

	Mintage	BU	PF
1997,	1,500	$235.00	
1997, Proof	3,106		$310.00
1998	3,286	235.00	

Gold Issues
Feathered Serpent (1/4, 1/2, and 1 oz.)

The design depicted on the three gold coins is a detail from the Temple of Quetzalcóatl in Teotihuacán. The Serpiente Emplumada (Feathered Serpent) was one of the most powerful gods of the Teotihuacán culture, and the subject of special rituals. The repeated element in the coin's border is based on a design found in an image of the goddess Chalchiuhtlicue.

Gold coins in this design were issued in 1997 in both Brilliant Uncirculated and Proof, in three weights: 1/4 ounce (denominated 25 pesos), 1/2 ounce (50 pesos), and 1 ounce (100 pesos). These weights and denominations were also issued in 1998, in Brilliant Uncirculated only.

Quetzalcóatl sculpture, Teotihuacán.

1/4-oz. gold, 25 pesos. 1997, 1998. BW-936, KM-624.
Brilliant Uncirculated and Proof.

Proof.

Composition: 0.999 gold. *Weight:* 7.7758 g. *Obverse:* On a horizontal oval field, the national coat of arms with the eagle facing left, its feathers resembling plates of armor. Above, the legend **ESTADOS UNIDOS MEXICANOS**; below, a half-wreath of oak and laurel. Surrounding the field, an ornamental border; below the border, **1/4 ONZA DE ORO / LEY 0.999**. *Reverse:* At the center of the field, the feathered serpent-god Quetzalcóatl. To the left, the date; to the right, the mintmark M̥; in the exergue below, **SERPIENTE EMPLUMADA**. Surrounding the field, an ornamental border with **$25** below. *Diameter:* 23 mm. *Edge:* Reeded.

	Mintage	BU	PF
1997	500	$475.00	
1997, Proof	206		$785.00
1998	500	475.00	

1/2-oz. gold, 50 pesos. 1997, 1998. BW-937, KM-625.
Brilliant Uncirculated and Proof.

Proof.

Composition: 0.999 gold. *Weight:* 15.5517 g. *Obverse:* On a horizontal oval field, the national coat of arms with the eagle facing left, its feathers resembling plates of armor. Above, the legend **ESTADOS UNIDOS MEXICANOS**; below, a half-wreath of oak and laurel. Surrounding the field, an ornamental border; below the border, **1/2 ONZA DE ORO / LEY 0.999**. *Reverse:* At the center of the field, the feathered serpent-god Quetzalcóatl. To the left, the date; to the right, the mintmark M̥; in the exergue below, **SERPIENTE EMPLUMADA**. Surrounding the field, an ornamental border with **$50** below. *Diameter:* 29 mm. *Edge:* Reeded.

	Mintage	BU	PF
1997	500	$950.00	
1997, Proof	206		$1,550.00
1998	500	950.00	

1-oz. gold, 100 pesos. 1997, 1998. BW-938, KM-626.
Brilliant Uncirculated and Proof.

Proof.

Composition: 0.999 gold. *Weight:* 31.1035 g. *Obverse:* On a horizontal oval field, the national coat of arms with the eagle facing left, its feathers resembling plates of armor. Above, the legend **ESTADOS UNIDOS MEXICANOS**; below, a half-wreath of oak and laurel. Surrounding the field, an ornamental border; below the border, **1 ONZA DE ORO / LEY 0.999**. *Reverse:* At the center of the field, the feathered serpent-god Quetzalcóatl. To the left, the date; to the right, the mintmark M̥; in the exergue below, **SERPIENTE EMPLUMADA**. Surrounding the field, an ornamental border with **$100** below. *Diameter:* 34.5 mm. *Edge:* Reeded.

	Mintage	BU	PF
1997	500	$1,900.00	
1997, Proof	206		$3,100.00
1998	500	1,900.00	

TOLTEC COLLECTION

Released in 1998, the sixth and final collection in the Pre-Columbian Series honored the complex Toltec civilization, which was centered around the city of Tula in the current state of Hidalgo. With a population of around 40,000, the Toltecs were at their height from the mid-9th century to the 12th century. They left a legacy of a vast wealth and beauty in a majestic archaeological zone; the ruins include ball courts, pyramids, and residences. The most renowned remaining architecture is the Temple of Tlahuizcalpantecuhtli (Morning Star), or the Pyramid of Quetzalcóatl. It features four sculptures called the Atlantean figures: Toltec warriors, each wearing a butterfly-shaped breastplate and carrying an atlatl (spear-thrower). Carvings along the base of the pyramid include jaguars, coyotes, and eagles eating human hearts.

The Toltecs established an advanced educational system that attracted students from as far away as what is now Central America. Their crops included maize and cotton—which legend says grew in bright colors without being dyed. (Modern science confirms the existence of naturally colored cotton in the Americas as early as 5,000 years ago.) One of the Toltecs' main trade partners was Chichén Itzá, a major Mayan city-state in the Yucatán area. As militarism played a significant role in the Toltec civilization, their major trade item was obsidian, which they used to manufacture weapons. Seen in the Atlantean figures, military attire consisted of breastplates, shields, spears, and headdresses.

The Toltecs, like other Mesoamericans, had a polytheistic religion. They worshipped the feathered serpent god Quetzalcóatl; Tezcatlipoca, god of the night and darkness; Tlaloc, god of the rain and vegetation; Centeotl, god of corn; Itzpapalotl ("Obsidian Butterfly"), a fearsome warrior goddess; and Tonatiuh, or the sun god. Their religious rituals included human sacrifice, which, from the carvings seen along the Temple of Tlahuizcalpantecuhtli, was performed by extraction of the heart, although possibly by other methods as well.

Much of what is known about the Toltecs comes from ancient texts of the Aztecs and Maya, who often combined both history and legend. One such legend is that of Quetzalcóatl, who was not only the feathered serpent god, but was apparently believed to have come to the Toltecs as a man. He eventually left the people, but was prophesied to return; later stories claim the Aztecs thought the return had finally happened when Hernán Cortés arrived (see the Aztec Collection section). Similarities between the art and architecture of the Toltec pyramids and that of the Mayan El Castillo in Chichén Itzá indicate that a relationship of more than just trade may have existed between the two cultures.

The decline of the Toltecs and their city of Tula came in the 12th century with the burning of the city, possibly due to invasion by the Chichimec tribes. Legend says the remaining Toltec people were led by Huemac, the last Toltec ruler, to the city of Chapultepec, where Toltec ruins have been discovered. The city of Tula was found in the 1940s by Mexican archaeologist Jorge Acosta, who was excavating a nearby village.

Silver Issues

Jaguar (1/4, 1/2, and 1 oz.)

The three silver coins depict a bas-relief sculpture from the National Museum of Anthropology; carved into the stone is a jaguar, an animal revered by the Toltecs. The geometric figure repeated throughout the border of the field is inspired by an element in a column of the Quetzalcóatl-Tlahuizcalpantecuhtli temple.

Silver 1-ounce coins in this design were issued in 1998 in both Brilliant Uncirculated and Proof, in three weights: 1/4 ounce (denominated 1 peso), 1/2 ounce (2 pesos), and 1 ounce (5 pesos).

Jaguar, bas-relief fragment; National Museum of Anthropology.

1/4-oz. silver, 1 peso. 1998. BW-939, KM-661.
Brilliant Uncirculated and Proof.

Brilliant Uncirculated.

Composition: 0.999 silver. *Weight:* 7.7700 g. *Obverse:* On a trapezoidal field with convex sides, the national coat of arms with the eagle facing left, its feathers resembling plates of armor. Above, the legend **ESTADOS UNIDOS MEXICANOS**; below, a half-wreath of oak and laurel. Surrounding the field, an ornamental border; below the border, **1/4 ONZA DE PLATA / LEY 0.999**. *Reverse:* At the center of the field, a sculpture of a jaguar. To the left, **1998**; to the right, mintmark M̥; below, **JAGUAR**. Surrounding the field, an ornamental border with **$1** below. *Diameter:* 27 mm. *Edge:* Reeded.

	Mintage	BU	PF
1998	6,400	$24.00	
1998, Proof	4,000		$28.00

1/2-oz. silver, 2 pesos. 1998. BW-940, KM-662.
Brilliant Uncirculated and Proof.

Brilliant Uncirculated.

Composition: 0.999 silver. *Weight:* 15.5517 g. *Obverse:* On a trapezoidal field with convex sides, the national coat of arms with the eagle facing left, its feathers resembling plates of armor. Above, the legend **ESTADOS UNIDOS MEXICANOS**; below, a half-wreath of oak and laurel. Surrounding the field, an ornamental border; below the border, **1/2 ONZA DE PLATA / LEY 0.999**. *Reverse:* At the center of the field, a sculpture of a jaguar. To the left, **1998**; to the right, the mintmark M̥; in the exergue below, **JAGUAR**. Surrounding the field, an ornamental border with **$2** below. *Diameter:* 33 mm. *Edge:* Reeded.

	Mintage	BU	PF
1998	6,600	$32.00	
1998, Proof	2,200		$55.00

1-oz. silver, 5 pesos. 1998. BW-941, KM-663.
Brilliant Uncirculated and Proof.

Brilliant Uncirculated.

Composition: 0.999 silver. *Weight:* 31.1030 g. *Obverse:* On a trapezoidal field with convex sides, the national coat of arms with the eagle facing left, its feathers resembling plates of armor. Above, the legend **ESTADOS UNIDOS MEXICANOS**; below, a half-wreath of oak and laurel. Surrounding the field, an ornamental border; below the border, **1 ONZA DE PLATA / LEY 0.999**. *Reverse:* At the center of the field, a sculpture of a jaguar. To the left, **1998**; to the right, the mintmark M̥; in the exergue below, **JAGUAR**. Surrounding the field, an ornamental border with **$5** below. *Diameter:* 40 mm. *Edge:* Reeded.

	Mintage	BU	PF
1998	5,800	$65.00	
1998, Proof	4,300		$85.00

Quetzalcóatl (1 oz.)

This silver 1-ounce coin depicts the birth of Ce Acatl Topiltzin Quetzalcóatl, as shown on a bas-relief housed in the National Museum of Anthropology. Tradition relates that Quetzalcóatl was a leader of the Toltecs and led them to build a great city, dominating several territories with military power and wealth once they were established. He established the cult of the serpent and discontinued human sacrifices during his reign. The emblem repeated throughout the border is found on a belt in a depiction of Quetzalcóatl.

Silver 1-ounce coins in this design, denominated 5 pesos, were issued in 1998 in Brilliant Uncirculated and Proof.

1-oz. silver, 5 pesos. 1998. BW-941.1, KM-665. Brilliant Uncirculated and Proof.

Relief sculpture of Ce Acatl Topiltzin Quetzalcóatl; National Museum of Anthropology.

Brilliant Uncirculated.

Composition: 0.999 silver. *Weight:* 31.1030 g. *Obverse:* On a trapezoidal field with convex sides, the national coat of arms with the eagle facing left, its feathers resembling plates of armor. Above, the legend **ESTADOS UNIDOS MEXICANOS**; below, a half-wreath of oak and laurel. Surrounding the field, an ornamental border; below the border, **1 ONZA DE PLATA / LEY 0.999**. *Reverse:* At the center of the field, a sculpture of the birth of Quetzalcóatl. To the left, **1998**; to the right, the mintmark M̥; in the exergue below, **QUETZALCOATL**. Surrounding the field, an ornamental border with $5 below. *Diameter:* 40 mm. *Edge:* Reeded.

	Mintage	BU	PF
1998	7,100	$65.00	
1998, Proof	3,900		$85.00

Priest (1 oz.)

This coin design, Sacerdote (Priest), depicts one of the great Toltec Atlantean figures (carved stone columns in the shapes of warriors), this one in the form of a priest. Priests within the Toltec culture had a very important social status. They had a direct relation with the gods they venerated and adopted the names and virtues of the gods they represented. The emblem repeated in the coin's surrounding border is inspired by a design on the priest's vest.

Silver 1-ounce coins in this design, denominated 5 pesos, were issued in 1998 in Brilliant Uncirculated and Proof.

1-oz. silver, 5 pesos. 1998. BW-941.2, KM-664. Brilliant Uncirculated and Proof.

Brilliant Uncirculated.

Illustration of Sacerdote statue.

Composition: 0.999 silver. *Weight:* 31.1030 g. *Obverse:* On a trapezoidal field with convex sides, the national coat of arms with the eagle facing left, its feathers resembling plates of armor. Above, the legend **ESTADOS UNIDOS MEXICANOS**; below, a half-wreath of oak and laurel. Surrounding the field, an ornamental border; below the border, **1 ONZA DE PLATA / LEY 0.999**. *Reverse:* At the center of the field, an Atlantean priest figure. To the left, **1998**; to the right, the mintmark M̊; in the exergue below, **SACERDOTE**. Surrounding the field, an ornamental border with **$5** below. *Diameter:* 40 mm. *Edge:* Reeded.

	Mintage	BU	PF
1998	7,800	$65.00	
1998, Proof	3,800		$85.00

Serpent With Skull (1 oz.)

The Serpiente con Craneo (Serpent With Skull) motif shows a detail of the Coatepantli, or "Serpent Wall," found at the Tula site in Hidalgo. The sculpture is a bas-relief of a serpent devouring a human skull. The emblem repeated in the border encircling the coin's field is from the armor on a figure of the god Quetzalcóatl.

Serpiente con Craneo (Serpent With Skull) motif; Tula, Hidalgo.

Silver 1-ounce coins in this design, denominated 5 pesos, were issued in 1998 in Brilliant Uncirculated and Proof.

1-oz. silver, 5 pesos. 1998. BW-941.3, KM-666. Brilliant Uncirculated and Proof.

Brilliant Uncirculated.

Composition: 0.999 silver. *Weight:* 31.1030 g. *Obverse:* On a trapezoidal field with convex sides, the national coat of arms with the eagle facing left, its feathers resembling plates of armor. Above, the legend **ESTADOS UNIDOS MEXICANOS**; below, a half-wreath of oak and laurel. Surrounding the field, an ornamental border; below the border, **1 ONZA DE PLATA / LEY 0.999**. *Reverse:* At the center of the field, a serpent devouring a human skull. To the left, **1998**; to the right, the mintmark M̥; in the exergue below, **SERPIENTE CON CRANEO**. Surrounding the field, an ornamental border with $5 below. *Diameter:* 40 mm. *Edge:* Reeded.

	Mintage	BU	PF
1998	8,700	$65.00	
1998, Proofs	4,100		$85.00

Atlantes Figures (5 oz.)

The silver 5-ounce Toltec coin depicts three of the Atlantes statues, found in the temple of Quetzalcóatl in the archaeological zone of Tula in central Mexico. The statues, which overlook an ancient city dating back to 713 BCE, are Toltec warriors; they hold in their right hands weapons that fire darts, and in their left hands, several arrows. Each warrior wears a chest shield in the shape of a butterfly, a skirt tied in front with a wide belt, and a circular back shield representing the sun. The butterfly-shield motif is repeated in the border surrounding the field.

Atlantes figures; Tula, Hidalgo.

Silver 5-ounce coins in this design, denominated 10 pesos, were issued in 1998 in Brilliant Uncirculated and Proof.

5-oz. silver, 10 pesos. 1998. BW-942, KM-634.
Brilliant Uncirculated and Proof.

Proof.
Shown reduced; actual size 65 mm.

Composition: 0.999 silver. *Weight:* 155.7300 g. *Obverse:* On a trapezoidal field with convex sides, the national coat of arms with the eagle facing left, its feathers resembling plates of armor. Above, the legend **ESTADOS UNIDOS MEXICANOS**; below, a half-wreath of oak and laurel. Surrounding the field, an ornamental border; below the border, **5 ONZAS DE PLATA / LEY 0.999**. *Reverse:* At the center of the field, two Atlantean warrior figures with pillar. To the left, 1998; to the right, the mint-mark M̥; in the exergue below, **ATLANTES**. Surrounding the field, an ornamental border with **$10** below. *Diameter:* 65 mm. *Edge:* Reeded.

	Mintage	BU	PF
1998	5,560	$235.00	
1998, Proof	3,650		$310.00

Gold Issues

Eagle (1/4, 1/2, and 1 oz.)

The Águila (Eagle) design on the three gold coins of the Toltec Collection is based on a bas-relief at the Tula site: an eagle devouring a human heart. The eagle was one of the Toltecs' most revered creatures. The encircling border design is based on an ornament found on the arm of a Chaac-Mool.

Gold coins in this design were issued in 1998 in both Brilliant Uncirculated and Proof, in three weights: 1/4 ounce (denominated 25 pesos), 1/2 ounce (50 pesos), and 1 ounce (100 pesos).

Águila (Eagle) motif; Tula, Hidalgo.

1/4-oz. gold, 25 pesos. 1998. BW-943, KM-667. Brilliant Uncirculated and Proof.

Proof.

Composition: 0.999 gold. *Weight:* 7.7758 g. *Obverse:* On a trapezoidal field with convex sides, the national coat of arms with the eagle facing left, its feathers resembling plates of armor. Above, the legend **ESTADOS UNIDOS MEXICANOS**; below, a half-wreath of oak and laurel. Surrounding the field, an ornamental border; below the border, **1/4 ONZA DE ORO / LEY 0.999**. *Reverse:* At the center of the field, an eagle devouring a heart. To the left, 1998; to the right, the mintmark M̥; in the exergue below, **AGUILA**. Surrounding the field, an ornamental border with $25 below. *Diameter:* 23 mm. *Edge:* Reeded.

	Mintage	BU	PF
1998	303	$475.00	
1998, Proof	303		$785.00

1/2-oz. gold, 50 pesos. 1998. BW-944, KM-668.
Brilliant Uncirculated and Proof.

Proof.

Composition: 0.999 gold. *Weight:* 15.5517 g. *Obverse:* On a trapezoidal field with convex sides, the national coat of arms with the eagle facing left, its feathers resembling plates of armor. Above, the legend **ESTADOS UNIDOS MEXICANOS**; below, a half-wreath of oak and laurel. Surrounding the field, an ornamental border; below the border, **1/2 ONZA DE ORO / LEY 0.999**. *Reverse:* At the center of the field, an eagle devouring a heart. To the left, **1998**; to the right, the mintmark M̥; in the exergue below, **AGUILA**. Surrounding the field, an ornamental border with **$50** below. *Diameter:* 29 mm. *Edge:* Reeded.

	Mintage	BU	PF
1998	303	$950.00	
1998, Proof	303		$1,550.00

1-oz. gold, 100 pesos. 1998. BW-945, KM-669.
Brilliant Uncirculated and Proof.

Proof.

Composition: 0.999 gold. *Weight:* 31.1035 g. *Obverse:* On a trapezoidal field with convex sides, the national coat of arms with the eagle facing left, its feathers resembling plates of armor. Above, the legend **ESTADOS UNIDOS MEXICANOS**; below, a half-wreath of oak and laurel. Surrounding the field, an ornamental border; below the border, **1 ONZA DE ORO / LEY 0.999**. *Reverse:* At the center of the field, an eagle devouring a heart. To the left, **1998**; to the right, the mintmark M̥; in the exergue below, **AGUILA**. Surrounding the field, an ornamental border with **$100** below. *Diameter:* 34.5 mm. *Edge:* Reeded.

	Mintage	BU	PF
1998	303	$1,900.00	
1998, Proof	303		$3,100.00

Appendix A

Bullion Values of Gold and Silver Coins

The following charts show the values of common-date silver and gold Mexican coins, based purely on their precious-metal content; their values as collectibles are *not* included in the figures here.

SILVER COINS

	Fineness	Oz. Silver	Silver Price per Ounce						
			$14	$15	$16	$17	$18	$19	$20
1905 Coinage Reform									
10¢, .800 (T1)	0.800	0.0643	$0.90	$0.96	$1.03	$1.09	$1.16	$1.22	$1.29
10¢, Little .800 (T2)	0.800	0.0466	0.65	0.70	0.75	0.79	0.84	0.89	0.93
10¢, .720 (T4)	0.720	0.0386	0.54	0.58	0.62	0.66	0.69	0.73	0.77
20¢, .800 (T1)	0.800	0.1286	1.80	1.93	2.06	2.19	2.31	2.44	2.57
20¢, Little .800 (T2)	0.800	0.0907	1.27	1.36	1.45	1.54	1.63	1.72	1.81
20¢, .720 (T4)	0.720	0.0772	1.08	1.16	1.24	1.31	1.39	1.47	1.54
25¢, Scales (T1)	0.300	0.0321	0.45	0.48	0.51	0.55	0.58	0.61	0.64
50¢, .800 (T1)	0.800	0.3215	4.50	4.82	5.14	5.47	5.79	6.11	6.43
50¢, Reduced .800 (T2)	0.800	0.2330	3.26	3.50	3.73	3.96	4.19	4.43	4.66
50¢, .720 (T3)	0.720	0.1928	2.70	2.89	3.08	3.28	3.47	3.66	3.86
50¢, .420 (T4)	0.420	0.1077	1.51	1.62	1.72	1.83	1.94	2.05	2.15
50¢, Cuauhtemoc (T5)	0.300	0.0643	0.90	0.96	1.03	1.09	1.16	1.22	1.29
$1, Caballito (T1)	0.903	0.7859	11.00	11.79	12.57	13.36	14.15	14.93	15.72
$1, .800 (T2)	0.800	0.4662	6.53	6.99	7.46	7.93	8.39	8.86	9.32
$1, .720 (T3)	0.720	0.3857	5.40	5.79	6.17	6.56	6.94	7.33	7.71
$1, Little Morelos (T4)	0.500	0.2251	3.15	3.38	3.60	3.83	4.05	4.28	4.50
$1, General Morelos (T5)	0.300	0.1286	1.80	1.93	2.06	2.19	2.31	2.44	2.57
$1, Constitution (T6)	0.100	0.0514	0.72	0.77	0.82	0.87	0.93	0.98	1.03

Bullion Values of Gold and Silver Coins • 435

$1, .100 (T7)	0.100	0.0514	$0.72	$0.77	$0.82	$0.87	$0.93	$0.98	$1.03
$2, Victoria (T1)	0.900	0.7716	10.80	11.57	12.35	13.12	13.89	14.66	15.43
$5, Cuauhtemoc (T1)	0.900	0.8681	12.15	13.02	13.89	14.76	15.63	16.49	17.36
$5, Railroad (T2)	0.720	0.6430	9.00	9.65	10.29	10.93	11.57	12.22	12.86
$5, Hidalgo (T3)	0.720	0.6430	9.00	9.65	10.29	10.93	11.57	12.22	12.86
$5, Hidalgo/Wreath (T4)	0.720	0.6430	9.00	9.65	10.29	10.93	11.57	12.22	12.86
$5, Hidalgo/Chico (T5)	0.720	0.4179	5.85	6.27	6.69	7.10	7.52	7.94	8.36
$5, Constitution (T6)	0.720	0.4178	5.85	6.27	6.68	7.10	7.52	7.94	8.36
$5, Carranza (T7)	0.720	0.4179	5.85	6.27	6.69	7.10	7.52	7.94	8.36
$10, Hidalgo Grande (T1)	0.900	0.8359	11.70	12.54	13.37	14.21	15.05	15.88	16.72
$10, Constitution (T2)	0.900	0.8359	11.70	12.54	13.37	14.21	15.05	15.88	16.72
$10, Hidalgo/Madero (T3)	0.900	0.8359	11.70	12.54	13.37	14.21	15.05	15.88	16.72
$25, Olympics (T1)	0.720	0.5093	7.13	7.64	8.15	8.66	9.17	9.68	10.19
$25, Juarez (T2)	0.720	0.5093	7.13	7.64	8.15	8.66	9.17	9.68	10.19
$100, Morelos	0.720	0.6428	9.00	9.64	10.28	10.93	11.57	12.21	12.86
Una Onza	0.925	1.0000	14.00	15.00	16.00	17.00	18.00	19.00	20.00
1992 Coinage Reform									
N$10, silver center (T-A1)	0.925	0.1667	$2.33	$2.50	$2.67	$2.83	$3.00	$3.17	$3.33
N$20, silver center (T-A1)	0.925	0.2500	3.50	3.75	4.00	4.25	4.50	4.75	5.00
N$50, silver center (T-A1)	0.925	0.5000	7.00	7.50	8.00	8.50	9.00	9.50	10.00

GOLD COINS

	Fineness	Oz. Gold	Gold Price per Ounce						
			$1,100	$1,200	$1,300	$1,400	$1,500	$1,600	$1,700
1905 Coinage Reform									
$2	0.900	0.0482	$53.02	$57.84	$62.66	$67.48	$72.30	$77.12	$81.94
$2.50	0.900	0.0603	66.33	72.36	78.39	84.42	90.45	96.48	102.51
$5	0.900	0.1206	132.66	144.72	156.78	168.84	180.90	192.96	205.02
$10	0.900	0.2411	265.21	289.32	313.43	337.54	361.65	385.76	409.87
$20	0.900	0.4822	530.42	578.64	626.86	675.08	723.30	771.52	819.74
$50	0.900	1.2057	1,326.37	1,446.84	1,567.41	1,687.98	1,808.55	1,929.12	2,049.69

Appendix B
The Calendar Stone on Mexican Coinage

The size of the Calendar Stone is more obvious with someone next to it for perspective. It is pictured here, against the right wall, in the museum in Mexico City, ca. 1890.

Moctezuma II is believed to have commissioned the Aztec Sun Stone (in Spanish, Piedra del Sol or Piedra de los Soles) sometime after 1500 but before the Spanish defeat of the Aztecs in 1521, when the Spaniards defaced the surface of the stone and buried it. It was rediscovered in 1790, nearly 12 feet in diameter and weighing 24 tons, buried three feet beneath the surface of Mexico City's main square, or *zócalo*. Since then it has become both a symbol of Mexico and one of the most famous archeological remnants in the world.

Modern scholars agree that, although many of the stone's devices are Aztec pictographs representing units of time, it was never intended to be a calendar. More likely it was a sacrificial altar depicting the Nahuatl story of the history of the world and glorifying the sun god Tonatiuh. Even so, it is often called the Aztec Calendar Stone; and since this term is the one used by the Banco de México and the Casa de Monéda, *Aztec Calendar Stone* is the term used in this encyclopedia.

This appendix defines and explains the devices and ornaments from the Calendar Stone that appear on Mexican coinage. The terms for these designs can be confusing, in part because the descriptions used in popular culture, archaeology, and numismatics are often contradictory. "Ring of Quincunxes," for example, can refer strictly to the narrow circlet of five-dotted squares, or it can describe everything from the quincunxes outward, excluding the Ring of Serpents. Moreover, even among scholars there is disagreement about the *meaning* of many of the designs—for example, although the face at the center is commonly accepted to be that of Tonatiuh, scholars have argued that it is the earth deity Tlaltecuhtli, or the god of the night sun, Yohualtecuhtli; or that it represents the severed head of a sacrificial offering, perhaps human, perhaps a god.

For simplicity's sake, this encyclopedia uses the most commonly accepted interpretations, and, where applicable, the terms collectors are accustomed to using to describe the coins. This appendix provides as much history as necessary to explain the symbols; thorough coverage of the stone's history and of Aztec cosmology are outside the scope of this volume. An excellent summary reference on the subject, for those who would like to learn more, is *The Aztec Calendar Stone*, edited by Khristaan D. Villela and Mary Ellen Miller (Getty Research Institute, 2010).

Most of the rings of the Calendar Stone can be broken down into the following small units (noted in boldface). One that has already been mentioned is the **quincunx** (*quincunce* in Spanish)—a square with a dot in the center and one in each corner. The Aztecs used the symbol to denote something of great value. They associated the quincunx with greenstone (jade or other green mineral), which was precious to the Aztecs and was used in jewelry and art.

Quincunx.

The many small, U-shaped loops represent **eagle feathers**, and in fact the Calendar Stone is itself an eagle vessel, or *cuauhxicalli*—a basin or altar for conveying a sacrifice to the gods. The eagle represented both the sun and the Aztec people.

Eagle-feather loops.

The small, single circlets placed regularly around the rings of the stone represent **greenstone beads**. The slightly larger double-circlets represent **numbers**; one double-circlet represents the number 1; two together, the number 2; and so on, up to 13. Other symbols were used to depict higher numbers.

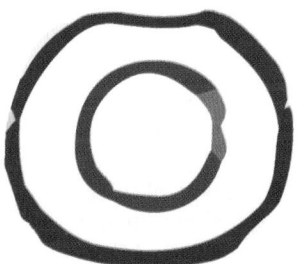

Greenstone bead.

The number 1.

Colorized diagram of the Aztec Calendar Stone. Tonatiuh and the four suns are in light pink; the Ollin symbol, outlined in magenta; the Ring of Days, shaded yellow; the Ring of Quincunxes, medium orange; the Ring of Sacrifice, lighter orange; the Ring of Serpents, purple.

Sun-ray.   Blade of a perforator.   Handle of a perforator.   Three drops/splashes of blood.

The four large points with curved bases are believe to signify **sun-rays**, while the smaller ones may be sun-rays or **perforators** (knives used for ceremonial blood-letting and sacrifices). Smaller still are the three-cornered points, slightly wishbone-shaped, that may represent **blood droplets**. Amid the circle of blood droplets and perforators are compound symbols consisting of a single quincunx topped by three eagle feathers, with a greenstone bead atop those; the emblem is thought to represent the decorated **handles** of the perforators.

These repeated symbols are combined with singular images to create the central disk of the Calendar Stone and the stone's border, the Ring of Serpents. Beginning at the center of the stone is the face of the sun god **Tonatiuh** (shaded pale pink in the diagram), his protruding tongue shaped like a flint knife. The first ring outward from Tonatiuh, also in pink, includes four rectangular elements representing the four previous "suns," or epochs, of the world.

Tonatiuh, the sun god.

The fifth and current epoch is represented by the symbol Ollin, which in the diagram is outlined in magenta. On the Calendar Stone, Tonatiuh, his claws, and the

Fire-butterfly. Reed (13 Acatl). Serpent's fire-feathers.

past epochs have been placed to fill the sections of the Ollin symbol. Between the two upper rectangles is a sharp perforator blade; between the two lower rectangles, a larger representation of the handle, consisting of two quincunxes, five eagle feathers, and a jade bead. The rounded shapes to the left and right of Tonatiuh's face are his claws.

Moving outward is the Ring of Days (Anillo de los Días), tinted yellow. Each of the 20 rectangles in this ring contains one of the Aztec glyphs for a day of the month. An Aztec month consisted of these 20 days; a year consisted of eighteen 20-day months. The presence of the Ring of Days gave early researchers the idea that the stone was used as a calendar. Modern scholars hold that the day-signs are simply part of the comprehensive repository of Aztec knowledge that the stone is believed to convey.

The next ring, which comprises the diagram's two orange areas, is the Ring of Splendor (Anillo del Resplandor). The darker-orange Ring of Quincunxes (Anillo de los Quincunces) includes the four large sun-rays; the lighter-orange Ring of Sacrifice (Anillo del Sacrificio) includes the eagle feathers, perforators, and handles. The Ring of Splendor is sometimes described as a *solar ring* or *sun disk*, and versions of the design (excluding the central area in pink) appear on other sacrificial disks, like the Stone of Tizoc.

The outermost ring, in purple, is the Ring of Serpents (Anillo de los Serpientes): two *xiuhtecoatl*, or fire-serpents, nose-to-nose and tail-to-tail, encircle the solar area. Emerging from their mouths at the bottom of the stone are Tonatiuh (right) and the fire god Xiuhtecuhtli (left). At the top of the stone, where the serpents' tails meet and turn inward, is a trapezoidal device bearing the emblem called **Reed** (the Aztec date "13 Acatl"). The lengths of the serpents' bodies are decorated with the **fire-butterfly** emblem; from their backs, toward the center, protrude feathery **flames**.

The entire face of the Calendar Stone is depicted on the 1-kilo silver Libertad and on the 20 pesos of 1917. Nearly all the separate elements of the Calendar Stone have appeared on Mexican coinage; examples are as follows.

A border of quincunxes and points (either blades or rays) on a 5 centavos (Type 1, 1911).

A border of eagle-feather loops and simplified blade handles on a 50 centavos (Type A1, 2000).

Two coins with a border of blood drops and stone beads: a 50 pesos (Type 1, 1982) and a 10 centavos (Type A1, 2000).

On the stainless-steel outer rim of the Type A2 two-peso coin (2000), 10 emblems from the Calendar Stone's Ring of Days.

A detailed representation of the Ring of Splendor on the 5 centavos (Type 1, 1938). The same depiction also appears on the 10 centavos, Type 5. Note the fragments of the Ring of Serpents: at the edge, the feathery flames; at the top, the tips of the serpents' tails; and at the bottom, their curled-up snouts.

Sun-rays on the 5 centavos (Type A1, 1995); note the rounded bases.

On the stainless-steel outer ring, a simplified version of the Ring of Splendor on the 1 peso (Type A2, 2010).

A partial border of repeating Reed symbols on the 20 centavos (Type A1, 2009).

Tonatiuh and the four previous suns, enclosed within the Ollin (fifth sun) symbol.

The round number-symbol, depicted on the gold 500-peso Pre-Columbian Series (Aztec) coin of 1992.

Appendix C
Eagle Styles on Mexican Coinage

During the colonial era, the eagle emblem appeared only on proclamation medals. The designs of circulating coinage referred solely to Spain and the current monarch. Since the War of Independence, of course, Mexican coinage has featured the eagle as the national emblem, nearly always perched on a cactus sprouting from a rock, and usually with water below. With the exception of the coins from the brief empire of Iturbide, the eagle clasps a snake between its beak and right claw.

A thorough study of each element in the emblem is beyond the scope of this appendix, and indeed, beyond the scope of this book. (The possible origins of the snake, for example, have been widely disputed, and could fill several chapters on their own.) Instead, we will examine the history of the stylistic depiction of the emblem—not only for the simple appreciation of the design's beauty, but to call attention to the way design choices reflect the national character at the time, as well as to explain terms that might be unfamiliar (e.g., "blade-like" versus "leaf-like" feathers) elsewhere in the book. Although 19th-century coinage is not covered in-depth in this volume, its eagle designs are included here for historical perspective (e.g., blade-like feathers, which one would reasonably associate with modern coinage, first appeared on certain Hookneck Eagle obverses).

Any discussion of the eagle design must begin with the artwork with which the Aztecs explained their history and culture to the Spanish conquerors—the images in the codices, particularly the Codex Mendoza. On the opening page of the latter, we see the eagle facing to the right, wings spread; it is perched on a cactus atop the Aztec glyph for "rock." Below the rock is a shield backed by arrows—the Aztec glyph for war. The round white balls of eagle down (the *ihuiteteyo*) on the shield represent the power of Tenochtitlán; they appear on many of Mexico's coinage designs, although they frequently go unnoticed by catalogers. (For more information on the Codex Mendoza, see page 2).

The Mexican eagle as depicted in the Codex Mendoza, ca. 1541.

Eagle Anatomy

The following discussion requires a bit of knowledge about the anatomy of Mexico's national symbol, and a few specialized terms. These are explained and illustrated here.

The secondary wing feathers (A) cover the upper edge of the wing from the elbow (not visible) to the upper curve of the wing (B), which is the equivalent of the human wrist. Although the feather placement does have a sort of design, this appendix uses the word *random* to distinguish between nature's pattern and patterns that appear to be machine made. The primary wing feathers (D), or "flight feathers," along with the tail feathers, are more regular in their placement.

One might not expect an eagle to have a knee (C), but it does; an engraver who depicts this part of the leg on the coinage has observed the animal closely.

The tail-feather spread (E) is like a fan, with the ends of the feathers rounded and more or less separated, depending on the flight position. The body feathers (F), like the secondary wing feathers, are, in effect, randomly arranged. The crest feathers (G) are a lighter gold than those on the body. When an eagle is provoked, the crest feathers stand up much like the hair on a cat's back.

This book refers to the hollow central "stalk" of the feather (H) as the *quill,* while the smooth, parallel parts that constitute the "flat" of the feather are called *barbs,* for the tiny barbules along their length that hold them in place. Feathery parts that lack barbs do not cling together and are called down (J), which is not depicted on the coinage except symbolically (the dots that represent the shield-dots from the Codex).

In the final photo, which is unlabeled, a handler displays the feet of a captive eagle. Note the width of the toes, similar to human fingers, and the length of the claws. Each foot has three toes in front and an opposing hind toe. Feet styles vary widely on the coinage.

THE IMPERIAL EAGLE

The eagle made a brief appearance during the War of Independence, on the 1811 coinage of the Supreme National Congress of America. However, it was Emperor Augustín de Iturbide who was the first to place the *full* motif of eagle, cactus, and rock on coins in Mexico.

Supreme National Congress. 8 reales (silver), 1811, BW-153.1, KM-206, 39 mm.

Unlike the bird in the Codex Mendoza, the eagle on these coins faces forward, wings outstretched; its body is generally angled to the left, with the head turned back to the right. With its left foot, it perches on a pad of a nopal cactus; its right foot is lifted, toes curled. The draftsmanship is inaccurate—the body and neck have a thin, stretched appearance, and the wings are anatomically improbable. Nonetheless, realism seems to have been the objective, and the design is drawn in full, textured relief. The body feathers are randomly placed, and the barbs (i.e., the "feathery" parts of the feather) are visible on the body and wing feathers of well-struck examples. The feet are in proportion to the body, and are anatomically correct. On the more skillful engravings, the legs are correct as well, complete with knees. Although the eagle appears rather scrawny and decidedly non-regal by modern standards, its dynamic posture suggests a fierce creature that is ready for action.

Iturbide 8 reales, 1822-M̊ BW-166.8, KM-310, 39 mm.

THE PROFILE OR "HOOKNECK" EAGLE

For a brief time after the 1823 abdication of Iturbide, before the new national emblem had time to be fully disseminated on the coinage (see "The Upright Eagle," following), a few mints produced the 8 reales and 8 escudos with the Profile (or "Hookneck") Eagle design. As the names suggest, the eagle is posed fully in profile to the left, its neck arched into a hooked shape as it fights a snake—a new addition to the emblem—that is clenched between its beak and its raised right claw. The wings are open high behind the body, nearly parallel to one another, and the outer edge of the nearest wing curves more or less inward. The realistically styled foot, with long toes and claws, may be placed on a cactus pad or directly on the rock, which on most examples emerges from water.

Upper left: Profile Eagle, 8 reales, Submissive Snake. 1824-D♀.
Lower left: Profile Eagle, 8 escudos, Curved Tail (Type I) on snake.

The Profile Eagle is a good example of two of the terms used in this book to describe the devices. *Naturalistic* simply means the design attempts to mimic nature; and *stylized* means the design conforms to the vision of the designer rather than to nature. In the Codex Mendoza, for example, the eagle is depicted naturalistically (if somewhat crudely), whereas the rock-glyph is a deliberately stylized element.

On some of the Profile Eagle coins, the depiction is entirely naturalistic. The feathers are molded in full relief, with distinct barbs emerging from both sides of the central quill. The body feathers are placed randomly, as in nature, and the wing feathers follow a natural, structural pattern. On other examples, the body feathers are somewhat stylized: their *placement* is essentially natural (i.e., random), but each feather is suggested by an outlined edge and one or two lines down the center. This particular type of stylized feather is described as blade-like in this encyclopedia, because it resembles the blade of a short, double-edged knife.

On all of the Profile Eagle coinage, the rock, cactus, and water are also depicted naturalistically, rather than as glyphs or symbols.

THE UPRIGHT EAGLE

On April 14, 1823, a new national emblem was decreed—without, of course, a crown. The eagle is very similar to Iturbide's eagle: the position is the same, with the breast mostly to the fore, wings stretched outward, the body angled to the left, the head turned to the right, and the right foot raised; the feathers are naturalistic; and the eagle is still thin through the body and wings. The legs and feet are correct and in proportion. Now, however, it is much more accurately rendered, and like the Profile Eagle, it holds a snake between its beak and its right foot. Its left foot, placed on the pad of a cactus emerging from a rock in the water, is turned toward the left. For the most part, the wings curve inward (one exception is on an 8 escudos of Chihuahua, which depicts the wing tips bending outward). State and federal coppers of the era follow the same general pattern, but with considerably more variation in style.

Upright Eagle, 8 reales, 1883/2-M, MH.

The new official emblem made its debut on coinage in 1824 and essentially remained the standard until the turn of the century.

THE REGENCY EAGLE

Obverse of the 1 centavo issued by the French Regency, 1864-M, Small Letters.

Reverse of the 1 peso issued by Emperor Maximilian, 1866-M.

1-peso reverse, close up.

The eagle lost its crown after the abdication of Iturbide, but regained it during the French Intervention under the brief rule of Emperor Maximilian. The eagle on the early Regency coinage, without the effigy of Maximilian, is more-or-less the earlier Upright Eagle design, with the addition of a crown. On the coins decreed by Maximilian, with his effigy on the obverse, the eagle on the reverse is enclosed in an Imperial shield. The crown is set above the shield, and the eagle is more vertical and formal in style.

THE FORWARD-FACING EAGLE

Two eagle styles predominated on post-Maximilian decimal coinage. One is basically a continuation of the Upright Eagle design used on the reales coinage, but achieved with greater accuracy by the engravers (e.g., the wing feathers are fuller and longer). The wing tips curve outward to varying degrees. The feet, seen from the front, have the correct number of toes and are generally proportional to the body (or slightly larger).

The other eagle still faces, not *essentially* forward, but entirely forward. The rendering is still realistic, but the eagle stands more erect, and its silhouette is nearly symmetrical. Porfirio Díaz is said to have promoted this formal, French-influenced style.

The eagle generally seen on Balance Scale coinage, in this example a 1-peso issue, 1903-C$_N$, FV.

Since the War of Independence, the eagle had displayed an air of fierceness; its slightly angled stance (including the feet turned away from the viewer, in the direction the eagle was leaning) suggested the bird was about to take flight. Now, with the eagle turned fully forward, the feet are turned forward as well. The pose still suggests strength, but of a more dignified sort, seeming to claim a place alongside the emblems of the European nations. Note also the size of the head with respect to the body: on those early Hookneck Eagles, the head is large and the face is anthropomorphized, displaying human fierceness and anger. The same was

The more formal eagle style favored by Porfirio Díaz (on a 50 centavos of 1905).

true of the Profile Eagles, but slightly more refined, as if the emotions of the engravers were being directed into a less-personal, but still proud, view of the Mexican nation. By the time of Díaz's formalized eagle, the head of the eagle is very small in proportion to the rest of the body, suggesting that the might of the Republic is much greater than that of the states and the individual citizen.

On coinage, this eagle remained the standard for most denominations into the 1930s and even beyond. In this encyclopedia, *forward-facing eagle* refers to this style.

EAGLE IN PROFILE

The original Aztec symbols, including the eagle's profile position, were restored to Mexico's coat of arms in 1916 by President Venustiano Carranza. In nearly every respect, the new emblem embraces the pre-European past: the depiction of the rock-glyph, the suggestion of the down feathers from the shield, the restoration of the eagle's head to full size, with a fierce expression, and ruffled feathers at the back of the neck. Interestingly, the species of snake is changed from a water snake to a rattlesnake. Scholars have disputed the reasons for the change, and in fact, for the reasons a snake was ever included at all; here, we will simply make note of the change and move onward.

Due to political issues, the new coat of arms was not made official, and thus did not make its way to the coinage, until the 1930s. In this encyclopedia, *eagle in profile* refers to this design.

THICK, DETAILED FEATHERS

The first modern coins with the eagle in profile were the 5 and 10 centavos and the 1 peso. The style in this generation of eagles is slightly less realistic than in earlier years. The feathers are placed in deliberate, manmade rows; the body feathers almost seem to merge with the wing feathers, and all are rendered with distinct barbs, like the teeth of a comb. For these three coins, the feathers are described herein as *thick, detailed feathers*. The ends of the tail feathers form a short, smooth fan—the fan being a detail required by law, but variously interpreted over the years. The edge of the wing follows the curve of the eagle's back, with the stiff primary feathers pointing downward. The legs are feathered all the way to the ankle; the left foot is

An example with the modern eagle in profile, designed with thick, detailed feathers (1 peso, 1949).

large and is turned in the same direction as the eagle. The splayed toes are short and thick, with very short claws. On the left foot, two front toes and the rear toe are visible; on the right foot, gripping the snake, the three front toes are visible. Curiously, the eagle's knees seem to have disappeared. In general, the stylistic choices suggest a yearning for a modern identity—still proudly, distinctly Mexican, but embracing the possibilities of the future.

BLADE-LIKE FEATHERS

Between 1942 and 1952, the 5- and 20-centavo and 5-peso denominations received a further stylized eagle. The general outline remains the same, but the feathers are quite different: the body feathers are much shorter, and quite straight; and all the feathers are smooth and barbless, having only a lengthwise stripe down the center to suggest the quill of a real feather. In this encyclopedia, we refer to these feathers as blade-like, since they resemble the blade of a two-edged knife. The feathers remain rigid, the edge of the wing curving inward, as with the previous style. The toes are much the same as on the eagle with thick, detailed feathers, and the eagle still has no knees.

The eagle in profile with blade-like feathers (5 pesos, 1947).

Leaf-like Feathers

In the 1950s and 60s, the eagle design took on a slightly "looser" appearance, at least with respect to the feathers and the restoration of the knee. The short body-feathers are randomly placed. Both the body feathers and the longer wing feathers curve in random directions, with the tips of the primary wing feathers curled away from the body and the leg feathers blown back toward the tail—details giving the appearance that the eagle is facing into the wind. The pointed feathers are completely smooth, although they are still raised in sculptural relief above the field. Due to the feathers' smooth surface and pointed tips, this encyclopedia describes them as *leaf-like*.

The eagle in profile with leaf-like feathers (5 pesos, 1959).

At the beak and the feet, the designer and naturalism part company entirely. The beak is unusually thick and its curve is squared off into a cruel, L-shaped hook. The left foot is nearly as large as the rock it stands on, and is in such strong profile it almost appears to have only a single front toe; the stubby claws resemble rose thorns. The simple outline of the foot makes it seem more a part of the stylized rock than of the realistic eagle.

Outlined Feathers

In keeping with the design of the coat of arms, most of the denominations in the 1970s were given a highly stylized obverse makeover. The eagle and other devices are drawn with raised outlines on a perfectly flat field, with no modeling of the shapes. Instead of curling forward over its prey, the eagle appears to stand more upright. Although the stylized feathers have a rigid appearance, the wing tips resemble streamers. The left leg is completely straight, such that the foot seems to emerge from the tapered body; and on the left foot, two of the front toes and the hind toe are visible.

The eagle in profile with outlined feathers and other devices (100 pesos, 1979).

Armor-like Feathers

The final design change to date took place in the 1980s. It retains the straight posture, rigid feather-placement, and streaming wing tips of the previous design, along with the sense that the left foot emerges directly from the body rather than from a leg. The major change is that a simple but fully modeled relief has been restored to all the design elements. The eagle's feathers hark back a bit to the blade-like feathers of the 1940s, with a straight center quill and no barbs, but now the feathers were more tapered. The newest body feathers almost appear to be clipped from sheets of metal, as if part of a suit of armor. The left foot is large but not outlandishly so, with two front toes and one hind toe being visible.

The eagle in profile with feathers resembling plates of armor (5,000 pesos, 1988).

GLOSSARY
PART I: GENERAL TERMS

alloy—A combination of two or more metals.

alpaca—A copper-nickel alloy, sometimes containing zinc, that mimics sterling silver; also known as *German silver*.

annulet—Literally, "little circle"; a decoration that resembles a small ring. On Mexican colonial coinage, a small ring with a dot in the center.

armored—Describes a portrait in which the subject wears armor, to indicate military strength.

assayer mark—The initials or other mark of an assayer, placed on a coin to guarantee its metallic composition.

assayer—One who analyzes and certifies metallic composition.

Azteca—The gold 20 pesos with the Aztec Calendar Stone reverse, first minted in 1917.

Balance Scale design—A coinage motif consisting of a small radiant liberty cap above a crossed sword and balance scale; between the pans of the scale is a scroll bearing the word LEY (law). Commonly used on Republic decimal coinage.

bas relief—A type of sculpture in which the design is raised above, but still attached to, the field behind it. Commonly found on architecture and sometimes seen on medallic art.

blank—A disc of metal before it is impressed with the design of a coin or medal.

bolo—A christening medal; common during the 19th and early 20th centuries in Mexico.

bullion—Pure, unalloyed metal in bulk form (bars, ingots, etc.).

bullion coinage—Coins struck from pure or nearly pure precious metal, for sale to collectors and investors at a small premium above their metal value.

bust—A term that loosely describes a portrait that is smaller than half-length (i.e., from the chest up). Generally assumes that at least part of one shoulder is included, but some numismatists apply the term to portraits that end at the neck.

Bust coinage—See "Portrait coinage."

BW-number—Bailey-Whitman number (from the *Whitman Encyclopedia of Mexican Money*, by Don and Lois Bailey).

cabo de barra—literally, "the end of the bar." In the cob-coinage era, planchets were clipped from the end of a bar of refined gold or silver, then weighed and, if necessary, filed or clipped to bring them to the proper weight before striking.

cacahoat—Cacao beans, a medium of exchange in the Anáhuac era.

cacahuapinol—Flour made of corn and cacao used as a medium of exchange in the Anáhuac era.

canutillos—The hollow quills of large feathers, filled with gold dust and sealed at each end; used as a medium of exchange in the Anáhuac era.

Casa de Moneda de México—The official mint of Mexico.

cast coinage—Coins made by the pouring of liquid metal into a mold made from an original coin; usually cruder in appearance than struck coinage.

centavo—The smallest fraction of a peso; 1 peso equals 100 centavos.

Centenario—The gold 50 pesos with the *Ángel de la Independencia* on the reverse, commemorating the 100th anniversary of the War of Independence; first struck in 1921.

chiampinoli—A kind of plant meal used as a medium of exchange in the Anáhuac era.

chopmark—The unique mark of a Chinese bank or money-changer, stamped into the surface of a coin to guarantee its precious-metal content.

cob—An early type of coin, struck with a hammer; in Mexico, cobs were issued from about 1580 to 1732. As no restraining collar was used, the planchets spread into irregular shapes when struck.

collar—An outer ring that confines a blank or planchet, such that it does not spread as it is struck by the coin press. The collar can have a design or lettering that is impressed into the edge of the coin.

commemorative coin—A legal-tender coin struck to honor or celebrate an event, a person, a place, or an idea. A commemorative coin can be circulating or non-circulating legal tender; the latter are sold at a premium above their face value.

coppers—Early copper coins of low face value.

counterstamp—A mark struck onto the obverse or reverse of an existing coin to "claim" it for use by a different government, or to change its value.

cuartilla—Silver quarter-real.

cud—A raised portion of metal at the edge of a coin where the edge of its die was broken; when the coin was struck, the metal flowed into the broken area.

cuentas—Jade beads used as a medium of exchange in the Anáhuac era.

currency—The system of money in general use in a given country. In numismatics, *currency* often refers to paper money.

decimal coinage—A coinage system whose base unit is divided into sub-units of 10, 100, or 1,000.

die variety—A minor alteration of a coin's basic design.

die—The piece of metal that imparts the design to the planchet when it is struck. Both the design and the relief are reversed, because they will be transferred in mirror image to the coin.

diesinker—One who engraves coinage dies.

dineros—A medieval measurement of fineness, in which pure silver was designated 12 *dineros*. One dinero equals 24 *granos*.

dot—A coin ornament consisting of a small, filled circle. It may be used as punctuation or simply as a word or line divider.

doubled die—A coinage die that has received two misaligned impressions, which are passed on to the coins struck from that die. Also refers to the resulting coins.

draped—Describes a portrait in which the subject is draped in a loose, flowing garment, reminiscent of ancient gods or rulers.

eagle in profile—Refers to the left-facing eagle design on Mexican coinage from 1916 to date. A broad descriptive term rather than a formal design type; not to be confused with the historic Profile ("Hookneck") Eagle of 1823–1825.

edge—The "third side" of the coin, often impressed with lettering or ornaments.

effigy—In numismatics, a depiction of a specific person on a coin.

error—A malformed or other incorrectly made coin caused by a mistake during the cutting or striking of the blank.

escudo—The base unit of Mexican pre-decimal gold coinage; 1 gold escudo equaled 16 silver reales.

essay (French *essai*)—Any coin that is struck with official mint dies but is not a regular issue.

exergue—The portion of a coin beneath the main design, often separated from the design by a line. Often used for the date or the engraver's name.

experimental strike—A sample strike performed by the mint to test a possible change in planchet diameter, format, shape, thickness, etc.

fantasy coin—A coin struck with official mint equipment and facilities, but without the mint's authorization, for the purpose of financial or other reward.

field—The plain background against which a coin's design is visible.

fineness—The purity of the precious metal in a coin. Expressed in thousandths: e.g., 99.9% or .999.

flan—A blank or planchet.

forward-facing eagle—Refers to the eagle design on Republic decimal coinage up until 1916. A broad descriptive term rather than a formal design type; not to be confused with the historic Upright Eagle design on Republic reales coinage.

G-number—Grove number (from the numerous references by F.W. Grove).

GB-number—Guthrie-Bothamley number (from *Mexican Revolutionary Coinage, 1913–1917*, by H. Guthrie and M. Bothamley).

German silver—A copper-nickel alloy, sometimes containing zinc, that mimics sterling silver; also known as *alpaca*.

grain—A unit of mass equal to 64.79891 milligrams. In the Medieval system of describing fineness, 24 *granos* equaled 1 *dinero*; pure silver was graded 12 *dineros*.

gramos—Grams.

granos—Grains (weight); see *grain*.

hammered coinage—Coins made by striking the planchet between the two dies with a large hammer.

Hand on Book design—Suspended over an open book, a hand holding a staff with a liberty cap on the point; the book is usually inscribed LA LIBERTAD EN LA LEY. The design was prominently used on gold escudos of the Republic.

hoe money—A flat, one-piece metal blade used as a medium of exchange in the Anáhuac era. Also called "Aztec hoe money," "ax money," or *tajaderas* (Spanish for "chopping knives").

Hookneck Eagle design—See Profile Eagle design.

incuse—Describes a design that is pressed into the surface of the coin, as opposed to raised above it (i.e., in relief).

jolas—Half-real coins issued under Spanish rule in San Fernando de Bexar (now San Antonio, Texas) in 1817 and 1818.

juego de pelota—Ball game.

jugate—Describes two overlapping portraits; the proximity signifies a close association. See also *trigate, quadragate*.

KM-number—Krause-Mishler number (from the *Standard Catalogue of World Coins*, by Chet Krause and Clifford Mishler).

laureate—Laureled; a portrait in which the head wears a laurel wreath, indicating the subject is victorious.

legal tender—The official money of a government or authorizing body.

legend—An inscription on a coin.

lettered edge—An edge design in words, rather than the usual reeding or other ornament.

ley—Law (e.g., as used in the Hand on Book design); fineness, when joined with the precious-metal content in a coin's legend (e.g., "Ley .999").

Libertad—The name given to the standard Mexican bullion series authorized in the late 20th century; also, any coin of that series.

Liberty Cap design—A coin design consisting solely of a liberty cap, usually surrounded by radiance. Does not apply to designs that incorporate a liberty cap into a complex motif (e.g., the Hand on Book design). Used prominently on silver reales coinage of the Republic.

liberty cap—In ancient Rome, the brimless cap, or *pileus*, worn by emancipated slaves. Widely adopted as a symbol of freedom; often inscribed with the word "Liberty" (in Spanish, "Libertad").

lozenge—A coinage ornament resembling a diamond shape.

mailed—Describes a portrait in which the subject wears mail (chain armor) to indicate military strength.

maravedi—A small denomination during the era of Carlos and Johanna; coins were struck in 2 and 4 maravedies.

mascle—A coinage ornament consisting of a lozenge with a smaller diamond shape in the center.

medio—Half; a half-real coin.

milled coinage—In general, any coinage that is struck by machine instead of by hand; in particular, the screw-press coinage issued from 1732 through 1821, supplanting cob (stamped) coinage.

mintmark—A symbol on a coin indicating the mint at which it was struck.

monogram—Coin design in which the denomination is set very large and is the main design feature of the reverse.

mule—A coin struck from two dies that were not originally meant to be paired.

non-circulating legal tender (NCLT)—A coin that is legally valid for commercial use but is not intended for that purpose and is never or almost never seen in circulation. Proof and commemorative coins, for example, are NCLT coinage; they are struck with extra care and are sold to the public at a premium above their face value.

nuevo peso—New peso, a transitional denomination devised in 1992; the decimal point in the value was moved three places to the left of its former location, and the new denomination was indicated with an N before the peso symbol (e.g., N$5).

OAX-number—Reference number from *La Venta Oaxaca*, by C. Woodworth.

obverse—The front, or "heads," side of the coin. In Mexican numismatics, the obverse typically (but not always) is the side bearing the coat of arms.

octavo—A 1/8-real coin.

off metal—A strike on a metal other than the one intended for circulation.

onza—Ounce. See also *Una Onza*.

oro—Gold.

overdate—A die on which some or all of the numerals in the date are superimposed over older ones. Also, a coin struck from such a die.

overstrike—An impression struck on an already-struck coin, but with a different die.

patolquechtli—Pieces of cotton fabric used as a medium of exchange in the Anáhuac era.

pattern—A coinage sample, officially sanctioned but not for circulation, created to test a new or revised design, denomination, or metal.

peso—The base unit of Mexican decimal coinage.

piece of eight—A Spanish milled 8-real coin.

Pillar coinage—Spanish-colonial coins issued in Mexico from 1732 through 1771, bearing on their obverse the Spanish coat of arms flanked by two columns or pillars known as the Pillars of Hercules.

Pillars of Hercules—Two pillars representing the western-most limit of the travels of Hercules as he completed his 12 labors of penance; this Greek myth was extended during the Renaissance era with the notion that the pillars were inscribed "Ne Plus Ultra" ("Nothing Farther Beyond")—a warning to sailors to turn back and go no farther. On Spanish coinage, with the motto "Plus Ultra" ("Farther Beyond"), the pillars represent the challenge to travel beyond the boundaries of the known world.

pilón—A small copper coin of Ferdinand VII, with the value of 1/16 real.

planchet—A disc of metal intended to be struck with a coin design.

plata—Silver.

platino—Platinum.

Plus Ultra (Latin)—A popular colonial-era coin inscription meaning "Farther Beyond," or, more loosely, "there are lands farther beyond these." Often written as PLVS VLTRA, as in Latin inscriptions.

pomegranate—An ornament commonly found on Spanish-colonial coins. In Christian symbolism, the fruit represents many things, including fertility, the suffering and resurrection of Jesus, and the bringing together of many individuals in one church.

Portrait coinage—Spanish-colonial coins issued in Mexico from 1772 through 1821, bearing on their obverse a portrait of the issuing king. Also called "Bust coinage."

Profile Eagle design—The design of the first reales coinage of the Republic, issued from 1823 to 1825. In the national coat of arms on the obverse, the eagle faces to the left, in profile, with its neck bent forward and its wings raised above its back; often called the "Hookneck Eagle" due to the pronounced curve of the eagle's neck. Not to be confused with "eagle in profile" (see related definition).

Proof—Coins struck with special care for sale to collectors at a premium above their face value.

pura—Pure.

quadragate—Describes four overlapping portraits; the proximity signifies a close association. See also jugate, trigate.

quatrefoil—A coinage ornament resembling a four-petaled flower.

quincunce—Quincunx (a square, five-dot pattern with one dot in each corner and one in the center).

real—The base unit of Mexican pre-decimal silver coinage.

relief—The portion of a coin's design that is raised above the surface.

reverse—The back, or "tails," side of a coin. In Mexican numismatics, the reverse typically (but not always) holds the date, mintmark, and value.

rim—The raised portion around the perimeter of a coin's obverse or reverse, which protects the design from wear.

rondule—A coin ornament that resembles a small ring with an empty center.

royal strikes—Perfectly round cob coins with unusually sharp strikes. They may have been intended as proof of workmanship for the king.

screw press—An early pressing machine of simple design, in which the upper plate is driven toward the lower plate by means of a large, perpendicular screw.

seigniorage—The difference between a coin's production cost and its face value.

señal—A small copper coin of Ferdinand VII, with the value of 1/4 real.

tajadera—See "hoe money."

Texas jolas—Half-real coins issued under Spanish rule in San Fernando de Bexar (now San Antonio, Texas) in 1817 and 1818.

tlaco—A small copper coin of Ferdinand VII, with the value of 1/8 real.

token—A privately issued coin-like object used in trade; not an official government issue.

trigate—Describes three overlapping portraits; the proximity signifies a close association. See also jugate, quadragate.

truncation—The sharply cut-off edge at the bottom of a bust or portrait.

Una Onza—The Mexican silver one-ounce bullion series issued in 1949, 1978–1980, and 1989.

Upright Eagle design—The style of the national coat of arms on most of the Republic real and escudo coinage, save for a brief time during which the Profile Eagle was used. The Upright Eagle stands with head up and turned to the right, its breast facing forward and its wings spread open to the sides.

vellón—A system of small-value coins created to facilitate business transactions and record-keeping.

Winged Victory—In general, another name for the *Ángel de la Independencia* motif; specifically, the NCLT commemorative 200 pesos of 2010.

PART II: BANCO DE MÉXICO CATALOG TERMS

When perusing Mexican coin products offered by a U.S. retailer, English speakers seldom have a problem. A knowledgeable dealer will be well acquainted with the terminology, mintages, and other data. When attempting to go directly to the source for original information and research, however, the non-Spanish-speaking collector will encounter roadblocks. Although many of the pages on the Web sites of the Banco de México and the Casa de Moneda de México are available in English, some are Spanish-only; smaller Web sites will rarely have English-language versions. And online translation tools, while sometimes accurate, often produce results that range from amusing to downright misleading.

The following are some Spanish terms commonly found on retail Web sites and in product catalogs. A word of caution: terminology can vary from source to source—one site may describe a coin as *mate-brillo* (prooflike) while another may describe it as *espejo* (Proof). Always consult someone knowledgeable before making a purchase.

acabado—Surface finish (e.g., acabado mate-brillo, "prooflike"; acabado espejo, "Proof"; acabado satín, "Brilliant Uncirculated"; acabado ordinario, "Uncirculated").

acuñacion—Mintage.

acuñar—To mint; *acuñada*, "minted."
anverso—Obverse.
billetes—Bank notes.
bimetálica—Bimetallic.
certificado de acuñación—Certificate of authenticity.
cifras—Figures (e.g., in Banco de México mintage reports, *Cifras: piezas* means "Figures: Pieces"; *Cifras: Miles de piezas*, "Figures: Thousands of pieces").
colección—Collection.
conmemorativa—Commemorative.
cuño(s) corriente(s)—Current mintage; current mintage figures.
denominación—Denomination.
diámetro—Diameter.
disposable—Available.
espejo—Proof.
gramos—Grams.
granos—Grains (weight).
juego—In the context of the mint catalog, a coin set.
juegos de monedas en acabado espejo—Proof coin sets.
ley—Fineness, in the context of the mint catalog.
libro-folleto—Booklet.
mate-brillo—Prooflike.
medalla—Medal.
metales finos—Precious metals.
moneda—Coin.
monedo de curso—Legal-tender coin.
onza—Ounce.
oro—Gold.
piezas—Pieces.
piezas de prueba—Trial strikes.
plata—Silver.
platino—Platinum.
pura—Pure.
reverso—Reverse.
set—Coin set (e.g., *set individual*, "individual set"; *set de dos monedas*—"two-coin set"; etc.). See also *juego*.
sin circular—Uncirculated.
tamaño real—Actual size.

BIBLIOGRAPHY

Amaya Guerra, Carlos Abel. *Illustrated Price Guide of the Modern Mexican Coins, 1905 to Date, Including Errors and Varieties*. Mexico City: Author, 2008.

Banco de México. *The History of Coins and Banknotes in Mexico*. Mexico City: Author, 2014.

Banco de México web site: www.banxico.org.mx.

Berdan, Frances F., and Patricia Rieff Anawalt. *The Essential Codex Mendoza*. Berkeley: University of California Press, 1997.

Buttrey, T.V., and Clyde Hubbard. *A Guide Book of Mexican Coins 1822 to Date* (6th ed.). Iola, Wisc.: Krause, 1992.

Casa de Moneda de México web site: www.cmm.gob.mx.

Grove, Frank W. *Coins of Mexico*. Lawrence, Mass.: Quarterman, 1981.

Krause, Chester L., and Clifford Mishler. *2014 North American Coins & Prices: A Guide to U.S., Canadian, and Mexican Coins*. Iola, Wis.: Krause, 2013.

Villela, Khristaan D. Villela, and Mary Ellen Miller, eds. *The Aztec Calendar Stone*. Los Angeles: Getty Research Institute, 2010.

IMAGE CREDITS

2. Codex Mendoza—Wikimedia Commons.
4. Castaing machine—Encyclopedia, or a Systematic Dictionary of the Sciences, Arts, and Crafts, by Denis Diderot. France: ca. 1760.
9. Benziger Bros.—Walter Grutchfield.
9. Birmingham Mint—Osoom.
9. New Orleans Mint—Library of Congress.
9. San Francisco Mint—Southern Methodist University.
9. Denver Mint—Library of Congress.
9. Philadellphia Mint—Library of Congress.
11. nopal farm—Jaec.
27. Benito Juárez García—*Mexico: A History of Its Progress and Development in One Hundred Years*, by Marie Robinson Wright. Philadelphia: G. Barrie & Sons, 1911.
33. Pyramid of the Sun—Allan T. Kohl.
36. Francisco Madero—Flickr-Commons.
42. Cuauhtémoc—El Comandante.
44. Palenque—Carlos Adampol Galindo.
44. Pakal the Great—Wikimedia Commons.
50. José María Morelos—Wikimedia Commons.
55. *El Angel*—Ari Helminen.
60. steam engine—Wikimedia Commons.
61. Parish Church of Dolores Hidalgo—José Juan Figueroa.

Image Credits

65. Quetzalcóatl—Marcelosan.
69. Hidalgo, Steel—Arturo Claros.
77. Coyolxauhqui—David Moran.
81. Venustiano Carranza—*Carranza and Mexico*, by Carlo de Fornaro. New York: M. Kennerly, 1915.
85. Juana de Asbaje—Wikimedia Commons.
88. *Fuente de Petroleos*—Eneas de Troya.
109. Vicente Guerrero—Wikimedia Commons.
112. Guadalupe Victoria—Wikimedia Commons.
130. Ignacio Zaragoza—Library of Congress.
133. Xiuhtecuhtli—Wikimedia Commons.
135. Octavio Paz—Royalwrote.
137. Belisario Domínguez Palencia—Flickr-Commons.
138. Armed Forces logo—Wikimedia Commons.
143. Constitution page—Tarlton Law Library, University of Texas School of Law.
167. *Don Quixote* title page—Wikimedia Commons.
184. Monument of the Revolution—Rob Young.
188. Lázaro Cárdenas—Wikimedia Commons.
198. coats of arms—Wikimedia Commons.
199. coats of arms—Wikimedia Commons.
205. Codex eagle—Wikimedia Commons.
206. Caracara—Andy Morffew.
206. golden eagle standing—Toshihiro Gamo.
206. golden eagle bristling—Michael Jansen.
261. *Calavera Quijotesca*—Wikimedia Commons.
263. Miguel de Cervantes—Wikimedia Commons.
268. People to University, University to People—Wikimedia Commons.
268. Rectory Tower—Adán Eduardo Pedraza.
268. Central Library—scanudas.
273. *La Adelita*—Flickr-Commons.
274. Revolutionaries on train—Southern Methodist University.
275. *soldaderas*—Library of Congress.
303. Nunnery—Jennifer Bjarnason.
304. Church—Sybz.
305. Observatory—H. Michael Miley.
306. Warriors—Pascal.
306. Pyramid—Celso Flores.
308. El Castillo—Cornell University.
308. Nunnery—Cornell University.
317. screw press—Encyclopedia, or a Systematic Dictionary of the Sciences, Arts, and Crafts, by Denis Diderot. France: ca. 1760.
340. Ixtaccíhuatl and Popocatépetl—Lorenzo Tlacaelel.
373. Eagle Warrior—Dennis Jarvis.
377. Brazier Effigy—Dennis Jarvis.
379. God of Fire—Gilardo Sánchez.

381. God of Flowers—Dennis Jarvis.
383. Tizoc Stone—Wikimedia Commons.
384. Jaguar—OtisT.
387. ball-court wall carving—Alejandro Linares Garcia.
389. *ulama* player—Manuel Aguilar-Moreno.
392. Smiling Face—OtisT.
393. Old Man With Brazier—Allen.
394. Pyramid of the Niches—MorGwenn.
398. Chaac-Mool—Alberto Melograna.
400. Lintel 26—Michael Wal.
401. Pakal drawing—Wikimedia Commons.
402. Mask of the God Chaac—OtisT.
404. Personage of Jaina—Thomas Aleto.
407. Master of the Limes—O. Cadena.
409. Jaguar-Man—Wikimedia Commons.
411. Wrestler—Wikimedia Commons.
412. Ceremonial Ax—Walters Museum.
413. Olmec colossal head—Southern Methodist University.
414. Priest bas-relief—Olivier Bruchez.
417. Disc of Death—Wikimedia Commons.
422. Pyramid of the Sun—Allan T. Kohl.
423. Quetzalcóatl—Marcelosan.
425. Jaguar bas-relief—Wikimedia Commons.
427. Ce Acatl Topiltzin QuetzalcOatl bas-relief—Wikimedia Commons.
429. Serpent With Skull bas-relief—Wikimedia Commons.
430. Atlantes Figures—Alejandro Linares Garcia.
431. Eagle relief—HJPD.
436. Archaeological Museum, Mexico City, 1890—Cornell University.
441. Mexican eagle—Wikimedia Commons.
442. eagle-anatomy photos—Tony Hisgett.
442. eagle feet—Virginia State Park staff.

Acknowledgments

The authors would like to thank the following individuals and organizations for their invaluable help in bringing this book together:

Diane Alatorre
Carlos Abel Amaya Guerra
American Numismatic Association's Edward C. Rochette Money Museum
Banco de México
Robert Briggs
Dave Busse
Casa de Moneda de México
Roger Charteris Reyes
Juan Cristóbal Díaz Negrete
Duane Douglas
Cory Frampton
Fundación Carlos Slim
Manuel Galán Medina
Ira Goldberg
Larry Goldberg
Luis M. Gómez-Wulschner
Russel H. Goodyear
Heritage Auctions
Ann Hernandez
Alberto Hidalgo
Max Keech
Jeff Lewis
Richard A. Long
Greg B. Meyer
Alfonso Miranda
Museo Soumaya
Ignacio Pineda
Kent Ponterio
Richard Ponterio
Ponterio & Associates
Elmer Powell
J.R. Rollo
Cori Sedwick Downing
Daniel Frank Sedwick
Alex Siegel
Spink America
Stack's Bowers Galleries
Cathy Stovall
Mike Stovall
Pat Stovall

We would also like to give special thanks to Scott Doll, who was tireless in his assistance with varieties, mintages, valuations, images, and manuscript review.

Our sincerest apologies if, by some oversight, we've failed to acknowledge any of the contributors to this book.

Whitman Publishing would like to thank Kenneth Bressett, Beth Deisher, Robert Lemke, Diana Plattner, and José Luis Ramirez-Damian, for their contributions to this project.

About the Authors

Born and reared in south-central Michigan, Don Bailey joined the Marine Corps during the Korean War. When he retired from the Marines, he lived in Yuma, Arizona, where he was introduced to the vastly interesting history of Mexico. He started collecting U.S. coins in the early 1960s, but soon turned exclusively to Mexican numismatics, concentrating at first on the coinage of Maximilian and the French Intervention. Since 1979 he has been very active in the Mexican numismatic field as a full-time dealer, attending most of the major coin shows in the United States and Mexico. His wife, Lois, has been his full-time business and research partner.

In 1967, Don started the Maximilian Numismatic and Historical Society, which prospered for several years until burnout and a waning of collector interest in specialty organizations took their toll. He published his first article, on the subject of Mexican numismatics, that same year. Since then he has written on other subjects (including the story of the 1980s forger and murderer Mark Hoffman), but Mexican history and numismatics have always been his focus. He has written articles and columns for *World Coin News*, *Coin World*, and other publications, and served as *Coin World*'s "Mexican Trends" analyst. He has also been a contributor to major references on Mexican numismatics, including the *Standard Catalog of Mexican Coins*,

Standard Catalog of World Coins, and *Tokens of Latin America;* Frank W. Grove's numerous volumes on medals, decorations, and tokens of Mexico; and the *Guide Book of Mexican Coins*, by T.V. Buttrey and Clyde Hubbard, to name a few.

Don has been a member of, and an officer in, many numismatic organizations. He is a life member of the American Numismatic Association and has been a member of the Sociedad Numismatica de México for more than 40 years, serving for a number of those years as the society's official representative in the United States. He has worked with the Banco de México and the Casa de Moneda de México to promote their products and numismatic materials, and in 1974 he was appointed to the U.S. Assay Commission.

Don has been the recipient of the ANA's Presidential Award, the Sociedad Numismatica's José Tamborrel Jr. Award (twice), and the Sociedad's Alberto Francisco Pradeau Award. *Numismatic News* named him a Numismatic Ambassador in 1980. On September 27, 2001, Don received the Orden Mexicana del Águila Azteca (Mexican Order of the Aztec Eagle), the highest honor bestowed on a foreigner by the government of Mexico.

In June of 1997, Don, Joe Flores, and Sal Falcone organized the United States Mexican Numismatic Association, and Don served for many years as its executive director and the editor of its quarterly publication, the *Mexican Numismatic Journal*. The Sociedad Numismatica honored the association with the Dr. Alberto Francisco Pradeau award for promoting Mexican numismatics.

According to Don, "These fifty years have been a ball. Fifty years of working, if one can use that term, in a field that you really enjoy is all that one can ask. My wife, Lois, is a vital part of the operation. Without her assistance and encouragement the goals we have achieved would have been impossible to reach."

ABOUT THE FOREWORD WRITER

Beth Deisher for 27 years was editor of *Coin World*, the world's largest and most widely circulated news weekly specializing in coverage of collectible coins, medals, paper money, exonumia, and any item once used as money. She joined the *Coin World* staff in 1981 as news editor and also served as executive editor before being tapped to lead the editorial team in 1985.

Deisher is a Fellow of the American Numismatic Society and holds memberships in many state, regional and national numismatic organizations, including the American Numismatic Association. She is the recipient of numerous awards for her work within the hobby community. She is the author of the award-winning *Cash In Your Coins: Selling the Rare Coins You've Inherited*.

ABOUT THE RESEARCH EDITOR

Diana Plattner is a writer and editor who previously served as editorial director at Whitman Publishing. One of her proudest achievements at Whitman was her nine-year association with *A Guide Book of United States Coins* (a.k.a. the Red Book), for which she served as project manager, manuscript editor, and data wrangler. She currently operates an independent book-packaging company in Atlanta, Georgia, where she lives with her husband, Andy.

INDEX

The following is a general subject index. Formally named commemorative series are listed in a separate "Index to Commemorative Series" at the end. If the desired subject is not found in the main index, try the separate commemorative listings.

1-kilogram gold, 369

1-kilogram silver, 357

Acosta, Jorge, 425

"La Adelita," 273

Aguascalientes
  Emblematic circulating coins, 155
  Emblematic NCLT coins, 238, 249
  Heraldic circulating coins, 154
  Heraldic NCLT coins, 226, 237

Aldama, Juan, 131

Alemán, Miguel, 60

Alfaro Siqueiros, David, 268

Allende, Ignacio, 21, 131, 132
  on circulating coins, 82, 110–111, 183

Alta California, 141

American Bank Note Company, 264

Americas
  discovery of, 191–192
  first coinage of, 1

Amistad Dam, 157, 240, 251

Andrés Molina Enríquez, 118–119

Ángeles Ramirez, Felipe, 140

Angel of Freedom monument, Chihuahua, 156, 239, 250

Angel of Independence monument, Mexico City. *See El Ángel del la Independencia*

El Ángel del la Independencia, 55
  on circulating coins, 56, 75–76
  on NCLT coins, 272

Anillo de las Dias. *See* Ring of Days

Anillo de las Quincunces. *See* Ring of Quincunxes

Anillo de las Serpientes. *See* Ring of Serpents

Anillo del Resplandor. *See* Ring of Splendor

Anillo del Sacrificio. *See* Ring of Sacrifice

aqueduct of Querétaro, 162, 204, 245, 256

aqueducts, Aztec, 372

Arc de Triomphe, 184

Argentina, 198

Arizpe, Miguel Ramos, 102–103

Armada de México, 201

Armed Forces, 138

Army of the Three Guarantees, 105

Asbaje, Juana Inés de, 84–85

Atlan, 86–87

Atlantes figures, 425, 429, 430–431

Avenue of the Dead, 416

ax/hatchet, ceremonial
  Central Veracruz, 395–397
  Olmec, 412

Aztec Calendar Stone
  on bullion coins, 357
  on circulating coins, 17, 19, 23, 26, 70
  discovery of, 436
  on NCLT coins, 180–181
  rings explained, 438
  selected as theme for new-peso designs, 89, 95–99
  See also appendix B

Aztec/Nahuatl glyphs
  bundle (of kindling), 379–381
  crocodile, 381–382, 383–384
  hand, 377–379
  knife, 373–377
  rock, 2, 441, 445
  war, 2

Aztecs,
  cosmology, 126, 133, 438–439
  defeat of Totonacs, 387

enemies of, 42
history of, 438–439
money of, 1
Spanish defeat of, 373

Azueta, Lieutenant, José, 139

Baja California, 141
Emblematic circulating coins, 155
Emblematic NCLT coins, 238, 249
Heraldic circulating coins, 154
Heraldic NCLT coins, 226, 237

Baja California Sur
Emblematic circulating coins, 155
Emblematic NCLT coins, 238, 249
Heraldic circulating coins, 153
Heraldic NCLT coins, 225, 236

Banco de México, 80th anniversary of on circulating coins, 168–169

banknote, 264

Barber, Charles, 47

barbs, feather, 442, 443, 446

Barrera, Juan de la, 142

"Battle Hymn of the Republic," 142

Battle of Puebla, 128–129

Benziger Brothers, 9–10

Bernal's Hill (Cerro de Bernal), Tamaulipas, 164, 247, 258

Bicentenario gold bullion, 369

bighorn sheep, 155, 238, 249

bimetallic coinage, hoarded for silver content, 90, 143, 215

Birmingham Mint, 9–10

black bear, 210

Black Power salute, 73

blood drops, 438, 440

bloodletting, ritual, 372, 407

Boari, Adamo, 195

Bolivia, 198

box turtle, 157, 240, 251

"Boy Heroes," 141–142

Brandenburg Gate, 184

Bravo, Nicolás, 105–106, 112
at Chapultepec Castle, 142

brazier
effigy, 377–379
old man with, 393

Brazil, 198

Brehme, Hugo, 274

bullion, commemorative. *See in index to commemorative coin series*

Bustamante, Carlos María de, 100

butterfly, 203
monarch, 185, 186, 160, 243, 254

BV (bullion value), v

BW (Bailey-Whitman) numbers, v

Caballito peso, 46–47, 197, 281
pattern, 47

Cabañas Hospice, 159, 242, 253

cabo de barra, 1

Cabrera, Luis, 119

cacao, 1, 331

Calavera Quitojesca, 261

calendars
Aztec, 372
Olmec, 407
Totonac, 387
See also Aztec Calendar Stone

Campeche
Emblematic circulating coins, 156
Emblematic NCLT coins, 239, 250
Heraldic circulating coins, 153
Heraldic NCLT coins, 225, 236

"El Capricho," 320

Cárdenas, Lázaro, 60, 88, 188–189
on NCLT coins, 187, 188

Carlos and Johanna coinage, 2

Carlos, John, 73

Carranza, Venustiano, 80–81
on circulating coins, 57, 63, 79, 80, 82–83, 123
influence of, on coin design, 445–446
on NCLT coins, 183–184

"Carta Marina Nuova Tavola," 197

Casa de Moneda de México, 470th anniversary of
  on circulating coinage, 168

Castaing machine, 4

El Castillo, 308, 397, 425. *See also* Pyramid of the Castle

Castle of Chapultepec, 132

Catedral de Santa Prisca, 158, 241, 252

Catedral de Santiago del Saltillo, 157, 240, 251

cave paintings, 155, 238, 249

Ce Acatl Topiltzin Quetzalcóatl, 428

Ceniceros, Severino, 295

Centenario (gold 50 pesos), 75–76
  Metcalf restrike, 76

Centeotl, 425

Central Library (UNAM), 204, 268

Central Veracruz culture, 387

Cervantes, Miguel de, 260–264
  eponymous annual literary award, 136
  See also Don Quijote a la Mancha

Cervantino Festival, 260

Chaac, mask of, 402

Chaac-Mool, 398–400

Chalchiuhtlicue, 421, 423

Chapultepec, 425

Chapultepec Castle, 142

Chapultepec Park, 142

charreada, 193

charrito, 200–201

charro, 193–194

Chiapas, 141
  Emblematic circulating coins, 156
  Emblematic NCLT coins, 239, 250
  Heraldic circulating coins, 153
  Heraldic NCLT coins, 225, 236

Chichén Itzá, 164, 308, 397, 425
  Chaac-Mool, 399
  Church, 304
  Kukulcán Pyramid, 308 (*see also* Pyramid of the Castle)
  Nunnery, 303, 308
  Observatory, 204, 305
  Pyramid of the Castle (*see* Pyramid of the Castle)
  Temple of Warriors, 306

Chichimecas, 387, 425

Chihuahua, 141
  Emblematic circulating coins, 156
  Emblematic NCLT coins, 239, 250
  Heraldic circulating coins, 152
  Heraldic NCLT coins, 224, 235

Chile, 198

chinampas, 372

china poblana, 193

Chinelo, 160, 243, 254

chopmarked coinage, 5

Christ of the Noas, 157, 240, 251

Christopher Columbus

Cinco de Mayo, 129

civil-rights era, 73

cliff diver, 158, 241, 252

Coahuila
  Emblematic circulating coins, 157
  Emblematic NCLT coins, 240, 251
  Heraldic circulating coins, 152
  Heraldic NCLT coins, 224, 235

Coahuila y Tejas, 141

Coatepantli, 430

Coatlicue, 77

cob coinage, 1

Codex Mendoza, 2–3, 133, 205–206
  eagle depicted in, 441, 444
  See also Mexican eagle

Coinage Reform of 1905, 7, 8. *See also chapters 2 and 4*

Coinage Reform of 1905, 100th anniversary of, 166
  on circulating coinage, 167–168

Coinage Reform of 1992, 7, 89. *See also chapters 3 and 4*

Index • 463

coins, historic, commemorated on modern coins
  Balance Scale coinage, 291
  Bolita peso, 282
  Bust or Portrait coinage, 283, 299, 278, 283, 296, 302
  Caballito peso, 281, 197
  Campo Morado coinage, 289
  Cap and Rays coinage, 280, 292
  Carlos and Johanna coinage, 181, 290, 302
  Charles III coinage, 278
  Charles IV coinage, 283, 299–300
  chopmarked coinage, 283, 292
  Cob coinage, 284
  counterstamped coinage, 283, 299
  Ferdinand VI coinage, 285
  Hand on Book coinage, 287
  Iturbide coinage, 294
  L.Y.S. coinage, 297
  L.V.O. coinage, 285, 301
  Maximilian coinage, 286
  Milled coinage, 283, 299, 278, 283, 296, 277
  Morelos coinage, 301
  Muera Huerta peso, 295
  Philip V coinage, 277, 296
  Pillar coinage, 277
  Railroad 5 pesos, 288
  Republic coppers, 300–301
  Republic decimal coinage, 291
  Republic reales coinage, 287, 292
  SUD coinage, 279, 301
  Supreme National Congress of America coinage, 290, 293
  Upright Eagle coinage, 300–301
  War of Independence, Royalist provisional coinage, 298

coins, minted outside Mexico, 9

Colima, 141
  Emblematic circulating coins, 157
  Emblematic NCLT coins, 240, 251
  Heraldic circulating coins, 152
  Heraldic NCLT coins, 224, 235

Colombia, 198

Columbus, New Mexico, 81

Columnaria design, 191

Conspiracy of Querétaro, 131

Constitution of 1824, 143

Constitution of 1857, 327, 329

Constitution of 1857, 100th anniversary of
  on bullion coins, 327–328
  on circulating coins, 51–52, 57, 62s, 67–68

Constitution of Apatzingán (1815), 104

Contreras, Calixto, 295

Convent of San Francisco, Tlaxcala, 164, 247, 258

Cornitán de Domínguez, 137

Cortés, Hernán, 65, 195, 373

Cos, José María, 5 pesos, 104
  counterstamped coinage, 5

Coyolxauhqui, 74, 77–78

crocodile, 209
  on NCLT coins, 391

Cuauhtémoc, 42
  on bullion coins, 330–332
  on circulating coins, 41, 43, 45, 58

Cuauhtémoc (ship), 201

cuauhxicalli, 373, 437

Cuba, 198

Cuitláhuac, 42

Cult of Fire, 379

"Declaration of the Rights of the Child," 189

deer, 155, 238, 249

deer-dancer, 163, 246, 257

Denver Mint, 9–10

Diario del Hogar (newspaper), 117

Diario de México, 100

Díaz, Porfirio, 36, 55, 184, 195
  influence of, on coin design, 445

Disc of Death, 417–419

Distrito Federal
  Emblematic circulating coins, 157
  Emblematic NCLT coins, 240, 251
  Heraldic circulating coins, 151
  Heraldic NCLT coins, 223, 234

Dolores Hidalgo (city), 61

Domínguez Medal of Honor, 137

Domínguez, Miguel, 21

Domínguez Palencia, Belisario, 121, 136–137

Don Quijote de la Mancha, 400th anniversary of, 260–261
  on circulating coins, 166–167
  on NCLT coins, 261–263

doping, 73

dove, 158, 203, 241, 252

Durango, 141
  Emblematic circulating coins, 158
  Emblematic NCLT coins, 252, 241
  Heraldic circulating coins, 151
  Heraldic NCLT coins, 234, 223

Durango pine tree, 158, 241, 252

eagle
  anatomy, 442
  compared to caracara, 205–206
  feathers, 442 (*see also* feather styles)
  feet, 442
  knees, 442, 443, 446
  sculpture, 432–433
  See also obverse eagle styles

eagle-feather design (Aztec), 437, 439

eagle-warriors, 373–377

Ear of Corn design, 28

East Slope, 135

Ecuador, 198

endangered species, 157, 185, 190, 192, 207–214, 240, 251

Enriqueta Basilio, Norma, 73

ESAI (essay), 47

escudo de monja, 85

escultopintura, 268

Escutia, Juan, 142

Espinoza Barrera, María Luz, 276

Exedra monument, 155, 238, 249

Expropacion Petrolera. *See* oil industry, nationalization of

feathered serpent, 65, 414, 423–424. *See also* Kukulkán; Quetzalcóatl

feather styles, 444
  armor-like
  blade-like, 444, 446
  leaf-like, 447
  naturalistic vs. stylized, 444
  outlined, 447
  thick and detailed, 446

Federal District Building, 157, 240, 251

Fernando Montes de Oca, 142

El Ferrocarril del Sureste, 60

Filomeno Mata, 117

fire-butterfly, 439

fire, old god of, 379–381, 393

fisherman's jewel, 202

Fishermen Fountain, Tabasco, 163, 246, 257

Flores Magón, Ricardo, 116

Fort Guadalupe, 129, 130

Fort Loreto, 129, 130

Fort of San Juan de Ulúa, 112

Fosbury, Dick, 73

French Intervention, 6

French Regency, 129, 444

Fuente de Petróleos, 88, 188
  on circulating coins, 87–88
  on NCLT coins, 186, 187–188

futbol, modern, 389
  1986 World Cup, 170–182
  2006 World Cup, 269–270
  Olympic victory in, 196

Galeana, Hermenegildo, 103

Galeón de Acapulco, 194–195

gesta heroica, 139

giant panda, 323–324

god of flowers, 381–382

Gold Coins of Mexico Program, 332–334

golden eagle, 205–206

golfina turtle, 192

The Grammarian Monkey, 135

Grant, Ulysses S., 142

greenstone
  Aztec symbol for, 437
  sculpture, 412, 413

grito de Dolores, 21, 61, 131, 132
  "El Grito," 132

Guanajuato, 141
  Emblematic circulating coins, 158
  Emblematic NCLT coins, 241, 252
  Heraldic circulating coins, 151
  Heraldic NCLT coins, 223, 234

Guatemala, 198

guerras floridas, 381

Guerrero
  Emblematic circulating coins, 158
  Emblematic NCLT coins, 241, 252
  Heraldic circulating coins, 150
  Heraldic NCLT coins, 222, 233

Guerrero, Vicente, 108
  on circulating coins, 57, 63–64, 82, 110, 158, 183, 252
  on NCLT coins, 241
  statue of, 55

Gutiérrez, Eulalio, 119–120

Hand on Book coinage, 6

harpy eagle, 212–213

Hernández, Gerónimo, 273

Herrera, Petra, 275–276

Hidalgo, Estado de
  Emblematic circulating coins, 159
  Emblematic NCLT coins, 242, 253
  Heraldic circulating coins, 150
  Heraldic NCLT coins, 222, 233

Hidalgo y Costilla, Miguel, 4–5l, 21, 110, 131–132
  on bullion coins, 326–327
  on circulating coins, 56–58, 59–60, 61, 62, 66–67, 68–70, 82, 107–108, 158, 183, 252
  on NCLT coins, 241, 272
  recruitment of José María Morelos, 50
  statue of, 55
  See also grito de Dolores

History of Gold medallic coin, 329–330

hoe money, 1

Hookneck Eagle coinage, 6

Huehuetéotl, 133–134, 379–381, 422

Huemac, 425

Huerta, Victoriano, 36, 139, 140
  assassinations ordered by, 36, 81, 121, 123, 124, 136, 137
  See also Muera Huerta peso

Huitzilapán, 86

Huitzilopochtli, 372, 373

hyperinflation, 89

Iberoamerican Cooperation multi-national series, 197–199

Iglesia de Santa Rosa, 162, 245, 256

ihuiteteyo, 2, 441, 445

Independence Day, 132

Iturbide, Augustín de, 5, 21
  on circulating coin coin, 105
  coinage of, 5, 294, 443
  and eagle motif, 443

Itzpapalotl, 425

Ixtaccíhuatl, 159, 242, 253
  and Popocatépetl, legend of, 340–341

jaguar
  endangered species, 211–212
  on NCLT coins, 211–212, 384–386, 425, 426–427

jaguar-human (child), 407–409

Jaguar-Man, 409–410, 412
  artifact resembling, 413

Jaina figurines, 404

Jalisco, 141
  Emblematic circulating coins, 159
  Emblematic NCLT coins, 242, 253
  Heraldic circulating coins, 150
  Heraldic NCLT coins, 222, 233

Jarabe Tapatío, 193

Jara Corona, Heriberto, 115

Jardín de San Marcos, 155, 238, 249

Jiménez Torres, Omar, 202

"Josefa Grande," 17, 20

Juárez García, Benito, 6, 27, 51
  on circulating coins, 26–27, 51–52, 57, 62–63, 67–68, 74, 78–79, 328

Juárez García, Benito, birth bicentennial
  on circulating coins, 169
  on NCLT coins, 269

juego de pelota, 395

jugador de pelota, 421

K'iche' Maya, 397

KM (Krause-Mishler) numbers, v

Kukulkán, 65, 403. *See also* feathered serpent; Quetzalcóatl

Kukulkán Pyramid, 403. *See also* Pyramid of the Castle, 308

The Labyrinth of Solitude, 135

Lee, Robert E., 142

Legaria, 8

Libertads, gold
  1 kilo, 369
  Early, 358–364
  mini, 358–360
  "New," 366–369
  See also Gold Coins of Mexico Program

Libertads, platinum, 369–370

Libertads, silver, 339–357
  1-kilo, 357
  Aztec Calendar, 357
  Early, 340–346
  First Reverse Restyling, 345–346
  "New," 346–357
  Obverse Restyled, 352–357
  Second Reverse Restyling, 351

Liberty Cap coinage, 6

Lintel 26, Yaxchilán, 400–401

lobo, 185

López Rayón, Ignacio, 99–100

Lo Que Dice, y Lo Que Se Hace, 100

Los Grandes Problemas Nacionales, 118

Macedonio Alcalá Theater, 161, 244, 255

Madero, Francisco, 36
  on circulating coins, 29, 34–35, 37–38, 68, 82–83, 84, 121–122, 183–184
  relationship with Venustiano Carranza, 80–81

Manatee, 211

Mariles, Humberto, 196

Márquez, Francisco, 142

mask
  of Chaac, 402
  funerary, 156, 239, 250, 419
  jaguar, 158, 241, 252
  See also Temple of the Masks

Matamoros, Mariano, 102

Maximilian coinage, 6, 444

Maya,
  history of, 397
  culture honored on circulating coin, 71
  See also Palenque

medallic coinage, gold, 326–332

medals
  commemorative, 129
  Iberoamericana, 198
  Olympic, 73
  proclamation, 4
  Sociedad Numismática de México, 301–302

Melgar, Augustín, 142

Mesoamerican ball game, 387
  history of, 388–389
  origins of, 407
  rules of, 389
  See also juego de pelota

Mesoamerican ball player
  on circulating coins, 71, 72, 174
  equipment worn by, 389
  modern, 389
  on NCLT coins, 196, 270, 421
  See also jugador de pelota

Metcalf, Edward H., 76

Mexcaltitlán de Uribe, 160, 243, 254

Mexica, 33, 86. *See also* Aztecs

Mexican eagle, 205–206
  in Codex Mendoza, 441
  history of use on coinage (*see appendix C*)

Mexican Hat Dance, 193

Mexican state federation, 141, 143, 215
  original states and territories, 141

Mexican State Federation Series, 141–165
  denominations in, 215
  Series 1: circulating, 143–154
  Series 1: NCLT, 215–226, 226–237
  Series 2: circulating, 154–165
  Series 2: NCLT, 237–248, 248–259

Mexica Triple Alliance, 372–373

Mexico
  first black president of, 110
  first president of, 111
  armed forces of, 100th anniversary, 138–139

Mexico City Mint, 1, 8

México, Estado de, 141
  Emblematic circulating coins, 159
  Emblematic NCLT coins, 219, 253
  Heraldic circulating coins, 149
  Heraldic NCLT coins, 221, 232

Mexico Mint, 8

Michoacán, 141
  Emblematic circulating coins, 160
  Emblematic NCLT coins, 243, 254
  Heraldic circulating coins, 149
  Heraldic NCLT coins, 221, 232

Miguel de Cervantes Award, 136

milled coinage, 277

milled edge, 4

Mina, Francisco Xavier, 55, 101

mining, 157, 240, 251

Mining Monument, Zacatecas, 165, 248, 259

Mint Sets
  current series, 311–312
  early series, 309
  late series, 310–311

Moctezuma I, 373

Moctezuma II, 65, 195, 373
  and Aztec Calendar Stone, 436

Montaño, Otilio, 5 pesos, 120–121

Montejo, Francisco de, 397

Monumento a la Independencia, 55. *See also El Ángel de la Independencia*

Monumento de la Revolucion, 86, 184
  on pattern 2000 pesos, 86

Morelia, 50

Morelos, Estado de, 51
  Emblematic circulating coins, 160
  Emblematic NCLT coins, 243, 254
  Heraldic circulating coins, 149
  Heraldic NCLT coins, 221, 232
  Revolutionary coinage, 301

Morelos, José María, 50–51
  on circulating coins, 46, 49, 51, 52–54, 79, 82, 108, 183
  on NCLT coins, 272
  places named for, 50–51
  statue of, 55
  See also Morelos coinage

Moreno, Pedro, 104–105

Mounted Liberty/Victory design, 180. *See also* Caballito peso

Múgica, Francisco J., 116–117

Museo Nacional de Antropologia. *See* National Museum of Anthropology, Mexico City

Museo del Templo Mayor. *See* Museum of the Great Temple, Tenochtitlan

Museum of Anthropology, Xalapa, 407, 413

Museum of the Great Temple, Tenochtitlan, 373, 377, 379

Nahui Ocelotl (4-Jaguar), 384–386

National Autonomous University (UNAM), 266–268
  motto, 268
  Olympic Stadium, 74
  research performed on Pyramid of the Sun, 33
  student protestors fired on in 1968, 73, 268

National History Museum, 142

National Museum of Anthropology, Mexico City, 381, 383, 384, 391, 392, 393, 395, 398, 402, 404, 409, 411, 417, 420, 422, 426, 428

Nava Power Plant, 157, 240, 251

Nayarit
  Emblematic circulating coins, 160
  Emblematic NCLT coins, 243, 254
  Heraldic circulating coins, 148
  Heraldic NCLT coins, 219, 231

Neri, Margarita, 275

New Fire ceremony, 133–134

New Orleans Mint, 9–10

new peso, 7, 89–90

new-peso denominations
  new 1 peso, 95, 389, 398
  new 2 pesos, 96–97, 376, 390, 399
  new 5 pesos, 98, 130, 376, 380–381, 390–394, 399–402s, 400–402
  new 10 pesos, 125, 384, 394–395, 403–404
  new 25 pesos, 395–396, 404–405
  new 50 pesos, 396, 405
  new 100 pesos, 396–397, 406

Nicaragua, 199

Nike, 54, 55

Niños Héroes (Boy Heroes), 141–142

Nobel Prize
  for Literature, 1990, 135, 136
  for Peace, 1965, 200

non-circulating legal tender (NCLT), defined, 170

nopal cactus, 11

Nuevo León, 141
  Emblematic circulating coins, 161
  Emblematic NCLT coins, 244, 255
  Heraldic circulating coins, 148
  Heraldic NCLT coins, 220, 231

nuevo peso, 7. *See also* new peso; new-peso denominations

numbers, Aztec, 437, 440

O'Gorman, Juan, 268

Oaxaca, 141
  Emblematic circulating coins, 161
  Emblematic NCLT coins, 244, 255
  Heraldic circulating coins, 148
  Heraldic NCLT coins, 220, 231

Obregón, Álvaro, 81, 113–114, 116

Obregón Santacilia, Carlos, 184

obsidian, 416, 425

obverse vs. reverse, v

obverse eagle styles
  forward-facing, 445–447
  Imperial, 443
  in profile, 445–446
  Profile or "Hookneck" Eagle, 443
  Upright Eagle, 444

Ocotlán Church, 164, 247, 258

oil industry, nationalization of, 87, 186–189

Oil Monument. See Fuente de Petroleos

old god of fire. *See* fire, old god of

Old Royal Treasury Building, San Luis Potosí, 162, 245, 256

olive ridley sea turtle, 192

llamaliztli, 388

Ollin, 126, 161, 244, 255, 438, 440

Olmec colossal head, 163, 246, 257, 406
  on circulating coins, 35
  on NCLT coins, 413–414

Olmecs, 406–407

Olympic Games
  on bullion coins, 324–325
  on circulating coins, 72
  on commemorative medal
  first ever hosted in Latin America, 73
  first televised, 73
  London (1948 and 2012), 196
  Mexican gold-medal disciplines in, 196
  Mexico City (1968), 73–74
  on NCLT coins, 196

Onza. *See* Una Onza

Open Chapel, Tlaxcala, 164, 247, 258

Orozco, Pascual, 36, 120

Ortega, Margarita, 275

Ortega Romero, Francisco, 202

Ortega, Rosaura, 275

Ortiz de Domínguez, Josefa, 21, 131
  on circulating coins, 17, 20, 22–23, 113
  See also "Josefa Grande," "White Josefa"

Our Lady of Sorrows, 61

oyamel tree, 185

Pachuca Monumental Clock, 159, 242, 253
Pakal the Great, 44, 156, 239, 250
  on circulating coins, 38, 45
  on NCLT coins, 401–402
Palace of Cortés, 160, 243, 254
Palacio de Bellas Artes, 195–196
Palenque, 44, 397
  Red Queen of, 44
  Tomb of Pakal, 401–402
  See also Pakal the Great
paper money
  on circulating coins, 168–169
  first issued, 5
  on NCLT coins, 264–265
Parada, Margarita Maza, 27
Paraguay, 199
Parish Church of Dolores Hidalgo, 61
  on bullion coins, 326–327
  on circulating coins, 59–60
  on NCLT coins, 271, 272
Paris Mint, 47
Parque Fundidora, 161, 244, 255
Paseo de la Reforma, 88
paso de la muerte, 193–194
patolquechtli, 1
Pattern Proof Sets, 313
Pavlova, Anna, 193
Paz, Octavio, 134–135, 268
pelota, 196. *See also juego de pelota*
People to University, University to People, 268
perforator (knife), Aztec design, 438
  blade, 438, 440
  handle, 438, 439
Peru, 199
Philadelphia Mint, 9–10
Philip IV coinage, 3
Philip V coinage, 3
piece of eight, 3
Piedra del Sol. *See* Aztec Calendar Stone
Pillar coinage, 5

pillar dollar, 3
Pillars of Hercules, 191
Pillet, Charles, 47, 197
piñata, 189
Pino Suárez, José María, 124
El Pipíla, Guanajuato, 158, 241, 252
Pirámide del Castillo. *See* Pyramid of the Castle
Pirámide de El Tajín. *See* Pyramid of El Tajín
Pirámide del Sol. *See* Pyramid of the Sun
pitahaya (dragonfruit), 163, 246, 257
Plan of Ayala, 120
Plan of Iguala, 112
platinum medallic coinage, 336–337
Plural (magazine), 135
poinsettia, 158, 241, 252
Popocatépetl, 159, 242, 253
  Ixtaccíhuatl, legend of, 340–341
Portrait (Bust) coinage, 5
Portugal, 199
Posada, J.G., 261
Prairie Dog, 214
Pre-Columbian Series, 199–200. *See also* chapter 10
Presentation Mint Sets (1992-93), 312
prickly pear, 11
priest sculpture
  Olmec, 414
  Toltec, 429
Primo de Verdad y Ramos, Francisco, 101–102
proclamation medals, 4
Profile Eagle coinage, 443
Pronghorn, 208
Proof Sets, 313–314
  of 1995, 314
  See also Rainbow Proof Sets, 314

Puebla, 141
  Emblematic circulating coins, 161
  Emblematic NCLT coins, 244, 255
  Heraldic circulating coins, 147
  Heraldic NCLT coins, 219, 230

Pyramid of the Castle, 307, 397
  on circulating coins, 165
  on NCLT coins, 248, 259, 307–308, 403–404

Pyramid of El Tajín. *See* Pyramid of the Niches

Pyramid of the Moon, 416
  on circulating coins, 159
  on NCLT coins, 242, 253

Pyramid of the Niches, 387, 394
  on circulating coins, 164
  on NCLT coins, 247, 258

Pyramid of Quetzalcóatl (Toltec), 425

Pyramid of the Sun, 33, 34, 416
  on circulating coins, 29, 31–34
  on NCLT coins, 422

La Quebrada Cliff, Guerrero, 158, 241, 252

Querétaro, 141
  Emblematic circulating coins, 162
  Emblematic NCLT coins, 245, 256
  Heraldic circulating coins, 147
  Heraldic NCLT coins, 219, 230

Quetzalcóatl, 65, 430
  on circulating coins, 57, 64
  legends concerning, 65, 373, 425
  on NCLT coins, 423
  See also Ce Acatl Topiltzin Quetzalcóatl; feathered serpent; Kukulkán; Temple of Quetzalcóatl

quill, feather, 442

quills, gold-filled, 1

quincunx, 437, 439

Quintana Roo
  Emblematic circulating coins, 162
  Emblematic NCLT coins, 245, 256
  Heraldic circulating coins, 147
  Heraldic NCLT coins, 219, 230

Railroad 5 pesos, 57, 59, 60

railways, 60

Rainbow Proof Sets, 314
  1/2-oz. gold Libertad, 363
  1/4-oz. platinum Libertad, 370

Ranchero Aguilar Bullring, 164, 247, 258

Rectory Tower (UNAM), 268

Red Queen of Palenque, 44

Reed (13 Acatl), 439, 440

Reforma del Norte, 27

Regeneracion (newspaper), 116

religion
  Aztec, 126, 133, 438–439
  Catholicism decreed sole in Mexico, 109
  Central Veracruz, 387
  freedom of, 329
  Maya, 397
  Olmec, 406–407
  Teotihuacán, 416
  Toltec, 425
  Totonac, 387

Republic decimal coinage, 6

Republic reales coinage, 5–6

Revolution, 75th anniversary of, 183–184
  on circulating coins, 82–83

Revolution, 100th anniversary of, 315–316
  on circulating coins, 113–124
  Mint Sets, 312
  on NCLT coins, 273–275
  Proof Sets, 314–315

Revolutionary heroes, 113–124
  interment locations, 184

Revolution, first shot fired in, 117

Ride of Death, 193–194

Ring of Days, 438, 439, 440

Ring of Quincunxes, 437, 438

Ring of Sacrifice, 438

Ring of Serpents, 438, 439, 440

Ring of Splendor, 439, 440

river crocodile, 208–209

river otter, 209–210

royal eagle, 207

rubber, 133
Ruíz, Diego, 387
Rural Defense Corps, 138
Ruscelli, Girolamo, 197
sacbeob, 397
sacrificial knife, 126
sacrificial offerings, 372, 387, 392, 397, 398, 416
Saddle Hill (Cerro de la Silla), Nuevo León, 161, 244, 255
saguaro cactus, 155, 163, 238, 246, 249, 257
San Antonio, Texas, 1
San Fernándo de Bexar, 1
San Francisco Mint, 9–10
San Lorenzo site, 406, 407, 413
San Luis Potosí, 141
 Emblematic circulating coins, 162
 Emblematic NCLT coins, 245, 256
 Heraldic circulating coins, 146
 Heraldic NCLT coins, 218, 229
 mint located at, 8
Santa Anna, Antonio Lopéz de, 27, 55, 142
Santa Fe de Nuevo México, 141
Santo Domingo de Palenque, 44
screw press, 3, 4, 277, 316–317
 basic design, 317
 on bullion coins, gold, 334–335
 on bullion coins, platinum, 336, 338
 on bullion coins, silver, 318–325
 on NCLT coins, 265–266
"Sentimientos de la Nacion," 50
Serdán, Carmen, 117–118
shells as money, 1
Sinaloa
 Emblematic circulating coins, 163
 Emblematic NCLT coins, 246, 257
 Heraldic circulating coins, 146
 Heraldic NCLT coins, 218, 229
skull motif, 417, 430
Smith, Tommie, 73

Sociedad Numismática de México, 301–302
solar ring, 439
soldadera, 275–276
 on circulating coins, 123–124
 on NCLT coins, 273–274
Sonora
 Emblematic circulating coins, 163
 Emblematic NCLT coins, 246, 257
 Heraldic circulating coins, 146
 Heraldic NCLT coins, 218, 229
Sonora y Sinaloa, 141
Spain, 199
SS *José M. Morelos*, 51
state copper coinage, 6
State Federation Series. *See* Mexican State Federation Series
stone beads (Aztec design), 440
Stone of Moctezuma I, 373–374, 377, 381
Stone of the Suns. *See* Aztec Calendar Stone
Suárez, Vicente, 142
SUD coinage, 50
sun-ray (Aztec design), 438, 440
Sun Stone. *See* Aztec Calendar Stone
Supreme National Congress coinage, 5, 443
Tabasco, 141
 Emblematic circulating coins, 163
 Emblematic NCLT coins, 246, 257
 Heraldic circulating coins, 145
 Heraldic NCLT coins, 217, 228
Tabasco Planetarium, 163, 246, 257
tajaderas, 1
El Tajín (city), 387–388, 394, 407. *See also* Central Veracruz Collection; Pyramid of the Niches
Talavera ceramics, 161, 244, 255
Taller (journal), 135
Tamaulipas, 141
 Emblematic circulating coins, 164
 Emblematic NCLT coins, 247, 258
 Heraldic circulating coins, 145
 Heraldic NCLT coins, 217, 228

tameme, 372

Teatro Juárez, Guanajuato, 158, 241, 252

Temple of Kabah, 402

Temple of Masks, 162, 245, 256

Temple of Quetzalcóatl (Teotihuacán), 416, 423

Temple of Quetzalcóatl (Tula), 425, 431

Temple of Tlahuizcalpantecuhtli, 425

Templo de San Antonio, 155, 238, 249

Tenochtitlán, 42, 86, 341, 372–373, 387, 441
   canals, 372
   founding of, 2–3

Teotihuacán, 33, 422
   history of, 416
   See also Pyramid of the Moon; Pyramid of the Sun

Teresa de Mier, Servando, 101, 106–107

Texas *jola*, 1

Texcoco, 372

Tezcatlipoca, 425

Tikal, 397

Tizoc, 383

Tizoc Stone, 383–384

Tlacopan, 372

Tlaloc, 372, 377–379, 425

Tlaltecuhtli, 437

Tlaxcala, 141, 141
   Emblematic circulating coins, 164
   Emblematic NCLT coins, 247, 258
   Heraldic circulating coins, 145
   Heraldic NCLT coins, 217, 228

Toltecs, history of, 425

Tonatiuh, 126, 425, 436, 437, 438–439
   Aztec design, 440
   on circulating coins, 125–128, 440
   on Calendar Stone, 438–439

Totonacs, 387–397

trade
   Aztec, 372

colonial Mexico and the Far East, 194
colonial Mexico and Spain, 332
Teotihuacán, 416

Tres Zapotes, 406, 407

Tula, Hidalgo, 425
   Atlantes figures
   eagle bas-relief, 431
   Serpent Wall, 430

Tulum ruins, 162, 245, 256

tuna (prickly pear), 11

ulama, 388–389

UNAM. *See* National Autonomous University (UNAM)

Una Onza, 316–320

UNICEF, 200

Upright Eagle coinage, 6, 300, 301, 444

Uribe, Virgilio, 139

Uruguay, 199

U.S. Constitution, 200th anniversary of
   on bullion coins, gold, 324–325
   on bullion coins, platinum, 337–338
   on bullion coins, silver, 321–323

Valdes, Francisco, 47

Valladolid, 50

vaquita marina, 190

Vasconcelos, José, 114, 268

Vega de Ochoa, Olga María, 202

Venezuela, 199

La Venta ruins, 406, 407, 414

Veracruz, Estado de, 141
   Emblematic circulating coins, 164
   Emblematic NCLT coins, 247, 258
   Heraldic circulating coins, 144
   Heraldic NCLT coins, 216, 227

Veracruz, Port of
   centennial of 1914 defense of, 139

vessel, anthropomorphic, 420

Vicario, Leona, 5 pesos, 107

Victoria, Guadalupe, 111
   on circulating coins, 70, 71–72, 112

Victoria ("Victory") motif, 55
 on circulating coins, 54, 56
 See also El Ángel de la Independencia;
  Mounted Liberty/Victory

Villa, Francisco "Pancho," 36, 80, 81
 birth name, 114
 on circulating coins, 82–83, 114–115,
  183–184
 raid on Columbus, New Mexico, 81

volcanoes, 157, 240, 251

volcano rabbit, 213–214

Vuelta (magazine), 135

War of Independence, 4–5
 beginning of, 131–132
 Insurgent coinage (*see* SUD coinage)
 Mint Sets, 312
 Proof Sets, 314–315
 Royalist coinage, Oaxaca, 5
 Royalist coinage, provisional (*see* L.V.O.
  coinage)
 statue commemorating, 55

War of Independence, 175th anniversary of
 on circulating coins, 82
 on NCLT coins, 183

War of Independence, 200th anniversary of
 on bullion coins, 369
 on circulating coins, 99–113
 Mint Sets, 312
 on NCLT coins, 271–273
 Proof Sets, 315–316

War of Independence, heroes of
 on circulating coins, 99–113
 interment locations, 55, 132

wheat-ear 1 centavo, 12, 14–15

"White Josefa," 17, 20

wolf, 185

World Cup Futbol Games
 Germany (2006), 269–270
 Mexico City (1986), 83, 170–182

wrestler sculpture, 411

Xinantecatl volcano, 159, 242, 253

xiuhtecoatl, 439

Xiuhtecuhtli, 133, 439, 439
 on coins, 133

Xochipilli, 381–382

Yaqui deer-dancer, 163, 246, 257

Yaxchilán, 400

Yohualtecuhtli, 437

Yucatán, 60, 141
 Emblematic circulating coins, 165
 Emblematic NCLT coins, 248, 259
 Heraldic circulating coins, 144
 Heraldic NCLT coins, 216, 227

Yucatec Maya, 397

Zacatecas, 141
 Emblematic circulating coins, 165
 Emblematic NCLT coins, 248, 259
 Heraldic circulating coins, 144
 Heraldic NCLT coins, 216, 227

Zacatecas, 100th anniversary of the taking
 of, 140

Zacatecas Cable Car, 165, 248, 259

Zacatecas Cathedral, 165, 248, 259

zacatuche, 213

Zapata, Emiliano, 36, 80, 81
 on circulating coins, 82–83, 122–123,
  183–184
 See also Zapatista coinage

Zapatismo, 122

Zapatista coinage
 1 centavo, 11, 12
 2 centavos, 15, 16

Zaragoza, Ignacio, 128, 130

Zebadúa, Delina, 137

INDEX TO COMMEMORATIVE COIN SERIES

This index lists non-circulating commemorative series, both bullion and legal tender. Circulating commemoratives are listed in the main index.

Aztec Collection, 372–386
 Guerrero Aguila, 373–377
 Brasero Efigie, 377–379
 Huehuetéotl, 379–381
 Xochipilli, 381–382
 Piedra de Tizoc, 383–384
 Jaguar / Stone of the Suns, 384–386

Bullion Commemorative Series
  gold issues, 324–325
  platinum issues, 337–338
  silver issues, 321–325

Central Veracruz Collection, 386–397
  Bajorrelieve de El TajIn, 387–391
  Palma con Cocodrilo, 391
  Carita Sonriente, 392
  Anciano con Brasero, 393
  Pirámide de El Tajín, 394–395
  Hacha Ceremonial, 395–397

Cervantino Festival, 33rd International, 260

Chichén Itzá 070707 Series, 303–307

Cultural Fusion Series, 330–331

Endangered Species in Mexico Collection, 207–214

FIFA World Cup, Germany, 2006, 269–270

Greatest Moments in the History of the [Olympic] Games, 324–325

Hidalgo y Costilla, Miguel, Birth Bicentennial, 326–327

Iberoamericana Series, 191–199

Independence, 175th Anniversary of, 183

Independence Bicentennial
  NCLT 20 pesos, 271–273
  bullion commemorative, 369

Mayan Collection, 397–406
  Chaac-Mool, 398–400
  Dintel 26, 400–401
  Lápida Tumba de Palenque, 401–402
  Mascarón del Dios Chaac, 402
  Pirámide del Castillo, 403–404
  Personaje de Jaina, 404–406

Mexican Monetary Anniversaries, 264–266

Mexican State Federation Series 1: Heraldic, 215–237

Mexican State Federation Series 2: Emblematic, 237–259

Millennium Collection, 201–204

National Autonomous University (UNAM), 100th anniversary of, 266–267

Nationalization of the Oil Industry, 50th Anniversary of, 186–189

Numismatic Heritage of Mexico Series, 276–301

Olmec Collection, 406–416
  Señor de las Limas, 407–409
  Hombre Jaguar, 409–410
  El Luchador, El, 411
  Hacha Ceremonial, 412
  Cabeza Olmeca, 413–414
  Sacerdote, 414–416

Reform of 1905, 100th Anniversary of, 266

Revolution, 75th Anniversary of, 183–184

Revolution Centennial, 273–275

Save the Children Fund, 189

Save the Giant Panda, 323–324

Teotihuacán Collection, 416–424
  Disco de la Muerte, 417–419
  Mascara, 419
  Vasija, 420
  Jugador de Pelota, 421
  Pirámide del Sol, 422
  Serpiente Emplumada, 423–424

Toltec Collection, 425–433
  Jaguar, 426–427
  Quetzalcóatl, 428–429
  Sacerdote, 429
  Serpiente con Craneo, 430
  Águila, 431–433
  Atlantes, 431–432

U.S. Constitution, 200th Anniversary of
  gold issues, 324–325
  platinum issues, 337–338
  silver issues, 321–323

UNICEF / For the Children of the World, 200–201

United Nations Environment Programme, 190

World Cup Futbol Games (1986), 170–182

World Wide Fund for Nature, 185–186